Foundation XML for Flash

Sas Jacobs

Foundation XML for Flash

ISBN (pbk): 1-59059-543-2

Printed and bound in the United States of America 9 8 7 6 5 4 3 2 1

Distributed to the book trade worldwide by Springer-Verlag New York, Inc., 233 Spring Street, 6th Floor, New York, NY 10013. Phone 1-800-SPRINGER, fax 201-348-4505, e-mail orders-ny@springer-sbm.com, or visit www.springeronline.com.

For information on translations, please contact Apress directly at 2560 Ninth Street, Suite 219, Berkeley, CA 94710. Phone 510-549-5930, fax 510-549-5939, e-mail info@apress.com, or visit www.apress.com.

The source code for this book is freely available to readers at www.friendsofed.com in the Source Code section.

Credis

Lead Editor
Chris Mills

Technical Reviewer
Kevin Ruse

Editorial Board
Steve Anglin, Dan Appleman
Ewan Buckingham, Gary Cornell
Tony Davis, Jason Gilmore
Jonathan Hassell, Chris Mills
Dominic Shakeshaft, Jim Sumser

Associate Publisher
Grace Wong

Project Manager
Pat Christenson

Copy Edit Manager
Nicole LeClerc

Copy Editor
Liz Welch

Assistant Production Director
Kari Brooks-Copony

Production Editor
Kelly Winquist

Compositor
Katy Freer

Proofreader
Lori Bring

Indexer
Broccoli Information Management

Artist
Katy Freer

Cover Designers
Corné van Dooren, Kurt Krames

Manufacturing Director
Tom Debolski

For my parents, David and Sherry-Anne, and my sister, Lucy. Thanks for all your support. I feel lucky to have been born into such a terrific family.

CONTENTS AT A GLANCE

CONTENTS

FOREWORD

If you work with Flash for anything other than creating animations, sooner or later you are going to run smack into XML. But the fact that you have this book in your hands right now means you already know this.

XML has been touted as the great equalizer, allowing seamless data transfer across platforms and programs. According to some, XML was going to save the world. While the world still needs some work, XML has gone a long way to improve communications between all kinds of systems.

Recognizing this some years ago, Macromedia put XML support into Flash 5, and with each version, this feature has seen remarkable improvements. If you are doing any kind of Flash application development, or even just building a dynamic website in Flash, you *need* to know about XML. Why? Because if you are moving data around and you don't know about XML, I can guarantee that you are wasting a lot of time and energy dealing with that data. Another reason is that, if it hasn't already happened, someday you're going to be asked to do a project that uses XML, or apply for a job where they ask you about it.

In the companies I have worked with, we *always* ask about a person's experience with XML and Flash. All too often the answer from beginning (and even intermediate) Flash users is something like, "XML—isn't that sort of like HTML?"

So, you need to learn XML to work with Flash. Why not just go grab any other book on XML? Well, that's what I did when I first started. They usually have a single, brush-off chapter on the makeup of XML itself, and then you start wading through DTDs, schemas, namespaces, XSLT, style sheets, and CSS, most of which doesn't have much relevance to working with XML in Flash—and most of which puts me to sleep. Moreover, the stuff you *do* need to know about—the Flash XML object and classes, Flash web service classes, XML sockets, and so forth—is not going to be covered by a general XML book.

However, the book you have in your hands is specifically tailored to teach you exactly what you need to know about XML for Flash applications. You are going to get a solid grounding in what XML is, why it is so cool, and how to use it in Flash. Just about every aspect of using XML as it relates to Flash is covered. Additionally, there are some very useful, real-world applications of generating XML from Microsoft Office documents. Although this may seem a bit odd at first, I can't tell you how many times I've been handed content from a client in a Word or Excel document and had to convert that to XML. (My solution has usually been to give it to an intern to convert by hand!)

As for the author, I've known Sas for some time and can vouch for both her knowledge of the subject and for her ability to communicate and teach about it in a clear, concise, and understandable way. She has given presentations about XML at Flash conferences throughout the world, and despite the way she pronounces *parse* (parze) and *data* (dahta), she has been very well received. (Sorry, Sas, you didn't think I going to be able to resist that, did you?) In addition, she has given Flash training sessions; written tutorials, manuals, and documentation; and done technical editing for a number of books. And all that's in addition to the Flash development business she runs. In short, she knows her stuff, so listen to what she has to say!

So, fire up your computer, start Flash, get comfortable, and prepare to become a Flash XML expert!

Keith Peters
Foundation ActionScript Animation: Making Things Move!
ISBN: 1590595181
friends of ED
`http://www.friendsofed.com/books/1590595181/index.html`

ABOUT THE AUTHOR

Sas Jacobs is a web developer who loves working with Flash. She set up her business, Anything Is Possible, in 1994, working in the areas of web development, IT training, and technical writing. The business works with large and small clients building web applications with ASP.NET, Flash, XML, and databases.

Sas has spoken at such conferences as Flash Forward, MXDU, and FlashKit on topics relating to XML and dynamic content in Flash.

In her spare time, Sas is passionate about traveling, photography, running, and enjoying life. One of her most fervent wishes is that Flash will take over the Web!

ABOUT THE TECHNICAL REVIEWER

Kevin Ruse (San Jose, California) is an enthusiastic instructor who has taught at the University of California Extension Program in Cupertino, as well as DeAnza Community College. He currently provides training to Fortune 500 companies throughout the United States. He has over 20 years of experience in the graphic design and production industry, from concept to finished product. Kevin is the author of *XML for Web Designers Using Macromedia Studio MX 2004* (Charles River Media, 2004) and *Web Standards Design Guide* (Charles River Media, 2005).

ABOUT THE COVER IMAGE

Corné van Dooren designed the front cover image for this book. Having been given a brief by friends of ED to create a new design for the Foundation series, he was inspired to create this new setup combining technology and organic forms.

With a colorful background as an avid cartoonist, Corné discovered the infinite world of multimedia at the age of 17—a journey of discovery that hasn't stopped since. His mantra has always been "The only limit to multimedia is the imagination," a mantra that is keeping him moving forward constantly.

After enjoying success after success over the past years—working for many international clients, as well as featuring in multimedia magazines, testing software, and working on many other friends of ED books—Corné decided it was time to take another step in his career by launching his own company, *Project 79*, in March 2005.

You can see more of Corné's work and contact him through `www.cornevandooren.com` or `www.project79.com`.

If you like his work, be sure to check out his chapter in *New Masters of Photoshop: Volume 2*, also by friends of ED (ISBN 1590593154).

ACKNOWLEDGMENTS

I just want to say a big thank you to the people who helped in putting together this book. First, thanks to Chris Mills at friends of ED for his guidance and humor. I'd also like to thank Kevin Ruse for some great suggestions during his technical reviews. Thank you to my copy editor, Liz Welch, for her accuracy and amazing knowledge of the English language. Finally, thanks to Pat Christenson, who oversaw the whole project and made things very easy for me as a first-time author—just don't mention Chapter 4 to her!

INTRODUCTION

This book should be subtitled "Everything you wanted to know about XML and Flash but were afraid to ask"! It introduces you to XML and shows you why, where, when, and how to use XML in Flash.

I wrote this book for both Flash designers and developers. It provides a great starting point if you haven't worked with XML before. You'll understand about the history of XML and learn about creating XML documents. I'll show you where XML fits into the web development world, and we'll look at some of the related recommendations including XPath, XML schemas, and Extensible Stylesheet Language Transformations (XSLT).

If you have Office 2003 for the PC, you'll also learn how Word, Excel, and Access 2003 can generate XML documents for use in Flash. Your clients can use these software packages to generate XML content for the Flash applications that you build.

The bulk of the book will work with XML in Flash. I'll show you the different ways that you can include XML content in your applications. We'll start by writing ActionScript to load and modify XML documents. Then we'll take a closer look at the data components that ship with Flash and use them with UI components like the List and DataGrid. Data components are great if you prefer to work visually. They can speed up the development process because you don't need to write any ActionScript. I'll also show you how to script these components.

The rest of the book looks at web services and XML sockets. I'll finish by showing a process that will help you to decide how to work with XML in Flash. By the end of the book, you'll have built several Flash XML applications that you'll be able to use in your work and personal projects.

The examples in the book assume a basic understanding of ActionScript, but you don't have to be an advanced coder to make them work. I've purposely kept the design of these applications very simple and used function-based code rather than ActionScript 2.0 classes. I believe this approach makes it easier for people who aren't full-time coders.

Although the book includes some server-side code examples, it doesn't aim to teach server-side coding. I'm a .NET developer so I've included VB .NET code. I've included a PHP version as well, and you can also create your own server-side files, written in other languages.

I hope you enjoy reading this book as much as I've enjoyed putting it together. During the writing process, I was continually amazed at the power of XML as a web technology. To me, the combination of Flash and XML is unbeatable, and I hope you'll discover the same thing. I see Flash as the future of the Web, and XML will help to cement that position.

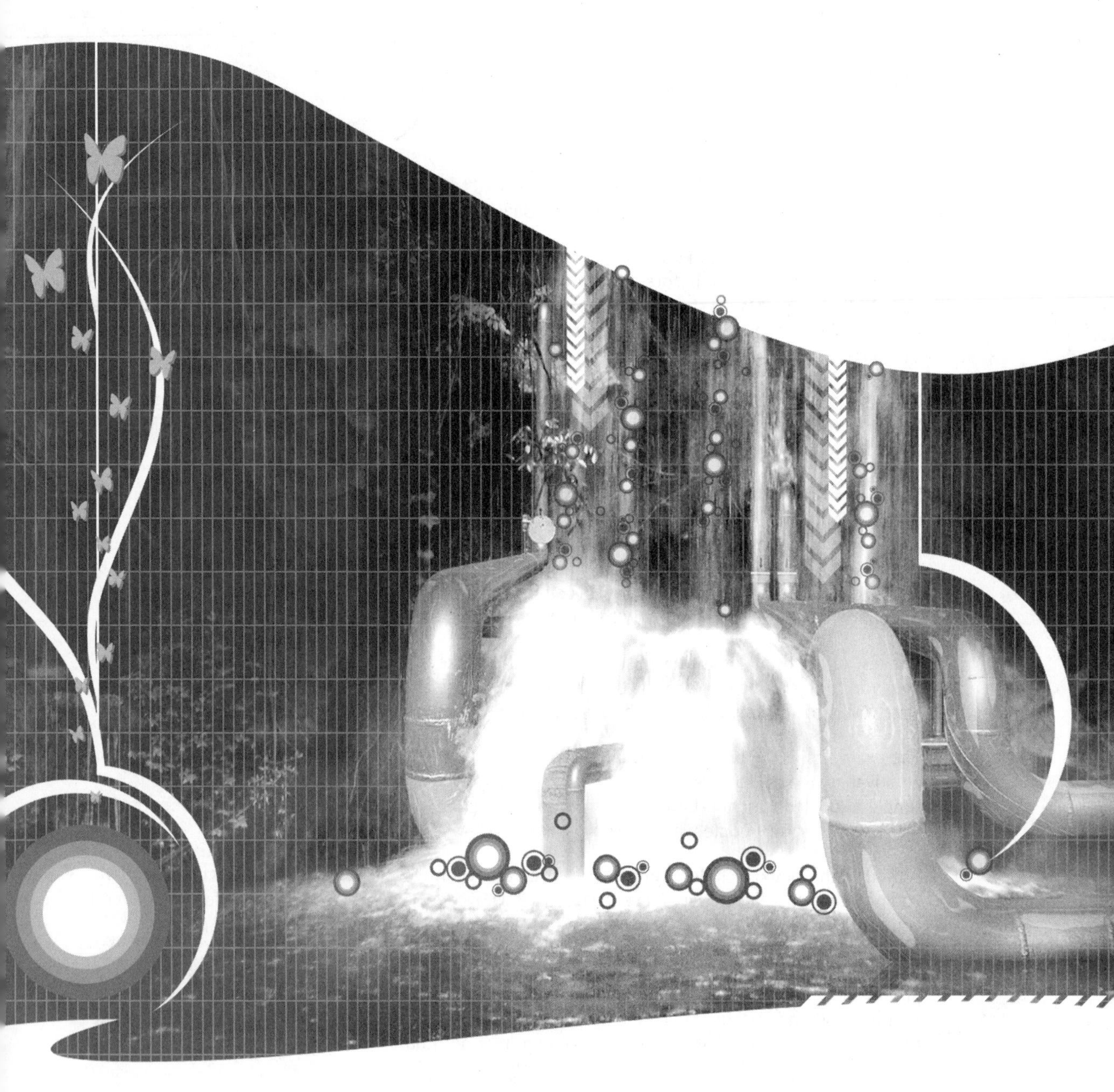

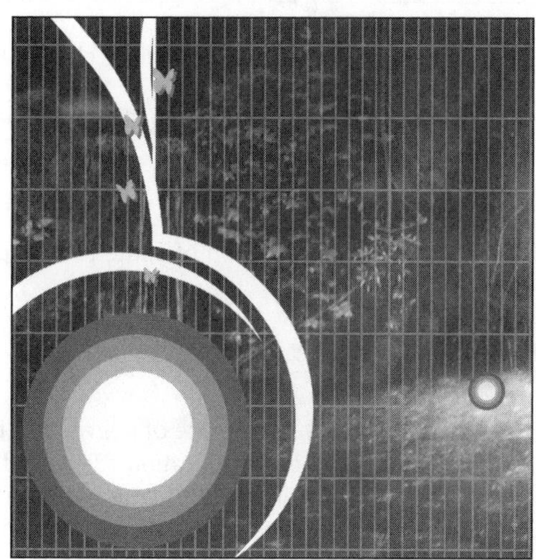

Chapter 1

FLASH AND XML

How can you create dynamic Macromedia Flash movies that share their content with other software applications and people? How can you store your data so that is simple to use but also adheres to web standards? The answer to both of these questions is to use Extensible Markup Language (XML) with your Flash movies. Storing your data in XML documents provides you with a flexible, platform-independent solution that is simple to implement in Flash.

This book is about using Flash with XML documents. Although it's not a substitute for an XML reference book, you'll learn the important points about working with XML. You'll also learn where and how to use XML documents within your Flash applications.

If you're new to XML, this book helps you to make your Flash movies more dynamic and interactive. Flash developers who've worked with dynamic content benefit by learning more about data binding with XML and Flash web services. Whatever your level, this book provides you with some new insights and ideas about Flash and XML.

Before we learn more about XML and its role within Flash, it's important to understand a little of the history of both areas. In this chapter, I look briefly at this history as well as the reasons why Flash can be a useful tool for working with XML information. I also show you some Flash applications that use XML to provide their data. Chapters 2 and 3 provide you with more detail about XML.

When you develop interactive websites, Flash provides many advantages over HTML web pages. Couple Flash with an external XML data source and you have a flexible and powerful solution for both web and stand-alone applications.

Some of the reasons you might choose Flash to work with XML documents are

- The multimedia capabilities of Flash
- The ability of Flash to visualize and interact with complicated information
- The ability of Flash to simplify the display of information
- The separation of content from presentation that is possible within Flash

Flash

Flash is an amazing piece of software. It began as a simple animation tool and has grown into a sophisticated, high-end application for web developers and designers alike. Most people are familiar with the powerful animation features that are available within Flash. It is a great alternative to animated GIFs and helps web designers avoid some of the cross-browser issues associated with using Dynamic Hypertext Markup Language (DHTML).

Nowadays, the uses for Flash are many and varied. Flash creates everything from simple animations to entire websites and applications, as well as broadcast-quality animations and content for mobile devices. Developers have used Flash for e-learning and online help applications. Flash even challenges Microsoft PowerPoint as a tool for creating online presentations.

The Flash Player is one of the most popular web browser plug-ins in the history of the Internet. In March 2005, Macromedia stated that Flash content had reached 98.3 percent of Internet viewers. This means that designers and developers can rely on some version of the Flash Player being available on most computers. You can find out more about the popularity of Flash compared with other plug-ins at `www.macromedia.com/software/player_census/flashplayer/`.

People are less familiar with the role of Flash in rich-media applications. Flash creates flexible and stylish front-ends for web applications as well as for stand-alone projects. The more recent releases of Flash include a range of tools for creating complex graphical user interfaces (GUIs). The standard UI components included with Flash make it easy for both designers and developers to create interactive movies. These components are also great for rapid prototyping of applications.

Flash movies can include dynamic content from a number of different sources—databases, text files, and XML documents. A Flash movie can work like a template where you fill in the blanks with the external data. To change the contents of a dynamic Flash movie, simply update the data source. You don't even have to open Flash.

While we've been watching Flash evolve, the area of web development has changed dramatically. We've seen a move from static, brochure-style websites to more interactive sites that offer real functionality to users. Think about the Internet banking applications that are available from most major banks.

Web pages have become increasingly complicated to cope with more sophisticated information and higher expectations from website visitors. The original HTML specification has struggled to meet the demands of modern web pages. As a result, different flavors of HTML have emerged, each tied to specific software packages and versions.

A high proportion of websites are now driven by content management systems. These systems allow website owners to maintain their own content without writing a single line of HTML. Increasingly, these sites draw content from sources such as database and mainframe systems. The role of website designer has changed from updating static web pages to creating systems that allow clients to update their own content.

XML

There have been many other changes in the workings of the World Wide Web, including the introduction of XML in 1998. Since that time, the World Wide Web Consortium (W3C) has released many different recommendations for working with XML documents. XML has become a standard for exchanging electronic data both on and off the Web. Software packages like databases and web browsers now offer the ability to work with XML documents. Even Microsoft Office 2003 for PCs offers support for information in XML format.

The W3C published the first XML specification back in 1998. XML provides a way to create new markup languages and sets out some strict rules for the creation process. In 2000, applying XML rules to the HTML recommendation created a new recommendation, Extensible Hypertext Markup Language (XHTML).

Since that time, XML has filtered into the web development world and its expansion looks set to continue. XML documents provide structured data for both humans and software applications to read. Websites can use XML documents to provide content. Web services allow us to share information across the Internet using an XML format.

XML is a powerful tool for use in building web applications. It is browser and platform independent, and isn't tied to any commercial organization. XML processing software is also available on virtually every platform.

Flash 5 was the first version to introduce XML support. It has remained an important tool in subsequent releases of Flash. The built-in XML parser means that Flash movies can include content from external XML documents. Flash can also generate XML to send to external files.

Flash MX 2004 included data components that automated the process of connecting to an XML document. Developers could incorporate XML content with a single line of ActionScript. The components also allowed for binding between XML content and UI components.

The advanced multimedia and GUI development tools within Flash make it a perfect front-end for applications that use XML documents. You can generate XML from diverse sources, and it's even possible to use Office 2003 on a PC to update the XML content in your Flash movies.

Before we continue, I need to point out that XML is not necessarily the best solution for all dynamic Flash movies. XML documents are a useful option, but other solutions might be more appropriate, such as storing content in a text file or database. Chapter 11 looks at some of the issues you need to consider when deciding which approach to use in your Flash movies.

Multimedia capabilities

Everyone is familiar with the multimedia capabilities within Flash. Flash movies can include sound, video, and animations, and you've probably seen at least one game or application built in Flash that uses these capabilities. One of the strengths of Flash is its ability to produce this multimedia content with relatively small file sizes.

Often, information is easier to understand when it is in a visual form. Everyone knows that a picture is worth a thousand words! The multimedia capabilities of Flash make it ideal for displaying some types of data. Flash also adds a level of interactivity that isn't easy to achieve when you use formats like HTML.

One of the common multimedia applications for Flash movies is the photo gallery. You've probably seen variations on this theme in several places on the Internet. My own website, `www.sasjacobs.com`, has a Flash photo gallery that I use to display my travel photos. You can see a screenshot in Figure 1-1.

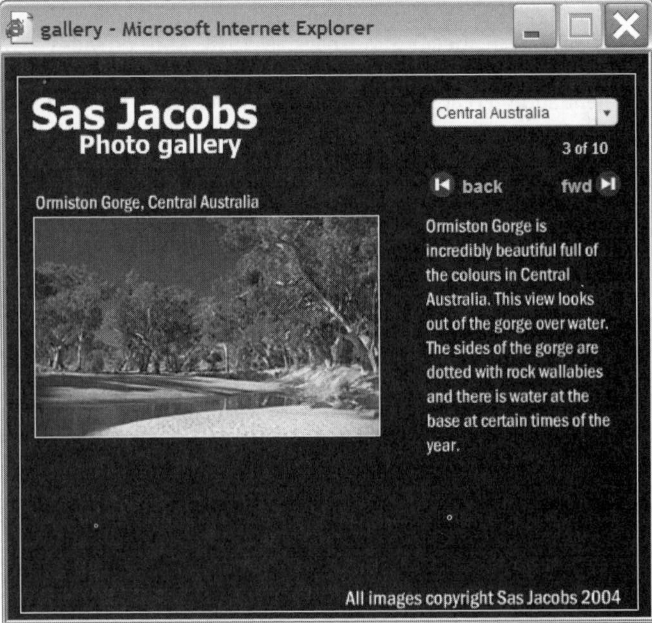

Figure 1-1. A Flash photo gallery application that uses content from an XML document

I use an XML file to store the information about my photos. The XML document includes a file name, category, caption, and description for each photo. The categories display in a ComboBox component. Users select a category and use the back and forward buttons to view each image. As the image loads, the relevant details from the XML document display in the Flash movie.

Each photo is loaded into the gallery only when the user requests the image. This makes the gallery operate much more quickly than if I displayed all photos on a single web page. I've also added a fade-in and fade-out, which would have been very difficult to achieve, cross-browser, with JavaScript and HTML.

I can update the photos in the gallery by changing the XML document. I use an XML editor and type in the changes. You'll learn how to build a similar photo gallery application later in this book.

You can see another variation on the Flash XML Photo gallery application at `www.davidrumsey.com/ticker.html`. Figure 1-2 shows a screenshot.

Figure 1-2. A ticker-style Flash photo gallery application

This is a new take on an old favorite and a clever way to display image thumbnails. The gallery uses a "ticker" to display image thumbnails, similar to a stock ticker. You can choose whether to view an ordered or random display. The information for the images in the ticker comes from an XML file. The application is simple to update and can easily be used for other image collections.

Visualizing complex information

Another strength of Flash is its ability to provide a visual representation of complex information. If you search for **Flash maps** in your favorite search engine, you'll find many commercial products that use Flash to display location maps. Some of these offer XML support for plotting specific points.

In another example, Bernhard Gaul has used Flash as an interface for a global airport weather web service. The information comes from the Cape Science GlobalWeather web service in XML format; Figure 1-3 shows a screenshot.

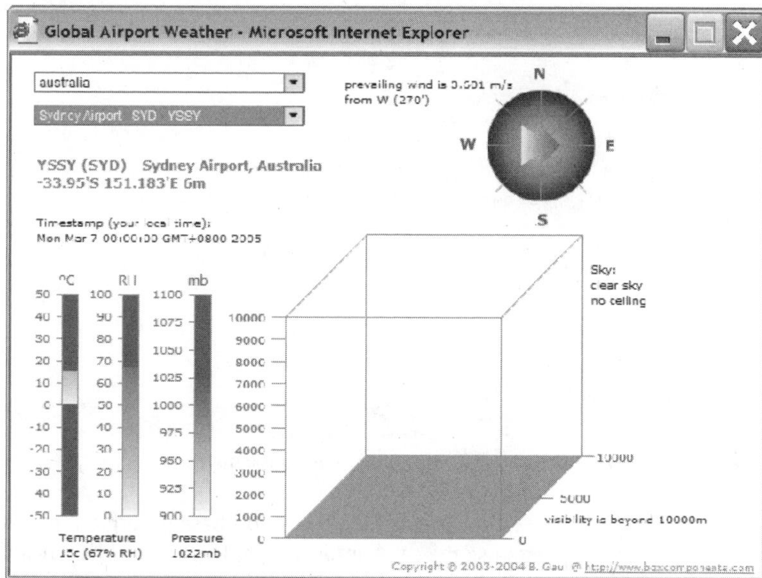

Figure 1-3. Global airport weather information displayed in a Flash movie with content from a web service

Strong visual elements show information such as wind direction, temperature, and pressure. It's much easier to get a sense of the weather from this Flash movie compared with reading a list of figures. You can find out more at `www11.brinkster.com/bgx/webservices/weather.html`.

You can also find this at `www11.brinkster.com/bgx/webservices/weather.html`. Open the website in your favorite browser and click the "View the Flash Visualization" link.

Another example of visualizing information is in the periodic table of elements. We've probably all seen this in high school science classes. Within the periodic table, the position of each element is based on the element's bonding abilities. It is a visual way to represent repeating patterns within elements.

Many web pages provide a visual representation of this table. A Flash representation of the same content makes the information much easier to access. In the Flash version shown in Figure 1-4, rolling the mouse over an element displays the element name. Clicking the element pops up more information about each element. You can see the example at the GalaxyGoo website at `www.galaxygoo.com/chemistry/PeriodicTable.htm`.

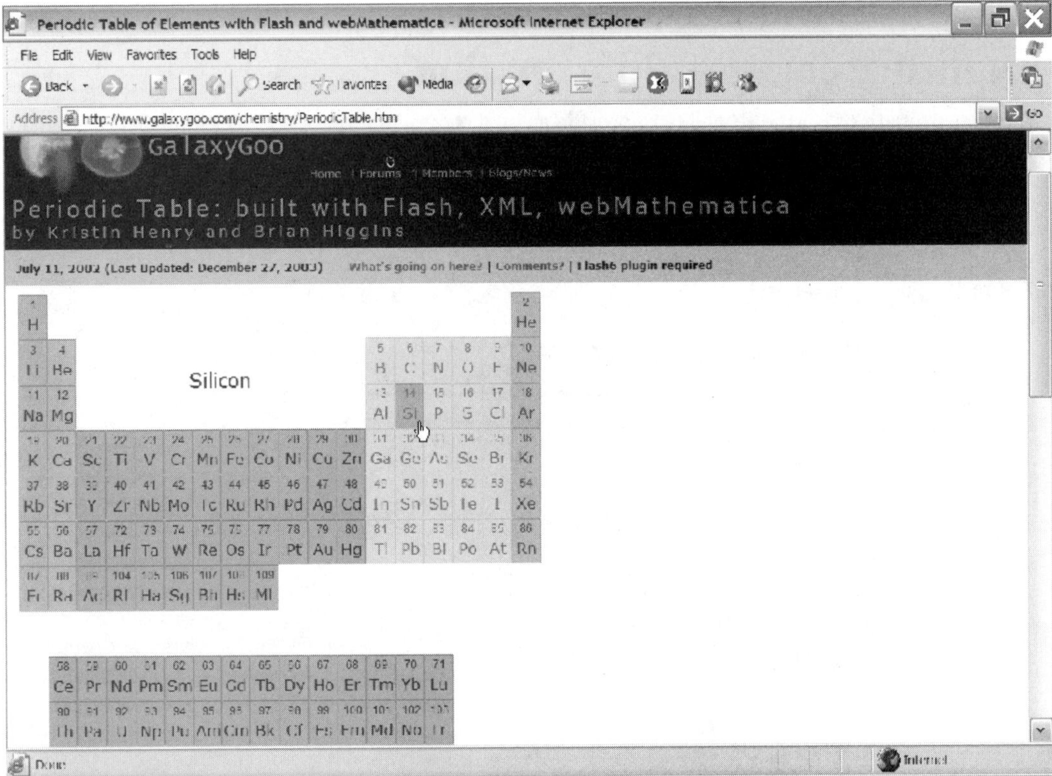

Figure 1-4. An interactive periodic table created in Flash, XML, and webMathematica

Incidentally, this example uses an XML document to provide the basic information about each element. That allows other applications to use the same information. The website also includes a spelling game (see `www.galaxygoo.com/games/tabletoy/tabletoy.html`) that uses the same XML content.

Simplifying the display of information

Information displayed in lists and tables can often be difficult to process. Humans are more comfortable with visual or summarized information that scans easily. Flash is very good at taking complicated information and displaying it in a simplified manner. It can alter the visual appearance by reducing the amount of information that displays. Flash can also add sorting, animation, or other kinds of visual cues to the data.

Displaying content from Office 2003 for PCs

Microsoft Office 2003 is a very popular PC software suite for business and personal users alike. At the time of writing, the latest version of Office for Macintosh users is Office 2004. The Mac version offers limited XML functionality only within Excel, so the example that follows isn't applicable to Macintosh users.

Organizations frequently store complicated tables of information in Excel spreadsheets. If the information is stored in these software packages, how can you make selected parts available to your clients? You may need to simplify a complex Excel structure into something more manageable. You might also have to restrict access to the full worksheet for commercial reasons.

One of my clients, Dura-lite, faced this problem. Dura-lite works with heat transfer products and maintains a complex set of related part numbers within an Excel workbook. The company uses Excel for complicated lookups between two different sets of numbering systems.

Dura-lite needed to make the lookup available to their clients. The existing structure was complicated and contained confidential information so they couldn't just send out their Excel workbook. The clients would have found it difficult to understand and use the content.

Dura-lite also wanted to place this information on their website and on a CD-ROM catalog that could be run offline. However, they felt most comfortable maintaining the data in their Excel workbook. They didn't want to re-create the data in a database and wanted to use the same content for both the website and CD-ROM.

I used Flash to create a catalog for the Excel information. The content for the catalog comes from the Excel workbook via an XML document. Dura-lite updates the workbook and from time to time saves the information from Excel in XML format. The catalog is available on the Dura-lite website in a password-protected area. They also distribute it on a CD-ROM.

The structure of the Excel workbook they use is relatively complex. It contains seven worksheets, each corresponding to a manufacturer. Each worksheet contains information about a model and engine with corresponding part numbers. An additional sheet provides a cross-lookup between part numbers.

Figure 1-5 shows the structure of the workbook. For commercial reasons, I've removed the data, but imagine the structure populated with long part numbers. It would be very difficult to read!

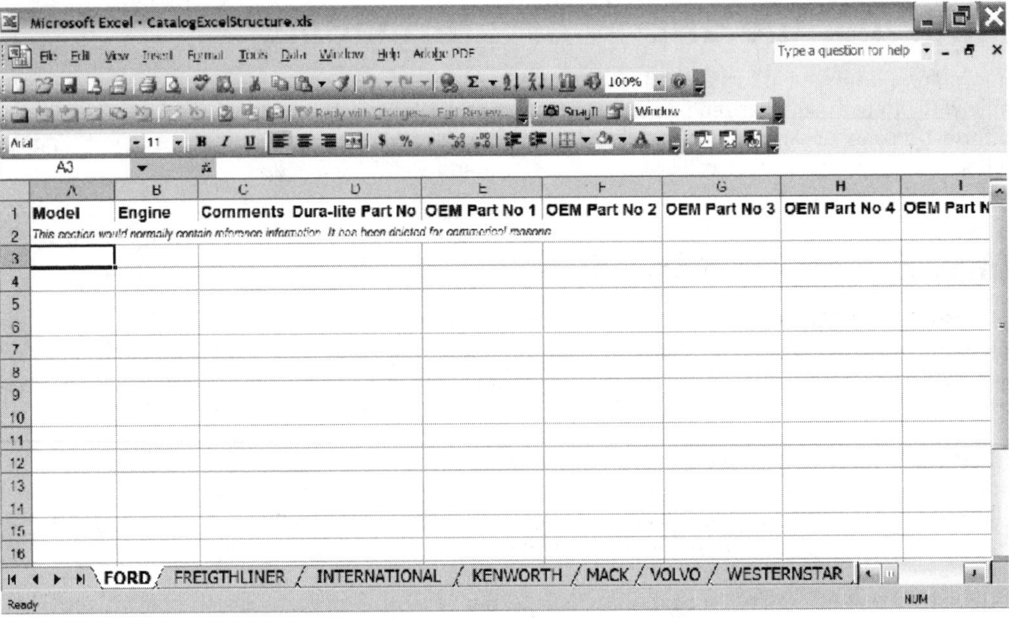

Figure 1-5. The Excel workbook structure for Dura-lite parts

Figure 1-6 shows the same content displayed in the Flash catalog.

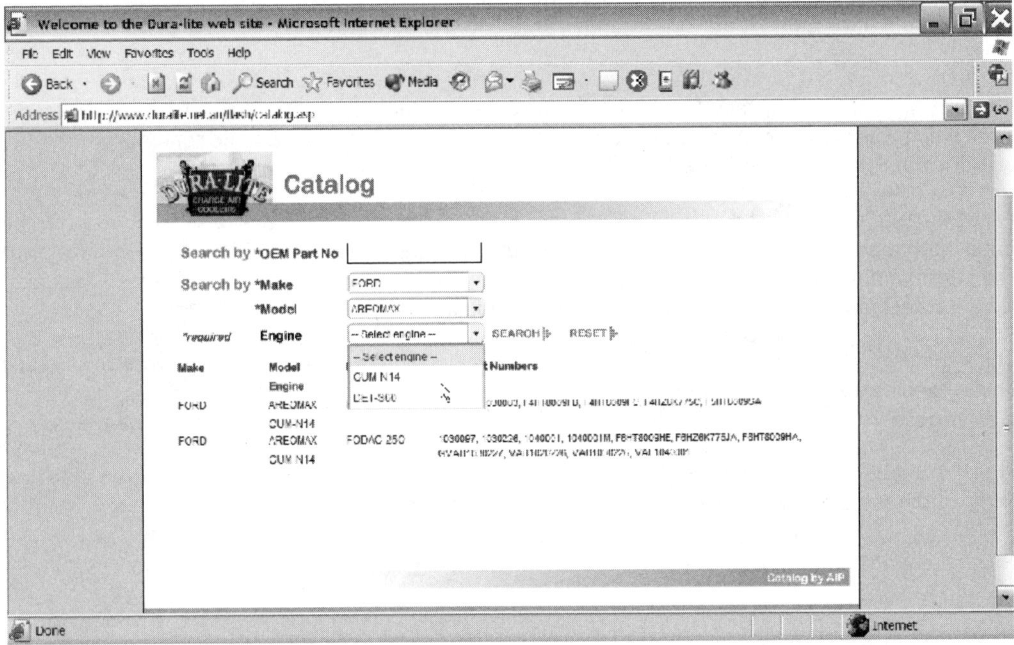

Figure 1-6. The Flash catalog for Dura-lite parts

There are two ways to use the catalog. If the user knows the original equipment manufacturer (OEM) part number, they enter it and click Search. Otherwise, they select a manufacturer from a drop-down list. This populates the Model drop-down list with all related models. The Engine drop-down list is then populated. The user can optionally choose an engine before they click Search.

The results display in a list below the search form. The text is selectable so that clients can copy and paste the part numbers. You can't see this example on the Web as it is in a password-protected area.

The Flash catalog is much easier to use than the Excel workbook. It simplifies the information available to the user and offers a simple but powerful means of searching for data. An XML document provides the link between Excel and Flash. Dura-lite can update their content at any time using their Excel file, and they don't need to rely on me to make changes for them. Likewise, I don't have to make numerous small updates on their behalf. I can leave control of the content up to Dura-lite and focus on design and development issues.

Displaying content from a web service

Web services provide another example where Flash simplifies the display of complex information. Many organizations make their data available to the public through web services. Data arrives in an XML document, and the built-in XML parser within Flash can translate this document into a simple visual display for users.

Earlier in the chapter, we saw an example of a web service that provides airport weather information. In the next example, we look at how Flash can consume a news service from Moreover. The new headlines update on a daily basis, but the structure of the XML document providing the information never changes. Users can view up-to-date news items any time they open the Flash movie.

Figure 1-7 shows a sample XML document from Moreover displayed in a web browser.

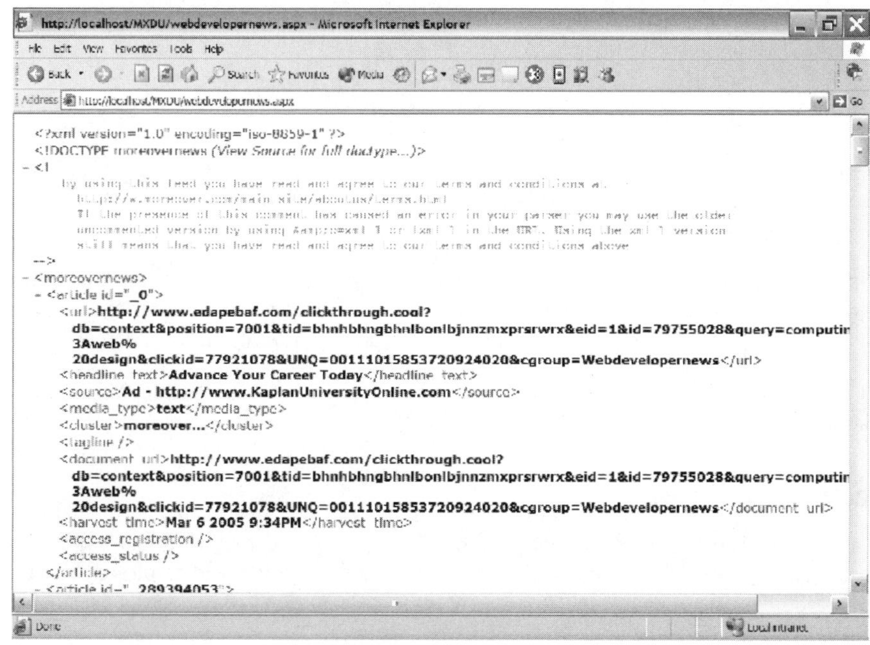

Figure 1-7. An XML document from Moreover news

I requested the daily web developer news and this XML document was provided. It contains a set of articles. Each article has related information such as an id, URL, and headline.

It's not easy for me to scan this document to read the news headlines. The document isn't designed to be read by humans. I can look through the list for the `<headline_text>` element but it's pretty hard work. If I want to see the news item in full, I'll have to copy the `<url>` text and paste it into the address line of a web browser.

Compare the XML document with Figure 1-8, which shows the same information displayed within a Flash movie.

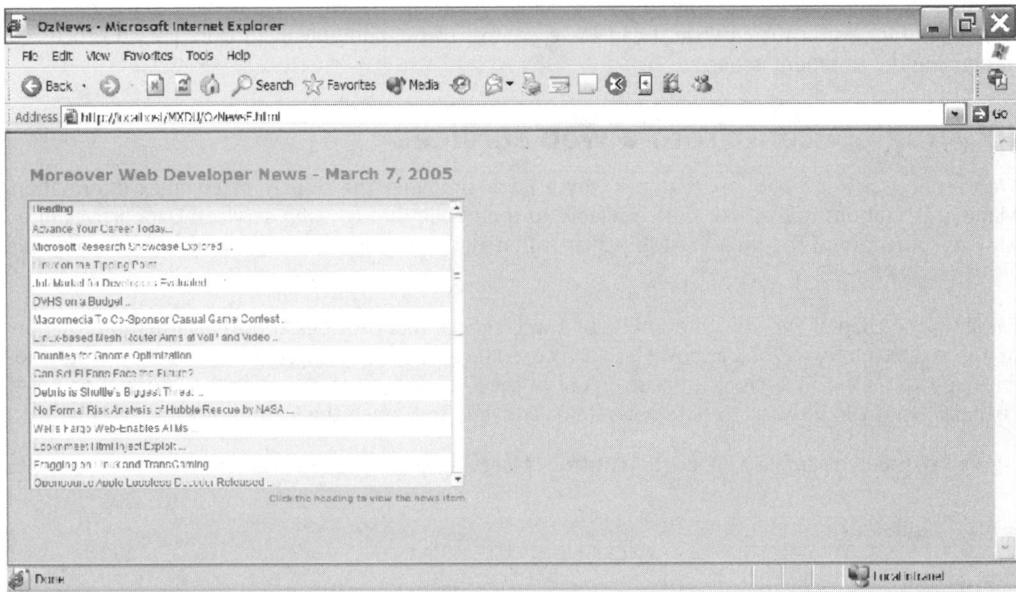

Figure 1-8. Moreover news headlines displayed in a Flash movie

Flash has extracted the relevant information and the headline displays in a DataGrid component. It has also colored every second line to make it easy to view the headlines. Each headline links to an HTML page that displays more detail when clicked.

I could change the display by adding extra columns or by using different colors. I could also make this movie more interactive. For example, the source for the news item could display as the user moves their mouse over the title. I could also add a button that allows me to look up news items from earlier dates.

Flash provides a presentation layer that makes the information much more accessible. You'll build something similar later in this book.

Accessing your computer

Another example of simplifying information with Flash is using it to interact with parts of your computer—for example, the files and folders. Flash can't interact with files and folders directly so you have to use a server-side file. This is important for security reasons—you don't really want a user being able to delete the contents of your hard drive by using a Flash movie.

Server-side languages like ColdFusion, PHP, and VB .NET allow you to work with folders and files on your computer. You could use them to generate a list of characteristics such as file and folder names, file sizes, or the last modified date of a document. You can also use server-side languages to edit and delete files and folders, as well as to change the contents inside text files.

Flash can use a server-side language to work with files and folders on a computer. The server-side file can generate an XML representation of your files and folders. Flash then has access to the information about them in a structured format.

So when would this be useful? Well, any time you wanted to create an up-to-date list of files for use within a Flash movie. In this book, one of the examples we'll look at is an MP3 player.

I've backed up most of my CDs in MP3 format so I can listen to them while I work. I have also built a Flash MP3 player that can play the files. The MP3 player loads the file list from an XML document.

I could type the names of all of my MP3s into an XML file and display the list in Flash. However, given the number of CDs I own, that's likely to take me a long time and I'd have to update the file each time I add new songs.

Instead, I wrote a server-side file that gets the details of the folders and MP3 files in my library, and creates the XML document automatically. However, the XML document doesn't exist in a physical file. Instead, it's generated as a stream of XML information whenever I open the Flash movie.

Figure 1-9 shows the XML document that I have generated from my folders and MP3 files. I used an ASP.NET file to create this document. At the time of writing, there were 542 lines in the file. I'd hate to have to maintain the list manually by typing the content myself!

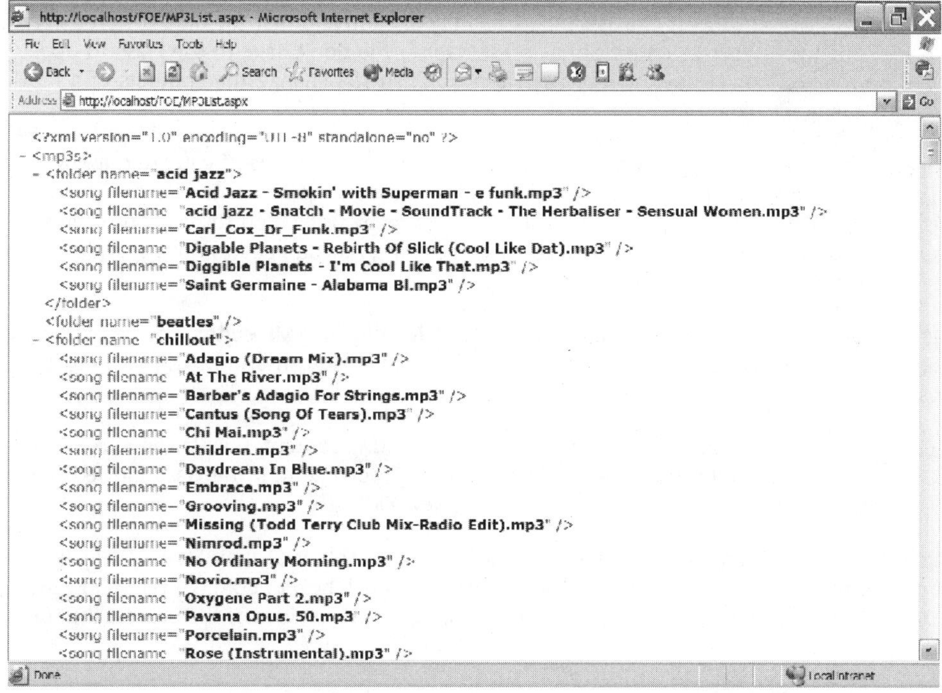

Figure 1-9. An XML document containing a list of MP3 files generated by an ASP.NET file

This XML document powers the Flash MP3 player shown in Figure 1-10.

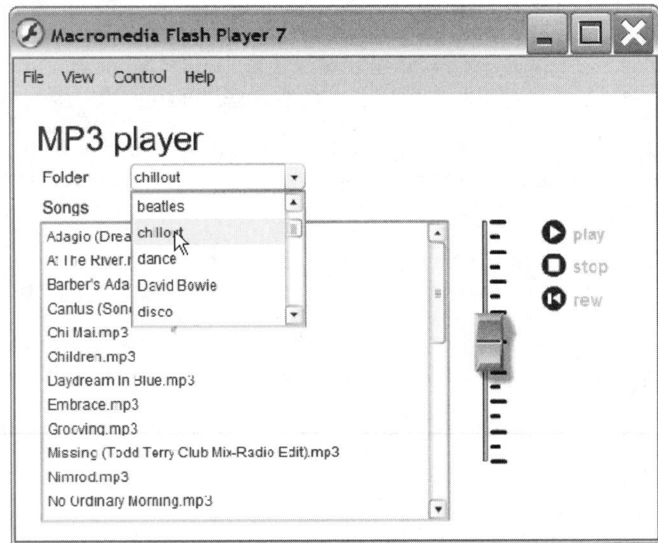

Figure 1-10. An MP3 player that uses an XML document listing the MP3 files

You'll learn how to build a very similar MP3 player a little later in this book.

Separating content and presentation

It's much more flexible for you to build Flash movies that include dynamic content. The term *dynamic content* means that the content changes independently of Flash and that the data is stored in a separate place. When you separate data from its presentation, you don't have to use Flash to update the content. Even if you don't know how to use Flash, you can still change the contents of a movie by changing the external data source.

This means your clients can update their own Flash content. For example, if you are drawing content from an XML or text file, they can open a text editor and edit the contents directly. They can also change the content in a database like MySQL or Access or by using web forms. Your clients are no longer reliant on you every time they want to make a change. All you need to do is provide them with a mechanism for updating the data source.

In the case of XML, clients could update content directly using an XML editor. This would be appropriate for data with a simple structure and confident clients. You can also provide a web form that allows clients to make updates.

You can even set up Office 2003 documents that generate XML content. Clients can make changes in Word, Excel, or Access and export the contents to an XML document. If the Flash movie is part of a website, they can then use a web form to upload the new XML file.

Going back to my Dura-lite example, the client maintains the content of their Flash catalog with Excel. They export the Excel file as an XML document. Figure 1-11 shows how to do this. I can't show the Dura-lite Excel file for commercial reasons, but the screenshot gives you an idea of the process they use.

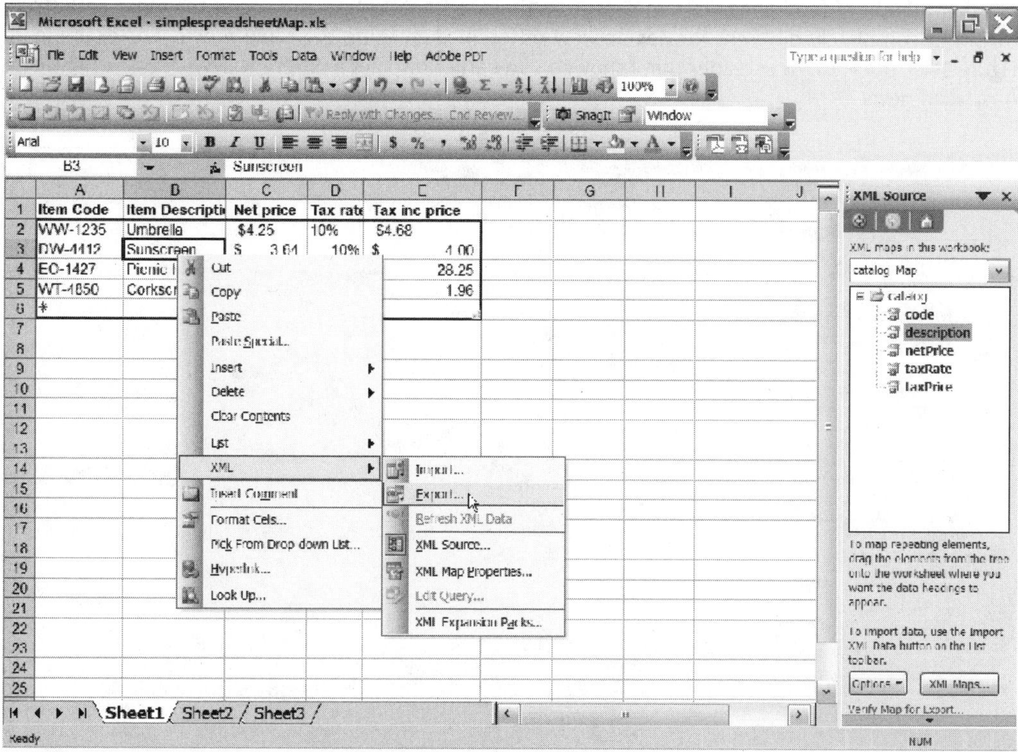

Figure 1-11. Exporting XML data from an Excel spreadsheet

Figure 1-12 shows the web interface that Dura-lite uses to upload a new XML file. This is in a password-protected area so I'm unable to provide a link to the page, but the screenshot should give you the general idea.

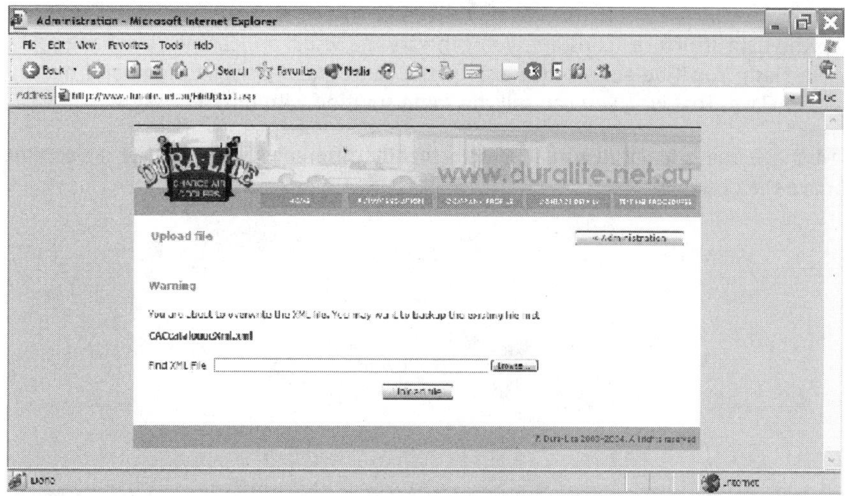

Figure 1-12. Dura-lite uses a web interface to upload their new XML files.

Another benefit of separating Flash movies from their content is that you can use the same data structure with completely different movies or view different data using the same movie. For example, in Figure 1-13, the Flash newsreader that I showed you earlier displays a different news feed—in this case Australian news.

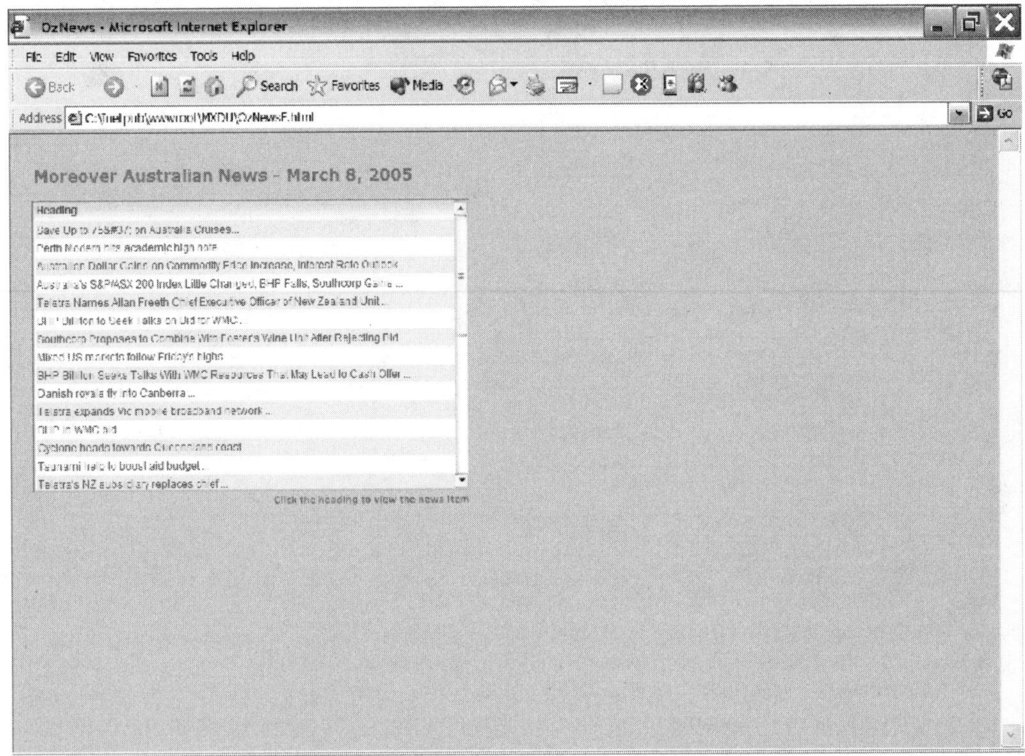

Figure 1-13. The same Flash movie can be used to access multiple sources of information.

If you keep the data structures constant, you can vary the visual appearance by changing Library elements within Flash. You'll be able to use exactly the same ActionScript to load and display the XML content within Flash. That way, you can sell the same solution with different skins.

Figure 1-14 shows the original newsreader with slightly different styling. I make no comment about how attractive the design is!

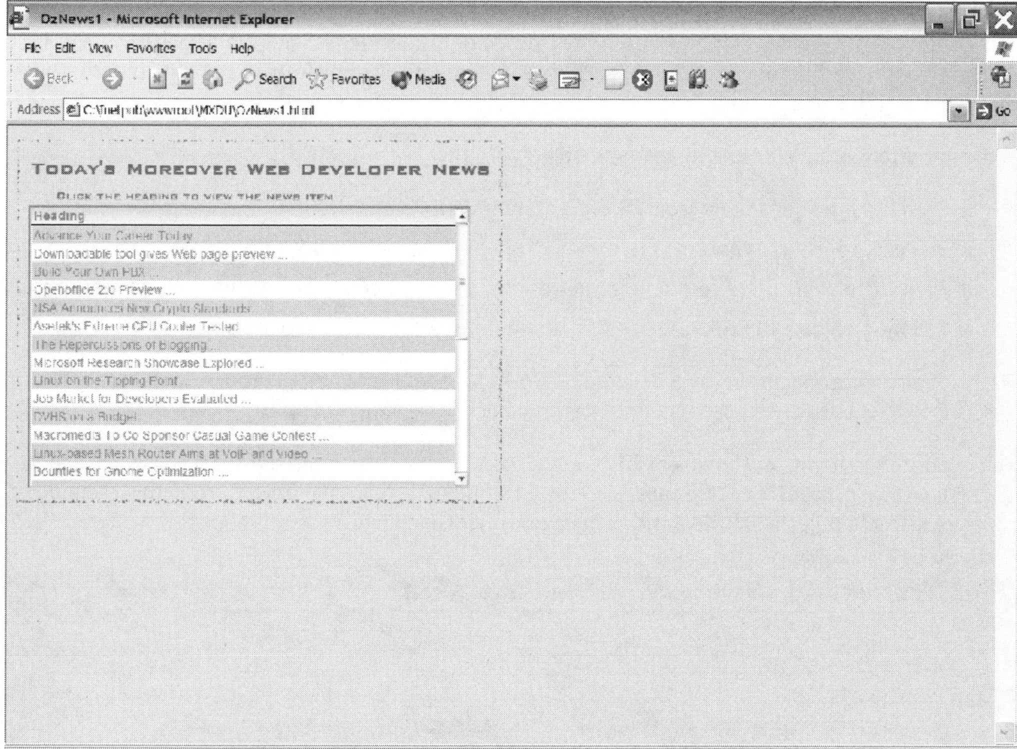

Figure 1-14. The same source of information can be used with different Flash movies.

Specific applications for Flash

Some applications are particularly well suited to Flash. XML-driven maps, stock tickers, and photo gallery examples abound on the Web.

E-learning is another area where Flash is proving very useful. Combining Flash with XML allows distribution of e-learning applications on CD-ROMs. You can run the applications in stand-alone mode without the need for an Internet connection or even a Flash Player. These applications have all the benefits of dynamic data with the flexibility of a portable format.

Flash as a learning tool

In my part of the world, there is a joint project to produce online content for students and teachers. The project, called the Le@rning Federation, is an initiative of the governments of Australia, the Australian states, and New Zealand. You can find out more about the project at `www.thelearningfederation.edu.au/`.

The project works in priority areas such as science, languages other than English, literacy, and numeracy. Content has been developed in each area to support specific learning objectives. The aim is to create a pool of resource materials for teachers and students. Schools can access the content online, through e-learning management systems or servers.

Some important principles for the learning objects are that

- Data is stored separately from its presentation.
- It is easy to modify content.
- Learning objects use a common framework for different contexts, i.e., they can be repurposed.
- Learning objects can operate as stand-alone objects that don't require server interaction.

Flash coupled with XML is an ideal delivery platform for these learning objects. A high proportion of learning objects already created use these technologies.

The website contains a showcase of sample content at `www.thelearningfederation.edu.au/tlf2/showMe.asp?nodeID=242#groups`. Figure 1-15 shows a learning object from the "stampede" series of learning objects that deal with languages other than English.

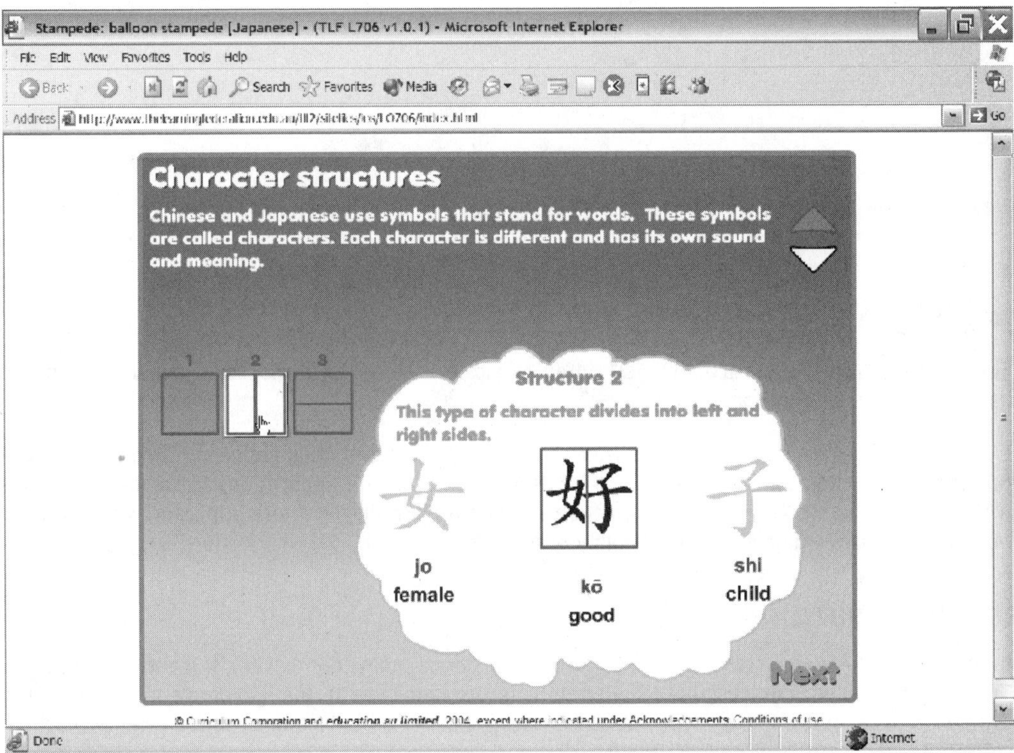

Figure 1-15. A learning object about understanding Chinese and Japanese characters

Creating Flash applications with Flex

Macromedia Flex is an alternative means of creating Flash applications. It is a presentation server that is installed on a web server. At the time of writing, Flex was only available for Sun's Java 2 Enterprise Edition (J2EE) application servers.

Flex includes a library of components and uses Macromedia's Maximum Experience Markup Language (MXML), an XML-based language to describe the interface for an application with ActionScript. MXML lays out the visual components and defines aspects like data sources and data bindings. You can also extend MXML with custom components.

You write the MXML in XML files using a text or XML editor. You can also use Macromedia's Flex Builder. Each MXML file must end with the file extension `.mxml`. Learning about XML will help you to use Flex to create applications.

I haven't covered Flex in this book as it could be an entire book in its own right. You can find out more about it at `www.macromedia.com/software/flex/`.

Summary

In this chapter, I covered a brief introduction to Flash and XML. I looked at some of the reasons why developers might use Flash with XML in their applications. I also showed you some sample applications that use Flash and XML together.

In the next chapter, I'll introduce you to XML and explain how to create XML documents. We'll look at the meaning of the word *well formed* and examine the differences between XML, HTML, and XHTML. Chapter 3 will go into more detail about XML documents and we'll look at Document Type Definitions (DTDs), XML schemas, and Extensible Stylesheet Language Transformations (XSLT). If you have experience in working with XML documents, you might want to skip ahead to Chapter 4, where we'll start to build Flash XML applications.

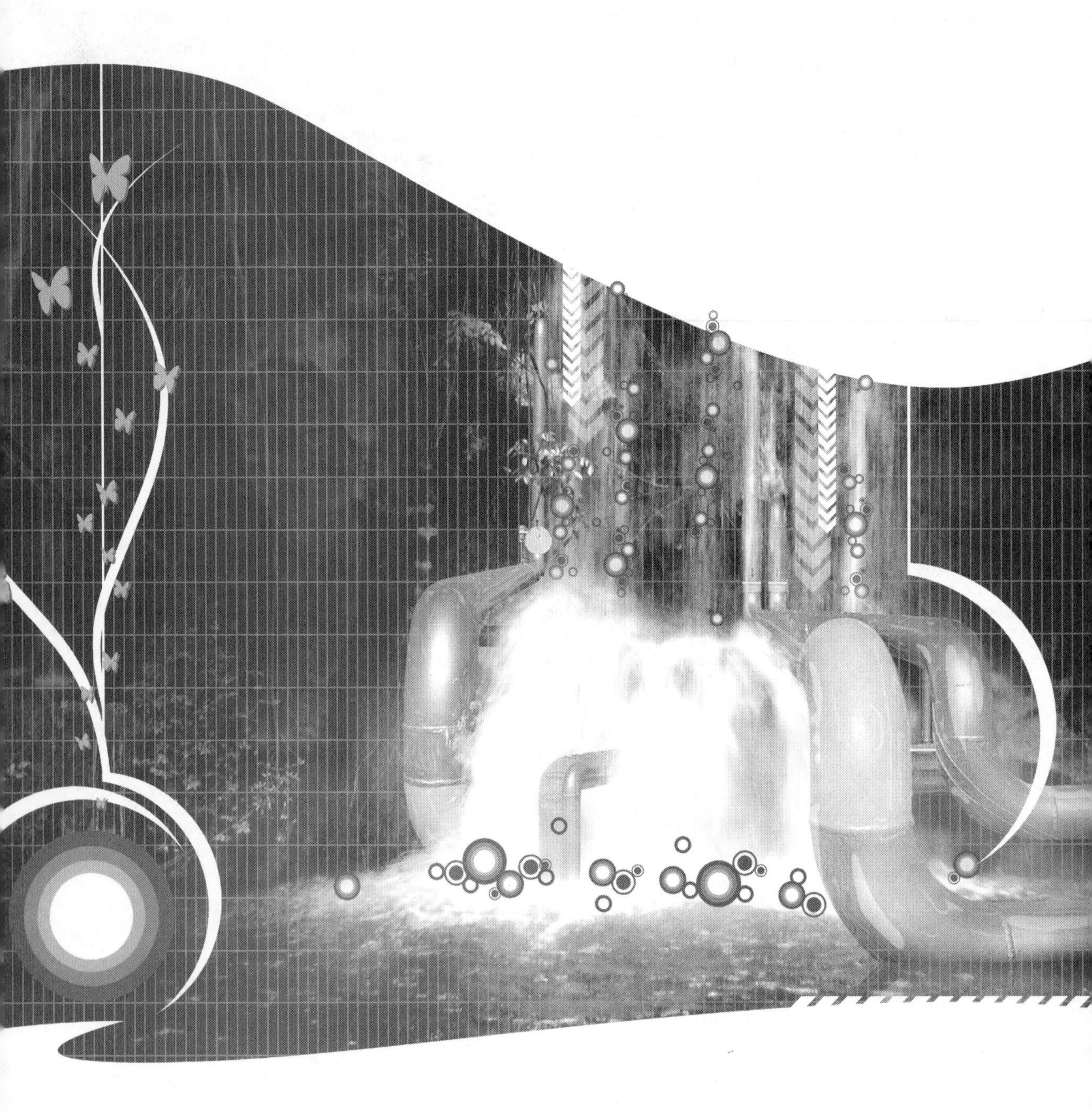

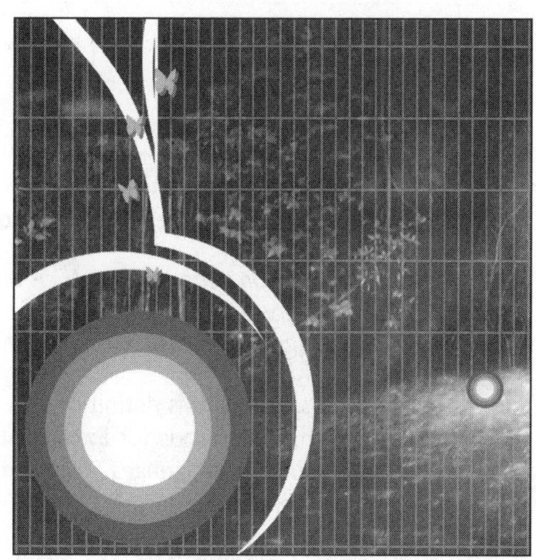

Chapter 2

INTRODUCTION TO XML

If you work in the web design or development area, you've probably heard of XML. You may have come across it when you were learning how to write web pages or when you started exploring web services. Many software programs share information using XML documents, and Office 2003 for PCs lets you work with XML documents. So what is all the hype about and why should you know about XML?

XML is rapidly becoming the standard for exchanging information between applications, people, and over the Internet. Both humans and computers can read XML documents, and as a format, XML is flexible enough to be adapted for many different purposes.

This chapter introduces you to XML. It explains some of the basic concepts, including the rules governing the structure of XML documents. You'll also learn about some of the uses for XML and the reasons why should you start to use XML in your projects. I show some examples of XML documents, and by the end of the chapter, you'll have a solid understanding of XML and related concepts.

I'll expand on the concepts covered here in Chapter 3, where we'll look at using an XML editor and creating XML content with Office 2003. I'll also look at some related topics—defining XML document rules with schemas and changing the appearance of XML documents with transformations.

What is XML?

Let's start by answering the most basic question: What is XML?

The World Wide Web Consortium (W3C) provides the following definition for XML in their glossary at `www.w3.org/TR/DOM-Level-2-Core/glossary.html`:

Extensible Markup Language (XML) is an extremely simple dialect of SGML. The goal is to enable generic SGML to be served, received, and processed on the Web in the way that is now possible with HTML. XML has been designed for ease of implementation and for interoperability with both SGML and HTML.

As you can see from this definition, it's very difficult to explain XML in a single sentence or paragraph. To start with, XML stands for **Extensible Markup Language**. Extensible means that you can use XML to create your own languages. The term markup means that the languages you create use tags to surround or mark up text.

XML is not a markup language like HTML. It is a meta-language that you can use to create other markup languages. The languages that you create work with structured data, and you use XML to invent tags that describe your data and the data structures. You can use different tags each time you create an XML document, or you can use the same tags for different documents.

Groups have created their own languages based on XML. This allows them to share information specific to their industry or area of expertise using a common set of markup tags and structures.

One example, Chemical Markup Language (CML), allows scientists to share molecular information in a standardized way. There are specific rules for structuring CML documents and referring to molecular information. MathML is another example of a standard language using XML. XML documents can use MathML to describe mathematical operations.

Extensible HTML (XHTML) is an example that is probably more familiar to you. XHTML was created when HTML was rewritten according to XML rules.

Think about the tags you use in XHTML—`<p></p>`, `<h1></h1>`. These tags mark up information on a web page, and you use them in a specific way, according to some predefined rules. For instance, one rule says that you can't include `<p></p>` tags in the `<head>` section of a web page.

Being familiar with these rules means that you can open any web page written in XHTML and understand the structure. It also means that any software package that knows the XHTML rules can display a web page.

By itself, XML doesn't do anything other than store information. It's not a programming language in its own right. XML documents need humans or software packages to process the information that they contain.

XML documents work best with structured information such as names and addresses, product catalogs, and lists of documents—anything with a standardized format. You can store hierarchical information within XML documents, a bit like storing information in a database. Instead of breaking the information into tables and fields, you use elements and tags to describe the data.

This concept is a little easier to explore with an example. Most of us have a phone book that we use to store contact information for our friends and colleagues. You probably have the information in a software package like Microsoft Outlook or Outlook Express.

Your phone book contains many different names but you store the same information about each contact — their name, phone number, and address. The way the information is stored depends on the software package you've chosen. If the manufacturer changed the package or discontinued it, you'd have to find a new way to store information about your contacts.

Transferring the information to a new software program is likely to be difficult. You'd have to export it from the first package, rearrange the contents to suit the second package, and then import the data. Most software applications don't share a standard format for contact data, although some can talk to each other. You have to rely on the standards created by each company.

As an alternative, you can use XML to store the information. You create your own tag names to describe the data; tags like `<contact>`, <phone>, and `<address>` provide clear descriptions for your information. Anyone else who looks at the file will be able to understand what information you are storing.

Because your phone book XML document is in a standard format, you can display the details on a web page. Web browsers contain an XML parser to process the XML content. You can also print out your contacts or even build a Flash movie to display and manage your contacts.

Your friends could agree on which tags to use and share their address books with each other. You can all save your contacts in the same place and use tags to determine who has contributed each entry. When you use a standardized structure for storage, the ways that you can work with the information are endless.

How did XML start?

XML has been around since 1998. It is based on Standard Generalized Markup Language (SGML), which in turn was created out of General Markup Language (GML) in the 1960s. XML is actually a simplified version of SGML.

SGML describes how to write languages, specifically those that work with text in electronic documents. SGML is also an international standard—ISO 8879. Interestingly enough, SGML was one of the considerations for HTML when it was first developed.

The first XML recommendation was released in February 1998. Since then, XML has increased in popularity, and it's now a worldwide standard for sharing information. Human beings, databases, and many popular software packages all use XML documents to store and share information. Web services also use an XML format to share information over the Internet.

The W3C developed the XML specification. This organization also works with other recommendations such as HTML and XHTML. Detailed information about the XML specification is available at the W3C's website at `www.w3c.org/XML/`. At the time of writing, the current specification was for XML 1.1. You can view this specification at `www.w3.org/TR/2004/REC-xml11-20040204/`.

Goals of XML

When it created XML, the W3C published the following goals at `www.w3.org/TR/REC-xml/#sec-origin-goals`:

1. XML shall be straightforwardly usable over the Internet.
2. XML shall support a wide variety of applications.
3. XML shall be compatible with SGML.
4. It shall be easy to write programs which process XML documents.
5. The number of optional features in XML is to be kept to the absolute minimum, ideally zero.
6. XML documents should be human-legible and reasonably clear.
7. The XML design should be prepared quickly.
8. The design of XML shall be formal and concise.
9. XML documents shall be easy to create.
10. Terseness in XML markup is of minimal importance.

In other words, XML should be easy to use in a variety of settings, by both people and software applications. The rules for XML documents should be clear so they are easy to create.

So how do we create XML documents?

Creating XML documents

Before we start, it's important to understand what we mean by the term *XML document*. The term refers to a collection of content that meets XML construction rules. When we work with XML, the term document has a more general meaning than with software packages. In Flash, for example, a document is a physical file.

While an XML document can be one or more physical files, it can also refer to a stream of information that doesn't exist in a physical sense. You can create these streams using server-side files; you'll see how this is done later in this book. As long as the information is structured according to XML rules, it qualifies as an XML document.

XML documents contain information and markup. You can divide markup into

- Elements
- Attributes
- Text
- Entities
- Comments
- CDATA

Elements

Each XML document contains one or more elements. Elements identify and mark up content, and they make up the bulk of an XML document. Some people call elements *nodes*.

Here is an element:

```
<tag>Some text</tag>
```

This element contains two tags and some text. Elements can also include other elements. They can even be empty, i.e., they contain no text.

As in HTML, XML tags start and end with less-than and greater-than signs. The name of the tag is stored in between these signs—<tagName>.

The terms element and tag have a slightly different meaning.

A tag looks like this:

```
<tagName>
```

whereas an element looks like this:

```
<tag>Some text</tag>
```

If an element contains information or other elements, it will include both an opening and closing tag—<tag></tag>. Empty elements can also be written in a single tag—<tag/>—so that

```
<tagname></tagname>
```

is equivalent to

```
<tagname/>
```

There is no preferred way to write empty tags. Either option is acceptable.

You can split elements across more than one line as shown here:

```
<contact>
  Some text
</contact>
```

Each element has a name that must follow a standard naming convention. The names start with either a letter or the underscore character. They can't start with a number. Element names can contain any letter or number, but they can't include spaces. Although it's technically possible to include a colon (:) character in an element name, it's not a good idea as these are used when referring to namespaces. You'll understand what that means a little later in the chapter.

You usually give elements meaningful names that describe the content inside the tags. The element name

```
<fullName>Sas Jacobs</fullName>
```

is more useful than

```
<axbjd>Sas Jacobs</axbjd>
```

You can't include a space between the opening bracket < and the element name. You are allowed to include space anywhere else, and it's common to include a space before the /> for empty elements. In the early days of XHTML, older browsers required the extra space for tags such as `<br />` and `<hr />`.

When an element contains another element, the container element is called the *parent* and the element inside is the *child*.

```
<tagname>
  <childTag>Text being marked up</childTag>
</tagname>
```

The family analogy continues with *grandparent* and *grandchild* elements as well as *siblings*.

You can also mix the content of elements, i.e., they contain text as well as child elements:

```
<tagname>
  Text being <childTag>marked up</childTag>
</tagname>
```

The first element in an XML document is called the *root element*, *document root*, or *root node*. It contains all the other elements in the document. Each XML document can have only one root element. The last tag in an XML document will nearly always be the closing tag for the root element.

XML is case sensitive. For example, <phoneBook> and </phonebook> are not equivalent tags and can't be used in the same element. This is a big difference from HTML.

Elements serve many functions in an XML document:

- Elements mark up content. The opening and closing tags surround text.
- Tag names provide a description of the content they mark up. This gives you a clue about the purpose of the element.
- Elements provide information about the order of data in an XML document.
- The position of child elements can show their importance.
- Elements show the relationships between blocks of information. Like databases, they show how one piece of data relates to others.

Attributes

Attributes supply additional information about an element. They provide information that clarifies or modifies an element.

Attributes are stored in the start tag of an element after the element name. They are pairs of names and related values, and each attribute must include both the name and the value:

```
<tagname attributeName="attributeValue">
  Text being marked up
</tagname>
```

Attribute values appear within quotation marks and are separated from the attribute name with an equals sign. You can use either single or double quotes around the attribute value. Interestingly enough, you can also mix and match your quotes in the same element:

```
<tagname attribute1="value1" attribute2='value2'>
```

You might choose to use double quotes where a value contains an apostrophe:

```
<person name="o'mahoney">
```

You would use single quotes where double quotes make up part of the value:

```
<photo caption='It was an "interesting" day'>
```

Keep in mind that tags can't be included within an attribute.

An XHTML image tag provides an example of an element that contains attributes:

```
<img src="logo.gif" width="20" height="15" alt="Company logo"/>
```

There is no limit to number of attributes within an element, but attributes inside the same element must have unique names. When you are working with multiple attributes in an element, the order isn't important.

Attribute names must follow the same naming conventions as elements. You can't start the name with a number, and you can't include spaces in the name. Some attribute names are reserved, and you shouldn't use them in your XML documents. These include

- xml:lang
- xml:space
- xml:link
- xml:attribute

You can rewrite attributes as nested elements. The following

```
<contact id="1">
  <name>Sas Jacobs</name>
</contact>
```

could also be written as

```
<contact>
  <id>1</id>
  <name>Sas Jacobs</name>
</contact>
```

There is no one right way to structure elements and attributes. The method you choose depends on your data. The way you're going to process the XML document might also impact on your choices. Some software packages find it harder to work with attributes compared with elements.

Text

Text refers to any information contained between opening and closing element tags. In the line that follows, the text Sas Jacobs is stored between the <fullName> and </fullName> tags:

```
<fullName>Sas Jacobs</fullName>
```

Unless you specify otherwise, the text between the opening and closing tags in an element will always be processed as if it was XML. This means that special characters such as < and > have to be replaced with the entities < and >. The alternative is to use CDATA to present the information, and I'll go into that a little later.

I've listed the common entities that you'll need to use in Table 2-1.

Table 2-1. Entities commonly used in XML documents

Character	Entity
<	<
>	>
'	'
"	"
&	&

Entities

Character entities are symbols that represent a single character. In HTML, character entities are used for special symbols such as an ampersand (&) and a nonbreaking space ( ).

Character entities replace reserved characters in XML documents. All tags start with a less-than sign so it would be confusing to include another one in your code.

```
<expression>3 < 5</expression>
```

This code would cause an error during processing. If you want to include a less-than sign in text, you can use the entity <:

```
<expression>3 &lt; 5</expression>
```

Some entities use Unicode numbers. You can use numbers to insert characters that you can't type on a keyboard. For example, the entity é creates the character **é**—an e with an acute accent. The number 233 is the Unicode number for the character **é**.

You can also use a hexadecimal number to refer to a character. In that case, you need to include an x in the number so the reference would start with &#x. The hexadecimal entity reference for **é** is é.

The Character Map in Windows tells you what codes to use. Open it by choosing Start ➤ All Programs ➤ Accessories ➤ System Tools ➤ Character Map. Figure 2-1 shows the Character Map dialog box.

The bottom left of the window shows the hexadecimal value. Don't forget to remove the trailing zeroes and add &#x to the beginning of the value. The right side shows the Unicode number. Again, you'll need to remove the first 0 from the code.

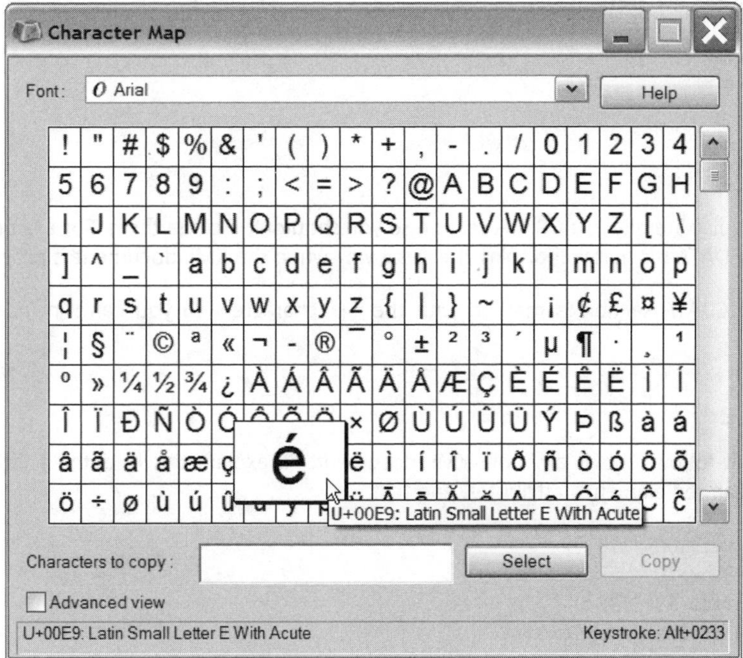

Figure 2-1. The character map in Windows displaying the small letter e with an acute accent

Comments

Comments in XML work the same as in HTML. They begin with the characters <!-- and end with -->:

```
<!-- here is a commented line -->
```

Comments are a useful way to leave messages for other users of an XML document without affecting the way the XML document is processed. In fact, processing software always ignores comments in XML documents. You can also use comments to hide a single line or a block of code.

The only requirements for comments in XML documents are that

- A comment can't appear before the first line XML declaration.
- Comments can't be nested or included within tag names.
- You can't include --> inside a comment.
- Comments shouldn't split tags, i.e., you shouldn't comment out just a start or ending tag.

CDATA

CDATA stands for character data. CDATA blocks mark text so that it isn't processed as XML. For example, you could use CDATA for information containing characters such as < and >. Any < or > character contained within CDATA won't be processed as part of a tag name.

CDATA sections start with `<![CDATA` and finish with `]]>`. The character data is contained within square brackets [ ] inside the section:

```
<![CDATA[
  3 < 5
  or
  2 > 0
]]>
```

Entities will display literally in a CDATA section so you shouldn't include them. For example, if you add `<` to your CDATA block it will display the same way when the XML document is processed.

The end of a CDATA section is marked with the `]]>` characters so you can't include these inside CDATA.

An example

The listing that follows shows a simple XML document. I'll explain this in detail a little later in the chapter. You can see elements, attributes, and text:

```
<?xml version="1.0"?>
<phoneBook>
  <contact id="1">
    <name>Sas Jacobs</name>
    <address>123 Some Street, Some City, Some Country</address>
    <phone>123 456</phone>
  </contact>
</phoneBook>
```

XML document parts

An XML document contains different parts. It will always start with a *prolog*. The remainder of the XML document is contained within the document root or root element.

Document prolog

The document prolog appears at the top of an XML document and contains information about the XML document as a whole. It must appear before the root element in the document. The prolog is a bit like the <head> section of an HTML document. It can also include comments.

XML declaration

The prolog usually starts with an XML declaration, although this is optional. If you do include a declaration, it must be the first line of your XML document. The declaration tells software applications and humans that the content is an XML document:

```
<?xml version="1.0"?>
```

The XML declaration includes an XML version, in this case 1.0. At the time of writing, the latest recommendation was XML 1.1. However, you should continue to use the `version="1.0"` attribute value for backward compatibility with XML processors. For example, adding a version 1.1 declaration causes an error when the XML document is opened in Microsoft Internet Explorer 6.

The XML declaration can also include the `encoding` and `standalone` attributes.

XML documents contain characters that follow the Unicode standard, maintained by the Unicode Consortium. You can find out more at `www.unicode.org/`.

Encoding determines the character set for the XML document. You can use Unicode character sets UFT-8 and UTF-16 or ISO character sets like ISO 8859-1, Latin-1 Western Europe. If no encoding attribute is included, it is assumed that the document uses UTF-8 encoding. Languages like Japanese and Chinese need UTF-16 encoding. Western European languages often use ISO 8859-1 to cope with the accents that aren't part of the English language.

The `encoding` attribute must appear after the `version` attribute:

```
<?xml version="1.0" encoding="UTF-8"?>
<?xml version="1.0" encoding="UTF-16"?>
<?xml version="1.0" encoding="ISO-8859-1">
```

The `standalone` attribute indicates whether the XML document uses external information, such as a Document Type Definition (DTD). A DTD specifies the rules about which elements and attributes to use in the XML document. It also provides information about the number of times each element can appear and whether an element is required or optional.

The `standalone` attribute is optional but must appear as the last attribute in the declaration. The value `standalone="no"` can't be used when you are including an external DTD or style sheet.

```
<?xml version="1.0" encoding="UTF-8" standalone="yes"?>
```

Processing instructions

The prolog can also include processing instructions (PI). These instructions pass information about the XML document to other applications.

Processing instructions start with <? and finish with ?>. The first item in a PI is a name, called the PI target. PI names that start with *xml* are reserved.

A common PI is the inclusion of an external XSLT style sheet. This PI must appear before the document root:

```
<?xml-stylesheet type="text/xsl" href="listStyle.xsl"?>
```

Processing instructions can also appear in other places in the XML document.

Document Type Definitions

Document Type Definitions (DTDs), or DOCTYPE declarations, appear in the prolog. These are rules about the elements and attributes within the XML document. A DTD provides information about which elements are legal in an XML document and tells you which elements are required and which are optional. In other words, a DTD provides the rules for a valid XML document.

The prolog can include a set of declarations about the XML document, a reference to an external DTD, or both. This code shows an external DTD reference:

```
<?xml version="1.0"?>
<!DOCTYPE phoneBook SYSTEM "phoneBook.dtd">
```

We'll look at DTDs in more detail in Chapter 3.

Tree

Everything that isn't in the prolog is contained within the document tree. This includes the elements, attributes, and text in a hierarchical structure. The root node is the trunk of the tree. You call the child elements of the root node branches.

As we've seen, elements can include other elements or attributes. They can also contain text values or a mixture of both. HTML provides good examples of mixed content.

```
<p>This is a paragraph element with an element <br/> inside</p>
```

This distinction becomes important when you use a schema to describe the structure of the document tree.

Document root

An XML document can have only one root element. All of the elements within an XML document are contained within this root element.

The root element can have any name at all, providing that it conforms to the standard element naming conventions. In HTML documents, you can think of the `<html>` tag as the root element.

White space

XML documents include white space so that humans can read them more easily. White space refers to spaces, tabs, and returns that space out the content in the document. The XML specification allows you to include white space anywhere within an XML document except before the XML declaration.

XML processors do take notice of white space in a document, but many won't display the spaces. For example, Internet Explorer won't display more than one space at a time when it displays an XML or XHTML document.

If white space is important, maybe for poetry or a screenplay, you can use the xml:space attribute in an element. There are two possible values for this attribute: default and preserve. Choosing the default value is the same as leaving out the attribute.

You can add the xml:space="preserve" attribute to the root node of a document to preserve all space within the document tree:

```
<phoneBook xml:space="preserve">
```

Namespaces

XML documents can get very complicated. One XML document can reference another XML document, and different rules may apply for each. When this happens, it's possible that two different XML documents will use the same element names.

In order to overcome this problem, we use *namespaces*. Namespaces associate XML elements with an owner. A namespace ensures that each element name is unique within a document, even if other elements use the same name.

You can find out more about namespaces by reading the latest recommendation at the W3C website. At the time of writing, this was the "Namespaces in XML 1.1" recommendation at www.w3.org/TR/2004/REC-xml-names11-20040204/.

It isn't compulsory to use namespaces in your XML documents, but it can be a good idea. Namespaces are also useful when you start to work with schemas and style sheets. We'll look at some examples of schemas and style sheets in the next chapter.

Each namespace includes a reference to a Uniform Resource Identifier (URI). A URI is an Internet address, and each URI must be unique in the XML document. The URIs used in an XML document don't have to point to anything, although they often will.

You can define a namespace using the xmlns attribute within an element. Each namespace usually has a prefix that you use to identify elements belonging to that namespace. You can't start your prefixes with *xml*, and they shouldn't include spaces.

```
<FOE:fullName xmlns:FOE="http://www.friendsofed.com/">
  Sas Jacobs
</FOE:fullName>
```

In the preceding element, the FOE prefix refers to the namespace http://www.friendsofed.com/. I've prefixed the element <fullName> with FOE, and I can use it with other elements and attributes.

```
<FOE:address>
  123 Some Street, Some City, Some Country
</FOE:address>
```

I'll then be able to tell that the <address> element also comes from the http://www.friendsofed.com/ namespace.

You can also define a namespace without using a prefix. If you do this, the namespace will apply to all elements that don't have a prefix or namespace defined.

The following listing shows how to use a namespace with no prefix in an XML element:

```
<contact id="1" xmlns="http://www.friendsofed.com/">
  <name>Sas Jacobs</name>
  <address>123 Some Street, Some City, Some Country</address>
  <phone>123 456</phone>
</contact>
```

The namespace applies to all the child elements of the <contact> element so the <name>, <address>, and <phone> elements will use the default namespace `http://www.friendsofed.com/`.

Namespaces will become clearer when we start working with schemas and style sheets in Chapter 3.

A simple XML document

So far, we've covered some of the rules for creating XML documents. We've looked at the different types of content within an XML document and seen some XML fragments. Now it's time to put these rules together to create a complete XML document.

The following listing shows a simple XML document based on the phone book that I talked about earlier. I use the example throughout the rest of this chapter.

```
<?xml version="1.0"?>
<phoneBook>
  <contact id="1">
    <name>Sas Jacobs</name>
    <address>123 Some Street, Some City, Some Country</address>
    <phone>123 456</phone>
  </contact>
  <contact id="2">
    <name>John Smith</name>
    <address>4 Another Street, Another City, Another Country</address>
    <phone>456 789</phone>
  </contact>
</phoneBook>
```

I've saved this document in the resource file `address.xml`.

The first line declares the document as an XML document. The declaration is not required, but it's good practice to include it. A software package that opens the file will immediately identify it as an XML document.

The remaining lines of the XML document contain elements. The first element, <phoneBook>, contains the other elements: <contact>, <name>, <address>, and <phone>. There is a hierarchical relationship between these elements.

There are two <contact> elements. They share the same *parent*, <phoneBook>, and are *child nodes* of that element. They are also *siblings* to each other.

The <contact> tag is a container for the <name>, <address>, and <phone> elements, and they are *child elements* of the <contact> tag. The <name>, <address>, and <phone> elements are *grandchildren* of the <phoneBook> element.

You'll notice that the last line is a closing </phoneBook> tag written with exactly the same capitalization as the first tag.

Each <contact> tag has a single attribute—id. Attributes normally provide extra information about a specific element, in this case a unique identifier for each <contact>.

As we saw earlier, the element

```
<contact id="1">
```

can be rewritten as

```
<contact>
  <id>1</id>
</contact>
```

In this document tree, the trunk of the tree is the <phoneBook> tag. Branching out from that are the <contact> tags, and each <contact> has <name>, <address>, and <phone> branches.

Figure 2-2 shows the relationship between the elements in the phone book XML document.

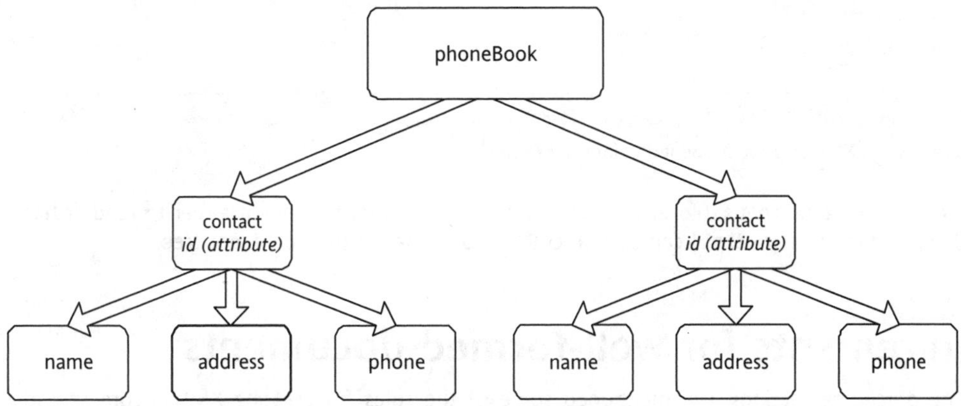

Figure 2-2. The hierarchy of elements within the phone book XML document

In this example, I've created my own tag names. The names I've chosen tell you about the type of information that I'm working with so it's easy to figure out what I'm describing.

If I want to share the rules for my phone book XML document with other people, I can create a DTD or XML schema to describe how to use the tags. Adding a reference to the DTD or schema will ensure that any XML documents that I create follow the rules. This process is called *validating* an XML document. I'll look at working with DTDs and schemas in the next chapter.

I can view an XML document by opening it in a web browser. Figure 2-3 shows `address.xml` displayed in Internet Explorer.

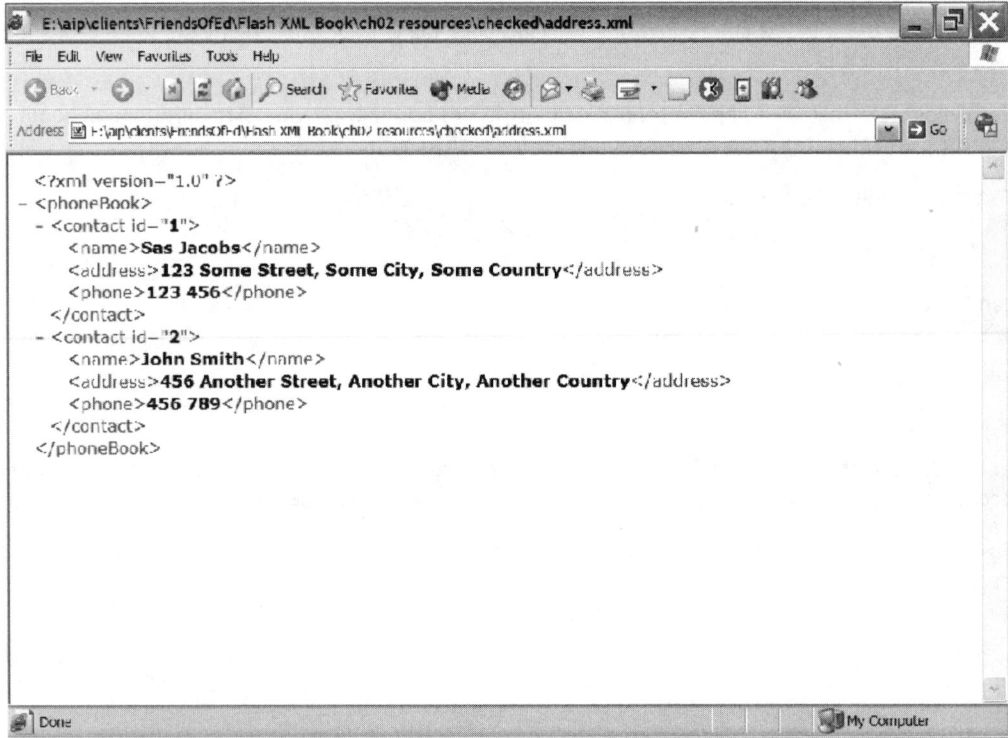

Figure 2-3. An XML document opened in Internet Explorer

You can see that Internet Explorer has formatted the document to make it easier to read. It has also added some minus signs that I can click to collapse branches of the document tree.

Requirements for well-formed documents

In the preceding sections, I've mentioned some of the rules for creating XML documents. In this section, we look at these rules in more detail. Documents that meet the requirements are said to be *well formed*.

XHTML provides us with a standard set of predefined tags. We have to use the `<ul> <li> </li> </ul>` tags when we want to create a list. Because there are no predefined tags in XML documents, it's important that the rules for creating documents are strict. You can create any tags you like, providing that you stick to these rules.

Well-formed documents meet the following criteria:

- The document contains one or more elements.
- The document contains a single root element, which may contain other nested elements.
- Each element closes properly.
- Start and end tags have matching case.
- Elements nest correctly.
- Attribute values are contained in quotes.

I'll look at each of these rules in a little more detail.

Element structure

An XML document must have at least one element: the document root. It doesn't have to have any other content, although in most cases it will.

The following XML document is well formed as it contains a single element <phoneBook>:

```
<?xml version="1.0"?>
<phoneBook/>
```

Of course, this document doesn't contain any information so it's not likely to be very useful.

It's more likely that you'll create an XML document where the root element contains other elements. The following listing shows an example of this structure:

```
<?xml version="1.0"?>
<phoneBook>
  <contact id="1">
    <name>Sas Jacobs</name>
    <address>123 Some Street, Some City, Some Country</address>
    <phone>123 456</phone>
  </contact>
</phoneBook>
```

As long as all of the elements are contained inside a single root element, the document is well formed.

This listing shows a document without a root element. This document is not well formed.

```
<?xml version="1.0"?>
<contact id="1">
  <name>Sas Jacobs</name>
</contact>
<contact id="2">
  <name>John Smith</name>
</contact>
```

Elements must be closed

You must close all elements correctly. The way you do this depends on whether or not the element is empty, i.e., whether it contains text or other elements.

You can close empty elements by adding a forward slash to the opening tag:

```
<name/>
```

In the case of a nonempty element, you have to add a closing tag, which must appear after the opening tag:

```
<name>Sas Jacobs</name>
```

You can also write empty elements with a closing tag:

```
<name></name>
```

As XML is case sensitive, start and end tag names must match exactly. The following examples are incorrect:

```
<name>Sas Jacobs</Name>
<Name>Sas Jacobs</name>
```

You would rewrite them as

```
<name>Sas Jacobs</name>
```

The following example is also incorrect:

```
<name>Sas Jacobs
<name>John Smith
```

The elements have an opening tag but no corresponding closing tag. This rule also applies to XHTML. In XHTML, you can't use the following code, which was acceptable in HTML:

```
<p>A paragraph of information.
<p>Another paragraph.
```

I'll talk about the differences between XML, HTML, and XHTML a little later in this chapter.

Elements must nest correctly

You must close elements in the correct order. In other words, child elements must close before their parent elements.

This line is incorrect:

```
<contact><name>Sas Jacobs</contact></name>
```

and should be rewritten as

```
<contact><name>Sas Jacobs</name></contact>
```

Use quotes for attributes

All attribute values must be contained in quotes. You can either use single or double quotes; these two lines are equivalent:

```
<contact id="1">
<contact id='1'>
```

If your attribute value contains a single quote, you have to use double quotes, and vice versa:

```
<contact name="O'Malley"/>
```

or

```
<contact nickname='John "Bo bo" Smith'/>
```

You can also replace the quote characters inside an attribute value with character entities:

```
<contact name="O&apos;Malley"/>
contact nickname='John &quot;Bo bo&quot; Smith'/>
```

Documents that aren't well formed

If you try to view an XML document that is not well formed, you'll see an error. For example, opening a document that isn't well formed in a web browser will cause an error message similar to the one shown in Figure 2-4. This is quite different from HTML documents; most web browsers will ignore any HTML errors such as missing </p> tags.

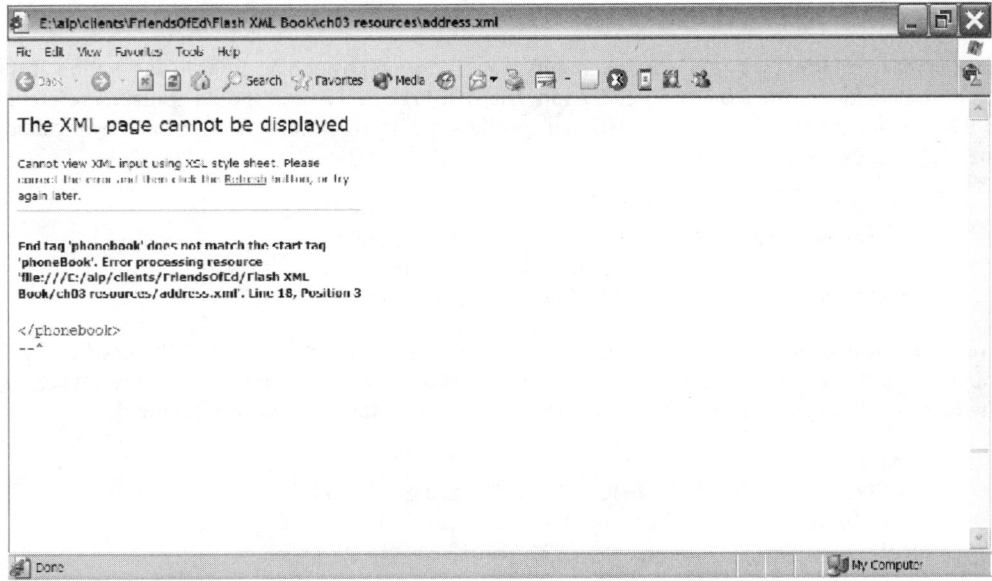

Figure 2-4. Internet Explorer displaying a document that isn't well formed

An XML editor such as XMLSpy often provides more detailed information about the error. You can see the same XML document displayed in XMLSpy in Figure 2-5.

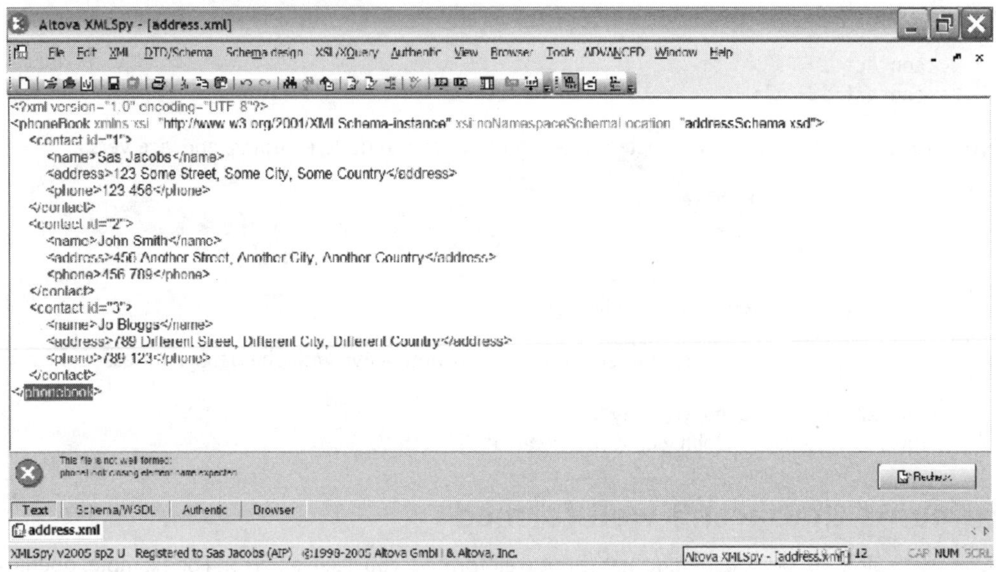

Figure 2-5. A document that is not well formed displayed in XMLSpy

The error message shows that the closing element name </phoneBook> was expected.

Well-formed XHTML documents

You can make sure that your XHTML documents are well formed by adding an XML declaration at the top of the file before the DOCTYPE declaration. The DOCTYPE declaration should contain a reference to the appropriate XHTML DTD. The DTD can specify strict or transitional conformance by including one of the following two declarations:

```
<!DOCTYPE html PUBLIC "-//W3C//DTD XHTML 1.0 Strict//EN"
"http://www.w3.org/TR/xhtml1/DTD/xhtml1-strict.dtd">
<!DOCTYPE html PUBLIC "-//W3C//DTD XHTML 1.0 Transitional//EN"
"http://www.w3.org/TR/xhtml1/DTD/xhtml1-transitional.dtd">
```

Strictly conforming documents must meet the mandatory requirements in the XHTML specification. If you are declaring a strictly conforming document, you should include a namespace in the <html> tag. The following listing shows the W3C recommendation for well-formed XHTML documents:

```
<?xml version="1.0" encoding="UTF-8"?>
<!DOCTYPE html PUBLIC "-//W3C//DTD XHTML 1.0 Strict//EN"
"http://www.w3.org/TR/xhtml1/DTD/xhtml1-strict.dtd">
<html xmlns="http://www.w3.org/1999/xhtml" xml:lang="en">
```

You can see this W3C recommendation at `www.w3.org/TR/xhtml11/conformance.html`.

Working with XML documents

You can work with XML documents in many different ways. To start with, you need to figure out how to create the document. For example, you can write the document yourself in a text editor or have it generated automatically by a software package. You can even create a stream of XML information by running a server-side web page through a web server.

You also need to consider how to work with your XML documents. Will you view them in a web browser? Will you display and update the document in Office 2003? Maybe you'll create a Flash movie that displays and updates the XML document.

Generating XML content

The simplest way to create an XML document is by typing the tags and data in your favorite text editor and saving it with an `.xml` extension. At the very minimum, you must follow the rules for well-formed XML content. You can also create a DTD or schema to describe the rules for your elements. This will allow you to ensure that your content is valid.

You can also use an XML editor to help create content. Many commercial XML editing tools are on the market. Search for **XML editors** in your favorite search engine to see a current list. I like to use XMLSpy, and I'll show you more about it in the next chapter. One advantage of XML editors is that they will color-code XML documents as well as provide code hints.

Software packages can generate XML documents automatically. Files written in PHP, ColdFusion, ASP.NET, or any other server-side language can generate XML from a database or another source. Microsoft Office 2003 for PCs also allows you to save an Office document in XML format.

Whenever you *consume* or use a web service, you'll receive the information that you request in an XML document. A web service is like an application that you can use across the Internet. Companies like Amazon and Google make some of their services available in this way. As you can imagine, Amazon doesn't want you poking around in their database so they provide web services that allow you to carry out various searches. They protect their data but still give you access.

To use a web service, you need to send a request to the provider. The request is formatted in a specific way, and there will be different requirements for each web service that you consume. You get the results back in XML format. We'll find out more about web services later in this book.

If you've used a news feed, the RSS (Rich Site Summary or Really Simple Syndication) format is an XML document. RSS uses XML to describe website changes and is really a type of web service. There are different RSS versions that you can use to provide a news feed from a website or organization. The specification for the most recent version, RSS 2.0, is at `http://blogs.law.harvard.edu/tech/rss`.

One example of an RSS feed is the news service from Macromedia. You can find out about the news feed from `www.macromedia.com/devnet/articles/xml_resource_feed.html` and view the content at `www.macromedia.com/devnet/resources/macromedia_resources.rdf`. This news feed provides information from the Macromedia Developer Center using RSS 1.0.

Using XML information

Software programs access the information in an XML document through the XML Document Object Model (DOM). The DOM is a W3C specification for programming languages that you use with XML documents. At the time of writing, version 3.0 of the DOM specification was available at `www.w3.org/TR/2004/REC-DOM-Level-3-Core-20040407/`.

The general term for any software package that processes XML documents is an *XML processor*. Many different software packages fall into this category. You can use them to view, extract, display, and validate your XML data. Word, Office, and Excel 2003 can exchange XML information and so are examples of XML processors.

XML parsers are one category of XML processors. Parsers can read through the content of an XML document and extract individual elements, attributes, and text. Parsers need to be able to separate processing instructions from elements, attributes, and text. Flash has a built-in XML parser that allows you to work with XML documents and include them in Flash movies.

XML parsers first check to see if a document is well formed. They can't use documents that aren't well formed. Earlier we saw an error message from Internet Explorer when it tried to open a document that wasn't well formed.

XML parsers fall into two categories—nonvalidating and validating parsers. All parsers check to see if a document is well formed. Validating parsers also compare the structure of the document with a DTD or XML schema to check that it is constructed correctly. A document that meets the rules listed within a DTD or schema is considered *valid* by the validating parser.

Most Web browsers are capable of displaying an XML file so that you can see the structure and content. They contain built-in parsers to process and display the XML document appropriately.

Both Internet Explorer and Mozilla Firefox contain nonvalidating XML parsers. They allow you to open and display an XML file just as you would any web page. When you open an XML file, the information structure displays using the default settings of the web browser.

Internet Explorer 6 contains version 3 of the MSXML Parser. You saw the file `address.xml` file as it appears when opened in Internet Explorer earlier in the chapter. Figure 2-6 shows the same file open in Firefox.

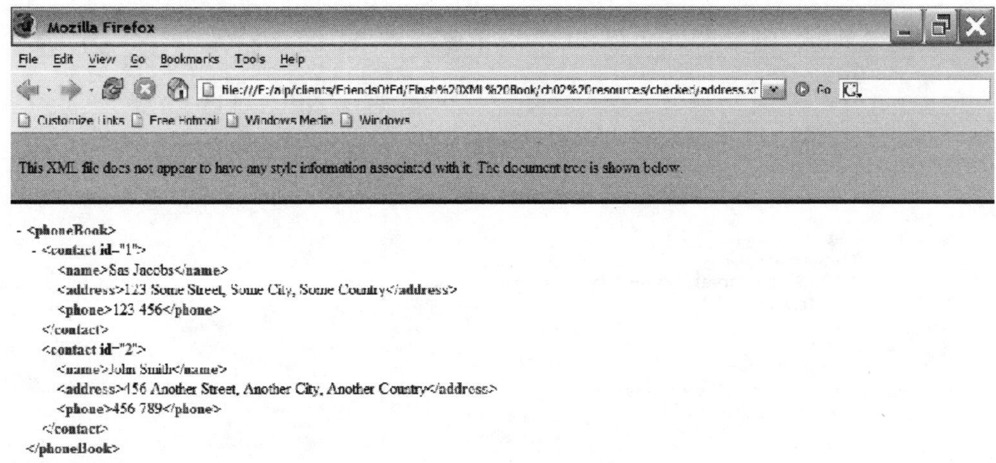

Figure 2-6. An XML file open in Firefox

You can download tools for Internet Explorer that will allow you to validate an XML file against an embedded schema. The download is called **Internet Explorer Tools for Validating XML and Viewing XSLT Output**; visit the Microsoft Download Center at `www.microsoft.com/downloads/search.aspx` for the relevant files.

By default, the tools install in a folder called `IEXMLTLS`. You'll need to right-click the `.inf` files in the folder and choose the Install option before the tools will be available within Internet Explorer.

After you have installed the IE XML tools, you can right-click an XML page that's open in Internet Explorer. The shortcut menu will have two extra options: Validate XML and View XSL Output. Figure 2-7 shows the context menu.

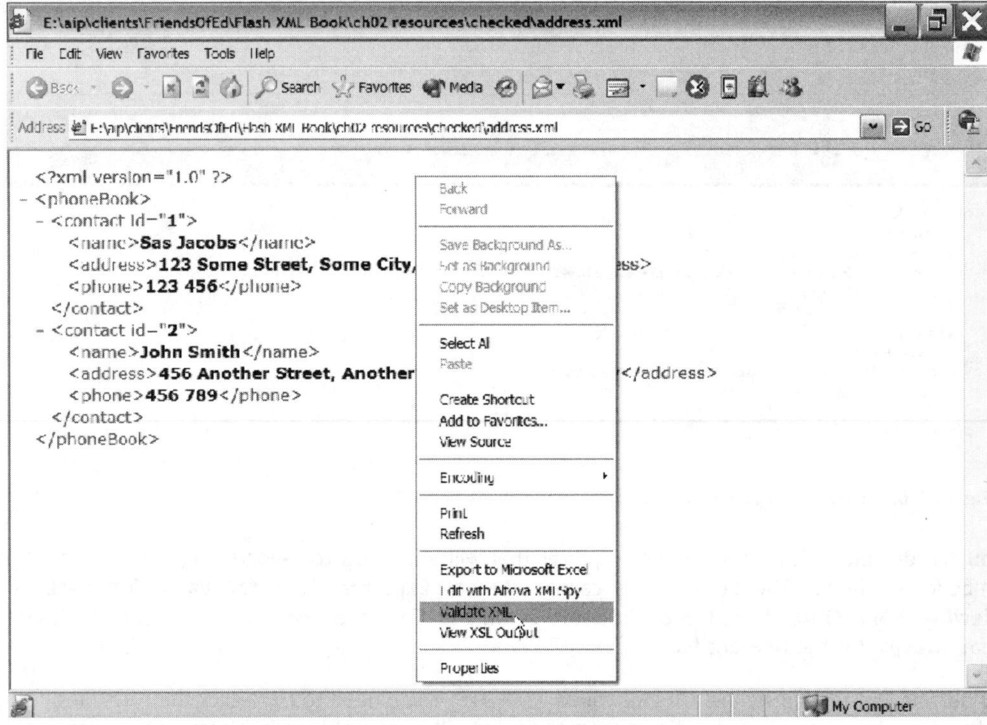

Figure 2-7. After installing the Internet Explorer XML tools, you can right click in the browser window to validate the XML or view XSL output.

Firefox contains a tool called the DOM Inspector, which displays information about the structure of the XML document. Choose Tools ➤ DOM Inspector to view the structure. Figure 2-8 shows this tool.

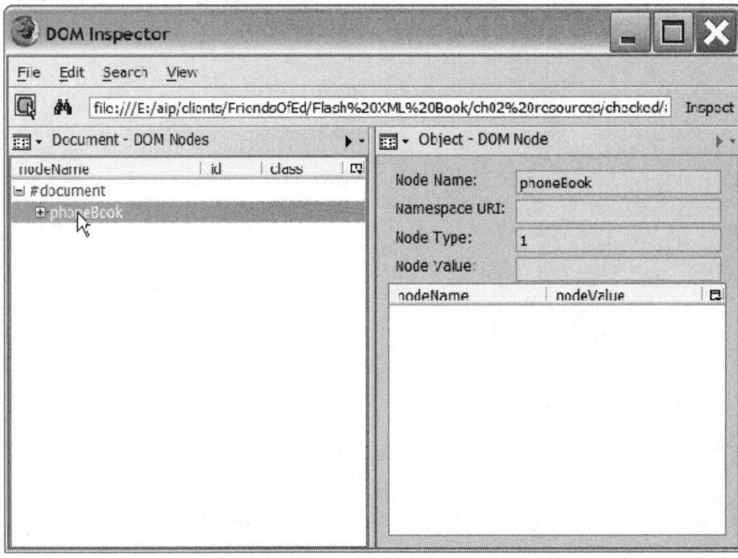

Figure 2-8. The DOM Inspector in Firefox

Flash contains a nonvalidating XML parser. This means that Flash won't check whether the XML document meets the rules set down in a DTD or XML schema. When you read in an XML document, Flash is able to convert the information into a document tree. You can then move around the tree to extract information for your Flash movie.

XML, HTML, and XHTML

Although the terms XML, HTML, and XHTML all sound similar, they're really quite different. XML and HTML are not competing technologies. They are both used for managing and displaying online information but both do different things. XML doesn't aim to replace HTML as the language for web pages. XHTML is a hybrid of the two languages.

HTML tags deal with both the information in a web page and the way it displays. In other words, HTML works with both presentation and content. It doesn't deal with the structure of the information or the meaning of different pieces of data. You can't use HTML to transform the display of information into a completely different layout. If you store information in a table, you can't easily change it into a list.

HTML was designed as a tool for sharing information online in web pages. The complex designs that appear in today's web pages weren't part of the original scope of HTML. As a result, designers often use HTML in ways that were never dreamed of when the language was first created.

The rules for using HTML aren't terribly strict. For example, you can add headings by using the tags `<h1>` to `<h6>`. The `<h1>` tag is the first level of heading, but there is no requirement to include heading tags in any particular order. The first heading in your HTML page could actually be enclosed in an `<h3>` or `<h4>` tag.

Web pages written in HTML can contain errors that don't affect the display of the information. For example, in many browsers, you could include two `<title>` tags and the page would still load. You can also forget to include a closing `</table>` tag and the table will still be rendered.

HTML is supposed to be a standard, but it works differently across web browsers. Most web developers know about the problems in designing a website so it appears the same way in Internet Explorer, Opera, Firefox, and Netscape Browser for both PCs and Macs.

Like XML, HTML comes from the Standard Generalized Markup Language (SGML). Unlike XML, HTML is not extensible. You're stuck with a standard set of tags that you can't change or extend in any way.

XML only deals with content. It describes the structure of information without concerning itself with the appearance of that information. An XML document can show relationships in your data just like a database. This just isn't possible in an HTML document.

XML content is probably easier to understand than HTML. The names of tags normally describe the data they mark up. In the example file `address.xml`, tag names such as <address> and <phone> tell you what data is contained in the element.

XML may be used to display information directly in a web page. It's more likely, though, that you'll use the XML document behind the scenes. It will probably provide the content for a web application or a Flash movie.

Compared with HTML, XML is much stricter about the way markup is used. There are rules about how tags are constructed, and we've already seen that XML documents have to be well formed. A DTD or schema can also provide extra rules for the way that elements are used. These rules can include the legal names for tags and attributes, whether they're required or optional, as well as the number of times that each element must appear. In addition, schemas specify what data type must be used for each element and attribute.

XML documents don't deal with the display of information. If you need to change the way XML data looks, you can change the appearance by using Cascading Style Sheets (CSS) or Extensible Stylesheet Language (XSL). XSL transformations offer the most power; you can use them to create XHTML from an XML document or to sort or filter a list of XML elements.

XHTML evolved so that the useful features of XML could be applied to HTML. The W3C says that XML *reformulated* HTML into XHTML. XHTML documents have much stricter construction rules and are generally more robust than their HTML counterparts.

The HTML specification provides a list of legal elements and attributes within XHTML. XML governs the way that the elements are used in documents. For example, in XHTML, you must close all tags. The HTML `<br>` tag has to be rewritten as `<br/>` or `<br></br>`. In XHTML, web designers can't use a single `<p>` tag to create a paragraph break as they could in HTML.

Another change is that you must write attribute values in full. For example

```
<input type="radio" value="JJJ" checked/>
```

has to be written as

```
<input type="radio" value="JJJ" checked="checked"/>
```

You can find the XHTML specification at `www.w3.org/TR/xhtml1/`. It became a recommendation in 2000 and was revised in 2002.

I've summarized the main changes from HTML to XHTML:

- You should include a DOCTYPE declaration specifying that the document is an XHTML document.
- You can optionally include an XML declaration.
- You must write all tags in lowercase.
- All elements must be closed.
- All attributes must be enclosed in quotation marks.
- All tags must be correctly nested.
- The `id` attribute should be used instead of `name`.
- Attributes can't be minimized.

The following listing shows the previous `address.xml` document rewritten in XHTML. I've done this so you can compare XHTML and XML documents.

```
<?xml version="1.0"?>
<!DOCTYPE html PUBLIC "-//W3C//DTD XHTML 1.0 Transitional//EN"
"http://www.w3.org/TR/xhtml1/DTD/xhtml1-transitional.dtd">
```

```
<html>
<body>
  <table>
  <tr>
    <td>Sas Jacobs</td>
    <td>123 Some Street, Some City, Some Country</td>
    <td>123 456</td>
  </tr>
  <tr>
    <td>John Smith</td>
    <td>4 Another Street, Another City, Another Country</td>
    <td>456 789</td>
  </tr>
</table>
</body>
</html>
```

Notice that the file includes both an XML declaration and a DOCTYPE declaration. You can see the content in the resource file `address.html`.

You're probably used to seeing information like this in web pages. A table displays the content and lists each contact in a separate row. Figure 2-9 shows this document opened in Internet Explorer.

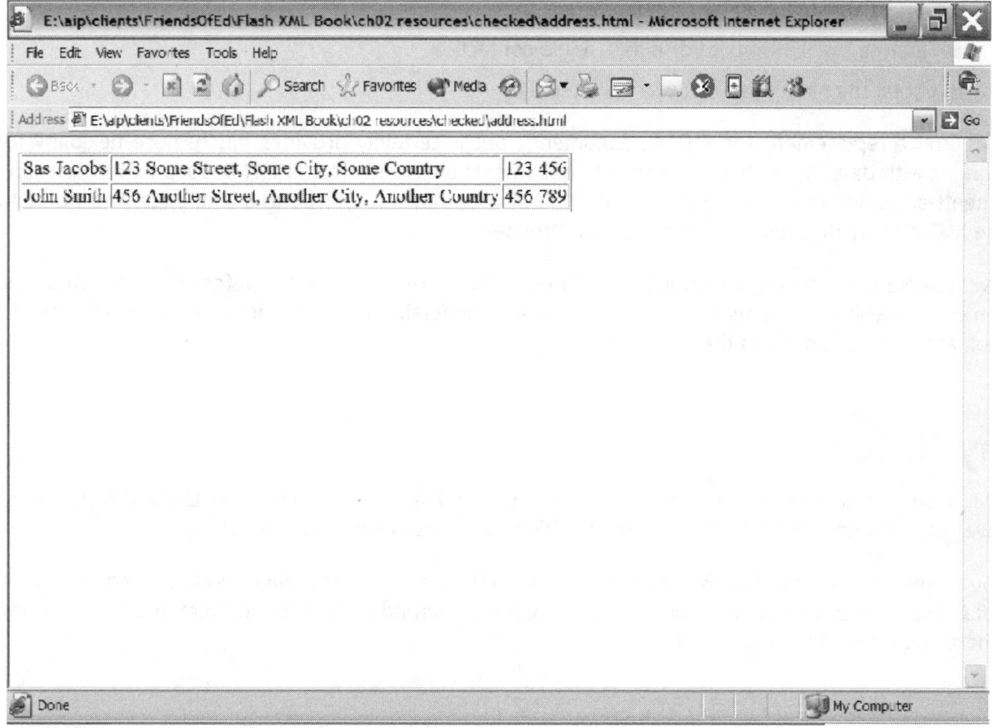

Figure 2-9. An HTML file displayed in Internet Explorer

I've rewritten the content in XHTML so that it conforms with the stricter rules for XML documents. However, the way the document is constructed may still cause some problems. Each piece of information about my contacts is stored in a separate cell within a table. The `<td>` tags don't give me any clue about what the cell contains. I get a better idea when I open the page in a web browser.

It would be difficult for me to use a software program to extract the content from the web page. I could remove the `<td>` tags and add the content to a database, but if the order of the table columns changed, I might end up with the wrong data in the wrong database field. There's no way to associate the phone number with the third column.

The web page controls the display of information. Although I can make some minor visual adjustments to the table using style sheets, I can't completely transform the display. For example, I can't remove the table and create a vertical listing of all entries without completely rewriting the XHTML.

Each time I print the document, it will look the same. I can't exclude information such as the address column from my printout. I don't have any way to filter or sort the information. I am not able to extract a list of contacts in a specific area or sort into contact name order.

Compare this case with storing the information in an XML document. I can create my own tag names and write a schema that describes how to use these tags. When I view the document in a web browser, the tag names make it very clear what information they're storing.

I can apply a transformation to change the appearance of an XML document, including

- Sorting the document into name order
- Filtering the contents to display a single contact
- Listing the names in a table or bulleted list

XML isn't a replacement for XHTML documents, but it certainly provides much more flexibility for working with data. You're likely to use XML documents differently from XHTML documents. XML documents are a way to store structured data that may or may not end up in a web page. You normally use XHTML only to display content in a web browser.

XML offers many advantages compared with other forms of data storage. Before I explore what you can do with XML documents, I think it's important to understand the benefits of working with XML. I'll look at this more closely in the next section.

Why XML?

XML is simple, flexible, descriptive, accessible, independent, precise, and free! Using it in Flash will save you maintenance time. What more incentive could you need to start working with it?

You've seen the advantages that XML offers over HTML and XHTML when working with structured data. Given the strong support for XML in Flash, there's bound to be some project in the near future where you'll need to use XML data.

Simple

The rules for creating XML documents are simple. You just need a text editor or another software package capable of generating XML. The only proviso is that you follow some basic rules so that the XML document is well formed.

Reading an XML document is also simple. Tag names are normally descriptive so you can figure out what data each element contains. The hierarchical structure of elements allows you to work out the relationships between each piece of information. When you use XML documents, you don't have to separate out extra style elements when reading an XML document.

Flexible

One key aspect of XML is its flexibility. As long as you follow some simple rules, you can structure an XML document in any way you like. The choice of tag names, attributes, and structures is completely flexible so you can tailor it to suit your data.

Unless you're working with an existing XML-based language such as XHTML, you are not restricted to a standard list of tags. For example, in XHTML, you have to use an `<h1>` tag to display a title on your web page; you can't create your own tag `<pageTitle>`.

You can share information about your XML-based language with other people by using a DTD or schema to describe the "grammar," or rules, for the language. While both types of documents serve the same purpose, schemas use XML to describe the syntax. So if you know XML, you know the basic rules for writing schemas.

Software programs can also use DTDs and schemas. This allows them to map XML elements and work with specific parts of XML documents. For example, Excel 2003 for PCs uses schemas when exporting XML documents. The schema describes the name for each tag, the type of data it will contain, and the relationships among each of the elements.

XML documents provide data for use in different applications. You can generate an XML document from a corporate software package, transform it to display on a website, share it with staff on portable devices, use it to create PDF files, and provide it to other software packages. You can reuse the same data in several different settings. The ability to repurpose information is one of XML's key strengths.

The way XML information displays is also flexible. You can display any XML document in a web browser to see the structure of elements. You can also use other technologies or software packages to change the display quite dramatically. For example, you could transform your phone book XML document into

- A printed list of names and numbers sorted into name order
- A web page displaying the full details of each entry in a table
- A Flash movie that allows you to search for a contact

I'm sure you can think of many more ways to use a phone book XML document.

Descriptive

Because you can choose your own tag names, your XML document becomes a description of your data. Some people call XML documents *self-describing*.

It's easy for humans to understand the content of an XML document just by looking at the tag names. It's also unambiguous for computers, providing they know the rules and structures in the XML document.

In our XHTML page, we could only describe each table cell using the tag `<td>`. The corresponding XML document used tags like <name>, `<address>`, and <phone>, so it was easy to determine what information each element contained.

The hierarchy in elements means that XML documents show relationships between information in a similar way to a database. The hierarchies in the phone book document tell me that each contact has a name, address, and phone number and that I can store many different contacts.

Accessible

XML documents separate data from presentation so you can have access to the information without worrying about how it displays. This makes the data accessible to many different people, devices, and software packages at the same time. For example, my phone book XML document could be

- Read aloud by a screen reader
- Displayed on a website
- Printed to a PDF file
- Processed automatically by a software package
- Viewed on a mobile phone

XML documents use Unicode for their standard character sets so you can write XML documents in any number of languages. A Flash application could offer multilingual support simply by using different XML documents within the same movie. Switch to a different XML document to display content in an alternative language. The Le@rning Federation example referred to in Chapter 1 does exactly that.

Independent

XML is platform and device independent. It doesn't matter if you view the data on a PC, Macintosh, or handheld computer. The data is still the same and people can exchange it seamlessly. Programmers can also use XML to share information between software packages that otherwise couldn't communicate with each other.

You don't need a specific software package to work with XML documents. You can type the content in just about any package capable of receiving text. The document can be read in a web browser, text editor, or any other XML processor. XML documents can query databases to provide a text-based alternative. In the case of web services, XML is an intermediary between you and someone else's database.

XML doesn't have "flavors" that are specific to a single web browser, version, or operating system. You don't have to create three different versions of your XML document to cater for different viewing conditions.

Precise

XML is a precise standard. If you want your XML document to be read by an XML parser, it must be well formed. Documents that aren't well formed won't display. Compare this with HTML files. Even when it contains fundamental errors, the web page will still display in a web browser.

When a schema or DTD is included within an XML document, you can validate the content to make sure that the structure conforms to the rules you've set down. Less strict languages like HTML don't allow you to be this precise with your content. XML documents with schemas provide standards so there is only one way that the data they contain can be structured and interpreted.

Free

XML is a specification that isn't owned by any company or commercial enterprise. This means that it's free to use XML—you don't have to buy any special software or other technology. In fact, most major software packages either support XML or are moving so that they will support it in the future.

XML is a central standard in a whole family of related standards. These recommendations work together to create an independent framework for managing markup languages. Table 2-2 shows some of the other related recommendations from the W3C.

Table 2-2. Some of the main XML-related recommendations from the W3C

Recommendation	Purpose
XML Schema Definition (XSD)	Schemas describe the structure and syntax of an XML document.
Extensible Stylesheet Language (XSL)	XSL determines the presentation of XML documents. It uses XSL Transformations (XSLT), XML Path Language, and XSL Formatting Objects (XSL-FO).
XSL Transformations (XSLT)	XSLT transforms one XML document into another XML document.
XML Path Language (XPath)	XPath navigates or locates specific parts of XML documents.
XSL Formatting Objects (XSL-FO)	XSL-FO specifies formatting to be applied to an XML document.
XML Linking Language (XLink)	XLink describes the links between XML documents.
XML Pointer Language (XPointer)	XPointer describes references between XML documents so you can use them in links or in other documents.

Continued

Table 2-2. *Continued*

Recommendation	Purpose
XML Query (XQuery)	XQuery queries XML documents to extract information. At the time of writing, it was a working draft rather than a recommendation of the W3C.
XForms	XForms are an XML-based replacement for XHTML forms.
Simple Object Access Protocol (SOAP)	SOAP is a standard protocol for requesting information from a web service.
Web Services Description Language (WSDL)	WSDL describes web services using an XML structure.

I'll look a little more closely at DTDs, XML schemas, and XSLT in Chapter 3 of this book.

What can you do with XML?

So far I've introduced you to XML and given you some background information on how to construct XML documents. You've also seen how XML is different from HTML and XHTML. Now it's time to explore how you can use XML documents.

Remember that the primary purpose for XML documents is the storage of data. XML allows people to share information using a self-describing document. The data is easy to read and interpret. Software packages can also read XML documents and use them as a medium for information exchange.

An XML document is portable and doesn't require the purchase of any specific software or technology. You can use the same XML documents for many different purposes. Best of all, XML documents are completely platform independent.

Common uses for XML documents include

- Storing and sharing information
- Querying and consuming web services
- Describing configuration settings
- Interacting with databases
- Interacting with Office 2003 documents

Storing and sharing information

The most important use for XML documents is in storing information. XML documents provide a way to describe structured data within a text file. The advantage of XML over other storage formats is that it is a standard so you can use the same content in many different ways. The same XML file could provide content for a website, a Flash movie, and a printed document. You save time because you need to create the XML file only once to use it in these varied settings.

Each XML document that you create will probably have a different structure designed to meet the needs of the people or software who will use the information. The element names will describe the data they contain, and the element structures will show how blocks of information relate to each other.

An XML document doesn't need any specific software or operating system, which means you can share it with other people and software applications. XML documents can also provide information to other web-based applications, including websites and Flash applications.

If you are working in an industry group, you can design your own language for sharing information. By creating DTDs or schemas, you ensure that everyone understands how the language works and that their XML documents conform to a standard set of rules. CML and MathML are good examples of common languages.

The listing that follows shows a MathML document taken from the examples at www.mathmlcentral.com/Tools/FromMathML.jsp. The listing shows how **sin(x^2)** could be described using MathML elements.

```
<math xmlns="http://www.w3.org/1998/Math/MathML">
  <mrow>
    <mi>sin</mi>
    <mo>&#8289;</mo>
    <mo>(</mo>
    <msup>
      <mi>x</mi>
      <mn>2</mn>
    </msup>
    <mo>)</mo>
  </mrow>
</math>
```

You can find out more about MathML at www.w3.org/Math/.

Another useful standard relates to graphics. Scalable Vector Graphics (SVG) is an XML-based language that describes two-dimensional graphics. If you want to find out more, the SVG recommendation is at www.w3c.org/Graphics/SVG/.

The following listing shows a sample SVG document. I've saved the document as shapes.svg (in your resource files) if you want to have a closer look. The elements describe a yellow rectangle, blue ellipse, and green triangle.

```
<?xml version="1.0" encoding="iso-8859-1" standalone="no"?>
<!DOCTYPE svg PUBLIC "-//W3C//DTD SVG 1.0//EN"
"http://www.w3.org/TR/SVG/DTD/svg10.dtd">
<svg>
  <desc>Shapes</desc>
  <rect x="5" y="5" width="100" height="50" fill="yellow"/>
  <ellipse cx="200" cy="100" rx="100" ry="40" fill="blue"/>
  <polygon points="110,140 40,300 120,250" fill="green"/>
</svg>
```

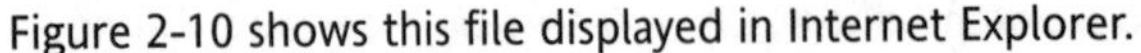

Figure 2-10 shows this file displayed in Internet Explorer.

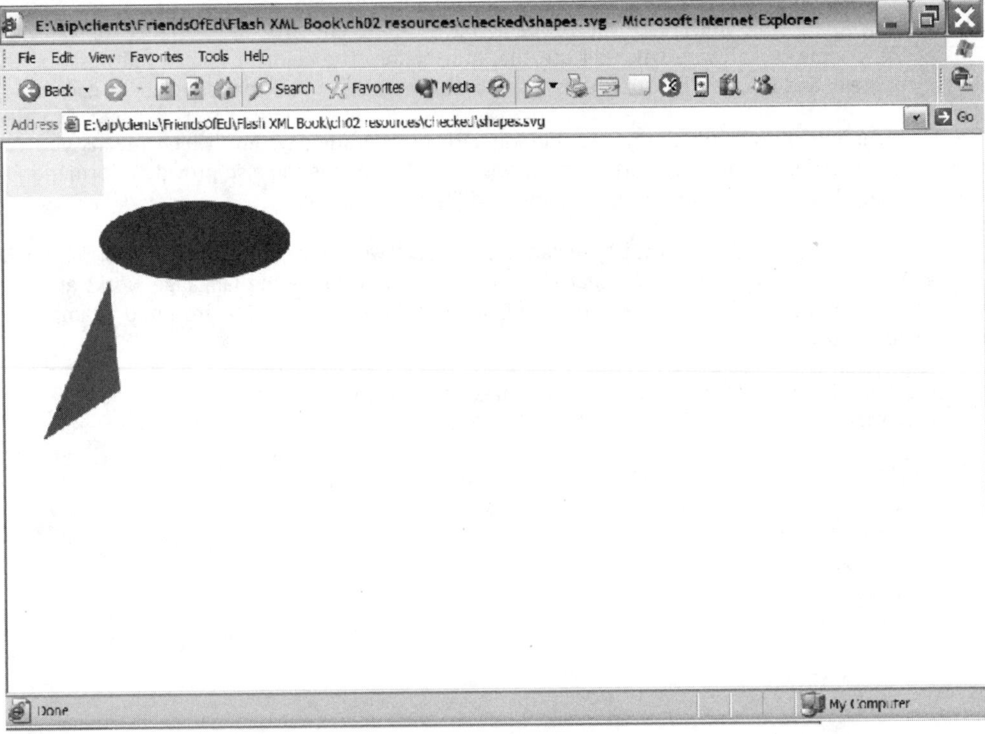

Figure 2-10. The sample SVG document displayed in Internet Explorer

Querying and consuming web services

XML documents are the standard way to share information through web services. Web services are public functions that organizations make available. For example, you can use web services to calculate currency exchange transactions, look up weather details, read news feeds, and perform searches at Amazon or Google.

When you send a request to a web service, you'll often use SOAP, an XML format. You'll also receive the information from the web service in an XML document. We'll look at web services in more detail later in this book.

Describing configuration settings

Many software packages use XML documents to describe their configuration settings. For example, an XML document format is used to configure .NET applications. The settings for a .NET application are stored in a file called `web.config`. The file uses standard XML elements to store settings such as debugging, authentication, error handling, and global variables. The following listing shows a sample `web.config` file. You can also see the saved `web.config` file within your resources.

```
<?xml version="1.0" encoding="UTF-8" ?>
<configuration>
  <appSettings>
    <add key="fileSaveLocation" value="D:\Hosting\website\images\"/>
  </appSettings>
  <system.web>
    <customErrors mode="Off"/>
    <compilation debug="true"/>
  </system.web>
</configuration>
```

The file contains a global variable or *key* location for saving files: `fileSaveLocation`. There are also some settings for customized errors and debugging.

Interacting with databases

Many common databases allow you to work with XML documents. SQL Server and Oracle both offer support for XML interaction. XML documents can query a database and return results. For example, in SQL Server, you can construct a SELECT statement that returns the results as an XML fragment:

```
SELECT * FROM BOOKS FOR XML AUTO
```

XUpdate is an XML-based language that describes updates to an XML document tree. It is not a W3C recommendation but uses the XPath specification. XUpdate is one way to manage XML document and database updates. Flash uses XUpdate in the XUpdateResolver data component.

You can find out more about XUpdate at `http://xmldb-org.sourceforge.net/xupdate/xupdate-wd.html`. There are some useful examples of XUpdate statements at `www.xmldatabases.org/projects/XUpdate-UseCases/`.

Interacting with Office 2003 documents

One exciting new application for XML is its role in Microsoft Office 2003 documents. For PC users, this means that you can save Word, Excel, and Access 2003 documents in XML format. Office 2003 can generate XML documents that you can use in other software packages, such as Flash. You can also display and update XML documents in Office 2003.

The Save As command converts Word and Excel 2003 documents into XML format using either **WordprocessingML** or **SpreadsheetML**. These are XML-based languages created by Microsoft to describe Word and Excel structures and formatting. You can also apply your own schema so that you can modify the XML documents produced by Office 2003.

Unfortunately, this functionality is only available for PC users. There is limited XML functionality in Excel 2004 for Macintosh users. Office XP for PCs also offers some XML support, but it is limited compared with Office 2003.

Why is XML important to web developers?

XML is an important tool for all web developers, even those who don't use Flash. XML provides the basis for much of the content on the Internet, and its importance will only increase over time. Many people consider XML the *lingua franca* of the Internet as it provides the standards for data exchange between humans and machines in many different settings.

Web developers use XML to create their own languages to store, structure, and name data. XML content is the perfect mechanism for self-describing data. This makes XML documents ideal for sharing with other developers and IT specialists.

As a developer, you can use the same XML content for many different purposes. For example, you could use a single XML document to power a .NET application as well as a Java version. You could also transform the content into an XHTML document, a Flash movie, or a PDF file.

XML-related technologies also let you sort and filter the data within an XML document. Style sheet transformations allow you to reshape your data any way you want. You can then show the transformed content in a web browser, read it aloud, print it out, or send it to a mobile phone.

A physical XML document provides portability over and above that of a database. Creating an XML document enables you to distribute database content offline. For example, you can use the XML file with a stand-alone Flash movie and distribute it on a CD-ROM. In addition, providing an XML layer between a user and a database is a good way to prevent access to sensitive corporate data.

The built-in support for XML within Flash allows Flash developers to use XML data within any Flash movie. Using the content from XML documents enables you to update your movies without ever having to open Flash. You can store your Flash application settings in an XML file so that you can configure the application with simple changes to the document. If you're not comfortable with ActionScript, you can use the data components to add XML content to your movies. You can work with the panels in Flash so that you don't have to write any ActionScript.

You can save maintenance time by allowing your clients to manage their own content. It's often not practical for them to learn how to use Flash, and in reality, you probably don't want to give your clients access to the Flash movies that you've created. Instead, you provide mechanisms for clients to update an XML file and the Flash movie will update accordingly.

I have clients who update the content of their Flash movies using Office 2003. They make the changes within Word, Access, or Excel 2003; export the content in XML format; and replace the existing XML file with the new file they've just created. They can use a web page to upload the new XML file to their website, or they can burn it to a CD-ROM with a stand-alone Flash file.

These clients have the flexibility to change their Flash movie content whenever they like, and I've found that most clients are very comfortable working this way. It also saves me from continually editing their Flash movies each time the content changes.

Summary

In this chapter, you've learned about XML and the contents of XML documents. You've also learned about the differences between XML, HTML, and XHTML. As a developer or designer, I hope I've shown you the advantages of working with XML in your applications.

The importance of XML cannot be overstated. As a technology, it allows organizations to create their own mechanisms for sharing information. At its simplest, XML provides a structured, text-based alternative to a database. More complex uses of XML might involve data interactions between corporate systems and outside consumers of information. The most important thing to remember is that an XML document can provide a data source for many different applications.

The widespread adoption of XML by major software companies such as Microsoft and Macromedia ensure its future. Most of the popular database packages provide XML support. If it's not already there, expect XML to become part of most software packages in the near future.

The next chapter looks at working with XML content in XML editors and in Office 2003. It also looks more closely at consuming web services. I'll cover creating DTDs and XML schemas as well as transforming XML documents with XSLT. We'll finish by creating an XML document and schema from scratch.

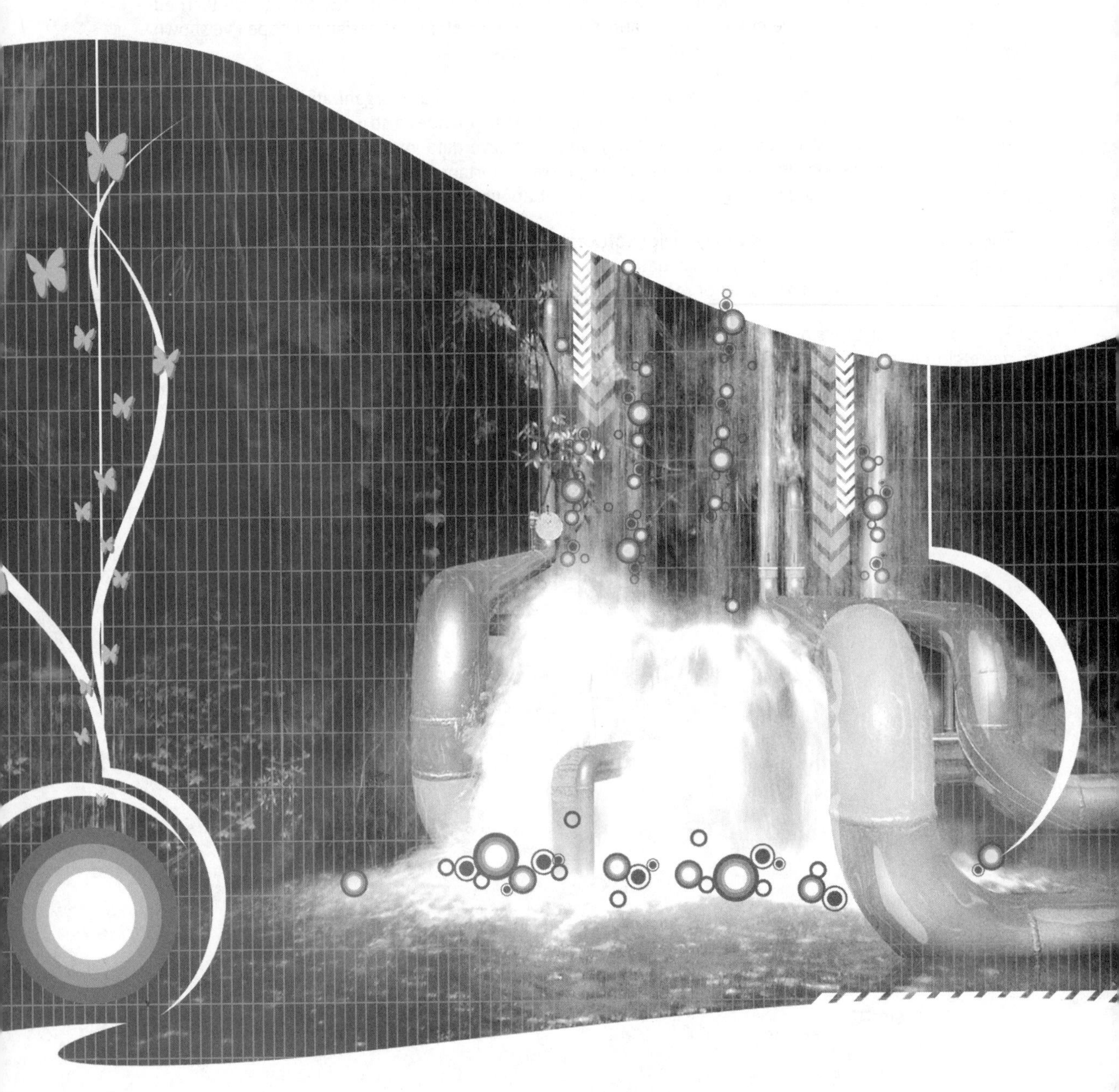

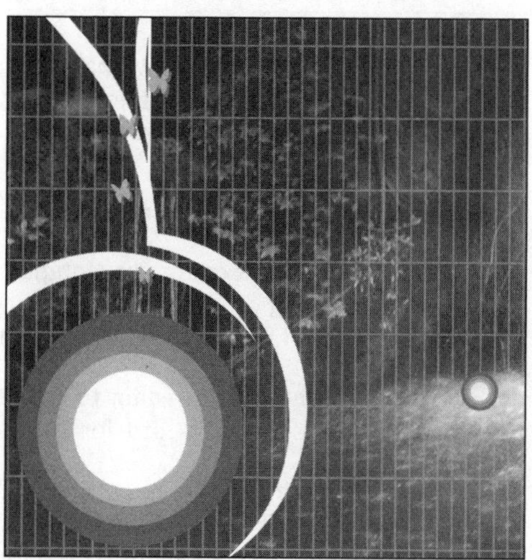

Chapter 3

XML DOCUMENTS

Before you can start working with XML content in Flash, you have to create the XML documents that you'll be using. This chapter looks at the different ways you can do this. I'll show you how you can generate content in a text or XML editor, from Office 2003 and by consuming web services. I'll have a quick look at querying Amazon and Google and receiving XML responses. You'll build applications that work with web services later in the book.

I'll also look at how you can transform XML documents using CSS and XSL style sheets. I'll cover creating Document Type Definitions (DTDs) and schemas that describe the rules for your XML documents. At the end of the chapter, we'll create an XML document and schema that we'll use in an application in the next chapter.

Remember that an XML document doesn't have to be a physical file. There's nothing to stop you from creating a text file with an `.xml` extension to store your XML content, and we'll look at different ways to do this. However, the term *XML document* can also refer to XML information that comes from a software package or web application.

Creating XML content

You can create XML content in many different ways, including

- Typing XML content in a text or XML editor
- Generating XML content with a server-side file
- Extracting XML content from software such as Office 2003
- Consuming XML generated by a web service or news feed

Each of the XML documents that you create will have different content and structure. The only thing they'll have in common is the rules that you use to create them. At the very minimum, all XML documents must be well formed. Later on, we'll look at creating valid documents with a DTD or schema.

Using a text editor

You can use a text editor like Notepad or SimpleText to type your XML content. You'll need to enter every line using your keyboard, which could take a long time if you're working with a large document. When you've finished, save the file with an `.xml` extension and you'll have created an XML document.

You can also use a text editor to create a DTD, schema, or XSL style sheet. Just remember to use the correct file extension—`.dtd` for DTDs, `.xsd` for schemas, and `.xsl` for XSL style sheets.

Don't forget that if you're using Notepad, you'll probably need to change Save as type to All Files before you save the document. Otherwise, you could end up with a file called `address.xml.txt` by mistake. Figure 3-1 shows the correct way to do this.

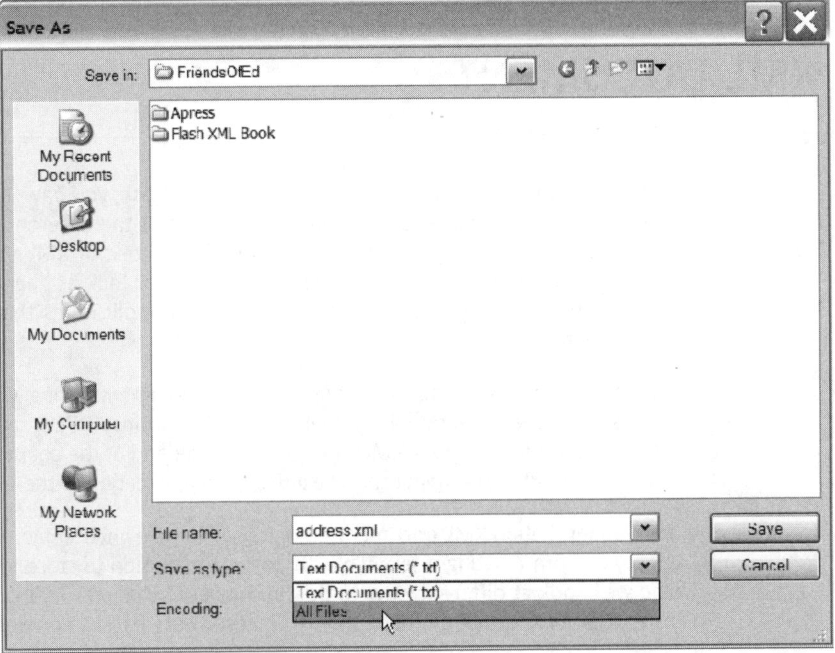

Figure 3-1. Saving an XML document in Notepad

Text editors are easy to use, but they don't offer any special functionality for XML content. Text editors won't tell you if your tag names don't match, if you've mixed up the cases of your element names, or if you've nested them incorrectly. There are no tools to check if your XML document meets the rules set down in a DTD or schema. Text editors don't automatically add color to your markup. In fact, you may not find any errors in your XML documents until you first try to use an XML parser.

You can also use HTML editors like HomeSite and BBEdit to create XML documents. The advantage of these over text editors is that they can automate the process a little. HTML editors often come with extensions for working specifically with XML documents. For example, they can add the correct declarations to the file and auto-complete your tag names. They'll also add coloring to make it easier to read your content.

However, you'll still have to type in most of your content line by line. Again, most HTML editors don't include tools to validate content and to apply transformations. You can only expect that functionality from an XML editor.

XML editors

An XML editor is a software program designed to work specifically with XML documents. Most XML editors include tools that auto-complete tags, check for well-formedness, and validate XML documents. You can use XML editors to create XSL style sheets, DTDs, and schemas.

The category "XML editors" includes both free and for-purchase software packages. With such a range of great XML tools available, you'd have to wonder why people would want to create XML documents with a text or HTML editor.

Common XML editors include

- Altova XMLSpy
- SyncRO Soft <oXygen/>
- WebX Systems UltraXML
- XMLEditPro (freeware)
- RustemSoft XMLFox (freeware)

You can find a useful summary of XML editors and their features at `www.xmlsoftware.com/editors.html`.

Although it isn't mandatory to use an XML editor when creating XML documents, it's likely to save you time, especially if you work with long documents.

Altova XMLSpy 2005 is one of the most popular XML editors for PCs. You can download a free home user edition of the software from `www.altova.com/download_spy_home.html`. You can also purchase a version with additional professional level features.

As we'll be using XMLSpy in this section of the book, it's probably a good idea to download it and install it on your computer. If you're working on a Macintosh, you'll need to get access to a PC if you want to try out the examples.

You can work with any type of XML content in XMLSpy, including XHTML documents. It includes a text editor interface as well as graphical features. XMLSpy offers features such as checking for well-formedness and validity. It also helps out with tag templates if you've specified a DTD or schema.

You can use XMLSpy to create DTDs and schemas as well as XSL style sheets. It also allows you to apply style sheets to preview transformations of your XML documents.

We'll look at some of the features of this software package in a little more detail as an illustration of what's possible with XML editing software.

To start with, when you create a new document, XMLSpy allows you to choose from many different types. Figure 3-2 shows you some of the choices.

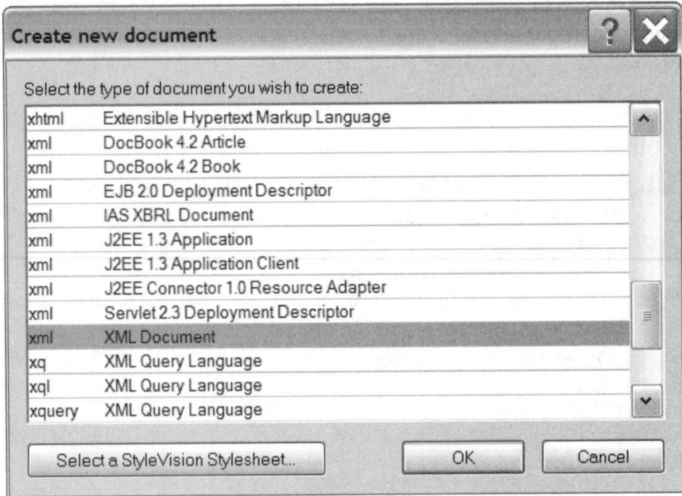

Figure 3-2. Options available when creating a new document with XMLSpy

Depending on the type of document you choose, XMLSpy automatically adds the appropriate content. For example, choosing the type XML Document automatically adds the following line to the new file:

```
<?xml version="1.0" encoding="UTF-8"?>
```

When you create a new XML document, XMLSpy will ask you if you want to use an existing DTD or schema. Figure 3-3 shows the prompt.

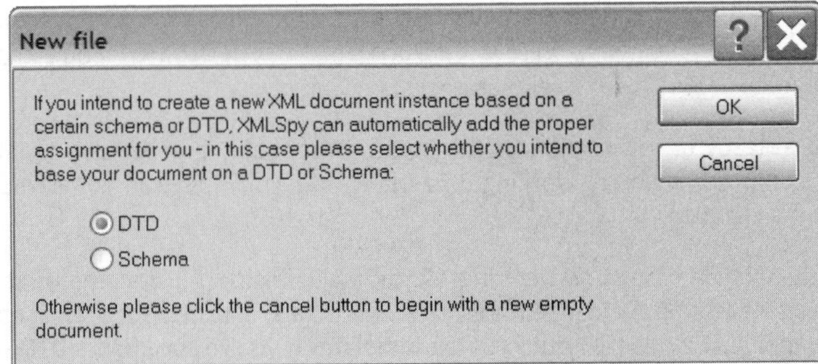

Figure 3-3. When you create a new XML document, XMLSpy prompts for a DTD or schema reference.

If you choose either a DTD or schema and select a file, XMLSpy will create a reference to it in your XML document:

```
<phoneBook xmlns:xsi="http://www.w3.org/2001/XMLSchema-instance"
xsi:noNamespaceSchemaLocation="addressSchema.xsd">
```

If you don't include a DTD or schema reference, you can always add one later by using the DTD/Schema menu.

You can use XMLSpy in Text view, like a text editor, or in Authentic view, which has WYSIWYG features. Schemas can also use the Schema/WSDL view, a graphical presentation that simplifies the creation process. The final option is Browser view, which simulates how a document would display in a web browser.

XML documents with a referenced DTD or schema will show you extra information when you work in Text view. Clicking on an element or attribute in the main window will display information about it in the Info panel on the left side. You can see this in Figure 3-4.

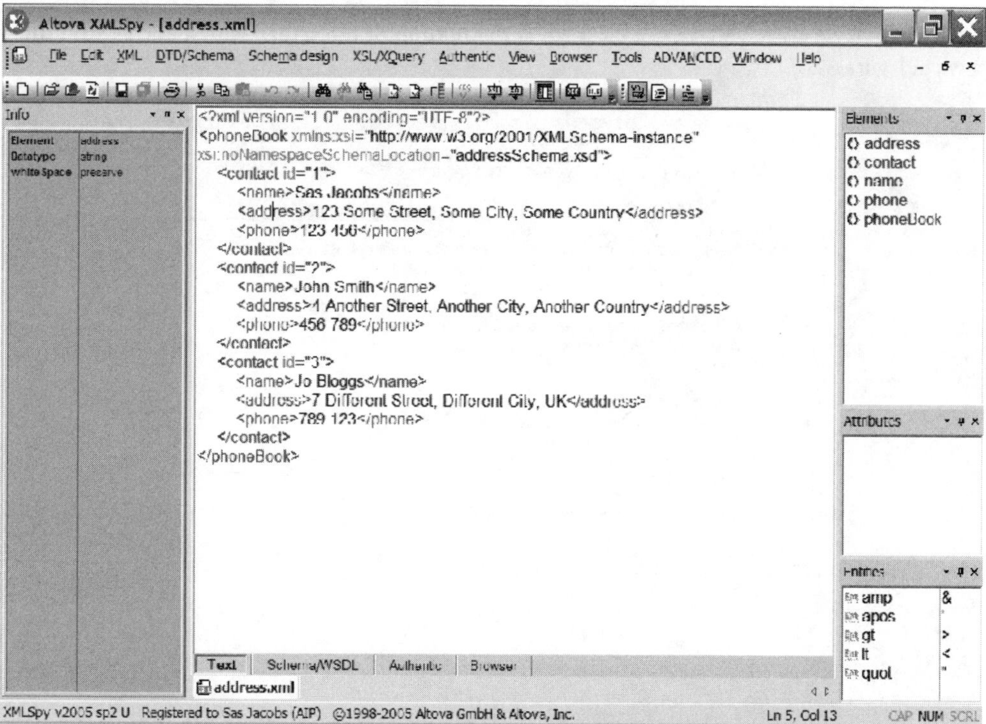

Figure 3-4. When a schema or DTD is referenced, XMLSpy displays information about the selected element or attribute. Entry Helpers are included on the right side of the screen.

The Entry Helpers panel on the right shows a list of the available elements. The panel also shows you common entities. One very useful feature is the ability to add an element template to the main window from the Elements panel.

Position your cursor in the XML document, double-click the appropriate tag name, and XMLSpy adds an element template to the code. This is very handy if the element you've chosen contains child elements as XMLSpy adds the complete tree from that point, including attributes.

Open the resource file `address.xml` in XMLSpy to test these features. Click to the left of the closing </phoneBook> tag and press *Enter*. Position your cursor in the blank line and double-click the <contact> element in the Elements panel. XMLSpy will insert a <contact> element, complete with child elements, into the document.

Another feature of XMLSpy is checking whether an XML document is well formed. If you are using a text editor, you'd have to do this by loading the document into an XML parser and checking for errors. Not only is this time consuming, but the error messages are often not as detailed as you'd like them to be!

In XMLSpy, you can check the document by clicking the button with the yellow tick or by using the *F7* key. XMLSpy then checks all the requirements for well-formed documents, including a single root node, tag case, element ordering, and quotes on attributes. I covered the requirements for well-formed documents in Chapter 2.

If XMLSpy finds an error, you'll see a message at the bottom of the screen with a Recheck button, as shown in Figure 3-5.

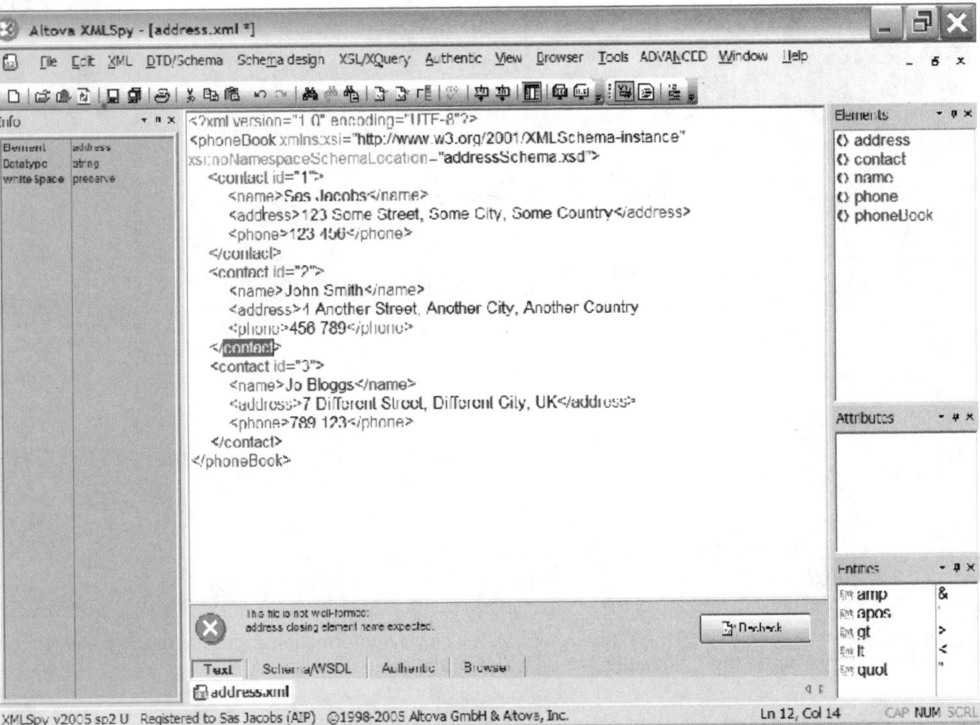

Figure 3-5. Using XMLSpy to check whether a document is well formed

If you want to see it in action, change the address.xml file to introduce a deliberate mistake and check it again for well-formedness. You could change the case of one of the closing tags or remove the apostrophes from an attribute. You'll see a detailed error message that will help you to pinpoint where you went wrong.

XMLSpy can also check if an XML document is valid against a DTD or schema. Click the button with the green tick or use the *F8* key. Figure 3-6 shows an invalid document after it's been checked in XMLSpy.

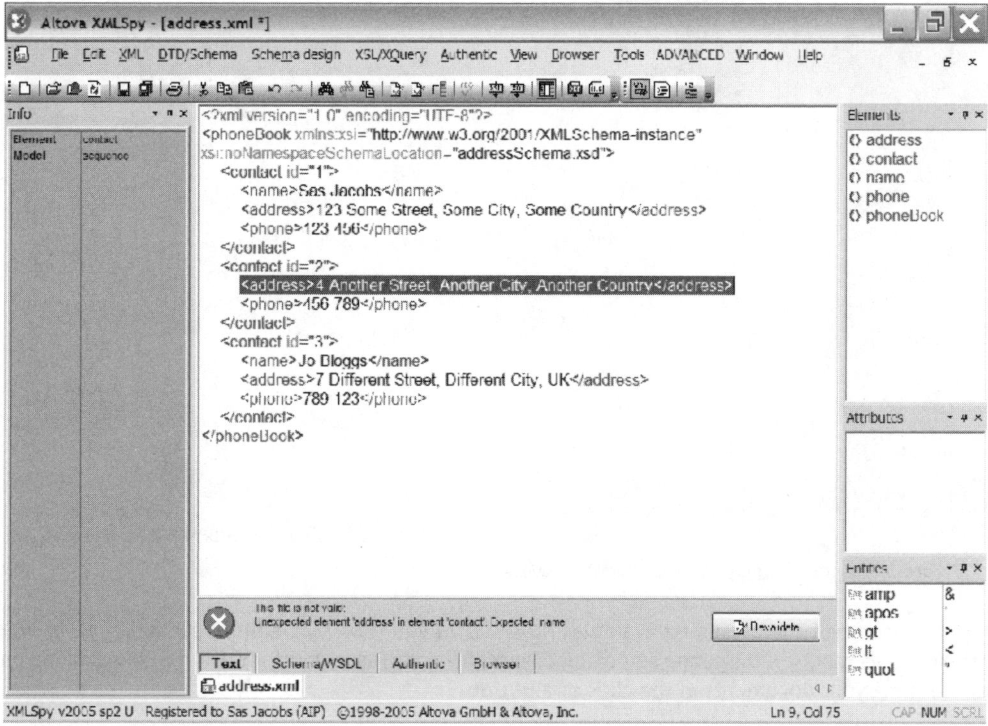

Figure 3-6. Checking validity in XMLSpy

You can test this feature by checking if address.xml is valid against its schema addressSchema.xsd. You might want to open up the schema file to have a look at the content. It will make a lot more sense to you later in the book!

Finally, if you're going to transform your XML document with XSLT, you can use XMLSpy to create the style sheet and to preview the transformation.

Once you've added a style sheet reference to your XML document, use the *F10* key to apply the transformation. XMLSpy will create an XSLOutput.html file and display your transformed content.

You can add a style sheet reference by choosing XSL/XQuery ➤ Assign XSL and selecting the file listStyle.xsl. Make sure you check the Make path relative to address.xml check box before clicking OK. XMLSpy adds the style sheet reference to the XML document.

```
<?xml-stylesheet type="text/xsl" href="listStyle.xsl"?>
```

Press the *F10* key to see the transformation. Figure 3-7 shows the `XSLOutput.htm` file created by XMLSpy.

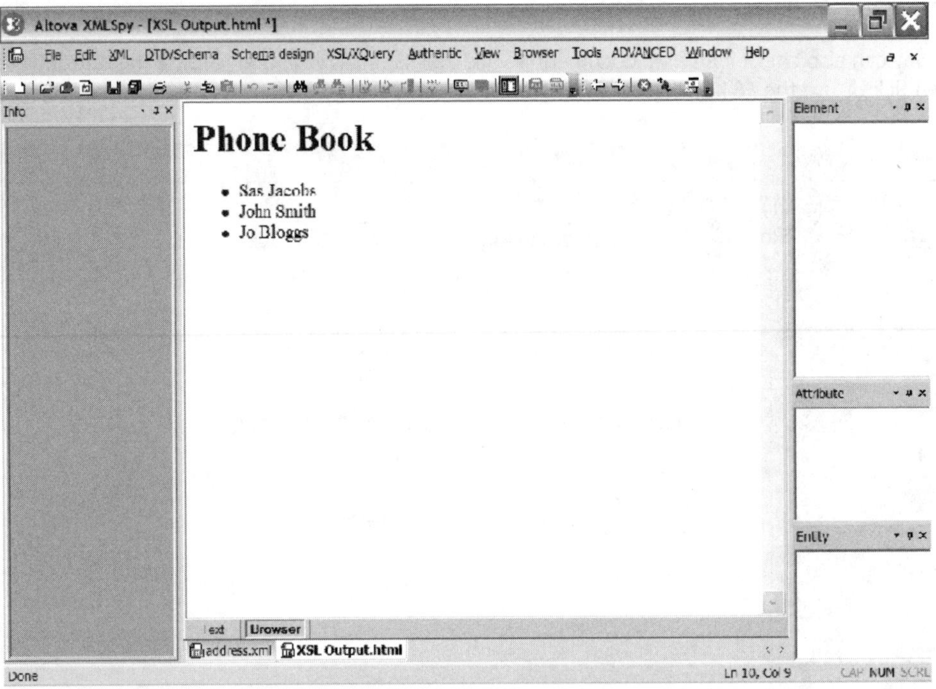

Figure 3-7. A transformed XML document in XMLSpy

Hopefully, some of the preceding examples have shown you how XML editors can help you to work with XML documents. A full-featured product like XMLSpy can save you a lot of time by validating and transforming your documents in the click of a button.

Server-side files

You can use content from any server-side file that generates XML. That means you can use a ColdFusion, PHP, or .NET file to create the XML content for you dynamically. For example, you might query a database and receive the response as an XML document. You might also use a server-side file to query the files and folders within your computer. Server-side code can create an XML document that describes the folder structures and file names.

The following listing shows some VB .NET code that generates a list of folders and files in XML format. The resource file `MP3List.aspx` contains the complete listing.

```
<%@ Page Language="vb" Debug="true" %>
<%@ import Namespace="System" %>
<%@ import Namespace="System.IO" %>
<%@ import Namespace="System.XML" %>
<script runat="server">
```

```
    Dim strDirectoryLocation as String = "e:\mp3z\"
    Dim dirs As String(), fileInfos as String()
    Dim i as Integer, j as Integer
      sub Page_Load
        Dim MP3Xml as XmlDocument = new XmlDocument()
        Dim folderElement as XMLElement
        Dim songElement as XMLElement
        Dim writer As New XmlTextWriter(Console.Out)
        writer.Formatting = Formatting.Indented
        MP3Xml.AppendChild(MP3Xml.CreateXmlDeclaration("1.0", "UTF-8", ➥
        "no"))
        Dim RootNode As XmlElement = MP3Xml.CreateElement("mp3s")
        MP3Xml.AppendChild(RootNode)
        if Directory.Exists(strDirectoryLocation) then
          dirs = Directory.GetDirectories(strDirectoryLocation)
          for i = 0 to Ubound(dirs)
            dirs(i) = replace(dirs(i), strDirectoryLocation, "")
          next
          Array.sort(dirs)
          for i=0 to Ubound(dirs)
            folderElement = MP3Xml.CreateElement("folder")
            folderElement.SetAttribute("name", dirs(i))
            RootNode.AppendChild(folderElement)
            fileInfos = Directory.GetFiles(strDirectoryLocation & ➥
            dirs(i) & "\", "*.mp3")
            for j = 0 to Ubound(fileInfos)
              fileInfos(j) = replace(fileInfos(j), strDirectoryLocation ➥
              & dirs(i) & "\", "")
            next
            Array.sort(fileInfos)
            for j = 0 to Ubound(fileInfos)
              songElement = MP3xml.CreateElement("song")
              songElement.SetAttribute("filename", fileInfos(j))
              folderElement.AppendChild(songElement)
            next
          next
        End If
        dim strContents as String = MP3Xml.outerXML
        response.write (strContents)
      end sub
  </script>
```

The server-side file returns a list of folders and MP3 files in an XML document. Figure 3-8 shows how the file looks when viewed in a web browser. Note that because the file contains server-side code, you'll have to run it through a web server like Microsoft Internet Information Services (IIS). If you check the address bar in the screenshot, you'll see that the file is running through `http://localhost/`.

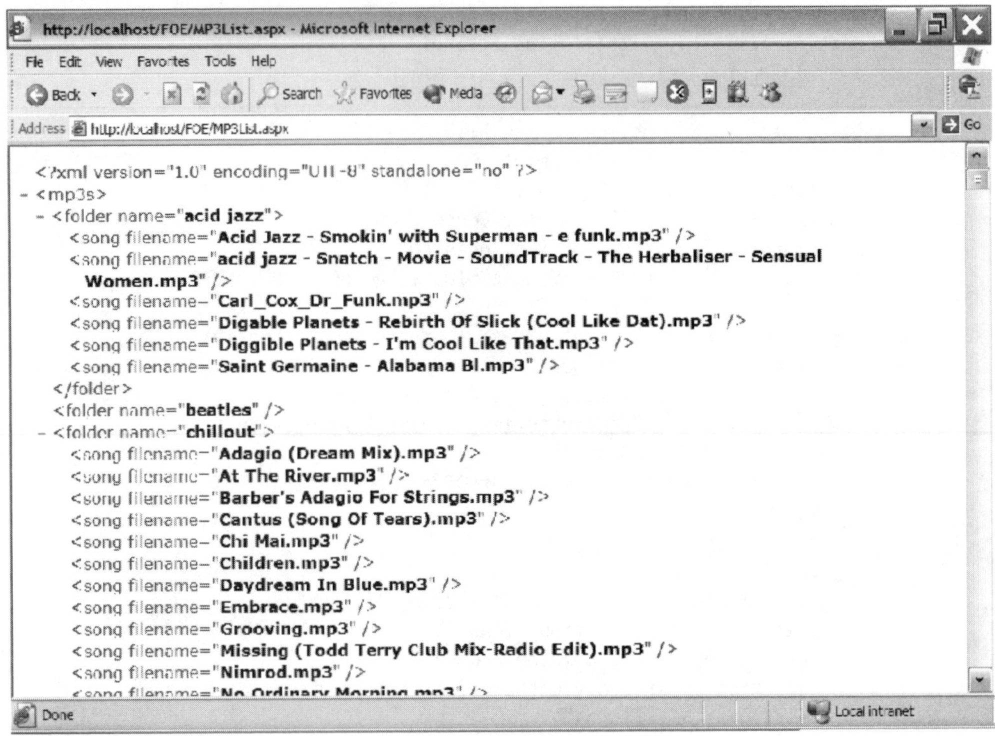

Figure 3-8. XML content generated by a server-side file, displayed in Internet Explorer

This is an example of an XML document that doesn't exist in a physical sense. I didn't save a file with an `.xml` extension. Instead, the server-side file creates a stream of XML data. The VB .NET file transforms the file system into an XML document.

Office 2003/2004

Believe it or not, Microsoft Office can be a source of XML content. For PCs, Microsoft Office 2003 has built-in XML support within Word, Excel, and Access. Unfortunately for Macintosh users, Office 2004 doesn't provide the same level of support. Macintosh users can use Excel 2004 to read and write XML documents, but they can't use schemas and style sheets.

Most people wouldn't think of Office documents as containers for structured XML information. Normally, when we work with Office documents we are more concerned with the appearance of data. Word, Excel, and Access 2003 all offer support for information exchange via XML. These applications can open, generate, and transform XML documents.

Word 2003 creates **WordprocessingML** (previously called WordML) while Excel writes **SpreadsheetML**. Both are markup languages that conform to the XML specification. You can find out more about these languages at `www.microsoft.com/office/xml/default.mspx`.

Whenever you use Save as and select XML format in Word or Excel, you're automatically generating one of those markup languages. Unfortunately, both languages are quite verbose as they include tags for everything—document properties and styling as well as the data itself. The resulting XML document can be quite heavy.

An alternative is to use a schema or XSL style sheet to format the output. You can extract the data to produce a much more concise XML document. Applying a schema to Word or Excel allows other people to update the content in Office without seeing a single XML tag.

Access also allows you to work with data in XML format, but it doesn't have its own built-in XML language. You just export straight from a table or query into an XML document that replicates the field structure.

In this section, I'll show you how to generate XML from Office 2003. The examples use sample files from the book's resources, so you can open them and follow along if you'd like. They are illustrations of the functionality that is available in Office 2003 rather than step-by-step tutorials. We'll do some more hands-on work with Office 2003 XML in Chapters 5, 6, and 7.

Word 2003

The stand-alone and professional versions of Word 2003 provide tools that you can use to work with XML documents. The trial edition of Word doesn't give you the same functionality. Let's look at the different ways that you can create and edit XML information in Word.

Creating an XML document using Save As

The simplest way to generate an XML document from Word 2003 is to use the File ➤ Save As command and choose XML Document as the type. Figure 3-9 shows how to do this.

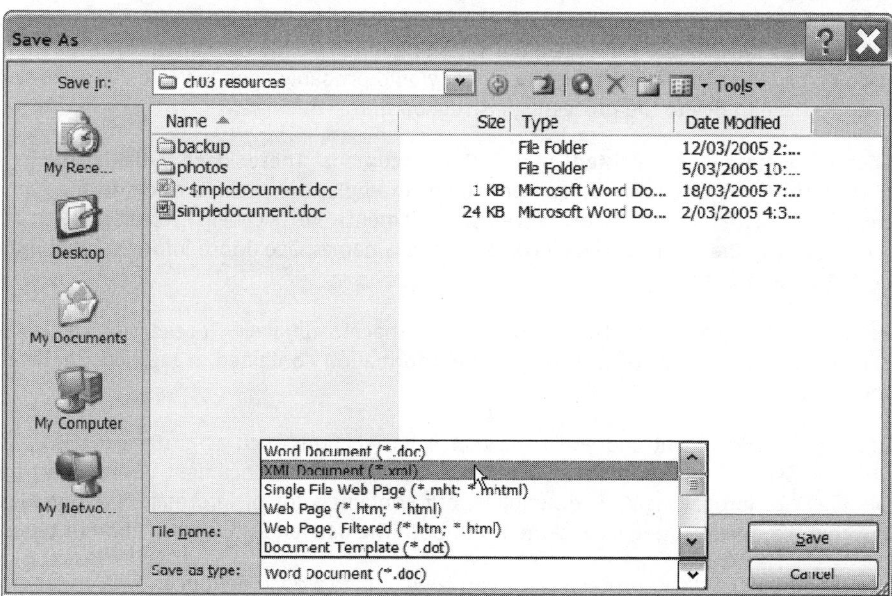

Figure 3-9. Using Save as type to generate an XML document

You can see a before and after example in your resource files. I've saved the Word document `simpledocument.doc` as `simpledocument.xml`. The source Word file contains three lines, each a different heading type. You can open `simpledocument.xml` in Notepad or an XML editor, to see the WordprocessingML generated by Word.

The following listing shows the first few lines of `simpledocument.xml`:

```
<?xml version="1.0" encoding="UTF-8" standalone="yes"?>
<?mso-application progid="Word.Document"?>
<w:wordDocument xmlns:w="http://schemas.microsoft.com/office/word/
2003/wordml" xmlns:v="urn:schemas-microsoft-com:vml"
xmlns:w10="urn:schemas-microsoft-com:office:word"
xmlns:sl="http://schemas.microsoft.com/schemaLibrary/2003/core"
xmlns:aml="http://schemas.microsoft.com/aml/2001/core"
xmlns:wx="http://schemas.microsoft.com/office/word/2003/auxHint"
xmlns:o="urn:schemas-microsoft-com:office:office"
xmlns:dt="uuid:C2F41010-65B3-11d1-A29F-00AA00C14882"
w:macrosPresent="no" w:embeddedObjPresent="no" w:ocxPresent="no"
xml:space="preserve">
<o:DocumentProperties><o:Title>Heading 1</o:Title>
<o:Author>Sas Jacobs</o:Author>
```

The listing I've shown doesn't display all of the content of the Word document; it only lists the introductory declarations. Feel free to repeat the test yourself to see the enormous amount of XML generated by Word.

You'll notice that there is a processing instruction on the second line of the XML document that instructs it to open in Word. If you double-click the file name, the XML document will probably open in Word 2003. As I have XMLSpy installed, this doesn't happen on my computer. However, if I tried to use this XML document within Flash, the document would probably open in Word 2003 and skip Flash altogether. I'd have to delete the processing instruction first.

A number of namespaces are listed in the XML document. These identify the elements in the document. Each namespace has a unique prefix. For example, the prefix o refers to the namespace `urn:schemas-microsoft-com:office:office`. The elements `<o:DocumentProperties>`, `<o:Title>`, and `<o:Author>` use the prefix o so they come from this namespace. More information about namespaces is available in Chapter 2.

The document also includes a declaration to preserve space: `xml:space="preserve"`. The last lines in the listing are elements, and you'll recognize the information contained in tags like `<o:Title>` and `<o:Author>`.

Scroll through the document and you'll see that it has sections such as `<o:DocumentProperties>`, `<w:fonts>`, `<w:styles>`, and `<w:docPr>`. The actual content of the document doesn't start until the `<w:body>` tag. WordprocessingML is descriptive, but contains a lot of information about the styling applied within the document. It is concerned with both the data and the presentation of the data.

If you knew how to write WordprocessingML, you could create a document in an XML editor and open it in Word. You could also edit the WordprocessingML from the Word document in your XML editor as an alternative way to make changes to the document.

Working with the XML Toolbox

You can download a tool to work with XML directly in Word 2003. It is a plug-in called XML Toolbox, which you can download from the Microsoft website at `www.microsoft.com/downloads/details.aspx?familyid=a56446b0-2c64-4723-b282-8859c8120db6&displaylang=en`. You'll need to have a full version of Word 2003 and the .NET Framework installed before you can use the Toolbox. Installing the plug-in is very simple. You need to accept the license agreement and click the Install button.

Once you've installed the Toolbox, you'll have an extra toolbar called the Word XML Toolbox. Figure 3-10 shows this toolbar. You can use XML Toolbox to view the XML elements within a document or to add your own content.

Figure 3-10. The XML Toolbox toolbar in Word 2003

Choose the View XML command from the XML Toolbox drop-down menu to see the WordprocessingML from within Word 2003. Figure 3-11 shows the XML source.

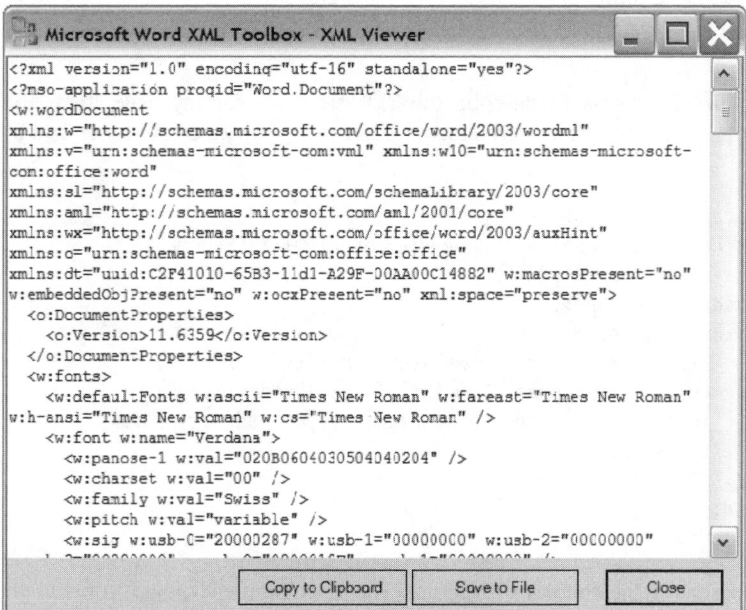

Figure 3-11. The WordprocessingML viewer in Word 2003

You can use the XML document generated by Word 2003 in other applications. For example, you could use Word to manage content for a web application or a Flash movie.

You're a little limited in the types of XML documents that Word 2003 can produce. Word doesn't handle data that repeats very well. You'd be better off to use Excel 2003 or Access 2003 instead. It's better to use Word 2003 documents as a template or form for XML data. You can create the document structure and set aside blank areas for the data.

Creating XML content by using a schema

If you have the stand-alone or professional versions of Word 2003, you'll be able to use schemas to ensure that an XML document created in Word is valid according to your language rules. A schema will also allow you to reduce the number of XML elements created from the document.

You need to follow these steps to create an XML document in Word 2003 using a schema:

1. Create a schema for the XML document.
2. Create a Word 2003 template that uses the schema.
3. Create a new document from the template and save the data in XML format.

The result is a valid XML document that is much smaller than its WordprocessingML relative.

Let's look at this more closely in an example. Chapter 5 provides you with the step-by-step instructions that you'll need to work through an example. The next section gives you an overview of the main steps and isn't intended as a tutorial.

Creating the schema

I used the following schema to describe the XML structure for my news item. The resource file `newsSchema.xsd` contains the complete schema. You'll learn how to create schemas a little later in this chapter.

```
<?xml version="1.0"?>
<xsd:schema xmlns:xsd="http://www.w3.org/2001/XMLSchema">
  <xsd:element name="news">
    <xsd:complexType>
      <xsd:sequence>
        <xsd:element name="newsDate" type="xsd:string"/>
        <xsd:element name="newsTitle" type="xsd:string"/>
        <xsd:element name="newsContent" type="xsd:string"/>
      </xsd:sequence>
    </xsd:complexType>
  </xsd:element>
</xsd:schema>
```

The schema describes the following structure. The root element `<news>` contains the `<newsDate>`, `<newsTitle>`, and `<newsContent>` elements. There can only be one of each of those elements, and they must be included in the order specified. The elements all contain `string` data.

Creating the Word 2003 template

I've created a simple template called `newsXML.dot` to show a news item. It is made up of three form fields to capture the date, title, and content of the news item. If you have Word 2003, you can open the file to see how it looks. Use the *Ctrl-Shift-X* shortcut key to toggle the display of the XML tags.

This template already has the schema applied, but I've included the instructions here in case you want to re-create it yourself. We'll cover this in more detail in Chapter 5. After you open the template, you'll need to unlock it if you want to make any changes. Choose Tools ➤ Unprotect Document.

To apply the schema to a Word 2003 template, choose Tools ➤ Templates and Add-Ins and select the XML Schema tab. Click the Add Schema button and navigate to the schema file. Enter a URI or namespace for the schema and an alias, as shown in Figure 3-12.

Figure 3-12. Entering schema settings in Word 2003

When you've finished, the schema alias should appear in the Templates and Add-Ins dialog box, as shown in Figure 3-13.

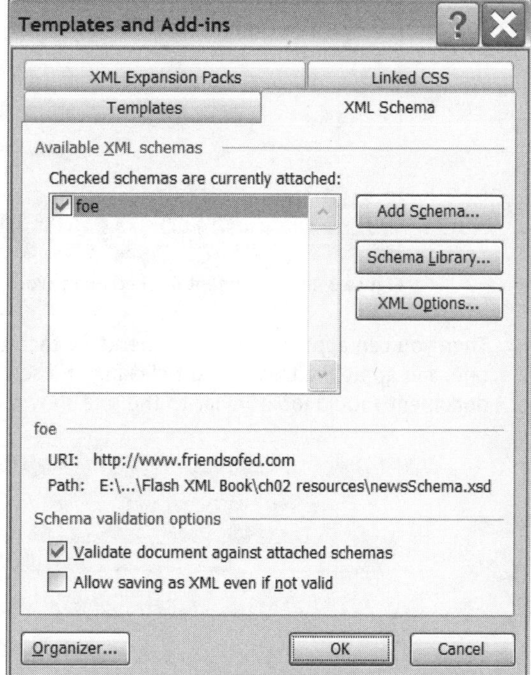

Figure 3-13. Attached schemas in Word 2003

To streamline the XML produced by this document, click the XML Options button and choose the Save Data Only option. This excludes formatting information from the output. Make sure that Validate document against attached schemas is also checked.

You can only apply the XML tags if you have selected the Show XML tags in the document option in the Task Pane. If you can't see the Task Pane, choose View ➤ Task Pane and choose XML Structure from the drop-down menu at the top.

First, you need to apply the root element to the entire document. Select all of the content, right-click, and choose Apply XML element. Select the news element. When prompted choose Apply to Entire Document. You should see the content surrounded by a shaded tag, as shown in Figure 3-14.

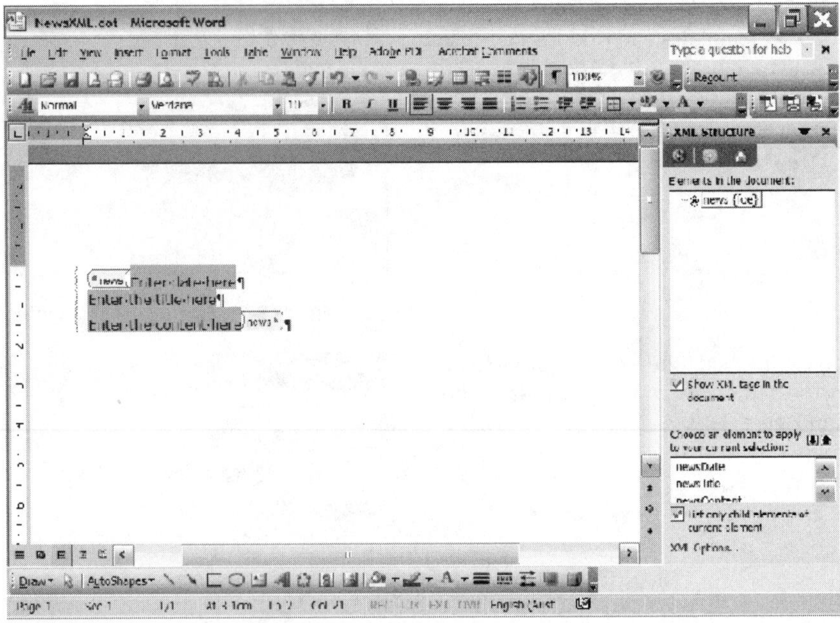

Figure 3-14 The content marked up in Word 2003

Then you can apply the other elements to each part of the Word document. Select the fields, one by one, and apply the tags by right-clicking and selecting Apply XML element. When you've finished, the document should look similar to the one shown in Figure 3-15.

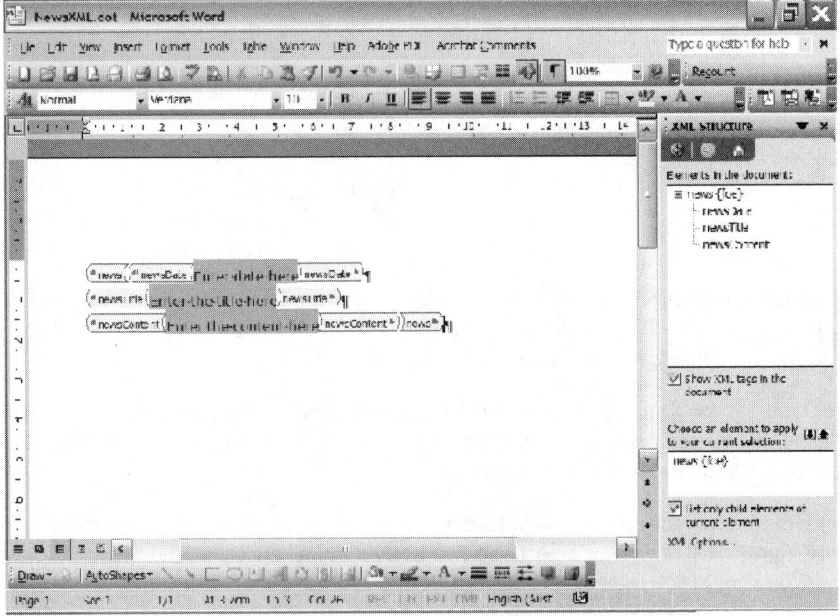

Figure 3-15. The completed template in Word 2003

The result is a template that maps to an XML schema. Don't forget to lock the fields before you save and close the template. Choose View ➤ Toolbars ➤ Forms and click the padlock icon.

Creating XML content from a new document

Once you've created the template, you can generate XML content from documents based on this template. Choose File ➤ New and select the news template. When the new document is created, all you have to do is fill in the fields. You can hide the XML tags by deselecting the Show XML tags in the document option in the Task Pane.

Output the XML by choosing File ➤ Save and selecting the XML document type. Make sure you check the Save data only option before you save. You'll see the warning shown in Figure 3-16. Click Continue.

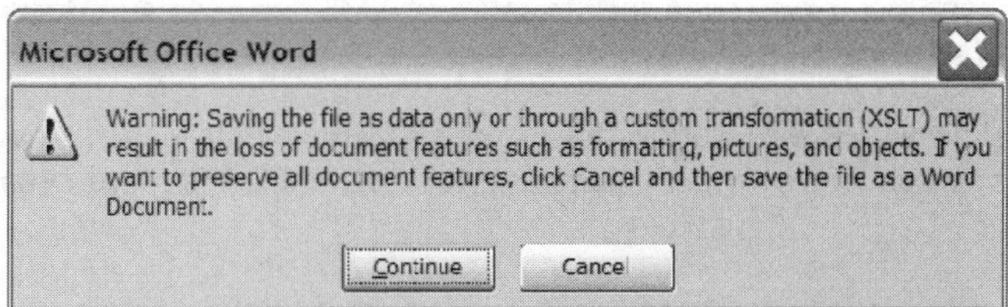

Figure 3-16. You'll see this warning when saving in XML format with a schema in Word 2003.

The resource file `NewsItem.xml` contains the competed XML document from Word 2003. The following listing shows the content:

```
<?xml version="1.0" encoding="UTF-8" standalone="no"?>
<news xmlns="newsSchema">
  <newsDate>July 4, 2005</newsDate>
  <newsTitle>Fireworks extravaganza!</newsTitle>
  <newsContent>US expats in Australia celebrated the 4th of July
  with firework demonstrations throughout the country.</newsContent>
</news>
```

Compare the structure and content of this XML document with the one that didn't use a schema, `simpledocument.xml`. The tag names in this document are more descriptive, and it is significantly shorter than the WordprocessingML document. It would be very easy to use this XML document within a Flash movie. Using `simpledocument.xml` would be much harder.

We'll cover the step-by-step instructions for creating XML from Word 2003 in much more detail in Chapter 5.

Excel

If you own Excel Professional or Enterprise edition, you'll be able to work with XML documents. Again, you can't use the trial edition of Excel 2003. As with Word, you can save an Excel file in XML format so that you can use it on the Web or in Flash. You can also use Excel to open an XML document so that you can update or analyze the information.

Excel document structures are very rigid. They always use a grid made up of rows and columns. This means that the structure of XML data generated from Excel will match this format. In Word, it's possible for you to include elements within other elements or text. For example, you could display this XML structure using Word:

```
<title>
  This is a title by
  <author>Sas Jacobs</author
</title>
```

In Excel, the smallest unit of data that we can work with is a cell. Cells can't contain other cells, so our XML document structure with mixed content can't display properly in Excel. Any XML document generated from Excel will include grid-like data.

Excel uses a document map to describe the structure of XML documents. A document map is like a simpler version of a schema.

In this section, I'll show you how to work with existing XML documents in Excel. It's an overview of the functionality that's available rather than a complete tutorial. You'll find more detailed information in Chapter 6.

Creating an XML document using Save As

As with Word, the easiest way to create an XML document from Excel is to save it using the XML document type. Choose File ➤ Save As and select XML in the Save as type drop-down box. I've done this with the file `simplespreadsheet.xls`; you can see the resulting XML document saved as `simplespreadsheet.xml`.

You'll notice that a simple Excel document has created a large XML document. This listing shows the first few lines of the XML document:

```
<?xml version="1.0"?>
<?mso-application progid="Excel.Sheet"?>
<Workbook xmlns="urn:schemas-microsoft-com:office:spreadsheet"
xmlns:o="urn:schemas-microsoft-com:office:office"
xmlns:x="urn:schemas-microsoft-com:office:excel"
xmlns:ss="urn:schemas-microsoft-com:office:spreadsheet"
xmlns:html="http://www.w3.org/TR/REC-html40">
<DocumentProperties xmlns="urn:schemas-microsoft-com:office:office">
  <Author>Sas Jacobs</Author>
  <LastAuthor>Sas Jacobs</LastAuthor>
```

The second line of the file is a processing instruction that instructs the file to open in Excel:

```
<?mso-application progid="Excel.Sheet"?>
```

As with Word, a number of namespaces are referenced in the XML document. The element names `<DocumentProperties>` and `<Author>` are self-explanatory. The XML document includes information about each sheet in a `<Worksheet>` element. There are descriptions for `<Table>`, `<Column>`, `<Row>`, `<Cell>`, and `<Data>`, and Excel methodically describes the contents of each worksheet by column and by row. This is how Excel translates the grid style of Excel documents into XML. What we're most interested in is the contents of the `<Data>` elements; they contain the values from each cell.

As with Word, you'll notice that Excel generates a long XML document. It's hard for humans to read, and extracting the content would be a lengthy process. Again, using a schema will reduce the quantity of data generated by Excel 2003.

You can use Excel to open an existing XML document. Before displaying the data, Excel will ask you how you want to open the file, as shown in Figure 3-17. The process will be a little different depending on whether the document references a schema.

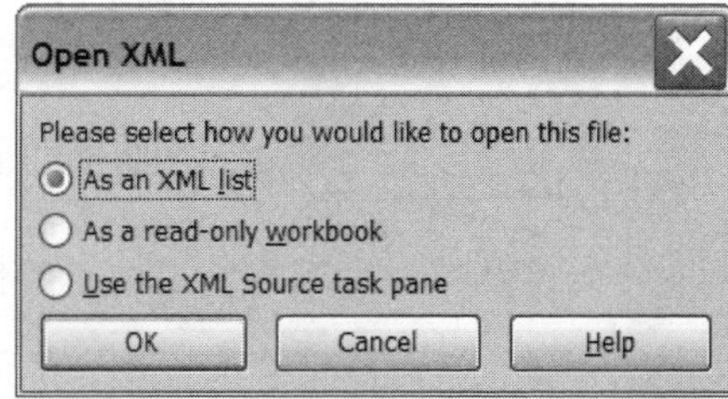

Figure 3-17. Excel 2003 asks how an XML file should be opened.

Opening an XML document with a schema

You use these steps to work with an XML document in Excel:

1. Optionally create a schema for the XML document.
2. Open the file in Excel.
3. Make changes to the content and export the XML file.

If you open the file as an XML list, Excel will use any related schema to determine how to display data. The following listing shows `address.xml`. It uses the schema `addressSchema.xsd`. Figure 3-18 shows how this file translates when opened in Excel.

```
<?xml version="1.0" encoding="UTF-8"?>
<phoneBook xmlns:xsi="http://www.w3.org/2001/XMLSchema-instance"
xsi:noNamespaceSchemaLocation="addressSchema.xsd">
  <contact id="1">
    <name>Sas Jacobs</name>
    <address>123 Some Street, Some City, Some Country</address>
    <phone>123 456</phone>
  </contact>
  <contact id="2">
    <name>John Smith</name>
    <address>4 Another Street, Another City, Another Country</address>
    <phone>456 789</phone>
  </contact>
  <contact id="3">
    <name>Jo Bloggs</name>
    <address>7 Different Street, Different City, UK</address>
    <phone>789 123</phone>
  </contact>
</phoneBook>
```

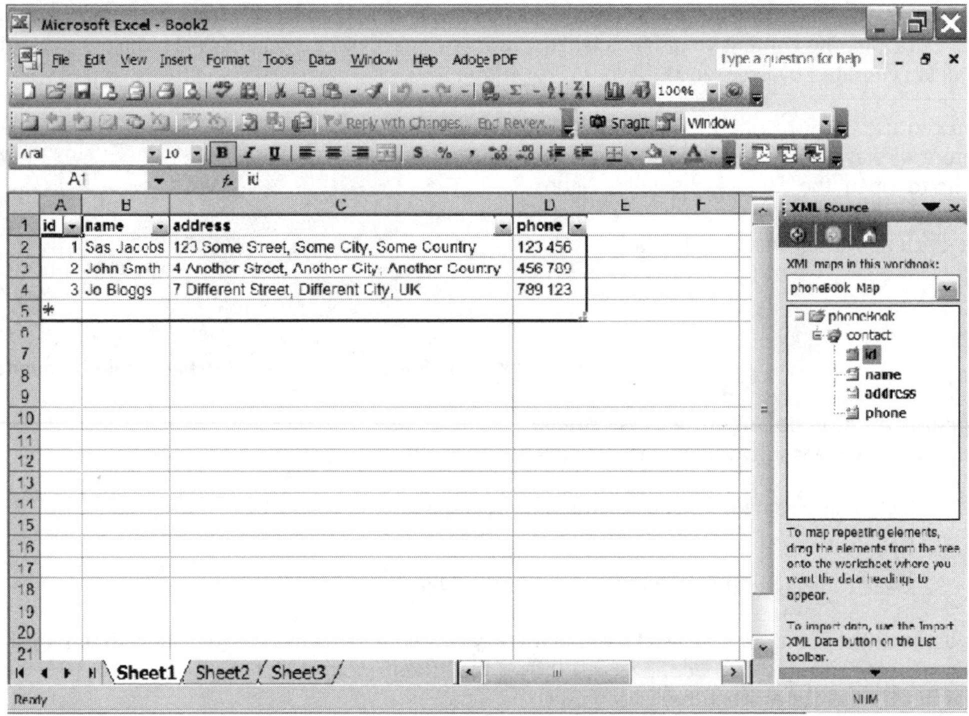

Figure 3-18. An XML document displayed in Excel 2003

Excel automatically creates a document map for the elements from the schema. You can see the document map in the XML Source Task Pane. Excel has also added an automatic filter to the column headings. You can select specific content from the XML document by choosing values from the drop-down lists.

You can make changes to the existing data in Excel or even add new data. Be careful how you generate the XML document. If you use Save As and choose the XML type, you'll re-create the current content using SpreadsheetML. It will produce a large document that doesn't match your schema. Instead, you should export the data as shown in the next section.

Exporting XML data with a document map

Before exporting the data, you'll want to make sure the changes you've made are valid against the schema. Right-click inside your data and choose XML ➤ XML Map Properties. Check the Validate data against schema for import and export option. This option isn't checked by default. You can also find XML Map Properties in the Data ➤ XML menu. Figure 3-19 shows the XML Map Properties dialog box.

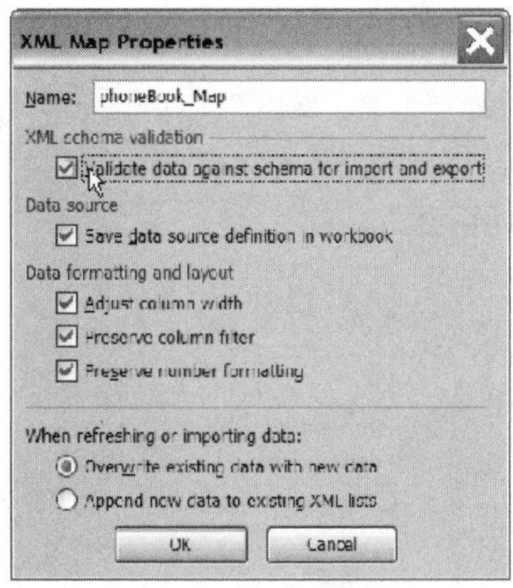

Figure 3-19. The XML Map Properties dialog box in Excel 2003

To export the XML document, right-click in the data and choose XML ➤ Export. Enter a file name, choose a location, and click Export. Excel will generate an XML document that is valid according to your schema.

I used Excel to update the `address.xml` file and exported the data to the resource file `addressExportedFromExcel.xml`. If you look at the XML structure, you'll see that it's almost identical to that of the `address.xml` file. Figure 3-20 shows them side by side in XMLSpy.

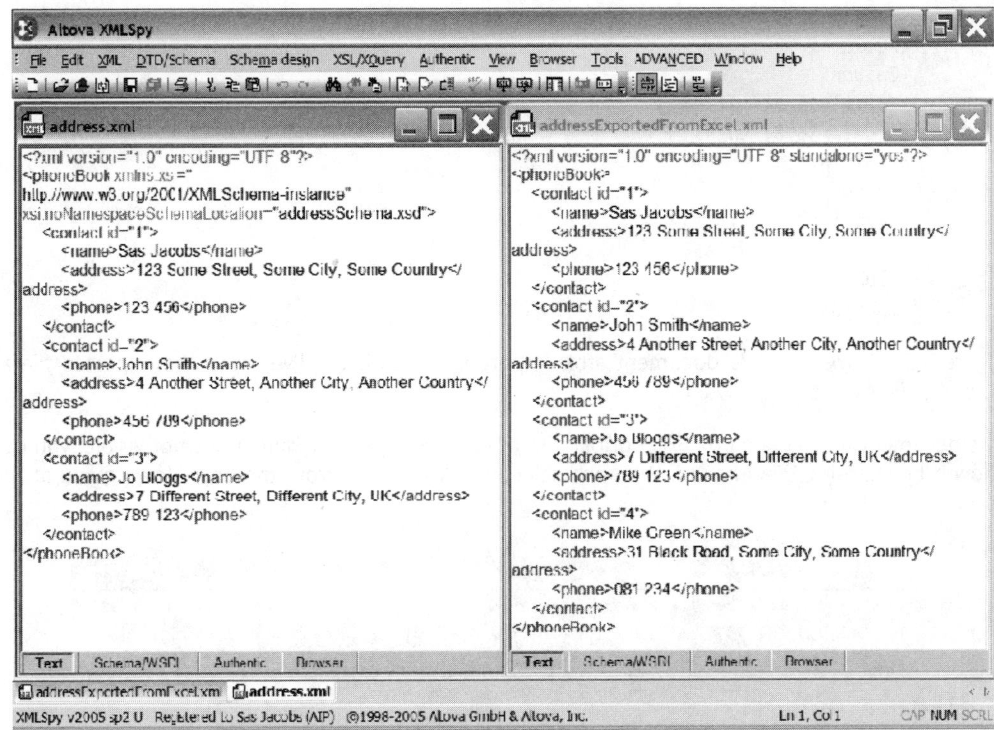

Figure 3-20. The original and updated XML documents open in XMLSpy

Opening an XML document without a schema

If you open an XML document that doesn't specify a schema, Excel will create one based on the data. Figure 3-21 shows the warning that Excel will display.

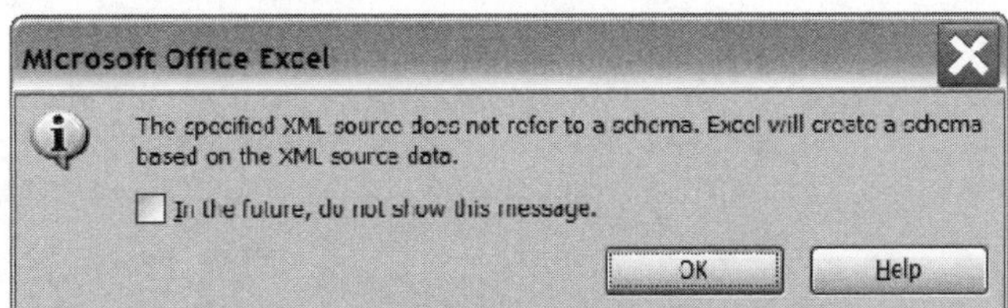

Figure 3-21. Excel 2003 will create a document map for an XML file if a schema doesn't exist.

When the data is imported, Excel creates a document map and figures out how to display the data. You can try this with the resource file `excelImport.xml`. This listing shows a simple XML document without a schema:

```
<?xml version="1.0">
<ImportData>
  <Column>
    <title>Jan</title>
    <data>1234</data>
  </Column>
  <Column>
    <title>Feb</title>
    <data>5678</data>
  </Column>
  <Column>
    <title>Mar</title>
    <data>9123</data>
</Column>
</ImportData>
```

Figure 3-22 shows the XML document after importing it into Excel. I've saved the imported file as resource file `excelImport.xls`.

The document map created by Excel displays in the XML Source Task Pane. If it's not visible, you can show it by choosing View ➤ Task Pane and selecting XML Source from the drop-down menu at the top of the Task Pane.

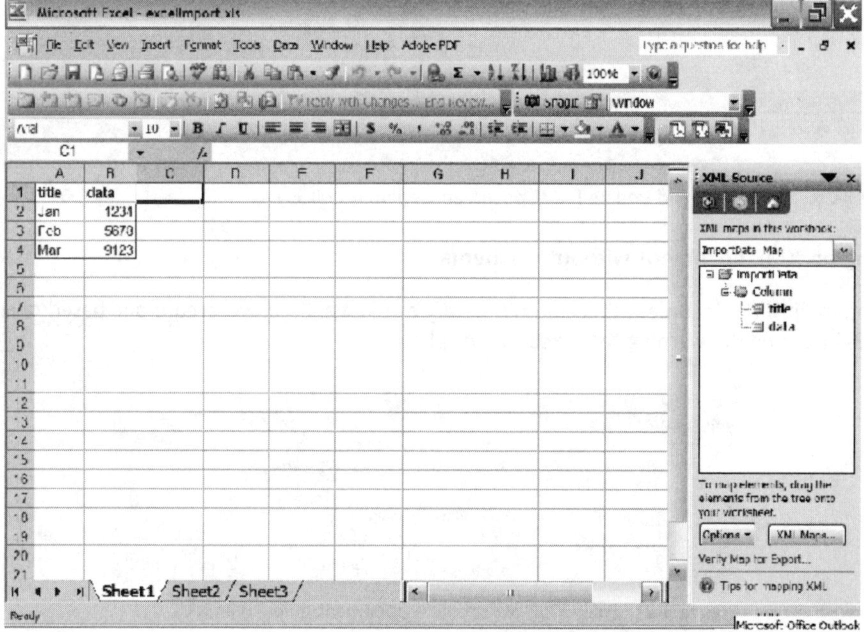

Figure 3-22. An XML file without a schema imported into Excel 2003

Working with mixed elements

If you use Excel to open an existing XML document, make sure that it conforms to a grid structure. Excel will have difficulty interpreting the structure of an XML document that contains text and child elements together in the same parent element.

This listing shows the file `addressMixedElements.xml`. As you can see, this document includes mixed content in the <address> element. It contains both text and a child element, <suburb>.

```
<?xml version="1.0" encoding="UTF-8"?>
<phoneBook>
  <contact id="1">
    <name>Sas Jacobs</name>
    <address>123 Some Street,
      <suburb>Some City</suburb>
    , Some Country</address>
    <phone>123 456</phone>
  </contact>
  <contact id="2">
    <name>John Smith</name>
    <address>4 Another Street,
      <suburb>Another City</suburb>
    , Another Country</address>
    <phone>456 789</phone>
  </contact>
</phoneBook>
```

Figure 3-23 shows the file opened in Excel 2003. The <address> element and text is missing; only the child element <suburb> displays.

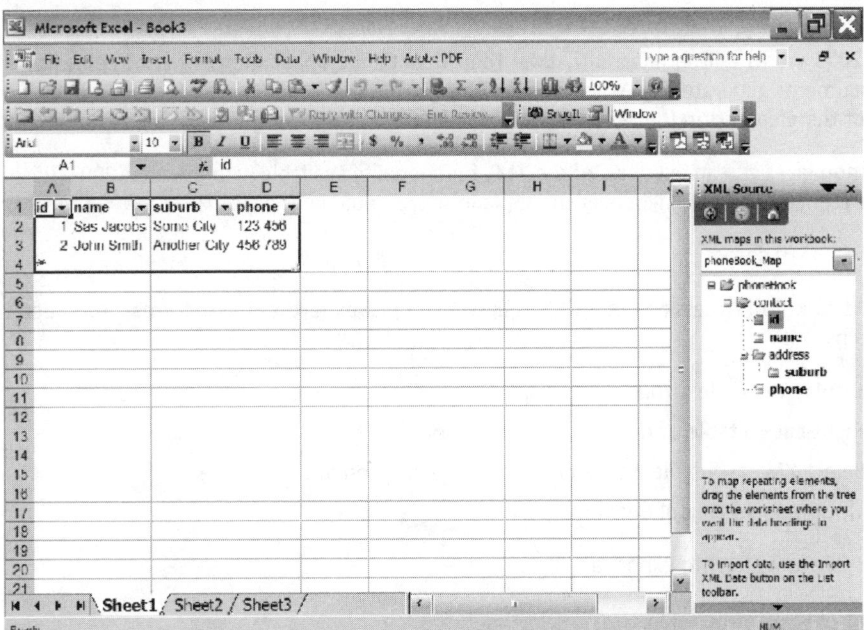

Figure 3-23. An XML document with mixed elements doesn't display correctly in Excel 2003.

If you export the data to an XML document, Excel will only save the elements displayed. The following listing shows the exported file addressMixedElementsExported.xml:

```
<?xml version="1.0" encoding="UTF-8" standalone="yes"?>
<phoneBook xmlns:xsi="http://www.w3.org/2001/XMLSchema-instance">
  <contact id="1">
    <name>Sas Jacobs</name>
    <address>
      <suburb>Some City</suburb>
    </address>
    <phone>123 456</phone>
  </contact>
  <contact id="2">
    <name>John Smith</name>
    <address>
      <suburb>Another City</suburb>
    </address>
    <phone>456 789</phone>
  </contact>
</phoneBook>
```

The text within the <address> element is missing. Excel has also added a namespace to the root element.

Using Excel VBA and XML

You can use VBA to work with XML documents. For example, you could handle the importing of XML documents automatically. Excel 2003 recognizes the XMLMaps collection, and you can use the Import and Export methods to work with XML documents programmatically.

Access

Access 2003 works a little differently than the other Office applications when it comes to XML. The XML documents generated by Access come directly from the structure of your tables and queries. The names of the elements in the resulting XML document come from the Access field names.

This section gives you an overview of the XML functionality available within Access 2003. It isn't a complete reference or tutorial. I'll cover the topic in more detail in Chapter 7.

Exporting XML data

Getting data out of Access and into XML is easy—you just export it in XML format. You need to follow these steps:

1. Display the table or query objects.
2. Right-click a table or query and select Export.
3. Select XML as the file type and choose a destination and file name.
4. Optionally select options for export.

Figure 3-24 shows how to export a table.

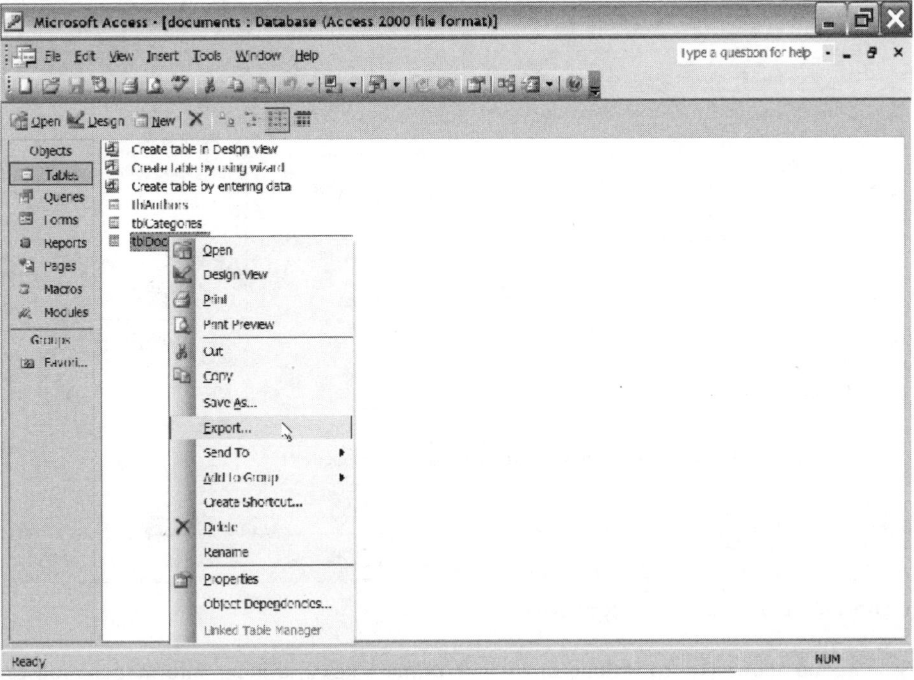

Figure 3-24. Exporting a table in Access 2003

After you chose the Export option, you'll have to enter a file name and choose a destination for the XML file. Don't forget to select XML from the Save as type drop-down list. When you click Export, you'll be asked to choose between exporting the data (XML), a schema (XSD), and presentation of the data (XSL). See Figure 3-25 for a view of the Export XML dialog box.

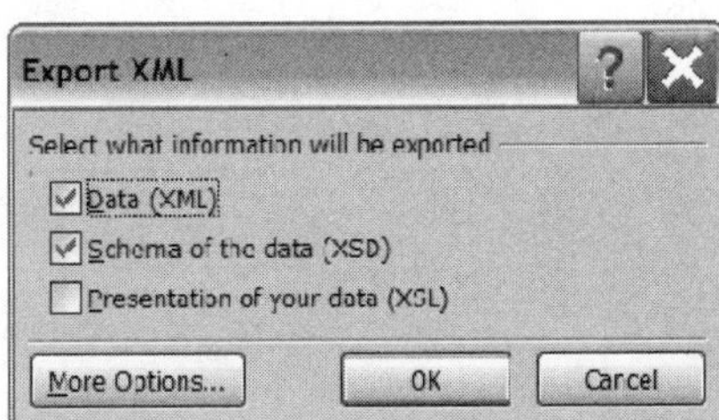

Figure 3-25. Export options in Access 2003

Setting export options

You have some extra options that you can view by clicking the More Options button. Figure 3-26 shows these options. You can also include related records from other tables and apply an XSL transformation to the data.

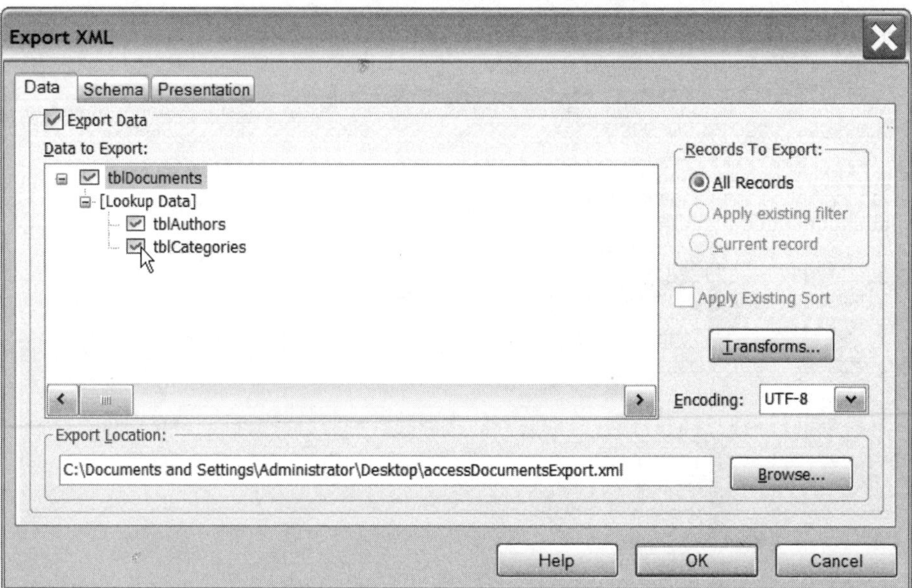

Figure 3-26. Export options in Access 2003

The Schema tab allows you to include or exclude primary key and index information. You can also embed the schema in your XML document or create an external schema. Figure 3-27 shows these options.

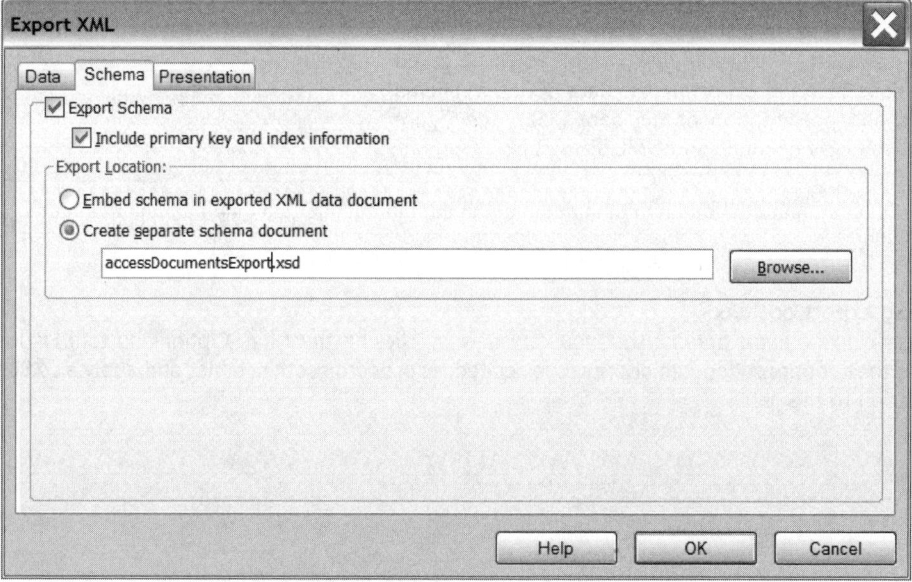

Figure 3-27. Schema export options in Access 2003

The Presentation tab, shown in Figure 3-28, allows you to generate HTML or ASP and an associated style sheet.

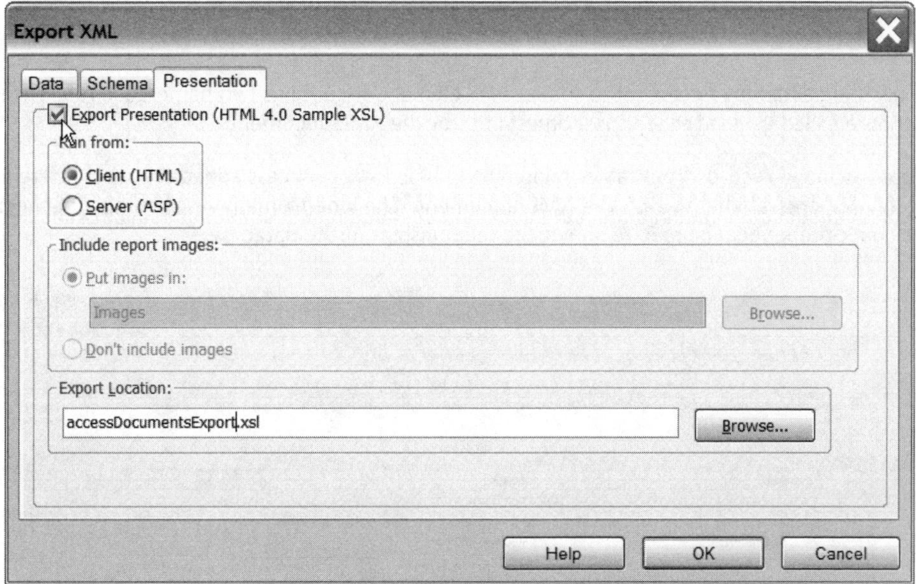

Figure 3-28. Presentation export options in Access 2003

I used the Access database documents.mdb and exported the records from tblDocuments. I included the related records from other tables and created both an XML and an XSD file. The resulting XML documents are called accessDocumentsExport.xml and accessDocumentsExport.xsd, respectively. If you have Access 2003, you can use the documents.mdb database to create the XML files yourself.

This listing shows a section of the sample XML document created by the export:

```
<?xml version="1.0" encoding="UTF-8"?>
<dataroot xmlns:od="urn:schemas-microsoft-com:officedata"
xmlns:xsi="http://www.w3.org/2001/XMLSchema-instance"
xsi:noNamespaceSchemaLocation="accessDocumentsExport.xsd"
generated="2005-03-04T18:10:06">
  <tblDocuments>
    <documentID>1</documentID>
    <documentName>Shopping for profit and pleasure</documentName>
    <authorID>1</authorID>
    <documentPublishYear>2002</documentPublishYear>
    <categoryID>4</categoryID>
  </tblDocuments>
  <tblAuthors>
    <authorID>1</authorID>
    <AuthorFirstName>Alison</AuthorFirstName>
    <AuthorLastName>Ambrose</AuthorLastName>
    <AuthorOrganization>Organization A</AuthorOrganization>
```

```
    </tblAuthors>
    <categoryID>4</categoryID>
      <category>Shopping</category>
    </tblCategories>
  </dataroot>
```

The only thing added by Access is the <dataroot> element. It contains two namespace references and an attribute called generated. This is a timestamp for the XML document.

Because I included records from tables related to tblDocuments, Access added the table references as separate elements at the end of the XML document. The one-to-many relationships between the tables aren't preserved. Figure 3-29 shows the relationships in the database.

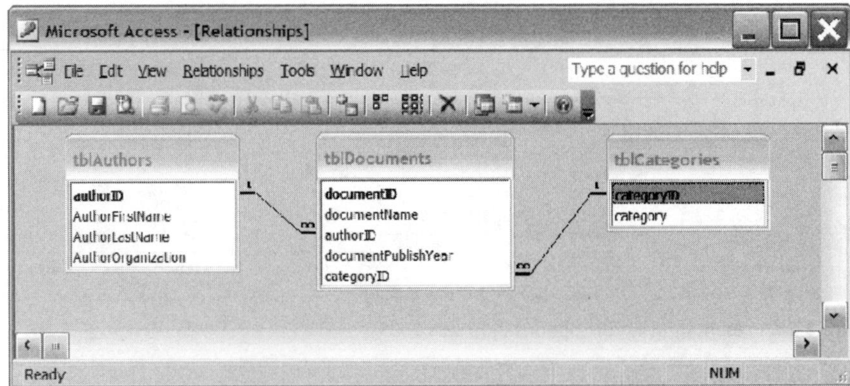

Figure 3-29. The relationships between tables in the documents.mdb database

Controlling the structure of XML documents

XML documents exported from Access are shorter than their Word and Excel equivalents. The elements in the XML document take their names from the field names in the table or query. Access replaces the spaces in field names with an underscore (_) character.

If you don't want to use the default field names in the table, an alternative is to create a query first that joins all the data and then export that to an XML document. Access won't give you the option to export data in linked tables, but the rest of the process is much the same as for exporting tables.

The following listing shows a trimmed-down version of the XML document, accessQryBookDetailsExport.xml. You can also look at the schema file, accessQryBookDetailsExport.xsd.

```
<?xml version="1.0" encoding="UTF-8"?>
<dataroot xmlns:od="urn:schemas-microsoft-com:officedata"
xmlns:xsi="http://www.w3.org/2001/XMLSchema-instance"
xsi:noNamespaceSchemaLocation="accessQryBookDetailsExport.xsd"
generated="2005-03-04T18:50:47">
  <qryBookDetails>
    <documentID>2</documentID>
    <documentName>Bike riding for non-bike riders</documentName>
    <authorID>4</authorID>
```

```
      <AuthorFirstName>Saul</AuthorFirstName>
      <AuthorLastName>Sorenson</AuthorLastName>
      <AuthorOrganization>Organization D</AuthorOrganization>
      <documentPublishYear>2004</documentPublishYear>
      <categoryID>5</categoryID>
      <category>Bike riding</category>
    </qryBookDetails>
  </dataroot>
```

This XML document organizes the data by document and shows the relationships between the related tables. You could also have organized the data by author or category.

For an example of documents organized by author, see the resource file `accessQryAuthorDocuments.xml`, shown in the listing that follows, and the resource file `accessQryAuthorDocuments.xsd`.

```
<?xml version="1.0" encoding="UTF-8"?>
<dataroot xmlns:od="urn:schemas-microsoft-com:officedata"
xmlns:xsi="http://www.w3.org/2001/XMLSchema-instance"
xsi:noNamespaceSchemaLocation="accessQryAuthorDocuments.xsd"
generated="2005-03-04T18:53:15">
  <qryAuthorDocuments>
    <authorID>1</authorID>
    <AuthorFirstName>Alison</AuthorFirstName>
    <AuthorLastName>Ambrose</AuthorLastName>
    <AuthorOrganization>Organization A</AuthorOrganization>
    <documentID>4</documentID>
    <documentName>Fishing tips</documentName>
    <documentPublishYear>1999</documentPublishYear>
  </qryAuthorDocuments>
  <qryAuthorDocuments>
   <authorID>1</authorID>
   <AuthorFirstName>Alison</AuthorFirstName>
    <AuthorLastName>Ambrose</AuthorLastName>
    <AuthorOrganization>Organization A</AuthorOrganization>
    <documentID>1</documentID>
    <documentName>Shopping for profit and pleasure</documentName>
    <documentPublishYear>2002</documentPublishYear>
  </qryAuthorDocuments>
</dataroot>
```

Writing queries still doesn't quite solve our problem. A better structure for the XML file from Access would have been to group the documents within each <authorID> element. Access doesn't do this automatically.

Using Access VBA and XML

You can automate XML importing and exporting with Access 2003 VBA. Access recognizes the `Application.ImportXML` and `Application.ExportXML` methods. You can trigger them from buttons on a form. It's important to note that VBA can't transform an XML document during the import process.

InfoPath

Office 2003 for PCs includes a new product called InfoPath that allows people to create and edit XML documents by filling in forms. The forms allow you to collect XML information and use it with your other business systems.

InfoPath is included in Microsoft Office Professional Enterprise Edition 2003, or you can buy it separately. There is no equivalent product for Macintosh Office 2004 users.

Office 2003 and data structure

Office 2003 can generate XML documents for use by other applications, including Flash movies. If you set up Word, Excel, or Access properly, your users can maintain their own XML documents using Office 2003. Most people are familiar with these software packages, so it's not terribly demanding for them to use them as tools for maintaining their data.

As you can see from the previous sections, each of the Office applications works with particular data structures. Word 2003 works best with nonrepeating information, a bit like filling in a form to generate the XML elements. Excel 2003 is best with grid-like data structures that don't include mixed elements. Access 2003 works with relational data, and you can write queries to specify which data to export. Using a schema in Word and Excel greatly simplifies the XML documents that they produce. We'll look at creating schemas a little later in this chapter.

Consuming a web service

You've probably heard the term *web services* mentioned a lot. The official definition from the W3C at `www.w3.org/TR/ws-gloss/#defs` is

A Web service is a software system designed to support interoperable machine-to-machine interaction over a network. It has an interface described in a machine-processable format (specifically WSDL). Other systems interact with the Web service in a manner prescribed by its description using SOAP-messages, typically conveyed using HTTP with an XML serialization in conjunction with other Web-related standards.

In simpler terms, a web service is a way for you to access data on another system using an XML format. Web services operate over the Internet and are platform independent. In order to use a web service, you request information and receive a response in an XML document.

You can use web services to look up a variety of information, including television guides, movie reviews, and weather updates. As an author, I can use Amazon's web service to find out the sales ranking and database details for any books that I've written.

When you start reading about web services, you'll see the terms UDDI, WSDL, SOAP, and REST. A glossary for the main terms associated with web services is at `www.w3.org/TR/2004/NOTE-ws-gloss-20040211/`.

You can find out what web services are available through a company's Universal Description, Discovery, and Integration (UDDI) registry. The UDDI contains a description of the web services that are available and the way that you can access them.

Web Services Description Language (WSDL) describes web services in a standard XML format. In case you're interested, most people pronounce this as *whizdle*. At the time of writing, the working draft for WSDL version 2 was available at `www.w3.org/TR/2004/WD-wsdl20-20040803/`.

The WSDL definition explains what is available through the web service, where it is located, and how you should make a request. It lists the parameters you need to include when requesting information, such as the fields and datatypes that the web service expects.

You can request information from a web service using a number of different protocols. The SOAP protocol is probably the most commonly used and has support within Flash. You can also use Representational State Transfer (REST), but Flash doesn't support this format natively.

SOAP, which stands for Simple Object Access Protocol, is a format for sending messages to web services. A SOAP message is an XML document with a specific structure. The request is contained within a part of the document called a SOAP Envelope.

You can find more about SOAP by viewing the note submitted to the W3C at www.w3.org/TR/2000/NOTE-SOAP-20000508/. This document isn't a W3C recommendation. At the time of writing, a working draft of SOAP version 1.2 was available at www.w3.org/TR/2002/WD-soap12-part1-20020626/.

REST is another way to work with web services. It is not a W3C standard; rather, REST is a style for interacting with web services. REST allows you to make requests through a URL rather than by sending an XML document request. Flash doesn't support REST requests, but you'll see a little later on that they can be very useful if you need to add data from a web service to a Flash movie.

Using web services to interact with Amazon

Amazon jumped into web services relatively early on. At the time of writing, the latest version of the Amazon E-Commerce Service (ECS) was version 4.0, which was released on October 4, 2004. You can find comprehensive information about ECS at www.amazon.com/gp/aws/landing.html. It's free to use, but you have to register with Amazon first to get a subscription ID before you can start making requests.

The ECS provides access to information about products, customer content, sellers, marketplace listings, and shopping carts. You could use ECS to build an Amazon search and purchase application on your own website.

The WSDL for the U.S. service can be found at webservices.amazon.com/AWSECommerceService/AWSECommerceService.wsdl. You can open the file in a web browser if you want to see what it contains. The schema for the U.S. service is at webservices.amazon.com/AWSECommerceService/AWSECommerceService.xsd. Again, you can view this file in a web browser. The other Amazon locations supported are the UK, Germany, Japan, France, and Canada.

The Application Programming Interface (API) for Amazon web services describes all the operations you can perform. This includes functions like ItemLookup and ItemSearch. You can also work with wish lists and shopping carts.

To make a REST query to search for an item at Amazon, you could use the following URL format:

```
http://webservices.amazon.com/onca/xml?Service=AWSECommerceService
&SubscriptionId=[YourSubscription ID Here]&Operation=ItemSearch
&SearchIndex=[A Search Index String]&Keywords=[A Keywords String]
&Sort=[A Sort String]
```

The request can include other optional parameters, and you can find out more in the online documentation. You can also get help by using the Help operation.

In the sample request that follows, I'm using my own name to search for books in the U.S. Amazon database. I have replaced my subscriptionID with XXXX; you'll need to use your own ID if you want to run the query.

```
http://webservices.amazon.com/onca/xml?Service=AWSECommerceService
&SubscriptionId=XXXX&Operation=ItemSearch&SearchIndex=Books
&Author=Sas%20Jacobs
```

If I enter the URL into the address line of a web browser, the request will run and the results will display in the browser window. All Amazon responses have the same structure, as shown in this listing:

```
<?xml version="1.0" encoding="UTF-8">
<rootTag xmlns="http://webservices.amazon.com/AWSECommerceService/ ➥
2004-03-19">
  <OperationRequest>
    ... XML header and HTTP request information
  </OperationRequest>
  <Items>
    ... XML data here
  </Items>
</rootTag>
```

The name of the root element will vary depending on the type of request that you made. For example, an ItemSearch request will use the root element name <ItemSearchResponse>. If there are any errors in your request, they'll be contained inside an <Errors> element.

When I made the preceding REST request, I received the response shown in the following listing. Note that I've removed the sections containing the subscriptionID from the listing. I've saved the results in the file AmazonQueryResults.xml.

```
<?xml version="1.0" encoding="UTF-8" ?>
<ItemSearchResponse xmlns="http://webservices.amazon.com/ ➥
AWSECommerceService/2005-02-23">
  <OperationRequest>
    <HTTPHeaders>
      <Header Name="UserAgent" Value="Mozilla/4.0 (compatible;
      MSIE 6.0; Windows NT 5.1; SV1; .NET CLR 1.1.4322)" />
    </HTTPHeaders>
    <RequestId>05BXE60PQPM6P687J1PA</RequestId>
    <Arguments>
      <Argument Name="Service" Value="AWSECommerceService" />
      <Argument Name="SearchIndex" Value="Books" />
      <Argument Name="Author" Value="Sas Jacobs" />
      <Argument Name="Operation" Value="ItemSearch" />
    </Arguments>
    <RequestProcessingTime>0.0390307903289795</RequestProcessingTime>
  </OperationRequest>
```

```
    <Items>
      <Request>
        <IsValid>True</IsValid>
        <ItemSearchRequest>
          <Author>Sas Jacobs</Author>
          <SearchIndex>Books</SearchIndex>
        </ItemSearchRequest>
      </Request>
      <TotalResults>2</TotalResults>
      <TotalPages>1</TotalPages>
        <Item>
          <ASIN>8931435061</ASIN>
          <DetailPageURL>http://www.amazon.com/exec/obidos/redirect?
          tag=ws%26link_code=xm2%26camp=2025%26creative=165953%26path=
          http://www.amazon.com/gp/redirect.html%253fASIN=8931435061%252
          location=/o/ASIN/8931435061%25253F
          </DetailPageURL>
          <ItemAttributes>
            <Author>Sas Jacobs</Author>
            <Author>YoungJin.com</Author>
            <Author>Sybex</Author>
            <ProductGroup>Book</ProductGroup>
            <Title>Flash MX 2004 Accelerated: A Full-Color Guide</Title>
        </ItemAttributes>
      </Item>
    </Items>
  </ItemSearchResponse>
```

It's common to query web services using a SOAP request. Usually some kind of server-side script generates the request for you. The WebServiceConnector data component in Flash can also generate SOAP requests.

Google provides an example of a web service that you can query with SOAP. At the time of writing, Google provided three different operations: doGetCachedpage, doSpellingSuggestion, and doGoogleSearch. You can see the WSDL at `http://api.google.com/GoogleSearch.wsdl`.

The W3C provides a sample SOAP message for Google at `www.w3.org/2004/06/03-google-soap-wsdl.html`. This listing shows an example based on the W3C sample. It does a search for the term Flash XML books:

```
<?xml version='1.0' encoding='UTF-8'?>
<soap11:Envelope xmlns="urn:GoogleSearch"
xmlns:soap11="http://schemas.xmlsoap.org/soap/envelope/">
  <soap11:Body>
    <doGoogleSearch>
      <key>00000000000000000000000000000000</key>
      <q>Flash XML books</q>
      <start>0</start>
      <maxResults>10</maxResults>
      <filter>true</filter>
```

```
        <restrict></restrict>
        <safeSearch>false</safeSearch>
        <lr></lr>
        <ie>latin1</ie>
        <oe>latin1</oe>
      </doGoogleSearch>
    </soap11:Body>
  </soap11:Envelope>
```

This listing shows a sample result XML document from the W3C site. I've shown the first result only to simplify the output:

```
<?xml version='1.0' encoding='UTF-8'?>
<soap11:Envelope
  xmlns="urn:GoogleSearch"
  xmlns:google="urn:GoogleSearch"
  xmlns:soapenc="http://schemas.xmlsoap.org/soap/encoding/"
  xmlns:soap11="http://schemas.xmlsoap.org/soap/envelope/">
  <soap11:Body>
    <doGoogleSearchResponse>
      <return>
        <documentFiltering>false</documentFiltering>
        <estimatedTotalResultsCount>3</estimatedTotalResultsCount>
        <directoryCategories soapenc:arrayType=
        "google:DirectoryCategory[0]">
        </directoryCategories>
        <searchTime>0.194871</searchTime>
        <resultElements soapenc:arrayType="google:ResultElement[3]">
          <item>
            <cachedSize>12k</cachedSize>
            <hostName></hostName>
            <snippet>Snippet for the first result would appear here
            </snippet>
            <directoryCategory>
              <specialEncoding></specialEncoding>
              <fullViewableName></fullViewableName>
            </directoryCategory>
            <relatedInformationPresent>true</relatedInformationPresent>
            <directoryTitle></directoryTitle>
            <summary></summary>
            <URL>http://hci.stanford.edu/cs147/examples/shrdlu/</URL>
            <title><b>SHRDLU</b></title>
          </item>
        </resultElements>
        <endIndex>3</endIndex>
        <searchTips></searchTips>
        <searchComments></searchComments>
        <startIndex>1</startIndex>
        <estimateIsExact>true</estimateIsExact>
```

```
      <searchQuery>shrdlu winograd maclisp teletype</searchQuery>
    </return>
  </doGoogleSearchResponse>
 </soap11:Body>
</soap11:Envelope>
```

We'll look more closely at using Flash to generate SOAP requests later in the book.

You can use the data-binding capabilities in Flash to display the results from the web service. The downside to creating a SOAP request using Flash is that you have to include your key as a parameter in the movie. This is not really a very secure option.

For security reasons, you often can't query a web service using a REST request within Flash. You need some kind of server-side interaction to make the request and pass the results into Flash. You can also use Flash Remoting to work with web services.

REST is a useful tool for Flash developers. As part of its security restrictions, recent Flash players will only let you run SOAP requests on a web service that contains a cross-domain policy file specifying your address. You can imagine that Amazon isn't going to do this for every Flash developer in the world! REST requests are a good workaround; you can use a server-side language to work with the information locally or *proxy* the information. Again, we'll cover this in more detail in Chapter 9.

Transforming XML content

Keeping XML content separate from its presentation allows you to apply many different looks to the same information. It lets you present the XML data on different devices. The requirements for displaying an XML document on a website are likely to be very different from those for printing it out or displaying it on a mobile telephone, even though the data will be the same.

Transformations are a powerful way to change the presentation of your data. Transforming means displaying, sorting, filtering, and printing the information contained within an XML document. You can use Cascading Style Sheets (CSS) to change the way your XML elements display in a web browser. XSL transformations allow you to change the display as well as include more advanced options such as sorting and filtering.

CSS

An easy way to transform the visual appearance of XML documents is by using CSS. CSS is a recommendation from the W3C. You can find out more at `www.w3c.org/Style/CSS/`.

CSS and XML work together in much the same way as CSS and HTML. You can use CSS to redefine the way XML tags display in a web browser. You include a reference to an external style sheet by adding a processing instruction below your XML declaration:

```
<?xml version="1.0"?>
<?xml-stylesheet href="styles.css" type="text/css"?>
```

This is much the same as the HTML instruction:

```
<link href="styles.css" rel="style sheet" type="text/css">
```

As with HTML pages, you can include multiple style sheet links:

```
<?xml-stylesheet href="globalstyles.css" type="text/css"?>
<?xml-stylesheet href="newsstyles.css" type="text/css"?>
<?xml-stylesheet href="homestyles.css" type="text/css"?>
```

The style declarations contained with the style sheets change the appearance of the XML elements. Each style declaration refers to a different element in the XML document. They are the same CSS declarations that you would use in HTML pages, so you can change font characteristics, borders, and colors for each element.

In addition to the standard style declarations, you need to consider whether the element is a block-level or inline element. In HTML, tables and headings are block-level elements while <span> is an inline element. Block-level elements automatically display with white space. In XML, all elements are inline by default. You'll need to declare block-level elements explicitly using the style declaration `display: block`.

This listing shows style declarations from the `addressCSS.xml` file:

```
contact {
  display: block;
  margin: 5px;
}
name {
  display: block;
  font-weight: bold;
  font-size: 16px;
  color: #0033CC;
  font-family: Verdana, Arial, sans-serif;
}
address {
  font-weight: normal;
  font-size: 12px;
  font-family: Verdana, Arial, sans-serif;
}
phone {
  display: block;
  font-weight: normal;
  font-size: 12px;
  color: #0033CC;
  font-family: Verdana, Arial, sans-serif;
}
```

The style sheet is saved as `styles.css`. Note that the file contains a style declaration for every element in the XML document.

Figure 3-30 shows the file `addressCSS.xml` file opened in a web browser. It looks very different from the raw XML document.

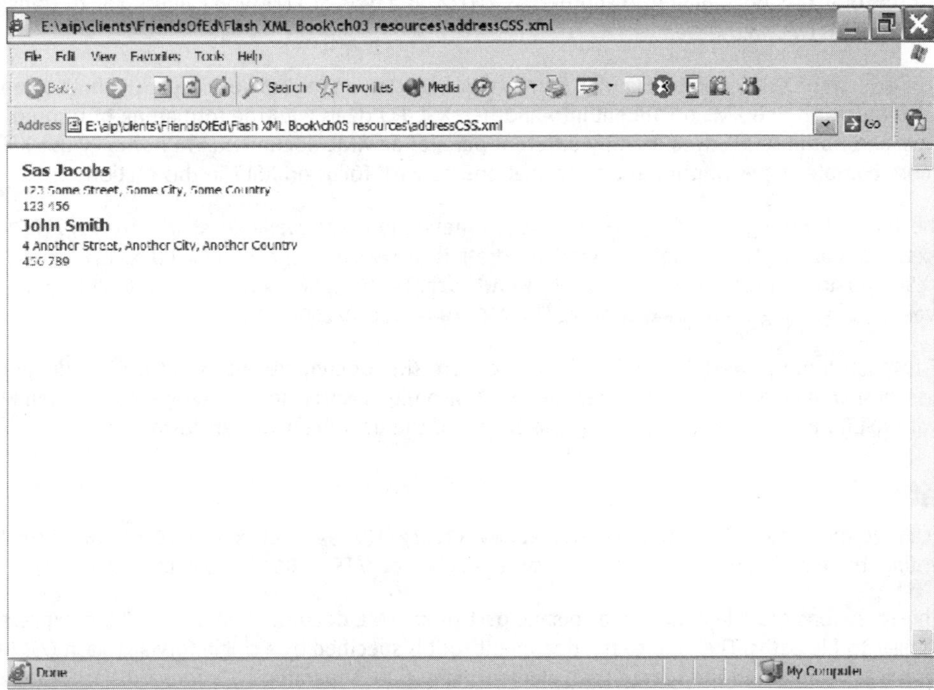

Figure 3-30. Internet Explorer showing an XML document transformed with CSS

As you can see in this example, I had to specify a style for each of my XML elements. In a large XML file, this is likely to be time consuming. CSS displays the XML elements in the same order that they appear in the XML document. I can't use CSS to change this order of the elements.

The W3C has released a recommendation titled "Associating Style Sheets with XML Documents" at `www.w3.org/TR/xml-stylesheet/`.

CSS changes the way that an XML file renders in the web browser. It doesn't offer any of the more advanced transformations that are available through XSL Transformations (XSLT). CSS may be of limited value because, unlike HTML pages, XML documents aren't always designed to be displayed in a web browser.

Bear in mind also that search engines and screen readers are likely to have difficulty when working with XML pages displayed with CSS. Search engines use the `<title>` tag, which isn't likely to be present in the same way in most XML documents. Screen readers normally require a system of headings—`<h1>`, `<h2>`, and so on—to make sense of content. It will be difficult for people using a screen reader to make sense of a document that uses nonstandard tag names.

XSL

Extensible Stylesheet Language (XSL) is another way to change the display of XML documents. XSL transforms one XML document into another. As XHTML is a type of XML, you can use XSL to transform XML into an XHTML web page.

XSL is made up of XSLT and XSL-FO (XSL Formatting Objects), and relies heavily on XPath. You can use XSLT to transform one XML document into another. XSL-FO deals with the formatting of printed documents, and both use XPath to identify different parts of an XML document. We normally use XSL-FO for more complex types of printed transformations, so we'll focus on XSLT in this section.

At the time of writing, the XSL version 1 recommendation was available at `www.w3.org/TR/2001/REC-xsl-20011015/`. The version 1.1 working draft is at `www.w3.org/TR/2004/WD-xsl11-20041216/`. The XSLT version 1 recommendation is at `www.w3.org/TR/1999/REC-xslt-19991116`, and you'll find the version 2 working draft at `www.w3.org/TR/2005/WD-xslt20-20050211/`.

XSLT is much more powerful than CSS; it can convert XML documents into valid XHTML documents for use by search engines and screen readers. XSLT also filters, sorts, and rearranges data. When working with XSLT, XPath expressions identify which part of the document to transform.

XPath

You can see the XPath 1.0 recommendation at `www.w3.org/TR/1999/REC-xpath-19991116`. At the time of writing, the working draft for version 2 was at `www.w3.org/TR/2005/WD-xpath20-20050211/`.

XPath expressions provide a path to a specific part of an XML document. In a way, XPath expressions are similar to file paths. The path to the document root is specified by a single forward slash (/). As we dig into each element in the source tree, element names are separated by a forward slash, for example, /phoneBook or /phoneBook/contact.

This listing shows our simple XML phone book example:

```
<phoneBook>
  <contact id="1">
    <name>Sas Jacobs</name>
    <address>123 Some Street, Some City, Some Country</address>
    <phone>123 456</phone>
  </contact>
  <contact id="2">
    <name>John Smith</name>
    <address>4 Another Street, Another City, Another Country</address>
    <phone>456 789</phone>
  </contact>
</phoneBook>
```

To refer to the <address> elements, use the following path:

```
/phoneBook/contact/address
```

In other words, start at <phoneBook>, move to <contact>, and finish at the <address> element. You can also use references relative to the current location.

Two slashes allow you to start the path anywhere in the XML document. The following code snippet specifies all <contact> elements, wherever they are located:

```
//contact
```

XPath expressions can target a specific element, for example, the first <contact> element.

```
/phoneBook/contact[1]
```

You can use the text() function to refer to the text inside an element:

```
/phoneBook/contact/address/text()
```

XPath recognizes wildcards, so we can specify **all** elements in an XML document by using the asterisk (*) character. This example shows all child elements of <phoneBook>:

```
/phoneBook/*
```

You can refer to attributes with the @ symbol, for example, the id attribute of <contact>:

```
/phoneBook/contact/@id
```

There is a lot more to the XPath specification than we've covered here, but this will provide a good starting point for the examples that will follow.

XSLT

Many people use the terms *XSL* and *XSLT* interchangeably. An XSLT stylesheet is an XML document that contains transformation rules to apply to an XML source document. We call the original XML document the *source tree*. The transformed document is the *result tree*. A style sheet is an XML document so you use the same rules for well-formedness.

XSLT style sheets start with a declaration followed by a document root. XSLT documents have a root element of either <stylesheet> or <transform>. We also need to include a reference to the namespace.

```
<?xml version="1.0"?>
<xsl:stylesheet version="1.0"
xmlns:xsl="http://www.w3.org/1999/XSL/Transform">
```

or

```
<?xml version="1.0"?>
<xsl:transform version="1.0"
xmlns:xsl="http://www.w3.org/1999/XSL/Transform">
```

It's more common to use <stylesheet> than <transform>. The closing tag in the style sheet will need to match this declaration.

In the previous examples, the namespace uses the xsl prefix so the elements are written <xsl:stylesheet> or <xsl:transform>. The code that follows also uses the xsl prefix as we're working in the same namespace.

Transforming content

XSLT documents can include an <template> and an <output> element. The <template> element shows how to transform the XML elements:

```
<xsl:template match = "Xpath expression">
```

The attribute match specifies which elements the template should affect.

The <output> element defines the format for the output document:

```
<xsl:output method="html" version="4.0" indent="yes"/>
```

We use an XPath expression to target each element or group of elements to be transformed. This listing shows a transformation of the phone book XML document into an HTML document:

```
<xsl:template match="/">
  <html>
  <body>
  <h1>Phone Book</h1>
  <ul>
  <xsl:for-each select="/phoneBook/contact">
    <li><xsl:value-of select="name" /></li>
  </xsl:for-each>
  </ul>
  </body>
  </html>
</xsl:template>
```

In the example, the document root is identified and transformed to create the <html>, <body>, and <ul> elements. For simplicity, no DTD or <head> section has been included in HTML in this example.

Each contact creates a <li> element that contains the value of the <name> element.

We can use a for-each statement to work with elements that appear more than once in the XML source document. It's a way to loop through a collection of elements. The example loops through the <contact> elements using the XPath expression /phoneBook/contact as the value of the select attribute.

The value-of statement returns the value of an element so that it can be included with the transformed HTML. In our example, value-of retrieves the value of the <name> element and includes it as a list item. Because the statement is inside a for-each loop, the <name> element uses a relative reference. It is a child of the <contact> element.

I've saved the complete style sheet as the resource file listStyle.xsl. It's a valid XML document, so you can display it in a web browser as shown in Figure 3-31.

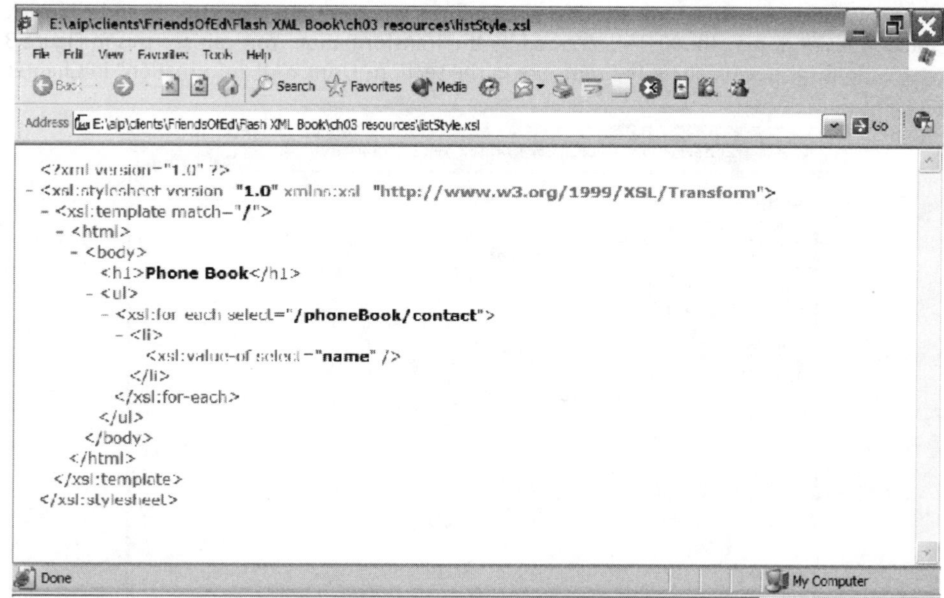

Figure 3-31. Internet Explorer showing the XSLT file

The following line applies the XSLT style sheet to the source XML document `addressXSL.xml`. It is included below the XML declaration:

```
<?xml-stylesheet type="text/xsl" href="listStyle.xsl"?>
```

Figure 3-32 shows the source document displayed in Internet Explorer after the transformation.

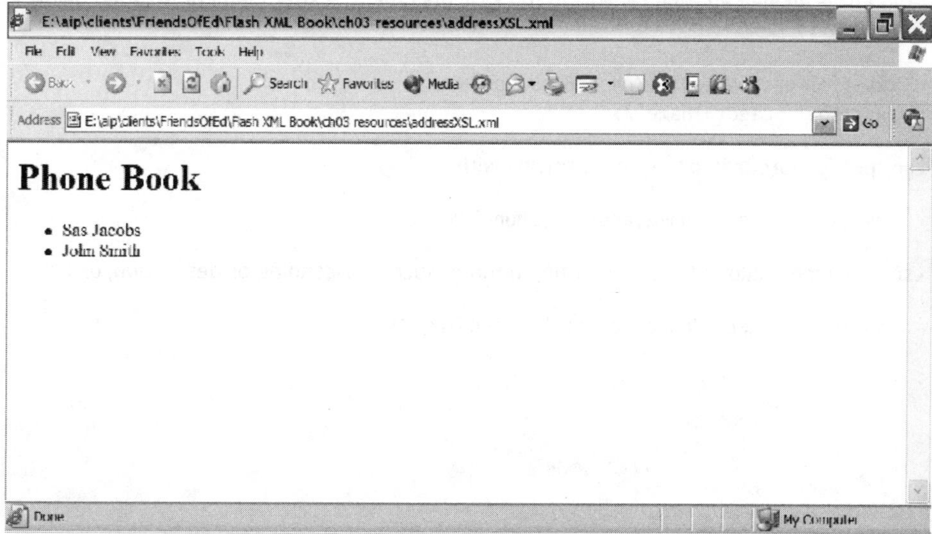

Figure 3-32. The transformed XML file in Internet Explorer

If you have installed the XML tools for Internet Explorer, you can right click the file and choose View XSL Output. It will display the XHTML created by the transformation. You can see this in Figure 3-33. The instructions for downloading the tools are in the section "Using XML information" in Chapter 2.

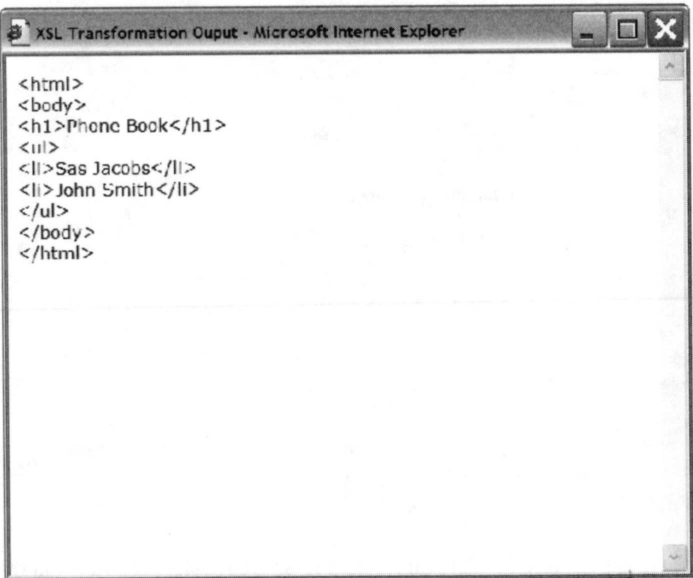

Figure 3-33. The XSL output in Internet Explorer.

Sorting content

You can sort XML documents at the same time that they are transformed. Sorting is only relevant where you have an element that repeats in the XML document. A `sort` element is added below a `for-each` element:

```
<xsl:for-each select="/phoneBook/contact">
<xsl:sort select="name"/>
```

You can specify more than one level of sorting with

```
<xsl:sort select="name,address,phone"/>
```

The `<sort>` element allows for other sorting options, such as ascending or descending `order`:

```
<xsl:sort select="name" order="descending"/>
```

Filtering content

XSLT transformations can also filter XML documents using XPath expressions. A filter criterion is added to the select attributes in the for-each statement:

```
<xsl:for-each select="/phoneBook/contact[name='Sas Jacobs']">
```

This XPath expression uses [name='Sas Jacobs'] to specify which contact should be selected. This is called a *predicate*. This criterion would only display the contact with a <name> value of Sas Jacobs. You can also use != (not equal to), < (less than), and > (greater than) in filter criteria.

Conditional content

The <if> element is used to conditionally include content in the result tree:

```
<xsl:for-each select="/phoneBook/contact">
  <xsl:if test="@id&gt;1">
    <li><xsl:value-of select="name" /></li>
  </xsl:if>
</xsl:for-each>
```

This example only includes contacts where the id attribute is greater than 1. Notice that I used the entity > to replace the > sign. This is necessary because using the > sign would indicate that the element should be closed.

You can specify alternative treatment for elements using <choose>, as shown here:

```
<xsl:for-each select="/phoneBook/contact">
  <xsl:choose>
    <xsl:when test="@id&gt;1">
      <li><xsl:value-of select="name" /></li>
    </xsl:when>
    <xsl:otherwise>
      <li><xsl:value-of select="address" /></li>
    </xsl:otherwise>
  </xsl:choose>
</xsl:for-each>
```

This listing uses <when> to test whether the contact attribute id is greater than 1. If so, the value of the <name> element displays. If not, the <otherwise> element specifies that the value of the <address> element should display. It's a nonsensical example, but I think you'll get the idea.

An example

XSLT will probably become clearer when we look at another example. I'll use XSLT to transform the phone book XML document into a table layout. The example will sort the XML document into name order. Each contact will display in a new row and the name, address, and phone details in a different cell.

Figure 3-34 shows how each XML element maps to XHTML content.

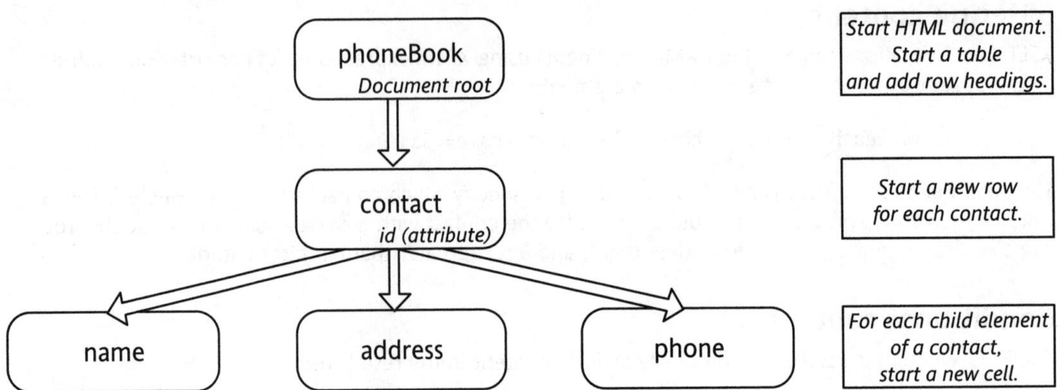

Figure 3-34. Mapping elements from the source tree to the result tree

In addition, the transformed content will be styled with a CSS style sheet.

I've called the completed XSLT file `tableStyle.xsl` (which you'll find in the resource files). The following listing shows the style sheet. Note that I've simplified the structure of the final HTML document.

```
<?xml version="1.0"?>
<xsl:stylesheet version="1.0"
xmlns:xsl="http://www.w3.org/1999/XSL/Transform">
  <xsl:template match="/">
    <html>
      <head>
      <title>Phone Book</title>
      <link href="tablestyles.css" type="text/css" rel="stylesheet"/>
    </head>
    <body>
    <h1>Phone Book</h1>
    <table>
    <tr>
      <th>Name</th>
      <th>Address</th>
      <th>Phone</th>
    </tr>
    <xsl:for-each select="/phoneBook/contact">
    <xsl:sort select="name" />
    <tr>
      <td><xsl:value-of select="name" /></td>
      <td class="shading"><xsl:value-of select="address"/></td>
      <td><xsl:value-of select="phone" /></td>
    </tr>
    </xsl:for-each>
    </table>
    </body>
    </html>
  </xsl:template>
</xsl:stylesheet>
```

The style sheet starts with an XML declaration and a style sheet processing instruction. It indicates a template starting at the root element. The transformation creates the HTML document, a page head, and a title. It also creates a reference to a CSS style sheet called `tablestyles.css`. Within the body, a table with a row of headings is created.

The transformation sorts each <contact> element by name and displays it in a table row. Table cells are created for the <name>, <address>, and <phone> elements.

The XML document `address_tableXSL.xml` uses this style sheet. Figure 3-35 shows the transformed file in Internet Explorer.

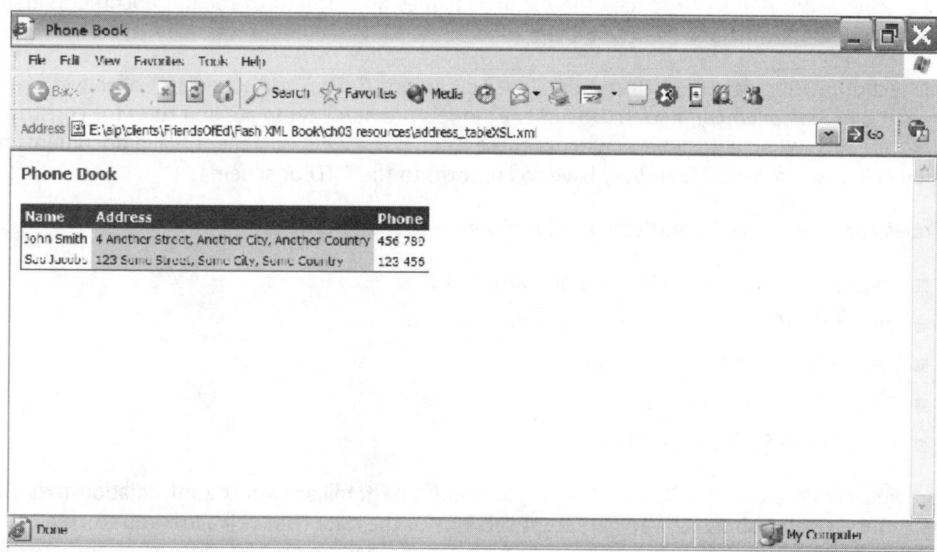

Figure 3-35. The transformed XML file in Internet Explorer

Other methods of applying transformations

You can use JavaScript to apply an XSLT transformation. This is an alternative if you don't want to include a reference to an XSLT file in your source XML document. For example, you might consider this if you want the transformations to be browser specific after detecting the browser version.

JavaScript can use the XML DOM of a web browser to transform the source tree. For example, in Internet Explorer, the `Microsoft.XMLDOM` includes the `transformNode` method. The following listing loads the XML source document and XSLT style sheet, and uses JavaScript to apply the transformation:

```
<script type="text/javascript">
  var xmlSourceDoc = new ActiveXObject("Microsoft.XMLDOM");
  xmlSourceDoc.async = false;
  xmlSourceDoc.load("address_tableXSL.xml");
  var xslTransformDoc = new ActiveXObject("Microsoft.XMLDOM");
  xslTransformDoc.async = false;
  xslTransformDoc.load("tableStyle.xsl");
  document.write(xmlSourceDoc.transformNode(xslTransformDoc));
</script>
```

Open the resource file `transform.htm` in a web browser to see the transformation in action. It looks just like the previous example, but we achieved the look in a different way.

You can also use languages like PHP, ASP.NET, and ColdFusion to apply a transformation server-side and deliver formatted XHTML to the web browser.

Determining valid XML

Earlier in this chapter, we worked with Office 2003 documents and converted them to an XML format. Using a schema allowed us to specify the element names and structures for the documents that we created. Schemas also helped to determine if data in the XML document was valid.

In this section, we'll create both Document Type Definitions (DTDs) and schemas. Collectively, we call DTDs and schema *document models*. Document models provide a template and rules for constructing XML documents. When a document matches these rules, it is a *valid* document. Valid documents must start by being well formed. Then they have to conform to the DTD or schema.

The rules contained in DTDs and schemas usually involve the following:

- Specifying the name of elements and attributes
- Identifying the type of content that can be stored
- Specifying hierarchical relationships between elements
- Stating the order for the elements
- Indicating default values for attributes

Before you create either a DTD or schema, you should be familiar with the information that you're using and the relationships between different sections of the data. This will allow you to create a useful XML representation. I find it best to work with sample data in an XML document and create the DTD or schema once I'm sure that the structure of the document meets my needs.

It's good practice to create a DTD or schema when you create multiple XML documents with the same structure. Document models are also useful where more than one author has to create the same or similar XML documents. Finally, if you need to use XML documents with other software, there may be a requirement to produce a DTD or schema so that the data translates correctly.

If you're writing a one-off XML document with element structures that you'll never use again, it's probably overkill to create a document model. It will certainly be quicker for you to create the elements as you need them and make changes as required without worrying about documentation.

Comparing DTDs and schemas

The DTD specification is older than XML schemas. In fact, DTDs predate XML documents and have their roots in Standard Generalized Markup Language (SGML). Because the specification is much older than XML, it doesn't use an XML structure.

On the other hand, schemas use XML to provide descriptions of the document rules. This means that it's possible to use an XML editor to check whether a schema is a well-formed document. You don't have this kind of checking ability with DTDs.

Schemas provide many more options for specifying the type of data for elements and attributes than DTDs. You can choose from 44 built-in datatypes so, for example, you can specify whether an element contains a string, datetime, or Boolean value. You can also add restrictions to specify a range of values, for example, numbers greater than 500. If the built-in types don't meet your needs, you can create your own datatypes and inherit details from existing datatypes.

The datatype support within XML schemas gives you the ability to be very specific in your specifications. You can include much more detail about elements and attributes than is possible in a DTD. Schemas can apply more rigorous error checking than DTDs.

Schemas also support namespaces. Namespaces allow you to identify elements from different sources by providing a unique identifier. This means that you can include multiple schemas in an XML document and reuse a single schema in multiple XML documents. Organizations are likely to work with the same kinds of data, so being able to reuse schema definitions is an important advantage when working with schemas.

One common criticism of XML documents is that they are verbose. As XML documents, the same criticism could be leveled at schemas. When compared with DTDs, XML schemas tend to be much longer. It often takes several lines to achieve something that you could declare in a single line within a DTD.

Table 3-1 shows the main differences between DTDs and schemas.

Table 3-1. The main differences between DTDs and schemas

DTDs	XML Schema
Non-XML syntax.	XML syntax.
DTD can't be parsed.	XSD document can be parsed.
No support for data typing.	Datatypes can be specified and custom datatypes created.
DTDs can't inherit from one another.	Schemas support inheritance.
No support for namespaces.	Support for namespaces.
One DTD for each XML document.	Multiple schema documents can be used.
Less content.	More content.

Document Type Definitions

A DTD defines an XML document by providing a list of elements that are legal within that document. It also specifies where the elements must appear in the document as well as the number of times the element should appear.

You create or reference a DTD with a DOCTYPE declaration; you've probably seen these at the top of XHTML and HTML documents. A DTD can either be stored within an XML document or in an external DTD file.

```
<!DOCTYPE html PUBLIC "-//W3C//DTD XHTML Basic 1.0//EN"
"http://www.w3.org/TR/xhtml-basic/xhtml-basic10.dtd">
```

The simplest DOCTYPE declaration includes only a reference to the root element of the document:

```
<!DOCTYPE phoneBook>
```

This declaration can also include other declarations, a reference to an external file, or both. DTD declarations are listed under the XML declaration:

```
<?xml version="1.0"?>
<!DOCTYPE documentRoot [element declarations]>
```

All internal declarations are contained in a DOCTYPE declaration at the top of the XML document. This includes information about the elements and attributes in the document. The element declarations can be on different lines:

```
<!DOCTYPE documentRoot [
<!ELEMENT declaration 1>
<!ELEMENT declaration 2>
]>
```

External file references point to declarations saved in files with the extension .dtd. They are useful if you are working with multiple documents that have the same rules. External DTD references are included in an XML document with

```
<!DOCTYPE documentRoot SYSTEM "file.dtd">
```

DTDs contain declarations for elements, attributes, and entities.

Elements

You declare an element in the following way:

```
<!ELEMENT elementName (elementContents)>
```

Make sure that you use the same case for the element name in both the declaration and XML document.

Elements that are empty—that is, that don't have any content—use the word EMPTY:

```
<!ELEMENT elementName (EMPTY)>
```

Child elements appear in a list after the parent element name. The order within the DTD indicates the order for the elements in the XML document:

```
<!ELEMENT elementName (child1, child2, child3)>
```

Elements can also include modifiers to indicate how often they should appear in the XML document. Children that appear once or more use a plus + sign as a modifier:

```
<!ELEMENT elementName (childName+)>
```

The pipe character (|) indicates a choice of elements. It's like including the word *or*.

```
<!ELEMENT elementName (child1|child2)>
```

You can combine a choice with other elements by using brackets to group elements together:

```
<!ELEMENT elementName ((child1|child2),child3)>
<!ELEMENT elementName (child1, child2|(child3,child4))>
```

Optional child elements are shown with an asterisk. This means they can appear any number of times or not at all.

```
<!ELEMENT elementName (childName*)>
```

A question mark (?) indicates child elements that are optional but that can appear a maximum of once:

```
<!ELEMENT elementName (childName?)>
```

Elements that contain character data include CDATA as content:

```
<!ELEMENT elementName (#CDATA)>
```

You can also use the word ANY to indicate that any type of data is acceptable:

```
<!ELEMENT elementName (ANY)>
```

The element declarations can be quite complicated. For example:

```
<!ELEMENT elementName ((child1|child2|child3),child4+,child5*,#CDATA)>
```

This declaration means that the element called elementName contains character data. It includes a choice between the child1, child2, or child3 elements, followed by child4, which can appear once or more. The element child5 is optional.

Table 3-2 provides an overview of the symbols used in element declarations.

Table 3-2. An explanation of the symbols used in element declarations within DTDs

Symbol	Explanation
,	Specifies the order of child elements.
+	Signifies that an element has to appear at least once, i.e., one or more times.
|	Allows a choice between elements.
()	Marks content as a group.
*	Specifies that the element is optional and can appear any number of times, i.e., 0 or more times.
?	Specifies that the element is optional, but if it is present, it can only appear once, i.e., 0 or 1 times.
	No symbol indicates that element must appear exactly once.

Attributes

Attributes declarations come after the elements. Their declarations are a little more complicated:

```
<!ATTLIST elementName attributeName attributeType defaultValue>
```

The `elementName` is the element that includes this attribute. Table 3-3 shows the main values for `attributeType`.

Table 3-3. The main attributeType values

Attribute Type	Comments
CDATA	Character data
ID	A unique identifier
IDREF	The id of another element
IDREFS	A list of ids from other elements
NMTOKEN	A valid XML name, i.e., doesn't start with a number and has no spaces
NMTOKENS	A list of valid XML names
ENTITY	An entity name
ENTITIES	A list of entity names
LIST	A list of specific values, e.g., (red | blue | green)

Most commonly, attributes are of the type CDATA.

The `defaultValue` indicates a default value for the element. In the following example, the XML element <address> will have an <addressType> attribute with a default value of home. In other words, if the attribute isn't included in the XML document, a value of home will be assumed.

```
<!ATTLIST address addressType CDATA "home">
```

Using `#REQUIRED` will force a value to be set for the attribute in the XML document:

```
<!ATTLIST address addressType CDATA #REQUIRED>
```

You can use `#IMPLIED` if the attribute is optional:

```
<!ATTLIST address addressType CDATA #IMPLIED>
```

If you always want to use the same value for an attribute and don't want it to be overridden, use `#FIXED`:

```
<!ATTLIST address addressType CDATA #FIXED "home">
```

You can also specify a range of acceptable values separated by a pipe character |:

```
<!ATTLIST address addressType (home|work|mailing) "home">
```

You can declare all attributes of a single element at the same time within the same ATTLIST declaration:

```
<!ATTLIST address
  addressType (home|postal|work) #REQUIRED
  addressID CDATA #IMPLIED
  addressDefault (true|false) "true">
```

The declaration lists a required addressType attribute, which has to have a value of home, postal, or work. The addressID is a CDATA type and is optional. The final attribute, addressDefault, can have a value of either true or false with the default value being true.

You can also declare attributes separately:

```
<!ATTLIST address addressType (home|postal|work) #REQUIRED>
<!ATTLIST address addressID CDATA #IMPLIED >
<!ATTLIST address addressDefault (true|false) "true">
```

Entities

Entities are a shorthand way to refer to something that you want to use in more than one place or in more than one XML document. You also use them for specific characters on a keyboard. If you've worked with HTML, you've probably used entities for nonbreaking spaces ( ) and the copyright symbol (©).

You declare an entity as follows:

```
<!ENTITY entityName "entityValue">
```

Whenever you want to use the value of the entity in an XML document, you can use &entityName;.

In the following example, I've declared two entities, email and author:

```
<!ENTITY email "sas@aip.net.au">
<!ENTITY author "Sas Jacobs, AIP">
```

I could refer to these entities in my XML document using &email; or &author;. The entities mean sas@aip.net.au and Sas Jacobs, AIP.

Entities can also reference external content; we call these *external entities*. They are a little like using a server-side include file in an HTML document.

```
<!ENTITY address SYSTEM "addressBlock.xml">
```

The XML document would use the entity &address; to insert the contents from the addressBlock.xml file. You could also use a URL like http://www.friendsofed.com/addressBlock.xml. The advantage here is that you only have to update the entity in a single location and the value will change throughout the XML document.

A sample DTD

The following listing shows a sample inline DTD. The DTD describes our phone book XML document:

```
<!DOCTYPE phoneBook[
  <!ELEMENT phoneBook (contact+)>
  <!ELEMENT contact (name,address,phone)>
  <!ELEMENT name (#PCDATA)>
  <!ELEMENT address (#PCDATA)>
  <!ELEMENT phone (#PCDATA)>
  <!ATTLIST contact id CDATA #REQUIRED>
  ]>
```

I've saved the XML document containing these declarations in the resource file `addressDTD.xml`. Figure 3-36 shows this file validated within XMLSpy.

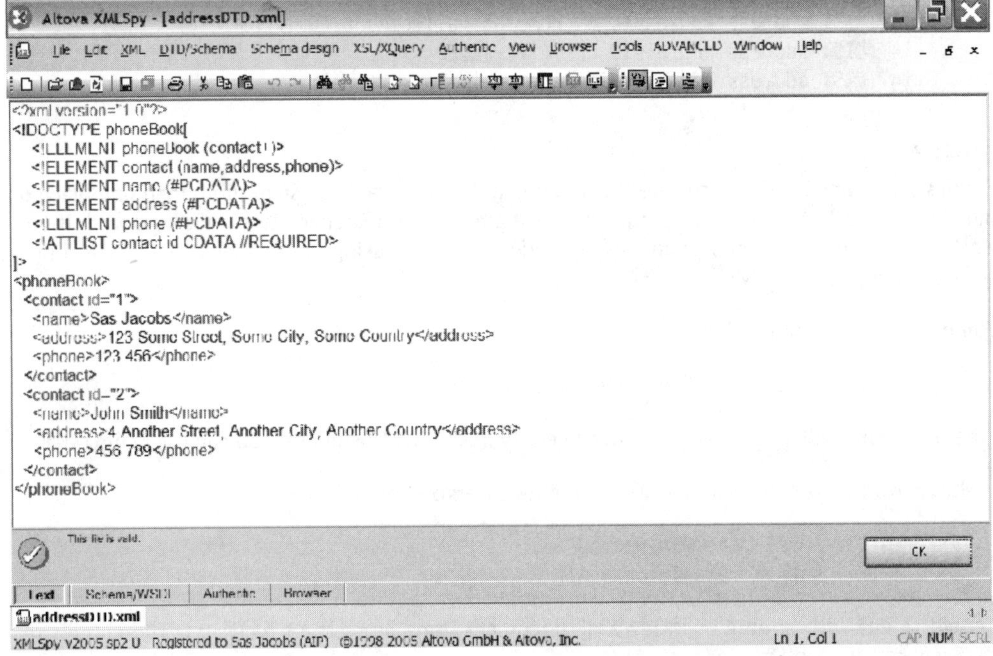

Figure 3-36. The file addressDTD.xml contains an inline DTD, which can be used to validate the contents in XMLSpy.

The file `addressEDTD.xml` refers to the same declarations in the external DTD. If you open the resource file `phoneBook.dtd` you'll see that it doesn't include a DOCTYPE declaration at the top of the file. This listing shows the content:

```
<!ELEMENT phoneBook (contact+)>
<!ELEMENT contact (name,address,phone)>
<!ELEMENT name (#PCDATA)>
<!ELEMENT address (#PCDATA)>
```

```
<!ELEMENT phone (#PCDATA)>
<!ATTLIST contact id CDATA #REQUIRED>
```

This DTD declares the root element phoneBook. The root element can contain a single element contact, which can appear one or more times. The contact element contains three elements—name, address, and phone—each of which must appear exactly once. The data in these elements is of type PCDATA or parsed character data.

The DTD includes a declaration for the attribute id within the contact element. The type is CDATA, and it is a required attribute.

Designing DTDs can be a tricky process, so you will probably find it easier if you organize your declarations carefully. You can add extra lines and spaces so that the DTD is easy to read.

XML schemas

An XML schema is an XML document that lists the rules for other XML documents. It defines the way elements and attributes are structured, the order of elements, and the datatypes used for elements and attributes.

A schema has the same role as a DTD. It determines the rules for valid XML documents. Unlike DTDs, however, you don't have to learn new syntax to create schemas because they are another example of an XML document. Schemas are popular for this reason. Some people find it strange that DTDs use a non-XML approach to define XML document structure.

At the time of writing, the current recommendation for XML schemas was at www.w3.org/TR/2004/REC-xmlschema-1-20041028/. You'll find the Datatypes section of the recommendation at www.w3.org/TR/2004/REC-xmlschema-2-20041028/. The working drafts for XML Schema version 1.1 are at www.w3.org/TR/2005/WD-xmlschema11-1-20050224/ and www.w3.org/TR/2005/WD-xmlschema11-2-20050224/.

Schemas offer several advantages over DTDs. Because schemas can inherit from each other, you can reuse them with different document groups. It's easier to use XML documents created from databases with schemas because they recognize different datatypes. You write schemas in XML so you can use the same tools that you use for your other XML documents.

You can embed a schema within an XML document or store it within an external XML file saved with an .xsd extension. In most cases, it's better to store the schema information externally so you'll be able to reuse it with other XML documents that follow the same format.

An external schema starts with an optional XML declaration followed by a <schema> element, which is the document root. The <schema> element contains a reference to the default namespace. The xmlns declaration shows that all elements and datatypes come from the namespace http://www.w3.org/2001/XMLSchema. In my declaration, elements from this namespace should use the prefix xsd.

```
<?xml version="1.0"?>
<xsd:schema xmlns:xsd="http://www.w3.org/2001/XMLSchema">
```

As with a DTD, a schema describes the document model for an XML document. This can consist of declarations about elements and attributes and about datatypes. The order of the declarations in the XSD document doesn't matter.

You declare elements as either simpleType or complexType. They can also have empty, simple, complex, or mixed content. Elements that have attributes are automatically complexType elements. Elements that only include text are simpleType.

I've included a sample schema document called addressSchema.xsd with your resources to illustrate some of the concepts in this section. You'll probably want to have it open as you refer to the examples that follow. You can see the complete schema at the end of this section.

In the sample schema, you'll notice that the prefix xsd is used in front of all elements. This is because I've referred to the namespace with the xsd prefix, that is, xmlns:xsd=http://www.w3.org/2001/XMLSchema. Everything included from this namespace will be prefixed in the same way.

Simple types

Simple type elements contain text only and have no attributes or child elements. In other words, simple elements contain character data. The text included in a simple element can be of any datatype. You can define simple element as follows:

```
<xsd:element name="elementName" type="elementType"/>
```

In our phone book XML document, the <name>, <address>, and <phone> elements are simple type elements. The definitions in the XSD schema document show this:

```
<xsd:element name="name" type="xsd:string"/>
<xsd:element name="address" type="xsd:string"/>
<xsd:element name="phone" type="xsd:string"/>
```

There are 44 built-in simple types in the W3C Schema Recommendation. You can find out more about these types at www.w3.org/TR/xmlschema-2/. Common simple types include string, integer, float, decimal, date, time, ID, and boolean.

Attributes are also simple type elements and are defined with

```
<xsd:attribute name="attributeName" type="elementType"/>
```

All attributes are optional unless their use attribute is set to required:

```
<xsd:attribute name="attributeName" type="elementType" use="required"/>
```

The id attribute in the <contact> element is an example of a required attribute:

```
<xsd:attribute name="id" type="xsd:integer" use="required"/>
```

A default or fixed value can be set for simple elements by using

```
<xsd:attribute name="attributeName" type="elementType"
default="defaultValue"/>
```

or

```
<xsd:attribute name="attributeName" type="elementType" fixed="fixedValue"/>
```

You can't change the value of a simple type element that has a fixed value.

Complex types

Complex type elements include attributes and/or child elements. In fact, any time an element has one or more attributes it is automatically a complex type element. The `<contact>` element is an example of a complex type element.

Complex type elements have different content types, as shown in Table 3-4.

Table 3-4. Complex content types

Content	Explanation	Example
Empty	Element has no content.	`<recipe id="1234"/>`
Simple	Element contains only text.	`<recipe id="1234">Omelette</recipe>`
Complex	Element contains only child elements.	`<recipe><food>Eggs</food></recipe>`
Mixed	Element contains child elements and text.	`<recipe>Omelette<food>Eggs</food></recipe>`

It's a little confusing. An element can have a complex type with simple content, or it can be a complex type element with empty content. I'll go through these alternatives next.

A complex type element with empty content such as

```
<recipe id="1234"/>
```

is defined in a schema with

```
<xsd:element name="recipe">
  <xsd:complexType>
    <xsd:attribute name="id" type="xsd:positiveInteger"/>
  </xsd:complexType>
</xsd:element>
```

The `<recipe>` element is a `complexType` but only contains an attribute. In the example, the attribute is declared. We could also use a `ref` attribute to refer to an attribute that is already declared elsewhere within the schema.

A complex type element with simple content like

```
<recipe id="1234">
  Omelette
</recipe>
```

is declared in the following way:

```
<xsd:element name="recipe">
  <xsd:complexType>
    <xsd:simpleContent>
      <xsd:extension base="xsd:string">
        <xsd:attribute name="id" type="xsd:positiveInteger"/>
      </xsd:extension>
    </xsd:simpleContent>
  </xsd:complexType>
</xsd:element>
```

In other words, the complex element called `<recipe>` has a complex type but simple content. The content has a base type of `string`. The element includes an attribute called `id` that is a `positiveInteger`.

Complex types have content that is either a sequence, a list, or a choice of elements. You must use either `<sequence>`, `<all>`, or `<choice>` to enclose your child elements. Attributes are defined outside of the `<sequence>`, `<all>`, or `<choice>` elements.

A complex type element with complex content such as

```
<recipe>
  <food>
    Eggs
  </food>
</recipe>
```

is declared as follows:

```
<xsd:element name="recipe">
  <xsd:complexType>
    <xsd:sequence>
      <xsd:element ref="food"/>
    </xsd:sequence>
  </xsd:complexType>
</xsd:element>
```

A complex type element with mixed content such as

```
<recipe>
  Omelette
  <food>
    Eggs
  </food>
</recipe>
```

is defined with

```
<xsd:element name="recipe">
  <xsd:complexType mixed="true">
```

```
      <xsd:sequence>
        <xsd:element name="food" type="xsd:string"/>
      </xsd:sequence>
    </xsd:complexType>
  </xsd:element>
```

The mixed attribute is set to true so that the <recipe> element can contain a mixture of both child elements and text or character data.

If an element has children, the declaration needs to specify the names of the child elements, the order in which they appear, and the number of times that they can be included.

Ordering child elements

The sequence element specifies the order of child elements:

```
<xsd:element name="elementName">
  <xsd:complexType>
    <xsd:sequence>
      <xsd:element name="childElement1" type="xsd:string"/>
      <xsd:element name="childElement2" type="xsd:string"/>
      <xsd:element name="childElement3" type="xsd:string"/>
    </xsd:sequence>
  </xsd:complexType>
</xsd:element>
```

You can replace sequence with all where child elements can be written in any order but each child element must appear only once:

```
<xsd:all>
  <xsd:element name="childElement1" type="xsd:string"/>
  <xsd:element name="childElement2" type="xsd:string"/>
  <xsd:element name="childElement3" type="xsd:string"/>
</xsd:all>
```

The element choice indicates that only one of the child elements should be included from the group:

```
<xsd:choice>
  <xsd:element name="childElement1" type="xsd:string"/>
  <xsd:element name="childElement2" type="xsd:string"/>
</xsd:choice>
```

Element occurrences

The number of times an element appears within another can be set with the minOccurs and maxOccurs attributes:

```
<xsd:element name="food" type="xsd:string" minOccurs="0"
maxOccurs="1"/>
```

In the previous example, the element is optional but if it is present, it must appear only once. You can use the value unbounded to specify an unlimited number of occurrences:

```
<xsd:element name="food" type="xsd:string" minOccurs="0"
maxOccurs="unbounded"/>
```

When neither of these attributes is present, the element must appear exactly once.

Creating undefined content

If you're not sure about the structure of a complex element, you can specify any content:

```
<xsd:element name="elementName">
  <xsd:complexType>
    <xsd:any minOccurs="0" />
  </xsd:complexType>
</xsd:element>
```

The author of an XML document that uses this schema will be able to create an optional child element.

You can also use the element anyAttribute to add attributes to an element:

```
<xsd:element name="elementName">
  <xsd:complexType>
    <xsd:element name="childElement" type="xsd:string"/>
    <xsd:anyAttribute />
  </xsd:complexType>
</xsd:element>
```

Annotations

You can use annotations to describe your schemas. An <annotation> element contains a <documentation> element that encloses the description. You can add annotations anywhere, but it's often helpful to include them underneath an element declaration:

```
<xsd:element name="recipe">
  <xsd:annotation>
    <xsd:documentation>
      A description about the element
    </xsd:documentation>
  </xsd:annotation>
  ... more declarations
</xsd:element>
```

Including a schema

You can include a schema in an XML document by referencing it in the document root. Schemas always include a reference to the XMLSchema namespace. Optionally, they may include a reference to a target namespace:

```
<phoneBook xmlns:xsi="http://www.w3.org/2001/XMLSchema-instance"
xsi:noNamespaceSchemaLocation="addressSchema.xsd">
```

The reference uses noNamespaceSchemaLocation because the schema document doesn't have a target namespace.

An example

The topic of schemas is very complicated. There are other areas that I haven't discussed in this chapter. An example that relates to the phone book XML document should make things a little clearer.

This listing shows the complete schema from the resource file addressSchema.xsd:

```
<?xml version="1.0"?>
<xsd:schema xmlns:xsd="http://www.w3.org/2001/XMLSchema">
 <xsd:element name="phoneBook">
   <xsd:complexType>
     <xsd:sequence>
       <xsd:element ref="contact" minOccurs="1"
       maxOccurs="unbounded"/>
     </xsd:sequence>
   </xsd:complexType>
 </xsd:element>
 <xsd:element name="contact">
   <xsd:complexType>
     <xsd:sequence>
       <xsd:element name="name" type="xsd:string"/>
       <xsd:element name="address" type="xsd:string"/>
       <xsd:element name="phone" type="xsd:string"/>
     </xsd:sequence>
   <xsd:attribute name="id" type="xsd:integer" use="required"/>
   </xsd:complexType>
 </xsd:element>
</xsd:schema>
```

The schema starts by declaring itself as an XML document and referring to the http://www.w3.org/2001/XMLSchema namespace. The first element defined is <phoneBook>. This is a complexType element that contains one or more <contact> elements. The attribute ref indicates that I've defined <contact> elsewhere in the document.

The <contact> element contains the simple elements <name>, <address>, and <phone> in that order. Each child element of <contact> can appear only once and is of type string. The <contact> element also contains a required attribute called id that is an integer type.

The schema is saved as resource file addressSchema.xsd. The XML file that references this schema is addressSchema.xml. You can open the XML file in XMLSpy or another validating XML editor and validate it against the schema.

We haven't covered everything there is to know about XML schemas in this section, but there should be enough to get you started.

XML documents and Flash

Flash can use XML documents from any source providing that they are well formed. The most straightforward method is to use a file saved with an `.xml` extension. This document can be something that you've written in NotePad, SimpleText, or XMLSpy. It can also be an Office 2003 document, perhaps from a Word template or Excel spreadsheet.

Flash can also consume XML documents provided by web services. You can do this either by using data components or by writing ActionScript. Your Flash movie can display parts of the XML document, perhaps by binding it to a UI component such as the DataGrid.

You can also use a server-side file to consume a web service using REST. The server-side file accesses a URL and receives the XML content. The file can then provide the XML document to Flash.

In Flash version 5, a measurable speed difference was caused by different XML document structures. Information in attributes parsed more quickly than information contained in elements. As a result, early XML documents created for Flash used attributes quite a bit. I'm not sure if there is still a noticeable speed difference with later Flash players.

One useful piece of advice that I can give you is that if you're going to write ActionScript to work with XML, it will really benefit you to keep the element structures in your XML document as simple as possible. Try to avoid deeply nested elements as the document will be much harder to process than if you use flatter structures.

Creating an XML document

I'd like to finish this chapter by creating an XML document from scratch. We'll also create a schema for the document so that we can update it in Office 2003 later.

I'll work through some of the decisions that we'll need to consider when creating our XML document. For this example, you can use either a text editor or an XML editor like XMLSpy. I've used XMLSpy as you'll see from my screenshots.

We'll be creating an XML document to describe photographs for an XML photo gallery that we'll create in Chapter 4. The photos that we're going to use are stored with the resource files in the `photos` folder. To make things easier, they are all landscape photos that are exactly the same width and height. In case you're interested, they're all photos that I've taken during my travels.

Our task is to design an XML document that will store information about these photos. We'll need to store the file name of the photo, a caption, and a description. If you look at the photo names, you'll see that they all have a two-letter prefix indicating where they were taken. There are photos from Australia, Europe, the United Kingdom, the United States, and South Africa.

You can see a working example of this photo gallery at `www.sasjacobs.com`. Click the photo gallery link on the home page. The online example uses transitions between each photo.

Before we start typing, let's consider the relationships between the pieces of data that we're going to store. The photo gallery contains many photos. Each photo comes from an area or location, and more than one photo can be associated with an area.

Figure 3-37 shows the relationships that we'll need to capture in our XML document.

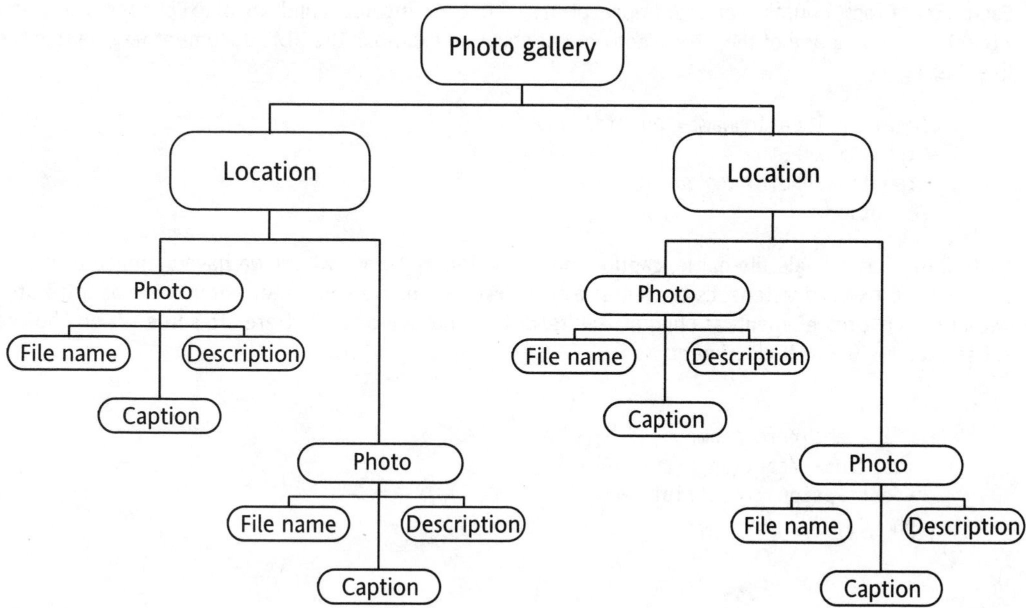

Figure 3-37. The data structure for the photo gallery

Let's start at the top and work down. We'll need to begin with an XML declaration. Actually, Flash doesn't need this, but it's a good habit for you to get into.

```
<?xml version="1.0" encoding="UTF-8" standalone="yes" ?>
```

All of the information in this XML document is contained inside the photo gallery, so we'll use that for the document root:

```
<photoGallery></photoGallery>
```

The photo gallery has multiple locations for the photos. Each location has its own name. I'll create an element with an attribute for the location name. This listing shows the XML document with the list of locations—Australia, Europe, the United Kingdom, the United States, and South Africa:

```
<?xml version="1.0" encoding="UTF-8" standalone="yes"?>
<photoGallery>
  <location locationName="Australia"></location>
  <location locationName = "Europe"></location>
  <location locationName = "South Africa"></location>
  <location locationName = "UK"></location>
  <location locationName = "US"></location>
</photoGallery>
```

You'll notice that I called the attribute `locationName` instead of just `name`. There's nothing wrong with using the word `name`; it's just not very specific and could easily refer to other elements. More importantly, `name` is often a reserved word in programming languages. Even though Flash will probably let us use the word `name`, it may color it incorrectly in the Actions panel.

Each <location> contains one or more photos, so we'll include child <photo> elements in each <location>. Using one of the <location> elements as an example, the XML document fragment looks like this:

```
<location locationName="Australia">
  <photo></photo>
  <photo></photo>
</location>
```

Each photo has a single file name, caption, and description. Here's where we have a choice to make. Photos have two characteristics as well as a text description. We can either enter these as attributes within the <photo> element, as child elements, or as a mixture of both. Here are some of the choices for structuring the XML document:

```
<photo>
  <filename></filename>
  <caption></caption
  <description></description>
</photo>
```

or

```
<photo filename="xxx" caption="yyy" description="zzz"/>
```

or

```
<photo filename="xxx" caption="yyy">
  Text displayed inside the photo element
</photo>
```

All of these choices are valid structures for the XML documents; however, the implications of each will be different.

The first choice, where all elements are child elements of <photo>, creates a clearly defined hierarchy in our elements. In the schema, we can specify the datatypes for each element as well as the order in which the elements are to appear. Actually, the order probably doesn't really matter. What is important is that there is only one occurrence of each element.

However, the first option creates a structure that nests more deeply than either of the other two examples. This means we'll need a little extra code to display the data within Flash.

The second option isn't too bad, but the description could be a problem. We'll probably want to enter quite a long description for some photos, and this might make the attribute difficult to read. We may also want to add some basic HTML tags for display within Flash, and we can't do that inside an attribute.

I favor the third option. Logically, the file name and caption are attributes of a <photo> element. Placing the text description inside the <photo> element allows us to enclose it within a CDATA declaration to preserve any HTML tags. There are no child elements within the <photo> element, which means it will be easier to process this document within Flash.

This listing shows the completed <location> element for the photographs of the United States:

```
<location locationName = "US">
  <photo filename="us-grandcanyon.jpg" caption="The Grand Canyon">
    <![CDATA[Flying through the <b>Grand Canyon</b> in a helicopter
    was an amazing experience.]]>
  </photo>
  <photo filename="us-timessquare.jpg" caption="Times Square">
    <![CDATA[There is <b>no</b> place in the world like Manhattan.]]>
  </photo>
</location>
```

Notice that I've included <b></b> tags in my description text. I'll be able to display these words as bold in Flash. I had to include the text as CDATA so that the <b></b> tags don't get parsed when the XML document is loaded.

I've saved the completed XML document as resource file `photoGallery.xml`. Figure 3-38 shows this document open in XMLSpy. I checked to see that the document was well formed.

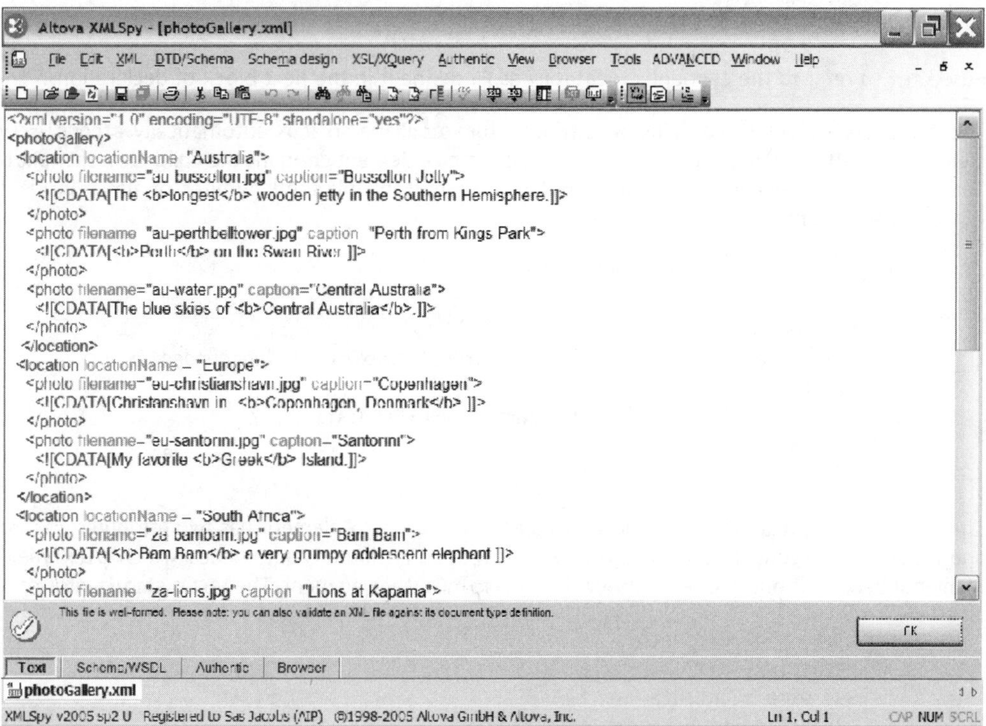

Figure 3-38. The complete file photoGallery.xml displayed in XMLSpy

Creating a schema

Now it's time to write a schema for this XML document. To start with, we'll need a new file containing an XML declaration and a root node that refers to the appropriate namespace:

```
<?xml version="1.0"?>
<xsd:schema xmlns:xsd="http://www.w3.org/2001/XMLSchema">
</xsd:schema>
```

I'll need to add declarations, starting with <photoGallery>, the document root of photoGallery.xml. This is a complexType element because it contains <location> elements. Each <location> element has to occur at least once and there is no upper limit for the number of repeats.

```
<xsd:element name="photoGallery">
  <xsd:complexType>
    <xsd:sequence>
      <xsd:element ref="location" minOccurs="1"
      maxOccurs="unbounded"/>
    </xsd:sequence>
  </xsd:complexType>
</xsd:element>
```

I used ref to refer to the element <location> as I'll define it in the next block of declarations.

The <location> element contains an attribute locationName so it is automatically a complexType element. The attribute is of string type. The <location> element contains the child element <photo>. This element must occur at least once but can appear an unlimited number of times inside the <location> element.

```
<xsd:element name="location">
  <xsd:complexType>
    <xsd:sequence>
      <xsd:element ref="photo" minOccurs="1" maxOccurs="unbounded"/>
    </xsd:sequence>
    <xsd:attribute name="locationName" type="xsd:string"/>
  </xsd:complexType>
  </xsd:element>
```

The final block will deal with the <photo> element. Each <photo> element has two attributes: filename and caption—and contains only text. An element with an attribute is automatically a complexType element, but because it only has text content, it is a simpleContent element. The text is string information.

```
<xsd:element name="photo">
  <xsd:complexType>
    <xsd:simpleContent>
      <xsd:extension base="xsd:string">
        <xsd:attribute name="filename" type="xsd:string"/>
        <xsd:attribute name="caption" type="xsd:string"/>
      </xsd:extension>
    </xsd:simpleContent>
  </xsd:complexType>
</xsd:element>
```

The following listing shows the complete schema. You can also see it in the resource file `photoGallerySchema.xsd`.

```
<?xml version="1.0"?>
<xsd:schema xmlns:xsd="http://www.w3.org/2001/XMLSchema">
  <xsd:element name="photoGallery">
    <xsd:complexType>
      <xsd:sequence>
        <xsd:element ref="location" minOccurs="1"
        maxOccurs="unbounded"/>
      </xsd:sequence>
    </xsd:complexType>
  </xsd:element>
  <xsd:element name="location">
    <xsd:complexType>
      <xsd:sequence>
        <xsd:element ref="photo" minOccurs="1" maxOccurs="unbounded"/>
      </xsd:sequence>
      <xsd:attribute name="locationName" type="xsd:string"/>
    </xsd:complexType>
  </xsd:element>
  <xsd:element name="photo">
    <xsd:complexType>
      <xsd:simpleContent>
        <xsd:extension base="xsd:string">
          <xsd:attribute name="filename" type="xsd:string"/>
          <xsd:attribute name="caption" type="xsd:string"/>
        </xsd:extension>
      </xsd:simpleContent>
     </xsd:complexType>
 </xsd:element>
</xsd:schema>
```

There are other ways that I could have arranged the declarations in the schema. For example, instead of using `ref`, I could have nested the element declarations within their parent elements. That's often referred to as a *Russian Doll* arrangement.

Linking the schema with an XML document

The final job is to link the schema with the `photoGallery.xml` file by adding a reference in the root element. I've done this in the resource file `photoGallerySchema.xml`. The root element in `photoGallerySchema.xml` has changed to

```
<photoGallery xmlns:xsi="http://www.w3.org/2001/XMLSchema-instance"
xsi:noNamespaceSchemaLocation="photoGallerySchema.xsd">
```

Figure 3-39 shows the completed file in XMLSpy, validated against the schema.

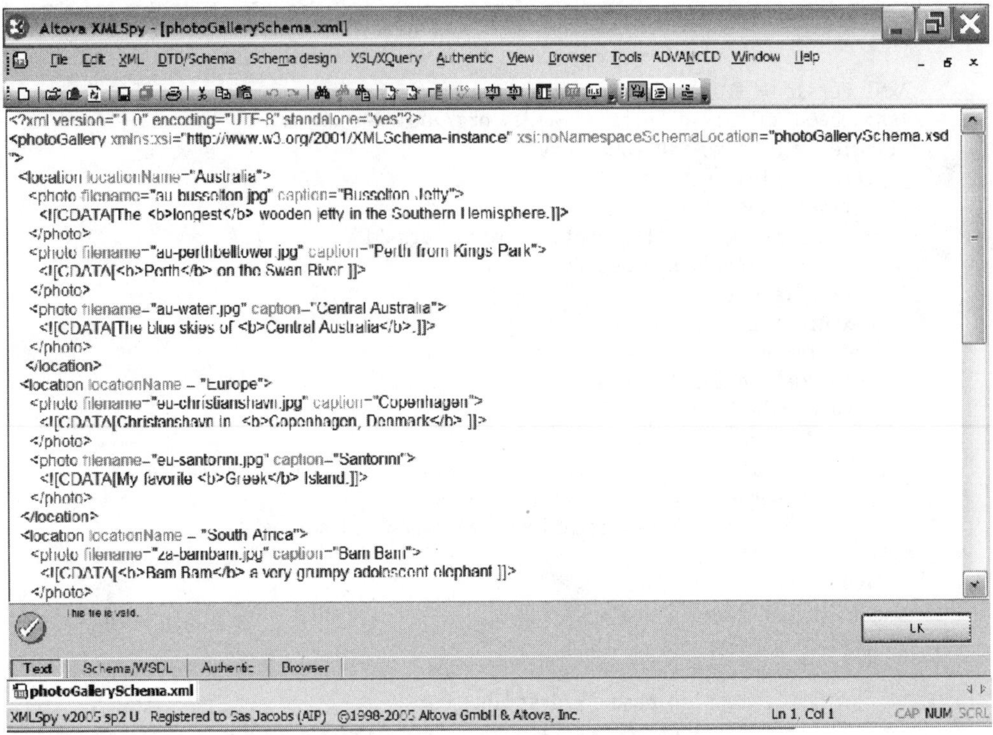

Figure 3-39. The complete file photoGallerySchema.xml displayed in XMLSpy

Summary

In this chapter, you looked at the different ways that you could create XML content. I covered the use of XMLSpy, Office 2003, and the role of server-side documents in generating XML. I also gave you a brief introduction to XPath, XSL transformations, DTDs, and XML schemas. We finished by creating an XML document and schema.

That's it for the theory behind XML documents. The rest of the book will focus on using Flash with XML documents. In Chapter 4, I'll look at the XML class and we'll create a photo gallery and MP3 player driven by XML data. Later in the book, we'll cover the data components that are included with Flash.

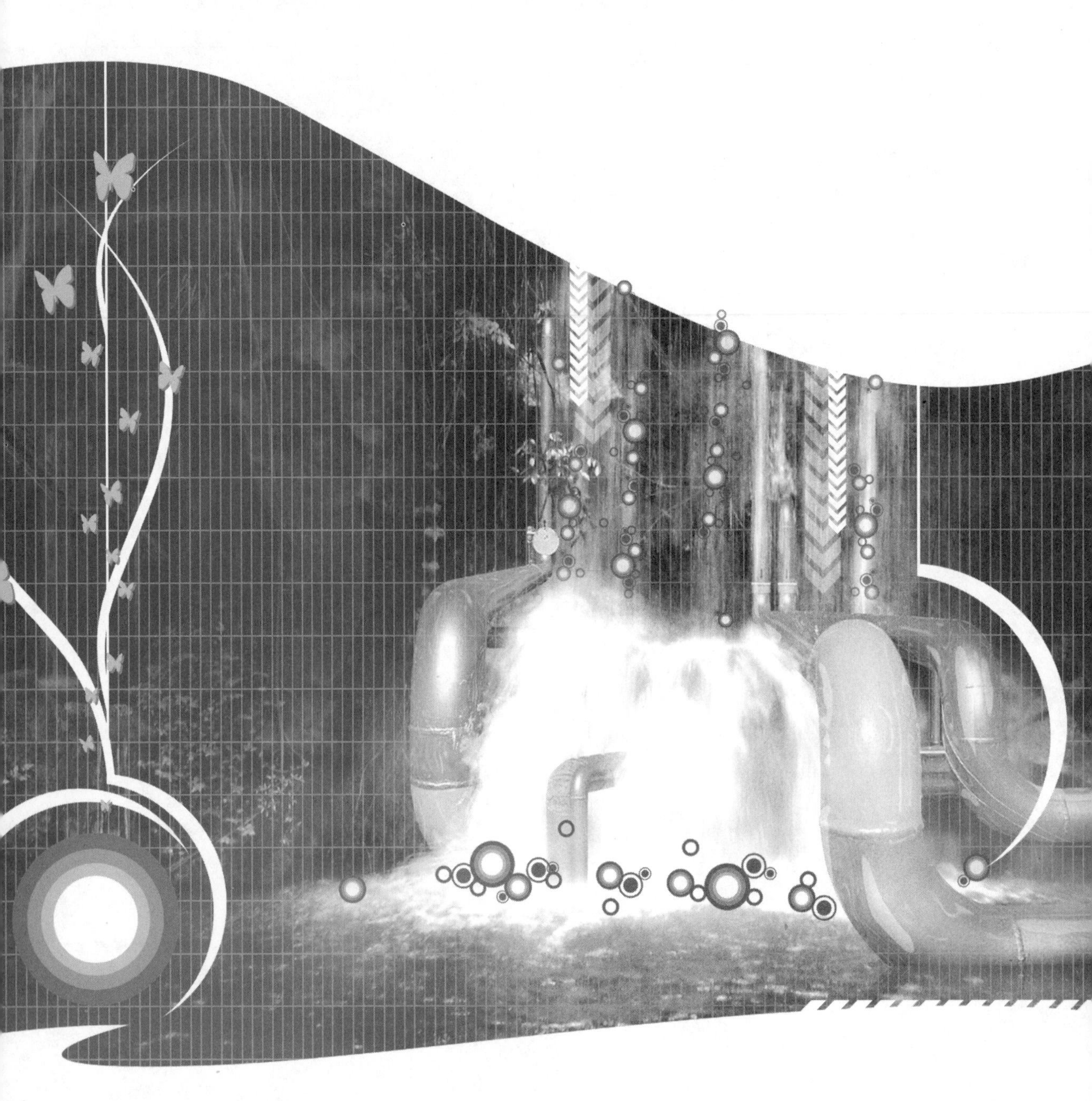

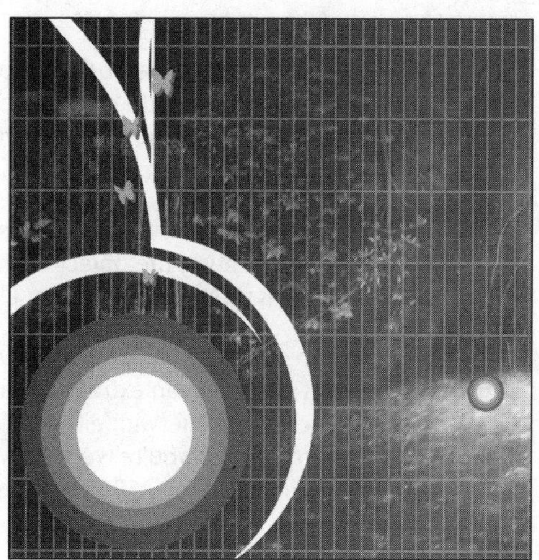

Chapter 4

USING THE XML CLASS

In the earlier chapters, you learned about XML and some of the related technologies. We covered the uses for XML and the advantages that it provides over other forms of data storage. In this chapter, we'll look at how to work with XML in Flash. You'll create Flash movies that include data from external XML documents. You'll also create and modify XML content within Flash and learn how to send it to other applications. We'll work through several examples so that you can practice what we cover.

This chapter will introduce you to the **XML** class—the most common way to work with XML documents in Flash. In Chapters 8 and 9, we'll look at another way to work with XML documents: by using data components.

If you're not familiar with object-oriented programming, the term *class* refers to the design of an object. It specifies the rules for the way the object works and lists all the methods and properties for the object. The XML class contains all the information needed for working with XML objects in Flash.

The XML class was introduced in Flash 5, and since that time, the ActionScript associated with it hasn't changed significantly. The XML class became a native object in Flash 6, which increased its speed compared with Flash 5. The XML class stores XML content in document trees within Flash. The class allows you to

- Create new XML documents or fragments
- Load external XML documents
- Modify XML content
- Send XML information from Flash

The XML class includes methods and properties to work with XML document trees. You'll also use a related class, the **XMLNode** class, which allows you to work with specific nodes in an XML document tree. You can find a summary of the methods, properties, and events of both classes in the tables at the end of this chapter.

When we create a new XML object from the XML class, we call the object an *instance* of the class, and the process of creating the object is known as *instantiation*. One way to view the difference is to see the XML class as a template that you use to create XML objects.

We'll start this chapter by learning how to load an external XML document into a Flash XML object. We'll look at how you can extract information from the document tree so you can add it to your Flash movie. You could do this with either a physical document saved with an `.xml` file extension or a stream of XML information. If you're working with an information stream, you can load XML content generated by a PHP, ColdFusion, or ASP.NET server-side page or from a web service. We'll cover web services in Chapter 9.

Loading an XML document into Flash

The process of loading an XML document into Flash involves the following steps:

1. Create an XML object.
2. Specify what happens after the XML document loads, that is, identify a function to deal with the loaded XML information.
3. Load the external document into the XML object. Flash parses the data into the XML document tree.

After the document has been loaded and parsed into an XML document tree, an event handler calls the function specified in step 2. Usually, this function checks first to see if the XML document has been loaded successfully. If so, the function extracts the information from the XML document and adds it to the Flash movie. It's common to use the XML document to populate UI components.

Using the load method

The following code demonstrates one way to load in an external XML document. It uses ActionScript version 2.0.

```
var myXML:XML = new XML();
myXML.ignoreWhite = true;
myXML.onLoad = functionName;
myXML.load("filename.xml");
```

On the first line, I create a new XML object called `myXML`. The second line sets the `ignoreWhite` property to true. This means that Flash will ignore white space such as tabs and returns in the XML document. If you forget to set this property, blank lines will be treated as nodes, which can cause problems when you're trying to extract information.

On the third line, I use the onLoad event handler to refer to the function that will be called after the file has loaded. In the example, I've used the name functionName. The last line loads the file called filename.xml. If this were a real example, I'd have to create the function called functionName to process the XML content from filename.xml after the file loads.

I can also load the XML document from a subdirectory of the current directory:

```
var myXML:XML = new XML();
myXML.ignoreWhite = true;
myXML.onLoad = functionName;
myXML.load("foldername/filename.xml");
```

Be aware that if your XML document includes file names and file paths, storing the XML document in a subfolder might cause you problems. When you try to use this information in a movie, Flash calculates the relative paths from the location of the .swf file. As this may be in a different location from the XML or .swf file, the movie may not be able to find the files at those locations. To avoid these potential problems, it's much easier if you keep your XML document in the same folder as your Flash movie.

In the code you've seen so far, I've used a file name ending with the .xml extension. However, you aren't limited to this type of file. You can load any type of file providing it results in an XML document. This means that you can load a server-side PHP, ColdFusion, Java, or ASP.NET file as long as it generates XML content.

If you do load a server-side file into your XML object, you'll need to include the full path so that the web server can process the server-side code. I've shown an example here; we'll learn more about working with server-side documents a little later in this chapter.

```
var myXML = new XML();
myXML.ignoreWhite = true;
myXML.onLoad = functionName;
myXML.load("http://localhost/webfolder/filename.aspx");
```

Understanding the order of the code

You may have noticed that, in the code samples above, I specified the load function before I loaded the XML document. On the surface, this doesn't make sense. Shouldn't I wait until the XML file loads and then specify which function to call?

In Flash, some ActionScript code doesn't run in a strict order. Lines don't necessarily wait for other lines to complete before they run. Much of the code that we write is in response to a specific event such as a mouse click. In this case, the event is the loading of an external XML file into an XML object. We call this *asynchronous* execution.

If we specified the load function after the load line, the XML file might have already finished loading before we set the function that should be called. This would mean that the onLoad function would be skipped completely. The only way to be sure that you call the function correctly is to set a reference to it before you load the XML file.

Understanding the onLoad function

After the XML document has finished loading, Flash calls the function that you specified in the onLoad line. The function is called by the onLoad *event handler*, and it runs after the XML document has been received by Flash and parsed into the document tree. You can assign the onLoad function with the following line:

```
myXML.onLoad = functionName;
```

If you've worked with ActionScript before, you'll notice that the function doesn't include those brackets that you're used to seeing after the function name, for example, functionName(). That's because we're not actually calling the function in this line; instead, we're assigning it to the onLoad event handler. The call will happen after the XML document is loaded and parsed.

Any onLoad function that you create automatically includes a parameter that tells you whether or not the file loaded successfully. The onLoad function should always test this parameter first before you start to process the XML document. You can also check the status property of the loaded document to see if there were any problems.

You can see this process in the following sample code:

```
var myXML:XML = new XML();
myXML.ignoreWhite = true;
myXML.onLoad = myFunction;
myXML.load("filename.xml");
function myFunction(success:Boolean):Void {
  if (success) {
    //process XML content
  }
  else {
    //display error message
  }
}
```

In these lines, I've defined the function myFunction with a parameter called success. You can use any name you like for this parameter. The important thing to remember is that the parameter is Boolean, so it can only have one of two values: true or false.

The first line in the function checks to see if the value of the parameter is true; that is, if the XML document has loaded successfully. If so, the function would normally then include lines that process the XML content. Otherwise, if the document didn't load successfully, we'd probably want to display an error message.

Using the line

```
if (success) {
```

is equivalent to using

```
if (success == true) {
```

I could also have used an inline function as shown here:

```
var myXML:XML = new XML();
myXML.ignoreWhite = true;
myXML.onLoad = function (success:Boolean):Void {
  if (success) {
    //process XML content
  }
  else {
    //display error message
  }
};
myXML.load("filename.xml");
```

Either of the two approaches shown here is acceptable. If you create the onLoad function separately, rather than inline, you will be able to reuse it when you load other XML documents. After all, if your XML documents have the same structure, you'll probably want to process them in the same way. Using the same function allows you to reuse the code and means that you'll only have to maintain one block of ActionScript. If you're loading a single XML document into your movie, it doesn't matter which method you choose.

The code shown so far uses the onLoad event handler. Flash provides another event handler for the XML object: onData. Both events trigger after the content has been loaded into Flash. The difference is that the onLoad event happens after the XML content has been parsed by Flash and added to the XML document tree. The onData event takes place before parsing, so you can use this event to access the raw XML from your external document. In most cases, you'll use the onLoad event handler.

> *In case you're wondering what the* :Void *means in* myFunction(success:Boolean):Void, *it indicates what type of information the function returns. In this case, nothing is returned, so I've used the word* Void. *You could also specify the datatype for the value returned by the function, for example,* String *or* Number.

After you load the XML content into an XML object, you'll need to add the data to your Flash movie. Before you do this, you should check that the document has loaded successfully.

Testing if a document has been loaded

You can test whether an XML document has been loaded by checking the loaded property of the XML object. The property returns a Boolean value and will display either true or false when traced in an Output window. Here's an example:

```
var myXML:XML = new XML();
myXML.ignoreWhite = true;
myXML.onLoad = function (success:Boolean):Void {
  trace (this.loaded);
};
myXML.load("filename.xml");
```

In the sample code, this refers to the XML object. I can use the keyword this because I'm inside the onLoad function for the XML object.

Note that the loaded property may return a value of true even when errors have occurred in parsing the XML content. Flash provides a mechanism for finding errors.

Locating errors in an XML file

When you load an external XML document into Flash, it's possible that it may not be well formed. Remember that well-formed documents meet the following requirements:

- The document contains one or more elements.
- The document contains a single root element, which may contain other nested elements.
- Each element closes properly.
- Start and end tags have matching case.
- Elements nest correctly.
- Attribute values are contained in quotes.

Where a document is not well formed, Flash may have difficulty in parsing it into the document tree. Flash may still indicate that the document has loaded successfully, even if it wasn't parsed correctly.

The XML class has a status property that indicates any problems that occurred when parsing the XML document. This property returns a value between 0 and -10; the values for each are shown here:

- 0—No error; the parse was completed successfully.
- -2—A CDATA section was not properly terminated.
- -3—The XML declaration was not properly terminated.
- -4—The DOCTYPE declaration was not properly terminated.
- -5—A comment was not properly terminated.
- -6—An XML element was malformed.
- -7—The application is out of memory.
- -8—An attribute value was not properly terminated.
- -9—A start tag was not matched with an end tag.
- -10—An end tag was encountered without a matching start tag.

Where a document contains multiple errors, the status property will only return one error value. Even though Flash may detect an error during parsing, it may still be possible to find information from all or part of the document tree.

To show you an example of the status numbers, let's load the resource file `address1.xml` file into Flash. The document is missing an ending </phoneBook> tag, as shown here:

```
<?xml version="1.0" encoding="UTF-8"?>
<phoneBook>
  <contact id="1">
    <name>Sas Jacobs</name>
    <address>123 Some Street, Some City, Some Country</address>
    <phone>123 456</phone>
  </contact>
```

I've saved this example in the resource file `simpleloadstatus.fla`. Figure 4-1 shows the status code that displays when I test the file. In this case, the code is `-9`, indicating a mismatch between start and end tags within the document.

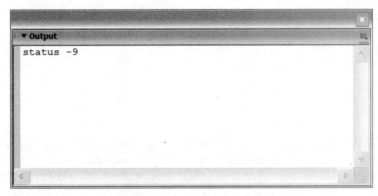

Figure 4-1. The Output window displaying the status property

So far, we've covered the theory behind loading external XML documents into Flash. We create an XML object and load a file, and Flash parses the contents into a document tree. We can then use a function to add the XML content to our movie.

Each time you load an external XML document, your code will probably start with the same steps:

1. Create the XML object.
2. Set the `ignoreWhite` property to true.
3. Specify the name of the function that will deal with the loaded XML document.
4. Load the XML document.
5. Within the load function, test whether the XML file has loaded successfully.
6. Display the document tree with a `trace` action to check the loaded contents.

We'll work through an example to illustrate these steps. We'll load an external XML document into Flash and display it in an Output window. When you do this, you should see the same content that is in the external document.

Exercise 1: Loading an external XML document

In this example, we'll create a simple Flash movie that loads the address.xml file and displays it in an Output window. You can see the completed example in the resource file simpleload.fla.

1. Create a new Flash movie and click frame 1 on the Timeline.
2. Save the document in the same folder as the address.xml file.
3. Add the following code into the Actions panel. You can open the panel by using the *F9* shortcut key.

```
var myXML:XML = new XML();
myXML.ignoreWhite = true;
myXML.onLoad = processXML;
myXML.load("address.xml");
function processXML(success:Boolean):Void {
  if (success) {
    trace(this);
  }
  else {
    trace ("Error loading XML file");
  }
}
```

In this example, I call the function processXML after the file address.xml loads. The function checks to see if the XML document loads successfully by checking the variable success. If so, I use the trace action to display the XML document tree in an Output window. If not, I display an error message in the Output window.

Because the function has been called by the onLoad event of the XML object, I can use the word this. In fact,

```
trace(this);
```

is the same as

```
trace(myXML);
```

4. Save the movie and test it with the *CTRL-ENTER* shortcut (*CMD-RETURN* on a Macintosh). You should see an Output window similar to the one shown in Figure 4-2. The Output window displays the document tree from the XML object. I've saved the sample file simpleload.fla with your resources.

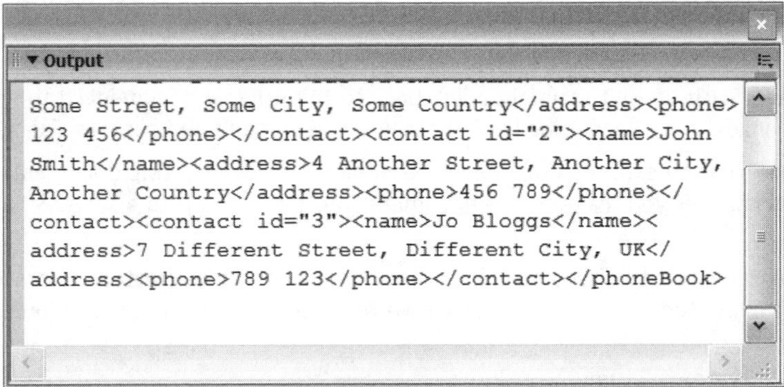

Figure 4-2. The Output window displaying XML content

5. If you see an error when you test the movie, it's most likely to be due to a misspelling. Check the XML document file name and the spelling of your success parameter within the function. A sample error is shown in Figure 4-3.

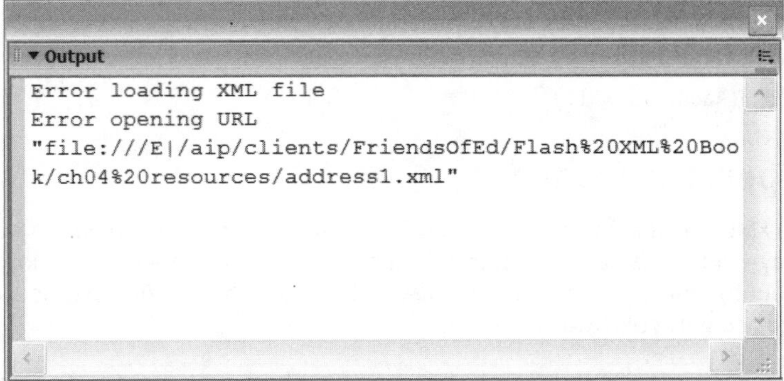

Figure 4-3. The Output window displaying an error message

In the previous exercise, we loaded the file `address.xml` into Flash. We tested that the document loaded successfully, and then we displayed the contents of the XML document tree in an Output window. Tracing the document tree can be a useful way to test that you've loaded the XML document correctly.

> *With most objects in Flash, you'll see* `[object Object]` *when you trace them in the Output panel. If you trace an* `XML` *or* `XMLNode` *object, Flash uses the* `toString` *method to display a text representation of the object. This is very useful when you want to view the XML document tree. Using*
>
> ```
> trace(myXML);
> ```
>
> *is the same as using*
>
> ```
> trace(myXML.toString());
> ```

Points to note from exercise 1

- It's possible for you to change the XML content within Flash independently of the external XML document. Flash doesn't maintain a link back to the original document. If the external document changes, it will have to be loaded again before the updated content displays within Flash.
- Flash can't update external documents. To update an external XML document, you'll have to send any changes you make to the document tree out of Flash to a server-side page for processing.
- Earlier in the chapter, I discussed inline onLoad functions. I've re-created the preceding example using an inline function. The code is shown here, and it's saved in the resource file simpleload2.fla:

```
var myXML:XML = new XML();
myXML.ignoreWhite = true;
myXML.onLoad = function(success:Boolean):Void {
  if (success) {
    trace(this);
  }
  else {
    trace ("Error loading XML file");
  }
};
myXML.load("address.xml");
```

Testing for percent loaded

Loading a large XML document might take some time, and it's useful to let the user know what's happening. You may want to display a message showing the user that the XML file is loading. The XML class allows you to find out how big the XML file is and how much has loaded, using the getBytesLoaded and getBytesTotal methods.

You can use these methods with the setInterval action to check progress at given time intervals. You can also use them in the onEnterFrame event handler of a movie. Loading small XML files is very quick, so these methods are only going to be useful when you're working with large XML files.

The following example is based on the code provided within the Flash help file. It shows how you can test for the percentage of an XML file loaded using the setInterval action. You can find the example in the resource file simpleloadpercent.fla.

```
var myXML:XML = new XML();
myXML.ignoreWhite = true;
myXML.onLoad = processXML;
var intervalID:Number = setInterval(checkLoad, 5, myXML);
myXML.load("large.xml");
function processXML(success:Boolean):Void {
  clearInterval(intervalID);
  if (success) {
    trace("loaded: " + this.getBytesLoaded());
    trace ("total: " + this.getBytesTotal());
  }
```

```
  else {
    trace ("Error loading XML file");
  }
}
function checkLoad(theXML:XML):Void {
  var loaded:Number = theXML.getBytesLoaded();
  var total:Number = theXML.getBytesTotal();
  var percent:Number = Math.floor((loaded/total) * 100);
  trace ("percent loaded: " + percent);
}
```

On my computer, despite loading an XML file of over 3 MB in size, the loading process only displays the total file size.

The following example shows the same methods used with the onEnterFrame event handler. You can see the example saved in the resource file `simpleloadEnterFrame.fla`.

```
var myXML:XML = new XML();
myXML.ignoreWhite = true;
myXML.onLoad = processXML;
var intervalID:Number = setInterval(checkLoad, 5, myXML);
myXML.load("large.xml");
this.onEnterFrame = function():Void {
  var loaded:Number = myXML.getBytesLoaded();
  var total:Number = myXML.getBytesTotal();
  var percent:Number = Math.floor((loaded/total) * 100);
  trace ("percent loaded: " + percent);
  if (percent == 100) {
    delete this.onEnterFrame;
  }
}
function processXML(success:Boolean):Void {
  if (success) {
    trace("loaded: " + this.getBytesLoaded());
    trace ("total: " + this.getBytesTotal());
  }
  else {
    trace ("Error loading XML file");
  }
}
```

Again, I am not able to get the percentage loaded value to display each time the movie enters a new frame. You may wish to use these methods with caution. In my work, using a preloader for XML documents has rarely been necessary. If required, an alternative approach might be to show and hide a movie clip that displays a loading message.

After you've loaded an external XML document, you'll need to display the contents within your Flash movie. The next section shows how you can extract information from an XML object. A little later, we'll use the techniques to populate UI components.

Navigating an XML object

In Chapter 2, I talked about XML parsers. You might remember that we use a parser to process an XML document. Once parsed, the software can work with the content from the XML document.

There are two types of parsers: validating and nonvalidating. The difference is that validating parsers compare an XML document against a schema or DTD to make sure that you've constructed the document correctly. Nonvalidating parsers don't do this.

Flash contains a nonvalidating parser. When you load an XML document into Flash, it processes the contents and creates an XML document tree. If you include a reference to a schema or DTD within an XML document, Flash won't check the document for validity before it is loaded.

The Flash document tree includes all elements from the XML document. Flash uses a family analogy to refer to different branches within the tree. Elements can be *children* of another *parent* element, or *siblings*.

Each element includes a collection of child elements called childNodes. The collection is an array so we can use the standard array methods. For example, we can determine how many elements are in the collection using the length property. Elements with no child elements will have a childNodes length of 0. We can also loop through the collection when we're processing an XML object.

In the address.xml file, shown here, the root element <phoneBook> has three child <contact> elements. We could programmatically work through each of the child elements, for example, adding them to a List component.

```
<?xml version="1.0" encoding="UTF-8"?>
<phoneBook>
  <contact id="1">
    <name>Sas Jacobs</name>
    <address>123 Some Street, Some City, Some Country</address>
    <phone>123 456</phone>
  </contact>
  <contact id="2">
    <name>John Smith</name>
    <address>4 Another Street, Another City, Another Country</address>
    <phone>456 789</phone>
  </contact>
  <contact id="3">
    <name>Jo Bloggs</name>
    <address>7 Different Street, Different City, UK</address>
    <phone>789 123</phone>
  </contact>
</phoneBook>
```

You can refer to a child element by its position in the collection. Because the childNodes collection is an array, the first element is at number 0. The following line refers to the first child element of the myXML object. You can also refer to children of an XMLNode object.

```
myXML.childNodes[0];
```

The firstChild and lastChild properties allow you to refer to the first and last items in the childNodes collection.

```
myXML.firstChild;
myXML.lastChild;
```

When you are processing an XML document tree, you usually start by referencing the root node of the document. This is the parent of all other elements and is the firstChild or childNodes[0] of the XML object.

All elements are children of the XML object, so you can refer to each one using its position within the XML object. It's a bit like a map. Start with the root node and move to the first child. Go to the second child node and find the third child. Finish at the first child of this node. You can end up with long paths as shown here:

```
myXML.firstChild.childNodes[1].childNodes[2].firstChild;
```

You'll learn a bit more about locating specific child nodes in a document later in this chapter. In the next section, I've shown the Flash notation for the XML elements in the file address.xml.

Mapping an XML document tree

I've shown the complete address.xml document here. Table 4-1 shows how you can refer to specific parts of this document once it's loaded into Flash. The table assumes that we've created an XML object called myXML.

```
<?xml version="1.0" encoding="UTF-8"?>
<phoneBook>
  <contact id="1">
    <name>Sas Jacobs</name>
    <address>123 Some Street, Some City, Some Country</address>
    <phone>123 456</phone>
  </contact>
  <contact id="2">
    <name>John Smith</name>
    <address>4 Another Street, Another City, Another Country</address>
    <phone>456 789</phone>
  </contact>
  <contact id="3">
    <name>Jo Bloggs</name>
    <address>7 Different Street, Different City, UK</address>
    <phone>789 123</phone>
  </contact>
</phoneBook>
```

Table 4-1. Mapping the XML document tree for address.xml

Element	Flash XML Element Path
`<?xml version="1.0" encoding="UTF-8"?>`	`xmlDecl` property
<phoneBook>	`myXML.firstChild` or `myXML.childNodes[0]`
`<contact id="1">`	`myXML.firstChild.firstChild` or `myXML.childNodes[0].childNodes[0]`
<name>	`myXML.firstChild.firstChild.firstChild` or `myXML.childNodes[0].childNodes[0].childNodes[0]`
<address>	`myXML.firstChild.firstChild.childNodes[1]` or `myXML.childNodes[0].childNodes[0].childNodes[1]`
<phone>	`myXML.firstChild.firstChild.lastChild` or `myXML.childNodes[0].childNodes[0].childNodes[2]`
`<contact id="2">`	`myXML.firstChild.childNodes[1]` or `myXML.childNodes[0].childNodes[1]`
<name> (within contact 2)	`myXML.firstChild.childNodes[1].firstChild` or `myXML.childNodes[0].childNodes[1].childNodes[0]`
<address> (within contact 2)	`myXML.firstChild.childNodes[1]. childNodes[1]` or `myXML.childNodes[0].childNodes[1].childNodes[1]`
<phone> (within contact 2)	`myXML.firstChild.childNodes[1].lastChild` or `myXML.childNodes[0].childNodes[1].childNodes[2]`
`<contact id="3">`	`myXML.firstChild.childNodes[2]` or `myXML.childNodes[0].childNodes[2]`
<name> (within contact 3)	`myXML.firstChild.childNodes[2].firstChild` or `myXML.childNodes[0].childNodes[2].childNodes[0]`
<address> (within contact 3)	`myXML.firstChild.childNodes[2].childNodes[1]` or `myXML.childNodes[0].childNodes[2].childNodes[1]`
<phone> (within contact 3)	`myXML.firstChild.childNodes[2].lastChild` or `myXML.childNodes[0].childNodes[2].childNodes[2]`

You can replace the myXML references with this if you're including the references in the onLoad function of the XML object. Placing any of the paths in a trace statement will display the complete element in an Output window. For example, the following onLoad function traces the second contact's <name> element from the address.xml file, as shown in Figure 4-4.

```
var myXML:XML = new XML();
myXML.ignoreWhite = true;
myXML.onLoad = processXML;
myXML.load("address.xml");
function processXML(success:Boolean):Void {
  if (success) {
    trace(this.firstChild.childNodes[1].firstChild);
  }
  else {
    trace ("Error loading XML file");
  }
}
```

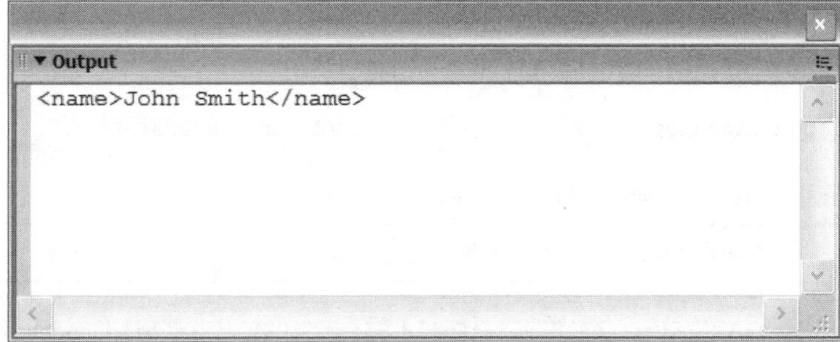

Figure 4-4. Tracing an element from the document tree

Understanding node types

The XML class stores XML content in a document tree. Earlier in the book, we learned that XML documents can contain

- Elements
- Attributes
- Text
- Entities
- Comments
- Processing instructions
- CDATA

Within an XML document tree, Flash recognizes only two types of nodes—XML elements and text nodes. You can access the attributes within an XML element but Flash ignores comments, processing instructions, and CDATA.

You can use the property nodeType to identify which type of element you're working with. The property returns a value of 1 for element nodes and 3 for text nodes. It's important to know which type you're working with because some properties of the XML class are specific to certain node types. This code shows how you can use the nodeType property to display the node type:

```
trace(myXML.nodeType);
trace(myXMLNode.nodeType);
```

You can find the name of an element node by using the nodeName property. This is the name of the tag included within the element, and you can use the property with an XML object or an XMLNode object.

```
trace(myXML.firstChild.nodeName);
trace(myXMLNode.nodeName);
```

Text nodes don't have a tag name, so the nodeName property will return a value of null.

A text node is the child of the parent element node. Instead of a nodeName, text nodes have a nodeValue, which displays the text content. To display the text inside an element, you can use

```
trace(myXML.firstChild.firstChild.firstChild.nodeValue);
```

The nodeValue property for an element node will display null.

Table 4-2 shows some examples of how to access the text from the file address.xml.

Table 4-2. Locating the text nodes within XML document tree for address.xml

Text	Flash XML Element Path
Sas Jacobs	myXML.firstChild.firstChild.firstChild.firstChild.nodeValue or myXML.childNodes[0].childNodes[0].childNodes[0].childNodes[0] .nodeValue
7 Different Street, Different City, UK	myXML.firstChild.childNodes[2].childNodes[1].firstChild.nodeValue or myXML.childNodes[0].childNodes[2].childNodes[1]. childNodes[0].nodeValue
456 789	myXML.firstChild.childNodes[1].childNodes[2].firstChild.nodeValue or myXML.childNodes[0].childNodes[1].childNodes[2].childNodes[0]. nodeValue

Again, you can replace the myXML references with this if you're including these references in an onLoad function. Adding any of the paths shown in Table 4.2 in a trace statement will display the complete element in an Output window.

The statements in the preceding table appear a little confusing. The paths are long, and it's not easy to figure out which element we're targeting with paths like firstChild.childNodes[1].childNode[2]. Your code will be much easier to read if you create XMLNode variables. These variables can act as signposts to specific parts of the XML document and make it easier to navigate the document tree.

Creating node shortcuts

As you've seen, writing a path to a specific element within the document tree can be an arduous process. It's much easier to use an XMLNode variable to provide a shortcut to a specific position in the document tree, as shown here:

```
var myXMLNode:XMLNode = myXML.firstChild.firstChild.firstChild;
```

By writing this line, you can use myXMLNode to refer to the element instead of the full path. If you use descriptive names for the XMLNode objects, you'll find it much easier to understand your code:

```
var NameNode:XMLNode = myXML.firstChild.firstChild.firstChild;
trace(NameNode);
```

You'd normally start this process by locating the root node of the document. Remember that each file has a single root node that contains all of the other elements.

Finding the root node

The root node of the tree is always the first child of the XML object, so you can locate it with the following code. Both lines are equivalent.

```
myXML.firstChild;
myXML.childNodes[0];
```

If you are referring to the first child within the onLoad function, you can also use

```
this.firstChild;
this.childNodes[0];
```

Displaying the firstChild of the XML document in an Output window is almost the same as displaying the entire XML document tree. The difference is that the firstChild doesn't include the XML declaration.

In the resource file simpleload.fla, replacing the line trace (this); with trace(this.firstChild); will show the document tree without the XML declaration.

```
var myXML:XML = new XML();
myXML.ignoreWhite = true;
myXML.onLoad = processXML;
myXML.load("address.xml");
function processXML(success:Boolean):Void {
  if (success) {
    trace(this.firstChild);
  }
  else {
    trace ("Error loading XML file");
  }
}
```

It can be useful to assign the root node to a variable so that you don't have to keep writing this.firstChild each time.

Setting a root node variable

It's often useful to set a variable for the root node. I like to use the variable name RootNode. You can use the variable type XMLNode so that you'll get code hints each time you type the variable name. These two lines are equivalent, and you can use either:

```
var RootNode:XMLNode = myXML.firstChild;
var RootNode:XMLNode = myXML.childNodes[0];
```

If you're referring to the root node from within the onLoad function, you can also use the word this:

```
var RootNode:XMLNode = this.firstChild;
var RootNode:XMLNode = this.childNodes[0];
```

Setting a variable provides a shortcut each time you want to refer to the root node. It saves you from having to write myXML.firstChild or myXML.childNodes[0].

To get to the first child of the root node, you could use either of these two lines:

```
this.firstChild.firstChild;
this.childNodes[0].childNodes[0];
```

You could also write

```
var RootNode:XMLNode = this.firstChild;
RootNode.firstChild;
```

or

```
var RootNode:XMLNode = this.childNodes[0];
RootNode.childNodes[0];
```

Using the descriptive name RootNode makes it much easier to identify your position within the XML document. You can use the same approach with other elements within the XML document tree.

Displaying the root node name

You can find out the name of the root node by using its nodeName property:

```
var RootNode:XMLNode = myXML.firstChild;
trace(RootNode.nodeName);
```

This is equivalent to the single line

```
trace (myXML.firstChild.nodeName);
```

You can try this with your resource file simpleload.fla. Modify the onLoad function as shown here:

```
function processXML(success:Boolean):Void {
  if (success) {
    var RootNode:XMLNode = this.firstChild;
    trace(RootNode.nodeName);
  }
```

```
    else {
      trace ("Error loading XML file")
    }
  }
```

When you test the movie, you should see an Output window similar to that shown in Figure 4-5.

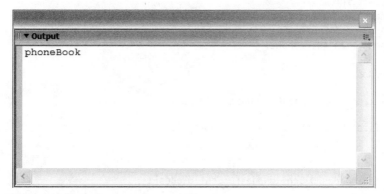

Figure 4-5. Displaying the root node name

You can see this example in the resource file `simpleprocess.fla`.

When you first start working with the XML class, it can be a very useful to trace the name of the root node as a first step. Making sure that the name is correct will help you to identify simple errors such as forgetting to set the `ignoreWhite` property value to true.

Once you've located the root node, you can start working your way through the document tree to find specific child nodes. Again, it's useful to create variables for positions within the document tree to make your code easier to understand.

Locating child nodes

Earlier in the chapter, you saw some examples of how to locate the child nodes within an XML object. Tables 4-1 and 4-2 provide some useful summaries. You started with the root element and used properties to find a specific node.

Working with specific child nodes

To refer to a specific node in your document tree, you need to construct a path. You can refer to each section of the path using properties like `firstChild` or a position in the `childNodes` collection such as `childNodes[2]`.

For example, in the XML fragment that follows, the <contact> element is the firstChild of the <phoneBook> root element, which is the firstChild of the XML object. The <name>, <address>, and <phone> elements are childNodes[0], childNodes[1], and childNodes[2], respectively, of the <contact> element.

```
<phoneBook>
  <contact id="1">
    <name>Sas Jacobs</name>
    <address>123 Some Street, Some City, Some Country</address>
    <phone>123 456</phone>
  </contact>
</phoneBook>
```

To refer to the <address> element, I could use the path

```
myXML.firstChild.firstChild.childNodes[1];
```

or

```
myXML.childNodes[0].childNodes[0].childNodes[1];
```

I could combine this with a root node variable to achieve the same result:

```
var RootNode:XMLNode = myXML.firstChild;
RootNode.firstChild.childNodes[1];
```

You can see an example of this in the resource file simpleprocess.fla.

I could use the following code to refer to the <phone> element:

```
myXML.firstChild.firstChild.lastChild;
```

or

```
myXML.childNodes[0].childNodes[0].childNodes[3];
```

The childNodes collection and the firstChild and lastChild properties are read-only. This means you can't use them to change the structure of the XML object.

Text elements are always the firstChild of the element that contains them. To refer to the text inside the <address> element, I could use the expression

```
myXML.firstChild.firstChild.childNodes[1].firstChild.nodeValue;
```

or

```
myXML.childNodes[0].childNodes[0].childNodes[1].firstChild.nodeValue;
```

I could also use the RootNode variable as shown here:

```
var RootNode:XMLNode = myXML.firstChild;
RootNode.childNodes[0].childNodes[1].firstChild.nodeValue;
```

Again, you can see an example of this in simpleprocess.fla. You may need to uncomment the relevant lines in the file.

All of the child nodes of an element live within the childNodes collection. This is an array of all the child nodes. As you'll often want to treat each childNode in a similar way, it makes more sense to work with the collection as a whole.

Working with the childNodes collection

It's more common to work with all childNodes in a collection rather than finding single nodes within the document tree. You can loop through the collection and perform similar actions on all of the nodes. The code that follows shows how to use a for loop in this way. We can determine how many children are in the collection of childNodes by using the childNodes.length property. This is the same as the length property of an array.

```
for (var i:Number=0; i < myXMLNode.childNodes.length; i++) {
  //do something
}
```

You can determine if an element has child nodes by testing the length property of the collection or by using the hasChildNodes method. You may want to perform one action for elements with child nodes and another for elements without children. Using the hasChildNodes method returns a value of either true or false, so it is often used within if statements, as shown in this code snippet:

```
if (RootNode.hasChildNodes()) {
  //do something with the child nodes
}
else {
  //do something else
}
```

The following example shows how we could display all of the names of the children of a specific node, in this case, the first <contact> element. I've shown the relevant lines in bold. You can also open the resource file simpleprocess.fla to test the example.

```
function processXML(success:Boolean):Void {
  if (success) {
    var RootNode:XMLNode = this.firstChild;
    var ContactNode:XMLNode = RootNode.childNodes[0];
    for (var i:Number=0; i < ContactNode.childNodes.length; i++) {
      trace (ContactNode.childNodes[i].nodeName);
    }
  }
  else {
    trace ("Error loading XML file");
  }
}
```

This code assigns the first contact node to an XMLNode variable called ContactNode. We can then loop through each of the child nodes of that variable and display their names.

If you test the movie, you should see an Output window similar to the one shown in Figure 4-6.

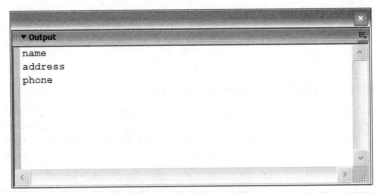

Figure 4-6. Displaying the child node names

Notice that I used an XMLNode variable called ContactNode to refer to the first <contact> element. The expression

```
ContactNode.childNodes[i].nodeName;
```

is much easier to understand than

```
myXML.firstChild.firstChild.childNodes[i].nodeName;
```

I could modify the function to display the text within each of the childNodes. Remember that the text within a node is always the firstChild of that node and that you can find the text using nodeValue. I've shown an example here; you can also see it in the simpleprocess.fla resource file.

```
function processXML(success:Boolean):Void {
  if (success) {
    var RootNode:XMLNode = this.firstChild;
    var ContactNode:XMLNode = RootNode.childNodes[0];
    for (var i:Number=0; i <ContactNode.childNodes.length; i++) {
      trace (ContactNode.childNodes[i].firstChild.nodeValue);
    }
  }
  else {
    trace ("Error loading XML file");
  }
}
```

Working your way through a complicated XML document can take some time. You have to understand the document structure and write code accordingly. An alternative way to work with the entire document tree is to use recursive functions. This can also be useful if you don't know the structure of the file or the names of the nodes.

Creating recursive functions

A *recursive function* is a function that calls itself. You can use a recursive function to extract the contents from the whole document tree. By calling the function again and passing the next branch of the tree, you can work your way through the entire XML object. You start by calling the function and passing the root node. If you find child nodes, you call the function again with each of the child nodes. You repeat the process until you've moved through the entire document tree.

This concept can be a little difficult to grasp, so I'll work through an example to help you understand it better.

Exercise 2: Processing an XML object with a recursive function

1. Create a new Flash file and save it in the same folder as the `address.xml` file.
2. Enter the following code. Instead of processing the XML object with the `processXML` function, I've used it to call another function called `showChildren`. The `showChildren` function takes one parameter, the root node of the XML object, which I've specified using `this.firstChild`.

```
var myXML:XML = new XML();
myXML.ignoreWhite = true;
myXML.onLoad = processXML;
myXML.load("address.xml");
function processXML(success:Boolean):Void {
  if (success) {
    showChildren(this.firstChild);
  }
  else {
    trace ("Error loading file");
  }
}
```

3. Add the `showChildren` function in the Actions panel, underneath the `processXML` function:

```
function showChildren(startNode:XMLNode):Void{
  if (startNode.nodeType == 1) {
    if (startNode.hasChildNodes()) {
      trace (startNode.nodeName + " has child elements:");
      for (var i:Number = 0; i < startNode.childNodes.length; i++) {
        if (startNode.childNodes[i].nodeType == 1) {
          trace ("element: " + startNode.childNodes[i].nodeName);
        }
        else {
          trace ("text: " + startNode.childNodes[i].nodeValue);
        }
        showChildren(startNode.childNodes[i]);
      }
    }
  }
}
```

The function looks confusing at first. It takes an XMLNode variable as a parameter and only proceeds if the XMLNode is an element node, that is, nodeType == 1. Text nodes can't have children.

The second if statement determines whether there are any childNodes of the current element node. If there are, the function traces the name of the node and the words has child elements.

Next, the function loops through the childNodes of the starting node. If the childNode is an element, the function traces the word element with the node name. Otherwise, for text elements, it traces the word text with the text content.

Finally, the function calls itself and passes the current childNode as a parameter. This repeats the process at the next level in the document tree. The function stops when it encounters a text node or when the current node has no childNodes.

4. Save the Flash file and test the movie. You should see an Output window similar to the one shown in Figure 4-7. You can find the completed file in your resources saved under the name recursive.fla.

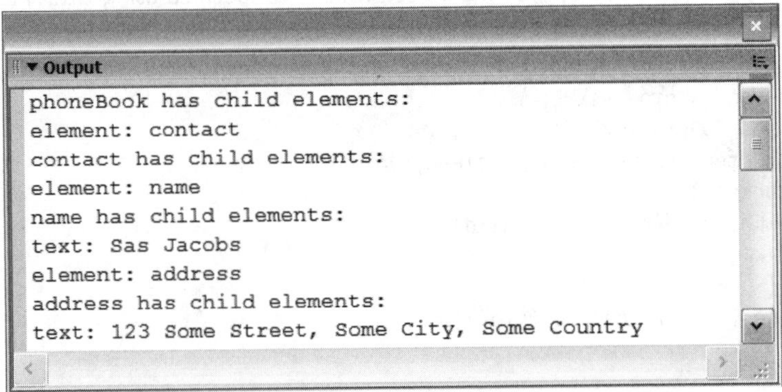

Figure 4-7. Displaying the contents of an XML document using a recursive function

Using a recursive function allows you to process the contents of the document tree without understanding the structure. It can also be a more efficient way to write code that processes the document tree.

So far, we've worked with child nodes, but it's useful to know that you can use ActionScript to find sibling nodes. These are nodes that share the same parent node.

Locating siblings

Flash provides two properties for dealing with siblings: nextSibling and previousSibling. These properties allow you to locate elements that share the same parent as the current node. You can refer to the previous and next siblings of the current node using

```
myXMLNode.previousSibling;
myXMLNode.nextSibling;
```

If there is no previous or next sibling, the property will return undefined, so you can't find the previousSibling of the first child node or the nextSibling of the last child node. As both of these properties are read-only, you can't use them to move nodes within the document tree.

The following example shows the processXML function modified to return the next and previous siblings of the second <address> element:

```
function processXML(success:Boolean):Void {
  if (success) {
    var RootNode:XMLNode = this.firstChild;
    var AddressNode:XMLNode = RootNode.childNodes[0].childNodes[1];
    trace ("current node: " + AddressNode.nodeName);
    trace ("previous: " + AddressNode.previousSibling.nodeName);
    trace ("next: " + AddressNode.nextSibling.nodeName);
  }
  else {
    trace ("Error loading XML file");
  }
}
```

I've included this example in the simpleprocess.fla resource file. If you test this file, you should see something similar to the Output window shown in Figure 4-8.

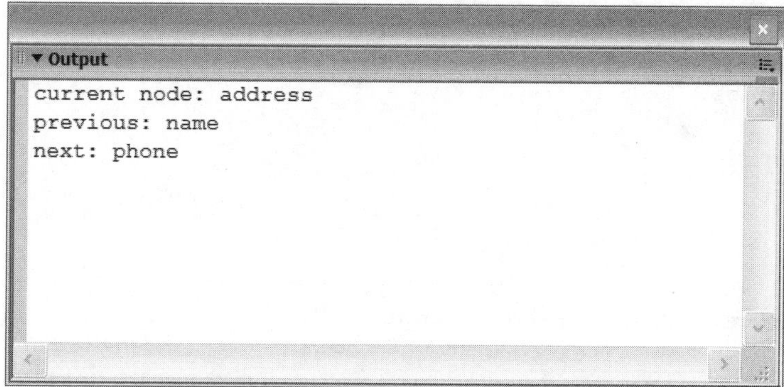

Figure 4-8. Displaying the previous and next sibling node names

As well as working with siblings, you can find the parent element of a node. This might be a quicker way to locate a node rather than writing a full path starting from the root node.

Locating parent nodes

You can refer to the parent of a current node using the parentNode property, as shown here:

```
myXMLNode.parentNode;
```

In this example, the processXML function displays the name of the parent of the second <address> element. I've made the relevant lines bold.

```
function processXML(success:Boolean):Void {
  if (success) {
    var RootNode:XMLNode = this.firstChild;
    var AddressNode:XMLNode = RootNode.childNodes[0].childNodes[1];
    trace ("parent node is " + AddressNode.parentNode.nodeName);
  }
  else {
    trace ("Error loading XML file");
  }
}
```

You can see the example in the simpleprocess.fla resource file. If you test the file, you should see an Output window similar to that displayed in Figure 4-9.

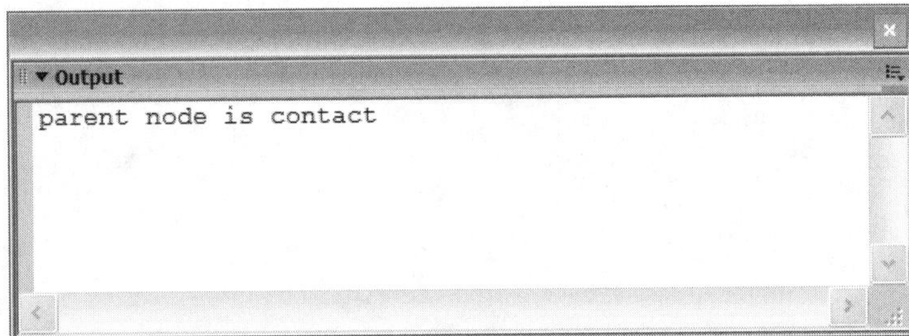

Figure 4-9. Displaying the parent node name

Note that the parentNode property is read-only, so you can't use it to change the structure of a document tree.

So far in this chapter, we've looked at how to extract information from both element and text nodes within an XML document. In the next section, I'll explain how you can work with attributes.

Extracting information from attributes

You refer to attributes differently compared with elements and text. Attributes aren't children of element. Rather, they are a collection, or array, within an element. Unlike the childNodes collection, the attributes collection is an associative array. This means that you can't use a position number. You have to refer to each attribute using its name.

The following lines show you how you can refer to the value of an attribute using its name. The two examples are equivalent. The first uses dot notation while the second uses associative array notation.

```
myXML.firstChild.attributes.attName;
myXML.firstChild.attributes["attName"];
```

In both examples, I'm finding the attribute called attName within the first child of the XML object called myXML.

In this XML fragment,

```
<?xml version="1.0" encoding="UTF-8"?>
<phoneBook>
  <contact id="1">
    <name>Sas Jacobs</name>
    <address>123 Some Street, Some City, Some Country</address>
    <phone>123 456</phone>
  </contact>
</phoneBook>
```

I could display the value of the id attribute of the <contact> element using the following code lines. Both the second and third lines are equivalent.

```
var RootNode:XMLNode = myXML.firstChild;
trace(RootNode.firsChild.attributes.id);
trace(RootNode.firstChild.attributes["id"]);
```

It's easy to refer to attributes when you know their names. However, there may be occasions when you don't know their names. In those cases, it can be useful to loop through the attributes collection, as shown here:

```
for (var theAtt:String in myXMLNode.attributes) {
  //reference the attribute name using theAtt
  //reference the value using myXMLNode.attributes[theAtt])
}
```

This code is equivalent to saying *for each attribute in the attributes collection.*

The next example shows the processXML function modified to show the attributes within the first <contact> element of the address.xml file. The function displays the name and value of each attribute. Unfortunately, the element only has one attribute so the loop repeats only once.

```
function processXML(success:Boolean):Void {
  if (success) {
    var RootNode:XMLNode = this.firstChild;
    var ContactNode:XMLNode = RootNode.childNodes[0];
    for (var theAtt:String in ContactNode.attributes) {
      trace(theAtt + " = " + ContactNode.attributes[theAtt]);
    }
  }
  else {
    trace ("Error loading file");
  }
}
```

In this example, we create a new XMLNode variable called ContactNode to refer to the first <contact> element. We use a for loop to move through the collection of attributes. Because I'm working with an associative array, I have to refer to the value of the attribute using ContactNode.attributes[theAtt]).

You can see this example in the simpleprocess.fla resource file. Uncomment the relevant lines and test the movie. You should see an Output window similar to the one shown in Figure 4-10.

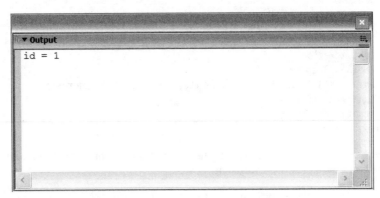

Figure 4-10. Looping through the attributes collection

You've learned a lot about loading external documents and extracting their values within Flash. We covered the various properties that you could use to move through the document tree. I showed you how to find the name of a node and the value of text within a node. The theory we've covered so far will make more sense when you work through an exercise.

Putting it all together

In this section, we'll put together everything we've covered so far in the chapter and create a simple XML application. We'll use the photoGallery.xml file that you created in Chapter 3. The application will load the content from the XML document and add the contents to create a photo gallery.

We'll work through the following steps to create our application. These steps are likely to be the same ones you use each time you load an external XML document.

1. Create the XML object.
2. Set the ignoreWhite property to true.
3. Specify the name of the function that will deal with the loaded XML document.
4. Load the XML document.
5. Within the load function, test whether the file has loaded successfully.
6. Display the document tree with a trace action to check that you've loaded the contents correctly.
7. Set a variable referring to the RootNode of the XML document.
8. Work through the document tree, adding content to the Flash movie.

The completed file gallery_completed.fla is included with your resources for Chapter 4 in case you want to see how the finished application works. Note that I've used ActionScript version 2.0 and version 2.0 components in the files, so you'll need at least Flash MX 2004 to complete the exercise.

Exercise 3: Creating an XML photo gallery

In this exercise, we'll create a simple Flash photo gallery that loads external images. We'll take the images from the photos folder included with the Chapter 4 resources. You can also use your own images if you'd prefer. Just add them to the photos folder and the XML document.

Setting up the environment

1. Move the photos folder, the starter file gallery.fla, and the photoGallery.xml file from the resources to the same directory on your computer.
2. Open gallery.fla. Figure 4-11 shows the interface.

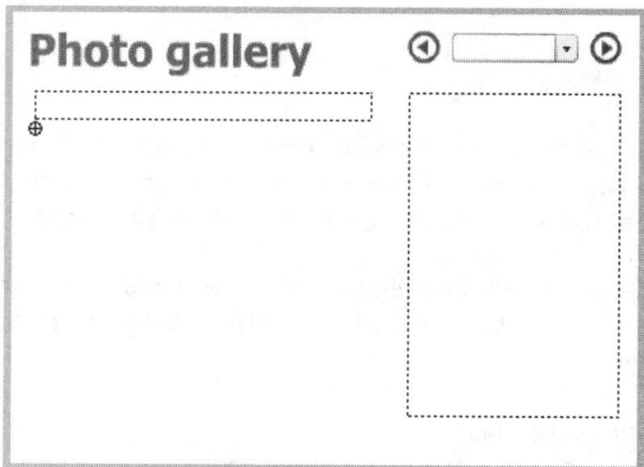

Figure 4-11. The gallery.fla interface

The interface includes a static text field containing the text Photo gallery. There are two dynamic text fields, one on the left for the caption and one on the right for the comments about the image. They have the instance names caption_txt and comment_txt, respectively.

There is an empty movie clip called empty_mc below the caption. We'll use this to display the photos. The top right of the interface includes a ComboBox component, gallery_cb, and two buttons, back_btn and forward_btn. Users will choose the gallery from the ComboBox component and navigate through the photos with the two buttons.

The XML document

We created the XML document photoGallery.xml in Chapter 3. The following code shows a summary of the document structure:

```
<?xml version="1.0" encoding="UTF-8" standalone="yes"?>
<photoGallery>
  <location locationName="galleryName">
    <photo filename="filename.jpg" caption="caption content">
      Text
    </photo>
    <photo filename="filename.jpg" caption="caption content">
      text
    </photo>
  </location>
  <location locationName="galleryName">
    <photo filename="filename.jpg" caption="caption content">
      Text
    </photo>
  </location>
</photoGallery>
```

The root element <photoGallery> contains one or more <location> elements. Each <location> has a single attribute locationName and contains one or more <photo> elements. The <photo> elements contain a filename and caption attribute as well as some descriptive text.

Feel free to update the XML document and photos folder with your own contents. The Flash movie is set up for landscape images with a width of up to 290 pixels, but you can change the movie if you're using differently sized images.

Loading the XML document into Flash

We'll load the XML document into the gallery.fla movie.

3. Create a new layer in the gallery.fla file and name it actions.
4. Click the first frame of the actions layer and open the Actions panel with the *F9* shortcut key.
5. Add the code shown here. This code loads the document photoGallery.xml into the photoXML object. When the loading is completed, the loadPhotos function displays the contents of the XML object.

```
var photoXML:XML = new XML();
photoXML.ignoreWhite = true;
photoXML.onLoad=loadPhotos;
photoXML.load("photoGallery.xml");
stop();
function loadPhotos(success:Boolean):Void{
  if (success) {
    trace (this);
  }
  else {
    trace("Error in loading XML file");
  }
}
```

6. Save the movie and test it with the *Ctrl-Enter* shortcut key (*Cmd-Return* on a Macintosh). You should see something similar to the image shown in Figure 4-12.

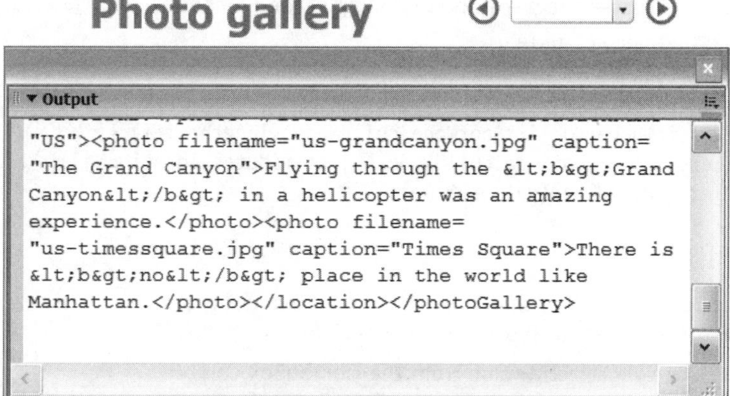

Figure 4-12. Testing that the XML document has been loaded into Flash

You'll notice that Flash has ignored the CDATA block from the XML document. Instead, the <b> tag has been converted to the HTML entities < and >. As we discovered earlier, Flash doesn't recognize CDATA.

Once the XML document has been loaded into the photoXML object, it's time to start populating the interface.

Loading the ComboBox component

We'll start by adding the names of each location to the ComboBox component. The name comes from the locationName attribute in the <location> element.

7. Create a new XMLNode variable called RootNode at the top of the actions layer. We create it outside of the loadPhotos function so that we can refer to the root node of the XML object anywhere within the Flash movie.

```
var RootNode:XMLNode;
```

8. Modify the loadPhotos function as shown here. I've indicated the new lines in bold. The function calls the loadCombo function after successfully loading the XML file.

```
function loadPhotos(success:Boolean):Void{
  if (success) {
    RootNode = this.firstChild;
    loadCombo();
  }
  else {
    trace("Error in loading XML file");
  }
}
```

9. Add the loadCombo function below the loadPhotos function. I've used the addItem method of the ComboBox component to add the locationName attribute values. Notice that I've done this inside a loop so that I can process all child elements of the root node in the same way. I have also added an item --Select-- at the beginning of the ComboBox.

```
function loadCombo():Void {
  var galleryName:String;
  gallery_cb.addItem("-- Select --");
  for (var i:Number=0; i< RootNode.childNodes.length; i++) {
    galleryName = RootNode.childNodes[i].attributes.locationName;
    gallery_cb.addItem(galleryName);
  }
}
```

10. Test the movie again. You should see the gallery names in the ComboBox component as shown in Figure 4-13.

At the moment, when we select a value from the ComboBox component, nothing happens. We actually want the first image from the selected gallery to be displayed on the Stage. To achieve that, we'll need to add an event listener to the ComboBox component.

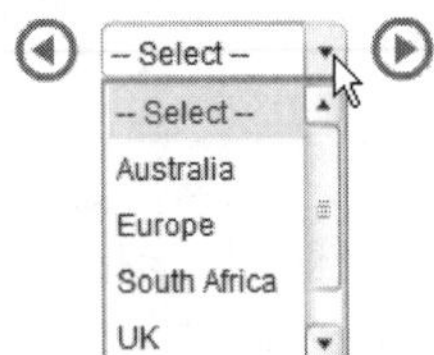

Figure 4-13. Testing that the ComboBox component has been populated

Adding an event listener to the ComboBox

ActionScript is an event-driven language. We use it to respond to events that occur in a movie, for example, the click of a button or selecting a value from a ComboBox. Because we want something specific to happen when these events occur, we can use an event listener. Event listeners listen for specific events and respond by calling a function.

We want an image to display when the value of the item in the ComboBox changes. We can only do this with an event listener that listens for the change event of the ComboBox. When the listener detects that event, it will call a function to deal with the changed value in the ComboBox.

11. Add the following code above the loadPhotos function. The code creates an object called CBOListener, which listens for the change event. When the event fires, the listener calls the loadGallery function.

```
var CBOListener:Object = new Object();
CBOListener.change = loadGallery;
gallery_cb.addEventListener("change", CBOListener);
```

12. Add the loadGallery function below the loadCombo function. The function receives the object that called it as a parameter, that is, the listener. It traces the label of the selected option using evtObj.target to locate the target of the event listener.

```
function loadGallery(evtObj:Object):Void {
  trace (evtObj.target.selectedItem.label);
}
```

13. Test the movie. You should see something similar to Figure 4-14 when you make a selection in the ComboBox.

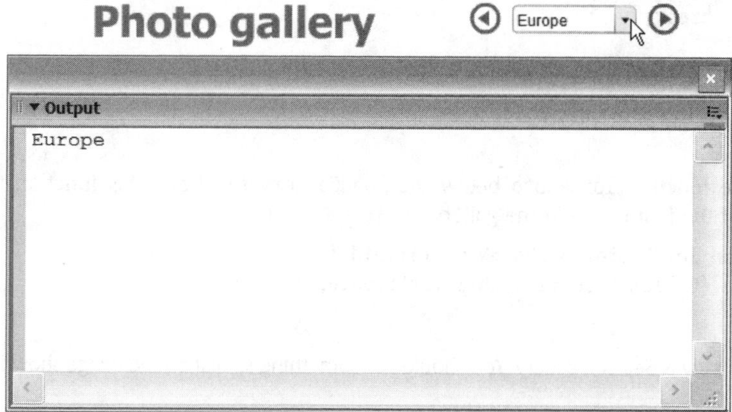

Figure 4-14. Testing the ComboBox listener

Once we have detected the selected gallery, we can move to that section of the document tree and load the first image.

Loading the photos

The first task is to move through the document tree and locate the selected gallery. We'll create some variables to help out.

14. Add new variables called selectedGallery, photoPosition, GalleryNode, and PhotoNode below the RootNode variable at the top of the Actions panel. Set the types to String, Number, and XMLNode, as shown here. These variables will have scope throughout the Flash movie because we haven't created them within a function.

```
var RootNode:XMLNode;
var selectedGallery:String;
var photoPosition:Number;
var GalleryNode:XMLNode;
var PhotoNode:XMLNode;
```

15. Modify the loadGallery function as shown here. The new lines appear in bold. The function finds if we've selected a gallery and sets the variable selectedGallery. It then finds the correct gallery and sets the position in the document tree within the variable GalleryNode. Finally, it calls the loadPhoto function, passing a value of 0 to indicate that the first image should display. The break statement ends the loop.

```
function loadGallery(evtObj:Object):Void {
  var galleryName:String;
  if (evtObj.target.selectedItem.label !="- Select -") {
    selectedGallery = evtObj.target.selectedItem.label;
    for (var i:Number=0; i< RootNode.childNodes.length; i++) {
      galleryName = RootNode.childNodes[i].attributes.locationName;
      if (galleryName ==  selectedGallery) {
```

```
                GalleryNode = RootNode.childNodes[i];
                photoPosition=0;
                loadPhoto(photoPosition);
                break;
            }
        }
    }
}
```

16. Add the function loadPhoto below the loadGallery function. This function traces the file name of the first image in the gallery.

```
function loadPhoto(nodePos:Number):Void {
  trace (GalleryNode.firstChild.attributes.filename);
}
```

17. Test the movie. Select a gallery. You should see something similar to the image shown in Figure 4-15.

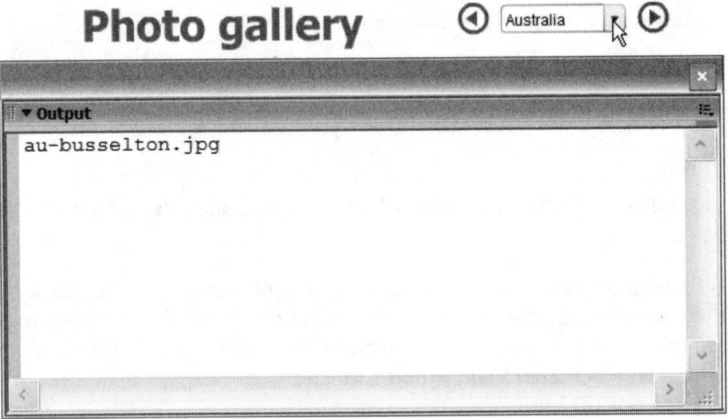

Figure 4-15. Testing the loadPhoto function

Now we need to use the file name to display the image from the photos folder in the empty movie clip. We also need to add text from the XML document to the caption and comment fields.

18. Modify the loadPhoto function as shown here. The function sets the PhotoNode variable and finds the file name, caption, and comments from the document tree. The loadMovie action loads the image from the photos folder into empty_mc. The text and htmlText properties display the caption and comments. Notice that we set the html property of the comment_txt field to true so that it can render the HTML tags from the CDATA section of the XML document.

```
function loadPhoto(nodePos:Number):Void {
  PhotoNode = GalleryNode.childNodes[nodePos];
  var filename:String = PhotoNode.attributes.filename;
  var caption:String = PhotoNode.attributes.caption;
  var comments:String = PhotoNode.firstChild.nodeValue;
  empty_mc.loadMovie("photos/" + filename);
  caption_txt.text = caption;
```

```
    comment_txt.html = true;
    comment_txt.htmlText = comments;
  }
```

19. Test the movie again and select an image gallery. You should see something similar to Figure 4-16.

Figure 4-16. Testing that the first image loads

If you select the other galleries, the first image from each will load. A problem arises when we choose the `-- Select --` option. The current image, caption, and comment remain. It would be better if this selection cleared the image and the text fields.

20. Change the `loadGallery` function as shown here. If we choose the `-- Select --` item, `empty_mc` is unloaded and the text fields are cleared.

```
function loadGallery(evtObj:Object):Void {
  var galleryName:String;
  if (evtObj.target.selectedItem.label !="-- Select --") {
    selectedGallery = evtObj.target.selectedItem.label;
    for (var i:Number=0; i< RootNode.childNodes.length; i++) {
      galleryName = RootNode.childNodes[i].attributes.locationName;
      if (galleryName ==  selectedGallery) {
        GalleryNode = RootNode.childNodes[i];
        photoPosition=0;
        loadPhoto(photoPosition);
        break;
      }
    }
  }
  else {
    empty_mc.unloadMovie();
    caption_txt.text = "";
    comment_txt.htmlText = "";
  }
}
```

21. Test the movie again. Select an image gallery and then choose the first option in the ComboBox. The interface should clear.

So far, we can view the first image in each image gallery. The next step is to configure the buttons so we can navigate through all of the photos in each gallery.

Configuring the buttons

The gallery movie includes two buttons: back_btn and forward_btn. When the back button is pressed, we should move to the previous image, if one exists. Conversely, the forward button should move us to the next image. We'll start by disabling the buttons so that we can't navigate until after we've selected an image gallery.

22. Enter the following lines above the photoXML variable declaration at the top of the actions layer:

```
back_btn.enabled = false;
forward_btn.enabled = false;
```

23. Change the loadGallery function. We'll need to enable the buttons after we have selected a gallery. We'll also need to disable the buttons when the -- Select -- option is chosen and clear the selectedGallery variable.

```
function loadGallery(evtObj:Object):Void {
  var galleryName:String;
  if (evtObj.target.selectedItem.label !="-- Select --") {
    selectedGallery = evtObj.target.selectedItem.label;
    for (var i:Number=0; i< RootNode.childNodes.length; i++) {
      galleryName = RootNode.childNodes[i].attributes.locationName;
      if (galleryName ==  selectedGallery) {
        GalleryNode = RootNode.childNodes[i];
        photoPosition=0;
        loadPhoto(photoPosition);
        back_btn.enabled = true;
        forward_btn.enabled = true;
        break;
      }
    }
  }
  else {
    empty_mc.unloadMovie();
    caption_txt.text = "";
    comment_txt.htmlText = "";
    selectedGallery = "";
    back_btn.enabled = false;
    forward_btn.enabled = false;
  }
}
```

24. Test the movie. Check that the buttons are enabled and disabled as you choose different gallery options.

Finally, we'll need to make the back and forward buttons work. We created the variable photoPosition earlier so we could keep track of the current photo number and the childNode within the selected gallery.

25. Enter the following lines above the loadPhotos function at the top of the actions layer. The onRelease functions test whether there is a previousSibling or nextSibling of the current PhotoNode. If so, we either decrement or increment the photoPosition variable and call the loadPhoto function.

```
back_btn.onRelease = function():Void {
  if (PhotoNode.previousSibling.nodeName != undefined) {
    photoPosition--;
    loadPhoto(photoPosition);
  }

forward_btn.onRelease = function():Void {
  if (PhotoNode.nextSibling.nodeName != undefined) {
    photoPosition++;
    loadPhoto(photoPosition);
  }
}
```

26. Test the movie for the last time and check that the gallery is functioning properly. Congratulations on completing the exercise. You can find the completed file saved as `gallery_completed.fla` in your resources for this chapter.

Points to note from exercise 3

- It's important to define variables in the appropriate place. If you'll only use a variable inside a function, you should define it inside that function using a var statement. When the function has finished running, the variable will cease to exist. This type of variable has *local* scope.

  If you want to use a variable in more than one function, you'll need to define it outside the functions. The variable will then have *timeline* scope, and it will be available to every block of code on the current timeline. I normally list these variables at the top of a layer for convenience.

  You can set, retrieve, and change the values of timeline variables within functions. The RootNode variable is a perfect example of a timeline variable. We declare the variable at the top of the actions layer but its value isn't set until we call the loadPhotos function.

- There is probably a more elegant way of dealing with the back and forward action of the buttons. For example, I could have disabled the back button if we were at the first photo and the forward button if we were at the last photo in the collection. Instead, I chose to use the previousSibling and nextSibling properties so you could see how they work.

- If you followed the example, you'll notice that, in each step, I wrote a little bit of code and then tested the movie. It's very important that you test your movie regularly. If you leave it too long before testing, it will be much harder to debug than if you have made only small changes each time. Sometimes, errors can compound and create strange results, making it hard to track down the cause of the problem.

- You probably also noticed that I was fairly specific about where you should place the code on the actions layer. In fact, you could have put the code in just about any order and the gallery would still have worked. I wanted you to keep your code in a logical order so you could compare your content with the completed file. That way it'll be easier for you to locate any errors in your code.

In the previous exercise, we created our first complete Flash XML application. We started by loading the XML document into Flash. We used it to populate a ComboBox component, and we added an event listener that responded when the user chose a gallery. The application displayed photos from the selected gallery, and we configured buttons so that the user could move to the next and previous photos. I broke the exercise into steps so you could see one approach that you could use to create the application.

If we didn't have a physical XML document with the photo information, we could have generated it from a database or by using a server-side file. These are examples of dynamic XML documents.

Loading dynamic XML documents

We refer to content stored in a physical document as *static* content. The content doesn't change each time we open the file, and we have to use a text or XML editor if we want to update the document. It's also possible to work with *dynamic* content. This type of content comes from a changing data source like a database.

In the previous example, we loaded information from a physical XML document into Flash. I saved the XML document with an `.xml` extension and stored it in the same folder as the Flash movie. You could view the file outside of Flash, in a text or XML editor.

As I mentioned earlier, it's also possible to load XML content from a server-side file that creates an XML stream. This is a dynamic source of XML. You can use PHP, ColdFusion, ASP.NET, or any other server-side file that creates XML content. In this section, I'll show you an example using ASP.NET.

Installing IIS

Before you can work with server-side files, you'll need to have a web server installed on your computer to process the files correctly. As I'm running Windows XP Professional, I have IIS (Internet Information Services) installed. This allows me to run server-side files written in ASP or ASP.NET. I can also install an extension that allows me to run PHP files.

Windows XP Professional doesn't install IIS by default, so you may need to install it yourself using the Windows XP CD-ROM that came with your computer. You can check whether IIS is installed by looking at the folders in your C drive. IIS adds a folder called `Inetpub` to the C drive, and that folder should contain a subfolder called `wwwroot`. The `wwwroot` folder is the location for your websites. You'd normally create a set of folders within `wwwroot`—one for each site or application.

If you don't have IIS installed, you'll need to choose Start ➤ Control Panel and select the Add or Remove Programs panel. Choose Add/Remove Windows Components on the left hand side and select the Internet Information Services (IIS) option. Click Next and follow the prompts to install IIS.

To work through the next exercise, you'll also need to download and install the free .NET Framework from the Microsoft website. You can check if it's installed by looking in the Add or Remove Programs Control Panel. If it's there, you should see an entry for Microsoft .NET Framework. If it's not, you can install it using Windows update at the Microsoft website. Make sure you install the .NET framework after you've installed IIS.

When you want to work with server-side files in Flash, the most important thing to remember is that the files must run through the web server first. This means that you have to use the full http:// path to the file. The web server will then process the server-side code before Flash receives the results. If you included the file name without the full path, Flash would read the server-side commands literally, without processing them first.

To work with server-side files in Flash, I have to copy them to the wwwroot subdirectory of the Inetpub folder. I usually create another folder in that area and copy all of my files there. For example, my files might live in the folder C:\Inetpub\wwwroot\FOE.

My web server has an address of http://localhost so I can open the files in a web browser by using the address http://localhost/foldername. When I use the full path, the web server processes the server-side code before sending the information to Flash.

You'll see an example of dynamic XML documents in the next exercise where we'll create an MP3 player. The movie uses ASP.NET to find out the names of MP3 files and folders. The server-side page converts the structure to XML before sending it to Flash. I've used an ASP.NET page written in Visual Basic (VB) as I don't work with other server-side languages. You could also use a page written in another language. You'll find a PHP version of the page and Flash movie with your resources.

If you don't want to use a server-side file, you can still follow along with the exercise. However, you'll need to create an XML file with the structure shown here. The root node <mp3s> contains a number of <folder> elements. Each <folder> has an attribute called foldername that indicates the name of the folder. The <folder> elements contain one or more <song> elements, and each <song> uses the attribute <filename> for the name of the MP3 file.

```
<?xml version="1.0" encoding="UTF-8" standalone="no" ?>
  <mp3s>
  <folder name="foldername">
    <song filename="filename.mp3" />
    <song filename="filename.mp3" />
  </folder>
  <folder name="foldername">
    <song filename="filename.mp3" />
    <song filename="filename.mp3" />
  </folder>
</mp3s>
```

If you don't use a server-side file, you'll need to replace the file name http://localhost/mp3s/MP3List.aspx with the name you choose for the XML file. You'll also need to change the file name if you're using a different server-side language.

Exercise 4: Creating an MP3 player

In this exercise, we'll use an ASP.NET page to create an XML representation of MP3 folders and files. Flash will load the content, and we'll create an application to play the files. After you complete the exercise, you'll have a fully functioning MP3 player built in Flash. You can change the playlist by adding MP3 files to selected folders. If you want to see what you're building, you can see the finished product in the resource file MP3s_completed.fla. For those of you who prefer to work in PHP, the resource file MP3sPHP_completed.fla refers to the PHP version MP3List.php.

This is a long exercise, and we'll work through the following steps to complete the application:

1. Setting up the environment
2. Testing the server-side page
3. Loading the XML content into Flash
4. Testing that the XML content loaded correctly
5. Loading the MP3 categories into a ComboBox component
6. Adding a listener to the ComboBox component
7. Loading the selected songs into a List component
8. Adding a listener to the List
9. Playing the selected song
10. Configuring the controls

Let's get started by setting up the environment. For copyright reasons, you'll need to use your own MP3 files for this exercise. You'll organize them into a set of subfolders to provide categories for the MP3 player.

Setting up the environment

1. Create a new folder in your web server called `MP3s`. The path to mine is `C:\Inetpub\wwwroot\MP3s`. You can find out more about web servers in the previous section.
2. Copy the files `MP3s.fla` and `MP3List.aspx` from the Chapter 4 resources to the new folder.
3. Create a set of subfolders for each song category in the `MP3s` folder. Copy MP3 files to each subfolder. Figure 4-17 shows how my folders are set up.

Figure 4-17. The folder structure for my MP3s

4. Open the starter file MP3s.fla from the folder in the web server. You can see the interface in Figure 4-18.

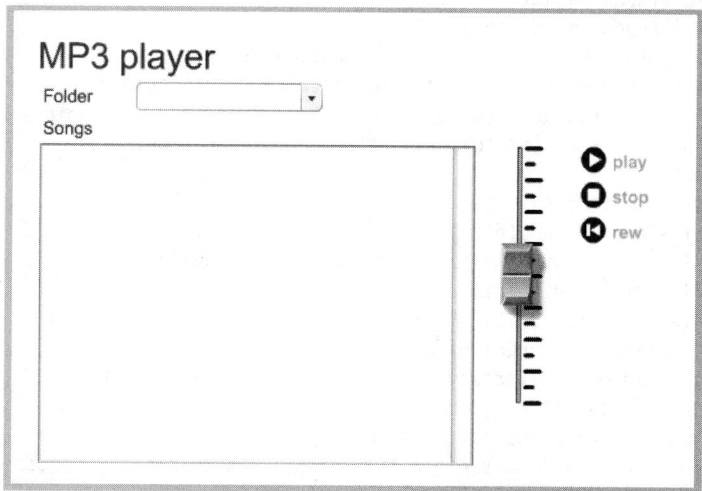

Figure 4-18. The MP3s movie interface

The interface contains a ComboBox component called folder_cb that will list the folders in the MP3s folder. There is also a List component called songs_list. We'll use this to display the songs in the selected folder. The interface also includes a sound volume slider and buttons to control the playback of songs.

Understanding the server-side page

I've created a server-side page in ASP.NET called MP3List.aspx. The page looks inside c:\inetpub\wwwroot\mp3s, finds the subfolders and MP3 files, and creates an XML document. You can find the PHP version of the page in the resource file MP3List.php. Note that these pages don't create a physical document, but just a stream of XML information. This is similar to the stream of information that you'd receive if you were consuming a web service. You'll find out more about web services in Chapter 9.

I've included the code from Mp3List.aspx here, and I'll explain how it works. Note that I've used ASP 1.1.

```
<%@ Page Language="vb" %>
<%@ import Namespace="System" %>
<%@ import Namespace="System.IO" %>
<%@ import Namespace="System.XML" %>
<script runat="server">
  Dim strDirectoryLocation as String = "c:\inetpub\wwwroot\mp3s"
  Dim dirs As String(), fileInfos as String()
  Dim i as Integer, j as Integer
  sub Page_Load
    Dim MP3Xml as XmlDocument = new XmlDocument()
    Dim folderElement as XMLElement
    Dim songElement as XMLElement
```

```
            MP3Xml.AppendChild(MP3Xml.CreateXmlDeclaration("1.0", "UTF-8", _
            "no"))
            Dim RootNode As XmlElement = MP3Xml.CreateElement("mp3s")
            MP3Xml.AppendChild(RootNode)
            if Directory.Exists(strDirectoryLocation) then
              dirs = Directory.GetDirectories(strDirectoryLocation)
              for i = 0 to Ubound(dirs)
                dirs(i) = replace(dirs(i), strDirectoryLocation, "")
              next
              Array.sort(dirs)
              for i=0 to Ubound(dirs)
                folderElement = MP3Xml.CreateElement("folder")
                folderElement.SetAttribute("foldername", _
                replace(dirs(i),"\",""))
                RootNode.AppendChild(folderElement)
                fileInfos = Directory.GetFiles(strDirectoryLocation _
                & dirs(i) & "\", "*.mp3")
                for j = 0 to Ubound(fileInfos)
                  fileInfos(j) = replace(fileInfos(j), strDirectoryLocation _
                  & dirs(i) & "\", "")
                next
                Array.sort(fileInfos)
                for j = 0 to Ubound(fileInfos)
                  songElement = MP3xml.CreateElement("song")
                  songElement.SetAttribute("filename", fileInfos(j))
                  folderElement.AppendChild(songElement)
                next
              next
            End If
            dim strContents as String = MP3Xml.outerXML
            response.write (strContents)
          end sub
        </script>
```

The first four lines of the code set up the language as Visual Basic and import the namespaces that the page will need to use. Next, I've created some variables, including the variable strDirectoryLocation, which sets the location of the folder that contains the MP3s. You can change this folder reference to point to other folders on your computer. You don't have to include the MP3s folder within the web server folder. I've also created two arrays: one for the directories in the folder and one for the files in each directory.

When the page loads, I create a new XMLDocument and some XMLElement variables. The page adds elements to the XMLDocument to create the XML page, and it starts by using the AppendChild and CreateXMLDeclaration methods to add the XML declaration. Then I create the RootNode element <mp3s> and append it to the document.

The page checks that the `MP3s` folder exists, and if so, it finds the directories inside and loops through them. The code removes the full path and adds the folder name to the `dirs` array. When the `dirs` array is completed, the page sorts it into alphabetical order.

Next, the page loops through the `dirs` array and creates the `<folder>` element, setting the `foldername` attribute. For each folder, we create an array of files called `fileInfos`, which is sorted into alphabetical order. The page loops through the `fileInfos` array and creates `<song>` elements with a `filename` attribute. At the end, the page writes the completed `XMLDocument` to the screen.

5. Test the ASP.NET file in a web browser by loading the URL `http://localhost/mp3s/MP3List.aspx`. You should see something similar to Figure 4-19. It's a good idea to check that this page works before you start working on the Flash movie.

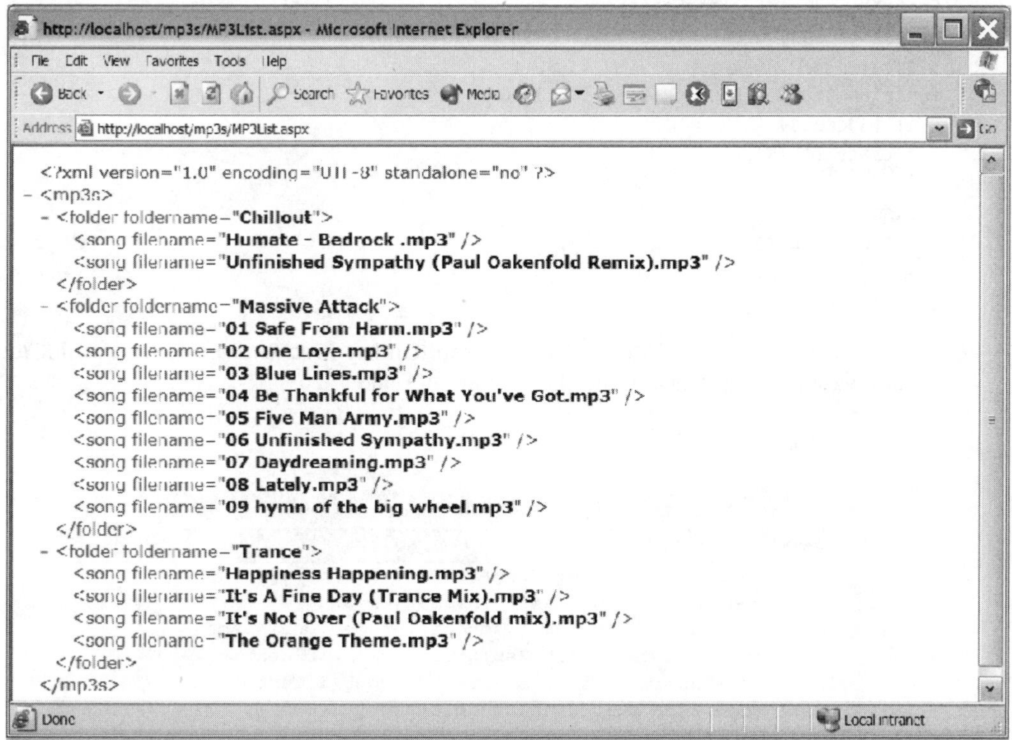

Figure 4-19. Displaying the page MP3List.aspx in a web browser

This is one example of how you could create an XML information stream from a server-side page.

Loading the XML information into Flash

We've created the XML document that we'll use. Now it's time to load the information into Flash.

6. Create a new layer in the Flash file and name it actions. Click frame 1 in the Timeline.
7. Open the Actions panel with the *F9* shortcut key and add the code here. The code loads the XML information stream from the URL `http://localhost/mp3s/MP3List.aspx` into the `SongsXML` object. When the loading is completed, the `loadSongs` function displays the contents of the XML object in an Output window. This is the same approach that we used in the previous exercise.

```
var SongsXML:XML = new XML();
SongsXML.ignoreWhite = true;
SongsXML.onLoad = loadSongs;
SongsXML.load("http://localhost/mp3s/MP3List.aspx");
stop();
function loadSongs(success:Boolean):Void {
  if (success) {
    trace (this);
  }
  else {
    trace ("Error loading file");
  }
}
```

8. Save the movie and test it with the *Ctrl-Enter* shortcut key (*Cmd-Return* on a Macintosh). You should see something similar to the image shown in Figure 4-20.

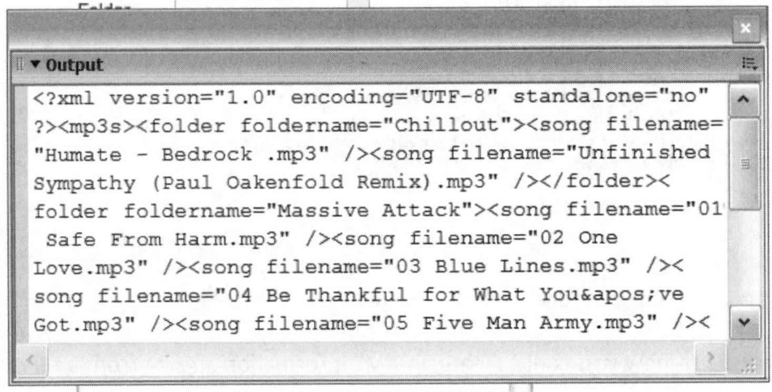

Figure 4-20. Testing that the XML content has been loaded into Flash

We now have to add the content from the XML document tree to the Flash interface. We'll start with the song categories.

Loading the ComboBox component

We'll add the information from the folderName attribute to the ComboBox component. This will display a list of all of the MP3 subfolders so that the user can select a song category.

9. Create a new XMLNode variable, RootNode, at the top of the actions layer. Because we create this variable outside of a function, we'll be able to use it anywhere within Flash. It has *timeline* scope.

```
var RootNode:XMLNode;
```

10. Modify the loadSongs function as shown here so it calls the loadCombo function when the XML information has been successfully loaded. I've indicated the new lines in bold.

```
function loadSongs(success:Boolean):Void{
  if (success) {
    RootNode = this.firstChild;
    loadCombo();
  }
  else {
    trace("Error loading file");
  }
}
```

11. Add the loadCombo function to the actions layer. It uses the addItem method to add the foldername attribute to the ComboBox.

```
function loadCombo():Void {
  var folderName:String;
  folder_cb.addItem("-- Select --");
  for (var i:Number=0; i< RootNode.childNodes.length; i++) {
    folderName = RootNode.childNodes[i].attributes.foldername;
    folder_cb.addItem(folderName);
  }
}
```

12. Test the movie. Figure 4-21 shows how it should appear.

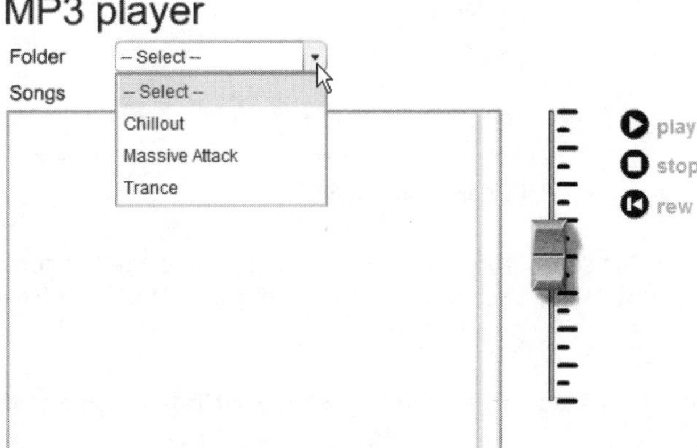

Figure 4-21. Testing the ComboBox component

When we select a folder from the ComboBox, we'll want to add the songs from that folder to the List component. If the user chooses the `-- Select --` option, we'll want to clear the list so nothing displays. The movie will need to listen for a change in the ComboBox and respond to the event.

Adding a listener to the ComboBox

13. Add the following code above the `loadSongs` function. The change event in the ComboBox will call the `loadList` function.

```
var CBOListener:Object = new Object();
CBOListener.change = loadList;
folder_cb.addEventListener("change", CBOListener);
```

14. Add the `loadList` function below the `loadCombo` function. The function traces the label of the selected option.

```
function loadList(evtObj:Object):Void {
  trace (evtObj.target.selectedItem.label);
}
```

The `loadList` function receives an event object as a parameter, and I've referred to it using `evtObj`. The event object contains information about the event. To refer to the ComboBox component, I can use `evtObj.target` and any of the properties of the ComboBox component. In this case, I've used `selectedItem.label` to find out which category the user selected.

15. Test the movie and choose a value from the ComboBox. You should see something similar to Figure 4-22.

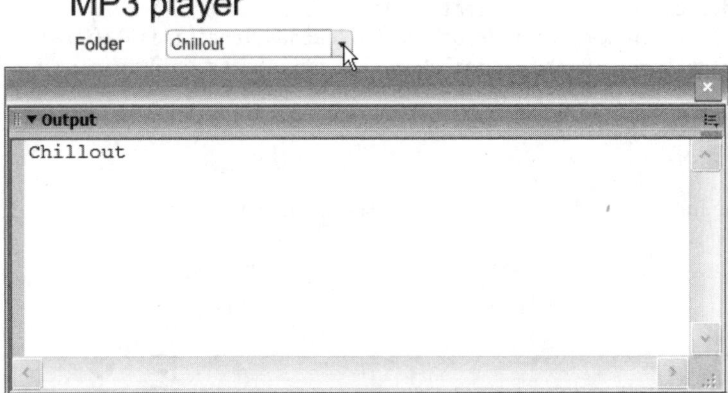

Figure 4-22. Testing the ComboBox listener

The next step is to load the songs from the selected category into the List component. The category comes from the `<folder>` element, so we'll start by creating a variable to refer to this element.

Loading the songs

16. Add a new variable called `FolderNode` below the `RootNode` variable at the top of the Actions panel.

```
var FolderNode:XMLNode;
```

17. Modify the `loadList` function as shown here. The new lines are in bold. If we've selected a folder, the function finds the node in the document tree and adds the child node songs within it to the List component. If we've chosen the `-- Select --` option, we clear the List using the `removeAll` method. I've also used the `removeAll` method before adding new songs so that we don't end up with a mix of new and old songs in the List.

```
function loadList(evtObj:Object):Void {
  var selectedFolderName:String;
  var currentFolderName:String;
  var songName:String;
  selectedFolderName = evtObj.target.selectedItem.label;
  if (selectedFolderName != "-- Select --") {
    songs_list.removeAll();
    for (var i:Number=0; i < RootNode.childNodes.length;i++){
      currentFolderName = RootNode.childNodes[i].attributes.foldername;
      if (selectedFolderName == currentFolderName) {
        FolderNode = RootNode.childNodes[i];
        for (var j:Number=0; j < FolderNode.childNodes.length; j++) {
          songName = FolderNode.childNodes[j].attributes.filename;
          songs_list.addItem(songName);
        }
      }
    }
  }
  else {
    songs_list.removeAll();
  }
}
```

18. Test the movie. Choose a folder and check that the List component populates correctly. Figure 4-23 shows how the interface should look at this stage.

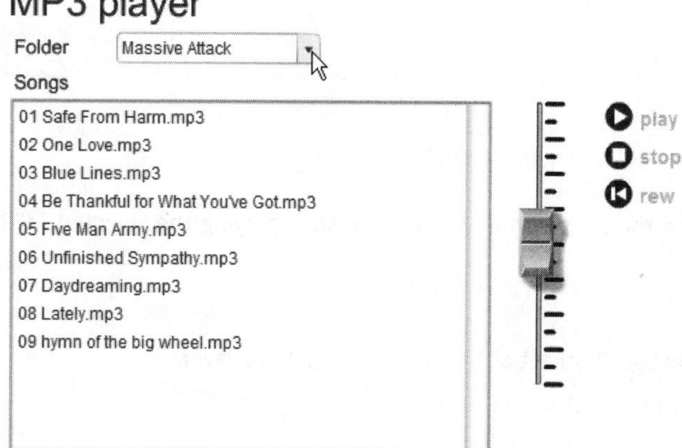

Figure 4-23. Testing that the List component is populated correctly

When we choose a song, we'll want it to play so we need to add an event listener to the List component. The event listener listens for the change event that occurs when the user makes a selection from the List. The listener then plays the selected song.

Adding a listener to the List

19. Add the following code below the ComboBox listener. It creates a listener for the List component that calls the playSong function when the selection changes.

```
var listListener:Object = new Object();
listListener.change = playSong;
songs_list.addEventListener("change", listListener);
```

20. Add the playSong function at the bottom of the actions layer. This function traces the selected song name.

```
function playSong(evtObj:Object):Void {
  trace(evtObj.target.selectedItem.label);
}
```

21. Test the movie, choosing a folder and a song. You should see something similar to Figure 4-24 when you select an MP3.

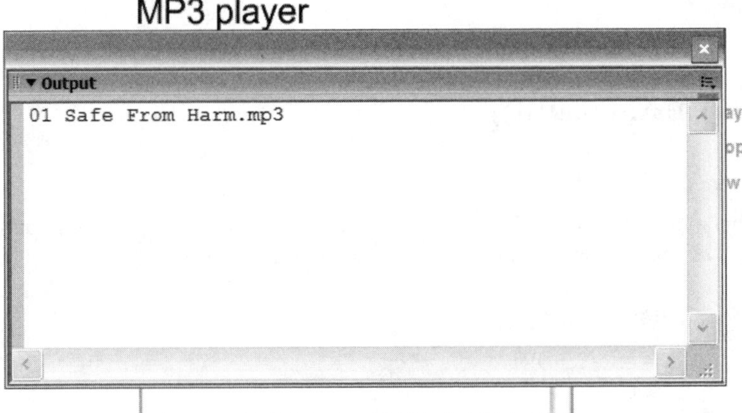

Figure 4-24. Tracing the song file name

Instead of displaying the song name, we want to start playing the selected MP3 file. We can do this using a Sound object.

Playing the song

22. Create a new Sound object at the top of the actions layer.

```
var MP3ToPlay:Sound = new Sound();
```

23. Modify the playSong function as shown here. The changed code is shown in bold. The function creates a variable, selectedSong, which contains the path and file name for the MP3. It stops any song that is currently playing and loads the selected MP3. When the new MP3 has loaded successfully, it starts playing the song at a volume of 50.

```
function playSong(evtObj:Object):Void {
  var selectedSong:String = evtObj.target.selectedItem.label;
  selectedSong = folder_cb.selectedItem.label + "/" + selectedSong;
  stopAllSounds();
  MP3ToPlay.onLoad = function(success:Boolean):Void {
    if (success) {
      MP3ToPlay.setVolume(50);
      MP3ToPlay.start();
    }
    else {
      trace ("Error opening mp3");
    }
  };
   MP3ToPlay.loadSound(selectedSong, false);
}
```

24. Test the movie and choose a song. Make sure your speakers are turned up so you can hear it playing. When you select a new song, the first song should stop before the second one starts.

At this point, you can play songs in the MP3 player but you can't use any of the other interface elements. To finish the application, we'll configure the volume slider and the Play, Stop, and Rewind buttons.

Configuring the buttons

25. Create a variable at the top of the layer called songOffset. We'll use this to store the position where a song stops when the Stop button is clicked.

```
var songOffset:Number;
```

26. Configure the Stop button by adding the following code below the event listeners. We store the song position in the variable songOffset. This is a measurement in milliseconds, starting from the beginning of the song.

```
stop_btn.onRelease = function():Void {
  songOffset = MP3ToPlay.position;
  MP3ToPlay.stop();
}
```

27. Add the following code for the Play button. The function stops any sounds that are currently playing and plays the selected song from the previously stopped position.

```
play_btn.onRelease = function():Void {
  stopAllSounds();
  MP3ToPlay.start(songOffset/1000);
}
```

28. Add the following code for the Rewind button. The function starts playing the song from the beginning.

```
rewind_btn.onRelease = function():Void {
  stopAllSounds();
  MP3ToPlay.start(0);
}
```

29. Test the movie. You should be able to select a song and use the Stop, Start, and Rewind buttons to control playback.

The last thing left to do is to set up the volume fader. If you look at the interface, you'll see that the fader contains two parts: a scale and a fader knob. Dragging the fader knob should change the volume between the values of 0 and 100.

Configuring the slider

30. Add the following code beneath the other button actions. When the fader button is clicked, the startDrag method allows you to drag it between the coordinates listed. When you release the button, the dragging stops and the function calculates the new volume based on the ending position of the button. Finally, it resets the volume of the song to the calculated value.

```
fader_btn.onPress = function():Void {
  this.startDrag(fader_mc, 406, 105, 406, 305);
}
fade_btn.onRelease = function():Void {
  this.stopDrag();
  var newVolume:Number = (200 - (this._y - 105))/2;
  MP3ToPlay.setVolume(newVolume);
}
```

I passed five parameters to the startDrag method. The first parameter specifies the target movie clip. The numbers specify the left, top, right, and bottom measurements used to constrain the draggable area.

I calculated the new volume using (200 - (this._y - 105))/2. The scale is exactly 200 pixels high and is placed at a y position of 105 pixels. I find the new y position relative to the scale—this._y - 105—and take it from the height of the scale—200 - (this._y - 105). This gives me the position using the scale of 200 pixels so I have to divide by 2 to get a volume out of 100.

31. Test the movie. You should be able to play a song and have full control of the volume. You should also be able to start, stop, and rewind the song. Congratulations, you've completed this exercise. You can find the completed file MP3s_completed.fla saved with your resources. You can also see the resource file MP3sPHP_completed.fla if you'd rather work with PHP.

Points to note from exercise 4

- The first few steps of exercise 4 were very similar to those in exercise 3. In fact, you'll probably perform similar steps each time you load external XML content into a Flash movie. These steps usually involve

  1. Creating a new Flash movie.
  2. Making sure that the Flash movie and external XML document are stored in the same location. You should also save the Flash movie before you start doing any testing.
  3. Loading the XML document.
  4. Creating a function to test for successful loading and tracing the XML object in the Output window.
  5. Adding content from the XML object to user interface components and configuring event listeners.
  6. Configuring other instances in the movie.

- It's a good idea to view dynamic XML documents within a web browser before you include them in a Flash movie. This is one way to test that a server-side file is creating the correct XML content. Don't forget to use the full path to the file in your browser, for example, http://localhost/FOE/MP3List.aspx.
- If you forget to include the full path to the server-side file in Flash, you may not see an error when loading the XML content. Flash will try to load the page content into the XML tree. You'll only find a problem when you start to work with the elements in the document. Tracing elements will return `null` values, as shown in Figure 4-25. You can use the `status` property to find whether there are any errors in the document.

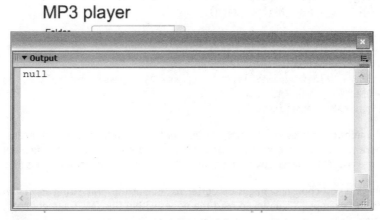

Figure 4-25. Tracing the root node when the full server path has been omitted

There are times when you'll need to create XML content in Flash without loading it from an external document. For example, we might need to generate XML that queries or logs into another application. In the next section, we'll look at how to generate XML from within Flash.

Creating XML content within Flash

You can use Flash to create XML content, without the need to load it first from an external file. You may want to do this to send an XML fragment to an external application. I've used this process to request information from external systems. The request required an XML document, so I created the content within Flash and used the `sendAndLoad` method to send the XML packet to the application. You'll learn more about sending information from Flash later in this chapter.

There are two ways to create XML content from Flash. Either you can create an XML string and add it to your XML object, or you can use methods such as `createElement` and `createTextNode` to generate the structure programmatically. We'll start by looking at the first approach.

Creating an XML string

The easiest way to create a simple XML fragment is by creating an XML string, as shown here. When you do this, Flash won't determine whether the XML is well formed or valid.

```
var myXML:XML = new XML("<name>Sas</name>");
```

In the example, the XML object contains a single XML node, <name>. Where the string is longer, it can be useful to add it to a variable, as shown here:

```
var XMLString:String;
XMLString = "<login><name>Sas</name><pass>1234</pass></login>";
var myXML:XML = new XML(XMLString);
```

You can also use the parseXML method to add content to an existing XML object:

```
var XMLString:String;
XMLString = "<login><name>Sas</name><pass>1234</pass></login>";
var myXML:XML = new XML();
myXML.parseXML(XMLString);
```

The parseXML method replaces any existing content within the XML tree, which means it isn't a good candidate where you need to preserve the current tree. My preference is for the first approach so that I don't overwrite any XML content by mistake, but either method will achieve the same result.

Whichever method you choose, it might be better to set out the XML string so that you can read it more easily. In this example, it's easier to read the nodes within the XML fragment compared with the earlier example:

```
XMLString =  "<login>";
XMLString += "<name>Sas</name>";
XMLString += "<pass>1234</pass>";
XMLString += "</login>";
```

The file createXMLstring.fla contains the example shown here. The XMLString variable stores the XML content in string format. The code adds the variable to the myXML object and displays it in the Output window.

```
var XMLString:String;
XMLString =  "<login>";
XMLString += "<name>Sas</name>";
XMLString += "<pass>1234</pass>";
XMLString += "<browser>IE</browser>";
XMLString += "<os>PC</os>";
XMLString += "</login>";
var myXML:XML = new XML(XMLString);
trace(myXML);
```

Figure 4-26 shows the movie when tested.

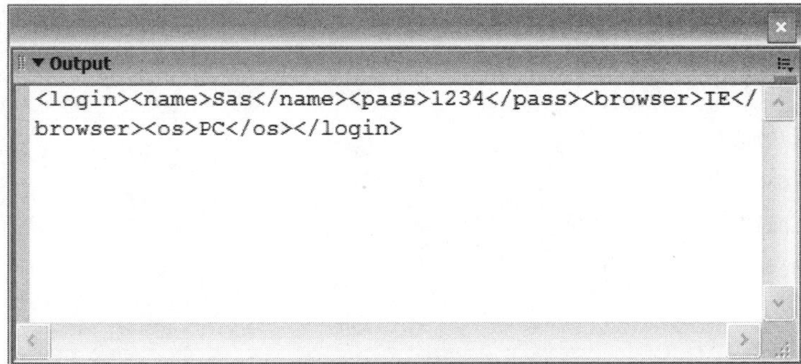

Figure 4-26. Displaying the contents of the XML object

Once you've created the XML object, you can extract the content using the properties discussed earlier. For example, the line that follows creates the output shown in Figure 4-27.

```
trace(myXML.firstChild.firstChild.firstChild.nodeValue);
```

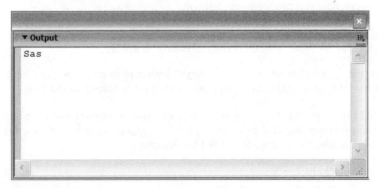

Figure 4-27. Displaying the contents from an XML object created in Flash

You need to be careful if your XML string includes attributes. Well-formed XML documents use quotation marks around attribute values, and these will cause problems in your code unless you escape them with the backslash character (\).

Here's an example. I've escaped the quotes around the attribute value `"first"` with backslashes so it reads `\"first\"`. You can find this example in the resource file `createXMLString.fla`.

```
var XMLQuotesString:String;
XMLString =  "<login>";
XMLString += "<name type=\"first\">Sas</name>";
XMLString += "<pass>1234</pass>";
XMLString += "</login>"
var myQuotedXML:XML = new XML(XMLString);
trace(myQuotedXML);
```

You can see that it's easy to create content using strings of XML information. An alternative method is to create XML content with ActionScript, using methods of the XML class.

Creating XML using methods

The methods of the XML class that you can use to create XML content include

- createElement
- createTextNode
- appendChild
- insertBefore
- cloneNode
- removeNode

We'll look at the cloneNode and removeNode methods later in the chapter when we look at modifying existing XML content.

Creating new elements

You add a new element by creating it and either appending or inserting it into your document tree. This example shows how you can create an element:

```
var myXML:XML = new XML();
var RootNode:XMLNode = myXML.createElement("login");
```

When you use the createElement method, it doesn't have a position in the document tree. You will have to use either the appendChild or insertBefore method to place it in the tree.

The appendChild method adds the node at the end of the current childNodes collection. The next example uses this method to add a new child to the XML object. In fact, as it's the first child of the XML object, we're adding the root node of the XML document.

```
myXML.appendChild(RootNode);
```

If you want to use the insertBefore method, the parent node will have to have at least one existing child node within the document tree. This example shows how to use insertBefore:

```
var BrowserNode:XMLNode = myXML.createElement("browser");
var OSNode:XMLNode = myXML.createElement("os");
RootNode.appendChild(OSNode);
RootNode.insertBefore(BrowserNode, OSNode);
```

In our earlier XML string example, we worked with the following XML structure:

```
<login>
  <name>Sas</name>
  <pass>1234</pass>
  <browser>IE</browser>
  <os>PC</os>
</login>
```

The next example uses the appendChild method to create the same XML structure. At the end, it traces the document tree in an Output window. You can see the example in the resource file `createXMLMethods.fla`.

```
var myXML:XML = new XML();
var RootNode:XMLNode = myXML.createElement("login");
var NameNode:XMLNode = myXML.createElement("name");
var PassNode:XMLNode = myXML.createElement("pass");
var BrowserNode:XMLNode = myXML.createElement("browser");
var OSNode:XMLNode = myXML.createElement("os");
myXML.appendChild(RootNode);
RootNode.appendChild(NameNode);
RootNode.appendChild(PassNode);
RootNode.appendChild(BrowserNode);
RootNode.appendChild(OSNode);
trace (myXML);
```

Figure 4-28 shows how the movie appears when tested. Note that the child elements are empty because we haven't yet added any text elements.

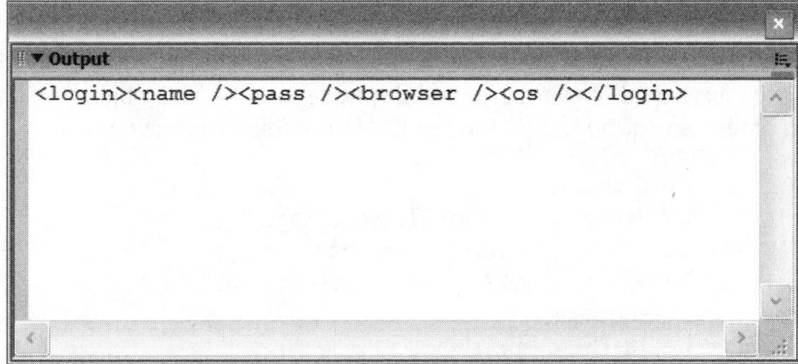

Figure 4-28. Displaying the XML document tree

I could have achieved the same result by using the `insertBefore` method. I've shown this in the example that follows, and it is also available in the `createXMLMethods.fla` resource file. You'll have to uncomment the relevant lines within the file if you want to test the code.

```
var myXML:XML = new XML();
var RootNode:XMLNode = myXML.createElement("login");
var NameNode:XMLNode = myXML.createElement("name");
var PassNode:XMLNode = myXML.createElement("pass");
var BrowserNode:XMLNode = myXML.createElement("browser");
var OSNode:XMLNode = myXML.createElement("os");
myXML.appendChild(RootNode);
RootNode.appendChild(OSNode);
RootNode.insertBefore(BrowserNode, OSNode);
RootNode.insertBefore(PassNode, BrowserNode);
RootNode.insertBefore(NameNode, PassNode);
trace (myXML);
```

If you traced the document tree code, it would appear identical to the output in Figure 4-28. The two methods achieve the same result, but there is one difference. Using insertBefore, I have to start with the last child node in the tree and work my way up through the child nodes. If I use appendChild, I start at the beginning and work my way down to the last child node. You can compare both examples in the resource file createXMLMethods.fla.

To complete the document tree, we need to add text to the child nodes. Text nodes are child nodes of the parent element node. In this line, for example, Child text is a child node of the <pElement> node:

```
<pElement>Child text</pElement>
```

In Flash, I'd refer to it using one of these two lines:

```
pElementNodeRef.firstChild;
pElementNodeRef.childNodes[0];
```

Creating new text nodes

You use the createTextNode method to add text to an element:

```
var myXML:XML = new XML();
var TextNode:XMLNode = myXML.createTextNode("Some text");
```

As with element nodes, when you first create a text node it has no position in the document tree. You will need to use the appendChild method to add this node into the XML object. In Flash, a text node is always a child of an element node. You can see this in the following example:

```
var myXML:XML = new XML();
var RootNode:XMLNode = myXML.createElement("login");
var ChildNode:XMLNode = myXML.createElement("name");
var NameTextNode:XMLNode = myXML.createTextNode("Sas");
myXML.appendChild(RootNode);
RootNode.appendChild(ChildNode);
ChildNode.appendChild(NameTextNode);
```

In the example, we've created a root node and child node and appended them to the document tree. The createTextNode method creates a text node containing Sas and appends it as a child of ChildNode. Figure 4-29 shows how myXML would appear if shown in the Output window.

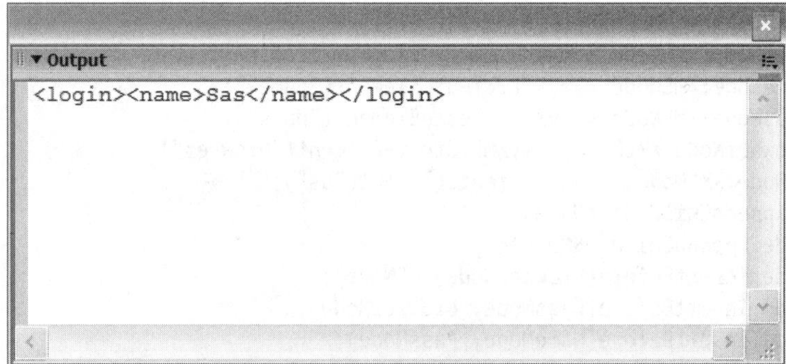

Figure 4-29. Displaying the XML document tree, including a text node

Earlier we created the structure for the login XML document. We generated the elements and the code here illustrates how you could add the text nodes. In this example, I've used the appendChild method for all nodes. I've shown the new lines in bold.

```
var myXML:XML = new XML();
var RootNode:XMLNode = myXML.createElement("login");
var NameNode:XMLNode = myXML.createElement("name");
var PassNode:XMLNode = myXML.createElement("pass");
var BrowserNode:XMLNode = myXML.createElement("browser");
var OSNode:XMLNode = myXML.createElement("os");
var NameTextNode:XMLNode = myXML.createTextNode("Sas Jacobs");
var PassTextNode:XMLNode = myXML.createTextNode("1234");
var BrowserTextNode:XMLNode = myXML.createTextNode("IE");
var OSTextNode:XMLNode = myXML.createTextNode("PC");
myXML.appendChild(RootNode);
RootNode.appendChild(NameNode);
RootNode.appendChild(PassNode);
RootNode.appendChild(BrowserNode);
RootNode.appendChild(OSNode);
NameNode.appendChild(NameTextNode);
PassNode.appendChild(PassTextNode);
BrowserNode.appendChild(BrowserTextNode);
OSNode.appendChild(OSTextNode);
trace (myXML);
```

You can find the example in the resource file `createXMLMethodsText.fla`. Figure 4-30 shows how this example appears when tested.

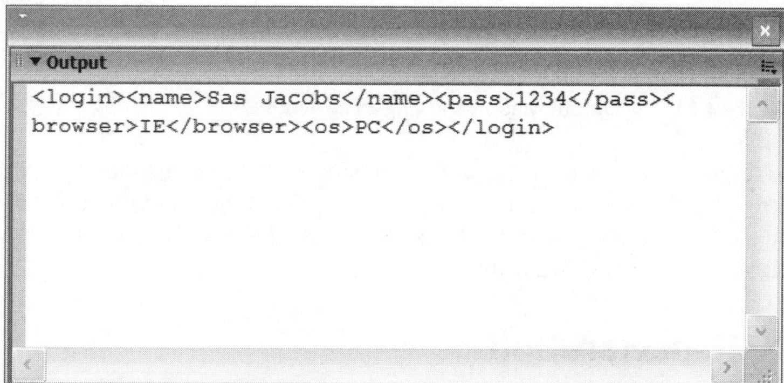

Figure 4-30. The completed example

If you compare the number of lines of code that it took to create this output with the example that used an XML string, you'll see that it's a much longer way of creating a new document tree. Given that it takes more work, why would you use XML methods to create a new document? Well, you can use the methods shown in this section to work with an existing document tree, so it's worthwhile getting a good understanding of how they work.

In the next section, I'll look at how you can add attributes to the document tree using ActionScript.

Creating attributes

Adding attributes to elements within Flash is very easy. You just set the name and value of the attribute as shown here:

```
var myXML:XML = new XML();
var RootNode:XMLNode = myXML.createElement("login");
var ChildNode:XMLNode = myXML.createElement("name");
myXML.appendChild(RootNode);
RootNode.appendChild(ChildNode);
ChildNode.attributes.type="first";
```

I could also have written the last line using associative array notation:

```
ChildNode.attributes["type"]="first";
```

You can see this example in the resource file `createXMLMethodsAttributes.fla`. Figure 4-31 shows the Output window that displays when testing the movie.

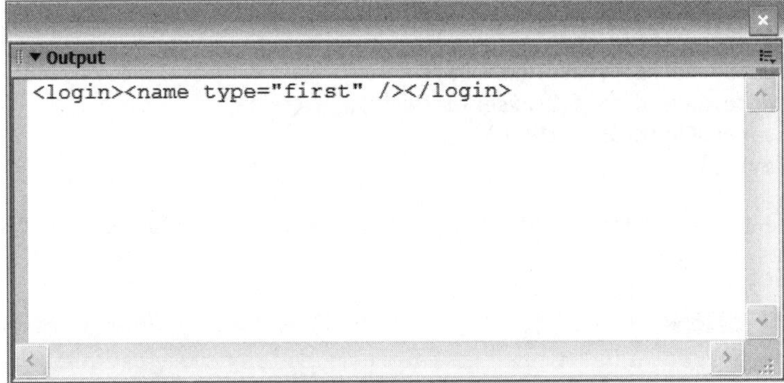

Figure 4-31. The Output window showing an attribute

In the examples we've worked with so far in this section, we haven't included an XML declaration in the document tree. You'll recall that this declaration is optional, but some external applications may require that you include it when you send XML content out of Flash. The next section shows you how to add this declaration to your XML packet.

Adding an XML declaration

The `xmlDecl` property allows you to set or read the XML declaration within the XML document tree. It doesn't matter whether you've created the document using an XML string or using XML methods. When you first create the document within Flash, the value of the `xmlDecl` property is set to `undefined`.

You can add an XML declaration by setting the property as shown here. Notice that I've escaped the quotation marks with a backslash character. If I don't do this, I'll get an error message in Flash.

```
var myXML:XML = new XML();
myXML.xmlDecl = "<?xml version=\"1.0\" encoding=\"UTF-8\"?>";
```

I don't need to place the declaration in the document tree as Flash will automatically add it in the appropriate place once I've set the value. You can see an example of this in the resource file createXMLExtras.fla. It's also shown in Figure 4-32 in the next section.

Adding a DOCTYPE declaration

Flash includes the docTypeDecl property so that you can read and set a reference to a DTD. A DTD allows you to validate your XML document, but Flash won't try to perform any validation when it detects a reference to this type of file. Flash can't validate XML documents as it contains a nonvalidating parser.

You can set a reference to a DTD by using the following code. As with the XML declaration, I had to escape the quotes in the declaration.

```
var myXML:XML = new XML();
myXML.docTypeDecl = "<!DOCTYPE documentRoot SYSTEM \"file.dtd\">";
```

Again, Flash automatically places this declaration at the correct position in the document tree. You can see an example in the resource file createXMLExtras.fla. Figure 4-32 shows the content of the document tree from the example file.

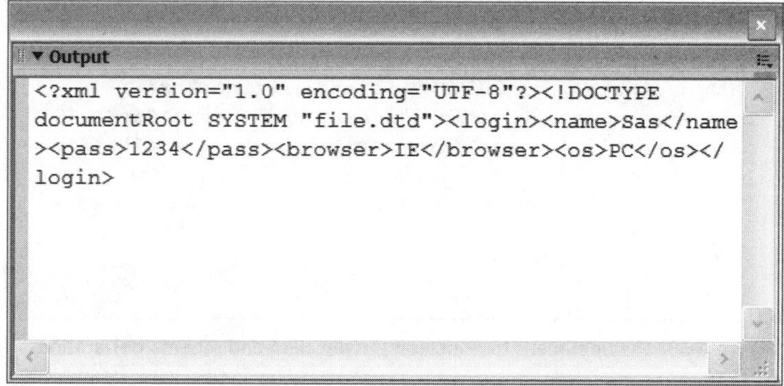

Figure 4-32. The document tree including XML and DTD declarations

You've seen two different approaches to generating XML content within Flash: using an XML string and using XML class methods. While the XML string approach is quicker, it will replace any existing content within an XML object. If you're manipulating an existing XML tree, you will have to rely on the methods of the XML class. There are some limits to these XML class methods.

Limits of XML methods

You may have noticed that we haven't used Flash methods to add XML processing instructions. That's because this is not possible in Flash. Unfortunately, it might be required if you need to create an XML document for an external application that includes a reference to a style sheet. To achieve this, you'll have to create the XML document using an XML string. Similarly, if you need to include namespaces or schema references in the XML document, you'll also have to use an XML string to create the document tree.

The next example shows how you can include these elements in your document tree. You'll need to escape the quotes in the style sheet declaration and in the schema declarations within the <login> element. You can see the example in the resource file `createXMLOther.fla`.

```
var XMLString:String;
XMLString = "<?xml-stylesheet type=\"text/xsl\" href=\"style.xsl\"?>";
XMLString +="<login ";
XMLString +="xmlns:xsi=\"http://www.w3.org/2001/XMLSchema-instance\"";
XMLString +="xsi:noNamespaceSchemaLocation=\"schema.xsd\">";
XMLString +="<login>";
XMLString +="<name>Sas</name>";
XMLString +="<pass>1234</pass>";
XMLString +="<browser>IE</browser>";
XMLString +="<os>PC</os>";
XMLString +="</login>";
var myXML:XML = new XML(XMLString);
```

Figure 4-33 shows the output when you trace the contents of `myXML`.

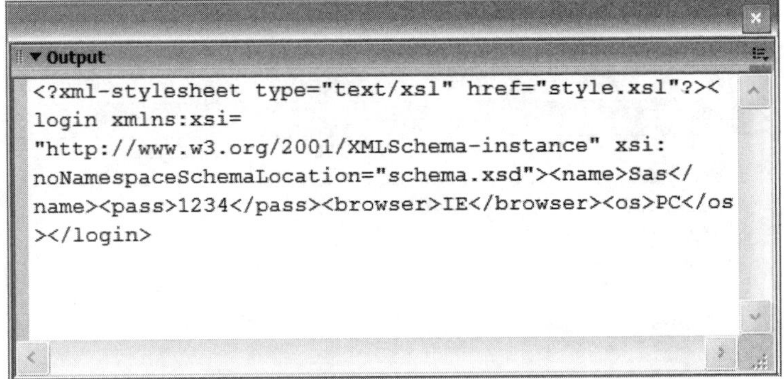

Figure 4-33. The document tree including style sheet and schema declarations

Putting it all together

In the preceding section, you learned how to create XML tree structures in two different ways. We used an XML string to add content to the document tree. We also used XML class methods to add elements programmatically.

In the example that follows, we'll use a combination of both approaches to create an XML document within Flash.

Exercise 5: Creating the address.xml file structure within Flash

In this example, we'll use Flash to create the XML document tree shown here. It is a cut-down version of the address.xml file that you've seen previously. We'll start by adding the XML declaration and root node using an XML string. We'll add the contacts using methods of the XML class.

```
<?xml version="1.0" encoding="UTF-8"?>
<phoneBook>
  <contact id="1">
    <name>Sas Jacobs</name>
    <address>Some Country</address>
    <phone>123 456</phone>
  </contact>
  <contact id="2">
    <name>John Smith</name>
    <address>Another Country</address>
    <phone>456 789</phone>
  </contact>
</phoneBook>
```

1. Create a new Flash document called createAddressXML.fla.
2. Name the first layer actions and add the following code to frame 1. The code creates an XML string and an XML declaration for the XML object myXML.

```
var XMLString:String = "<phoneBook/>";
var myXML:XML = new XML(XMLString);
myXML.xmlDecl = "<?xml version=\"1.0\" encoding=\"UTF-8\"?>";
trace (myXML);
```

3. Test the movie. You should see an Output window similar to the example shown in Figure 4-34. The window displays an XML declaration and an empty root node.

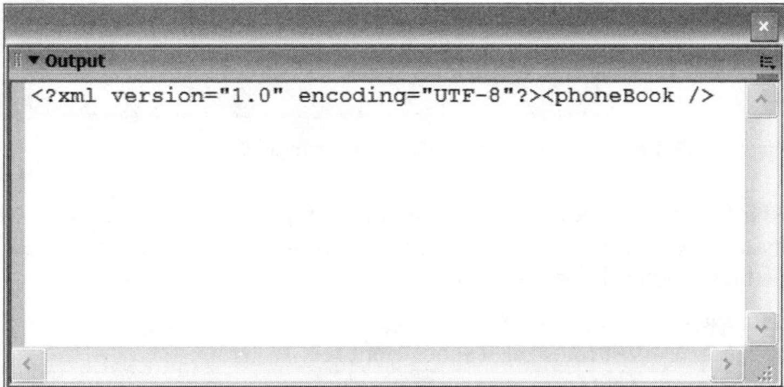

Figure 4-34. Displaying the XML declaration and root node

4. Add the following arrays to the actions layer. The arrays contain the content for the XML document. Storing the information in arrays allows us to add content to the XML tree within a loop.

```
var arrNames:Array = new Array("Sas Jacobs","John Smith");
var arrAddress:Array = new Array("Some Country", "Another Country");
var arrPhone:Array = new Array("123 456", "456 789");
```

5. Create the <contact> nodes as shown here. I've added the `id` attribute to the node and set it to be one more than the value of `i`. In other words, the `id` will start at `1`. I also created the variables that I'll need a little later.

```
var ContactNode:XMLNode;
var NameNode:XMLNode;
var AddressNode:XMLNode;
var PhoneNode:XMLNode;
var TextNode:XMLNode;
for (var i:Number=0; i < arrNames.length; i++) {
  ContactNode = myXML.createElement("contact");
  ContactNode.attributes.id = i + 1;
  myXML.firstChild.appendChild(ContactNode);
}
```

6. Test the movie. You should see something similar to the screenshot displayed in Figure 4-35.

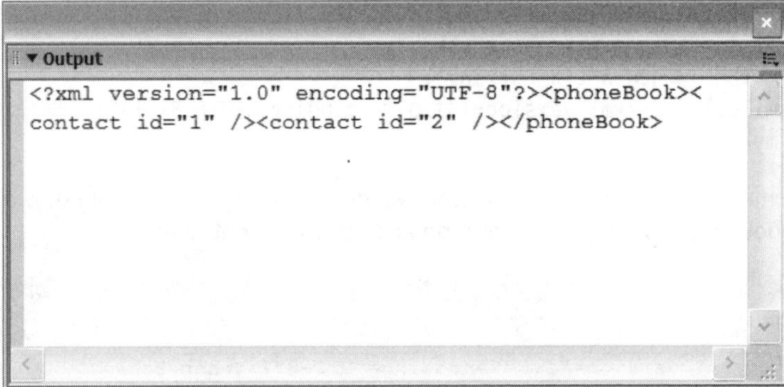

Figure 4-35. Displaying the contact nodes and attributes

7. Modify the `for` loop as shown in the bold lines in the following code. We've created the child elements and text elements and appended them to the <contact> nodes. I've added spaces to make the blocks easier to understand.

```
for (var i:Number=0; i < arrNames.length; i++) {
  ContactNode = myXML.createElement("contact");
  ContactNode.attributes.id = i + 1;
  myXML.firstChild.appendChild(ContactNode)

  NameNode = myXML.createElement("name");
  AddressNode = myXML.createElement("address");
  PhoneNode = myXML.createElement("phone");
```

```
        TextNode = myXML.createTextNode(arrNames[i]);
        NameNode.appendChild(TextNode);
        ContactNode.appendChild(NameNode);

        TextNode = myXML.createTextNode(arrAddress[i]);
        AddressNode.appendChild(TextNode);
        ContactNode.appendChild(AddressNode);

        TextNode = myXML.createTextNode(arrPhone[i]);
        PhoneNode.appendChild(TextNode);
        ContactNode.appendChild(PhoneNode);
    }
```

8. Test the movie. You should see something similar to the example shown in Figure 4-36. We've used Flash to create the XML document shown earlier. You can see the completed example in the resource file `createAddressXML.fla`.

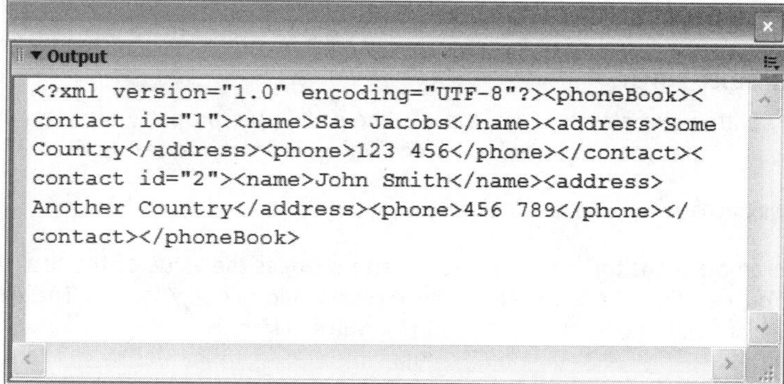

Figure 4-36. Displaying the finished XML file

In addition to creating XML document trees within Flash, it's important to be able to manipulate existing trees and modify the content that they contain. You might need to do this if you're allowing a user to change the values in your Flash XML application. You need to apply the changes to the document tree, so we'll look at that in the next section.

Modifying XML content within Flash

It's common to load an external XML file and update the structure and contents in a Flash application. Flash has methods such as `cloneNode` and `removeNode` that change the document structure. We'll look at these methods in this section.

Before we continue, however, it's important to recognize the limits of the XML class when updating XML documents. Flash allows you to manipulate the document tree inside a movie, but it can't modify an external XML document.

If you need to change an external file, you'll have to send the updated content from Flash to a server-side file for processing. Only server-side files have permission to update physical XML files. We'll look at how you can send XML content from Flash a little later in the chapter.

The modifications that we want to make to an XML document generally fall into these categories:

- Changing existing values
- Duplicating existing nodes
- Removing nodes
- Changing node structures

We'll look at each of these modifications in more detail.

Changing existing values

You can change the text or attributes associated with an XML document by assigning new values. You'll need to locate the node and enter the new value. You can also change the name of an element within Flash.

Changing a text node

If you're dealing with a text element, you can use the nodeValue property to assign updated text to the node. Remember that you can only use the nodeValue property on text nodes.

```
myNode.nodeValue = "Updated value";
```

The following example loads the file `address.xml` and changes the value of the first <name> element to `Jo Green`. You can find the example in the resource file `modifyXML.fla`. The example doesn't update the external file, but only the document tree within Flash.

```
var RootNode:XMLNode;
var NameNode:XMLNode;
var addressXML:XML = new XML();
addressXML.ignoreWhite = true;
addressXML.onLoad=loadAddresses;
addressXML.load("address.xml");
stop();
function loadAddresses(success:Boolean):Void {
  if (success) {
    RootNode = this.firstChild;
    trace ("before: " + RootNode.firstChild);
    NameNode = RootNode.childNodes[0].firstChild;
    NameNode.firstChild.nodeValue = "Jo Green";
    trace ("after: " + RootNode.firstChild);
  }
}
```

When you test the code, you'll see the Output window shown in Figure 4-37.

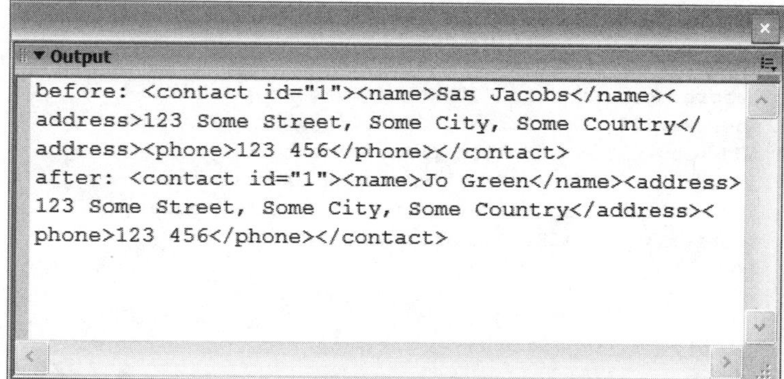

Figure 4-37. Displaying the first <name> element before and after the change

Changing an attribute value

Changing an attribute value is even easier. You assign the new value to the attribute using either of the two lines shown here. Both lines are equivalent.

```
myNode.attributes.attName = "Updated value";
myNode.attributes.["attName"] = "Updated value";
```

The next example changes the value of the first contact id of the loaded file `address.xml` from 1 to 99. I've highlighted the line in bold. You can find the example in the resource file `modifyXML.fla`. To test the file, you'll need to uncomment the code block.

```
var RootNode:XMLNode;
var NameNode:XMLNode;
var addressXML:XML = new XML();
addressXML.ignoreWhite = true;
addressXML.onLoad=loadAddresses;
addressXML.load("address.xml");
stop();
function loadAddresses(success:Boolean):Void {
  if (success) {
    RootNode = this.firstChild;
    trace ("before: " + RootNode.firstChild);
    RootNode.firstChild.attributes.id = "99";
    trace ("after: " + RootNode.firstChild);
  }
}
```

Figure 4-38 shows the Output window that displays when you test this code.

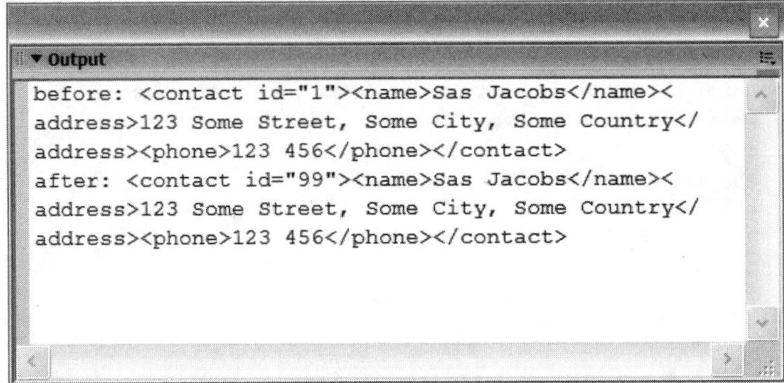

Figure 4-38. Displaying the <contact> element before and after the change

Changing a node name

You don't often need to change the name of a node in an XML document tree. External applications using the XML document often rely on a fixed set of XML tag names, which means changing the names within Flash may cause errors. If you need to change tag names, however, you can use the nodeName property:

```
myNode.nodeName = "New tag name";
```

Note that you can only change the name of element nodes as text nodes don't have names.

The next example loops through all <name> elements from the `address.xml` file and changes them to <fullName> elements. I've highlighted the relevant line in bold. You can find the code in the resource file `modifyXML.fla`. Again, you may need to uncomment the relevant code blocks within Flash to test the file.

```
var RootNode:XMLNode;
var NameNode:XMLNode;
var addressXML:XML = new XML();
addressXML.ignoreWhite = true;
addressXML.onLoad=loadAddresses;
addressXML.load("address.xml");
stop();
function loadAddresses(success:Boolean):Void {
  if (success) {
    RootNode = this.firstChild;
    for (var i:Number=0; i<RootNode.childNodes.length; i++) {
      NameNode = RootNode.childNodes[i].firstChild;
      trace ("before: " + NameNode);
      NameNode.nodeName = "fullName";
      trace ("after: " + NameNode);
    }
  }
}
```

When you test the code, you'll see something similar to Figure 4-39.

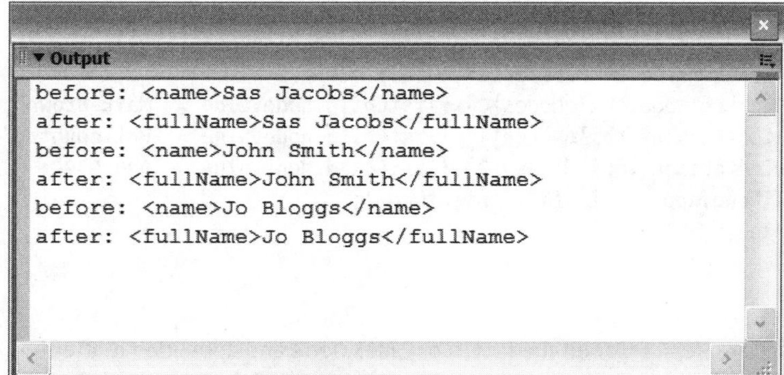
Output
before: <name>Sas Jacobs</name>
after: <fullName>Sas Jacobs</fullName>
before: <name>John Smith</name>
after: <fullName>John Smith</fullName>
before: <name>Jo Bloggs</name>
after: <fullName>Jo Bloggs</fullName>

Figure 4-39. Displaying changes to the <name> element

Duplicating an existing node

If you need to add a new node, a useful technique is to duplicate an existing node and change the values. When you duplicate a node, you can choose whether to duplicate the child nodes as well. This can save a lot of time when you're working with complicated node structures.

The cloneNode method allows you to duplicate a node. It takes one argument, deep, a Boolean value, that is, true or false, indicating whether or not to include the child nodes. A cloned node doesn't have a position within the document tree. Once you have cloned a node, you'll need to insert it into the document tree with either the appendChild or the insertBefore method.

The following code demonstrates how to clone a node with all of its children and append it to another node:

```
var myNewNode:XMLNode = myOldNode.cloneNode(true);
myParentNode.appendChild(myNewNode);
```

You could also have inserted it before an existing node:

```
var myNewNode:XMLNode = myOldNode.cloneNode(true);
RootNode.insertBefore(myNewNode, myParentNode);
```

The next example shows how you could duplicate a <contact> node from the address.xml file and change the values. You can see the example saved in the resource file cloneXML.fla.

```
var RootNode:XMLNode;
var ContactNode:XMLNode;
var addressXML:XML = new XML();
addressXML.ignoreWhite = true;
addressXML.onLoad=loadAddresses;
addressXML.load("address.xml");
stop();
function loadAddresses(success:Boolean):Void {
```

```
    if (success) {
      RootNode = this.firstChild;
      ContactNode = RootNode.firstChild;
      var NewContactNode:XMLNode = ContactNode.cloneNode(true);
      NewContactNode.attributes.id = "4";
      NewContactNode.childNodes[0].firstChild.nodeValue = "Mark Brown";
      NewContactNode.childNodes[1].firstChild.nodeValue = "Hot country";
      NewContactNode.childNodes[2].firstChild.nodeValue = "999 999";
      RootNode.appendChild(NewContactNode);
      trace (this);
    }
  }
```

In the previous example, we cloned the first <contact> node and appended it after the last <contact> node. We then changed the values to produce the following XML fragment at the end of the XML document tree:

```
<contact id="4">
  <name>Mark Brown</name>
  <address>Hot country</address>
  <phone>999 999</phone>
</contact>
```

Figure 4-40 shows the Output window that displays when you test the code.

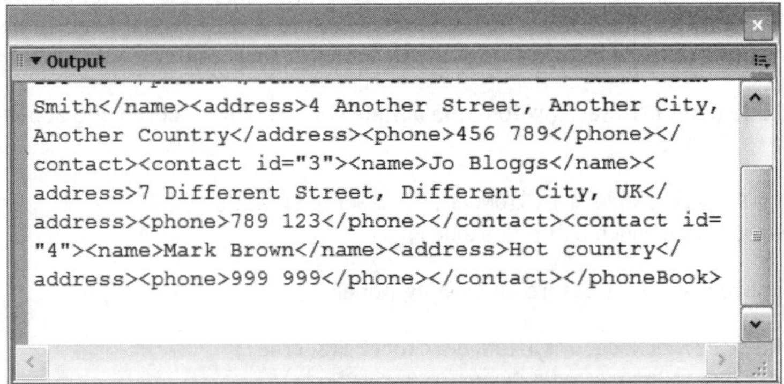

Figure 4-40. Displaying the cloned <contact> element

You may also need to delete an element from your XML document tree.

Deleting existing content

The removeNode method allows you to remove a node from the document tree within Flash. As with all of the other modification methods, these changes only affect the tree inside Flash and won't automatically update an external XML document.

```
myNode.removenode();
```

When you remove a node from the document tree, all child nodes and other descendants are removed at the same time.

The next example shows how you can remove the last <contact> element from the loaded `address.xml` file. You can see this example in the resource file `removeXML.fla`.

```
var RootNode:XMLNode;
var ContactNode:XMLNode;
var addressXML:XML = new XML();
addressXML.ignoreWhite = true;
addressXML.onLoad=loadAddresses;
addressXML.load("address.xml");
stop();
function loadAddresses(success:Boolean):Void {
  if (success) {
    RootNode = this.firstChild;
    ContactNode = RootNode.lastChild;
    trace ("before: " + RootNode.lastChild);
    ContactNode.removeNode();
    trace ("after: " + RootNode.lastChild);
  }
}
```

Figure 4-41 shows the resulting Output window when we test the movie.

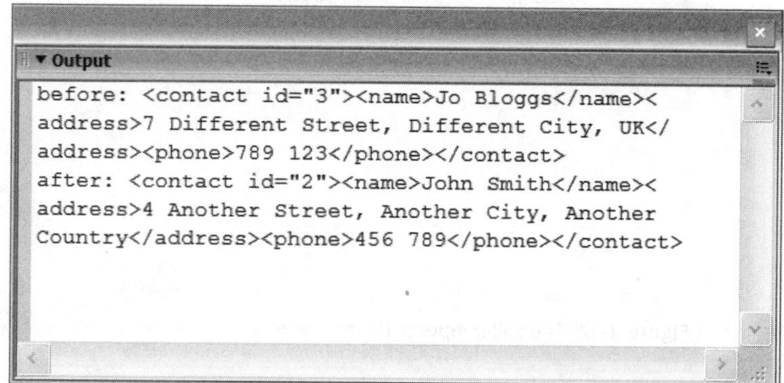

Figure 4-41. Displaying the last <contact> element in the document tree before and after the deletion

In the previous section, you saw some of the different ways that we can work with an XML document tree in Flash. We learned how to changes values, add new nodes, duplicate existing nodes with or without their child nodes, and delete nodes.

You can combine these methods to change your XML document tree within Flash. Bear in mind that although you carry out updates in Flash, you can't change the external document without using a server-side file. We'll see this a little later in the chapter.

We'll work through an example so you can see how we can update XML content within Flash using UI components in an application.

Putting it all together

Exercise 6: Adding a new image to the photo gallery XML tree

In this exercise, we'll load the external `photoGallery.xml` file into an XML object in Flash. We'll then use a form to add a new image to the document tree. We'll work through the following steps:

1. Setting up the environment
2. Validating the user changes
3. Updating the document tree

The exercise won't update the external XML document. We'll need a server-side file to do that, and we'll complete this step in the last exercise.

Setting up the environment

1. Open the starter file `galleryupdate.fla`. Figure 4-42 shows the interface. Make sure that the `photoGallery.xml` file is in the same directory.

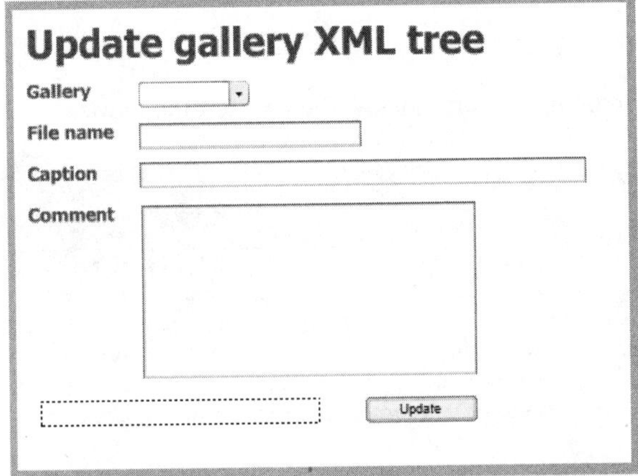

Figure 4-42. The galleryupdate.fla interface

The interface shows a ComboBox component, some text fields, an update button, and a dynamic text field that we'll use to display error messages. The user will select a gallery and fill in the details of the new photo.

2. Test the Flash movie, and you'll see that it loads the external XML file and populates the ComboBox component with photo gallery names.

Validating the form

We need to make sure that you've entered valid data before changing the structure of the XML document. You must have selected a gallery and entered a file name that ends in `.jpg`.

3. Add the following event handler to the actions layer. The event handler will call an inline function when you click the Update button. The function checks to see that you have selected a gallery and entered a file name ending with .jpg. If you have entered the relevant details, the function clears the error message text field.

```
update_btn.onRelease = function():Void {
  selectedGallery = gallery_cb.selectedItem.label;
  if (selectedGallery != "-- Select --" ){
    if (filename_txt.text == "") {
      error_txt.text = "Please enter a filename";
    }
    else if (filename_txt.text.indexOf(".jpg") == -1){
      error_txt.text = "Please enter a filename ending in jpg";
    }
    else {
      error_txt.text = "";
  }
  else {
    error_txt.text = "Please select a gallery before clicking update";
  }
}
```

Updating the XML document tree

After you've validated the data, you can find out the new values and use methods of the XML class to update the document tree.

4. Change the inline function as shown here. I've started by declaring some variables. The function finds the selected <location> node and creates a new <photo> node with the appropriate caption and filename attributes. It also adds a child text node containing the comment.

```
update_btn.onRelease = function():Void {
  selectedGallery = gallery_cb.selectedItem.label;
  var currentGallery:String;
  var comment:String;
  var NewPhotoNode:XMLNode;
  var NewPhotoCommentNode:XMLNode;
  if (selectedGallery != "-- Select --" ){
    if (filename_txt.text == "") {
      error_txt.text = "Please enter a filename";
    }
    else if (filename_txt.text.indexOf(".jpg") == -1){
      error_txt.text = "Please enter a filename ending in jpg";
    }
    else {
      error_txt.text = "";
      comment = comment_txt.text;
      for (var i:Number=0; i < RootNode.childNodes.length; i++) {
        currentGallery = RootNode.childNodes[i].attributes.➥
        locationName;
        if (selectedGallery == currentGallery){
```

```
            GalleryNode = RootNode.childNodes[i];
            NewPhotoNode = photoXML.createElement("photo");
            NewPhotoCommentNode = photoXML.createTextNode(comment);
            NewPhotoNode.attributes.caption = caption_txt.text;
            NewPhotoNode.attributes.filename = filename_txt.text;
            NewPhotoNode.appendChild(NewPhotoCommentNode);
            GalleryNode.appendChild(NewPhotoNode);
            trace (photoXML);
            break;
          }
        }
      }
    }
    else {
      error_txt.text = "Please select a gallery before clicking update";
    }
  }
```

5. Test the Flash movie. Enter values in the form and click the Update button. You should see an Output window displaying the new node. You can see an example in Figure 4-43. The completed file is saved as `galleryupdate_completed.fla` with your Chapter 4 resources.

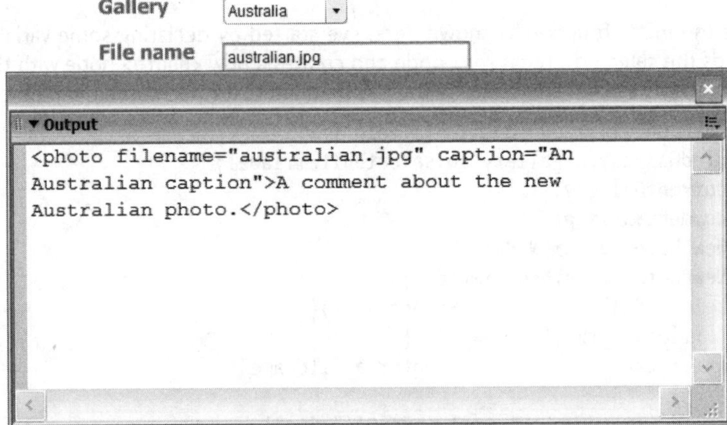

Figure 4-43. Displaying the new <photo> node

Figure 4-44 shows the competed form used to create the new <photo> node.

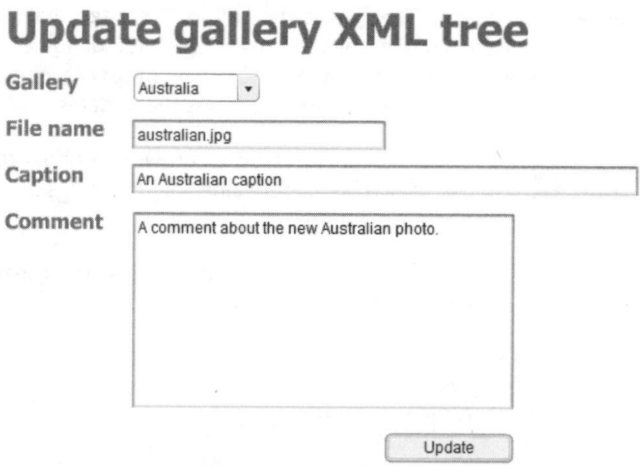

Update gallery XML tree

Gallery Australia

File name australian.jpg

Caption An Australian caption

Comment A comment about the new Australian photo.

Update

Figure 4-44. The form providing input for the new <photo> node

Don't forget that the `<photo>` node is added to the document tree within Flash but not to the external XML file. You'll need to send the updated XML tree from Flash to a server-side file before you can update the `photoGallery.xml` file.

So far, we've looked at how you can create new XML content and change the existing document tree within Flash. If the content originally came from an external file, changes that you make inside Flash don't update that file. For security reasons, Flash doesn't have the ability to update external documents. Imagine how dangerous it would be if a Flash movie could work directly with the files on your computer.

To update an external XML document, you'll need to send the document tree from Flash to a server-side file. The server-side file will then have to process the updates and save the changes to the external XML document. We'll look at this in more detail in the next section of this chapter.

Sending XML content from Flash

The XML class provides two methods for sending information from Flash: send and sendAndLoad. Both methods work in a similar way by sending the content to an external page for processing. The difference is that the sendAndLoad method also receives a response from the server-side page. Before you send the data out of Flash, you need to set the content type to `text/xml`. You'll see this next.

Using the send method

The send method sends XML content from Flash to a server-side page. If you are testing the Flash file in a web browser, the method uses POST to send the data, while GET is used from within Flash. This means that you might need to be careful about how you test any files using the send method of the XML class.

The send method has two parameters. The first is the URL of the page that will process the XML content. As this is normally a page written in ColdFusion, PHP, ASP.NET, or some other server-side language, you'll need to include the full path through the web server, http://localhost/FOE/page.aspx. If you forget this, the server-side page won't be able to process the updates.

The second parameter is optional and specifies the type of browser window to use to display the response from the server. You can use the HTML target values of _blank, _self, _parent, or _top. If you leave out the parameter, it's the same as using a value of _self.

Here's an example of the send method. Notice that the second line sets the contentType property to text/xml.

```
var myXML:XML = new XML("XML String");
myXML.contentType = "text/xml";
myXML.send("fullpathtopage.aspx", "_blank");
```

I've included a working example next, taken from the resource files sendXML.fla and sendXML.html. You can test the Flash movie if you have a web server with the .NET Framework installed. However, before you test the movie, you'll need to copy the showXML.aspx file to a directory named FOE in your web server. You don't need to place the Flash and HTML files in the FOE folder for the example to work correctly.

If you'd rather work with PHP, you can use the resource files showXML.php and sendXMLPHP.fla. You'll need a web server capable of parsing PHP.

You'll also need to test the resource file sendXML.html through a web browser, rather than through Flash itself. If you test the file within Flash, you'll get an error message.

```
var XMLString:String;
XMLString =  "<login>";
XMLString += "<name>Sas</name>";
XMLString += "<pass>1234</pass>";
XMLString += "<browser>IE</browser>";
XMLString += "<os>PC</os>";
XMLString += "</login>";
var myXML:XML = new XML(XMLString);
myXML.xmlDecl = "<?xml version=\"1.0\" encoding=\"UTF-8\"?>";
myXML.contentType = "text/xml";
myXML.send("http://localhost/FOE/showXML.aspx", "_blank");
```

The code creates an XML string and adds it to the myXML object. It adds an XML declaration and sets the content type to text/xml. Finally, it sends the document tree to the page showXML.aspx in the FOE folder in the web server. I had to use the full path to the showXML.aspx file. Figure 4-45 shows the results displayed in a web browser.

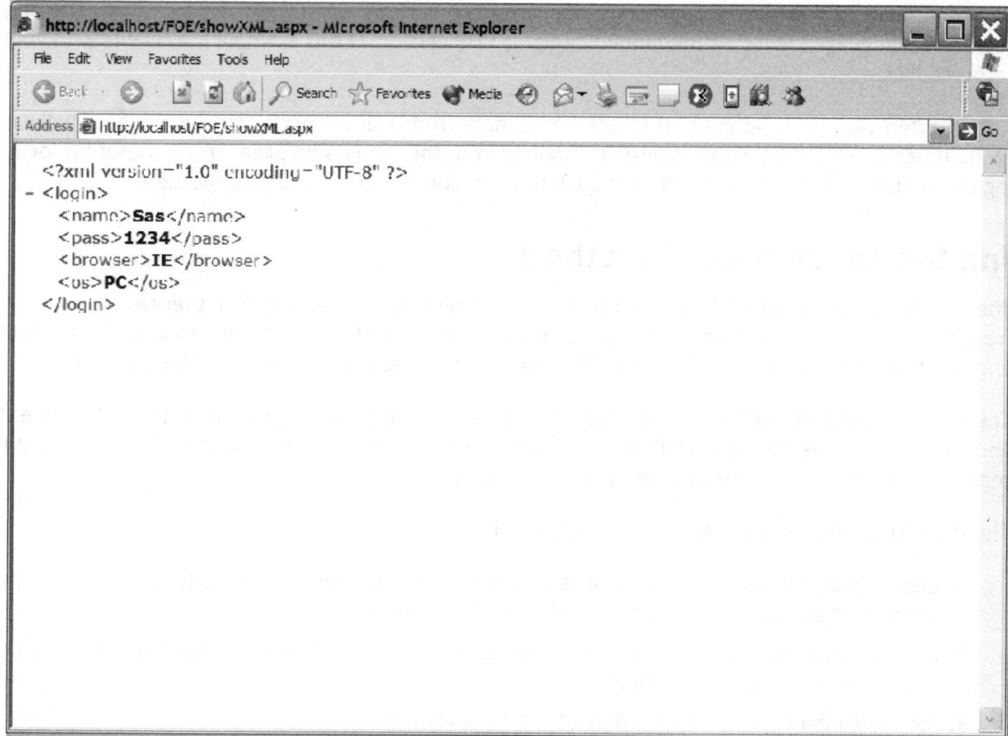

Figure 4-45. A web browser displaying XML sent from Flash

I used an ASP.NET file written in VB to process content from Flash. If you open the resource file `showXML.aspx`, you'll see this content:

```
<%@ Page Language="VB" validaterequest="false" ContentType="text/xml" %>
<%@ import Namespace="System" %>
<%@ import Namespace="System.IO" %>
<%@ import Namespace="System.XML" %>
<script runat="server">
  sub Page_Load(Source As Object, E As EventArgs)
    Dim xmlDocument As XmlDocument = New XmlDocument()
    Dim sr as StreamReader = new StreamReader(Request.InputStream)
    xmlDocument.Load(sr)
    response.write (xmlDocument.outerXML)
  end sub
</script>
```

The file sets the content type to `text/xml` and imports the relevant namespaces. When the page loads, a `StreamReader` takes the content from Flash and writes it to a new `XMLDocument`. This is not a physical document. The `outerXML` of the `XMLDocument` displays in the browser window. Note that this file doesn't include any error handling.

You could write similar code in any server-side language. I've chosen ASP.NET because that's the only server-side language I write. As mentioned earlier, a PHP version of this example is available with your resource files.

I don't often use the send method to send XML data from Flash. I prefer to use the sendAndLoad method because it allows me to receive a response from the server-side page. This is useful for locating server-side errors as they can be sent back to Flash and displayed in the application.

Using the sendAndLoad method

The sendAndLoad method works in a similar way to the send method except that it receives a response from the server-side page. Therefore, this method requires two XML objects: one to send the content and one to receive the response. The sendAndLoad method uses POST to send its XML content.

The sendAndLoad method has two parameters: the server-side page for processing the XML content and the name of the XML object that will receive the response. An event handler function for the receiving XML object processes the reply from the server.

The steps to use the sendAndLoad method are as follows:

1. Create two XML objects, one to send and one to receive. You may already have created the sending object when you first loaded the XML document.
2. If necessary, assign the XML document tree to the sending XML object. You won't need to do this if you are using an existing XML object.
3. Set the content type of the sending object to `text/xml`.
4. Set the onLoad handler for the receiving XML object.
5. Call the sendAndLoad method, using the full path to the server-side file and specifying the receiving XML object.
6. Create the onLoad function to deal with the response in the receiving XML object.

I've shown some sample code here:

```
var myXML:XML = new XML("<login>sas</login>");
var receiveXML:XML = new XML();
receiveXML.onLoad = replyFunction;
myXML.contentType = "text/xml";
myXML.sendAndLoad("fullpathtopage.aspx", receiveXML);
```

You can see an example of the sendAndLoad method in the resource file `sendAndLoadXML.fla`. I've also listed the code here. This time, you can test the file from within Flash. You'll just need to make sure that you're running a web server with the .NET Framework installed. You'll need to copy the server-side file `replyXML.aspx` to the `FOE` directory within the web server. Again, if you'd prefer, you can use the resource files `sendAndLoadXMLPHP.fla` and `replyXML.php`.

The following example sends the XML document tree to replyXML.aspx, which saves the updated content in a physical XML file:

```
var XMLString:String;
XMLString =  "<login>";
XMLString += "<name>Sas</name>";
XMLString += "<pass>1234</pass>";
XMLString += "<browser>IE</browser>";
XMLString += "<os>PC</os>";
XMLString += "</login>";
var myXML:XML = new XML(XMLString);
var replyXML:XML = new XML();
replyXML.onLoad = showResponse;
myXML.xmlDecl = "<?xml version=\"1.0\" encoding=\"UTF-8\"?>";
myXML.contentType = "text/xml";
myXML.sendAndLoad("http://localhost/FOE/replyXML.aspx", replyXML);
function showResponse(success:Boolean):Void {
  if (success) {
    trace (this);
  }
  else {
    trace ("Error receiving response");
  }
}
```

The replyXML.aspx page reads the XML content and saves it to a file called login.xml. The XML file is stored in the same location as the replyXML.aspx page—the FOE directory. Note that the physical file login.xml can only be created if you have permission to write to the FOE directory.

The server-side page also creates a message to send back to Flash. Flash receives it in the replyXML object. When Flash successfully receives a reply, the showResponse function displays it in an Output window. You can see the result in Figure 4-46. If you test the file, you'll see a new login.xml file created in the FOE directory of the web server.

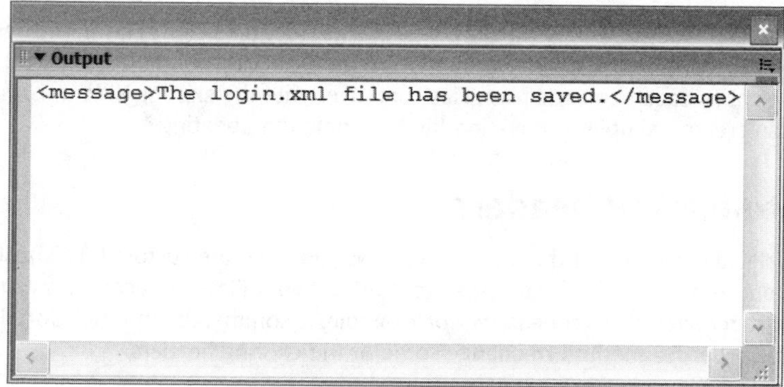

Figure 4-46. Displaying the server-side XML reply in Flash

The VB code that follows shows the contents of the server-side page in a web browser:

```
<%@ Page Language="VB" validateRequest="false" ContentType="text/xml"%>
<%@ import Namespace="System" %>
<%@ import Namespace="System.IO" %>
<%@ import Namespace="System.XML" %>
<script runat="server">
  sub Page_Load(Source As Object, E As EventArgs)
    Dim xmlDocument As XmlDocument = New XmlDocument()
    Dim xmlResponse AS XMLDocument = New XmlDocument()
    Dim strReader as StringReader
    Dim strXML as String
    Dim sr as StreamReader = new StreamReader(Request.InputStream)
    Try
      xmlDocument.Load(sr)
      xmlDocument.Save(Server.Mappath("login.xml"))
      strXML = "The login.xml file has been saved."
    Catch ex as exception
      strXML = ex.toString
    End Try
    strReader = new StringReader("<message>" & strXML & "</message>")
    xmlResponse.Load(strReader)
    response.write (xmlResponse.OuterXML)
  end sub
</script>
```

The page sets its type as text/xml and imports the relevant namespaces. It creates two new XMLDocuments, one to read the contents from Flash and the other to return XML content back to Flash. The page uses a StreamReader to access the content from Flash and load it into an XMLDocument. The Save method writes the content to the file login.xml.

A StringReader composes the return XML string. The second XMLDocument loads the StringReader and writes the outerXML to the browser window. If you know a different server-side language, you could write your own file to achieve the same functionality.

A different approach would be to send only the changed content from Flash. The server-side page would have to figure out what had changed and update the XML existing document. I think it's simpler to send the entire document tree from Flash and overwrite the existing XML document each time. It means you can create a simpler server-side file to handle the updating.

Adding custom HTTP headers

The addRequestHeader method of the XML class allows you to create custom HTTP headers when you send XML content from Flash. You might need to do this if your Flash application is working within an environment that requires custom headers, for example, a commercial intranet portal. You can also use the addRequestHeader method to change some of the existing headers.

To add a custom HTTP header, you need to specify the header name and a value. Note that string header values in the second parameter will need to use single quotes.

```
myXML.addRequestHeader("headerName", "'headerValue'");
```

You can't change the following standard HTTP headers with the addRequestHeader method:

- Accept-Ranges
- Age
- Allow
- Allowed
- Connection
- Content-Length
- Content-Location
- Content-Range
- ETag
- Host
- Last-Modified
- Locations
- Max-Forwards
- Proxy-Authenticate
- Proxy-Authorization
- Public
- Range
- Retry-After
- Server
- TE
- Trailer
- Transfer-Encoding
- Upgrade
- URI
- Vary
- Via
- Warning
- WWW-Authenticate

You've seen how to send XML information out of Flash so that it can be updated in a server-side file. In the next exercise, we'll use the sendAndLoad method to extend exercise 6 so that the form within the application updates the external file photoGallery.xml.

Putting it all together

Exercise 7: Saving the XML updates from Flash

In exercise 6, we used a form to update an XML document tree within Flash. In this exercise, we'll send the updated tree to a server-side page that updates the external XML file. You'll need to have a web server and the .NET Framework installed to complete this exercise. If you prefer to work with PHP, I've included the resource file `updateGallery.php`. You could also create your own server-side file to handle the updates. We'll start by setting up the environment.

Setting up the environment

1. If it doesn't already exist, create the folder `FOE` in the web server. If you're running IIS on Windows, the path to the web server is `C:\Inetpub\wwwroot`.
2. Copy the files `updateGallery.aspx, galleryXMLupdate.fla and photoGallery.xml` to the `FOE` directory.
3. Open the starter file `galleryXMLupdate.fla from the FOE folder`. This is the completed file from exercise 6. Figure 4-47 shows the interface.

Update gallery XML tree

Gallery -- Select --

File name

Caption

Comment

Update

Figure 4-47. Displaying the galleryXMLupdate.fla interface

You'll notice that the interface is populated with the existing gallery names from the XML document. We'll need to collect the data from the form to send to a server-side file for processing.

Sending the content from Flash

We'll use the `sendAndLoad` method of the XML class to send the information from Flash to a server-side page. The page will replace the existing `photoGallery.xml` file with an updated version. It will also send a message back to Flash.

4. Select frame 1 on the timeline and open the actions layer in the Actions panel with the *F9* shortcut key.
5. Change the `update_btn onRelease` function as shown here. The new line calls the function `updateContent`.

```
update_btn.onRelease = function():Void {
  selectedGallery = gallery_cb.selectedItem.label;
  var currentGallery:String;
  var comment:String;
  var NewPhotoNode:XMLNode;
  var NewPhotoCommentNode:XMLNode;
  if (selectedGallery != "-- Select --" ){
    if (filename_txt.text == "") {
      error_txt.text = "Please enter a filename";
    }
    else if (filename_txt.text.indexOf(".jpg") == -1){
      error_txt.text = "Please enter a filename ending in jpg";
    }
    else {
      error_txt.text = "";
      comment = comment_txt.text;
      for (var i:Number=0; i < RootNode.childNodes.length; i++) {
        currentGallery = RootNode.childNodes[i].attributes.➥
        locationName;
        if (selectedGallery == currentGallery){
          GalleryNode = RootNode.childNodes[i];
          NewPhotoNode = photoXML.createElement("photo");
          NewPhotoCommentNode = photoXML.createTextNode(comment);
          NewPhotoNode.attributes.caption = caption_txt.text;
          NewPhotoNode.attributes.filename = filename_txt.text;
          NewPhotoNode.appendChild(NewPhotoCommentNode);
          GalleryNode.appendChild(NewPhotoNode);
          updateContent();
          break;
        }
      }
    }
  }
  else {
    error_txt.text = "Please select a gallery before clicking update";
  }
}
```

6. Add the updateContent function, shown next, to the bottom of the actions layer. The function creates a new XML object called replyXML. It sets the content type for photoXML and sends the complete document tree to the server-side page updateGallery.aspx. The replyXML object receives the response from the server-side page and calls the showReply function.

```
function updateContent():Void {
  var replyXML:XML = new XML();
  replyXML.onLoad = showReply;
  photoXML.contentType = "text/xml";
  photoXML.sendAndLoad("http://localhost/FOE/updateGallery.aspx",➥
  replyXML);
}
```

7. Add the showReply function to the bottom of the actions layer. The function shows either the reply from the server or an error message.

```
function showReply(success:Boolean):Void {
  if (success) {
    trace (this);
}
  else {
    trace ("Error receiving reply");
  }
}
```

Testing the movie

8. Test the movie from within Flash and enter some values in the form. Figure 4-48 shows the values that I entered.

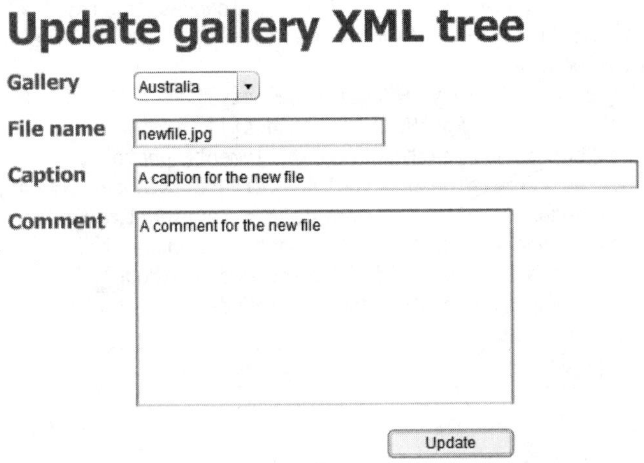

Figure 4-48. Displaying the form details

9. Click the Update button and Flash should process the update. Figure 4-49 shows the Output window displayed after the server-side file processes the update. In reality, I'd probably change the code so that the message displays in the interface.

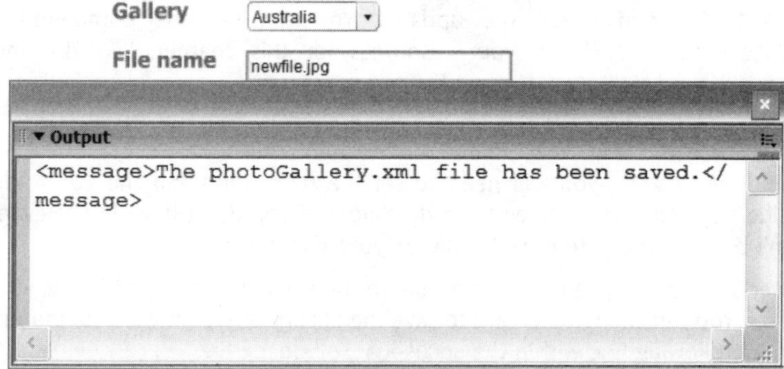

Figure 4-49. Displaying the response in Flash

10. Open the FOE folder.
11. Open the updated `photoGallery.xml` file. Figure 4-50 shows the updated contents in XML Spy. I've highlighted the new <photo> node.

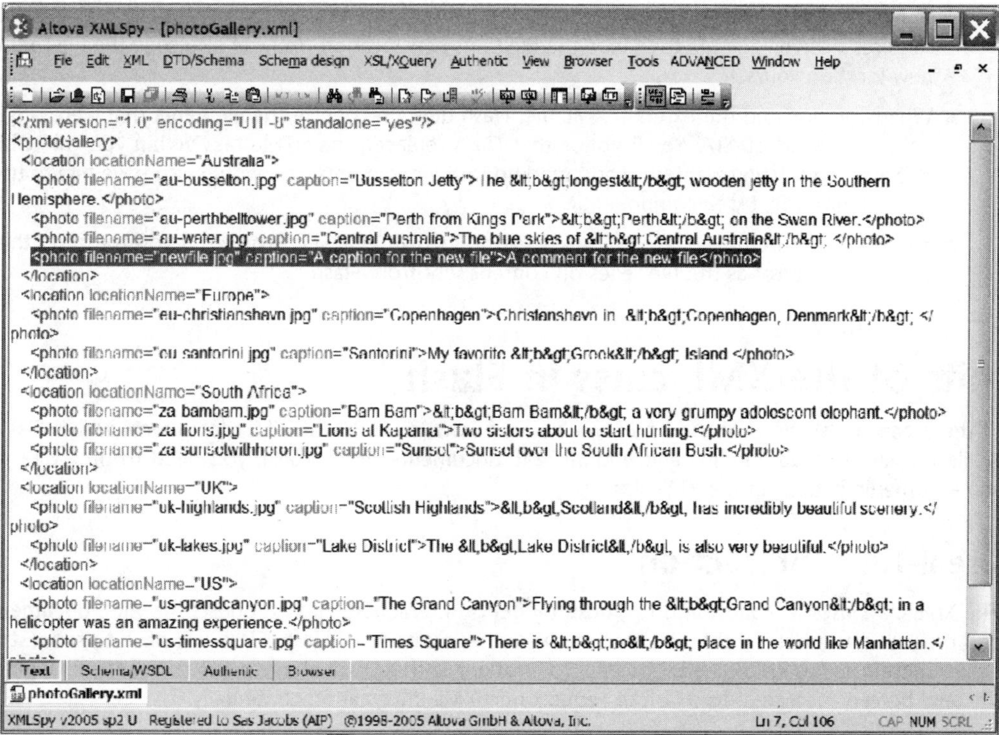

Figure 4-50. Displaying theupdated file in XMLSpy

In this exercise, we used a Flash XML application to add new information to an external XML file. Flash collated the information and generated a new XML node. We used the sendAndLoad method of the XML class to send the XML document tree to a server-side file for processing. We were able to open the XML file and check the updates. You can see the completed file saved as `galleryXMLupdate_completed.fla` in your resources for this chapter. I've also included a PHP version—`galleryXMLupdatePHP_completed.fla`.

Points to note from exercise 7

- As I mentioned earlier, you will need to set the permissions on the `FOE` folder so that the server-side page has access to write to the folder. If you don't have the relevant permissions, you won't be able to create the XML file on your computer.
- The server-side page saved the updated file to the current folder, that is, the `FOE` folder on the web server. You can change the path to save the file anywhere on your computer. You will need to alter the following line within the `updateGallery.aspx` file:

```
xmlDocument.Save(Server.Mappath("photoGallery.xml"));
```

For example, to save the file to `c:\flash\gallery\`, change the line to read

```
xmlDocument.Save("c:\flash\gallery\photoGallery.xml");
```

- When you entered the details in the form, the Flash movie didn't upload the image file at the same time. Flash can't do this for security reasons. You could use the new FileReference class to browse for the image file and determine the file name. However, the FileReference class still requires a server-side file to upload the file to its new location. You can also copy the file to the new location yourself.
- When you updated the external XML file, Flash didn't recognize the elements that were originally marked as CDATA. You'll notice that Flash replaced the HTML tags within your file with HTML entities. If you wanted to add markup to the comments, you would also have had to use entities in the TextArea component.
- You can't test the file `updateGallery.aspx` on its own in a web browser. If you try to do this, you'll see an error as the file relies on content sent from Flash.

Limits of the XML class in Flash

In the preceding sections of the book, you've seen how to work with XML documents within Flash. While it's easy to load, modify, and update XML documents within Flash, you need to be aware of some of the limitations of the XML class.

No real-time interaction

The XML class uses a request and response model of interaction. Flash requests the XML document and receives a response. If the XML document changes outside of Flash, Flash will have to request it again. Therefore, the XML class isn't useful for working with XML content that is constantly changing. It would be very inefficient for Flash to request new XML information continually.

If you need to work with real-time data, Flash provides the XMLSocket class. This class maintains a persistent connection with the server so data can be fed into a Flash movie. If you use this class, Flash doesn't need to request content or continually poll the server, checking for updates. You'll find out more about the XMLSocket class in Chapter 10.

No validation

Flash contains a nonvalidating XML parser so Flash can't check the contents of an XML document tree against a DTD or schema to check it is valid. This could cause problems when you want to update an external XML document. You don't have any way of checking that the XML is valid before you send it to a server-side page. You can get around this problem by adding validation to the server-side file that processes the updates.

Flash cannot update external XML documents

For security reasons, Flash isn't able to update external XML documents. You can manipulate the document tree within Flash, but as soon as you want to save the changes, Flash will need a server-side page and a web server.

If updating XML content in Flash is going to be a regular part of your work, you'll need to develop some skills in a server-side language like PHP, ColdFusion, or ASP.NET. An alternative is to work with a developer experienced in the area.

Security restrictions

Later versions of the Flash player restrict you to loading XML documents that come from the same domain as the Flash movie. If you store your SWF file at `http://www.mydomain.com`, by default you can only load an XML document from `http://www.mydomain.com`. Flash Players 7 and above don't allow you to load data from subdomains like `http://new.mydomain.com` or `https://www.mydomain.com`. You can't use an IP address that resolves to the same subdomain.

This restriction applies to all external data and affects the XML, LoadVars, and XMLSocket classes. It doesn't apply when you're working within Flash on your desktop machine. Rather, it comes into effect once you upload the movie to a web server.

If you need to include content from another domain or subdomain, you can create a cross-domain policy file. You can also *proxy* the data from another domain using a server-side file.

Creating a cross-domain policy file

When Flash requests data from a different domain, first it looks for the cross-domain policy file on the external web server. If the file exists and lists the current domain, Flash loads the external data. If not, the data cannot be loaded into the SWF file.

A cross-domain policy file is an XML document named `crossdomain.xml` that resides on the server providing the data. The file can list specific domains that can access the data, or it can provide blanket access to all domains. Policy files only work with the HTTP, HTTPS, or FTP protocols.

I've shown a sample crossdomain.xml file here. It contains a root element <cross-domain-policy> and a <allow-access-from> element. You can have more than one of these elements in your file to grant access to multiple domains.

```
<?xml version="1.0"?>
<cross-domain-policy>
  <allow-access-from domain="*.mydomain.com" />
</cross-domain-policy>
```

The file allows access from any subdomain in mydomain.com. I could also have listed a specific domain, http://www.mydomain.com, or an IP address. Using an asterisk grants access to all domains.

```
<?xml version="1.0"?>
<cross-domain-policy>
  <allow-access-from domain="*" />
</cross-domain-policy>
```

You can allow access from http domains to secure domains, that is, those using HTTPS, by adding an attribute to the <allow-access-from> element:

```
<?xml version="1.0"?>
<cross-domain-policy>
  <allow-access-from domain="www.mydomain.com" secure="false"/>
</cross-domain-policy>
```

If you don't include this attribute, the default value is true.

You usually place the crossdomain.xml file in the web server root directory. If you're using Flash Player 7 and above, you can also reference a custom location using the System.security.loadPolicyFile method. If you do this, you must set the location before you request data from the other domain.

```
var PF:String = "http://www.mydomain.com/policies/crossdomain.xml";
System.security.loadPolicyFile(PF);
```

An alternative solution is to proxy the data using a server-side file.

Proxying external data

Flash can load data from a server-side file in the same domain. You can use this type of file to request remote XML content and pass it to Flash. Macromedia provides code samples at www.macromedia.com/cfusion/knowledgebase/index.cfm?id=tn_16520. You will also see an example of proxying information in Chapter 9, when we look at web services.

Tips for working with XML in Flash

In this section, I'll give you some tips for working with XML documents in Flash. Factors such as the structure of your XML document, using the XMLNode class, and choosing the right approach can make it much easier to create Flash XML applications.

XML file structure

As you've discovered, extracting information from the XML tree can be a lengthy process. It's common for paths to specific nodes or attributes to be long and difficult to comprehend. Look at this example:

```
myXML.firstChild.childNodes[0].childNodes[0].firstChild.nodeValue;
```

The path refers to the text contained within a grandchild of the root node. The use of the `firstChild` property and the `childNodes[0]` array item don't provide much of a clue to the name of the node that we're interrogating.

Try to keep the structure of your XML document as shallow as possible. If you are able to limit the document to three or four levels of child elements, it will simplify the data extraction process greatly. It will also make it easier to manipulate the document tree within Flash.

Use the XMLNode class

Flash provides the XMLNode class to make it easier to work with specific locations in the document tree. You can create references to points within the XML tree using descriptive names, as shown here:

```
var NameNode:XMLNode = myXML.firstChild.childNodes[0].childNodes[0];
NameNode.firstChild.nodevalue;
```

The advantages of referring to `NameNode` are obvious. The paths to locations in the tree will be shorter, and the descriptive names will make these paths easier to understand.

Create XML with a string

If you need to create an XML document tree within Flash, you have two options: create an XML string or use the methods of the XML class. As you saw earlier in the chapter, it's much quicker to create your XML tree using a string of XML information.

Validate your XML documents

Valid XML documents are well formed and meet the criteria set down in either a DTD or schema. Chapter 3 provides more information about creating DTDs and schemas.

Flash doesn't check that a document is well formed before loading it into an XML object, so it's possible for Flash to load XML documents that are not well formed. You can easily check for the document by displaying the document in a web browser such as Internet Explorer or by using an XML editor. In fact, you should do this as a standard practice before you work with stand-alone XML documents in Flash.

Flash contains a nonvalidating parser. This means that Flash won't check whether your XML document has a valid structure. If you are using your XML document with other applications, it will be beneficial to check the validity of the XML document before you load it into Flash. You can use an XML editor such as XMLSpy to check an XML document against a DTD or schema.

Use the right tool for your dynamic content

XML is a hot topic in the web development world, and it can be tempting to assume that you should use XML for every Flash project requiring dynamic data. While the XML class makes working with XML documents in Flash easy, there may be some cases where a LoadVars class is a better solution.

XML documents are verbose by definition and have the potential to create large file sizes. If you're querying a database, it may be quicker to send the content into Flash using a variable pair string and the LoadVars class. You'll certainly be able to reduce the size of incoming information when compared with an XML document.

The XML class doesn't create a persistent connection to the web server. If you use the XML class in this situation, you'll have to poll the web server continually looking for changes. A better alternative in this case is to use the XMLSocket class. We'll look at this class in more detail in Chapter 10 of the book.

Summary of the properties, methods, and events of the XML class

This section provides a summary of the properties and methods of the XML class. Many of the properties and methods also apply to the XMLNode class, and I've noted this within the relevant tables. Table 4-3 shows a summary of the methods of the XML class.

Table 4-3. Summary of methods of the XML class

Method	Explanation	Applies to XMLNode
addRequestHeader	Adds a custom HTTP header or changes an existing HTTP header	
appendChild	Adds a child node at the end of the current collection of child nodes	Yes
cloneNode	Copies an existing node, optionally with all children	Yes
createElement	Creates a new XML element without positioning it in the document tree	
createTextNode	Creates a new child text node	
getBytesLoaded	Returns the number of bytes loaded from an external XML document	
getBytesTotal	Returns the total number of bytes in an external XML document	
getNamespaceForPrefix	Returns the namespace URI associated with the prefix of the node	Yes (XMLNode only)

Method	Explanation	Applies to XMLNode
getPrefixForNamespace	Returns the prefix associated with the namespace for the node	Yes (XMLNode only)
hasChildNodes	Returns a Boolean value indicating whether or not an element has child nodes	Yes
insertBefore	Inserts a child node before a specified child node	Yes
load	Loads an external XML document	
parseXML	Parses XML content into a document tree	
removeNode	Removes the specified node	Yes
send	Sends XML content to an external server-side page	
sendAndLoad	Sends XML content to an external server-side page and receives an XML reply in another XML object	
toString	Converts XML content to a string representation	Yes

Table 4-4 shows a summary of the properties of the XML class.

Table 4-4. Summary of properties of the XML class

Property	Explanation	Read-only	Applies to XMLNode
contentType	Sets the MIME type of the content		
docTypeDecl	Sets and returns the DOCTYPE declaration		
firstChild	Returns the first child in the collection of child nodes	Yes	Yes
ignoreWhite	Determines whether white space is preserved when an XML document is parsed		
lastChild	Returns the last child in the collection of child nodes	Yes	Yes
loaded	Returns a Boolean value indicating whether an external XML document has been loaded	Yes	
localName	Returns the full name of the XMLNode object i.e. the name without the prefix	Yes	Yes (XMLNode only)

Property	Explanation	Read-only	Applies to XMLNode
namespaceURL	Returns the URL of the namespace to which the XML node's prefix resolves	Yes	Yes (XMLNode only)
nextSibling	Finds the next sibling in the parent node's collection of child nodes	Yes	Yes
nodeName	Finds the name of an element node		Yes
nodeType	Finds the node type	Yes	Yes
nodeValue	Find the text within a text node		Yes
parentNode	Finds the parent node of the current child	Yes	Yes
prefix	Returns the prefix of the node name	Yes	Yes (XMLNode only)
previousSibling	Finds the previous sibling in the parent node's collection of child nodes	Yes	Yes
status	Returns a number providing information about the parsing of an XML document		
xmlDecl	Sets and returns the XML declaration		

Table 4-5 shows a summary of the events of the XML class.

Table 4-5. Summary of events of the XML class

Event handler	Explanation
onData	Triggered when external XML data is loaded, before it is parsed by Flash. Also triggered when an error occurs in loading XML data.
onHTTPStatus	Invoked when the load or sendAndLoad operation has ended. Returns the status code from the server e.g. 404 for page not found.
onLoad	Triggered after external XML data is loaded and parsed by Flash.

Both the XML and XMLNode classes include the collections listed in Table 4-6.

Table 4-6. Collections within the XML and XMLNode classes

Collection	Explanation	Read-only
`attributes`	Associative array of all attributes within a node	
`childNodes`	Array of child nodes within the current parent node	Yes

Summary

The XML class provides a flexible way to work with XML content in Flash. It allows you to load external XML documents into Flash and parse them into a document tree. Providing you know how to traverse this tree, it's easy to extract the data and add it to the interface of your movie. You can use the XML class to create XML content within Flash. You can either create an XML string or use methods and properties to create an XML document tree programmatically.

Flash also provides you with a number of methods for manipulating the structure of the XML tree. You can update the content of text nodes and attributes, add and remove nodes, and even change the names of a node. When you're ready to update an external file, the XML class provides methods for sending XML content.

Flash is an excellent tool for working with XML documents. In addition to the XML class, a number of built-in data components ship with the professional edition of Flash. These components enable you to configure your XML content using the Component Inspector. They also allow for data binding with UI components. The `XMLSocket` class allows you to work with XML using a persistent connection. It allows external data to trigger actions within Flash.

In the next three chapters, I'll look at how you can work with Flash and Office 2003. You can use Word, Excel, or Access 2003 to update content for your Flash movies.

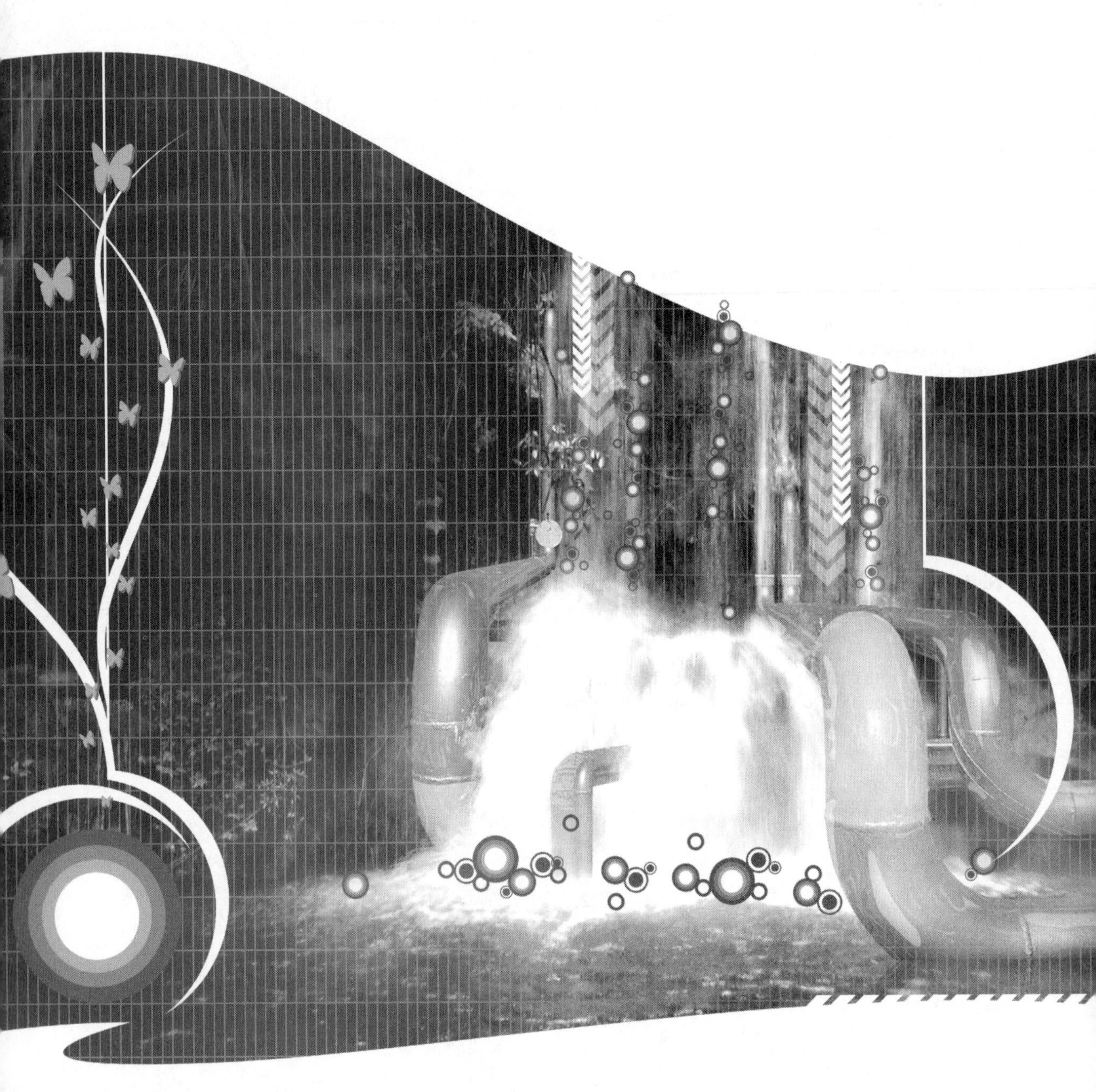

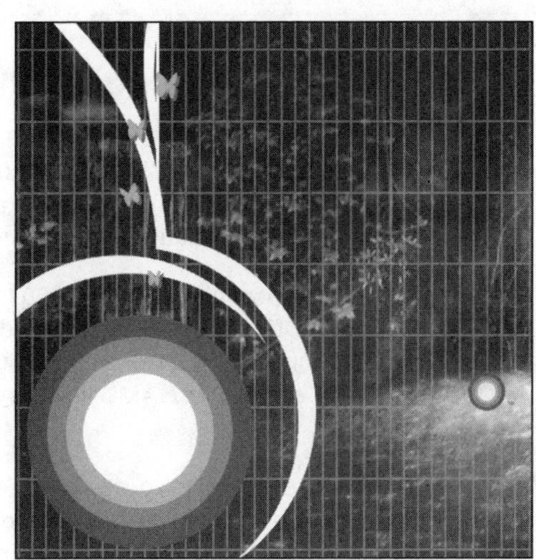

Chapter 5

WORKING WITH XML IN WORD 2003

In the previous chapter, you saw how to use the XML class in Flash. You can use this class to load external XML documents into Flash, to modify or generate new XML content, and to send XML from Flash to another application. If you want to include an external XML document in Flash, you'll need to generate the content somehow.

Earlier in the book, I showed you how to generate XML documents from XML editors, from server-side files, and even from Microsoft Office 2003 on a PC. In this chapter, I'll look more closely at how you can work with XML documents in Word 2003. By the end of this chapter, you'll have created a "Latest News" XML-driven application that you can update using Word 2003. I'll cover Excel and Access 2003 in the next two chapters.

You'll need a PC with a copy of Microsoft Office 2003 Professional or Enterprise edition before you can work through the examples. You won't be able to use a trial copy of the software, and unfortunately for Macintosh users, Office 2004 doesn't offer the same XML functionality. There is limited XML support in Excel 2004, but you won't be able to use it for the examples in the next chapter. If you're a Macintosh user, you might want to see if you can borrow a PC to work through the examples here.

The Microsoft website offers comprehensive support for Office 2003 and XML in the "XML in Office Development" section. You can visit `http://msdn.microsoft.com/office/understanding/xmloffice/default.aspx` to learn more.

Why use Microsoft Office?

Before we get started, you need to understand why you might want to use Office 2003 to generate XML content. Microsoft Office is one of the most popular software packages used by organizations. Most people have skills in working with at least Word and Excel, and many companies store a large portion of their information within Office documents.

XML makes it possible for Office 2003 to share information with other applications, including Flash. You can use Office to generate and update XML documents. You can use XML schemas and Extensible Stylesheet Language Transformations (XSLT) style sheets to change the way Office creates these documents. You can also use XML in external software packages to create and modify Word and Excel documents.

Documents serve two purposes within Office. First, they provide storage for data. This is particularly relevant for applications like Excel and Access. They also provide formatting information about the data they store. This is particularly important in packages like Word and Excel.

When you work with XML content, you're usually more interested in the data rather than its presentation. You'll normally add style and formatting to an XML document by transforming the content with an XSLT style sheet or by using Cascading Style Sheets (CSS). Flash can also provide a presentation layer for the data.

As developers, we often populate our dynamic Flash applications from XML documents. The actual content isn't important—we are more concerned with the structure of the data so we can include it in the application. Using external XML documents allows us to update the content of applications without opening Flash. If we're building applications for clients, we can either modify the XML documents ourselves each time the data changes or provide update mechanisms for our clients to use.

One option is to provide clients with an XML editor and teach them the tag structure of their XML documents. However, for many clients, the prospect of working with raw XML may be quite daunting. It's also very easy for them to make mistakes and generate documents that aren't well formed.

Another approach is to create web forms that allow clients to update XML content using server-side files. Most clients are quite comfortable filling in web forms in a web browser. It's a good solution, but someone has to build the web forms, which means the client ends up paying extra. The forms also have to run through a web server, so this approach won't work as easily in stand-alone applications, for example, those running from CD-ROMs.

You can use Office 2003 to provide another solution to this problem by treating Office 2003 documents as a storage mechanism for XML content. Clients can use packages like Word and Excel to update XML documents. Providing you set up Office correctly, clients need to learn only a few additional skills. If the Flash application is running on a web server, you can also build a web form that allows a client to upload the new XML content to the website.

I've used this approach successfully with a number of clients. Because they're comfortable with Office 2003, it's not too much of a stretch for them to work with data and generate XML content. You can find out more about one of my clients who uses this approach in Chapter 1.

If XML functionality is available in Word, Excel, and Access 2003, how do you decide which application you should use? In part, that depends on your client's skill levels, but it's also important to understand the data structures supported by each package.

Which Office packages can I use?

Within Microsoft Office 2003, both Word and Excel come with their own built-in XML vocabularies. Both packages can describe document structures and content using a set of predefined XML elements. Word 2003 uses WordprocessingML while Excel uses SpreadsheetML. Word and Excel can open XML documents written in WordprocessingML or SpreadsheetML as if they were `.doc` or `.xls` files.

You can find out more about these languages at `www.microsoft.com/office/xml/default.mspx`. You can also download the documentation for the XML schemas for Microsoft products from `www.microsoft.com/downloads/details.aspx?FamilyId=FE118952-3547-420A-A412-00A2662442D9&displaylang=en`. The schemas come with reference documentation in the form of a help file.

Access 2003 allows you to export existing data in XML format. Unlike the other Office applications, it doesn't have its own XML vocabulary. Other Microsoft applications have varying levels of XML support. PowerPoint 2003 and Outlook 2003 don't include XML features. Visio has had XML support since the release of the XP version. Visio 2003 uses the **DataDiagramingML** language and supports Scalable Vector Graphics (SVG), an XML-based standard for describing graphical elements. The Enterprise edition of Office 2003 includes an additional product, InfoPath, that works specifically with XML data. It uses forms to collect and manage information that the whole organization can share.

You can also use InfoPath, Word, Excel, and Access 2003 to consume SOAP-based web services. However, you'd need to install the Web Services toolkit from Microsoft and write some VBA code to make this happen. It's a little beyond the scope of this book, but if you're interested you can download the toolkit from `www.microsoft.com/downloads/details.aspx?familyid=fa36018a-e1cf-48a3-9b35-169d819ecf18&displaylang=en`. There's an article covering Excel at `http://msdn.microsoft.com/msdnmag/issues/05/02/ExcelWebServices/default.aspx`.

You don't have to use the built-in languages within Word and Excel 2003 in the XML documents that you generate. Instead, you can transform Office documents using XSLT style sheets and XML schemas. This allows you to extract the data from the document and ignore formatting information. In other words, you can create your own data structures for the XML documents. If you want to find out more about style sheets and schemas, refer back to Chapter 3.

Understanding data structures

You can structure data in many different ways. Some of it is list-based, and we often display this type of information in tables. Other data is relational in nature—we organize it according to the relationships between data items. The way the data is structured determines which Office 2003 application you should use to generate XML documents.

Word documents serve two purposes—they manage both style and content. We don't use Word to manage complicated tables of data—that's often best left to Excel. Instead, we're usually interested in template-style information, for example, a form letter or report. This gives you a clue about how best to use Word for generating XML documents.

Word 2003 doesn't generate repeating XML information particularly well, although there are some exceptions to this rule. Instead, you should treat Word as a template or form for generating XML content. You fill in the information and Word creates the XML document. This means that you should use Word for text-based Flash applications. An example of this is a latest news item display or a content management system, where the content is restricted to a fixed set of categories. We'll work through an example application later in this chapter.

Excel, on the other hand, is most concerned with data and data analysis. We often use Excel to manage flat-file or list databases. Although formatting the data is important, it is a secondary consideration. The grid structure within Excel makes it easy for us to format and manipulate list-based data.

The Excel interface gives you a good idea about the type of XML structures that it will support. Excel works best with grid-based content, particularly data that you can describe in terms of rows and columns. Excel isn't suited for data that contains large quantities of text—that's best left to Word. Later in the book, we'll see an example of using Excel 2003 to manage catalog data.

Access 2003 is a relational database so it works best with groups of data that are related. Although Access includes tools that deal with the layout of data, its primary concern is with content. In Chapter 7, we'll look at how you can search an existing database using Access and Flash.

In the rest of this chapter, I'll focus on Word 2003. You'll learn how to set up a Word document that generates XML content for use in Flash. We'll work through several examples to illustrate how Word treats XML data. We'll also work through a complete Flash application so that you can see the workflow from Word to Flash.

XML in Word 2003

Word 2003 includes XML as a native document format. This means that you can save any Word document in XML format. It also means that you can open and edit XML documents within Word.

Word 2003 includes an XML vocabulary called WordprocessingML. This language allows you to describe any aspect of a Word document using XML elements. You could create an entire Word document using WordprocessingML if you knew how to write the language. You can also generate WordprocessingML by saving a Word document in XML format.

Opening an existing XML document

Word's native XML capabilities mean that you can use it as a sophisticated XML editor. Open an existing XML document within Word 2003 and you'll see the document content marked up with tags. Each tag name is displayed in purple, with a different shape for start and end tags. Word also displays the XML Document pane so that you can start working with the content.

Figure 5-1 shows the `address.xml` document opened in Word. You can find this file with your resources if you want to try opening it in Word 2003.

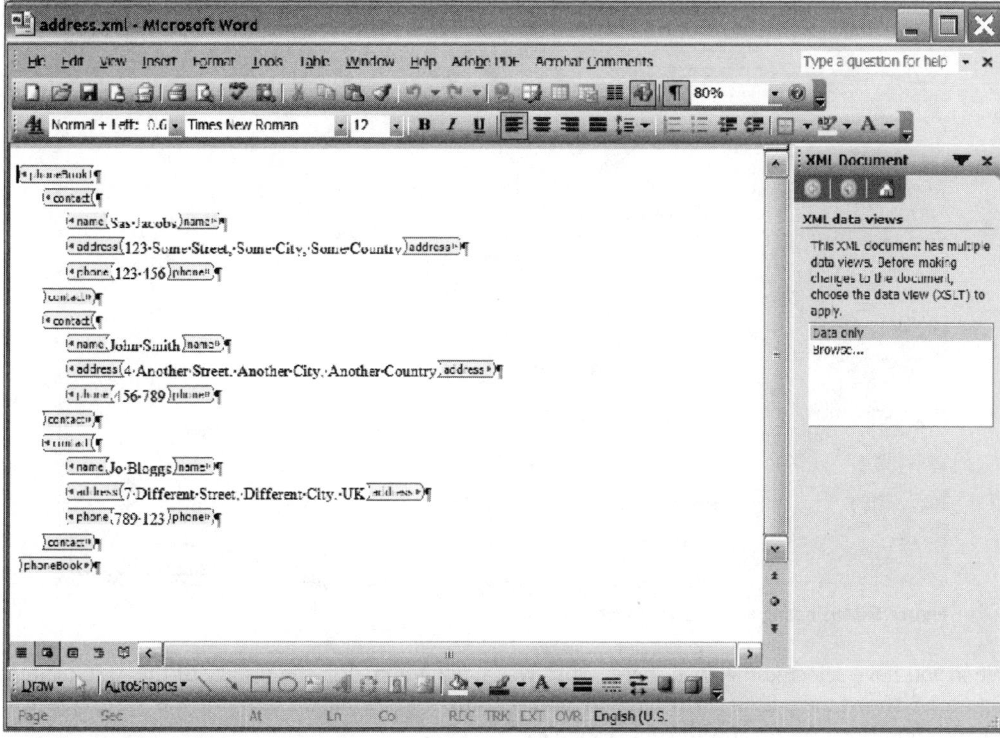

Figure 5-1. Opening an existing XML document in Word

The XML Document pane allows you to view the document in different ways. The screenshot in Figure 5-1 shows the Data only view.

Transforming the document view

When you open an XML document, you can apply an XSL transformation so that you can view the data in different ways. You can also apply a transformation to a document that is already open. An XSL transformation changes the original XML document tree into another type of XML document tree, called the result tree. For example, you can use XSL to generate new XML or HTML content from an existing XML document.

Once you've opened a file, the XML Document pane allows you to view Data only or apply an XSLT file. Clicking the Browse button allows you to search for an XSL file, as shown in Figure 5-2.

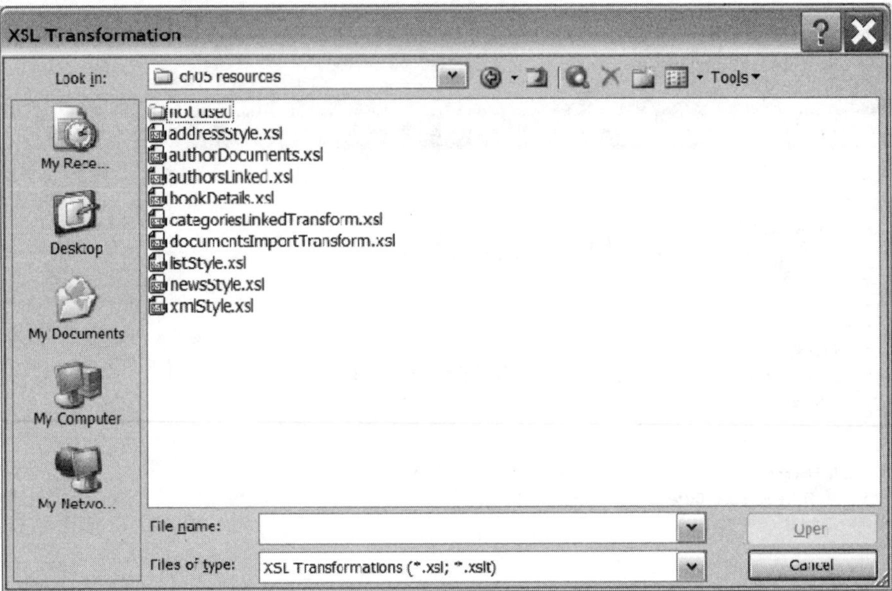

Figure 5-2. Selecting an XSL style sheet

When you have selected the style sheet, Word will apply it and alter the display of the XML content. Figure 5-3 shows the `address.xml` file after applying the transformation from the file `listStyle.xsl`. You can find this style sheet with your resources.

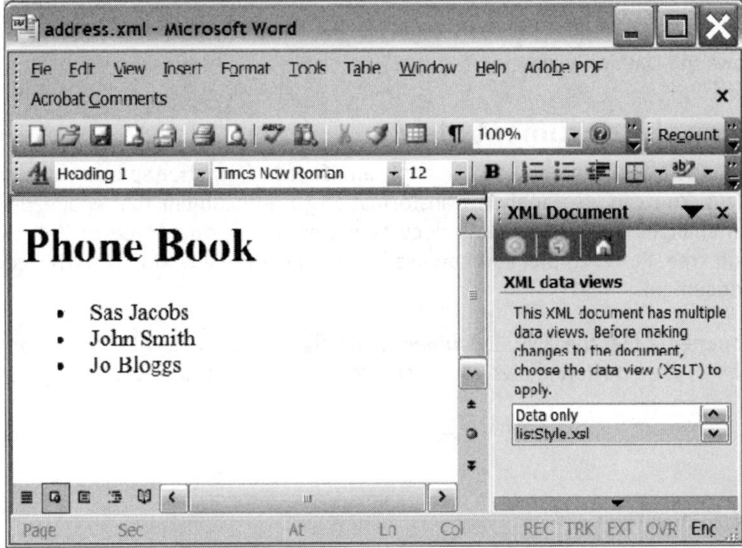

Figure 5-3. An XML document with an XSL style sheet applied

The style sheet transforms the content into an HTML document, containing a heading and a bulleted list. You can look at the contents of the style sheet if you want to see how the transformation works. You can learn more about transformations in Chapter 3.

You can also apply a transformation as you open an XML document by using the options you access by clicking the Open button. For example, in Figure 5-4, I've chosen to open an XML document with a transformation. When I choose this option, Word prompts me to locate the style sheet and opens the transformed XML document. I don't get the Data only view as an option in the XML Document pane.

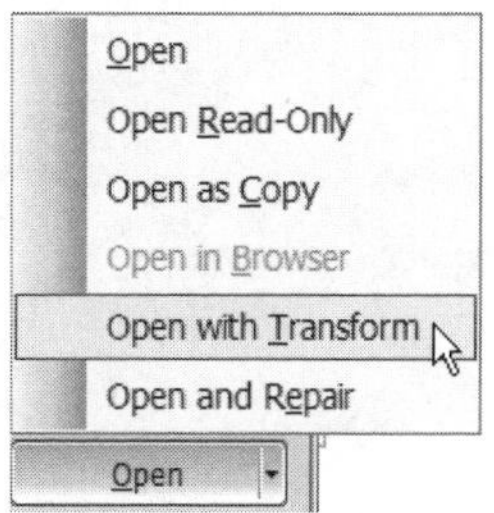

Figure 5-4. Opening an XML document and applying an XSL style sheet at the same time

If you choose Open with Transform, Word defaults to the `Templates` folder when searching for the style sheet. If the transformation results in an XML document, Word will display the XML Document pane. Figure 5-5 shows the `address.xml` document transformed with `xmlStyle.xsl`. You can find both documents with your resources. Compare this view with the one shown in Figure 5-1.

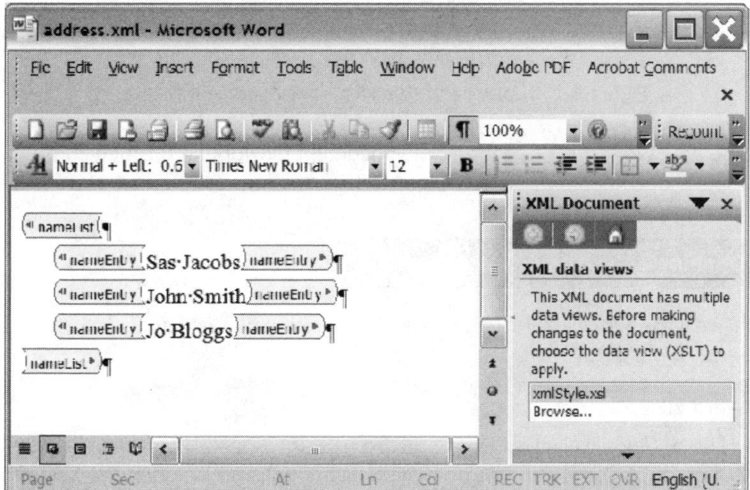

Figure 5-5. Applying an XSL style sheet to produce alternative XML content

Once open, you can apply more transformations to the XML document by clicking the Browse button.

Dealing with errors

Word 2003 won't open an XML document that is not well formed. If you try to open an XML document containing errors, you'll see an error message shown in Figure 5-6.

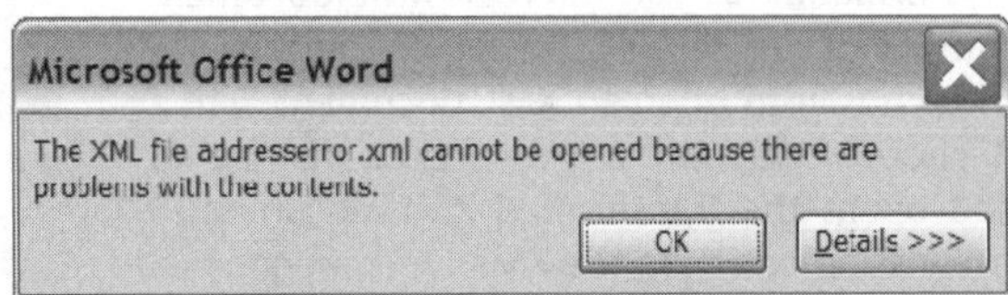

Figure 5-6. Trying to open a document that is not well formed

You can click the Details button to find out more about the error. Figure 5-7 shows the resulting detailed error message.

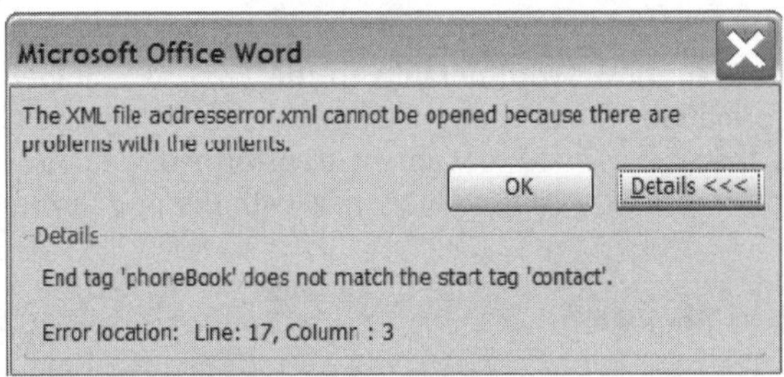

Figure 5-7. Displaying the detailed error message in Word

You'll understand how Word 2003 opens an XML document by working through an exercise. We'll practice opening an XML document with and without transformations to see how Word presents the data.

Exercise 1: Opening an existing XML document

In this exercise, we'll use Word 2003 to open the file address.xml. We'll apply transformations that create both XML and HTML output.

1. Open Word 2003.
2. Choose File ➤ Open, select `address.xml` from your resource files, and click Open. You should see XML tags displayed within the document. Word will also bring up the XML Document pane.
3. In the XML Document pane, click the Browse option and navigate to the xmlStyle.xsl document. Click Open and look at how Word transforms the content.
4. Click the Browse option again and navigate to the file `addressStyle.xsl`. Click Open and look at the different view of the data.
5. Click Browse again and choose the file `listStyle.xsl`. Click Open.
6. Double-click the different views in the XML Document pane and watch Word apply the transformations.
7. Close the `address.xml` file without saving and reopen it, choosing Open with Transform. Apply any of the style sheets listed in this exercise before opening the document.
8. Close the `address.xml` file without saving.

The exercise showed you how to open an XML document within Word 2003. You applied different transformations both after and during the open process. In the next section, we'll look at how you can generate XML content from Word.

Creating XML content with Save as

The easiest way to create an XML document in Word is to save an existing document in XML format. This will convert the document properties, content, and formatting to WordprocessingML. Figure 5-8 shows how you can save a document in XML format by selecting the file type XML Document.

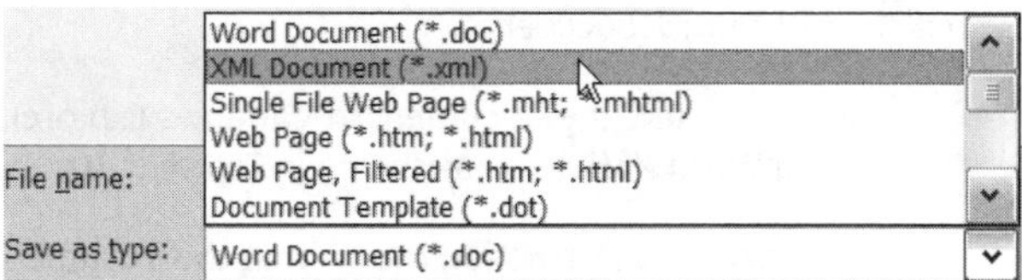

Figure 5-8. Using Save as type to generate an XML document

Word converts the document information into WordprocessingML and generates an XML document. Figure 5-9 shows the file `newsitem.doc` saved in XML format and opened in XMLSpy. You can see the files newsitem.doc and `newsitem.xml` with your resources.

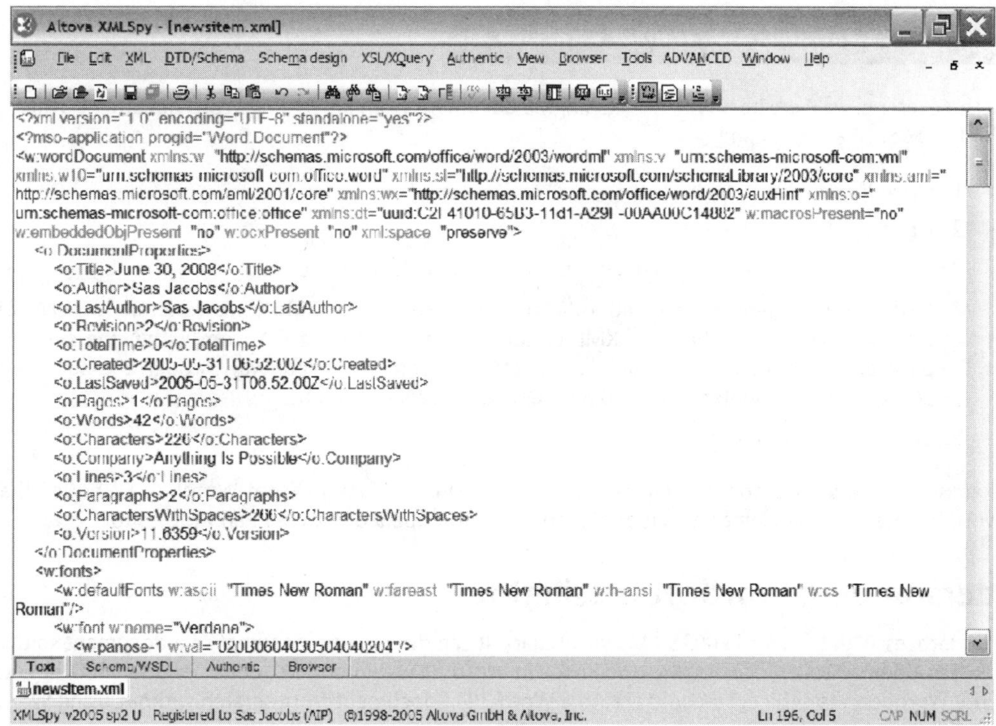

Figure 5-9. XML Spy showing an XML document generated by Word

You'll notice that Word generates a lot of content from a small document. The document shown in Figure 5-9 is 259 lines long in XMLSpy. This is because the XML document includes information about the document properties and formatting as well as the content. If you look through the file, you'll see that the document contains several sections. It starts by listing the document properties in the `<o:DocumentProperties>` element. It also lists the fonts and styles in the `<w:fonts>` and `<w:styles>` elements. It's not until we get to the `<w:body>` element on line 196 that we see the content of the document.

You'll also notice that, during the save process, Word adds a processing instruction at the top of the document, instructing the file to open within Word:

```
<?mso-application progid="Word.Document"?>
```

Figure 5-10. Viewing the Word XML icon in Windows Explorer

When you view the document in Windows Explorer, you'll see that it displays a Word XML icon, as shown in Figure 5-10.

The processing instruction means that the document automatically opens in Word when you double-click the icon. To open it in a different application, right-click the icon and choose Open with. You can also open the file from within another application. If you want to open the WordprocessingML document within Flash, you'll need to remove the processing instruction first. You can find out more about processing instructions in Chapter 2. We'll examine WordprocessingML more closely in the next exercise.

Exercise 2: Generating XML content with Save As

In this exercise, we'll create a WordprocessingML document from an existing Word document by using the File ➤ Save As command.

1. Open Word 2003 if necessary.
2. Open the file `newsitem.doc`.
3. Choose File ➤ Save As and change the type to XML Document.
4. Close the newsitem.xml file within Word and open it in an XML or text editor. You can use Notepad if you don't have an XML editor installed. Open the file from within the software package rather than double-clicking the XML file icon. Work your way through the document and see if you can interpret the document sections and elements.
5. Close the file without saving.

Exercise 2 showed you how to generate WordprocessingML content from Word. You'll notice that Word hid many of the elements that appeared when you opened the file in an XML editor.

Understanding WordprocessingML

WordprocessingML is Word 2003's XML vocabulary. It can describe every aspect of a document so that you can open a WordprocessingML document in Word or within an XML editor. If you knew how to write WordprocessingML, you could create a Word 2003 document from scratch without using Word.

Word XML documents always start with an XML declaration, processing instruction, and root element that references the Word namespaces. Here's an extract from a Word XML document:

```
<?xml version="1.0" encoding="UTF-8" standalone="yes"?>
<?mso-application progid="Word.Document"?>
<w:wordDocument
xmlns:w="http://schemas.microsoft.com/office/word/2003/wordml"
xmlns:v="urn:schemas-microsoft-com:vml"
xmlns:w10="urn:schemas-microsoft-com:office:word"
xmlns:sl="http://schemas.microsoft.com/schemaLibrary/2003/core"
xmlns:aml="http://schemas.microsoft.com/aml/2001/core"
xmlns:wx="http://schemas.microsoft.com/office/word/2003/auxHint"
xmlns:o="urn:schemas-microsoft-com:office:office"
xmlns:dt="uuid:C2F41010-65B3-11d1-A29F-00AA00C14882"
w:macrosPresent="no" w:embeddedObjPresent="no" w:ocxPresent="no"
xml:space="preserve">
```

A WordprocessingML document contains an <o:DocumentProperties> element that describes the properties of the document, including the title, author, creation, and revision dates and word counts There are <w:fonts> and <w:styles> elements that describe the formatting within the document. The content of the document is contained in a <w:body> element. This section is small relative to the remainder of the document. Each paragraph exists within a <w:p> element.

You could spend time learning how to write WordprocessingML so that you could write the XML by hand. You can also generate WordprocessingML by using the Save As command. If you're generating XML documents for use in Flash movies, WordprocessingML is not likely to be useful. It will include formatting information that is irrelevant to Flash. The XML document also uses a complicated element structure. For Flash developers, it's better to use an XML schema to streamline the XML document during the save process. You can apply this schema to either a document or template within Word 2003.

Structuring content within Word

Chapter 3 covered XML schemas and style sheets. Schemas provide the rules for constructing XML documents. You can use them to validate that an XML document has the correct structure. You can also use schemas within Word to dictate the structure of an XML document. Another alternative is to use XSLT style sheets to structure the XML output from Word.

The best way to work with either a schema or style sheet is to add it to the Word schema library. The library is specific to a computer rather than a document. Within Word, style sheets always have to refer to a schema document so you'll have to add at least one schema document to the library before you can include a style sheet. Word 2003 calls XSLT style sheets **solutions**.

These steps summarize how you can apply a schema and style sheet to a Word document. The next section covers each step in more detail.

1. Add the schema to the schema library.
2. Add a style sheet to the schema.
3. Attach the schema to a Word document.
4. Add XML tags to the Word document.
5. Save the data from the Word document in XML format.

Working with the schema library

You can access the schema library in Word by choosing Tools ➤ Templates and Add-Ins. You'll then need to select the XML Schema tab, as shown in Figure 5-11.

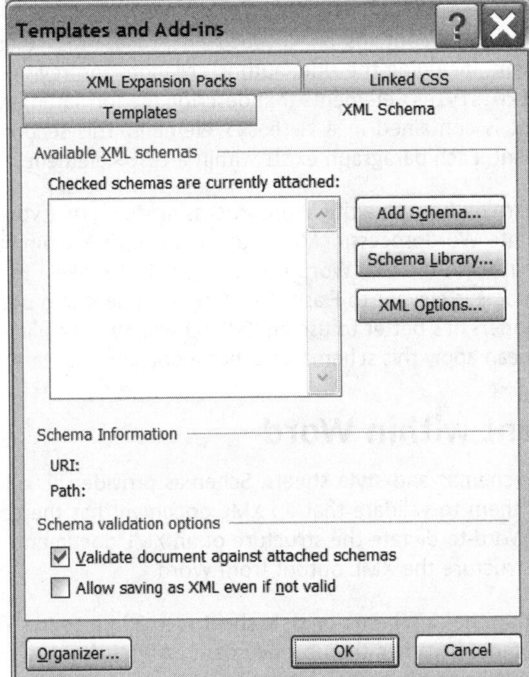

Figure 5-11. The XML Schema tab in the Templates and Add-Ins dialog box

The XML Schema tab shows all of the XML schemas attached to the current document. In Figure 5-12, the document has no schemas attached.

To access the schema library, click the Schema Library button. Figure 5-12 shows the Schema Library dialog box.

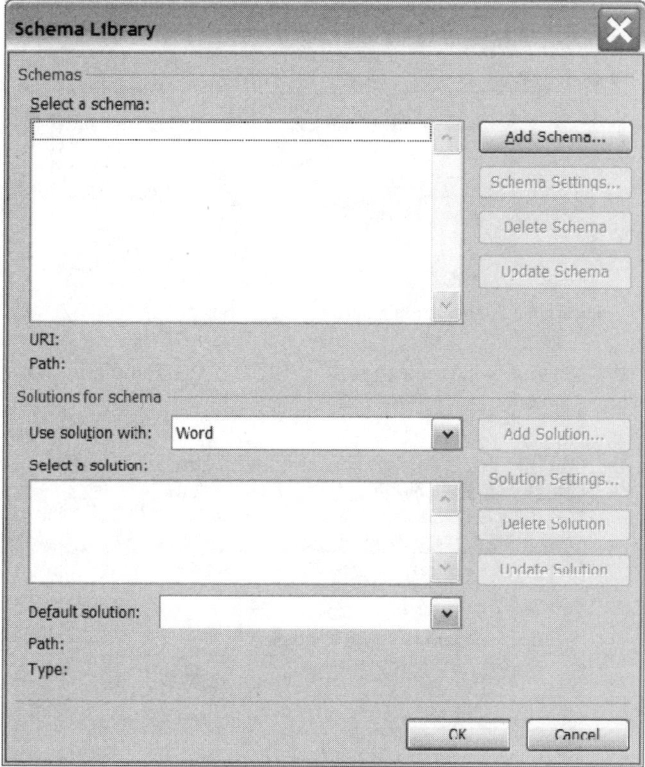

Figure 5-12. The Schema Library within Word 2003

You can use the dialog box to add a new schema as well as to update and delete existing schemas.

Adding a schema to the library

When you add an XML schema to the library, you'll be able to use it in more than one Word document. Prepare the schema outside of Word, perhaps in an XML editor such as XMLSpy. To add the schema, click the Add Schema button in the Schema Library dialog box. You could also click the same button in the XML Schema tab of the Templates and Add-Ins dialog box.

Locate the schema document and click Open. Word will show the Schema Settings dialog box. You'll need to enter a URI and an Alias. The URI is a unique value that identifies the schema. It should point to a valid web address; however, the location in the URI doesn't have to exist. The Alias is a short name that you can use to refer to the schema. You can see an example of the Schema Settings dialog box in Figure 5-13.

Figure 5-13. The Schema Settings dialog box

Once you've added the schema, you'll see the Alias listed in the Templates and Add-Ins dialog box. You can see this in Figure 5-14.

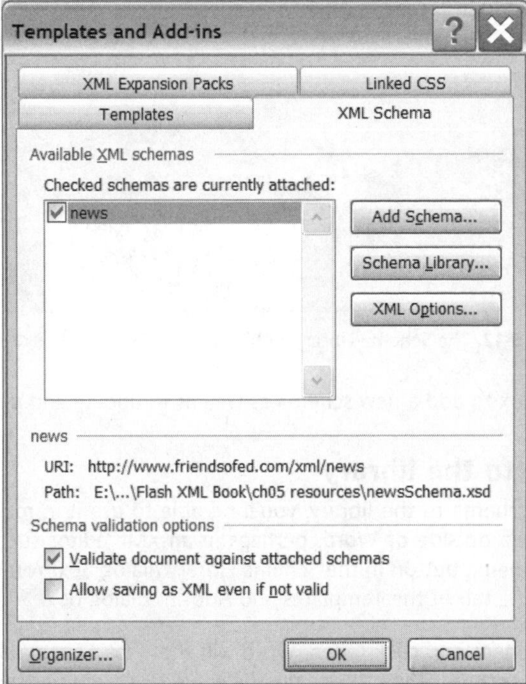

Figure 5-14. The Tempates and Add-Ins dialog box

The screenshot in Figure 5-14 shows that the news schema is checked. This means that this schema is attached to the current document.

Adding a transformation to a schema

If you have at least one schema in the schema library, you can add a related XSLT style sheet. Open the schema library and click the schema that contains the transformation, as shown in Figure 5-15.

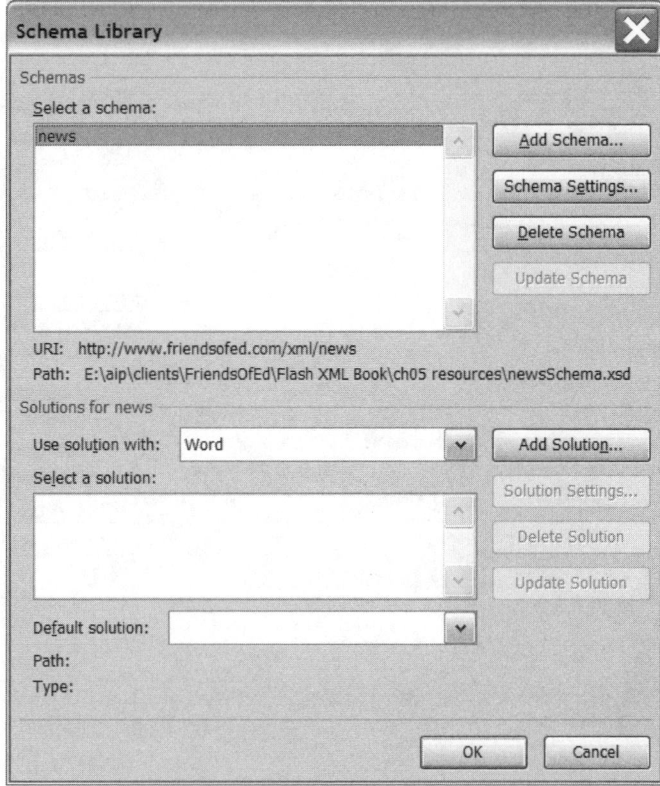

Figure 5-15. Selecting a schema from the Schema Library dialog box

Click the Add Solution button and select a style sheet. Enter a short name for the style sheet in the Alias field. Figure 5-16 shows a completed Solution Settings dialog box. Word has automatically added the XSL Transformation type.

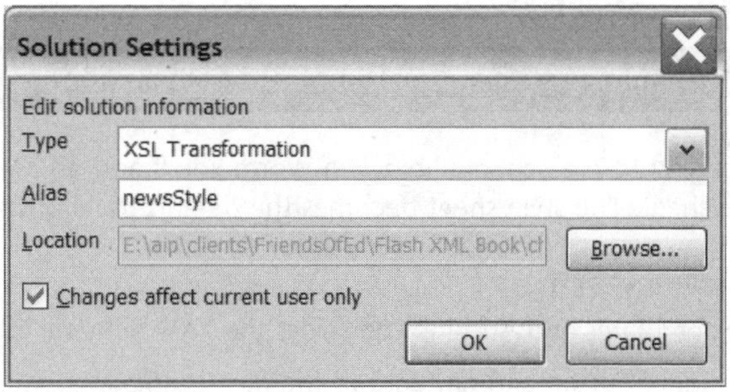

Figure 5-16. The Solution Settings dialog box

Click OK to return to the Schema Library dialog box. You'll see the solution listed, as shown in Figure 5-17.

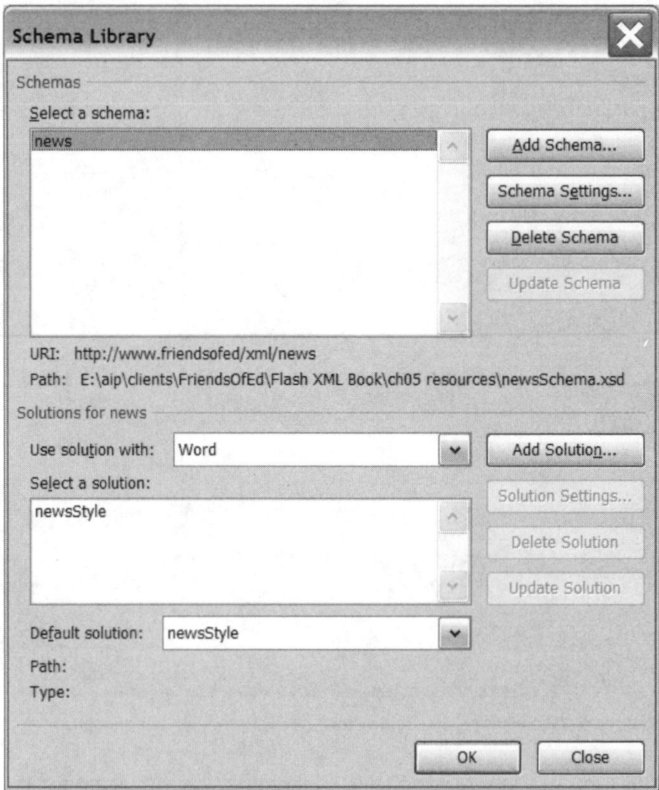

Figure 5-17. The Schema Library displaying an added solution

In the next exercise, you'll practice adding a schema and transformation to the schema library.

Exercise 3: Adding a schema and transformation to the schema library

Exercise 3 will introduce you to the schema library in Word. You'll add an XML schema to the library with an associated style sheet. The style sheet becomes the default transformation for Word.

1. Open Word 2003 if necessary.
2. Choose Tools ➤ Templates and Add-Ins and select the XML Schema tab.
3. Click the Add Schema button and navigate to the file `newsSchema.xsd`.
4. Enter http://www.friendsofed.com/xml/news in the URI field and news in the Alias field. Click OK.
5. Click the Add Solution button and navigate to the file `newsStyle.xsl`.
6. Enter newsStyle in the Alias field and click OK.
7. Click OK twice to close the Templates and Add-Ins dialog box.

Once you've added a schema and style sheet, you'll be able to apply them to your Word documents.

Creating a new Word XML document

You can create a new Word 2003 XML document by choosing File ➤ New and selecting XML document from the New Document pane. You can see this in Figure 5-18. When you choose this type, Word automatically displays the XML Structure pane with the blank document.

After you've created the blank XML document, the XML Structure task pane will display. The task pane allows you to attach a schema to the document.

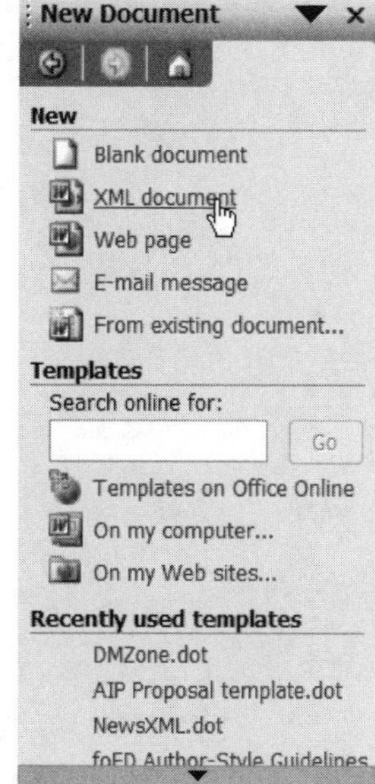

Figure 5-18. Creating a new XML document

Attaching a schema to a Word document

XML schemas describe the rules for creating XML documents. They list the valid elements and attributes, their datatypes, whether they're mandatory, and the number of times and the order in which they should appear. Schemas are useful for creating a shared XML vocabulary for people or applications working with XML documents. You can find out more about XML schemas in Chapter 3.

Word uses an XML schema so it can create a valid XML document. When you attach a schema, it stops Word from generating a WordprocessingML document. Instead, Word generates elements and structures that are consistent with the schema document. In a way, you're using the schema to teach Word how to write your XML document.

You can attach a schema to either a Word document or template so that you can structure the XML output from Word. The schema must be included within the schema library, and you can use it with a new document or a document that already contains content. You can also attach multiple schemas where different parts of the document are used for different purposes.

To attach a schema, choose Tools ➤ Templates and Add-Ins and select the XML Schema tab. Check the schema that you want to attach to the document, as shown in Figure 5-19.

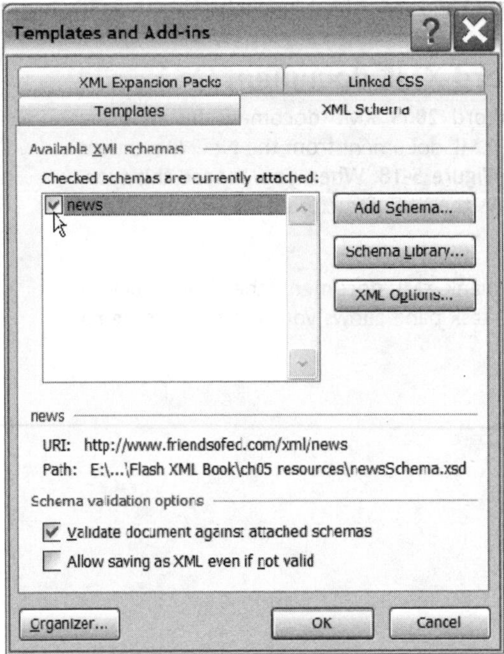

Figure 5-19. Attaching a schema to a Word document

When you attach a schema to an existing document, Word will automatically validate the content against the schema. Errors will display as a yellow cross in the XML Structure pane. Figure 5-20 shows an invalid news element. Word won't validate the contents if it can't locate the schema document.

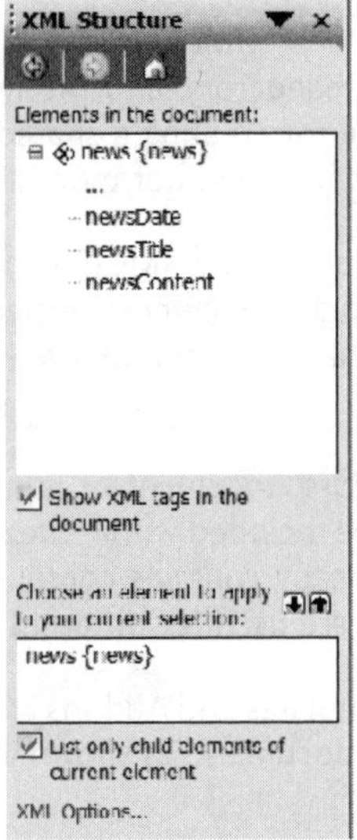

Figure 5-20. An invalid XML document in Word

After you've attached a schema, you'll need to mark up the content with XML tags from the schema document.

Adding XML tags to the document

Make sure that you can see the XML Structure pane in the right side of your document. If it is not showing, select View ➤ Task Pane and choose XML Structure from the drop-down menu at the top of the pane. Figure 5-21 shows how to do this.

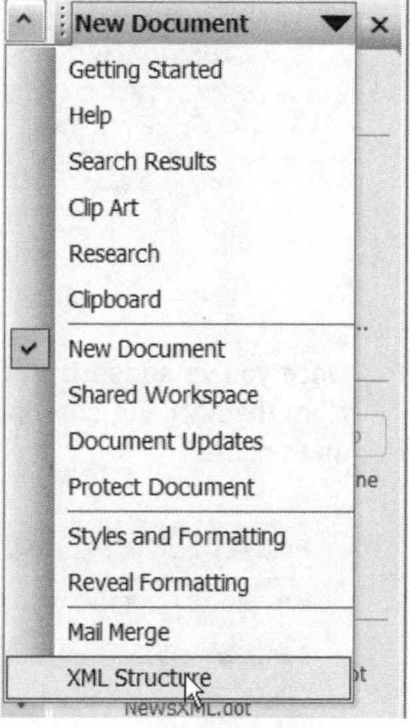

Figure 5-21. Displaying the XML Structure pane

Figure 5-22 shows the XML Structure pane. Notice that it includes an option for showing XML tags within the Word document—Show XML tags in the document. Make sure that you check this option. You'll probably want to uncheck the option later to hide the XML tags from users.

The XML Structure pane allows you to add the XML tags from the current schema to your document. You need to identify which portions of the document correspond to which tag names within the schema.

You'll notice that in Figure 5-22, only the root element displays in the list of elements. This is because you have to apply the root element first. Applying this element will make the other elements within the schema available in the XML Structure pane.

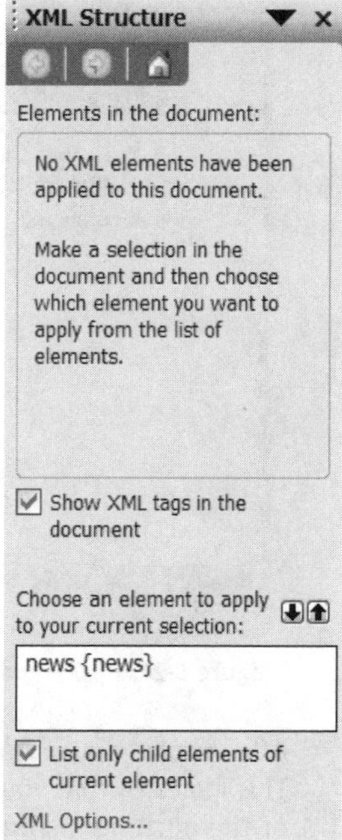

Figure 5-22. The XML Structure pane

Click the root element name in the XML Structure pane and choose the Apply to Entire Document option when prompted. Figure 5-23 shows the dialog box. You can apply the root element to a selection if you want to exclude the unselected content from the final XML document. You might do this to exclude an instruction or document title.

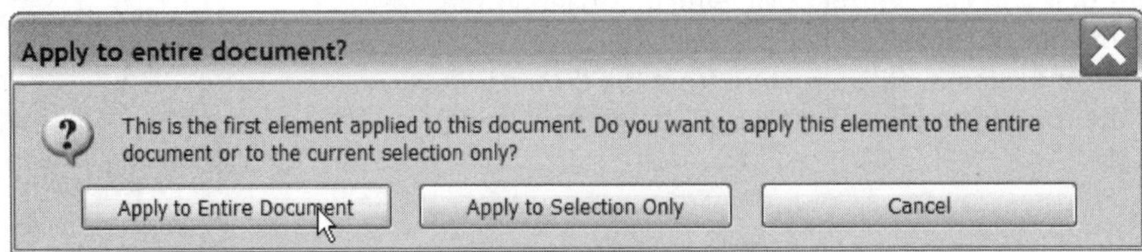

Figure 5-23. Applying the root element to the entire Word document

Once you've added the root element, you can select portions of the text and apply XML elements from the XML Structure pane. Figure 5-24 shows the process of highlighting text and clicking an element name.

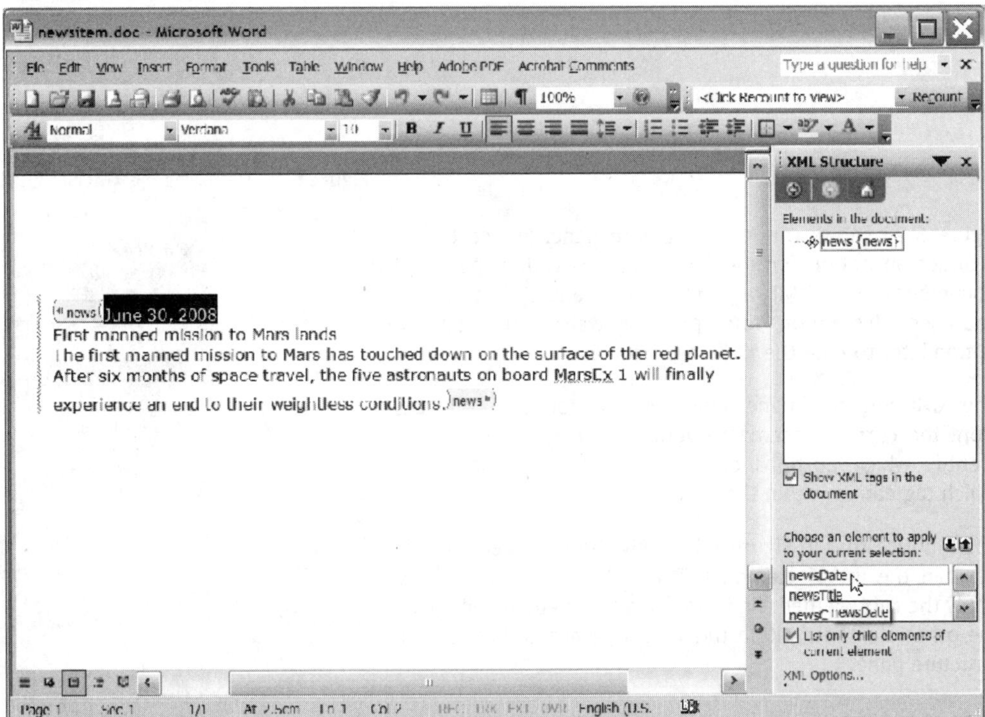

Figure 5-24. Applying an element to a portion of the Word document

After you've applied an XML element, that section of the Word document will display a purple tag. This indicates that you've applied the element. You can continue applying elements to the remainder of the document. You don't need to include all content from the Word document within your XML tags. Figure 5-25 shows the finished product.

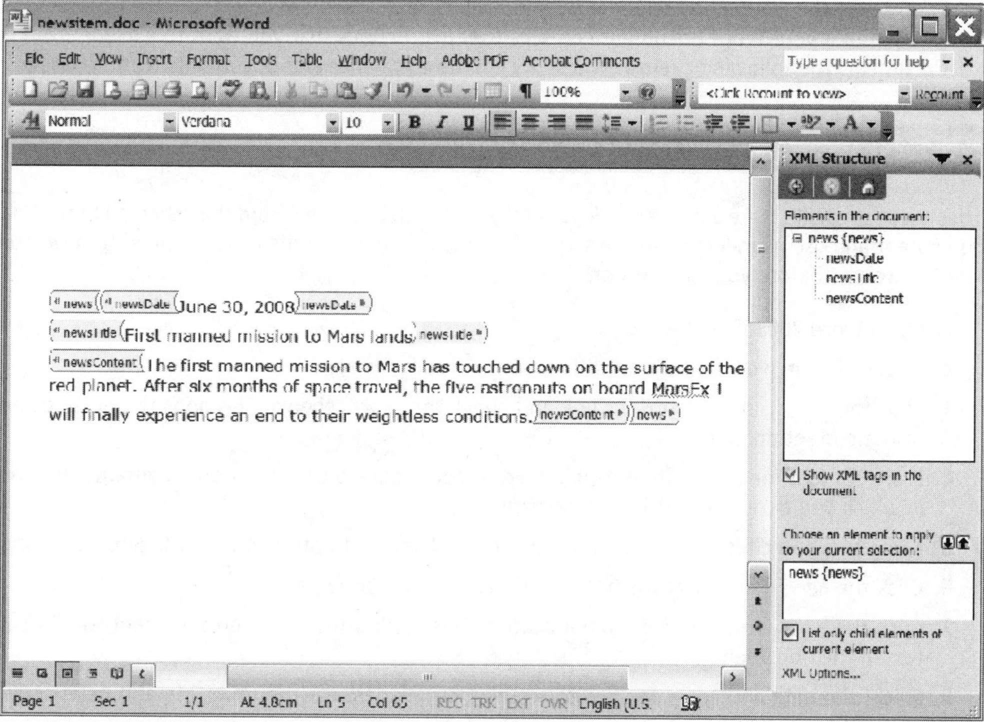

Figure 5-25. The Word document after applying all elements

If you don't mark up some text content within the root element, you'll create a mixed content element when you generate the XML document. Word preserves mixed content unless you tell it otherwise in the XML Options dialog box. Click the XML Options link in the XML Structure pane and check the Ignore mixed content check box, as shown in Figure 5-26.

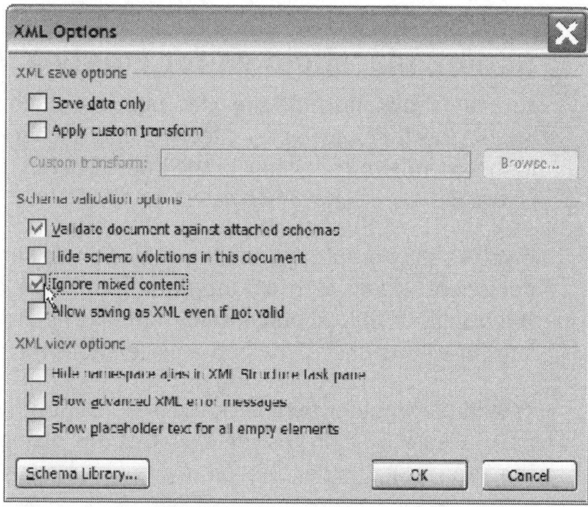

Figure 5-26. Selecting the Ignore mixed content option

When you select this option and save the data in XML format, Word excludes the mixed content. This might be useful if your Word document contains user instructions that you want to exclude from the XML document. The following exercise will show you how schemas and documents work together.

Exercise 4: Adding XML tags to a new Word document

In this exercise, we'll create a new XML document and attach a schema from the schema library. You'll add content and use elements from the schema to mark up the document. You'll need to have completed exercise 3 before you start this one.

1. Open Word 2003 if necessary.
2. Choose File ➤ New and select XML document from the New Document pane.
3. Click the Templates and Add-Ins link and check the news schema. This adds the news schema to the current document.
4. Enter content for a news item. You'll need to add a date, a title, and some content. The order in which you enter the text isn't important.
5. Make sure you check the Show XML tags in the document option in the XML Structure pane.
6. Click the news element at the bottom of the XML Structure pane.
7. Click the Apply to Entire Document button. This applies the root news element to all of the text in the document.
8. Select the date and apply the newsDate element. Repeat for the newsTitle and newsContent elements.
9. Save the document. The completed file should look like the example shown earlier in Figure 5-25. I've saved my completed document as `newsitem_tags.doc` with your resources.

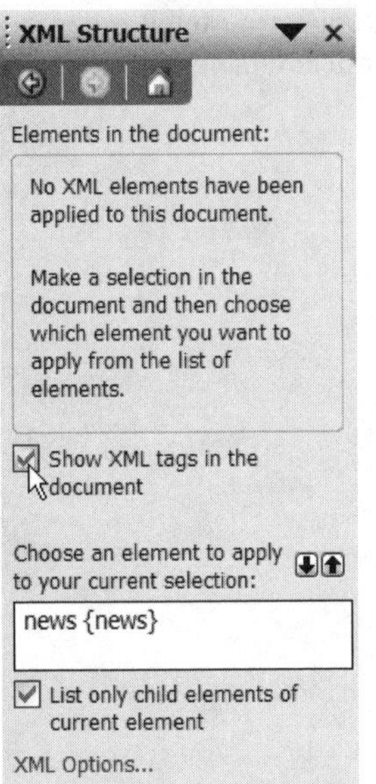

Figure 5-27. Showing the XML tags in a document

If you're working with an empty document, you won't be able to mark up existing text. Instead, you'll add tags without making a selection first. This means you might need to give some extra support to users who will add content to the document.

Adding placeholders for empty XML tags

You can show and hide the XML tags in a document by using the *Ctrl-Shift-X* shortcut keys or by checking and unchecking the Show XML tags in the document check box in the XML Structure pane. You can see this in Figure 5-27.

If you've shown the tags, the tag names display in purple within the Word document. If you turn off the option, only the content within each tag will display. If there's no content, nothing will display. This will be a problem for clients unless you add a placeholder for the tags.

To add placeholder text, click the XML Options link in the XML Structure pane. Figure 5-28 shows the XML Options dialog box that opens. Check the Show placeholder text for all empty elements option.

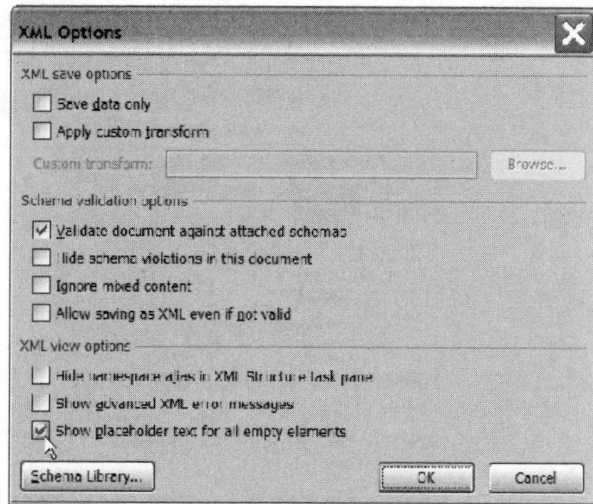

Figure 5-28. Setting the show placeholder text option

By default, placeholder text displays the name of an element. You can see an example of this in Figure 5-29.

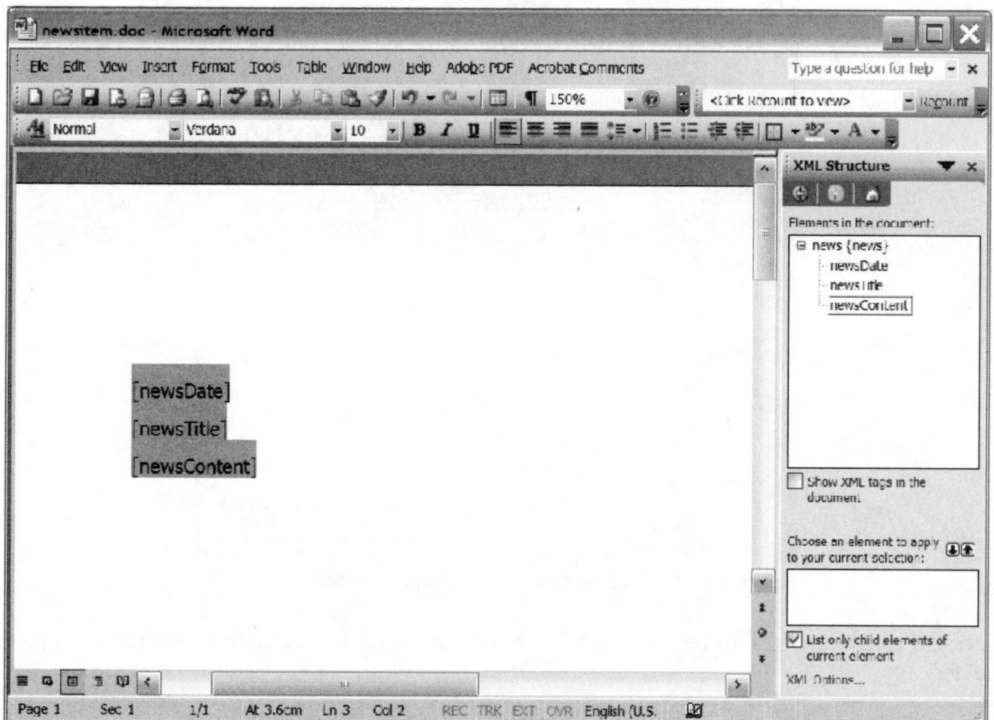

Figure 5-29. Displaying the default placeholder text for XML content in a Word document

Element names can't have spaces, so this type of placeholder may be difficult for clients to interpret. You can customize the placeholder text by right-clicking the element name in the XML Structure pane. You can see this in Figure 5-30.

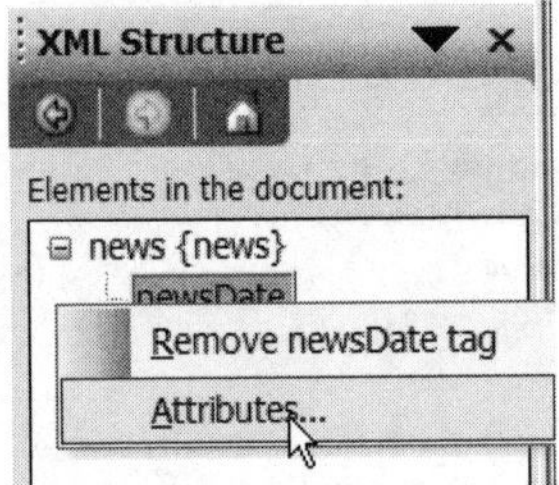

Figure 5-30. Customizing the display of placeholder text

Choose the Attributes option and enter new placeholder text at the bottom of the Attributes dialog box, as shown in Figure 5-31.

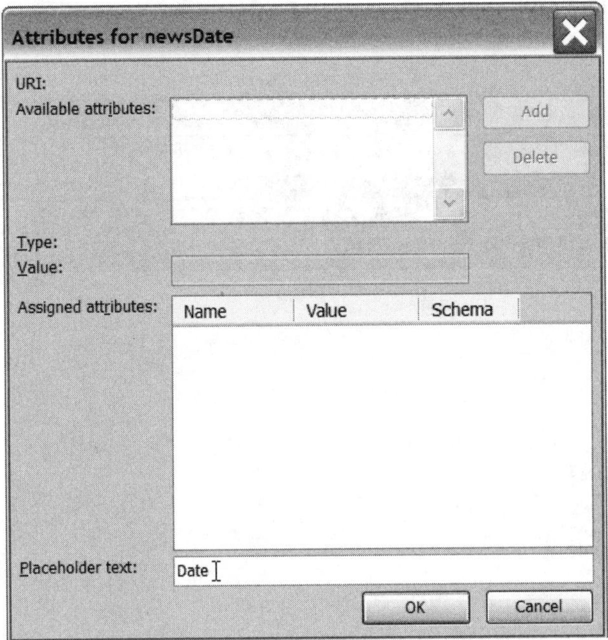

Figure 5-31. Entering custom text for the placeholder

Click OK to use the custom text. Figure 5-32 shows the completed document with renamed placeholders.

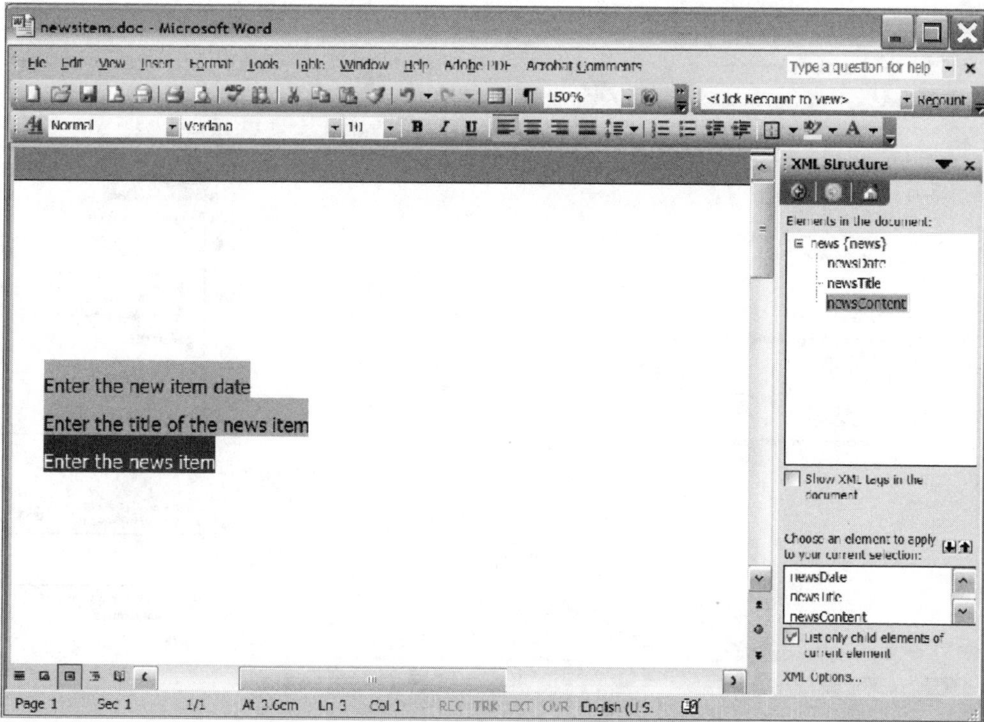

Figure 5-32. The changed placeholder names

In the example you just saw, we used the Attributes option to set placeholder text. You're probably wondering if we can use this to deal with XML attributes. In the next section, we'll look at how you can use Word with attributes.

Adding attributes

Working with attributes in Word 2003 is a little more difficult than working with elements. The only way to edit attributes is by using the Attributes dialog box. Unlike elements, a user can't just replace the content by typing within a Word document. This makes attributes a little trickier for users to update.

You can display the Attributes dialog box by right-clicking an element name in the XML Structure pane and selecting the Attributes option. You can see this in Figure 5-33.

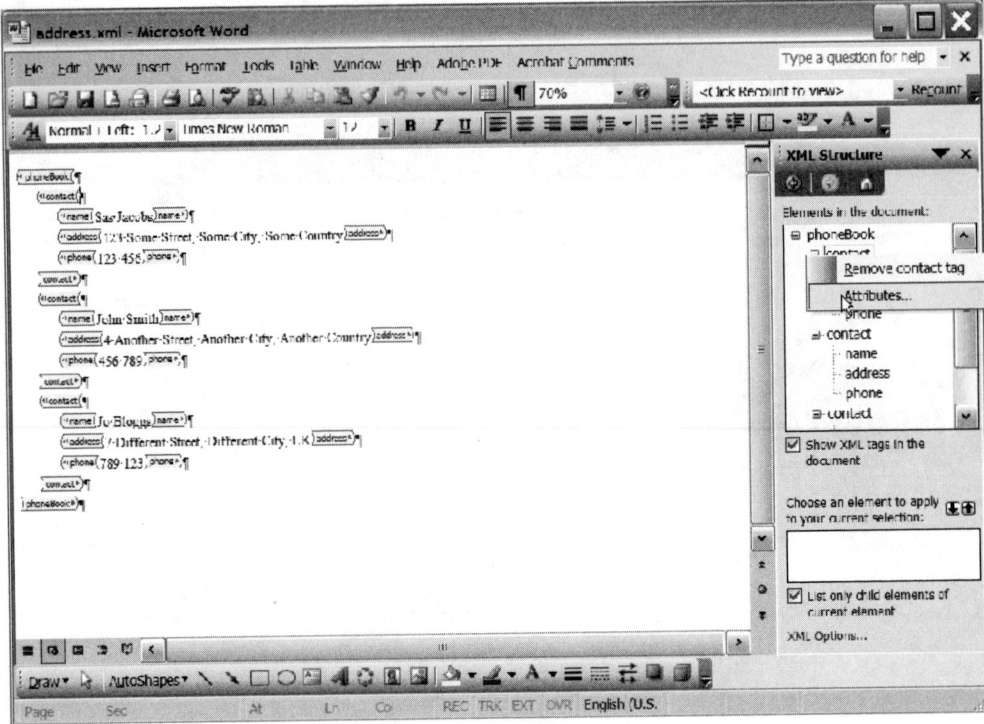

Figure 5-33. Viewing attributes from the XML Structure pane

The Attributes dialog box shows the existing attributes for the selected element. You can change the value of the attribute or delete it from the element. Figure 5-34 shows the Attributes dialog box.

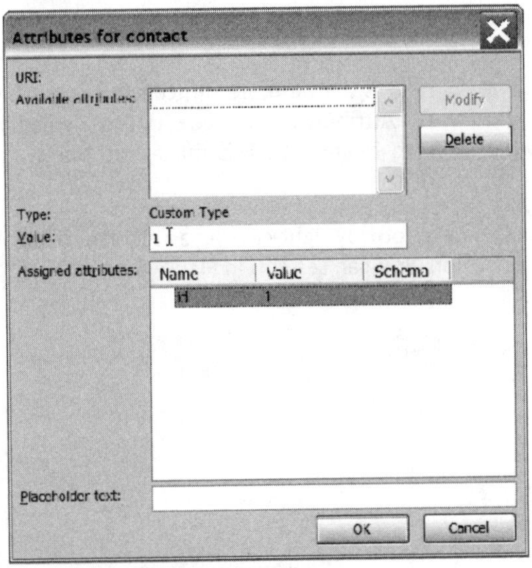

Figure 5-34. The Attributes dialog box

For some users, it may be too difficult to use the XML Structure pane to change the values of attributes. If you can't avoid using attributes in your Flash XML document, you can use other solutions to help your users. For example, you could apply a transformation that changes attributes to elements when the document is loaded. Of course, you'd have to translate these elements back to attributes when you save the document. A better solution may be to avoid using attributes.

Saving a structured XML document

Earlier, you saw the complicated XML structures generated when you used the Save As option to create a WordprocessingML document. Using a schema simplifies the XML document structure and allows you to save only the data from Word.

Make sure the document has an attached schema. Choose File ➤ Save As and select the XML Document type. Make sure you check the Save data only option before you click Save, as shown in Figure 5-35. If you don't do this, you'll generate a WordprocessingML document instead of creating your own XML structures based on the attached schema.

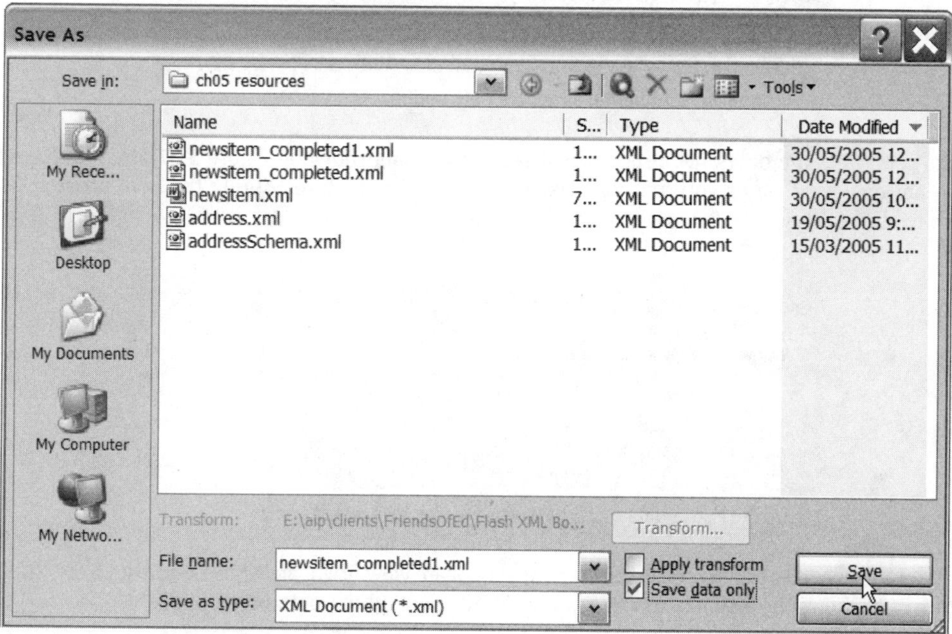

Figure 5-35. Saving a Word document in XML format

It's useful to turn on the Save data only option within Word so that it's always checked in the Save As dialog box. Click the XML Options link in the XML Structure pane and check the Save data only check box in the XML Options dialog box. You can see this in Figure 5-36.

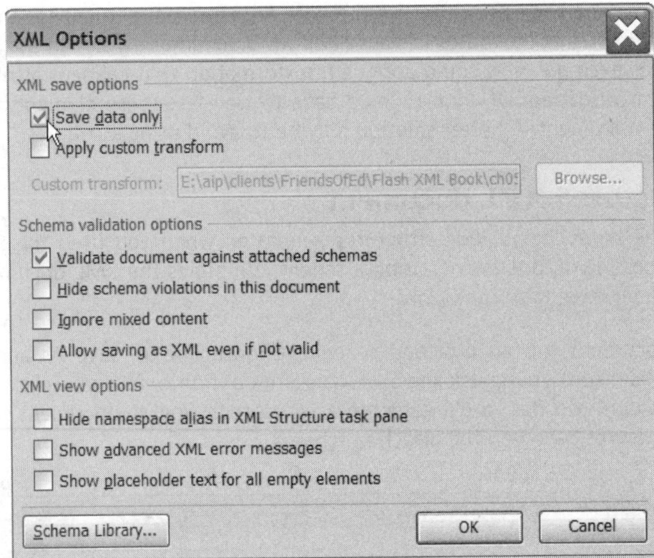

Figure 5-36. Setting the Save data only option

When you select the data only option, you'll see the warning shown in Figure 5-37 after you click the Save button. Word warns you that you may lose formatting features during the save process. You'll need to click Continue to generate an XML document.

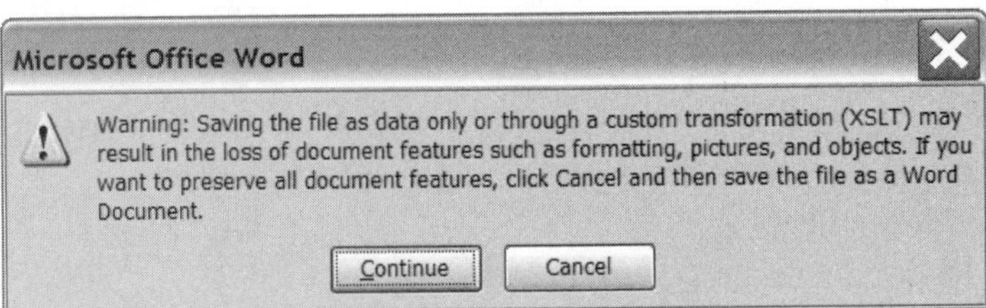

Figure 5-37. The default warning when saving XML content

Once you have created the XML document, you can view it in an XML editor such as XMLSpy. Figure 5-38 shows the XML document generated by selecting the data only option.

```
<?xml version="1.0" encoding="UTF-8" standalone="no"?>
<news xmlns="http://www.friendsofed/xml/news">
  <newsDate xmlns="">June 30, 2008</newsDate>
  <newsTitle xmlns="">First manned mission to Mars lands</newsTitle>
  <newsContent xmlns="">The first manned mission to Mars has touched down on the surface
of the red planet. After six months of space travel, the five astronauts on board MarsEx 1 will
finally experience an end to their weightless conditions.</newsContent>
</news>
```

Figure 5-38. The data only XML document created by Word

If you compare the content shown in Figure 5-39 with the equivalent WordprocessingML document, you'll notice that the new document contains significantly less content. The data only XML document contains no information about the properties of the Word document. It has no information about the formatting of the content.

Another way to generate structured XML content is by applying an XSLT transformation during the save process. If you do this, you can use the default transformation attached to the current schema. Remember that Word calls this a *solution* in the schema library. You can also apply a custom transformation.

Saving transformed XML content

You can use a transformation to change the names of the XML elements, streamline the XML elements generated, or switch elements and attributes during the save process. Choose File ➤ Save As and select the type XML Document. Make sure you check the Apply transform and Save data only options. Figure 5-39 shows how the Save As dialog box appears during a transformation.

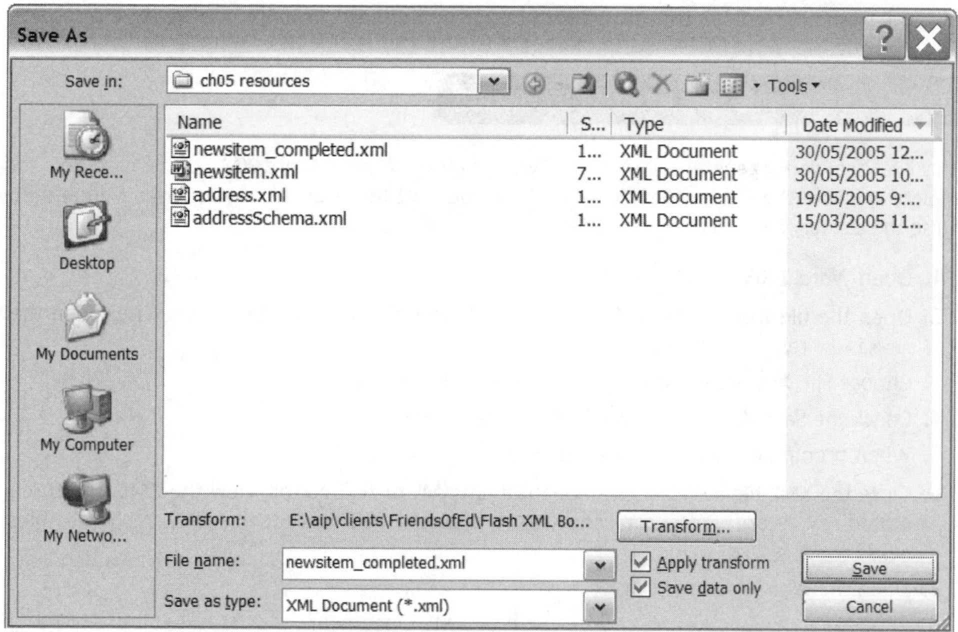

Figure 5-39. Saving a Word document with a transformation

Word will apply the default solution for the current schema. You can see this by opening the schema library. You could also use a different transformation by choosing Apply Custom Transformation in the XML Options dialog box.

Once you've saved and transformed the document, you can open it in an XML editor, as shown in Figure 5-40. Make sure you close the file in Word first.

```
<html>
<body>
<h1>First manned mission to Mars lands</h1>
<h2>June 30, 2008</h2>
<p>The first manned mission to Mars has touched down on the surface of the red planet. After
six months of space travel, the five astronauts on board MarsEx 1 will finally experience an end
to their weightless conditions.</p>
</body>
</html>
```

Figure 5-40. The transformed XML document

The screenshot displayed in Figure 5-40 shows the transformed content. The transformation applied within Word created HTML from the original XML document. You could also have used a transformation to add sorting or filtering to the XML document.

You'll understand Word 2003 transformations better by working through the next exercise.

Exercise 5: Generating structured XML content

In this exercise, you'll generate your own XML structures from a Word XML document. You should complete and save the file from exercise 4 before you start this exercise. If you haven't done this, you can use the starter file `newsitem_tags.doc`.

1. Open Word 2003 if necessary.
2. Open the file from exercise 4 if necessary. If you didn't complete the exercise, open the file `newsitem_tags.doc` instead.
3. Choose File ➤ Save As and select the type XML Document.
4. Check the Save data only check box and click Save.
5. When prompted, click the Continue button.
6. Close the XML file in Word and open it in an XML or text editor. View the XML structure generated by Word. You can see my completed file saved in your resource files as `newsitem_tags.xml`.
7. Open the Word document again.
8. Choose File ➤ Save As and choose the type XML Document.
9. This time, check both the Save data only and Apply transform check boxes. Change the name of the document so you can compare it with the one created in step 4. I saved mine as `newsitem_transform.xml`.
10. Click Save and when prompted, click the Continue button.
11. Close the XML file and open it in an XML or text editor.
12. Compare the two XML documents that you have created. You can see the two documents that I generated in the files `newsitem_tags.xml` and `newsitem_transform.xml`.

From this exercise, you can see that it's possible for you change the XML that Word creates during the save process. You can create multiple XSLT style sheets that create different XML documents from the same content. You can also use style sheets to change the output from XML to HTML.

Editing XML content in Word

You can use Word 2003 to edit an existing XML document. However, you'll need to take precautions to make sure that the editing process doesn't accidentally delete the XML tags. It can be useful to add protection to the Word document or template by locking the entire document and unprotecting the text that you need to edit.

You can protect a document by choosing Tools ➤ Protect Document. This displays the Protect Document pane, as shown in Figure 5-41. Check the Allow only this type of editing in the document: option and choose No changes (Read only) from the drop-down list. You can exempt text from the rule by selecting it and clicking the Everyone check box in the Exceptions area of the Protect Document pane.

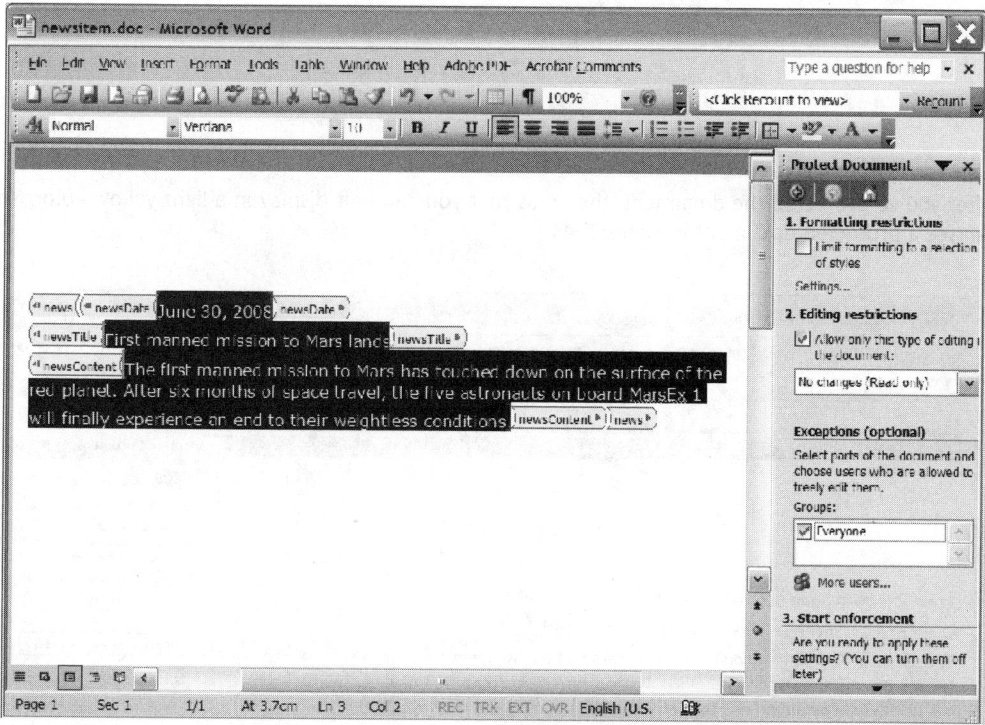

Figure 5-41. Protecting the Word document

In Figure 5-41, I've selected noncontinuous areas of the document by holding down the CTRL key to add new areas to the selection.

When you're ready to turn on the document protection, click the Yes, Start Enforcing Protection button in section 3 of the Protect Document pane. You can see this button in Figure 5-42. You may need to scroll down in the Protect Document pane before you see it.

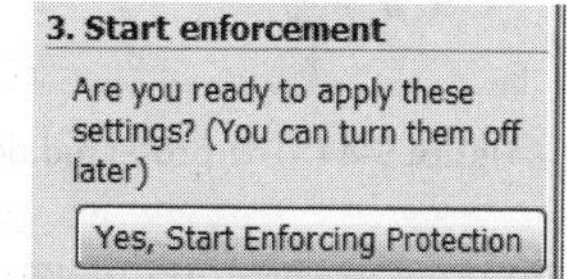

Figure 5-42. Enforcing protection in the Word document

You can add a password to secure the document and stop a user from unlocking the document. A password is optional. Figure 5-43 shows the Start Enforcing Protection dialog box.

Figure 5-43. The Start Enforcing Protection dialog box allows you to add a password.

After you've protected the document, the areas that you can edit display in a light yellow color. You can see a protected document in Figure 5-44.

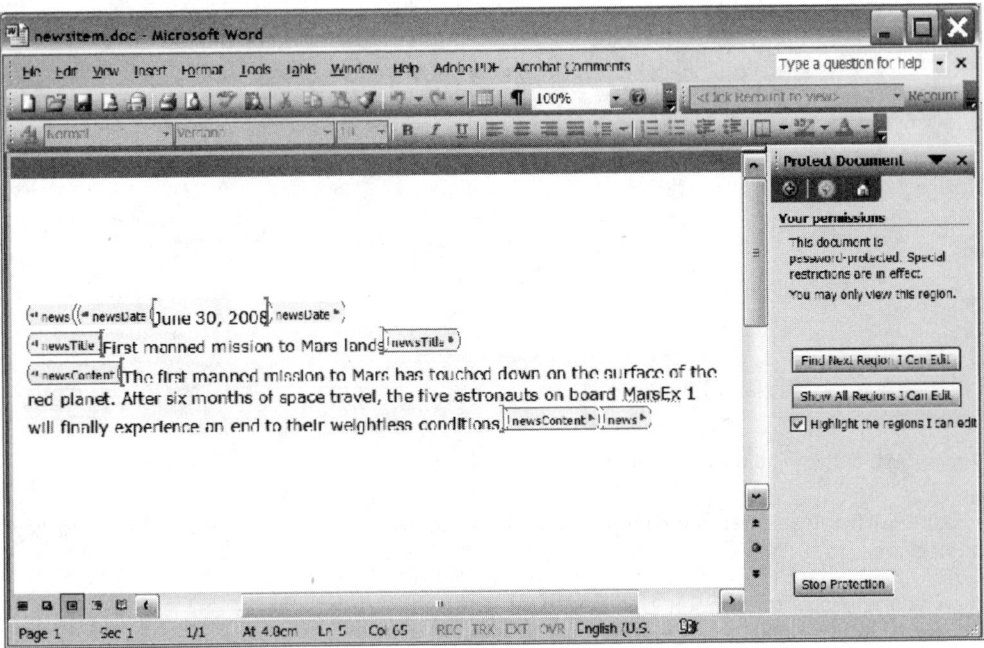

Figure 5-44. The protected document

Before you give this document to a user, it might be useful to turn off the display of the tags using the CTRL-SHIFT-X shortcut keys or by unchecking the option in the XML Structure pane. We'll cover placeholder text and document protection in the next exercise.

Exercise 6: Protecting the Word document

In this exercise, we'll add protection to the file we created in exercise 4. You should complete exercise 4 before starting this exercise. However, if you haven't done so, you can use the file `newsitem_tags.doc` instead.

1. Open Word 2003 if necessary.
2. Open the file from exercise 4 if necessary. If you haven't completed the exercise, you can use the file `newsitem_tags.doc`.
3. Make sure you can see the XML Structure pane.
4. Right-click the newsDate element and choose the Attributes option.
5. Add Enter date of news item as Placeholder text and click OK. Repeat the process for the newsTitle and newsContent elements, using appropriate text.
6. Choose Tools ➤ Protect Document.
7. In section 2 of the Protect Document pane, check the Allow on this type of editing in the document: option and select No changes (Read only) from the drop-down list.
8. Select the text within the document, using the Ctrl key to choose noncontinuous text blocks.
9. Check the Everyone check box in the Exceptions section of the Protect Document pane.
10. Click the Yes, Start Enforcing Protection button to turn on the document protection.
11. Enter a password and then reenter it again for confirmation. Click OK.
12. Display the XML Structure pane and uncheck the Show XML tags in the document check box.
13. Experiment with changing the text in the news item.
14. Remove the date to display the placeholder text.
15. Check the Show XML tags in the document check box to verify that you haven't accidentally deleted the XML tags from the document. You can see the completed document saved as `newsitem_protected.doc` in your resource files.

So far in the exercises, we've added a schema to the schema library and attached it to a new XML document. We've entered content that we've marked up with XML tags. We've generated an XML document and transformed the content. As a final stage, we added placeholder text and protected the XML tags against deletion.

The steps that you'll use to generate XML from a Word document are summarized here:

1. Add a schema to the schema library.
2. If necessary, add a style sheet to the schema.
3. Attach the schema to a Word document or template.
4. Mark up the document with XML tags from the schema, starting with the root element.
5. Add placeholder text for empty elements.
6. Protect the XML tags, if necessary.
7. Use Save As to generate XML content.

We'll use what we learned in the previous chapter to display the content of the news item in a Flash movie. We'll use Word to update the content and see how it changes within Flash.

Putting it all together

In the next exercise, we'll include the XML content generated by Word within a Flash movie. At the end of the exercise, we'll update the content in Word and see it changed within Flash.

Exercise 7: Adding the news item to a Flash movie

1. Open the starter file `newsItem.fla` in Flash. Figure 5-45 shows the interface. The movie contains a static text field with the title Latest news and a TextArea component named news_txt. The html property of the TextArea is set to true.

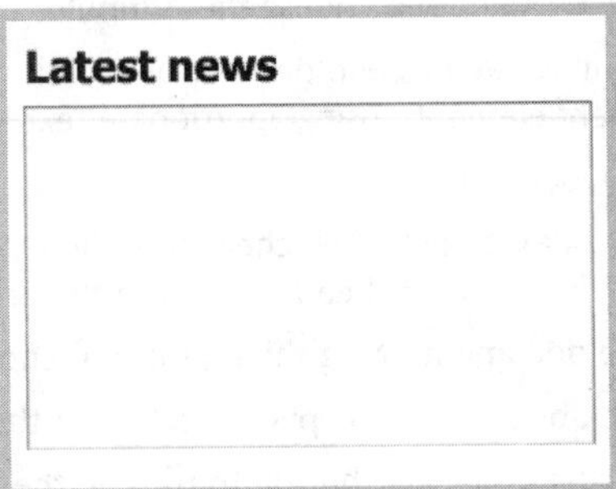

Figure 5-45. The Flash interface

2. Create a new layer called actions.
3. Open the file from exercise 6 in Word 2003. If you haven't completed the exercise, you can use the resource file `newsitem_protected.doc`.
4. Save the file in XML format, making sure that you choose the Save data only option. Enter the name `newsData.xml` for the file and save it in the same folder as the newsItem.fla file. Close the XML document in Word.
5. Switch back to Flash and add the following code on frame 1:

```
var RootNode:XMLNode;
var myXML:XML = new XML();
myXML.ignoreWhite = true;
myXML.onLoad = loadNews;
myXML.load("newsData.xml");
function loadNews(success:Boolean):Void {
  if (success) {
    RootNode = this.firstChild;
    trace (RootNode)
  }
}
```

The preceding code should look familiar to you from the previous chapter. I've created a new timeline variable for the root node as well as an XML object called `myXML`. The code loads the file `newsData.xml` and calls the `loadNews` function. The function tests for the successful loading of the XML document, sets the `RootNode` variable, and displays the contents in an Output window.

6. Test the Flash movie and you should see an Output window similar to that shown in Figure 5-46.

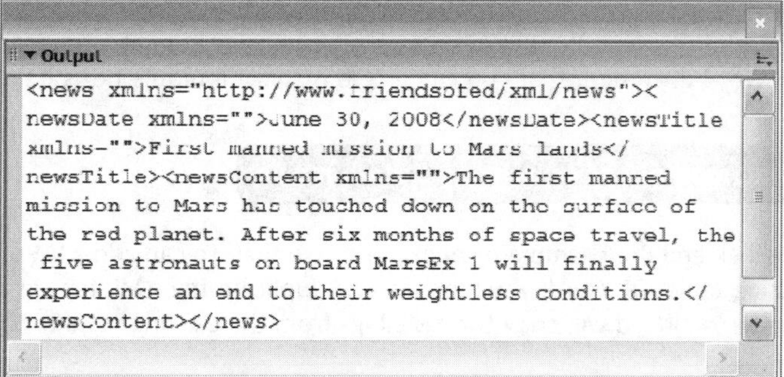
Output
<news xmlns="http://www.friendsofed/xml/news"><
newsDate xmlns="">June 30, 2008</newsDate><newsTitle
xmlns="">First manned mission to Mars lands</
newsTitle><newsContent xmlns="">The first manned
mission to Mars has touched down on the surface of
the red planet. After six months of space travel, the
five astronauts on board MarsEx 1 will finally
experience an end to their weightless conditions.</
newsContent></news>

Figure 5-46. Testing the Flash movie

7. Modify the loadNews function as shown here. The function creates a string variable called content_str that contains the complete news item. It then assigns the variable to the text property of the news_txt TextArea. Notice that I've included HTML <b> tags in the news item.

```
function loadNews(success:Boolean):Void {
  if (success) {
    RootNode = this.firstChild;
    var content_str:String = "<b>"+RootNode.childNodes[1].firstChild;
    content_str +="</b> ("+RootNode.childNodes[0].firstChild;
    content_str += ")<br>" + RootNode.childNodes[2].firstChild;
    news_txt.text = content_str;
  }
}
```

8. Test the movie. You should see something similar to the screenshot shown in Figure 5-47. You can see the completed file saved as `newsItem_completed.fla` in your resource files. You can also see the completed `newsData.xml` file.

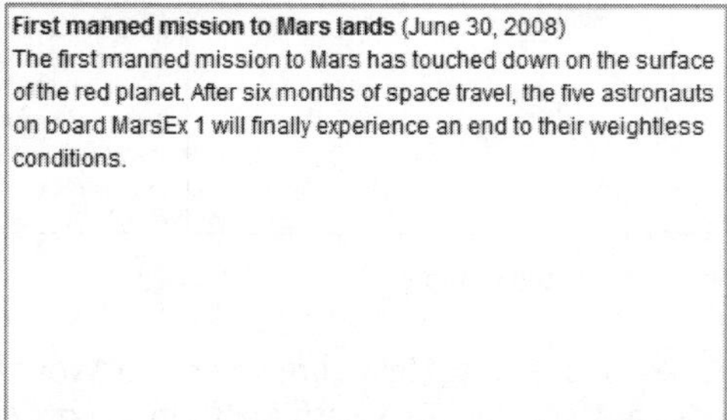
Latest news
First manned mission to Mars lands (June 30, 2008)
The first manned mission to Mars has touched down on the surface of the red planet. After six months of space travel, the five astronauts on board MarsEx 1 will finally experience an end to their weightless conditions.

Figure 5-47. The completed Flash movie

9. Make changes to the Word document and save it in XML format. Close the Word XML document and test the Flash movie again to see the updated content.

In exercise 7, we generated XML content from a Word document and used it within a Flash movie. You were able to use Word to update the contents of the Flash movie.

It would be more useful if you could display more than one news item at a time. In the next exercise, we'll create a new Word document that you can use to manage multiple news items.

Exercise 8: Adding multiple news items to a Flash movie

In this exercise, we'll extend the example from exercise 7 so that we can add a list of news items to the Flash movie. By using tables in Word, you'll be able to duplicate the XML tags in a Word document. Each time you add a row, Word will copy the XML tags from the existing rows to the new row.

Creating a new Word XML document and attaching a new schema

We'll start by creating a new Word document, attaching a new schema from the library, and adding sample content to a table.

1. Open Word 2003 if necessary and create a new XML document. You can use File ➤ New ➤ XML Document.
2. Click the Templates and Add-Ins link in the XML Structure pane and click the Add Schema button.
3. Navigate to the file `newsSchemaGroup.xsd` within your resources and click Open.
4. Enter http://www.friendsofed.com/xml/newsgroup in the URI field and newsGroup in the Alias field.
5. Click OK twice and check the newsgroup schema option. Click OK to attach the schema.

Adding XML tags to the Word document

Once you've attached the schema, you'll need to add content to the Word document. We'll add it in a table and mark up the content with XML tags from the schema.

6. Add a three-column table to the Word document. Enter a date in the first column, a news item title in the second column, and news content in the third. Figure 5-48 shows my news item.

June 30, 2008	First manned mission to Mars lands	The first manned mission to Mars has touched down on the surface of the red planet. After six months of space travel, the five astronauts on board MarsEx 1 will finally experience an end to their weightless conditions.

Figure 5-48. A news item within a table

7. Save the document as `newsTable.doc`. Make sure you select Word Document as the type and add it to the same folder as the completed Flash file from the previous exercise.
8. Click the news root element in the XML Structure pane and click the Apply to Entire Document button when prompted.
9. Select all of the text in the table row and apply the newsItem element.
10. Apply the newsDate, newsTitle, and newsContent elements to the contents of each cell within the table.

11. Add placeholder text for the XML tags.
12. Uncheck the Show XML tags in the document check box and save the document again.

Generate the XML and add to the Flash movie

You'll need to generate an XML document for use in the Flash movie. As the structure of the XML document generated has changed since exercise 7, we'll also need to update the Flash movie to display the information correctly.

13. Save the Word document in XML format, making sure that you check the Save data only option. Don't change the file name.
14. Close the Word XML document.
15. Switch to Flash and open the Flash file from the previous exercise. If you didn't complete the exercise, use the file `newsItem_completed.fla`. Make sure it is in the same folder as your `newsTable.xml` file.
16. Modify the code within the Flash file as shown here. I've indicated the new lines in bold.

```
var RootNode:XMLNode;
var myXML:XML = new XML();
myXML.ignoreWhite = true;
myXML.onLoad = loadNews;
myXML.load("newsTable.xml");
function loadNews(success:Boolean):Void {
  if (success) {
    RootNode = this.firstChild;
    var content_str:String="";
    var newsItem:XMLNode;
    var newsDetail:XMLNode;
    for (var i:Number=0; i<RootNode.childNodes.length;i++){
      newsItem = RootNode.childNodes[i];
      for (var j:Number=0; j<newsItem.childNodes.length;j++) {
        newsDetail=newsItem.childNodes[j];
        if (newsDetail.nodeName == "newsDate") {
          if (i > 0) {
            content_str += "<br><br>";
          }
          content_str += newsDetail.firstChild + " - ";
        }
        else if (newsDetail.nodeName == "newsTitle") {
          content_str += "<b>"+newsDetail.firstChild + "</b>";
        }
        else if (newsDetail.nodeName == "newsContent") {
          content_str += "<br>"+newsDetail.firstChild;
        }
      }
      news_txt.text = content_str;
    }
  }
}
```

The function loops through each of the child nodes of the <newsItem> node and adds the text to the content_str variable. If we're showing the second or subsequent news item, we add two line breaks above so we space out each news item.

17. Test the movie. You should see your first news item displayed in the Flash interface. I've shown my interface in Figure 5-49. Notice that I've changed the date and title display slightly compared with the previous example.

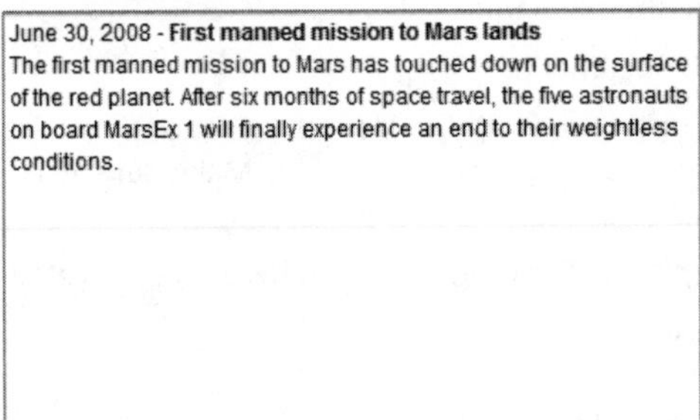

Latest news
June 30, 2008 - First manned mission to Mars lands
The first manned mission to Mars has touched down on the surface of the red planet. After six months of space travel, the five astronauts on board MarsEx 1 will finally experience an end to their weightless conditions.

Figure 5-49. The updated Flash interface

Update the XML content and check the Flash movie

18. Open the `newsTable.doc` document in Word 2003 and display the XML Structure pane. Turn off the Show XML tags in the document option if necessary.

19. Insert a row above the current row and check that the placeholder text displays. Add a news item.

20. Use File ➤ Save As to generate the data only XML content and close the file.

21. Test the Flash movie again. This time, you should see more than one news items displayed in the Flash interface, as shown in Figure 5-50.

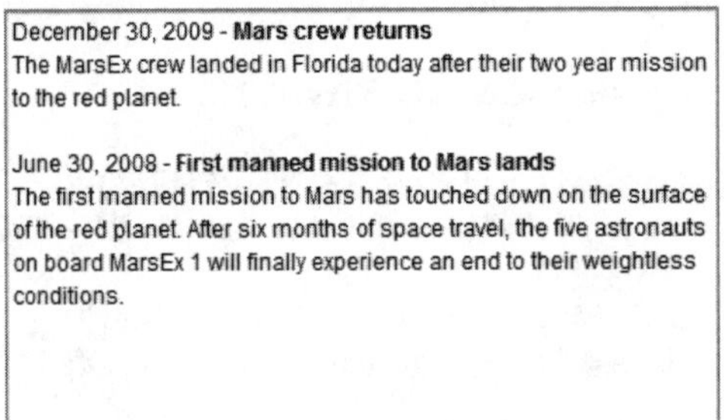

Latest news
December 30, 2009 - Mars crew returns
The MarsEx crew landed in Florida today after their two year mission to the red planet.
June 30, 2008 - First manned mission to Mars lands
The first manned mission to Mars has touched down on the surface of the red planet. After six months of space travel, the five astronauts on board MarsEx 1 will finally experience an end to their weightless conditions.

Figure 5-50. The completed Flash interface showing two news items

You can find the completed files for this exercise among your resource files saved as `newsTable.doc`, `newsTable.xml`, and `newsTable_completed.fla`. The exercise showed how to create a Word document that managed repeating items. You were able to use Word 2003 to manage the XML content for use in Flash.

Points to note from exercise 8

- In this exercise, we used a table to store the details of each news item. We added the XML tags to a row in a Word table. Each time you add a new row to the table, Word duplicates the XML tags. You could also sort the data within the table before you use it to generate XML content.
- You might notice that I didn't protect the XML tags in this Word document. Adding protection would have stopped me from adding more rows within the table and creating multiple news items.

Summary

In this chapter, we explored the ways in which Word 2003 can work with XML. We started by generating WordprocessingML from an existing Word document. During the chapter, we added a schema and style sheet and marked up the content using XML tags. We finished by generating XML from Word that we used in a Flash movie.

If you want to find out more about Word 2003 and XML, the Microsoft website provides online training at `http://office.microsoft.com/training/training.aspx?AssetID=RC011310811033`.

The site includes a quick reference card at `http://office.microsoft.com/training/Training.aspx?AssetID=RP011311071033&CTT=6&Origin=RC011310811033`. You can also find articles and other resources in the Office XML Developer Center at `http://www.msdn.microsoft.com/office/understanding/xmloffice/default.aspx`.

In the next chapter, we'll look at Excel 2003 and learn how to generate XML content from spreadsheets.

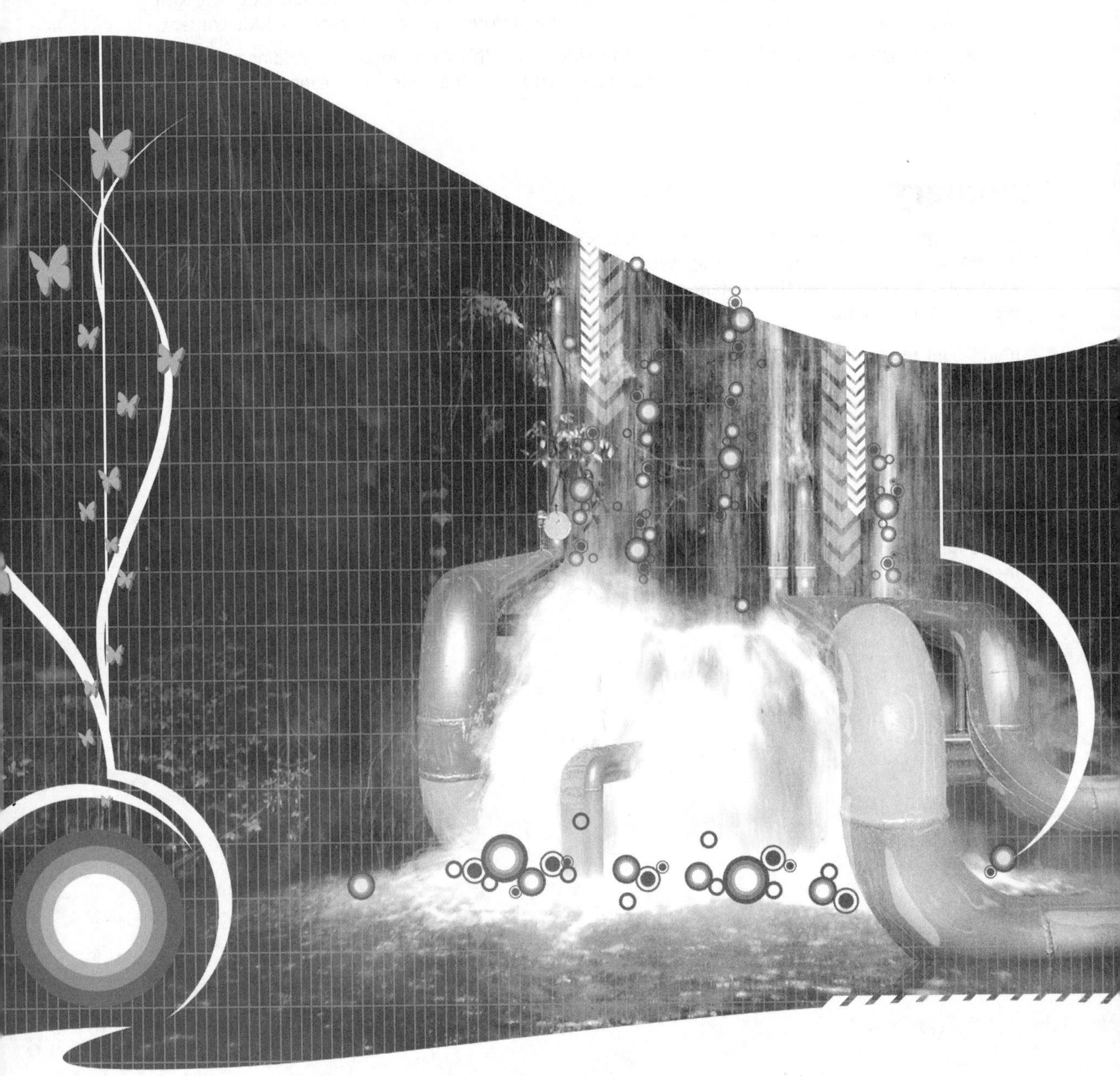

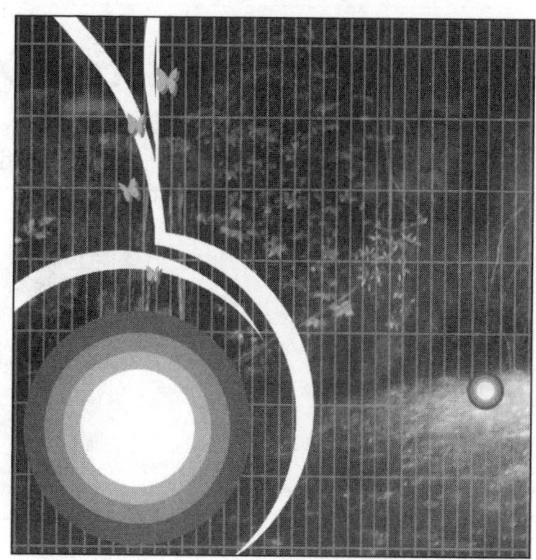

Chapter 6

WORKING WITH XML IN EXCEL 2003

In the previous chapter, you saw how to work with XML in Word 2003. I discussed why you might want to use Office 2003 to generate XML content. I also covered the data structures that are suitable for use in each of the Microsoft Office packages. Remember that Excel is most suitable for grid-like data. In this chapter, I'll show you how to use Excel to create and maintain XML documents.

Excel users have been able to work with XML since the release of Excel XP for Windows.. However, Excel 2003 extends the XML features available. The features discussed in this section are only available in the Professional or Enterprise edition of Excel 2003. There is limited support for XML in Excel 2004 for Macintosh users.

Excel 2003 includes an XML vocabulary called SpreadsheetML. This vocabulary allows you to describe anything within Excel using XML tags, including formatting and content. You can create SpreadsheetML documents in an XML editor or use Excel to generate a SpreadsheetML document.

Opening an existing XML document

Excel 2003 can open an existing XML document with the File ➤ Open command. If you are opening a SpreadsheetML document, Excel will display the contents immediately. Excel will ask how to open other types of XML documents. Figure 6-1 shows the Open XML dialog box that you'll see.

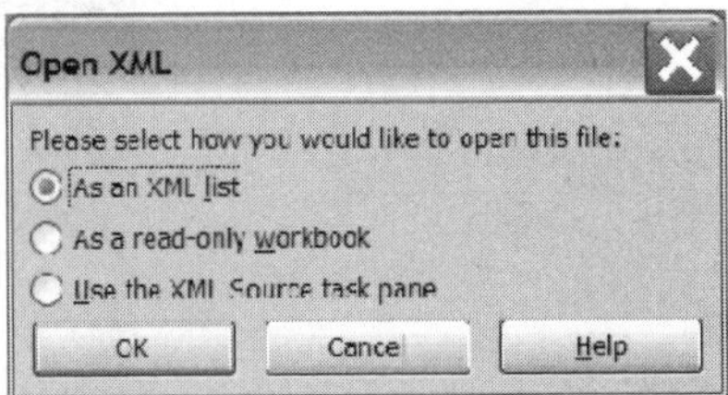

Figure 6-1. Excel asks how an XML document should be opened.

Opening as a list

When you open an XML document in Excel, you can open it as a list, as a read-only workbook, or by using the XML Source pane. If you choose the first option, As an XML list, Excel will check to see whether the document includes an XML schema reference. If Excel can't find a reference, it will create a schema, based on the data structure within the XML document. Figure 6-2 shows the message that Excel displays.

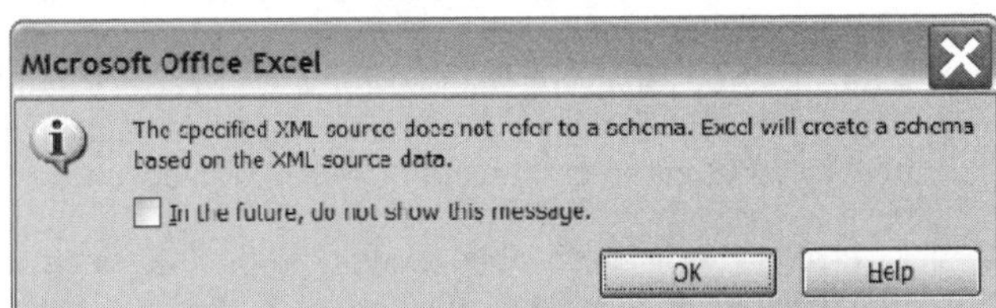

Figure 6-2. Excel will create a schema if one can't be found.

Excel imports the data from the XML document and adds it to the worksheet. The data displays in cells, and the first row of the data block contains the tag names. The row heading also includes automatic filter drop-down boxes so that you can view specific data.

Figure 6-3 shows the file `address.xml` open in Excel. You can see that the drop-down lists in the headings give you options for sorting and filtering the data by the selected column.

	A	B	C	D
1	id	name	address	phone
2	1	Sas Jacobs	123 Some Street, Some City, Some Countr	
3	2	John Smith	4 Another Street, Another City, Another Co	
4	3	Jo Bloggs	7 Different Street, Different City, UK	
5	*			
6				
7				
8				

Sort Ascending
Sort Descending
(All)
(Top 10...)
(Custom...)
123 456
456 789
789 123

Figure 6-3. An XML document opened in Excel

You might remember that in the address.xml file, the id is an attribute of the <contact> element. Excel displays this attribute in a column next to other elements from the document. Excel doesn't distinguish between the two types of data and adds the content in whichever order it appears in the XML document.

You can right-click anywhere within the data area to display the list-related functions. Figure 6-4 shows the List context menu.

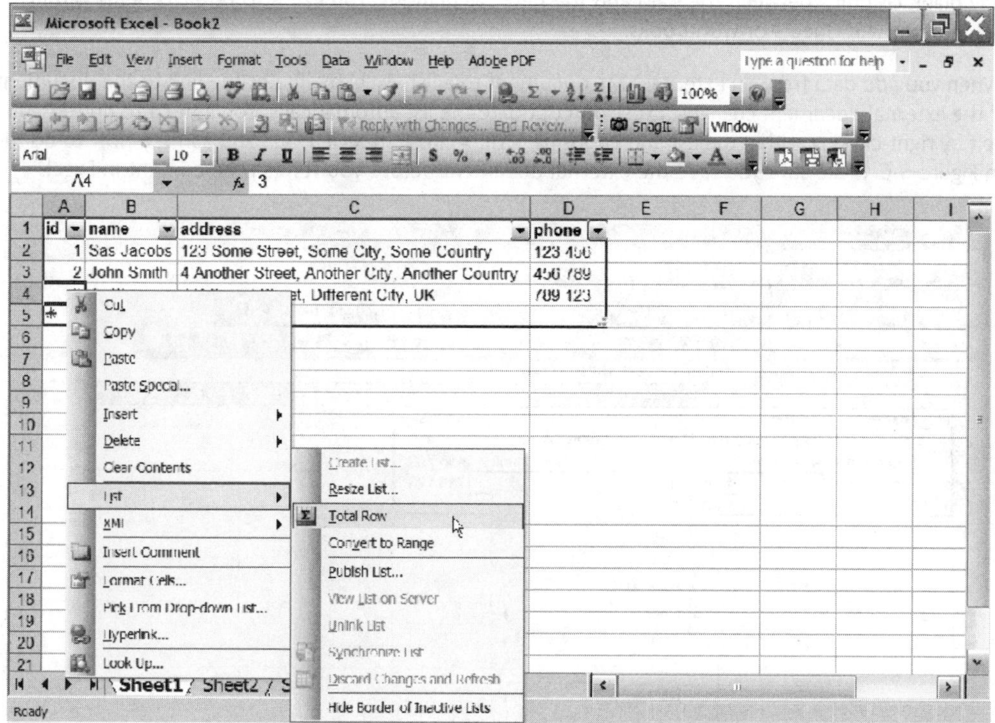

Figure 6-4. Right-click List options within Excel.

In Figure 6-4, I'm adding a total by choosing the Total Row option. Figure 6-5 shows the result.

	A	B	C	D
1	id	name	address	phone
2	1	Sas Jacobs	123 Some Street, Some City, Some Country	123 456
3	2	John Smith	4 Another Street, Another City, Another Country	456 789
4	3	Jo Bloggs	7 Different Street, Different City, UK	789 123
5	*			
6	Total			3

None
Average
Count
Count Nums
Max
Min
Sum
StdDev
Var

Figure 6-5. Displaying totals

Excel adds a SUBTOTAL function to the right-hand side column as well as a new row for totals. This function summarizes the data in the list by using an Average, Count, Sum, or another aggregate expression. I can't modify the formula within the formula bar, but I can choose a different type of summary function from the drop-down list. If I want to add a function for another column, I can click in the corresponding Total cell and make my selection.

It's useful to know that you can add calculated columns to the list. Just make sure that you don't leave any blank columns between the data and the new calculations. You can also refer to fields within the list in other worksheets or workbooks.

When you add data from an external XML document to a list, Excel maintains the link to the document. If the external document changes, Excel won't update the list automatically. You'll need to do this yourself by right-clicking within the list and choosing XML ➤ Refresh XML Data. You can see how to do this in Figure 6-6. Make sure you save the external document before you refresh the content in Excel.

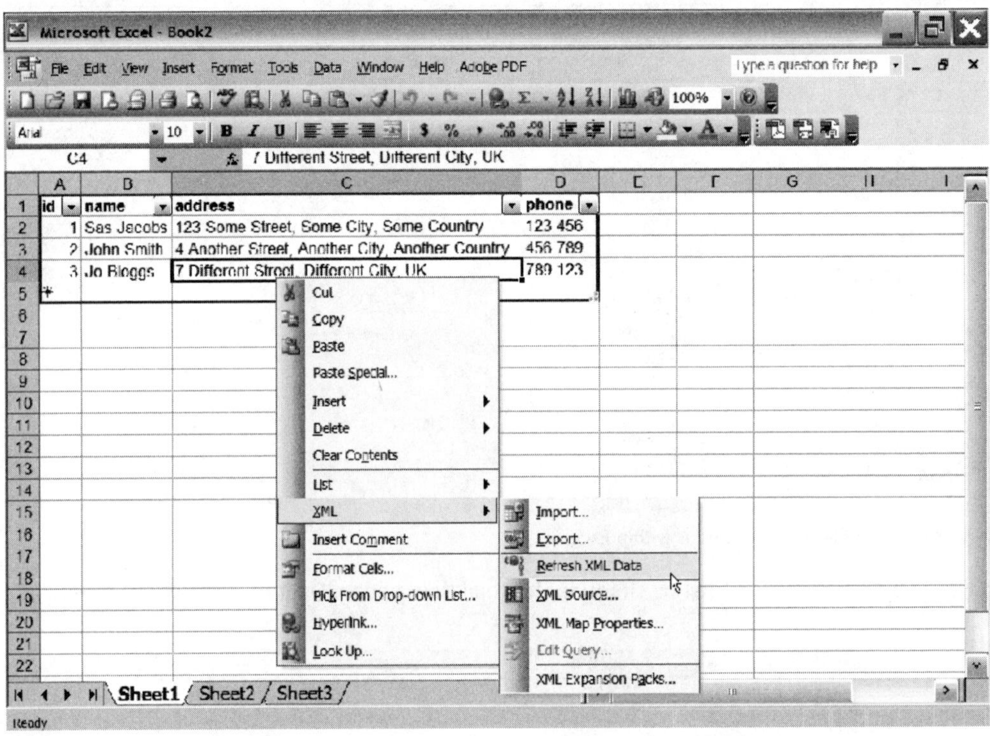

Figure 6-6. Refreshing the XML data in the Excel list

You can also edit the list in Excel and export the updated content. You'll see this a little later in the chapter.

Dealing with errors

If you try to import a document into Excel that is not well-formed, you'll see an error message. Figure 6-7 shows the error that occurs when you try to import this type of document as a list. You'll also see error messages if you try to import a document that isn't well-formed as a read-only workbook or using the XML Source task pane.

Figure 6-7. Excel cannot open a document that isn't well formed.

You can click the Details button to get more information about the error. Excel will display the XML Error dialog box, as shown in Figure 6-8.

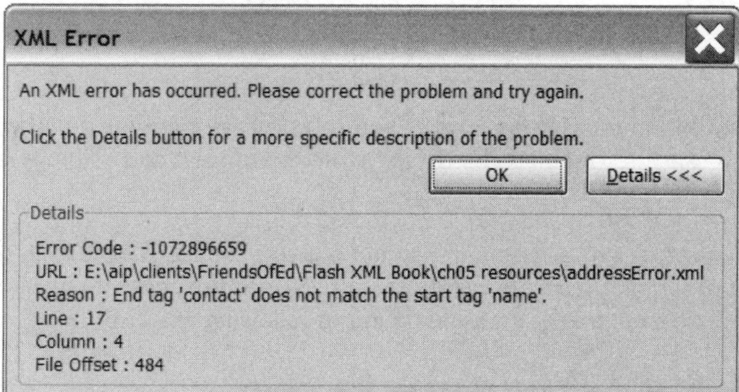

Figure 6-8. The XML Error dialog box

This error resulted from trying to open the file `addressErrror.xml` in Excel. You can find the file with your resources if you'd like to try and open it yourself. The message tells me that there's a missing end tag.

Opening as a read-only workbook

The second choice in the Open XML dialog box is As a read-only workbook. Figure 6-9 shows this choice after using File ➤ Open with an XML document.

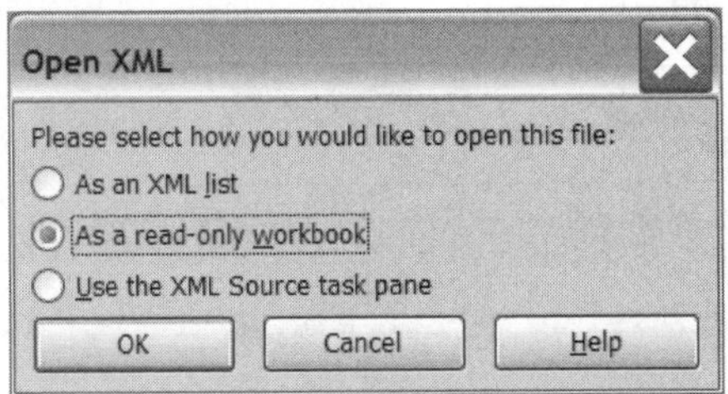

Figure 6-9. Opening an XML document as a read-only workbook

If you choose the second option, you'll see an entirely different view of the XML data, as shown in Figure 6-10. Excel displays the structure of the XML document in the headings using XPath statements. We discussed XPath in Chapter 3.

	A	B	C	D
1	/phoneBook			
2	/contact/@id	/contact/address	/contact/name	/contact/phone
3	1	123 Some Street, S	Sas Jacobs	123 456
4	2	4 Another Street, A	John Smith	456 789
5	3	7 Different Street, I	Jo Bloggs	789 123

Figure 6-10. A read-only view of XML data

Once you have the XML content in this format, you can process it as you would with any other Excel worksheet data. You can add formulas, change the structure of rows and columns, and add formatting to cells.

When you open a document as a read-only workbook, you can't export it back to the original XML document. The data itself isn't read-only, and you can still edit the content and save it to another file. You can see the two different views of XML data in the following exercise.

Exercise 1: Opening an existing XML document in Excel

In exercise 1, we'll open an existing XML document within Excel in two different ways: first as a list and then as a read-only workbook. We'll use the file `address.xml`.

1. Open Excel 2003.
2. Choose File ➤ Open and select `address.xml` from your resource files.
3. When prompted, choose the As an XML list option.
4. Click OK when Excel shows the schema message.
5. Experiment with the drop-down filters in the heading row.
6. Right-click within the list and add totals.

7. Close the document without saving and reopen it, this time as a read-only workbook.
8. Compare the document structure with the previous list view.
9. Close the document without saving.

Opening with the XML Source pane

The last option you have when opening an XML file is Use the XML Source task pane, shown in Figure 6-11. When you select this option without an attached schema, Excel will show the same schema prompt that you saw earlier.

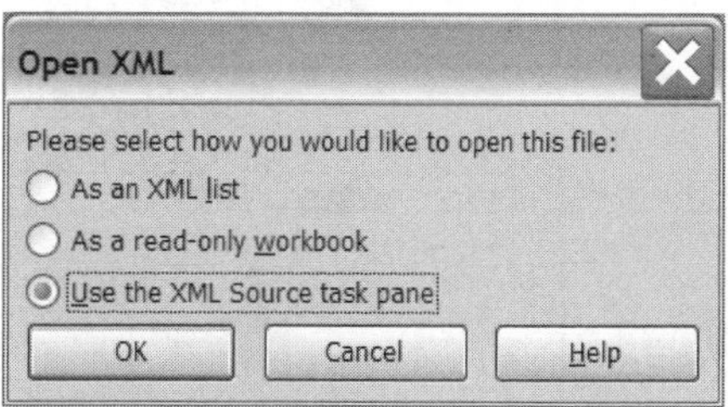

Figure 6-11. Using the XML Source task pane when opening an XML document

Excel creates an **XML map**, which is similar to a schema. The map displays in the XML Source pane, and shows the names of elements and attributes from the XML document. You can use the map to control the layout of the worksheet. You can choose which elements should appear in your list and the order of the columns. Figure 6-12 shows the document map for the `address.xml` file.

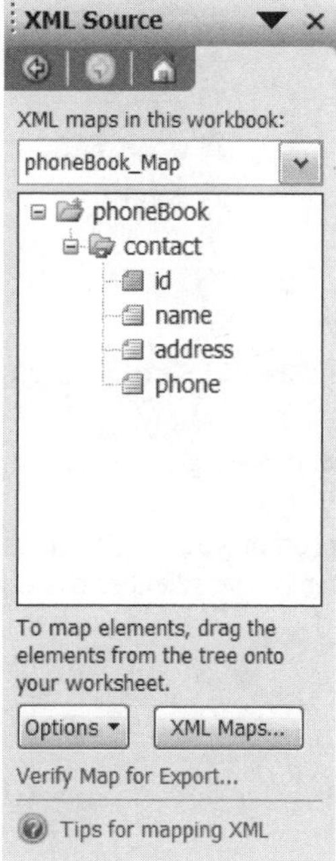

Figure 6-12. The XML map for the address.xml file

To set up your list, drag the elements from the map onto the worksheet. You'll notice that the process creates the structure for the data, rather than adding the content. Figure 6-13 shows the structure of a worksheet after adding elements from an XML map.

Figure 6-13. The list structure created from XML map elements

To add the data, you'll need to import it from the XML document. Right-click within the list structure and select the XML ➤ Import option. Make sure you click within the blue box. You can see how to do this in Figure 6-14.

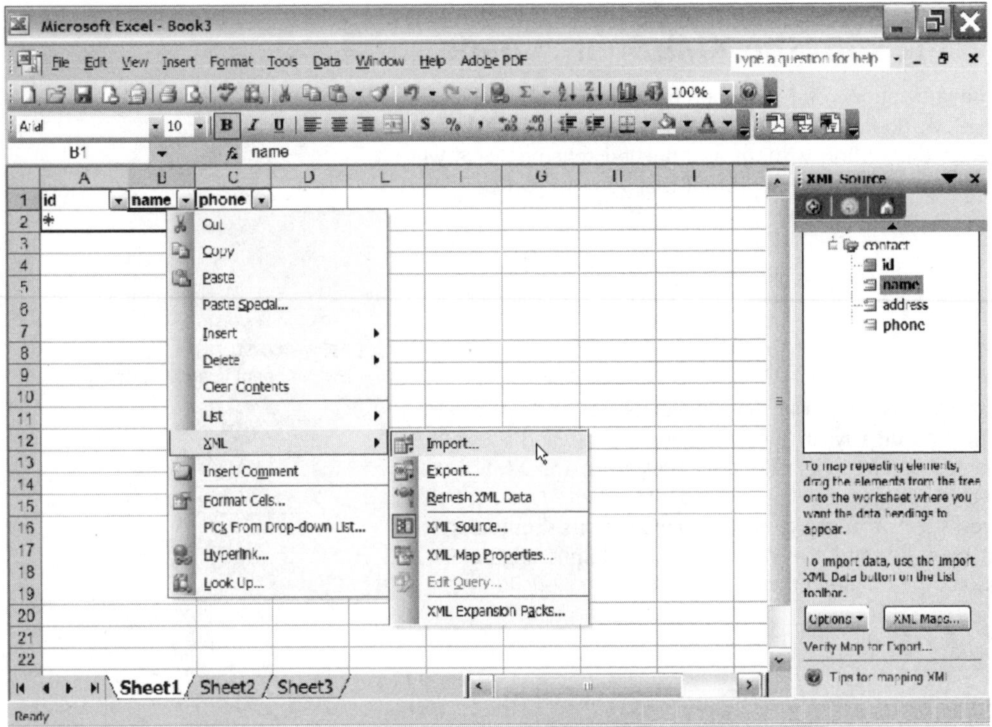

Figure 6-14. Importing XML data into the Excel list

Excel will prompt you for the location of the XML document containing the data that you want to import. After you've selected the document, Excel will add the data to your list, as shown in Figure 6-15.

	A	B	C
1	id	name	phone
2	1	Sas Jacobs	123 456
3	2	John Smith	456 789
4	3	Jo Bloggs	789 123

Figure 6-15. The imported data within Excel

Once the data is imported, you can work with it as described earlier in this section. You can sort the data, add totals, and enter new calculated columns. If the external XML document changes, you can update the contents in Excel by choosing XML ➤ Refresh XML Data.

It's worth bearing in mind that you can import data from an external document into your list at any time. Each time you import data, however, it will replace any existing content in the list.

Opening a document with a schema

When you open an XML document that references a schema, Excel displays the same three options for opening the document: As an XML list, As a read-only workbook, and Use the XML Source task pane. The only difference is that Excel won't prompt you about creating a schema for the document.

If Excel finds a schema, it will translate the contents into an XML map. You will be able to see the map in the XML Source pane. If the pane isn't shown, choose View ➤ Task Pane. Make sure that you select XML Source from the drop-down list at the top of the Task Pane, as shown in Figure 6-16.

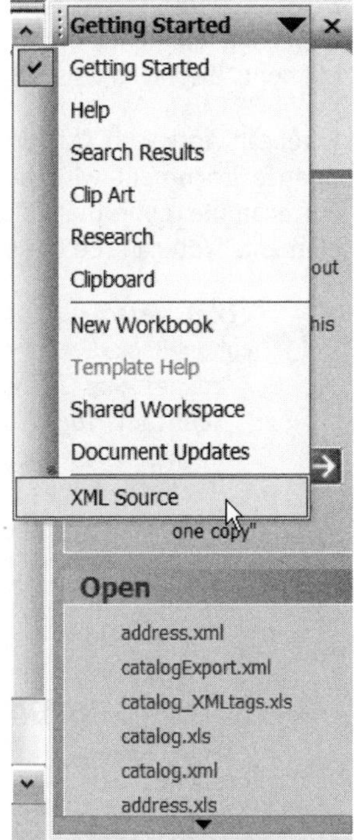

Figure 6-16. Dispaying the XML Source pane

Opening a document with an attached style sheet

If you open a document that references a style sheet, Excel will ask you whether to apply the transformation before opening. The Import XML dialog box is shown in Figure 6-17.

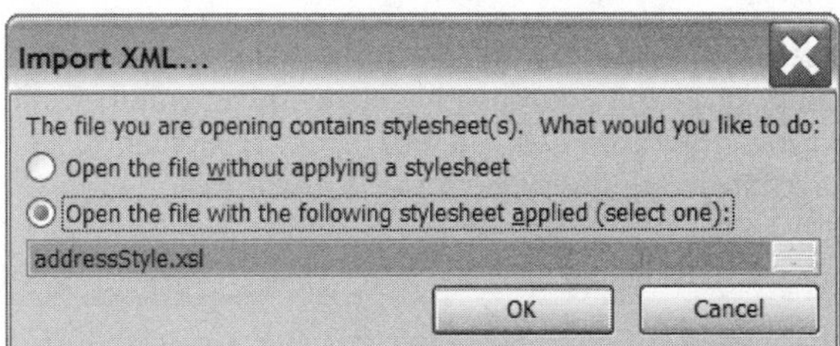

Figure 6-17. Opening an XML document that references a style sheet

You can apply the transformation or just open the XML document. If the transformation creates an XML document, Excel will prompt you about how to open the file and you can select from the same options: as a list, as a read-only workbook, or by using the XML Source pane.

Dealing with nonrepeating content

Excel recognizes two types of elements within an XML document: repeating and nonrepeating. Repeating elements occur more than once; nonrepeating elements appear only once. Repeating elements display in a list, and nonrepeating elements display in a single cell.

Excel can work with XML documents that contain a mixture of both types of elements. However, if you open a document with both types as an XML list, Excel will repeat any nonrepeating elements. For example, code that follows contains a nonrepeating <owner> element with repeating <contact> elements. You can see the content saved in the resource file `addressNonRepeating.xml`.

```
<?xml version="1.0" encoding="UTF-8"?>
<phoneBook>
  <owner>Sas Jacobs</owner>
  <contact id="1">
    <name>Sas Jacobs</name>
    <address>123 Some Street, Some City, Some Country</address>
    <phone>123 456</phone>
  </contact>
  <contact id="2">
    <name>John Smith</name>
    <address>4 Another Street, Another City, Another Country</address>
  <phone>456 789</phone>
  </contact>
</phoneBook>
```

Figure 6-18 shows the effect of opening this document as a list in Excel. Excel repeats the <owner> element in each row.

	A	B	C	D	E
1	owner	id	name	address	phone
2	Sas Jacobs	1	Sas Jacobs	123 Some Street, Some City, Some Country	123 456
3	Sas Jacobs	2	John Smith	4 Another Street, Another City, Another Country	456 789
4	*				

Figure 6-18. Opening a nonrepeating element in a list

A better solution is to select the Use the XML Source task pane option when you open this type of document. You can then position the nonrepeating elements separately from the repeating elements in the worksheet. When you import the data, the nonrepeating elements will appear only once. Figure 6-19 shows how you might structure this type of XML spreadsheet.

	A	B	C	D
1	Owne	Sas Jacobs		
2				
3	id	name	address	phone
4	1	Sas Jacobs	123 Some Street, Some City, Some Country	123 456
5	2	John Smith	4 Another Street, Another City, Another Country	456 789

Figure 6-19. Positioning nonrepeating items outside of the list

Using the XML Source pane allows you to position the elements appropriately within the worksheet and is a better option in this case.

Dealing with mixed content

So far, we've worked with simple XML documents that don't contain mixed content. You'll recall that mixed content occurs when an element contains both text and other elements as shown here:

```
<eName>Text<childName>Child text</childName> in an element</eName>
```

When you try to open a document containing mixed content, Excel can't easily place the content into a grid structure, so it must modify the content. This means that you'll lose some of the data from the original document.

I've shown the file addressMixedElements.xml next. The <address> element contains text as well as a <suburb> element, which means it is a mixed element.

```
<?xml version="1.0" encoding="UTF-8"?>
<phoneBook>
  <contact id="1">
    <name>Sas Jacobs</name>
    <address>123 Some Street,
      <suburb>Some City</suburb>
    , Some Country</address>
    <phone>123 456</phone>
  </contact>
  <contact id="2">
    <name>John Smith</name>
    <address>4 Another Street,
      <suburb>Another City</suburb>
    , Another Country</address>
    <phone>456 789</phone>
  </contact>
</phoneBook>
```

Figure 6-20 shows what happens when I open this document as a list in Excel.

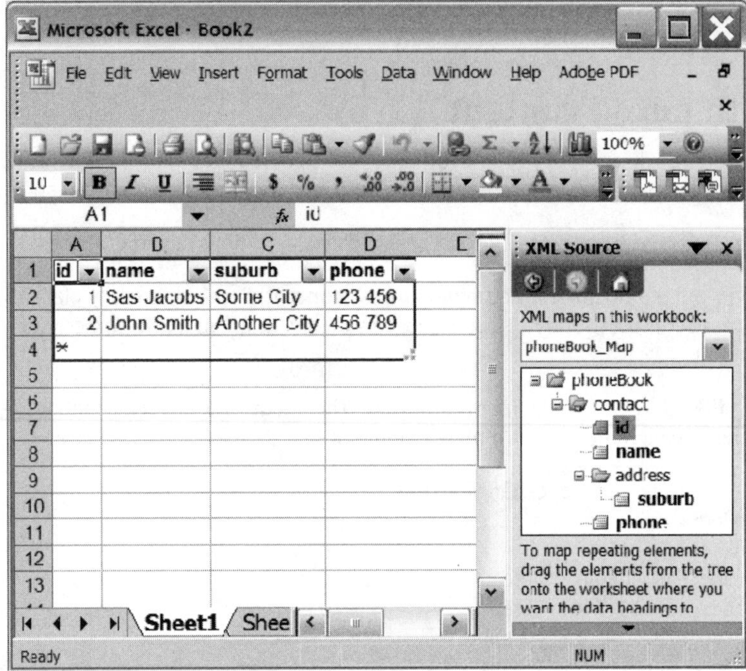

Figure 6-20. Opening an XML document with mixed content in Excel

The document map shows that the <address> element contains a <suburb> element. However, the list doesn't display the text within the <address> element. If I exported this list in XML format, I'd lose the text from the original <address> element. You'll learn more about exporting content from Excel a little later in the chapter.

The simple conclusion is that you can't work with mixed content in Excel. If you do, you'll lose some of the content when you export your data. For the purposes of Flash, it's much better to avoid mixed elements if you're going to use Excel to manage your content.

Dealing with complicated structures in a list

Another limitation of Excel is that it can't deal with complicated structures in XML lists. In the XML document shown here, I've stored <contact> elements in two different parents: the <friends> and <work> elements. You can see the content saved in the resource file `addressFixed.xml`.

```
<?xml version="1.0" encoding="UTF-8"?>
<phoneBook>
  <friends>
    <contact id="1">
      <name>Sas Jacobs</name>
      <address>123 Some Street, Some City, Some Country</address>
      <phone>123 456</phone>
    </contact>
    <contact id="2">
```

```
        <name>John Smith</name>
        <address>4 Another Street, Another City, Country</address>
        <phone>456 789</phone>
      </contact>
    </friends>
    <work>
      <contact id="3">
        <name>Jo Bloggs</name>
        <address>7 Different Street, Different City, UK</address>
        <phone>789 123</phone>
        </contact>
        </work>
  </phoneBook>
```

Excel gets a little confused when I try to open this document as a list. Figure 6-21 shows how Excel interprets the data.

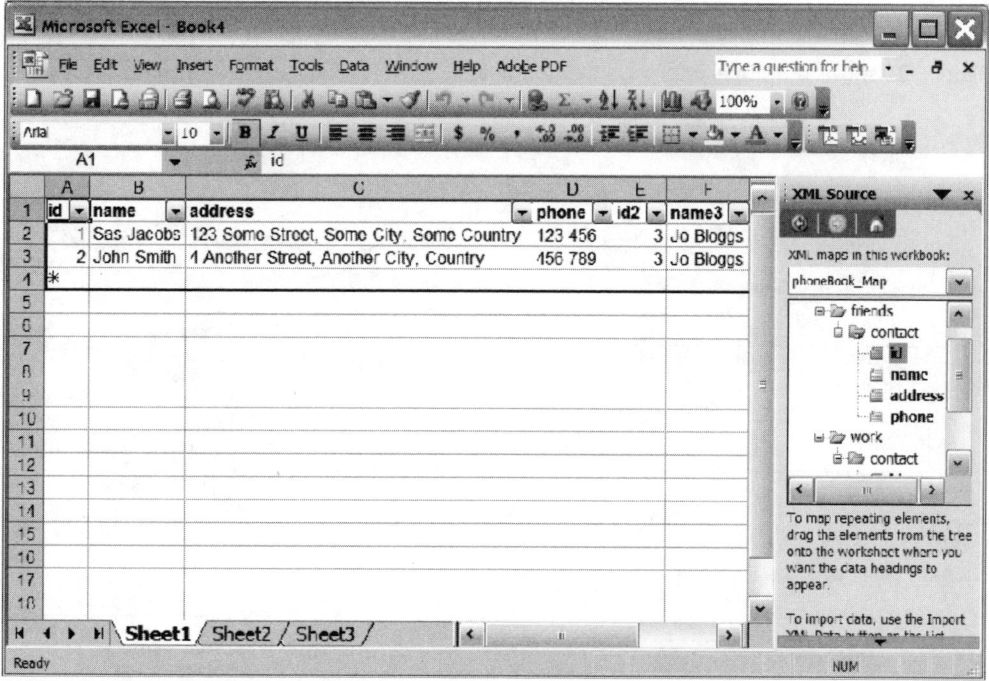

Figure 6-21. Excel has difficulty opening an XML document with a complex structure.

The <friends> and <work> elements from the XML map appear side by side. It would have made more sense to store them beneath each other with another column describing their category.

To achieve this outcome, I have to change the structure of the XML document. I've added the category as an attribute, as you can see this in the following XML document. You can see the content saved in the resource file `addressFixedAttributes.xml`.

```
<?xml version="1.0" encoding="UTF-8"?>
<phoneBook>
  <contact id="1" category="friends">
    <name>Sas Jacobs</name>
    <address>123 Some Street, Some City, Some Country</address>
    <phone>123 456</phone>
  </contact>
  <contact id="2" category="friends">
    <name>John Smith</name>
    <address>4 Another Street, Another City, Country</address>
    <phone>456 789</phone>
  </contact>
  <contact id="3" category="work">
    <name>Jo Bloggs</name>
    <address>7 Different Street, Different City, UK</address>
    <phone>789 123</phone>
  </contact>
</phoneBook>
```

Figure 6-22 shows how Excel interprets this content.

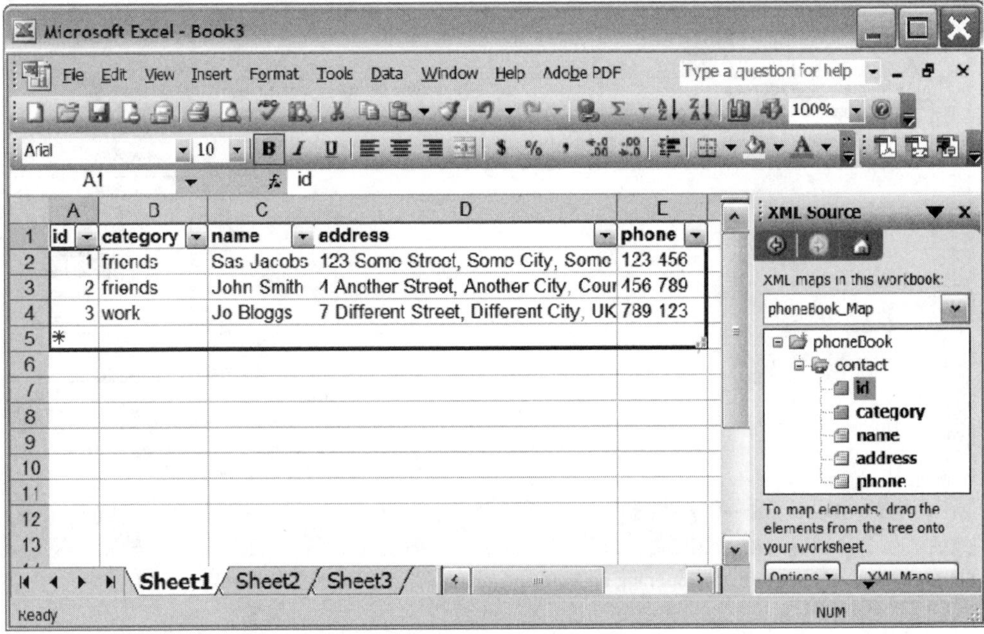

Figure 6-22. The list arising from the amended XML document structure

You can see that I had to simplify the XML document structure so that Excel could display the content in a list. The element structure is an important consideration if you're going to use Excel 2003 to manage the content for your Flash application.

In the next section, you'll complete an exercise that shows you how to open an XML document using the XML Source pane.

Exercise 2: Opening an existing XML document using the XML Source pane

In this exercise, we'll open the XML document addressNonRepeating.xml in Excel using the XML Source pane. The document contains both repeating and nonrepeating elements, and we'll use the XML Source pane to position the content appropriately. This approach provides more control over the structure of the worksheet compared with opening the XML document as a list.

1. Open Excel 2003 if necessary.
2. Choose File ➤ Open and select `addressNonRepeating.xml` from your resource files.
3. When prompted, choose the Use the XML Source task pane option and click OK. Click OK again so that Excel can create a schema from the document structure.
4. Enter the text Owner in cell A1. From the XML map, drag the owner element to cell B1.
5. Drag the id element to cell A3, the name element to cell B3, the address element to cell C3, and the phone element to cell D3, as shown in Figure 6-23. Notice that Excel automatically adds the column headings.
6. Right-click within the list structure and choose XML ➤ Import. Navigate to the file `addressNonRepeating.xml` and click Import. You may need to click OK as the list inserts rows within the worksheet.
7. Save the file as address.xls. You can see the completed file with your resources. Figure 6-23 shows the completed Excel spreadsheet.

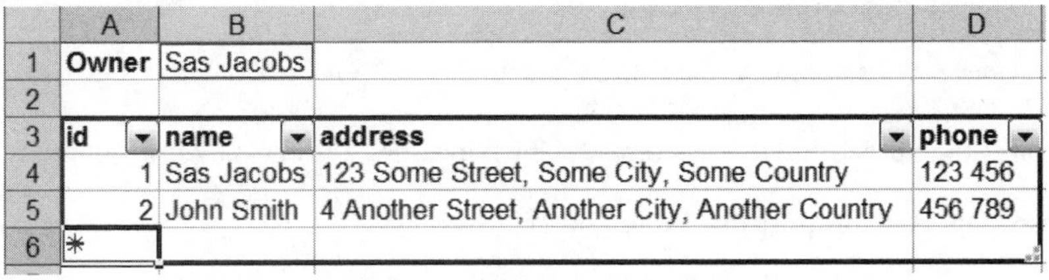

	A	B	C	D
1	**Owner**	Sas Jacobs		
2				
3	**id**	**name**	**address**	**phone**
4	1	Sas Jacobs	123 Some Street, Some City, Some Country	123 456
5	2	John Smith	4 Another Street, Another City, Another Country	456 789
6	*			

Figure 6-23. The completed Excel file from exercise 2

Using the XML Source pane provides you with much more control over the placement and structure of XML elements within your worksheet.

The process for opening an existing XML document within Excel 2003 is as follows:

1. Choose File ➤ Open and locate the XML document.
2. Select whether to open the document as an XML list, as a read-only workbook, or by using the XML Source task pane.
3. If you open an XML document that references a style sheet, choose whether to apply the transformation before opening the document.

In the next section, I'll show you how to create an XML document from an existing Excel spreadsheet. We'll generate a SpreadsheetML document and then create more structured content with a document map.

Creating XML content with Save As

You can convert any Excel spreadsheet into an XML document by using File ➤ Save As and choosing XML Spreadsheet as the file type. This command will create an XML document that describes both the structure and content of the spreadsheet using SpreadsheetML. Figure 6-24 shows how to create a SpreadsheetML document from Excel.

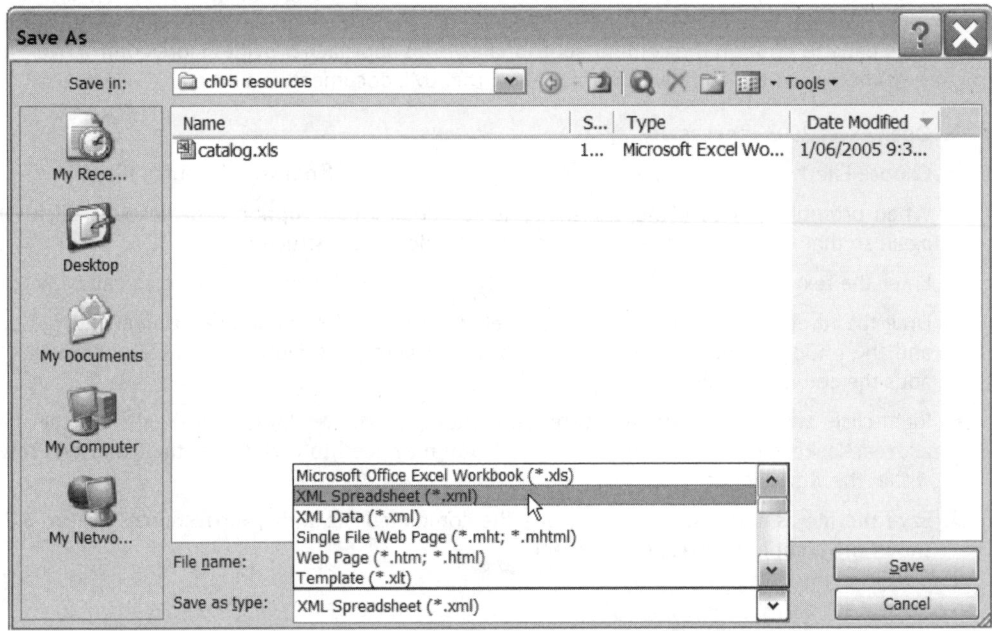

Figure 6-24. Using Save As to generate an XML document

Excel generates the SpreadsheetML document, which includes a processing instruction:

```
<?mso-application progid="Excel.Sheet"?>
```

Figure 6-25. The Excel XML icon

The processing instruction changes the icon in Windows Explorer and ensures that the document opens in Excel when you double-click the icon. If you want to open an Excel XML document in Flash, you'll need to remove the processing instruction first. You can see an example of the icon in Figure 6-25.

In Figure 6-24, you'll notice that there's an option to save XML Data in the Save as type drop-down box. You can only use this option where you have an XML map in the spreadsheet. We'll look at this option a little later.

Figure 6-26 shows XMLSpy displaying the SpreadsheetML generated by Excel.

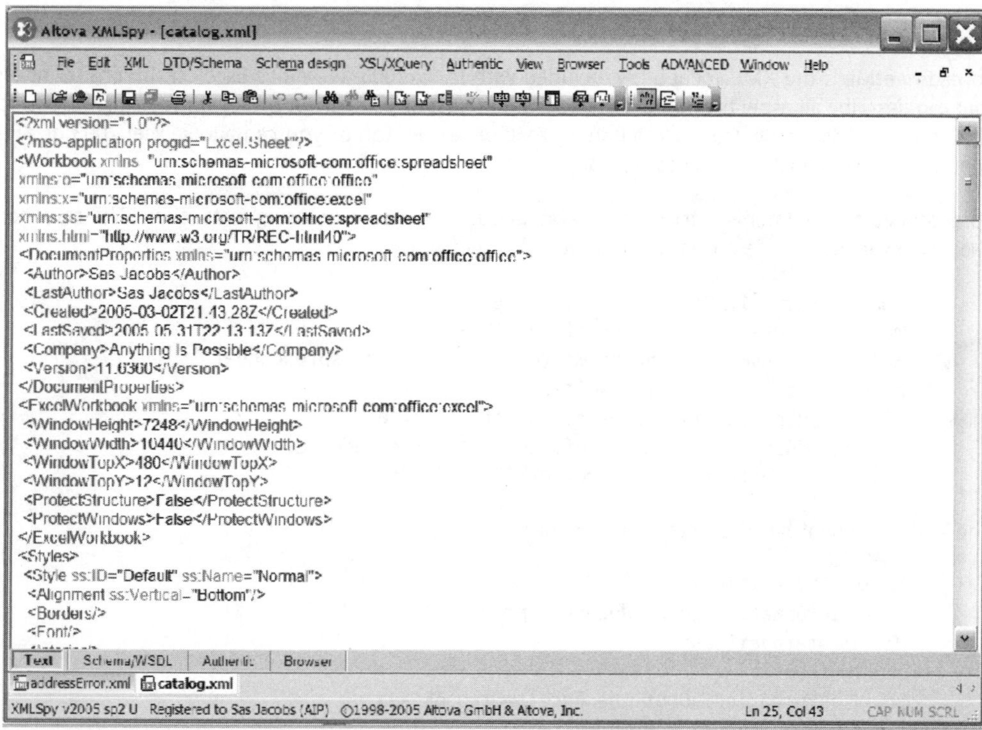

Figure 6-26. SpreadsheetML generated by Excel

You can see that this XML document is very long. It includes markup for the document properties and styles as well as the content. In the example shown in Figure 6-26, I've generated 172 lines of XML content from a single worksheet with 11 rows and 5 columns. We'll explore this further in exercise 3.

Exercise 3: Generating XML content with Save As

In exercise 3, we'll create a SpreadsheetML document by saving an existing Excel document as an XML spreadsheet.

1. Open Excel 2003 if necessary.
2. Choose File ➤ Open, and select `catalog.xls` from your resource files.
3. Choose File ➤ Save As and select the type XML Spreadsheet. Don't change the document name. Click Save. The XML document looks the same as any other spreadsheet when it is open in Excel. You can find the saved document `catalog.xml` in your resource files.
4. Close the XML file in Excel and reopen it in an XML or text editor.
5. Scroll through the file and look at the SpreadsheetML. Notice that some `<Cell>` elements have a formula attribute as well as the calculated value.
6. Close the file.

Understanding SpreadsheetML

SpreadsheetML is the XML vocabulary included with Excel 2003 as well as Excel XP. It consists of tags that can describe all aspects of an Excel spreadsheet. Just as you can with WordprocessingML, you can write the SpreadsheetML from scratch in an XML or text editor, or you can allow Excel 2003 or XP to generate the content for you automatically.

SpreadsheetML documents start with an XML declaration and processing instruction. The root node <Workbook> includes references to a number of namespaces.

```
<?xml version="1.0"?>
<?mso-application progid="Excel.Sheet"?>
<Workbook xmlns="urn:schemas-microsoft-com:office:spreadsheet"
 xmlns:o="urn:schemas-microsoft-com:office:office"
 xmlns:x="urn:schemas-microsoft-com:office:excel"
 xmlns:ss="urn:schemas-microsoft-com:office:spreadsheet"
 xmlns:html="http://www.w3.org/TR/REC-html40">
```

The XML document has the following structure:

```
<DocumentProperties>
  <!-- information about document properties -->
</DocumentProperties>
<ExcelWorkbook>
  <!-- information about the Excel workbook -->
</ExcelWorkbook>
<Styles>
  <!-- information about the styles -->
</Styles>
<Worksheet>
  <Table>
    <!-- multiple Column tags -->
    <Column />
    <!-- multiple Row blocks -->
    <Row>
      <Cell>
        <!-- Cell data type and contents -->
      </Cell>
      <!-- multiple Cell tags -->
    </Row>
  </Table>
  <WorksheetOptions>
  <!-- information about the Worksheet options -->
  </WorksheetOptions>
  <Sorting>
    <!-- information about sorting -->
  </Sorting>
</Worksheet>
```

The contents of the Excel worksheet are contained within the <Table> element. The element contains two attributes, ExpandedColumnCount and ExpandedRowCount, which indicate the table size. The <Table> element contains a number of <Row> elements, which in turn contain <Cell> elements. A <Data> child element contains the content of each cell. It has an attribute Type, which indicates the datatype of the contents. It's also possible for a <Cell> to include a Formula attribute that reflects the Excel formula used to generate the data.

When Excel opens a SpreadsheetML document, it won't prompt you about how to open the document. It opens the document natively, as if it was an Excel workbook. This is one of the advantages of working with SpreadsheetML documents. When you work with other XML documents, Excel prompts about how the file should be opened.

If you're using Excel to generate XML content for Flash, you may find the structure of a SpreadsheetML document a little unwieldy. It contains formatting information that you're unlikely to need, and all of the content for inclusion within Flash will be in the <Row> and child <Cell> elements. You'd be better off exporting the XML content from Excel using an XML map to refine the document structure.

Creating structured XML from an Excel document

Although SpreadsheetML is easy to understand and navigate, it is likely to be more useful to apply your own structures to Excel XML documents before you use them in Flash. You can do this by using an XML map in the document. We saw examples of XML maps earlier in this chapter.

You'll need to start by creating an XML schema for Excel to use as a document map. The schema specifies the valid elements and their relationship to each other. A schema document lists the rules for creating your XML document, and Excel uses this to generate structured XML data. You can find out more about XML schemas in Chapter 3.

Creating an XML map in Excel

An XML map is equivalent to a schema for a list of XML data within Excel 2003. Excel automatically generates the map from either a schema file or the structure of an existing XML document.

Before you create an XML map, you'll need to display the XML Source pane by choosing View ➤ Task Pane and selecting XML Source from the drop-down list at the top. Click the XML Maps button at the bottom right of the pane to bring up the XML Maps dialog box. You can see this in Figure 6-27.

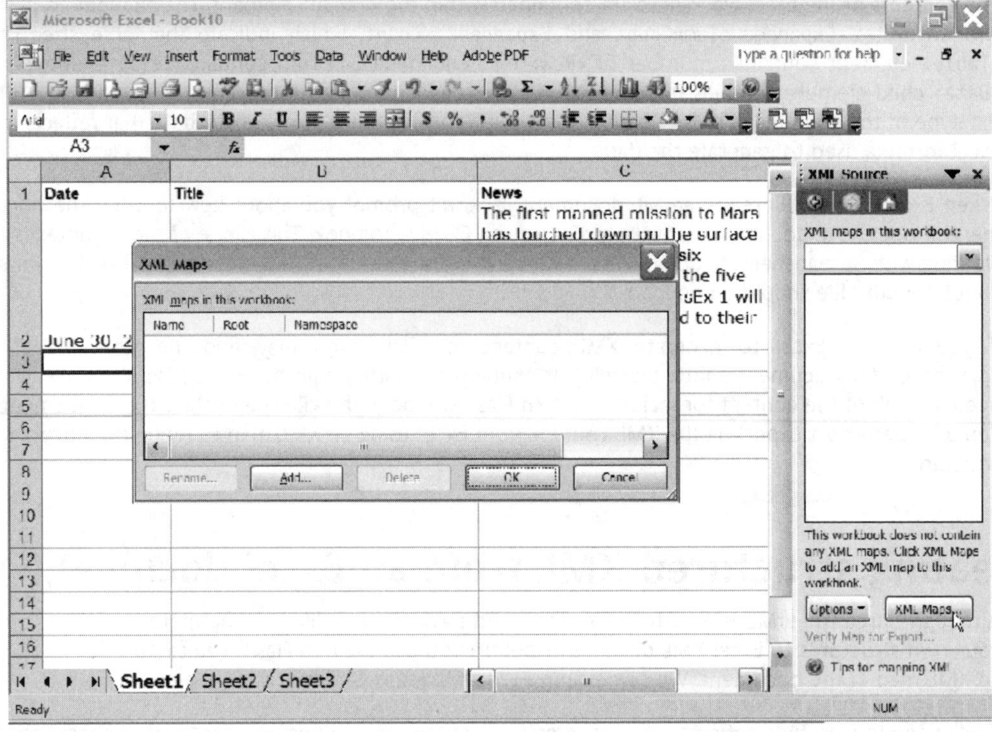

Figure 6-27. Displaying the XML Maps dialog box

You can add a map by clicking the Add button. Excel will prompt you for the location of an existing schema or XML file. It will then add the map to the XML Maps dialog box, as Figure 6-28 shows.

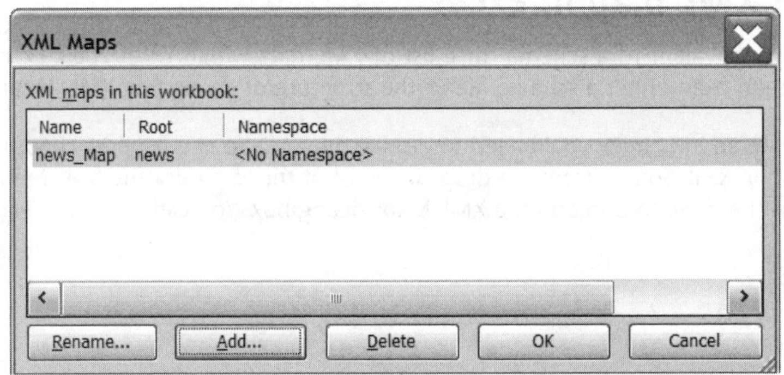

Figure 6-28. The completed XML Maps dialog box

Click OK to display the XML map in the XML Source pane. You can't modify the structure of the map, although you can rename and delete the map by clicking the XML Maps button in the XML Source pane. To change the structure, you'll need to alter the external file and then add it again.

Adding XML elements to Excel data

Once you've added the XML map to a document, you can drag the elements to sections of the worksheet. This creates the document structure. You can import data from an external XML document as described earlier in this section. You can also drag the elements to existing content. Whichever approach you use, it's useful to add headings to the worksheet to describe the contents.

To add an element to existing text, click the element name and drag it to the worksheet, as shown in Figure 6-29. You don't have to map all text within a worksheet to XML elements.

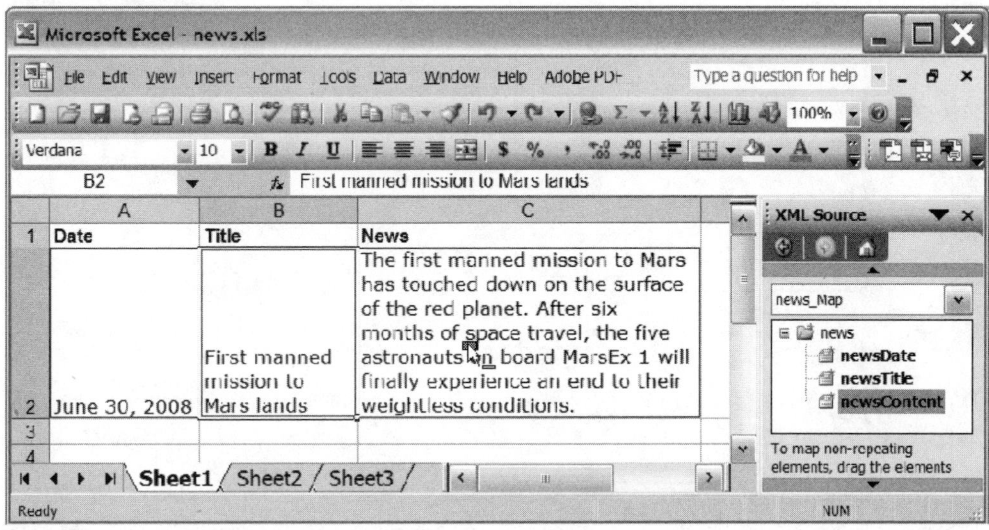

Figure 6-29. Dragging elements from the XML map to the worksheet

Excel provides options for dealing with headings, as shown in Figure 6-30. If you didn't enter a heading, you can ask Excel to insert one for you. You can also mark an existing heading row.

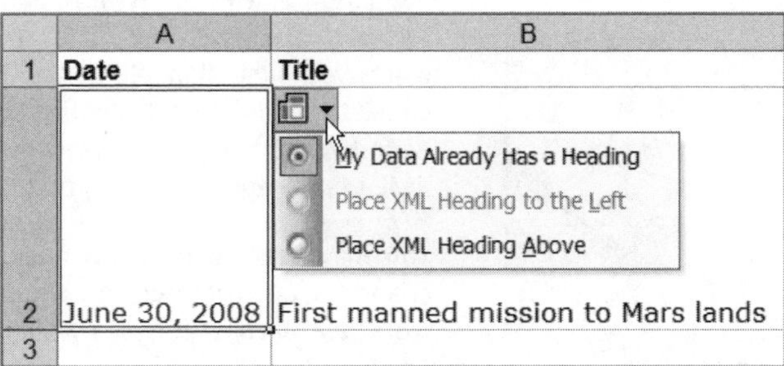

Figure 6-30. Selecting a heading option

You need to drag map elements to each area of data that you want to mark up. If you drag a nonrepeating element, Excel maps the element to a single cell. If you drag a repeating element, Excel will map the element to a list. Your document can have a mix of both repeating and nonrepeating elements. Make sure there aren't any blank rows and columns within your list.

You can modify the properties of the XML map by right-clicking within the list area and choosing XML ➤ XML Map Properties. This is shown in Figure 6-31.

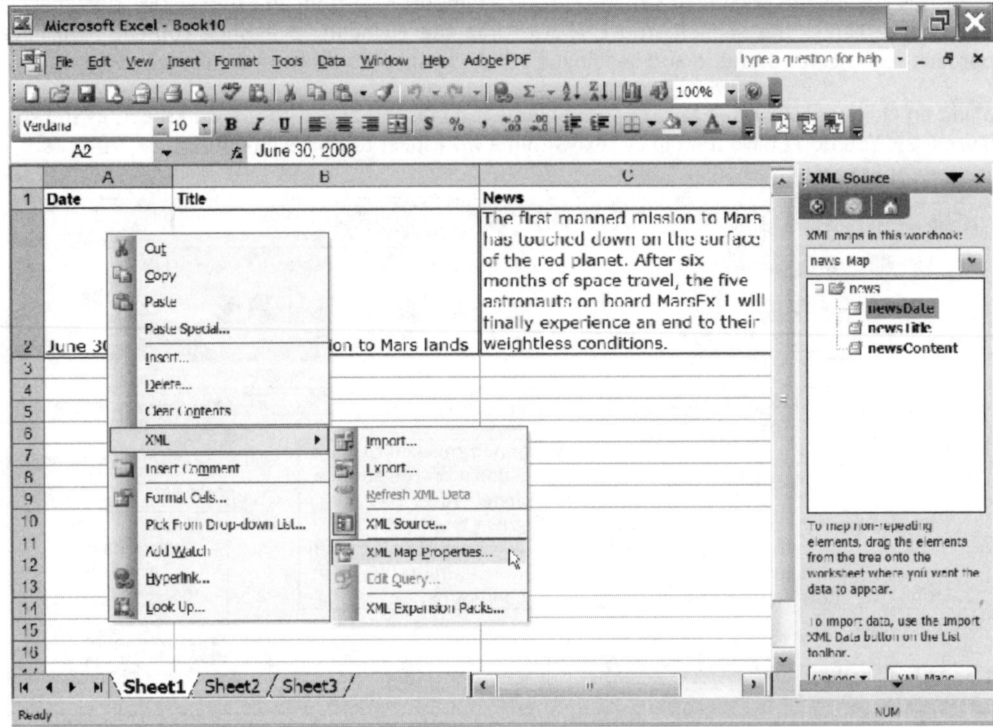

Figure 6-31. Choosing XML Map Properties

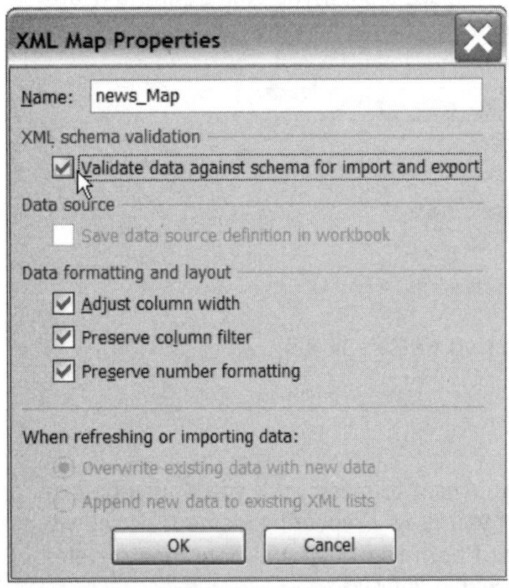

Figure 6-32. Enabling the validation option

You can use the XML Map Properties dialog box to turn validation on and off within the document. Validation will check if new data that you add conforms to the XML map. It also checks existing data when you first map elements. To enable validation, check the Validate data against schema for import and export option. Figure 6-32 shows the option in the XML Map Properties dialog box.

You may need to turn this option on and off as you change data structures and experiment with different worksheet layouts for your XML data.

Saving a structured XML document

Once you've added XML map elements to an Excel document, you can export structured XML data. Right-click within your data and choose XML ➤ Export, as shown in Figure 6-33.

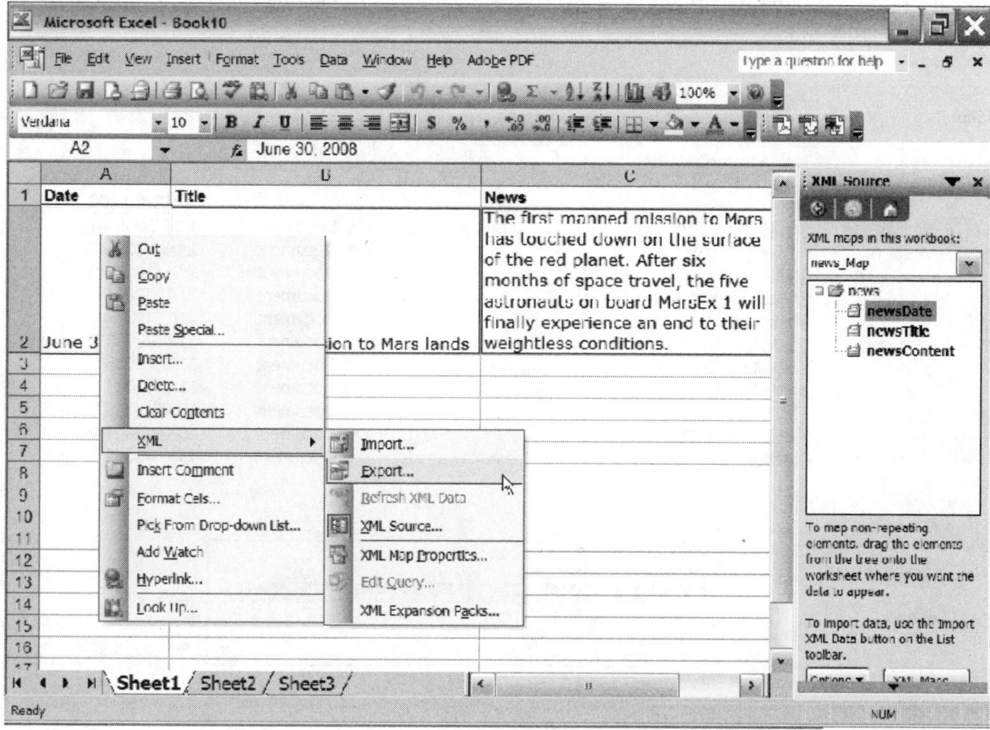

Figure 6-33. Exporting XML data from Excel

Exporting creates a document based on your schema or XML map. It will create a much smaller document than the equivalent SpreadsheetML content. The export process generates an XML declaration and XML element names from the document map. It is equivalent to selecting the Save data only option in Word 2003. Excel discards information about formatting and document properties during the export. Figure 6-34 shows the exported data opened in XMLSpy.

```
<?xml version="1.0" encoding="UTF-8" standalone="yes"?>
<news>
   <newsDate>June 30, 2008</newsDate>
   <newsTitle>First manned mission to Mars lands</newsTitle>
   <newsContent>The first manned mission to Mars has touched down on the surface of the red
planet. After six months of space travel, the five astronauts on board MarsEx 1 will finally
experience an end to their weightless conditions.</newsContent>
</news>
```

Figure 6-34. XML content exported from Excel

Because this document is considerably shorter than the SpreadsheetML equivalent, it's likely to be much easier to work with in Flash. As I pointed out earlier, you'll need to create an XML schema first. Each time you open the XML document in Excel, you'll be prompted about how the document should be opened, that is, as a list, as a read-only workbook, or using the XML Source pane.

You can create the same document by using File ➤ Save As and selecting the XML Data option. This is shown in Figure 6-35.

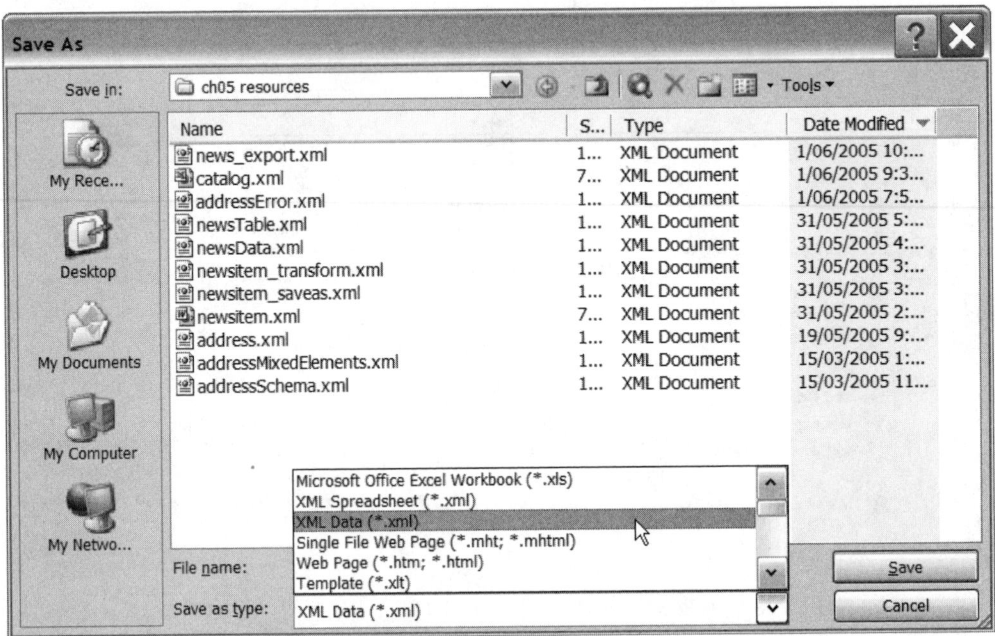

Figure 6-35. Using Save As with the XML Data option

When you click the Save button, you'll see the warning shown in Figure 6-36.

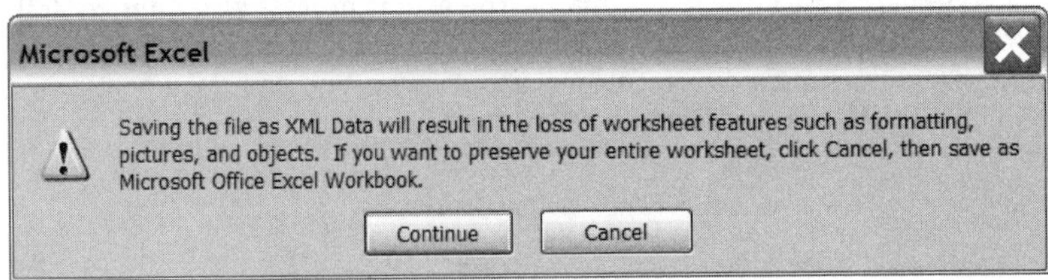

Figure 6-36. Loss of features warning when saving as XML data

Excel warns that you'll lose formatting information during the save process. You'll need to click the Continue button to save the data in XML format.

You've seen two methods of generating XML content from Excel. The first method used Save As to create a SpreadsheetML document from an Excel spreadsheet. You'd use this approach if you wanted to be able to preserve formatting and document properties in the XML document. Excel can open this document natively, as if it was an Excel spreadsheet.

The second approach used an XML schema to create a document map for the Excel file. This approach is useful if you need to have more control over the XML document created by Excel. Document maps allow you to structure elements and choose which content to export. You can also exclude unnecessary information such as cell and number formatting. If you're using the XML document in Flash, the second approach is usually the better option as it generates streamlined documents. The disadvantage is that Excel will prompt each time about how to open the XML document.

Let's work through an exercise so you can practice exporting XML data from Excel.

Exercise 4: Generating structured XML content from Excel

In this exercise, we'll add an XML map to an existing Excel document. You'll mark up elements within the spreadsheet and export the content.

1. Open Excel 2003 if necessary.
2. Choose File ➤ Open and select `catalog.xls` from your resource files.
3. If you can't see the XML Source pane, choose View ➤ Task Pane and select XML Source from the drop-down list at the top of the pane.
4. Click the XML Maps button in the XML Source pane.
5. Click the Add button in the XML Maps dialog box.
6. Select the file `catalogSchema.xsd` and click the Open button. Click OK. Figure 6-37 shows how the Excel document should appear at this point.

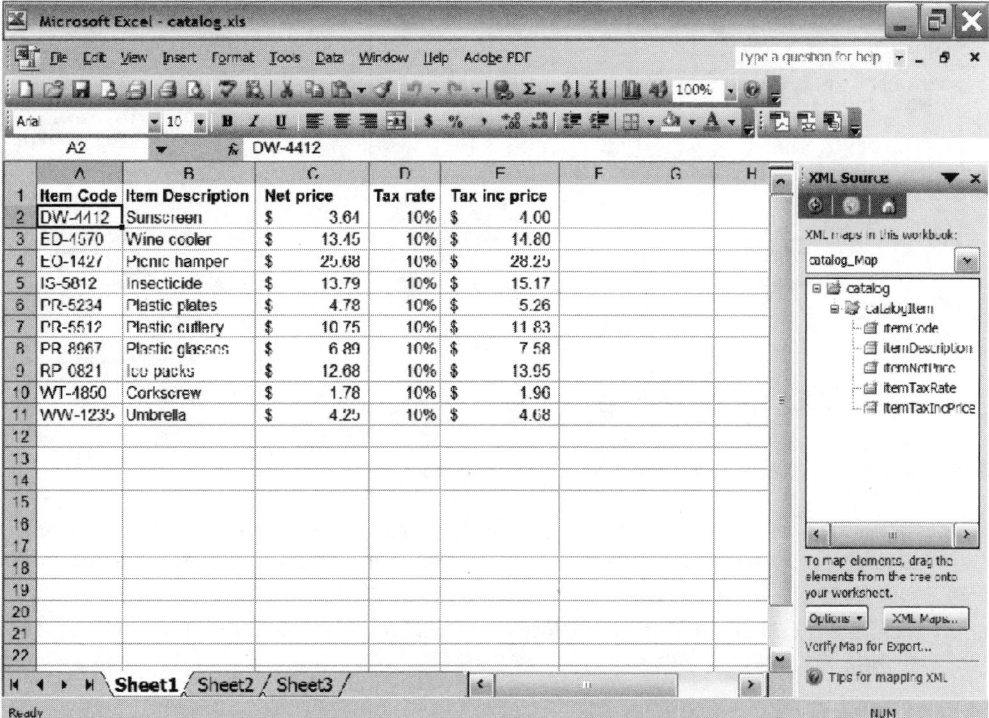

Figure 6-37. The catalog.xml file with XML map

7. Drag the <itemCode> element from the XML map to the Item Code heading in the spreadsheet. Repeat with the remaining elements. When you work with the <itemTaxRate> element, you'll see the message shown in Figure 6-38. Click the Use existing formatting button. The message occurred because the schema defines the content as a String datatype whereas Excel has formatted the cells as numbers.

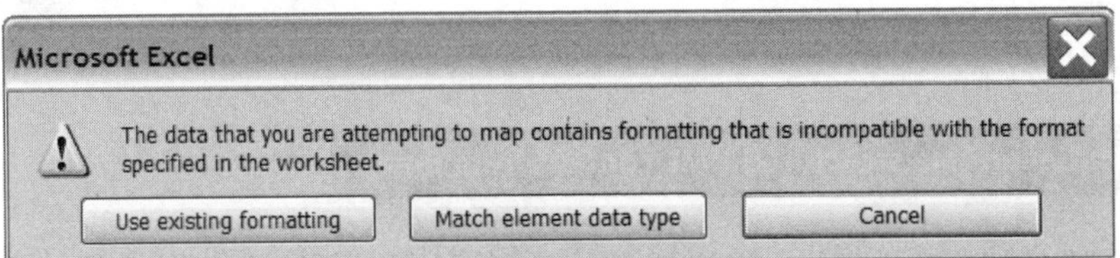

Figure 6-38. When a datatype mismatch is detected, Excel asks about cell formatting.

You can see the Excel file completed to this point in Figure 6-39.

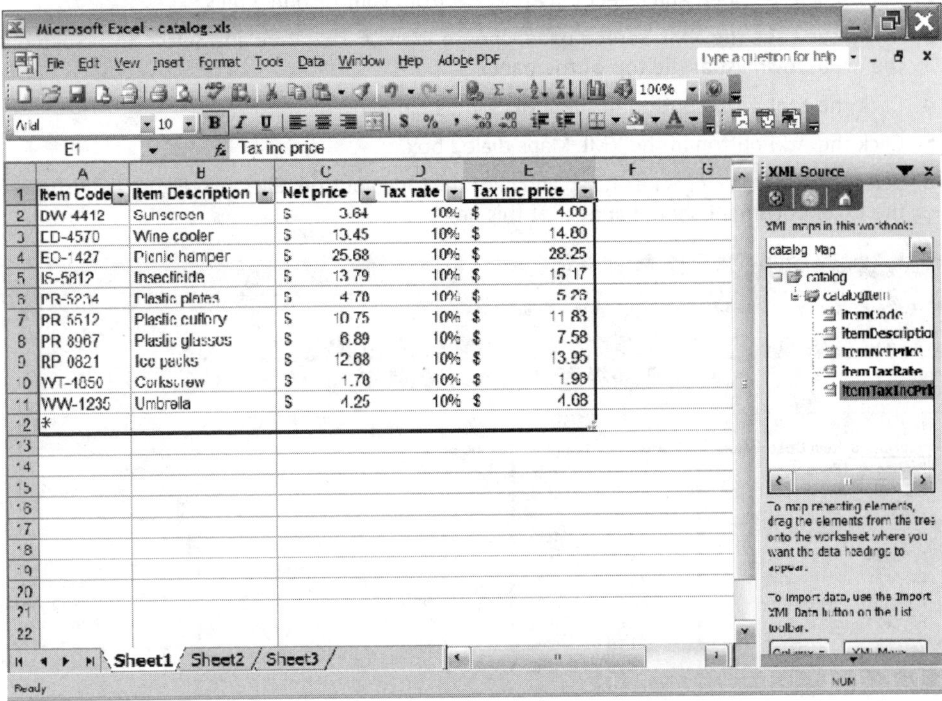

Figure 6-39. The catalog.xml file with XML elements mapped

8. Choose File ➤ Save As and choose the XML Data option. Change the file name to catalogExport.xml and click the Save button. You can see my completed file within your resources.

9. Click the Continue button and close the file. You can find the Excel file saved as `catalog_XMLtags.xls` with your resource files.

10. Open the `catalogExport.xml` file in an XML or text editor. Figure 6-40 shows the file in XMLSpy.

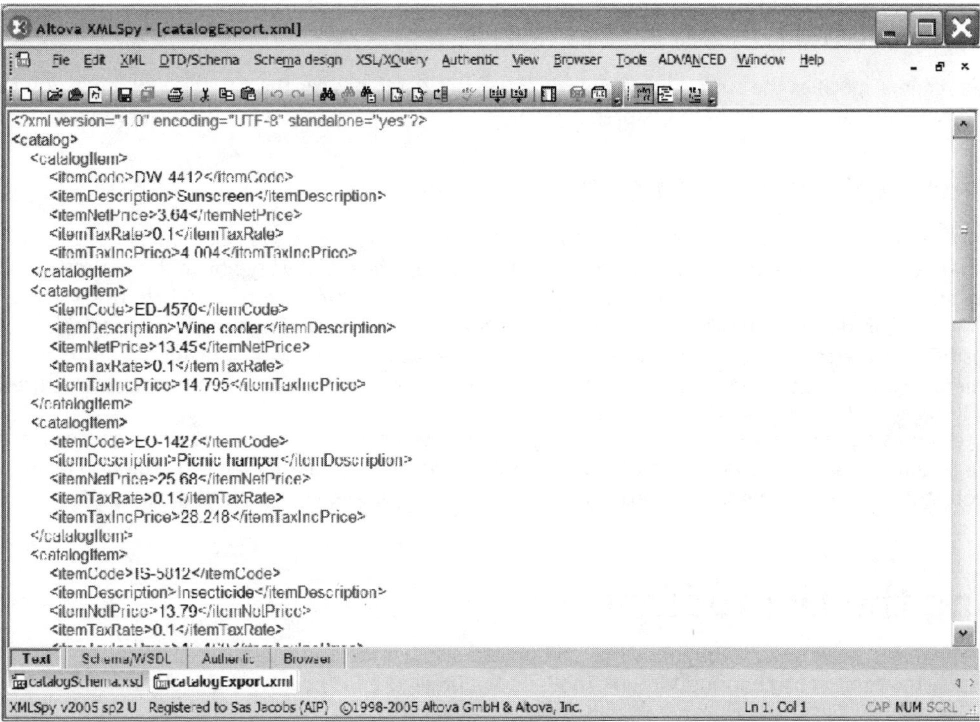

Figure 6-40. The structured XML file saved from Excel

Using an XML schema creates a much simpler, data-only version of the Excel worksheet. In case you're interested, the schema that generated the content is included as follows. You can also see it in the resource file `catalogSchema.xsd`.

```
<?xml version="1.0"?>
<xsd:schema xmlns:xsd="http://www.w3.org/2001/XMLSchema">
  <xsd:element name="catalog">
    <xsd:complexType>
      <xsd:sequence maxOccurs="unbounded">
        <xsd:element name="catalogItem">
          <xsd:complexType>
            <xsd:sequence>
              <xsd:element name="itemCode" type="xsd:string"/>
              <xsd:element name="itemDescription" type="xsd:string"/>
              <xsd:element name="itemNetPrice" type="xsd:decimal"/>
              <xsd:element name="itemTaxRate" type="xsd:string"/>
              <xsd:element name="itemTaxIncPrice" type="xsd:decimal"/>
            </xsd:sequence>
          </xsd:complexType>
        </xsd:element>
```

```
            </xsd:sequence>
          </xsd:complexType>
        </xsd:element>
      </xsd:schema>
```

The schema specifies the structure, element names, and datatypes for the catalog XML data. You can find out more about schemas in Chapter 3.

Editing XML content in Excel

If you have an XML list within Excel, you can edit the data by modifying the cell contents or by adding and deleting rows from the list. To add content at the end of the list, start typing in the last row, where the asterisk (*) appears. You can add rows within the list by selecting the row and choosing Insert ➤ Row. You can do the same with columns. Choose the Insert ➤ Column command after selecting the position for the column. Once you've edited the content within Excel, you can generate an XML document. You can either create a SpreadsheetML document or generate your own element structures.

Excel works a little differently from Word. As you can see, it's easier for users to add new content to the document, and you don't run the same risk of deleting or overwriting XML tags. You don't need to protect the document before you provide it to users, as you would with a Word document.

Using the List toolbar

The features we've seen throughout this section are also available through the List toolbar. You can display the toolbar by choosing View ➤ Toolbars ➤ List. Figure 6-41 shows the toolbar.

Figure 6-41. The List toolbar

The toolbar contains a number of useful features for working with XML documents. I've summarized the relevant icons in Table 6-1 as follows.

Table 6-1. Buttons used for working with XML data in the List toolbar

Button	Explanation
List ▾	Includes features for working with lists of data. See Figure 6-42 for the full range of options with this button.
Toggle Total Row	Displays and hides the totals row.
	Reloads the external XML document to refresh data. You need to do this because when you change an external XML document, it is not automatically updated within Excel. The process is covered earlier in this chapter.

Button	Explanation
	Imports XML data.
	Exports XML data.
	Allows you to work with the properties of the current XML map.

In the List drop-down box, you can find features for working with the list such as sorting and changing the list structure. Figure 6-42 shows the options in the drop-down List menu.

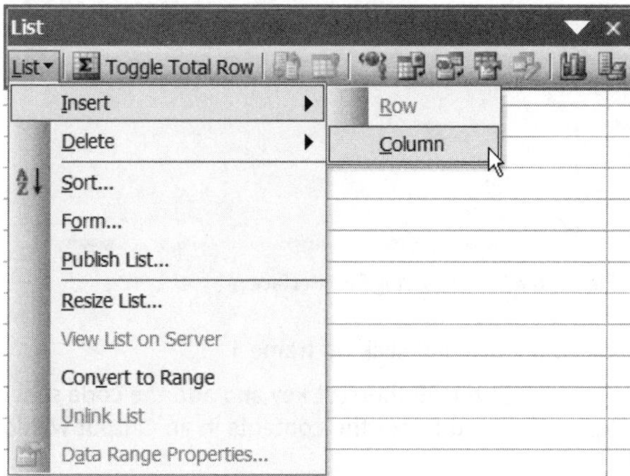

Figure 6-42. Options in the List drop-down box

You've seen how to work with XML data in Excel. Now it's time to put together what you've learned so that you generate XML documents for use within Flash.

Putting it all together

In the next exercise, we'll add the XML content from `catalog.xls` to a Flash movie. We'll make changes to the Excel workbook and see them reflected within the Flash application. You should complete exercise 4 before you start this exercise. If you haven't, you can use the `catalogExport.xml` and `catalog_XMLtags.xls` files from the resources.

Exercise 5: Creating a catalog using XML content from Excel

1. Open Flash if necessary.
2. Choose File ➤ Open and select `catalog.fla` from your resource files. Make sure the file is located in the same folder as `catalogExport.xml`. Figure 6-43 shows the Flash interface. It contains a List component and several TextInput components with some text labels.

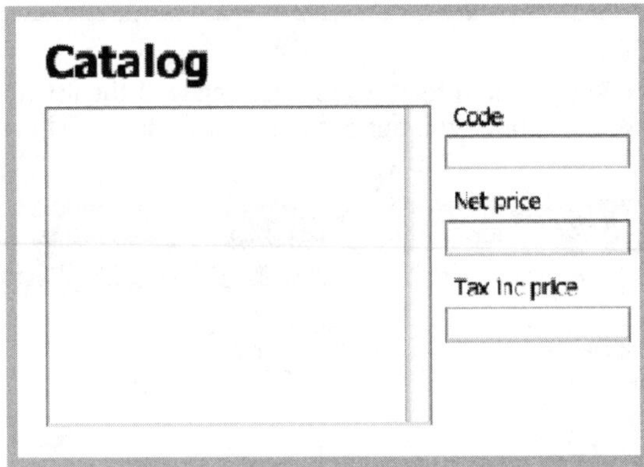

Figure 6-43. The catalog.fla interface

3. Add a new layer called actions and click on frame 1.
4. Open the Actions panel with the *F9* shortcut key and add the code shown here. The code loads the file `catalogExport.xml` and traces the contents in an Output window when the file is successfully loaded.

```
var RootNode:XMLNode;
var selectedItemNode:XMLNode;
var myXML:XML = new XML();
myXML.ignoreWhite = true;
myXML.onLoad = loadCatalog;
myXML.load("catalogExport.xml");
function loadCatalog(success:Boolean):Void {
  if (success) {
    trace (this);
  }
}
```

5. Test the movie. Figure 6-44 shows the Output window that you should see.

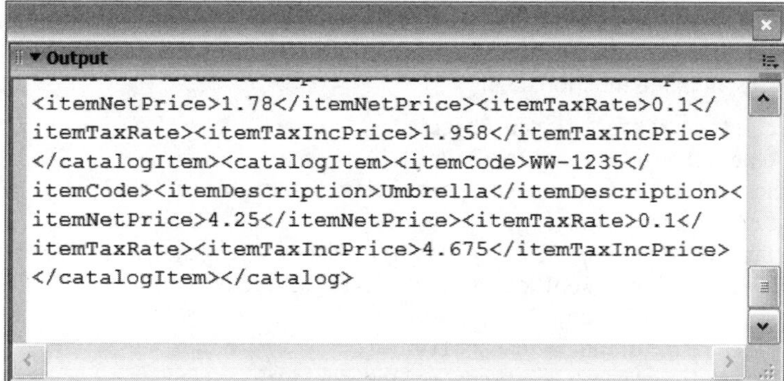

Figure 6-44. The Output window showing the contents from the XML document

6. Modify the `loadCatalog` function as shown here. I've indicated the changed lines in bold. The function extracts the description from each item and adds it to the `description_list` component using the `addItem` method. It then sorts the list into alphabetical order.

```
function loadCatalog(success:Boolean):Void {
  if (success) {
    RootNode = this.firstChild;
    var ItemDescriptionNode:XMLNode;
    for (var i:Number=0; i<RootNode.childNodes.length; i++) {
      ItemDescriptionNode = RootNode.childNodes[i].childNodes[1];
      description_list.addItem(ItemDescriptionNode.firstChild.nodeValue);
    }
    description_list.sortItemsBy("label");
  }
}
```

7. Test the movie. Figure 6-45 shows how the interface should appear at this point.

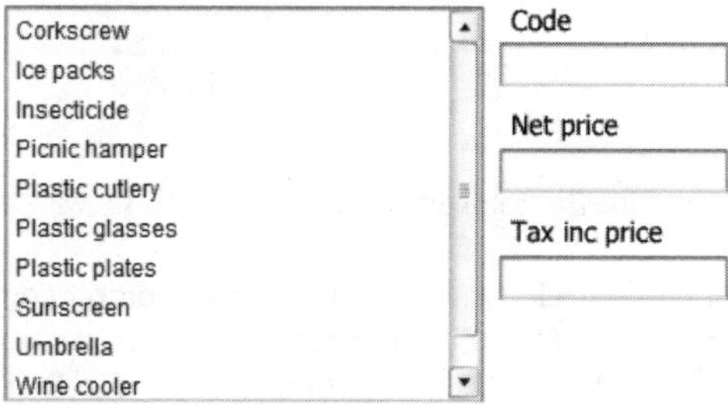

Figure 6-45. The Flash interface after populating the List component

8. Add the following code above the loadCatalog function. The code adds a listener to the List component that finds the selected item node and populates the TextInput components. The listener uses an inline function.

```
var ListListener:Object = new Object();
ListListener.change = function():Void {
  var chosenItem:String = description_list.selectedItem.label;
  var ItemDescription:String;
  for (var i:Number = 0; i < RootNode.childNodes.length; i++) {
    ItemDescription = RootNode.childNodes[i].childNodes[1].➥
    firstChild.nodeValue;
    if (ItemDescription == chosenItem) {
      selectedItemNode = RootNode.childNodes[i];
      break;
    }
  }
  code_txt.text=selectedItemNode.childNodes[0].firstChild.nodeValue;
  net_txt.text=selectedItemNode.childNodes[2].firstChild.nodeValue;
  gross_txt.text=selectedItemNode.childNodes[4].firstChild.nodeValue;
};
description_list.addEventListener("change", ListListener);
```

9. Test the movie and select a list item. Figure 6-46 shows the interface of the finished Flash file. You can see this file saved as catalog_completed.fla.

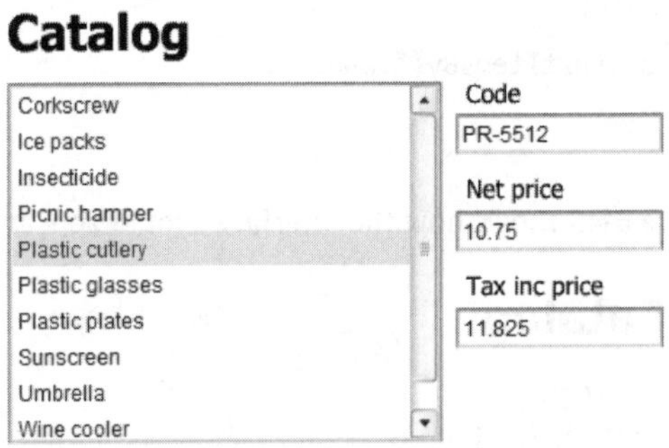

Figure 6-46. The completed Flash application showing a selected item

10. Switch to Excel and open your file from exercise 4. If you didn't complete the exercise, you can use the catalog_XMLtags.xls file from your resources. Add data to the row at the end of the list. Export the XML data as catalogExport.xml and close the Excel file. Test the Flash movie again to make sure that the content has updated.

In this exercise, you saw how to include XML content generated by Excel 2003 within a Flash application. You were also able to use Excel to update the data and the application. Once you understood the structure of the XML document, it was easy to add elements to the Flash interface. If the catalog contained a large quantity of data, users would probably find it easier to use the Flash application rather than searching through a long Excel file.

Summary

In this chapter, I covered the different ways that you can use Excel to work with XML content. We opened an existing XML document in Excel in three different ways: as a list, as a read-only workbook, and using the XML Source pane. We generated XML content from Excel using the Save As and Export commands. Throughout the chapter, we worked with XML maps that provided information to Excel about the XML structures within a document. In the last exercise, we included content from an Excel document within a Flash catalog application.

You can find out more about Excel XML at the Microsoft website. You might find it useful to complete the online training at `http://office.microsoft.com/training/training.aspx?AssetID=RC011310531033`. You can also find a quick reference card at `http://office.microsoft.com/training/Training.aspx?AssetID=RP011310601033&CTT=6&Origin=RC011310531033`. The Office XML Developer Center lists resources, including articles and downloads, and you can find it at `www.msdn.microsoft.com/zoffice/understanding/xmloffice/default.aspx`.

Access 2003 offers the simplest XML functionality of all the Office packages. One difference is that it doesn't have its own XML vocabulary. You can find out more about Access 2003 and XML in the next chapter.

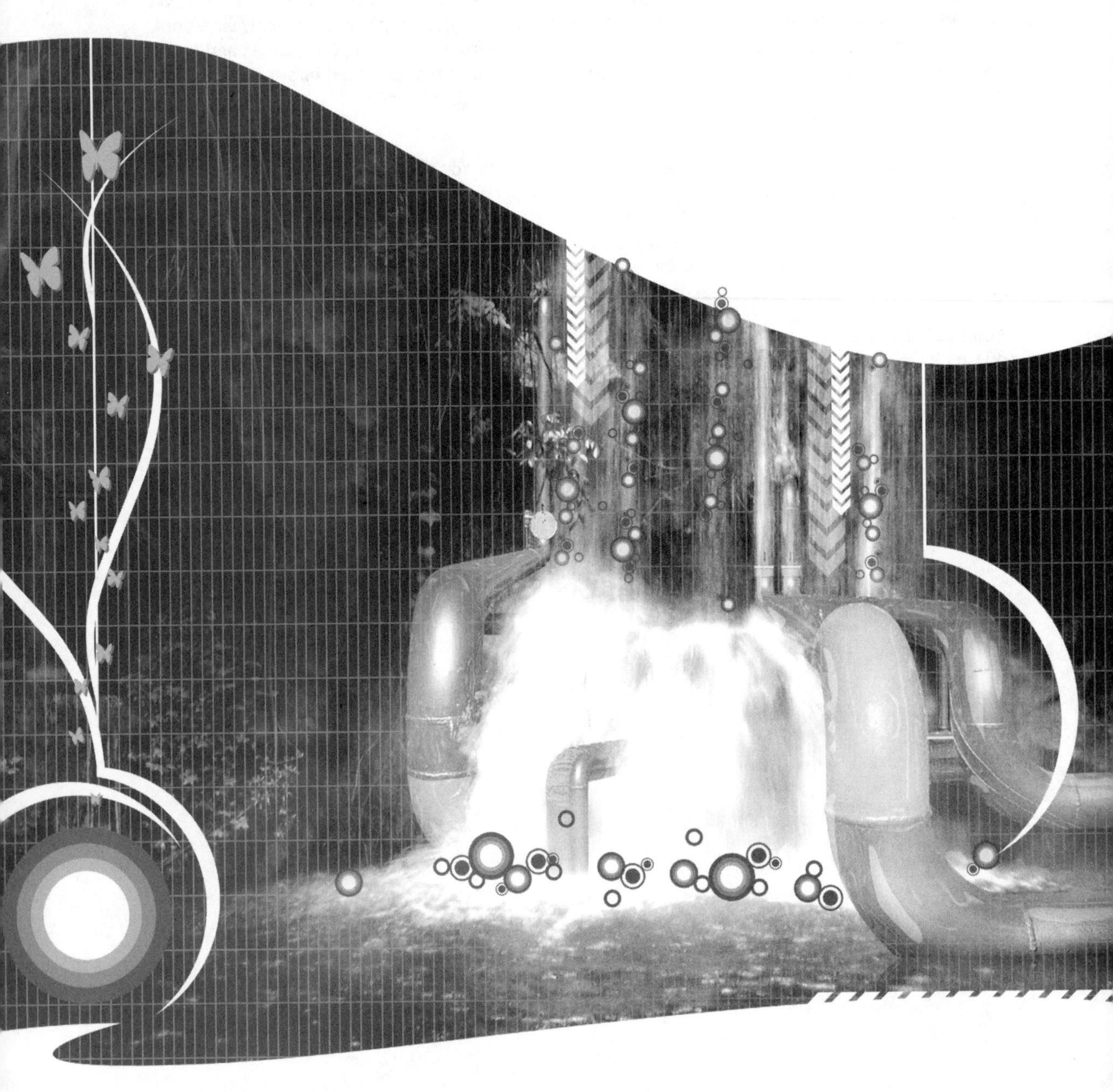

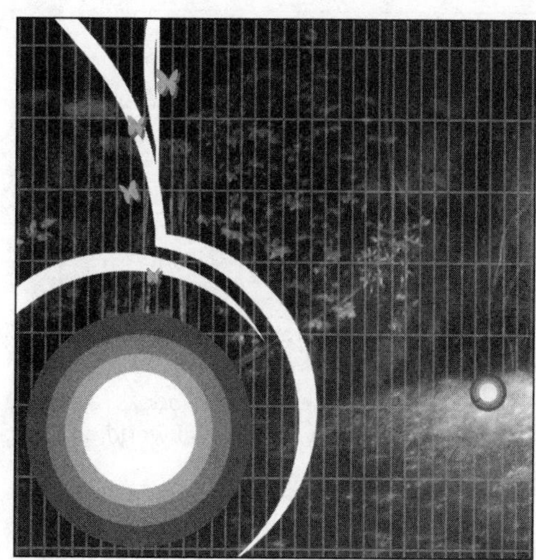

Chapter 7

WORKING WITH XML IN ACCESS 2003

In Chapter 5 you saw why you might want to use Office 2003 to generate XML content. In Chapters 5 and 6, I showed you how to work with XML in Word and Excel 2003. In both packages, you had a choice between using Microsoft XML vocabularies and creating your own XML structures. Access 2003 works a little differently: It uses XML to exchange data with other applications, and this mostly consists of exporting information from Access in XML format. Even though you're much less likely to use Access to import data, it's still possible.

Unlike Word and Excel 2003, Access doesn't have its own XML vocabulary. Rather, the XML content generated by Access is dependent on the database structures, particularly the field and table names. It's worth noting that Access doesn't work well with attributes. If you can't exclude attributes from your work, I'll show you a workaround later in this chapter.

Some of the concepts from relational databases aren't relevant in XML documents. For example, primary keys lie at the heart of Access databases, but they have no equivalent in XML documents. You'll also find that in XML documents it's hard to replicate the complicated data relationships that are often present in databases.

The best way to start working with Access XML is to export XML content. You can then examine the type of structures that Access generates. In the following section, we'll be working with the database `documents.mdb`. Figure 7-1 shows the relationships for this database.

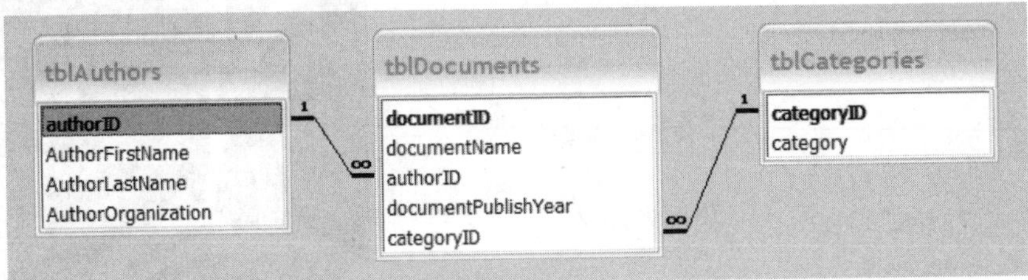

Figure 7-1. The relationships within documents.mdb

The database manages books, authors, and categories. For simplicity, each book has a single author and category. In the real world, the data relationships are likely to be more complicated.

Exporting content as XML

You can export an entire table from Access in XML format. You can also refine the contents of your database by exporting a query or report. Access uses the field names within the table or query to generate the tag names in the XML document.

Exporting a table object

Whichever type of database object you choose to export, the process is the same. You right-click the object and choose Export. Figure 7-2 shows Access exporting a table.

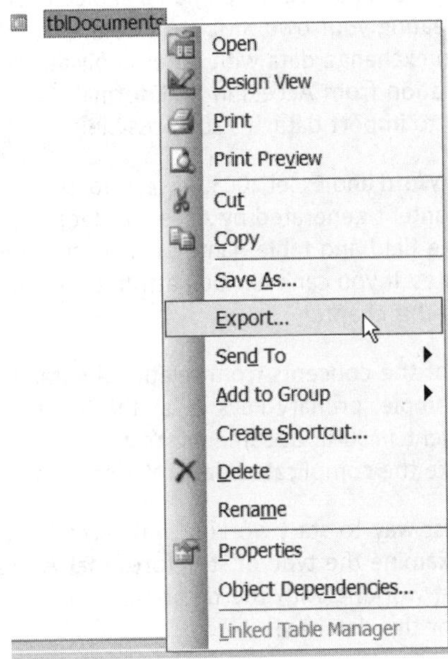

Figure 7-2. Exporting a table from Access

Access will prompt you for the type of data to export. Choose XML and enter a name and location for the XML document. When you click the Export button, Access asks which files you'd like to create; you can choose any of the following: Data, Schema of the data, or Presentation of your data. Figure 7-3 shows the Export XML dialog box.

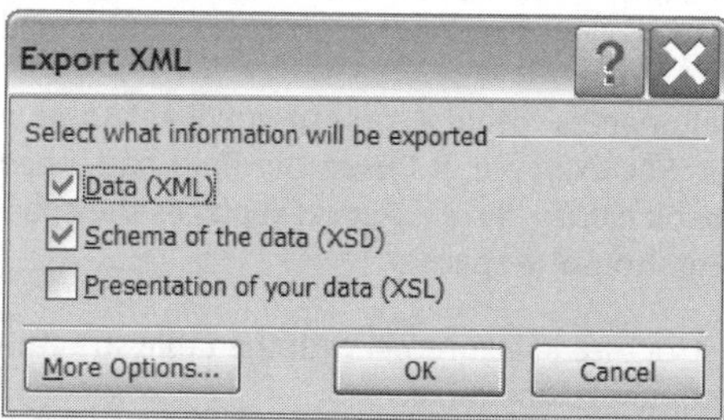

Figure 7-3. Choosing which files to export from Access

If you're exporting XML content for use in Flash, you'll only need to select the first option, Data (XML). Flash is unable to use either an XML schema or XSL style sheet. When you click OK, Access generates the files that you've selected. Figure 7-4 shows an exported XML document in XMLSpy.

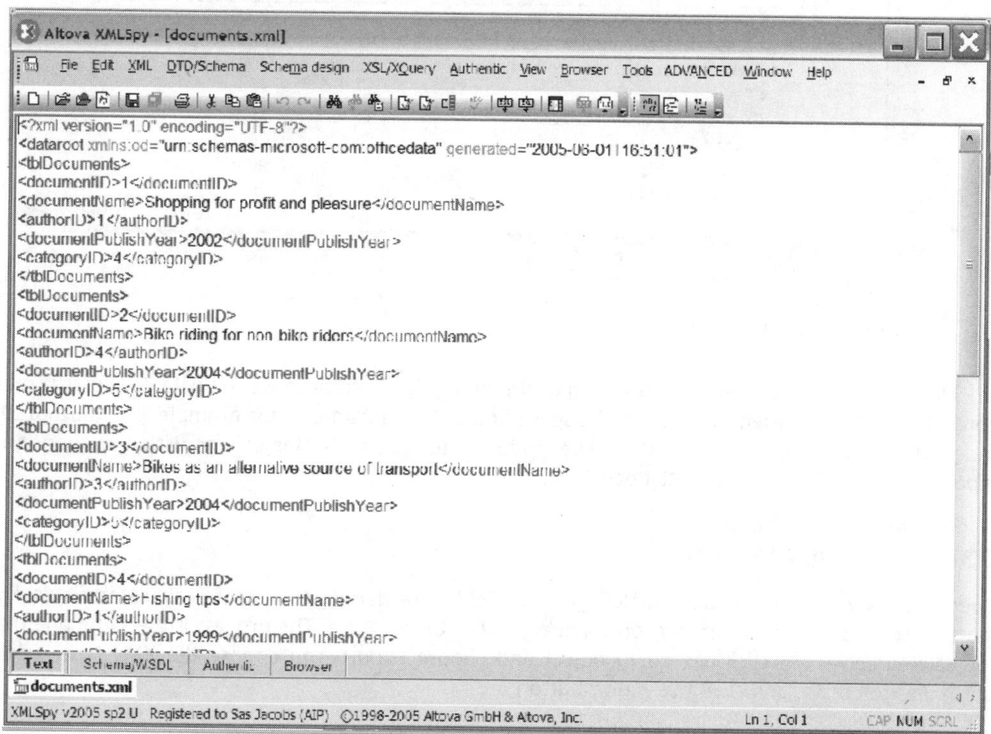

Figure 7-4. Exported XML content from Access displayed in XMLSpy

Access creates a root element called <dataroot> and adds a namespace and generated attribute containing a date and timestamp. This is the only content that Access creates in the XML document. All other content comes from existing data within Access. Each data row uses the table name for the tag, which, in the example in Figure 7-4, is <tblDocuments>. The child nodes use the field names from the table, and you can see the elements <documentID>, <documentName>, <authorID>, <documentPublishYear>, and <categoryID>.

Don't include spaces in the field names within Access or you'll get some unexpected results when you generate your XML document. For example, if I used the field name book Name, the XML document would include the element <book_x0020_Name>. Access replaces the space with _x0020_ (which is the hexadecimal Unicode representation of a space).

Compare the XML document structure in Figure 7-4 with the table structure that produced the content. Figure 7-5 shows the datasheet view of the table.

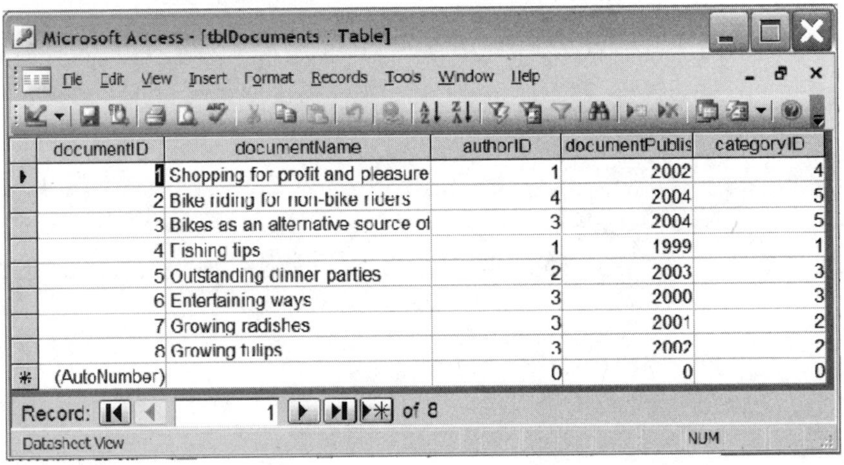

Microsoft Access - [tblDocuments : Table]

documentID	documentName	authorID	documentPublis	categoryID
1	Shopping for profit and pleasure	1	2002	4
2	Bike riding for non-bike riders	4	2004	5
3	Bikes as an alternative source of	3	2004	5
4	Fishing tips	1	1999	1
5	Outstanding dinner parties	2	2003	3
6	Entertaining ways	3	2000	3
7	Growing radishes	3	2001	2
8	Growing tulips	3	2002	2
(AutoNumber)		0	0	0

Record: 1 of 8

Datasheet View

Figure 7-5. The datasheet view of tblDocuments

The XML document is a direct reproduction of the table. However, because the data in Access is relational, some of the content may not make sense in the XML document, for example, the <authorID> and <categoryID> elements. An alternative option is to create the table joins within a query and export the query object to an XML document.

Exporting a query

Queries allow you to join related tables, give the fields new names, and create calculated fields. For these reasons, it's often better to export a query rather than a table. The process is the same one that you saw earlier—right-click the query object and choose Export. You choose the XML type, select which files to create, and click the Export button.

Figure 7-6 shows an Access query in Datasheet view.

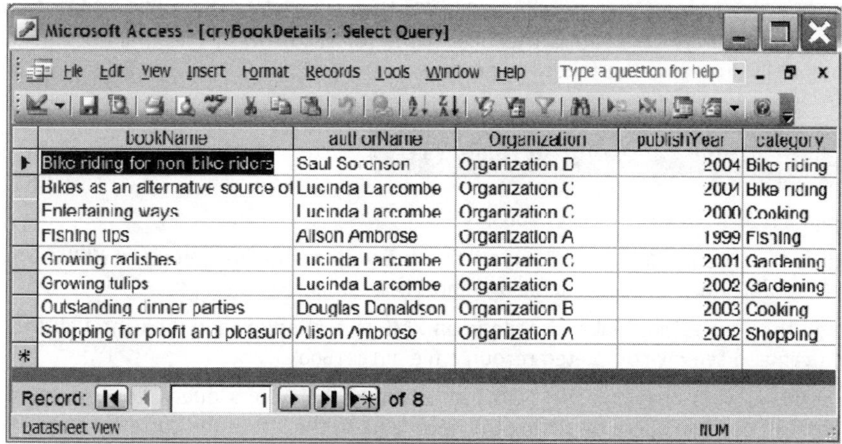

Figure 7-6. The Datasheet view of qryBookDetails

This query joins all three tables in the database and produces a simple list. The query also joins the author first name and last name into a single field and replaces the existing field names with more readable alternatives. Figure 7-7 shows the XML document produced by this query. You can see this content in the resource file bookDetails.xml.

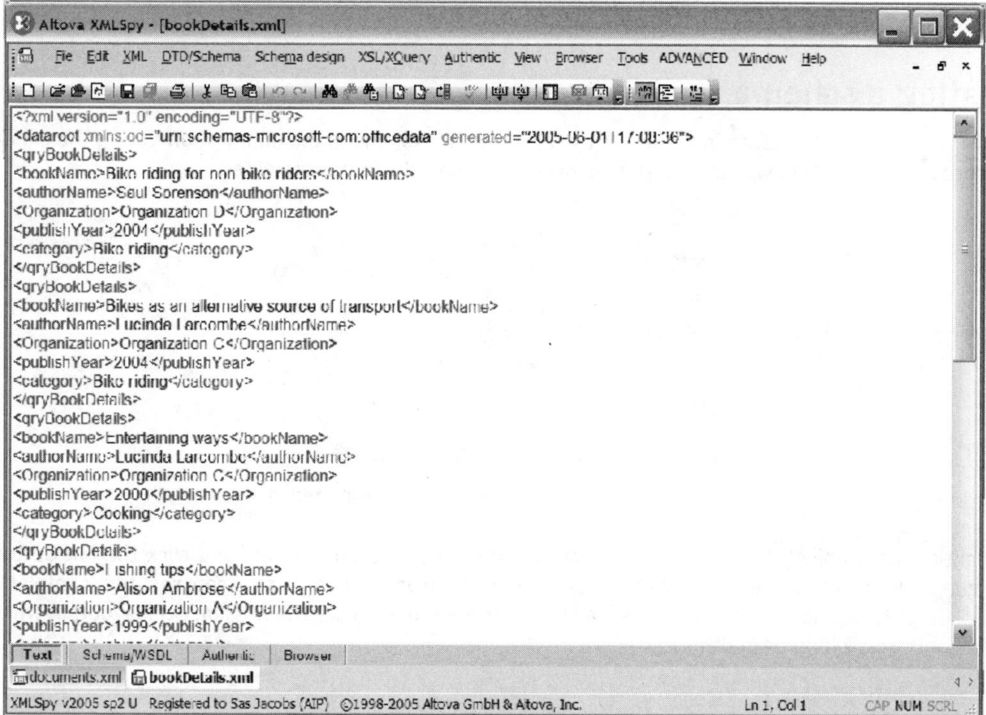

Figure 7-7. The qryBookDetails object exported in XML format

You might find this content more useful within Flash, compared to the table export. I could have renamed `qryBookDetails` to create a friendlier name for each row in the XML document. You can work through this process in the following exercise.

Exercise 1: Generating XML content from Access

1. Open `documents.mdb` in Access 2003.
2. Select the Queries objects and export the query qryAuthorDocuments in XML format. Select only an XML document and name it authorBooks.xml.
3. Open the new `authorBooks.xml` file in an XML or text editor and look through the contents. You can also see my completed resource file `authorBooks.xml`.
4. Experiment with changing the field names within the Access query. You can do this in the design view of the query by adding the new name to the left of the current name with a colon, for example, bookName: documentName. Export the file again to see the updated contents.

In this exercise, you've seen how to export XML content from an Access query. You've also seen how easy it is to change the names used within the XML document by changing the query field names.

Exporting a report

Access allows you to export reports just as you would tables and queries. The exported data will include all fields from the report, regardless of whether you can see them when the report prints out.

Creating a schema from Access

You can generate a schema from Access by selecting the Schema of the data option during the export process. Figure 7-8 shows the Export XML dialog box with this option selected.

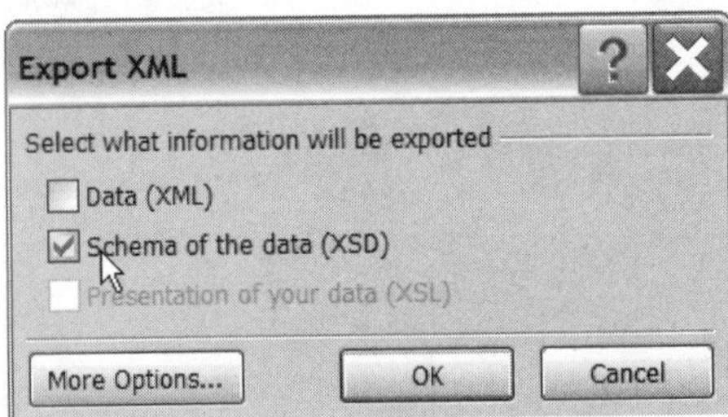

Figure 7-8. The qryBookDetails object exported in XML format

Right-click the object, choose Export, select the Schema of the data option, and click the OK button. Figure 7-9 shows the schema that Access generates from a query. You can see the completed `bookDetails.xsd` in your resource files. Notice that the schema uses the *Russian Doll* layout, in which elements nest within each other.

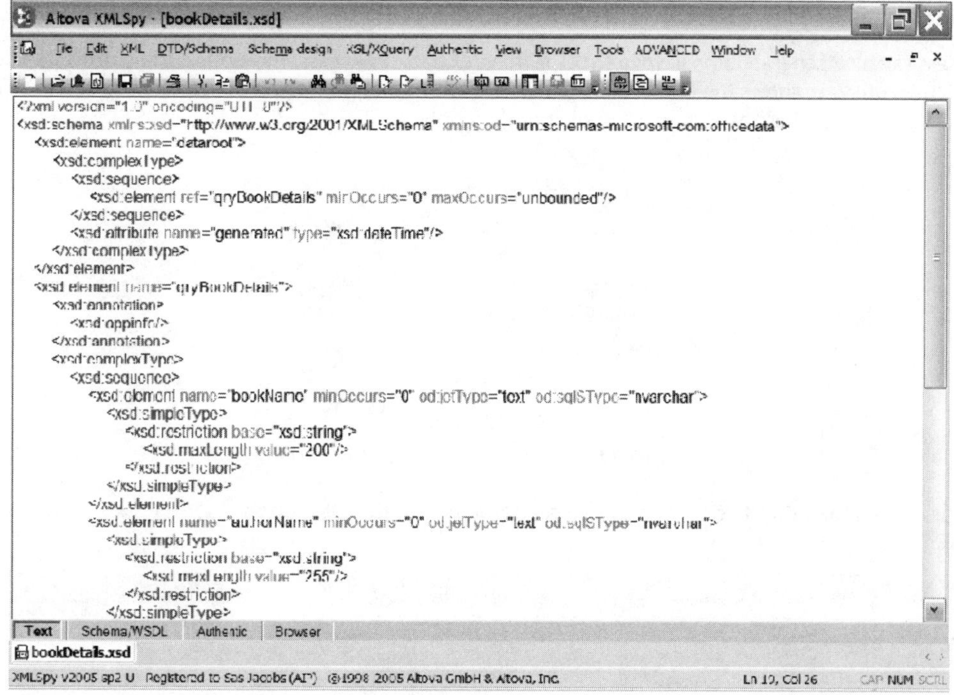

Figure 7-9. The schema document generated by Access

As Figure 7-9 shows, Access preserves the field-length restriction in an <xsd:maxLength> element. You can see an example in the <bookName> element here:

```
<xsd:element name="bookName" minOccurs="0" od:jetType="text"
od:sqlSType="nvarchar">
  <xsd:simpleType>
    <xsd:restriction base="xsd:string">
      <xsd:maxLength value="200"/>
    </xsd:restriction>
  </xsd:simpleType>
</xsd:element>
```

Access also extends the schema by adding its own namespace:

```
<xsd:schema xmlns:xsd="http://www.w3.org/2001/XMLSchema"
xmlns:od="urn:schemas-microsoft-com:officedata">
```

This allows the file to include declarations specific to Access. Within the file, declarations prefaced with the prefix od indicate those specific to Access:

```
<xsd:element name="bookName" minOccurs="0" od:jetType="text"
od:sqlSType="nvarchar">
```

The `od:jetType` attribute indicates the datatype within Access while the `od:sqlSType` represents the datatype within SQLServer.

Creating a style sheet from Access

Access can also generate an XSL style sheet from your data. In Access, this option transforms XML into HTML. Figure 7-10 shows the Export XML dialog box with this option checked. You'll need to check the Data option as well as the Presentation of your data option.

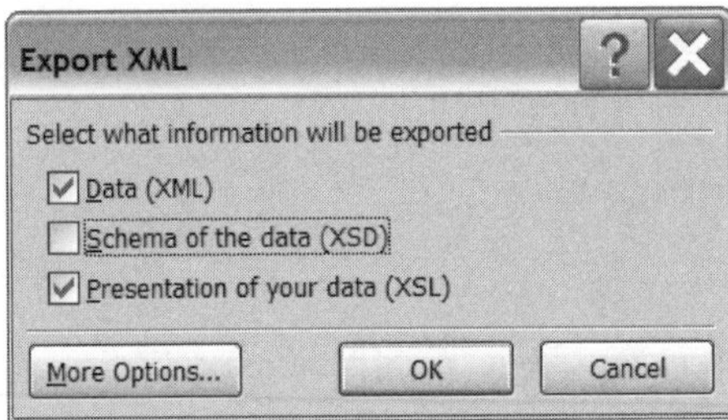

Figure 7-10. Generating a style sheet from Access

Figure 7-11 shows the style sheet generated after you click the OK button.

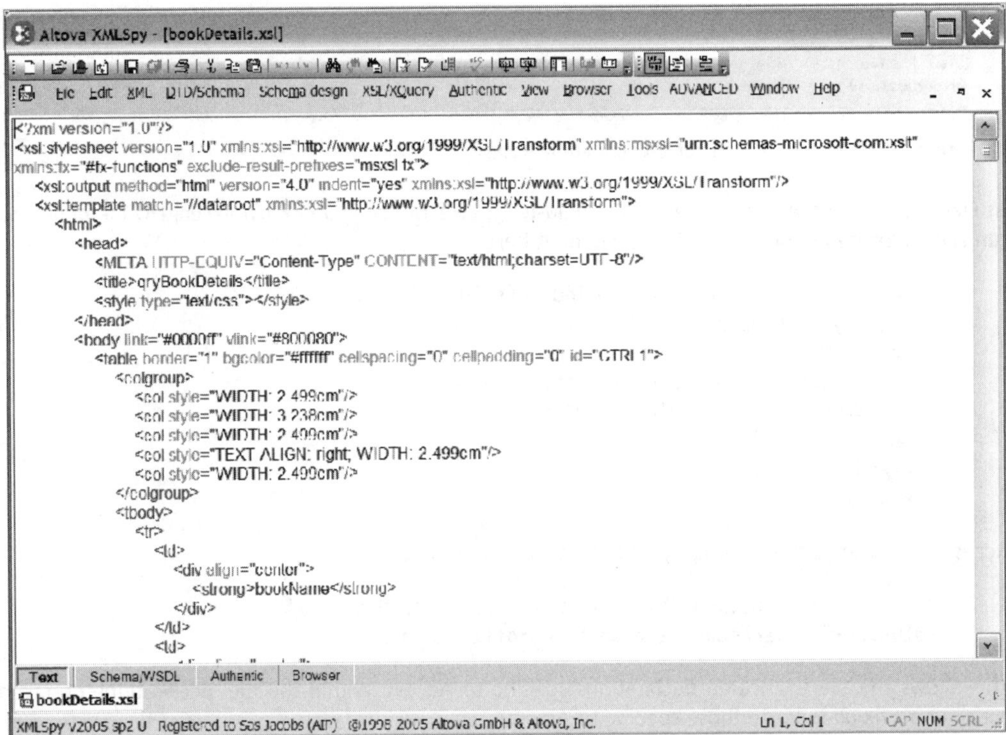

Figure 7-11. The style sheet generated from Access shown in XMLSpy

You'll notice that the style sheet transforms the XML data into HTML format. If you look through the transformed document, you'll see that the file includes CDATA that contains VBScript. The VBScript block lists a set of functions available to the transformation; you can see the content at the end of the file.

Access also generates the HTML document during the export. Figure 7-12 shows the transformed HTML file. I've included `bookDetails.xsl` and `bookDetails.htm` in your resource files.

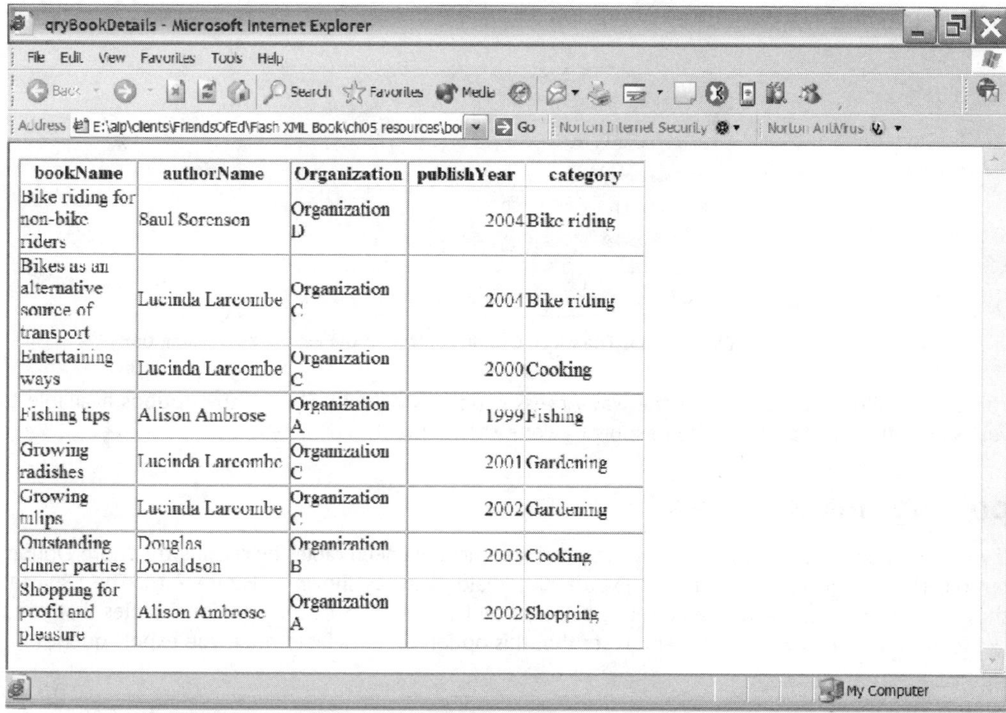

bookName	authorName	Organization	publishYear	category
Bike riding for non-bike riders	Saul Sorenson	Organization D	2004	Bike riding
Bikes as an alternative source of transport	Lucinda Larcombe	Organization C	2004	Bike riding
Entertaining ways	Lucinda Larcombe	Organization C	2000	Cooking
Fishing tips	Alison Ambrose	Organization A	1999	Fishing
Growing radishes	Lucinda Larcombe	Organization C	2001	Gardening
Growing tulips	Lucinda Larcombe	Organization C	2002	Gardening
Outstanding dinner parties	Douglas Donaldson	Organization B	2003	Cooking
Shopping for profit and pleasure	Alison Ambrose	Organization A	2002	Shopping

Figure 7-12. The transformed HTML document generated by Access

You'll notice that Access presents the data in a simple table format. The heading row shows the element names. You could create your own style sheet if you needed to create a custom transformation. We'll generate documents from an Access query in exercise 2.

Exercise 2: Generating XML content from Access

In this exercise, we'll generate an XML document, schema, and style sheet from an Access query.

1. Open `documents.mdb` in Access 2003 if necessary.
2. Export the query qryAuthorDocuments as an XML file, schema, and style sheet. Use the name authorDocuments for all the files.
3. Open the documents within an XML or text editor so you can see the contents.
4. Open `authorDocuments.htm` in a web browser so you can see the contents. You'll find my completed files `authorDocuments.htm`, `authorDocuments.xml`, `authorDocuments.xsd`, and `authorDocuments.xsl` with your resources.

In the examples you've seen so far, we haven't had much control over the XML content that Access generates. In the next section, I'll look at some of the options you have when exporting XML data.

Setting export options

You probably noticed the More Options button at the left of the Export XML dialog box each time you've exported XML content from Access (see Figure 7-13).

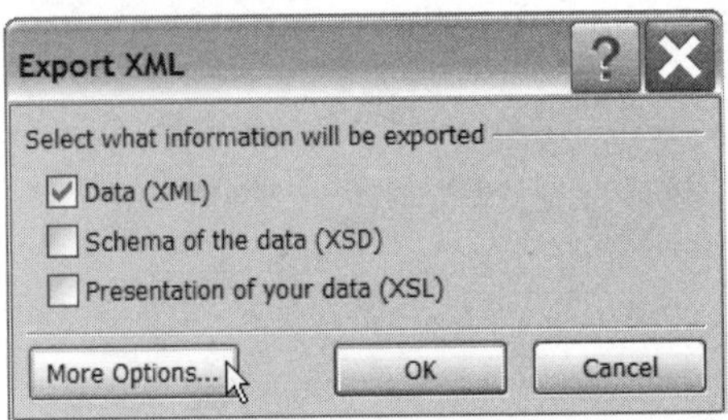

Figure 7-13. The More Options button in the Export XML dialog box

This button allows you to change the way Access exports XML data. One of the options available to you is including linked tables when exporting your XML content.

Exporting linked tables

If you are exporting a table from Access, you can also include linked tables by clicking the More Options button. This will display an expanded Export XML dialog box, as shown in Figure 7-14. The Data tab shows the tables that link to the currently selected table. Simply check the additional tables that you'd like to include in your XML document. Note that this option isn't available when you export queries.

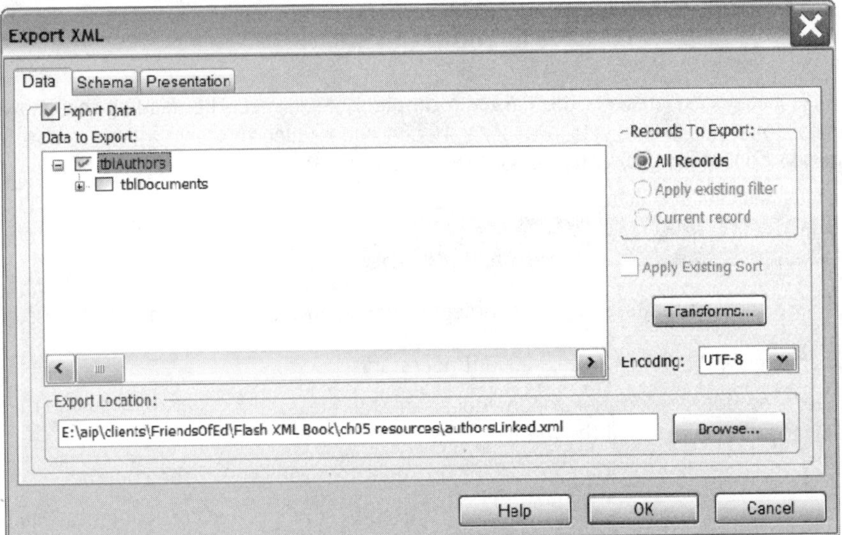

Figure 7-14. The Export XML extended dialog box allows you to select linked tables.

When you check the linked table name, the export will include related records from the linked table. Clicking OK will generate the linked data in XML format, as shown in Figure 7-15. You can view the data in the resource file `authorsLinked.xml`.

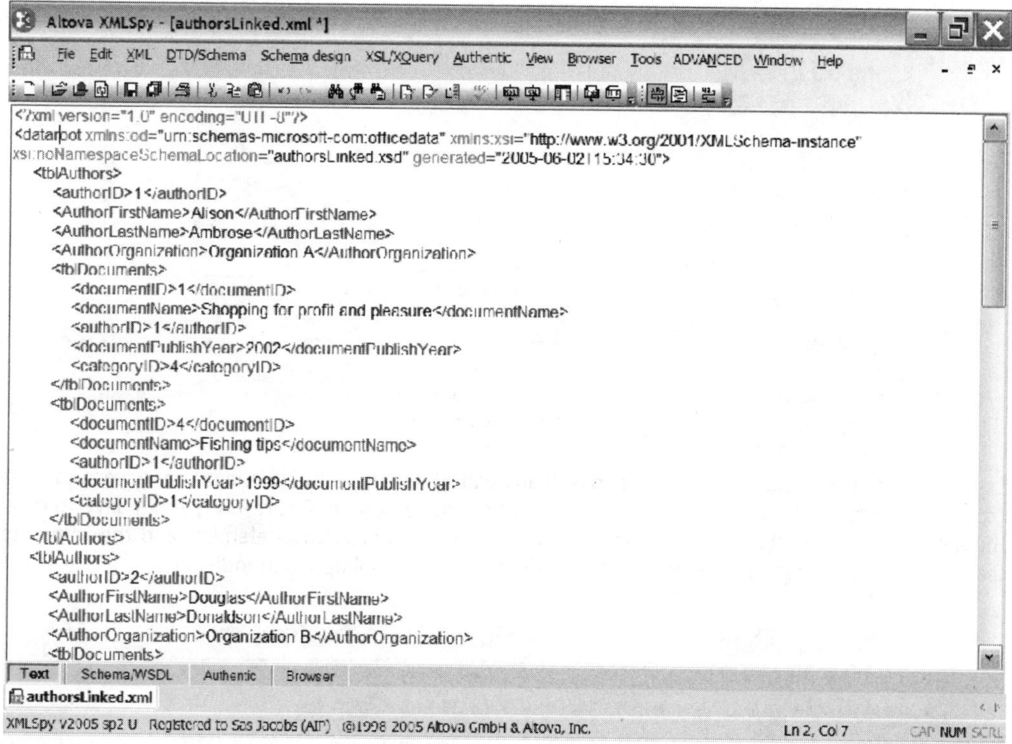

Figure 7-15. The linked tables exported in XML format

The XML file shown in Figure 7-15 includes records from both tblAuthors and tblDocuments. The documents that relate to an author are included as child elements within the `<tblAuthors>` element. This allows you to generate a hierarchical representation of the data within the XML document.

In this example, I've only shown the XML data generated from the linked tables. You could also have generated a schema and style sheet from the data. I've included `authorsLinked.xsl`, `authorsLinked.xsd`, and `authorsLinked.htm` in your resources so you can see the exported content.

Another option available to you is including the content from more than one linked table. You can drill down in the Export XML dialog box, as shown in Figure 7-16. Notice that the third linked table includes the text [Lookup Data].

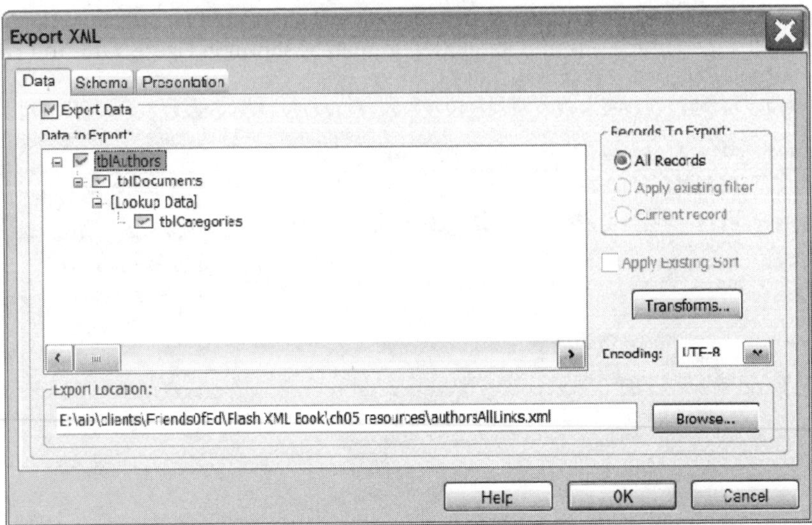

Figure 7-16. Selecting all linked tables from the Data tab

Exporting data in this way doesn't work so well. Instead of linking to the existing data, Access adds the content from the third table to the bottom of the XML document. In Figure 7-17, you'd have to make the link between the <categoryID> element within the <tblDocuments> element and the same element in the <tblCategories> element. That's what the text [Lookup Data] indicates.

Figure 7-17. The XML content produced from three linked tables

Given these difficulties, it's probably a good idea to stick with two linked tables and avoid including tables that show the text [Lookup Data]. We'll generate linked content in exercise 3.

Exercise 3: Generating linked XML content from Access

In exercise 3, we'll generate an XML document that contains data from a linked table.

1. Open `documents.mdb` in Access 2003 if necessary.
2. Export the table tblCategories as an XML file, including the linked tblDocuments table. Save the XML file with the name categoriesLinked.xml.
3. Open the `categoriesLinked.xml` file in an XML or text editor so you can see the contents. Within each category, you should see a list of child document elements. You can view the completed resource file `categoriesLinked.xml`.

Applying a custom transformation

You saw earlier that Access can generate a style sheet that transforms the XML document into an HTML representation. You can also apply your own custom transformation while exporting the data. Export the data as normal, making sure you click the More Options button. Click the Transforms button on the Data tab, as shown in Figure 7-18.

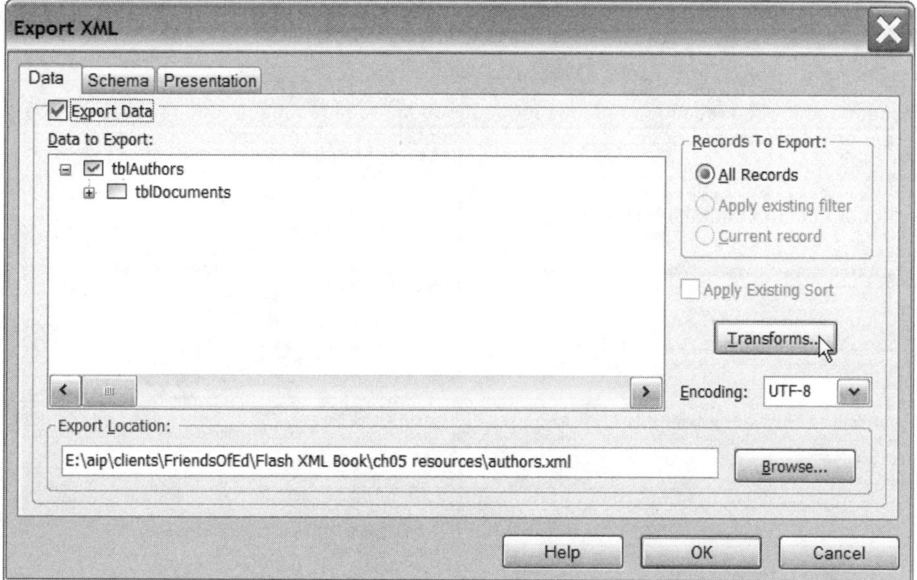

Figure 7-18. The Transforms button in the Export XML dialog box

Clicking this button brings up the Export Transforms dialog box, shown in Figure 7-19.

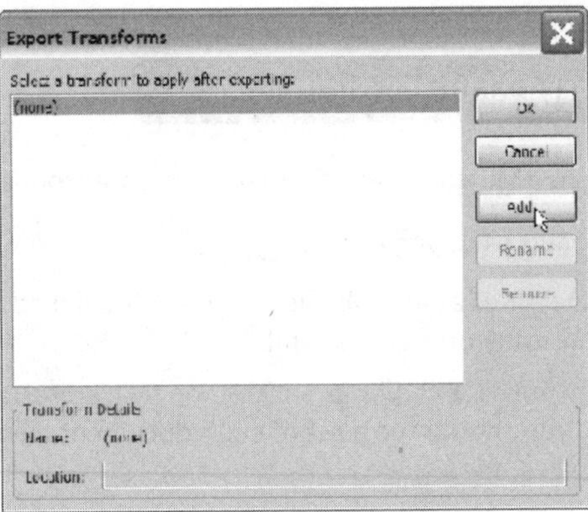

Figure 7-19. Adding a style sheet to the Export process

Click the Add button in the Export Transforms dialog box and select an XSLT style sheet. Once selected, the name of the style sheet will appear in the dialog box. Click OK to return to the Data tab of the Export XML dialog box. Click OK and Access applies the transformation as you export the data. Figure 7-20 shows a comparison of the transformed and untransformed data.

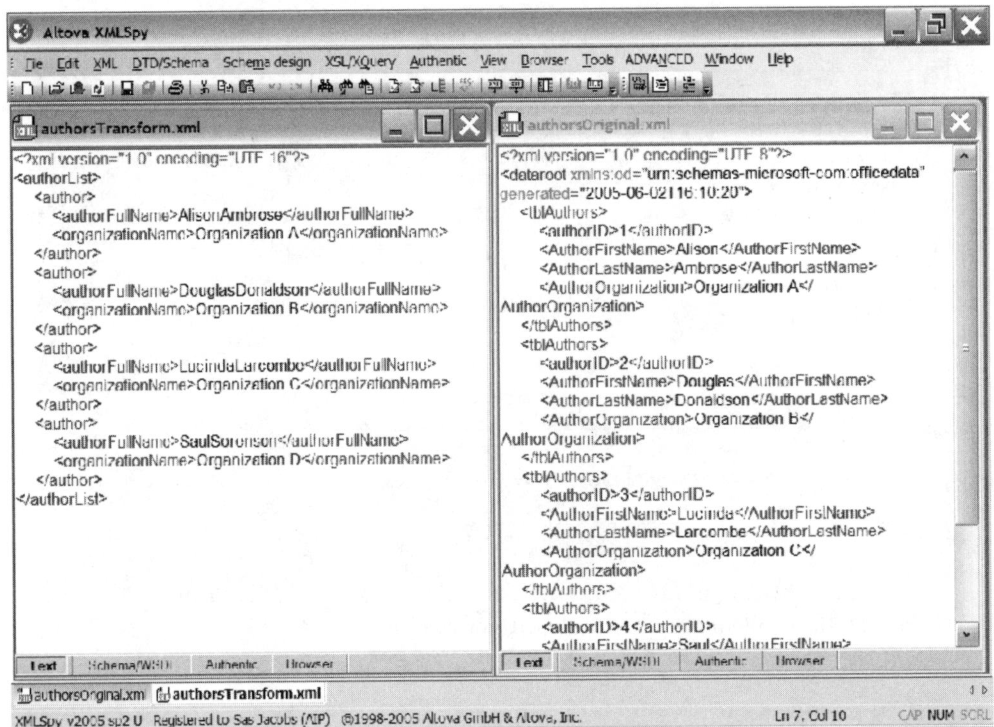

Figure 7-20. Comparing the transformed document (left) with the exported content

We'll complete an exercise so you can do the comparison yourself.

Exercise 4: Transforming XML content during export

In this exercise, we'll transform an XML document during the export process. The transformation will add new element names and apply sorting to the content.

1. Open `documents.mdb` in Access 2003 if necessary.
2. Export the table tblCategories as an XML file, including the linked tblDocuments table. Save the XML file with the name categoriesLinkedTransformed.xml.
3. Click the More Options button and then the Transforms button. Click the Add button, navigate to the file categoriesLinkedTransform.xsl, and click Add again.
4. Click the OK button twice to create the XML document. Open the file `categoriesLinkedTransformed.xml` in an XML or text editor. You can also see my completed file with your resources. You should see something similar to the screenshot shown in Figure 7-21. Notice that Access sorted the data during the export process.

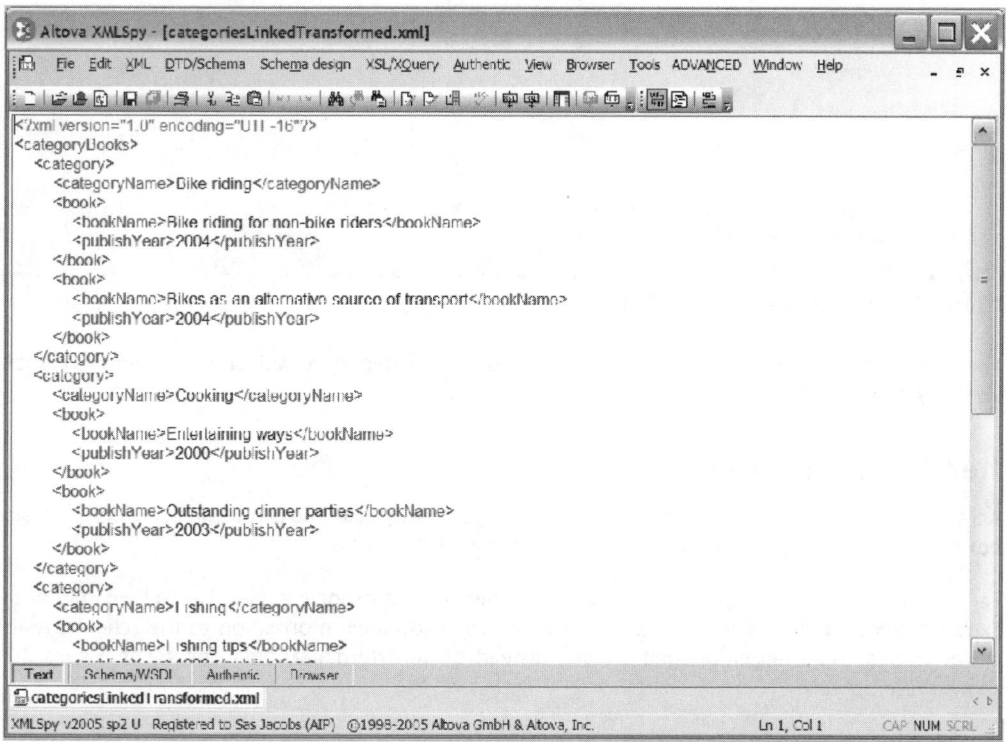

Figure 7-21. The transformed XML data from exercise 4

5. Open the file `categoriesLinkedTransform.xsl` in an XML or text editor to see the details of the transformation. Figure 7-22 shows the style sheet.

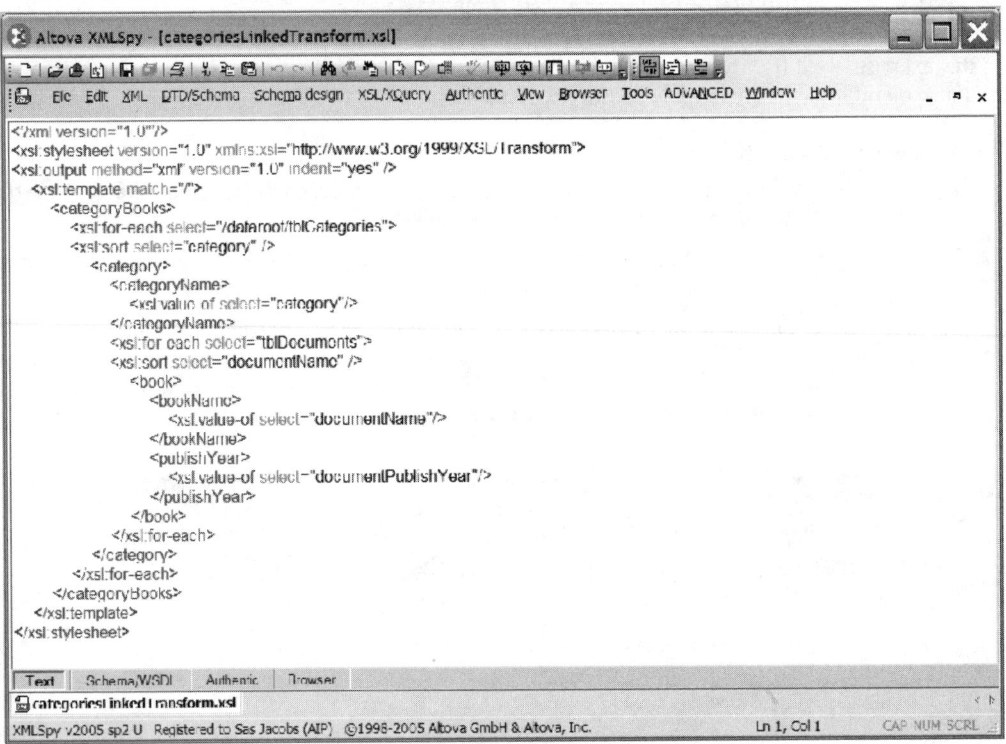

Figure 7-22. The XSLT style sheet used in the transformation

The transformation creates new element names for each category and document. Two `<xsl:sort>` elements sort by both `category` and `documentName`.

Other export options

Access provides some other export options in the Export XML dialog box. You can bring up this dialog box by clicking the More Options button during the export process.

Earlier, we saw how you could generate an XML schema while exporting data. The Schema tab in the Export XML dialog box allows you to add primary key and index information to the schema. It also allows you to create an embedded schema instead of an external schema document. Figure 7-23 shows these options.

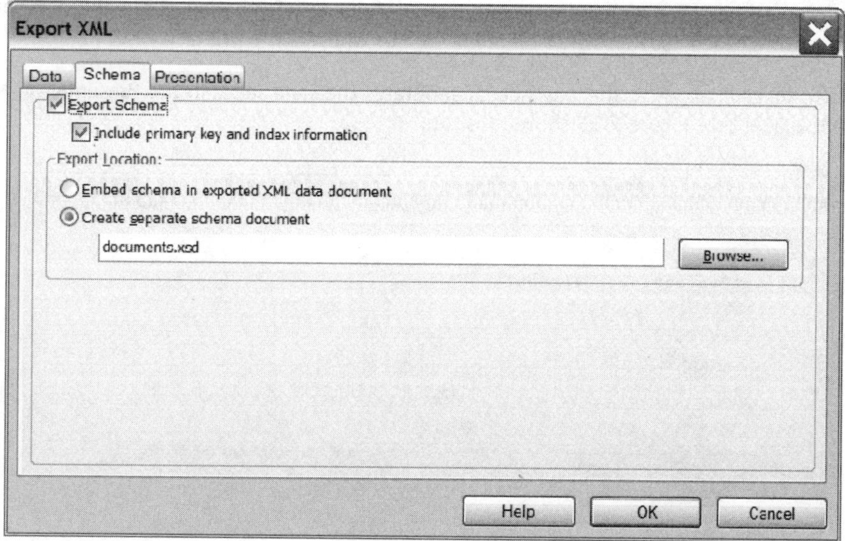

Figure 7-23. Options available on the Schema tab

You can see an XML document generated that includes the primary key and index information with an embedded schema in Figure 7-24. I've saved the resource file as `categoriesEmbeddedSchema.xml`.

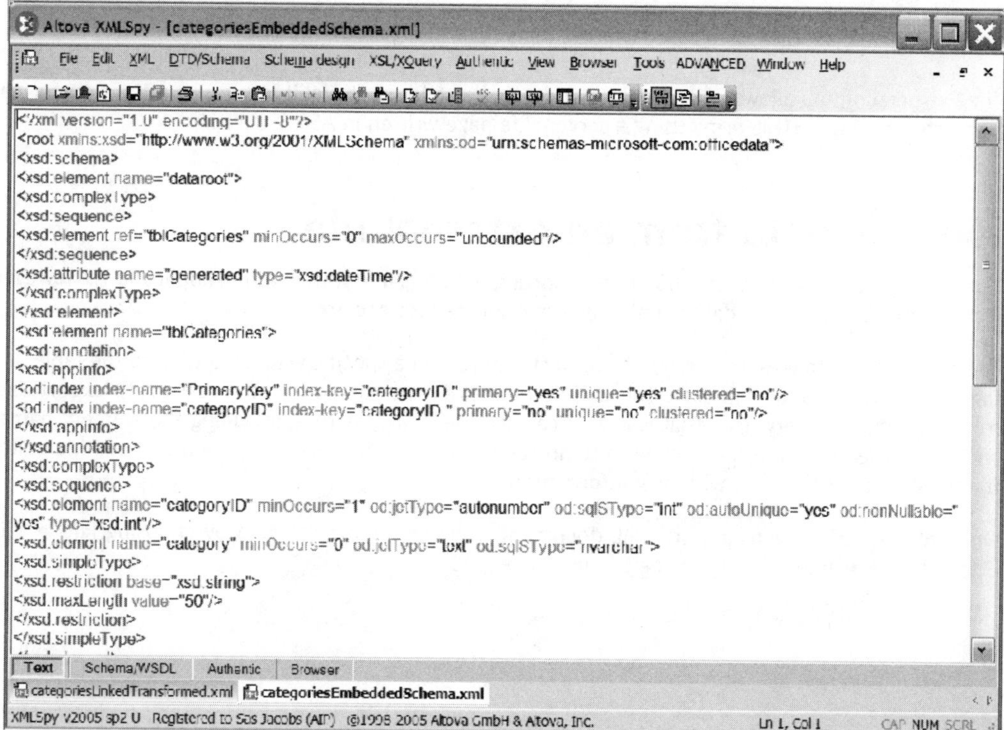

Figure 7-24. The exported XML document with an embedded schema

You'll notice that the schema includes an annotation showing information about the database. It lists two indexes within the <xsd:appinfo> element, one of which is the primary key.

You can also make changes to the way Access generates the style sheet in the Presentation tab of the Export XML dialog box. Figure 7-25 shows this tab.

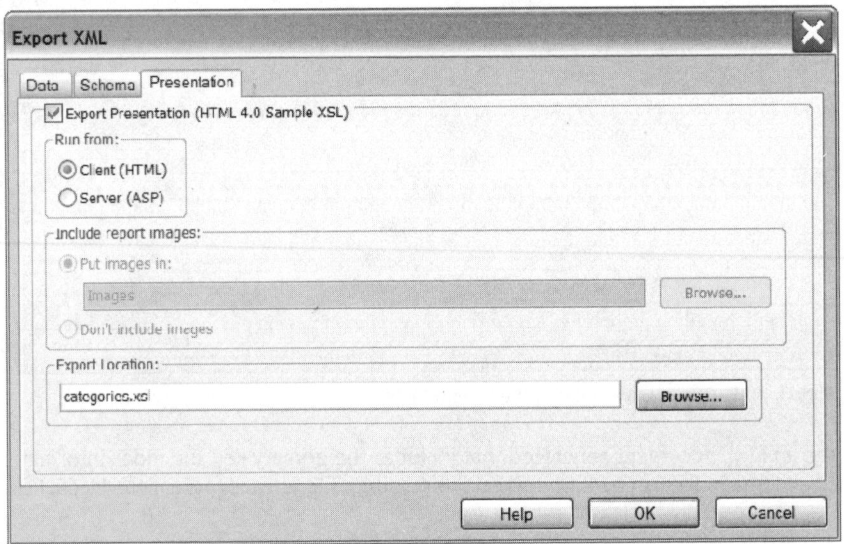

Figure 7-25. The Presentation tab in the Export XML dialog box

The Presentation tab allows you to export and name a style sheet file. It lets you run the transformation either through HTML or by using a server-side page written in ASP.

Importing data from an external file

The main use of XML in Access 2003 is in exporting data to share with external applications. However, it's also possible to import data from an external source into Access.

To import XML data into Access, you have to structure it in a specific way, according to the table and field names within your database. This can be hard to figure out, so it's often easiest to export data from the table or query first. That way, you can see the XML structure, including the element names and their order. By exporting, you get a template to use for your new data. Use a text or XML editor to replace the existing data with new information.

Once you've created your import XML document, you can import the data by choosing File ➤ Get External Data ➤ Import. You can see this in Figure 7-26.

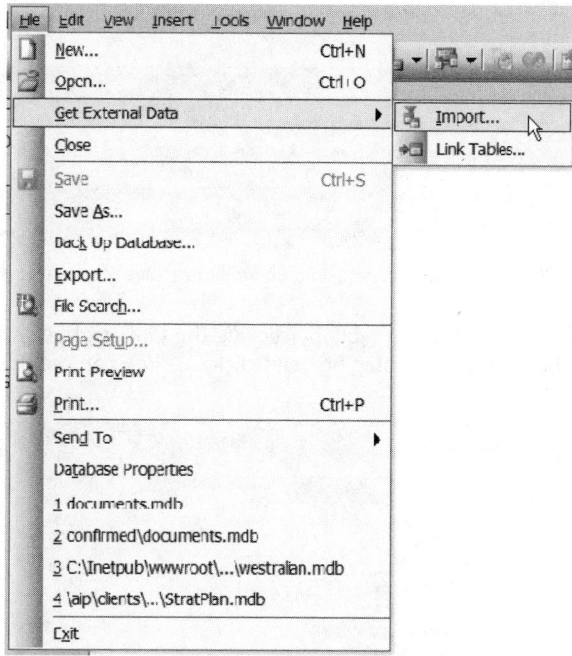

Figure 7-26. Importing external XML data into Access

Navigate to the XML document that you wish to import and click the Import button. When the Import XML dialog box appears, expand the structure to see the field names as shown in Figure 7-27.

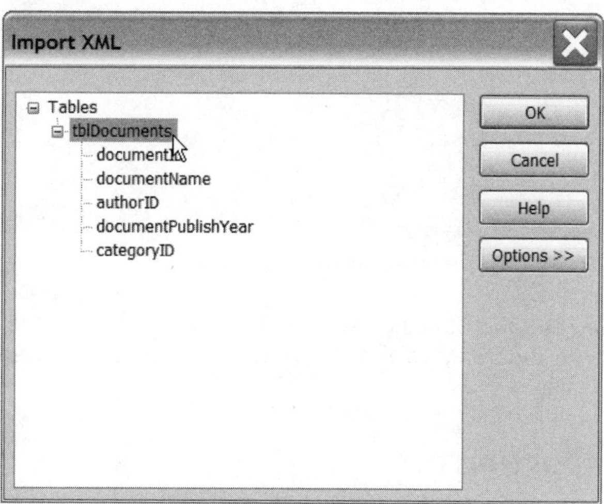

Figure 7-27. The Import XML dialog box

If you click OK now, Access will try to create a new table called tblDocuments. If you have an existing table with the same name, Access will name the new table tblDocuments1. This might be useful as you can check that the new data is compatible with the existing data before you combine the content.

Access shows a message to let you know that it has finished the import. You can see it in Figure 7-28.

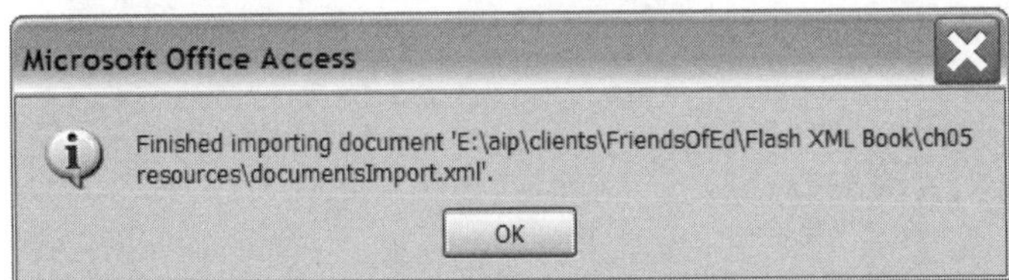

Figure 7-28. The Finished importing document message from Access

You can append the data to the existing table by clicking the Options button. Select Append Data to Existing Table(s) at the bottom of the dialog box and click OK. You can see this in Figure 7-29.

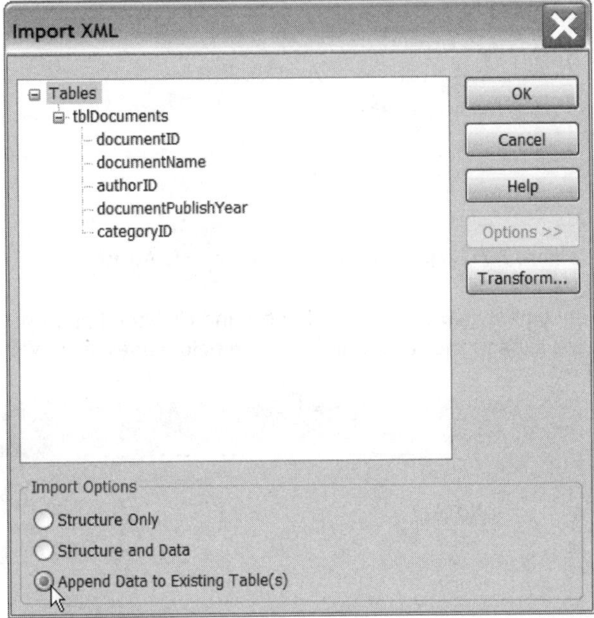

Figure 7-29. The Import XML dialog box

You can also create a new table structure without the data by choosing the Structure Only option before clicking OK in the Import XML dialog box. Again, if you choose an existing table name, Access will rename your new table.

Dealing with import errors

Access won't allow you to import XML data containing errors. If your XML document is not well formed, Access will display an error message similar to the one shown in Figure 7-30.

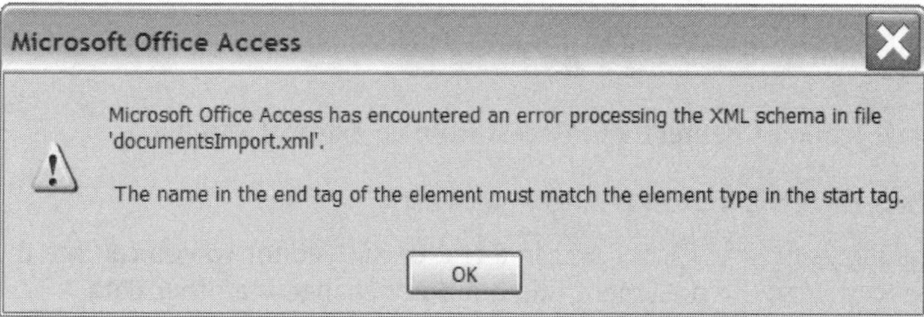

Figure 7-30. Access displays an error message if you try to import a document that is not well formed.

Access will also generate an error message if you try to import content that violates the data integrity rules within the database. It will store the error in a table called ImportErrors in the current database and display an error message dialog box. For example, Figure 7-31 shows the message that generates when you attempt to import a duplicate primary key value.

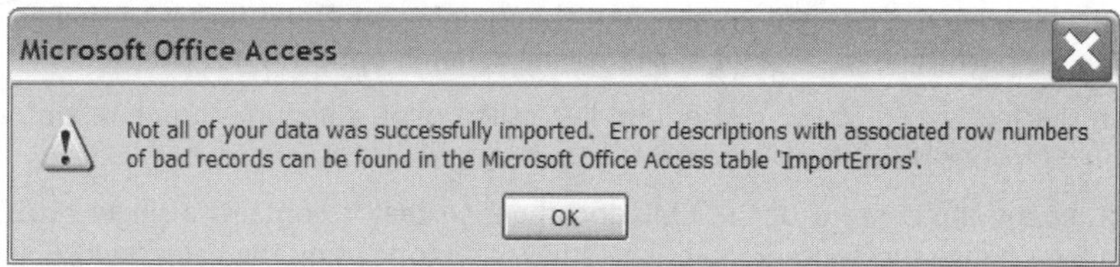

Figure 7-31. Access cannot import records that would cause an error.

The ImportErrors table contains the detailed error message. I've shown this in Figure 7-32 where the table is open in Datasheet view.

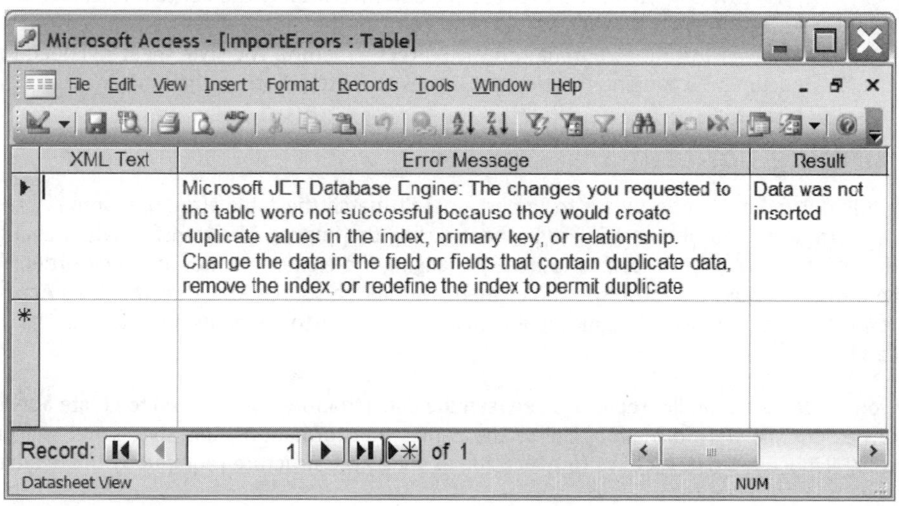

Figure 7-32. A detailed error message in the ImportErrors table

Let's do an exercise where Access imports content from an XML document.

Exercise 5: Importing XML content into Access

In this exercise, we'll import content into Access from an external XML file.

1. Open `documents.mdb` in Access 2003 if necessary.
2. Open the file `documentsImport.xml` in a text or XML editor so you can see the data template. Feel free to change the document title but don't change the other data.
3. Import the file documentsImport.xml from your resources into Access using File ➤ Get External Data ➤ Import. Don't forget to change the file type to XML before you click the Import button.
4. In the Import XML dialog box, select tblDocuments, click the Options button, and choose Append data to Existing Table(s). Click OK.
5. You should see a Finished import message. Click OK and open the table to check that it contains the new row.
6. Export tblCategories by right-clicking and choosing Export. Don't forget to change the file type to XML. Export the data, making sure that the Schema option is not checked.
7. Open the file in an XML or text editor. I've called mine categoriesStructure.xml, and you can find it with your resources.
8. We'll modify the content of the XML document so that it contains a single `<tblCategories>` element. Change the contents to create a new category, using the categoryID 6.
9. Import the new category and append it to tblCategories, following the same approach that you used earlier in steps 3–5.
10. Check that tblCategories contains your new data.

In this exercise, you saw how you could export a file and then modify the content to create an import document for Access. If you are exporting content from another application, you can easily create an XSLT style sheet to transform the content into the correct structure. The style sheet will need to transform the XML document, changing the element names to match those in the table.

Transforming content

If the XML document that you want to import doesn't match the table structure within Access, you can transform it by applying an XSLT style sheet during the import. The transformation changes the XML document from one format to another by changing the element names and their order. You can use the transformation to choose specific elements within the source XML document. As Access can't import attributes, the transformation can also change attributes to elements. We'll look at this in more detail a little later on.

Once you've identified the discrepancies between the data structures, you'll need to create a style sheet that carries out the transformation. Unlike the earlier transformations, this style sheet will produce another XML document. It will have to match the existing XML structure required by the database.

Once you've created the style sheet, choose File ➤ Get External Data ➤ Import and click the Transform button, as shown in Figure 7-33.

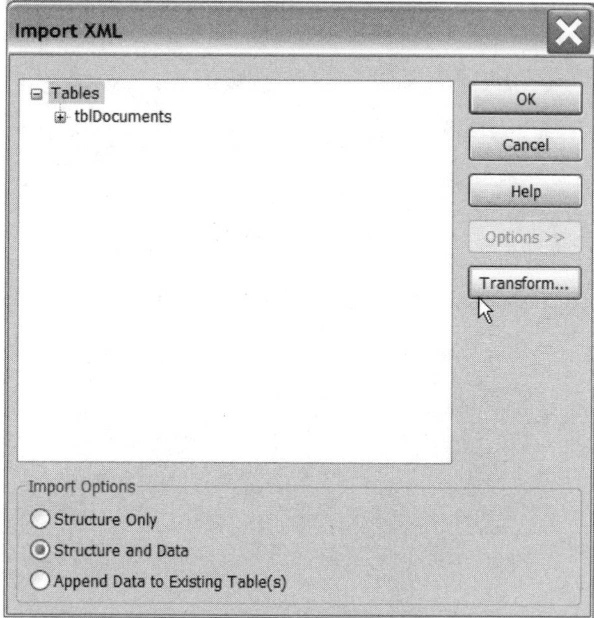

Figure 7-33. The Transform button in the Import XML dialog box

Click the Add button in the Import Transforms dialog box and navigate to the XSLT style sheet. Figure 7-34 shows the dialog box after the adding the style sheet. Click OK twice to import the transformed data.

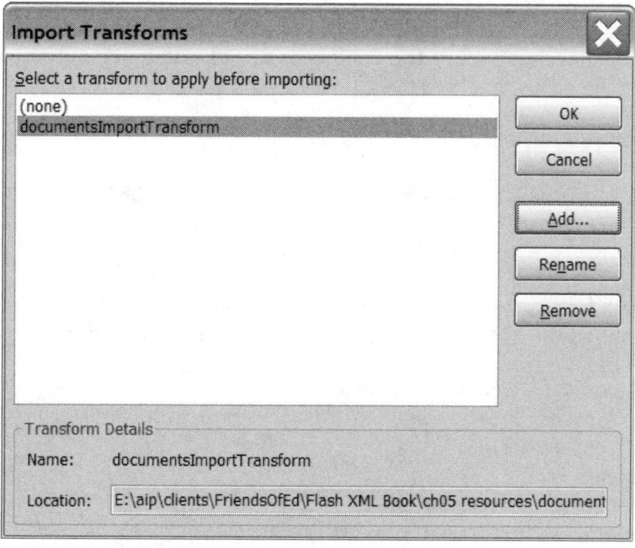

Figure 7-34. Adding a transformation

Access displays the message shown in Figure 7-35 when it completes the import.

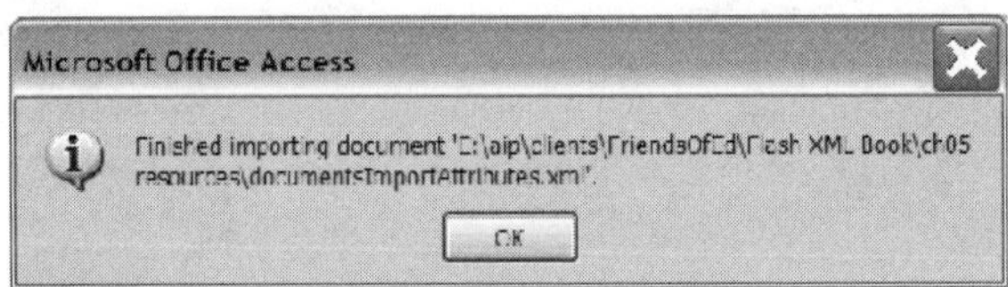

Figure 7-35. Access has completed the import.

If the transformation creates an XML document that Access can't import, you'll see the error message shown in Figure 7-36.

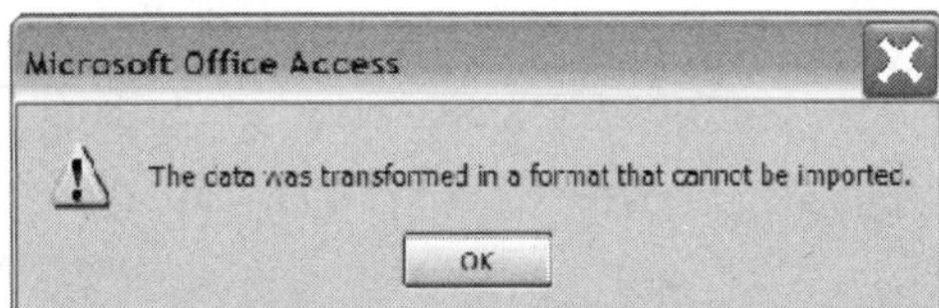

Figure 7-36. Tranformation errors prevent XML data from being imported in Access.

As previously mentioned, one of the reasons that you might need to transform data during the import process is if your XML document contains attributes. We'll look at importing attributes in the next section.

Using a style sheet to import attributes

Access can't deal with attributes in XML elements. If you need to import content that includes attributes, you'll have to use a transformation to change the content to elements before Access can include that content within a table. You can do this as part of the import process.

In the following XML document, all of the content is stored within attributes. You can see this content in the resource file `documentsImportAttributes.xml`.

```
<?xml version="1.0" encoding="UTF-8"?>
<allBooks>
  <book id="10" name="More great bike trips" authorID="4"
  publishYear="2005" categoryID="5" />
</allBooks>
```

To transform the data from attributes to elements, we'll need to apply a style sheet during the import process. This code shows the XML document structure that Access requires for imports:

```
<?xml version="1.0" encoding="UTF-8"?>
<dataroot xmlns:od="urn:schemas-microsoft-com:officedata"
generated="2005-06-03T06:55:34">
  <tblDocuments>
    <documentID>10</documentID>
    <documentName>More great bike trips</documentName>
    <authorID>4</authorID>
    <documentPublishYear>2005</documentPublishYear>
    <categoryID>5</categoryID>
```

```
  </tblDocuments>
</dataroot>
```

We can achieve the transformation by applying an XSLT style sheet. We'll work through an exercise to explore this further.

Exercise 6: Applying a transformation during import

In this exercise, we'll use an XSLT style sheet to transform an XML document containing attributes into a structure that Access can import.

1. Open `documents.mdb` in Access 2003 if necessary.
2. Import the file documentsImportAttributes.xml from your resources into Access. Click the Options button in the Import XML dialog box.
3. Add a transformation that uses the file `documentsImportTransform.xsl`. You can find this file in your resources. Append the data to the end of the existing table tblDocuments.
4. Open tblDocuments to check that Access has appended the data successfully.

I've shown the contents of the XSLT style sheet here. You can also view the resource file `documentsImportTransform.xsl`.

```
<?xml version="1.0"?>
<xsl:stylesheet version="1.0"
xmlns:xsl="http://www.w3.org/1999/XSL/Transform">
<xsl:output method="xml" version="1.0"/>
  <xsl:template match="/">
    <dataroot xmlns:od="urn:schemas-microsoft-com:officedata"
    generated="2005-06-03T06:00:01">
      <xsl:for-each select="/allBooks/book">
        <tblDocuments>
          <documentID>
           <xsl:value-of select="@id"/>
          </documentID>
          <documentName>
            <xsl:value-of select="@name"/>
          </documentName>
          <authorID>
            <xsl:value-of select="@authorID"/>
          </authorID>
          <documentPublishYear>
            <xsl:value-of select="@publishYear"/>
          </documentPublishYear>
          <categoryID>
            <xsl:value-of select="@categoryID"/>
          </categoryID>
        </tblDocuments>
      </xsl:for-each>
    </dataroot>
  </xsl:template>
</xsl:stylesheet>
```

The style sheet moves through each attribute and converts it to a named element. It uses the shorthand XPath notation @ to refer to each attribute. You can find out more about XPath statements in XSLT style sheets in Chapter 3.

Putting it all together

We'll finish the chapter by putting together what we've covered to create a Flash application that uses content from Access 2003. Access will export the data in XML format and Flash will use it in a document search application.

Exercise 7: Including data from Access in a Flash movie

In this exercise, we'll use Flash to search the contents of an Access database via XML documents. We'll export Access data into several different XML documents to populate the Flash interface. When the Flash movie loads, it will display all books from the Access database. Users will then be able to refine the list of books and filter the data by category or author. You can see the working example saved as `documents_completed.fla` in your resource files if you want to get a better idea of the application that you're building.

Generating the XML content

1. Open `documents.mdb` in Access 2003 if necessary.
2. Export the three tables from the database and save the XML documents as authorsList.xml, categoriesList.xml, and documentsList.xml. Make sure you uncheck the Schema option. You don't need to change any other settings.
3. Open the three documents in an XML or text editor to view the content.

Loading the XML documents into Flash

4. Open the starter file `documents.fla` in Flash. Figure 7-37 shows the interface. It contains two ComboBox components that you'll use to search for documents. It also contains a List component to display book details, as well as two Button components.

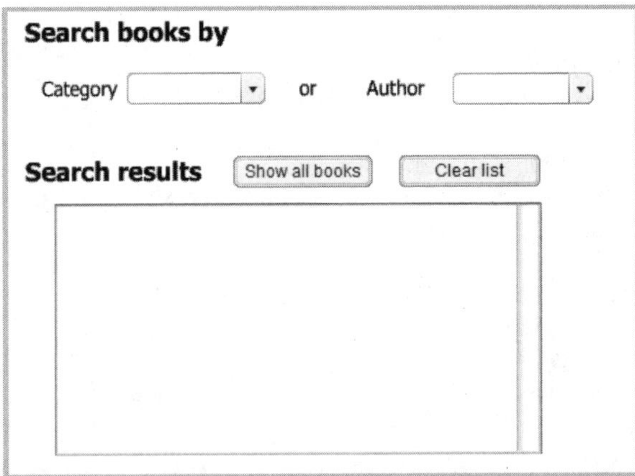

Figure 7-37. The documents.fla interface.

5. Create a new layer called actions and add the code show here on frame 1. The code creates three XML objects and loads the file documentsList.xml into one of the objects. The properties and onLoad event handlers are set for all three objects. When the document loads successfully, the DocsRootNode variable is set and Flash calls the loadCategoriesXML and loadAuthorsXML functions.

```
var DocsRootNode:XMLNode;
var catsXML:XML = new XML();
catsXML.ignoreWhite = true;
catsXML.onLoad = loadCategories;
var authorsXML:XML = new XML();
authorsXML.ignoreWhite = true;
authorsXML.onLoad = loadAuthors;
var docsXML:XML = new XML();
docsXML.ignoreWhite = true;
docsXML.onLoad = loadAllDocs;
docsXML.load("documentsList.xml");
function loadAllDocs(success:Boolean):Void {
  if (success) {
    DocsRootNode = this.firstChild;
    trace (DocsRootNode);
    loadCategoriesXML();
    loadAuthorsXML();
  }
}
```

6. Test the movie and you should see the DocsRootNode variable shown in an Output window.

7. Modify the loadAllDocs function as shown here. The new lines appear in bold. The function loads the remaining two XML documents into the catsXML and authorsXML objects.

```
function loadAllDocs(success:Boolean):Void {
  if (success) {
    DocsRootNode = this.firstChild;
    catsXML.load("categoriesList.xml");
    authorsXML.load("authorsList.xml");

  }
}
```

8. Add the following functions below the loadAllDocs function in the actions layer. When the new XML objects have successfully loaded, the contents display in an Output window. I've added a separator to make it easier to see the different XML trees in the Output window.

```
function loadCategories(success:Boolean):Void {
  if (success){
    var catsRootNode:XMLNode = this.firstChild;
    trace (catsRootNode);
  }
}
function loadAuthors(success:Boolean):Void {
  if (success){
```

```
      var authorsRootNode:XMLNode = this.firstChild;
      trace ("-----------");
      trace (authorsRootNode);
    }
  }
```

9. Test the movie and you should see the two root node variables in an Output window. Figure 7-38 shows this window.

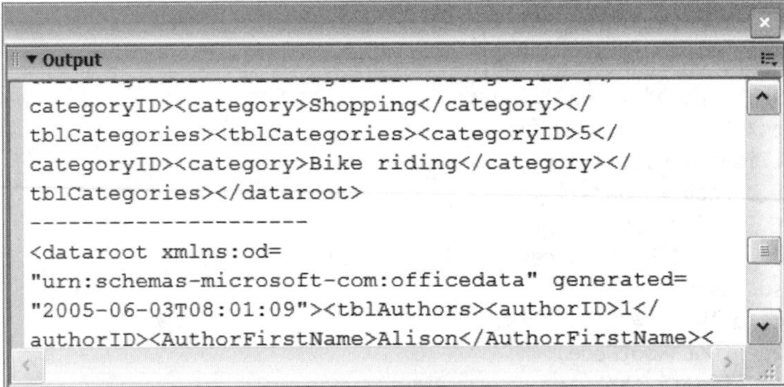

Figure 7-38. The Output window showing the XML trees

Populating the List component

10. Modify the loadAllDocs function to call the showAllDocs function. The showAllDocs function will populate the List component. I've created a function for this code so that we can call it again later when we click the Show all books button.

```
function loadAllDocs(success:Boolean):Void {
  if (success) {
    DocsRootNode = this.firstChild;
    catsXML.load("categoriesList.xml");
    authorsXML.load("authorsList.xml");
    showAllDocs();
  }
}
```

11. Add the showAllDocs function. This function populates the List component using the book title and publication year. It sorts the book names into alphabetical order.

```
function showAllDocs():Void{
  var BookNode:XMLNode;
  var ListItem_str:String;
  for (var i:Number = 0; i < DocsRootNode.childNodes.length; i++) {
    BookNode = DocsRootNode.childNodes[i];
    ListItem_str = BookNode.childNodes[1].firstChild.nodeValue;
    ListItem_str += ", "+BookNode.childNodes[3].firstChild.nodeValue;
    results_list.addItem(ListItem_str);
  }
  results_list.sortItemsBy("label");
}
```

12. Test the movie. Figure 7-39 shows the appearance of the movie at this point.

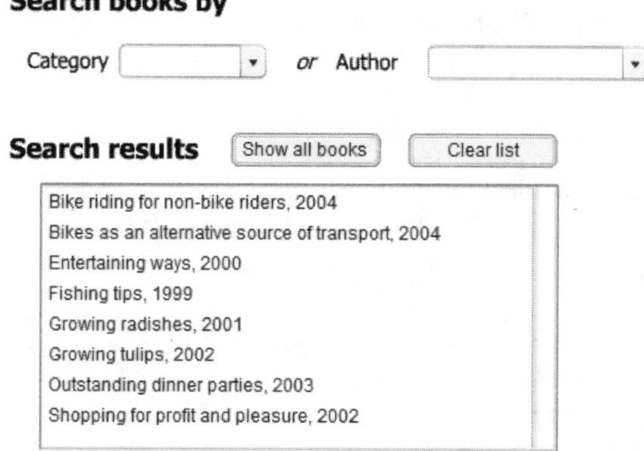

Figure 7-39. The populated List component

Configuring the buttons

13. Add the following code on the actions layer. The code configures the Show all books and Clear list buttons. When we click the Show all books button, we clear the existing contents and call the showAllDocs function. Clicking the Clear list button removes the contents of the List.

```
show_btn.onRelease = function():Void {
  results_list.removeAll();
  showAllDocs();
}
clear_btn.onRelease = function():Void {
  results_list.removeAll();
}
```

14. Test the movie and check that you can remove and show the contents within the List.

Configuring the ComboBoxes

15. Modify the loadCategories function as shown here so that it loads the categories in the category_cb ComboBox component. The function sorts the ComboBox and adds a Choose item at the top of the list.

```
function loadCategories(success:Boolean):Void {
  if (success){
    var catsRootNode:XMLNode = this.firstChild;
    var categoryNode:XMLNode;
    var category_str:String;
    var catID_int_int:Number;
    for (var i:Number = 0; i < catsRootNode.childNodes.length; i++) {
      categoryNode = catsRootNode.childNodes[i];
      category_str = categoryNode.childNodes[1].firstChild.nodeValue;
      catID_int = categoryNode.childNodes[0].firstChild.nodeValue;
```

```
        category_cb.addItem(category_str, catID_int);
      }
      category_cb.sortItemsBy("label");
      category_cb.addItemAt(0, "Choose ...");
      category_cb.selectedIndex = 0;
    }
  }
```

16. Modify the `loadAuthors` function as shown here. The new code appears in bold. Again, the function populates the ComboBox and adds a Choose item.

```
function loadAuthors(success:Boolean):Void {
  if (success){
    var authorsRootNode:XMLNode = this.firstChild;
    var authorNode:XMLNode;
    var author_str:String;
    var auID_int:Number;
    for (var i:Number = 0; i < authorsRootNode.childNodes.length; i++) {
      authorNode=authorsRootNode.childNodes[i];
      author_str=authorNode.childNodes[2].firstChild.nodeValue;
      author_str+=", "+authorNode.childNodes[1].firstChild.nodeValue;
      auID_int = authorNode.childNodes[0].firstChild.nodeValue;
      author_cb.addItem(author_str, auID_int);
    }
    author_cb.sortItemsBy("label");
    author_cb.addItemAt(0, "Choose ...");
    author_cb.selectedIndex = 0;
  }
}
```

17. Test the movie and check that Flash has loaded the ComboBoxes. Figure 7-40 shows how the interface should look at this point.

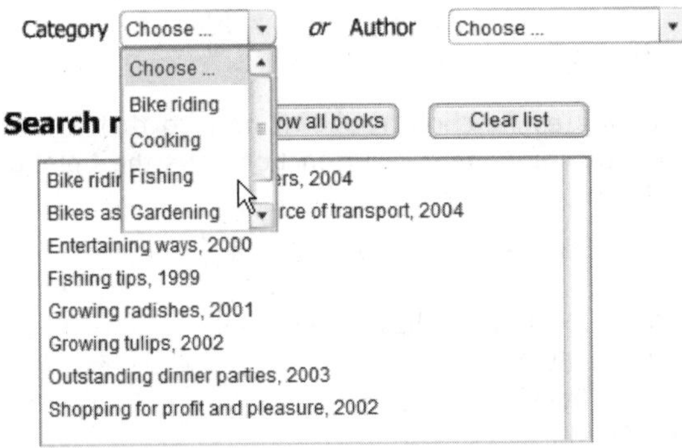

Figure 7-40. Testing that the ComboBox components have successfully loaded

Adding listeners to the ComboBoxes

18. Add the listeners shown here to the ComboBox components. The listeners listen for the change event and call the doFilter function, passing the name of the component and the selected value. Note that this only happens if the user selects an option other than Choose.

```
var CatListener:Object = new Object();
CatListener.change = filterResults;
category_cb.addEventListener("change", CatListener);

var auListener:Object = new Object();
auListener.change = filterResults;
author_cb.addEventListener("change", auListener);

function filterResults(evtObj:Object):Void {
  var componentName:String = evtObj.target._name;
  var componentValue:Number = evtObj.target.selectedItem.data;
  if (componentValue > 0) {
    doFilter(componentName, componentValue);
  }
}
```

Displaying the results

19. Add the following doFilter function. The function sets variables and removes the existing contents from the List. It determines which Combo we're working with and sets the child node number for use in the docsXML object. Child node 4, the fifth element, contains the author ID while number 2, the third element, contains the category ID. We then loop through the childNodes collection, that is, the books, and add any matching values to the List component. Finally, we sort the list into title order.

```
function doFilter(theComponent, theComponentValue){
  var nodeNum:Number;
  var BookNode:XMLNode;
  var nodeFilterID:Number;
  var ListItem_str:String;
  results_list.removeAll();
  if (theComponent._name == "category_cb") {
    nodeNum = 4;
    author_cb.selectedIndex = 0;
  }
  else {
    nodeNum = 2;
    category_cb.selectedIndex = 0;
  }
  for (var i:Number = 0; i <DocsRootNode.childNodes.length; i++) {
    BookNode = DocsRootNode.childNodes[i];
    nodeFilterID = BookNode.childNodes[nodeNum].firstChild.nodeValue;
    if (nodeFilterID == theComponentValue) {
      ListItem_str=BookNode.childNodes[1].firstChild.nodeValue;
      ListItem_str+=", "+BookNode.childNodes[3].firstChild.nodeValue;
```

```
      results_list.addItem(ListItem_str);
    }
  }
  results_list.sortItemsBy("label");
}
```

20. Modify the button functions as shown here. The new lines (which appear in bold) reset the ComboBox components back to the Choose option.

```
show_btn.onRelease = function():Void {
  results_list.removeAll();
  category_cb.selectedIndex = 0;
  author_cb.selectedIndex = 0;
  showAllDocs();
}
clear_btn.onRelease = function():Void {
  results_list.removeAll();
  category_cb.selectedIndex = 0;
  author_cb.selectedIndex = 0;
}
```

21. Test the movie. You should be able to filter the data by either category or author. You can see the completed `documents_completed.fla` within your resource files.

22. Modify the content in Access and export the files again. Check that the updated content appears in the Flash movie.

In this example, we were able to take the contents from Access tables and add them to a Flash application. There was only a small amount of content in the database, but the Flash movie would work the same way with larger amounts of data. The only thing to remember is that whenever you modify the Access database, you'll need to export the XML documents again to update the Flash movie. If your users aren't familiar with how to use Access, a Flash interface creates a more user-friendly means of interacting with the data.

Access XML resources

The Microsoft website contains resources for working with XML in Access 2003. You can find out more about working with XML in Access 2003 at `http://msdn.microsoft.com/office/understanding/xmloffice/articles/default.aspx?pull=/library/en-us/odc_ac2003_ta/html/odc_accessnewxmlfeatures.asp`. The Office XML Developer Center has useful articles; you can find it at `www.msdn.microsoft.com/office/understanding/xmloffice/default.aspx`.

Summary

In this chapter, you've seen how you can export and import XML data using Access 2003. You learned about the limits of working with XML in Access, and we worked through an exercise to include the database content in a Flash application. In Chapters 5 and 6, we covered Word and Excel 2003. If you've worked through all of these chapters, you'll have learned how to set up Office documents that can generate XML content for use in Flash.

It's important for you to learn Office 2003 XML skills so that you can incorporate them in your workflow. When you build XML Flash applications, you and your clients will need some way to maintain the XML content. You can create new Office documents or modify existing documents so that your clients can use Word, Excel, or Access 2003 to update XML Flash movies.

You may need to provide some training to your clients so that they can learn the extra import and export skills, but as you've seen, these techniques aren't difficult to grasp. The result is that your clients will have complete control over the content in their Flash applications without having to learn to use Flash.

Microsoft provides some excellent resources for learning XML with Office 2003 at its website. There are also a number of tools that you can download at `http://msdn.microsoft.com/office/understanding/xmloffice/tools/default.aspx`, including reference information for WordprocessingML and SpreadsheetML as well as add-ins for Word and Excel.

In the next chapter, I'll look at the data components that ship with Flash Professional. The components allow you to load and bind XML data directly to other data and user interface components. You'll learn how to incorporate XML content into Flash by writing a single line of ActionScript. You'll also see how you can script these components.

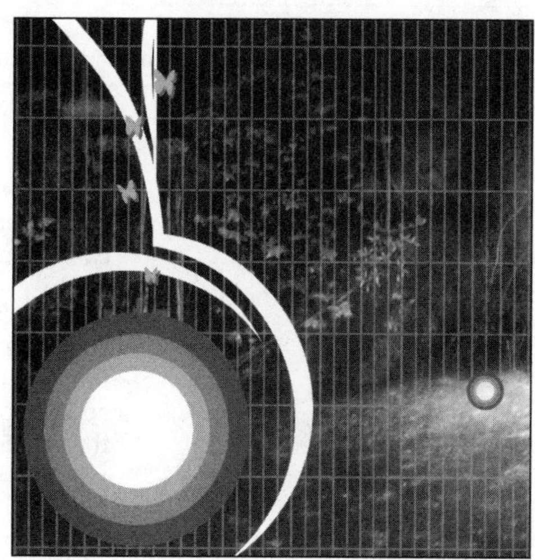

Chapter 8

USING THE DATA COMPONENTS WITH XML

In Chapter 4, you saw how to use ActionScript with the XML class. We loaded an XML document into Flash. We also created and modified XML content within Flash and sent it to a server-side file for processing. In Chapters 5, 6 and 7, we used Office 2003 for the PC to generate and manage the XML content for use in Flash.

Instead of writing ActionScript to work with XML content, you can use the data components supplied with Flash Professional. These components allow you to work visually. You drag the components into your movies and configure them using the Component Inspector panel. This can speed up your development process—you can include XML content without having to write a single line of ActionScript. The data components have no visual appearance in the published `.swf` file, so it doesn't matter where you place them.

Understanding data components

Flash Professional 8 includes a number of data components. Table 8-1 lists and explains the main purpose of each one.

Table 8-1. The data components shipped with Flash Professional

Component	Purpose
DataHolder	The DataHolder stores data and can be used to share information between other components. Unlike the DataSet, it doesn't track changes made by UI components.
DataSet	The DataSet also stores data that you can share with other components. The DataSet allows you to keep track of modifications that you make using UI components. You can then notify external applications of the changes made within Flash. We'll learn more about the DataSet component later in this chapter.
RDBMSResolver	The RDBMSResolver sends changes in data to an external data source. It works with database content.
WebServiceConnector	The WebServiceConnector consumes SOAP web services. You'll find out more about this component in Chapter 9.
XMLConnector	The XMLConnector connects to external XML documents. You can use the component to read and write XML data. You can use the component with the DataSet and XUpdateResolver components where you need to change external data using a server-side page. We'll learn more about the XMLConnector component in this chapter.
XUpdateResolver	The XUpdateResolver component creates XUpdate statements that describe changes made to your XML data within Flash. You use this component with the DataSet component. We'll explore this component later in this chapter.

You can download other data components, such as the RemotingConnector and MSSQLXMLConnector, from the Macromedia website.

In addition to the data components, Flash Professional 8 includes data-aware UI components such as the DataGrid, ComboBox, and List. This means that you can use data binding to connect the XML content from the XMLConnector directly to these UI components. You don't have to write ActionScript that loops through collections of `childNodes`. Instead, you configure the bindings visually through the Component Inspector and Flash does the hard work.

If you prefer to write ActionScript, you can also script the data components. You can use ActionScript to set all of the properties that are available through the Component Inspector. This may be useful if you're adding components to the Stage dynamically. However, scripting data binding between components can be a tricky proposition. You'll probably find it much easier to work with the Component Inspector.

There are some disadvantages to using the data components. First, you can only use these components in Flash Player 7 and above. The second disadvantage is the size of the components. Adding data components dramatically increases the size of your `.fla` files. Luckily, this size reduces again when you compile your `.swf` file.

In this chapter, I'll show you how to use the XMLConnector to load XML data into Flash. We'll bind the data to UI components and track changes through a DataSet component. We'll also look at the process of sending changes to an external data source with the XUpdateResolver component. I'll finish by showing you how to write ActionScript for the XMLConnector class. We'll create a simple address book application that lets you display and update XML content in Flash. Note that Flash can't update external data, so you'd still need to use a server-side file to update the external XML document.

Understanding the XMLConnector

The XMLConnector component is an alternative to the XML class. Instead of writing ActionScript to work with XML data, you can use the XMLConnector. The component can send, receive, and both send and receive XML content in the same way as the `load`, `send`, and `sendAndLoad` methods of the XML class. The most common use for the XMLConnector is to load an external XML document and bind the data to UI components.

One drawback of the XML class is that there is no support for XML schemas. You can't validate an XML document or view the required structures for your elements in Flash. This isn't the case with the XMLConnector. You can import sample XML data so that Flash displays a representation of the structure. Once you've done this, you can find the names of all elements and attributes as well as their datatypes in the Component Inspector panel.

The XMLConnector component allows you to bind data directly to UI components such as the TextInput, ComboBox, List, or DataGrid. Instead of writing ActionScript, you can configure the Component Inspector so that Flash automatically adds information from the external XML document to the UI components. You can add formatting to control how the content displays in your movie.

Binding directly to UI components means that a user cannot update the data. If you want users to update the data, you can track updates to the XML content by including a DataSet component and an XUpdateResolver. This is a more complicated process. I'll explain both processes in the next sections.

Displaying read-only XML data

If you are using Flash to display data from an external XML document, the process is simple. You load the XML document into Flash using an XMLConnector component. You then bind the XML content directly to one or more user interface components. You can also bind the data through the DataHolder or DataSet component, although this is less common. Figure 8-1 shows the process for displaying this type of data.

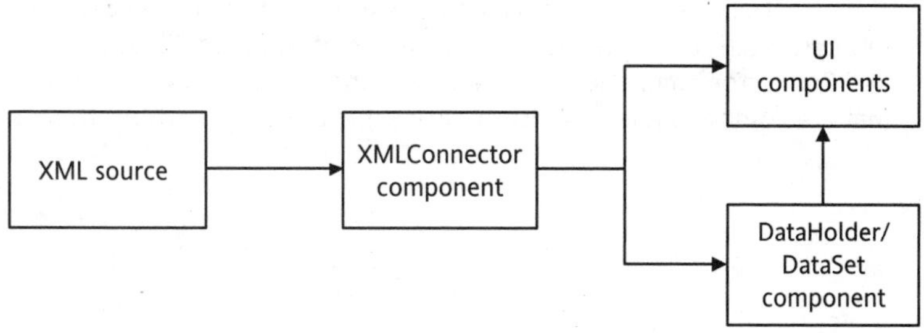

Figure 8-1. Using read-only XML data in Flash

Things become more complicated if you need Flash to track the changes made by the UI components. Flash can monitor these changes, but because it can't modify external content, you'll have to rely on server-side pages to update the external data source.

Displaying updatable XML data

You'll still use the XMLConnector to load the XML document. However, you'll need to bind the XML data to a DataSet component first before binding the DataSet to your UI components. The DataSet monitors changes made to the data by the UI components. The DataSet can then generate a list of all changes for the XUpdateResolver component. The XUpdateResolver converts the changes into statements for processing by a server-side file. Figure 8-2 shows this process.

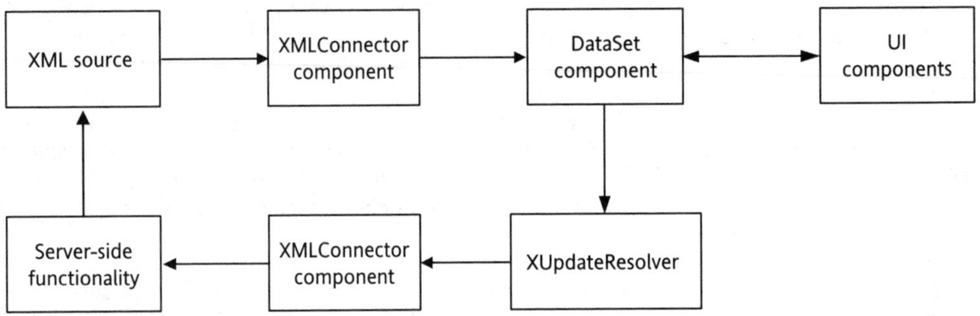

Figure 8-2. Using updatable XML data in Flash

Whichever process you use, you'll need to start by adding an XMLConnector and configuring it with the Component Inspector. You should note that all of the security restrictions on external data still apply to the XMLConnector component. You can find out more about these restrictions in Chapter 4.

Configuring the XMLConnector

Figure 8-3. The XMLConnector component icon

You can add an XMLConnector to your Flash movie by dragging it from the Components panel. I normally place these components off the Stage as they have no visual appearance in compiled Flash movies. Once you've added the component, you'll see the icon shown in Figure 8-3.

You can configure the settings for the XMLConnector in the Component Inspector. This panel allows you to specify the external XML document and configure other settings, such as white space. Don't forget that you'll also need to give the XMLConnector component an instance name. I usually use the suffix _xc to indicate that the component is an XMLConnector, for example, `instanceName_xc`.

Using the Component Inspector

Once you've added an XMLConnector to your Flash movie, you'll need to configure it with the Component Inspector. Figure 8-4 shows the Component Inspector panel.

The Component Inspector has three tabs that you'll use to work with the XMLConnector. To start with, you'll need to configure the Parameters panel so that you can set the connection properties. Table 8-2 shows a summary of the parameters in this panel and their purpose.

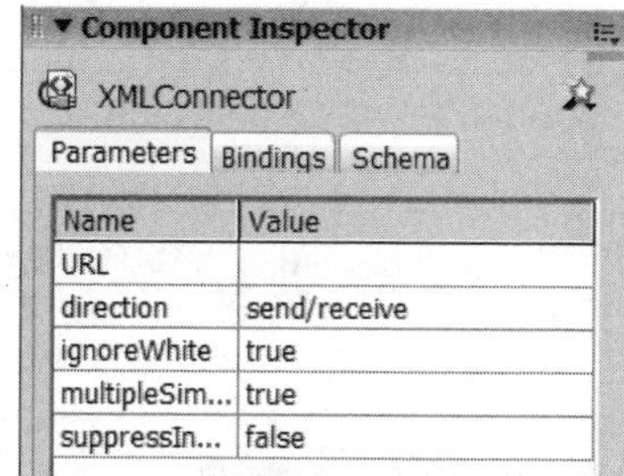

Figure 8-4. The Component Inspector panel

Table 8-2. The properties listed in the Parameters tab of the Component Inspector

Parameter	Purpose
URL	The path to an external XML document. This setting does not need to refer to a file ending with `.xml`. You can enter the path to a server-side file that results in an XML document. If you do this, you must remember to include the full server path, e.g., `http://localhost/XML/generateXML.aspx`.
direction	Determines whether you are sending, sending/receiving, or receiving the XML data. These values correspond to the `send`, `load`, and `sendAndLoad` methods of the XML class.
ignoreWhite	Determines whether white space is significant in the XML document. Note that this is set to true by default whereas the XML class has a default setting of false.
multipleSimultaneousAllowed	Specifies whether to allow multiple connections. If you set this property to false, when you are triggering one XMLConnector, further triggers are not possible.
suppressInvalidCall	Sets the behavior for invalid data parameters. If you set the value to true, the component won't be triggered if the parameters are invalid.

Most of the time, you'll only need to configure the first two settings: URL and direction.

After you've configured the parameters for the XMLConnector, you can import a sample XML document into Flash so you can see the XML element and attribute structures. This gives you a visual representation of the XML document structure and lists the names and datatypes of attributes and elements. Flash refers to this representation as a *schema*. Bear in mind that this is not the same as an XML schema. The next section covers the process of importing an XML structure into Flash.

Creating a schema from an XML document

The Schema tab in the Component Inspector allows you to generate a schema from an existing XML document. You choose a document with an .xml extension and Flash will find the names and datatypes of each element and attribute.

If you're using an XML file instead of a server-side file, you can generate a schema from the document that you're loading into Flash. You can also use a trimmed-down version of the file, as long as it contains at least two data elements. Note that you can't load a schema from a server-side file that results in an XML document.

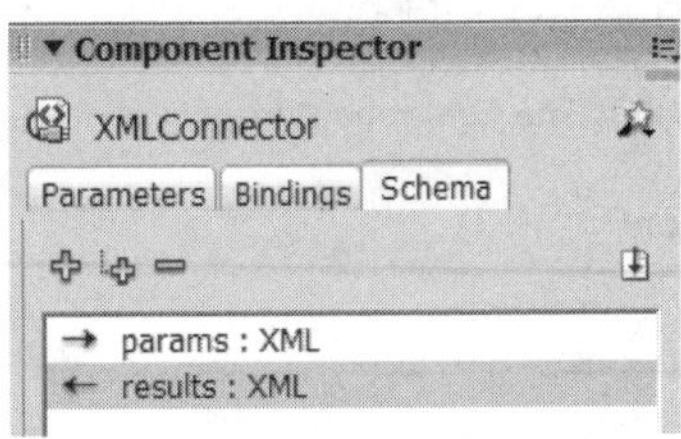

Figure 8-5. The Schema tab in the Component Inspector panel

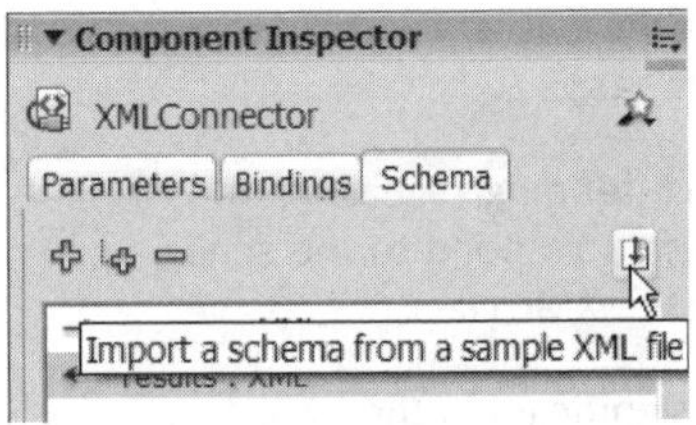

Figure 8-6. Importing a schema from a sample XML document

Flash allows you to generate two different types of schemas from external XML documents: one called params:XML and the other results:XML. The params type represents the structure of data being sent out of Flash while you use results for the structure of incoming XML data. Figure 8-5 shows both options. You can see their direction by looking at the arrows. The right arrow to the left of params indicates that XML data is outgoing while the left arrow indicates incoming data for results.

To create a schema, select either params or results and click the Import a schema button at the right side of the Schema tab. Figure 8-6 shows the button.

Click the button and navigate to the XML document. You must use a physical XML document rather than a server-side file that generates an XML document. Once you've imported the document, Flash will display the structure within the Schema tab.

I've used the resource file address.xml to generate the structure shown in Figure 8-7. The following listing shows the contents of the XML document:

```
<?xml version="1.0" encoding="UTF-8"?>
<phoneBook>
  <contact>
    <id>1</id>
    <name>Sas Jacobs</name>
    <address>123 Some Street, Some City, Some Country</address>
    <phone>123 456</phone>
  </contact>
  <contact>
    <id>2</id>
    <name>John Smith</name>
    <address>4 Another Street, Another City, Another Country</address>
    <phone>456 789</phone>
  </contact>
  <contact>
    <id>3</id>
    <name>Jo Bloggs</name>
    <address>7 Different Street, Different City, UK</address>
```

```
        <phone>789 123</phone>
      </contact>
    </phoneBook>
```

The address.xml document generates the Flash schema shown in Figure 8-7.

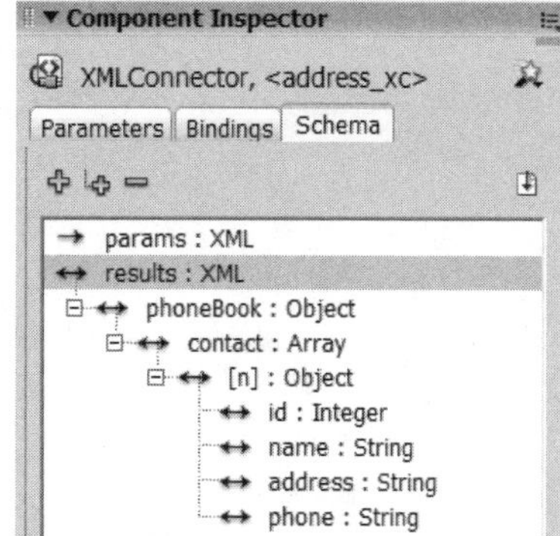

Figure 8-7. A sample results schema

Flash lists the name and datatype of each element in the Schema tab. In Figure 8-7, the root element is called phoneBook. It has an Object datatype. It contains an array of contact elements, equivalent to the childNodes collection in the XML class. The contact element contains id, name, address, and phone content.

You'll notice that the XML document shown in the previous listing is slightly different from the one we used in earlier chapters—it doesn't use attributes. In this version of the XML document, I've modified the id attribute and made it a child element of <contact>. The revised structure will make things easier as we bind data to UI components. Figure 8-8 shows a schema that contains attributes. They are prefaced by an @ sign.

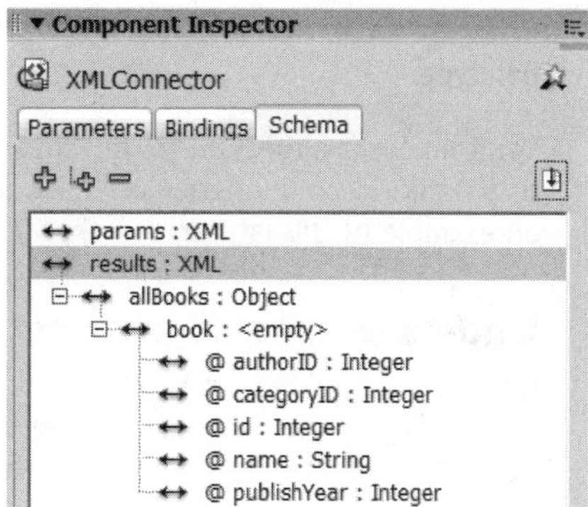

Figure 8-8. The results schema showing attributes

The schema shown in Flash is a representation of the bindable data structures within an XML document at the time of import. In other words, it shows what data you can bind to your other data components.

Flash doesn't maintain a link back to the XML document used to generate the results schema. If you change the XML document, you'll need to import the XML document again and regenerate the schema. You may also need to change your data bindings. It's probably not ideal to use the XMLConnector component if the structure of your XML document is likely to change.

If you don't have a sample XML document, you can create a schema in Flash manually.

Creating a schema by adding fields

While the usual method is to generate a schema by importing an existing XML document, it is possible for you to create the schema yourself. Select the parent element for your schema field and click the Add a field button, as shown in Figure 8-9. If you're adding the root element, you'll need to select either params or results first. For each subsequent element, you'll need to click the parent and add another field.

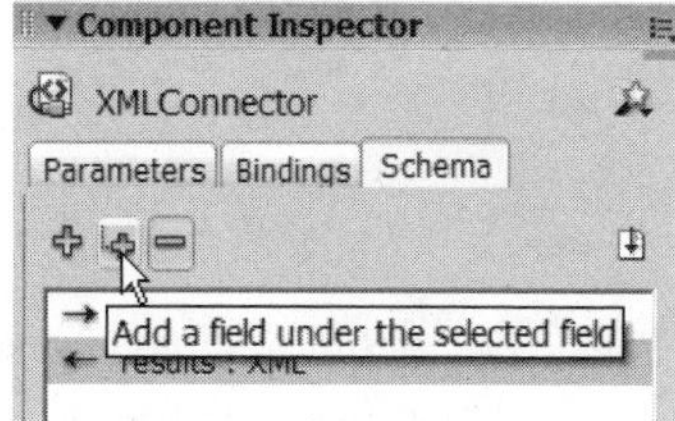

Figure 8-9. Clicking the Add a field button

Flash will add a new field underneath the selected element. You can configure the field using the settings at the bottom of the Schema tab. Figure 8-10 shows the properties that you can configure.

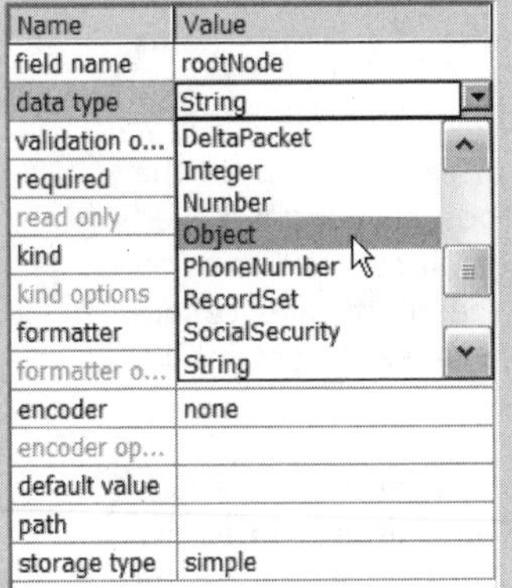

Figure 8-10. Configuring a new field

In Figure 8-10, I've entered the name rootNode for the new field and I'm selecting the Object datatype.

You can also use the Schema tab with the UI components. For example, if you're binding the XML data to a DataGrid component, you'll use the Schema tab to set the details for each column. I'll show you an example of this later in this chapter.

Understanding schema settings

Once you've created a schema for your XML document, you can configure the settings in the panel at the bottom of the Schema tab. The panel will display the settings for the currently selected schema item. Figure 8-11 shows the settings for an Array item called contact.

Name	Value
field name	contact
data type	Array
validation options	
required	true
read only	false
kind	none
kind options	
formatter	none
formatter options	
encoder	none
encoder options	
default value	
path	
storage type	array

Figure 8-11. The settings for an Array field

You don't often need to change the field properties within the Schema tab. Table 8-3 summarizes each setting and its purpose.

Table 8-3. Schema element settings

Setting	Explanation
field name	Lists the name of the field.
data type	Sets the datatype for the field. You can choose from Array, Attribute, Boolean, Custom, DataProvider, Date, DeltaPacket, Integer, Number, Object, PhoneNumber, SocialSecurity, String, XML, or ZipCode.
validation options	Specifies the validation for the field contents, for example, the number of characters within a String field. This option is only available for the following datatypes: Custom, Integer, Number, String, and XML.
required	Specifies whether the field is required.
read only	Specifies whether the content can be updated through data binding.
kind	Sets the kind of data at runtime. Select from none, AutoTrigger, Calculated, or Data. You could use a Calculated kind to create a calculation based on other field values.
kind options	Specifies any additional settings associated with the kind setting.
formatter	Details the name of a formatter to use when converting the field to a String type.
formatter options	Specifies any additional settings associated with the selected formatter.
encoder	Sets the encoding for the data at runtime. Select from Boolean, Compose String, Custom Formatter, Date, Rearrange Fields, or Number Formatter.
encoder options	Specifies any additional settings associated with the encoder.
default value	Specifies the default setting when the data is undefined or when you add a new item in Flash.
path	An optional setting specifying a path expression for the data.
storage type	The way data is stored. This setting relates to the data type chosen and is one of the following values: simple, attribute, array, or complex. You shouldn't need to change this setting.

Once you've configured the parameters and added a schema, you can trigger the XMLConnector component and test that it's working correctly. Triggering forces the XMLConnector to load data. After you've done that, you can bind the XML data to other components.

Triggering the component

You have to trigger the XMLConnector component before it sends or loads an XML document. One option is to trigger the XMLConnector after a button click. You can also trigger the component when the Flash movie first loads.

Triggering requires a single line of ActionScript that you can either write yourself or generate by adding a Behavior. Whichever method you choose, it's important to check that you've given the XMLConnector an instance name first. I'll start by showing you how you can trigger the component with a Behavior.

First, you'll need to show the Behaviors panel by using the *Shift-F3* shortcut key. Select frame 1 of the layer for the ActionScript. You can also select a button instance. Click the plus sign in the Behaviors panel, choose the Data category, and select Trigger Data Source. Figure 8-12 shows the selected option.

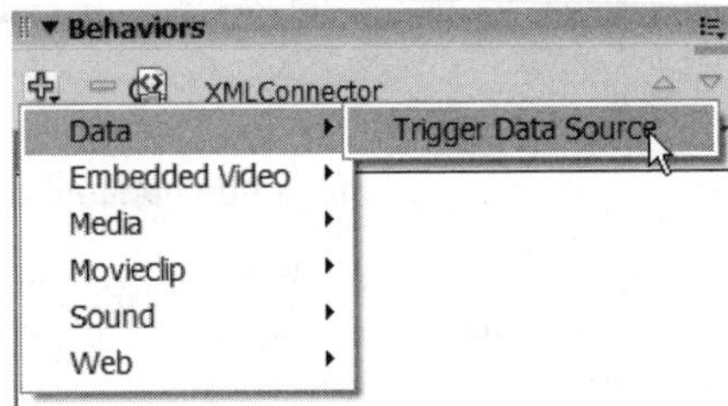

Figure 8-12. Adding a Behavior to trigger the XMLConnector

Flash will prompt you to select the component instance to trigger, as shown in Figure 8-13.

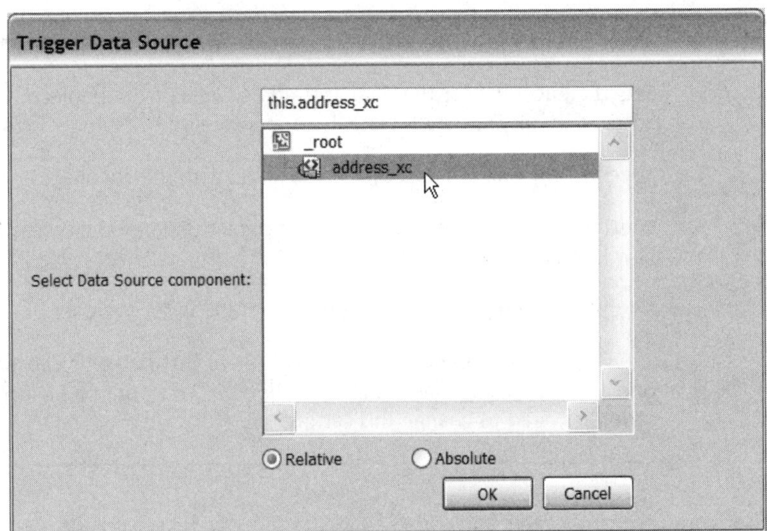

Figure 8-13. Selecting the XMLConnector component

Choose the instance and select whether you want a Relative or Absolute path. I normally leave the default Relative option selected. Click OK, and Flash will create a new Behavior to trigger the XMLConnector. Figure 8-14 shows the new Behavior in the Behaviors panel.

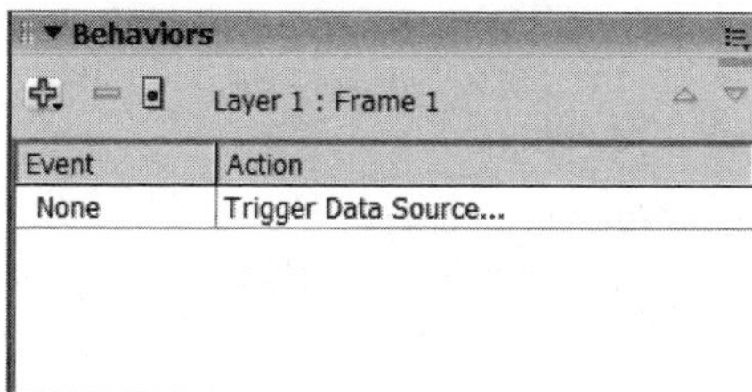

Figure 8-14. The Behaviors panel showing the new Behavior

Flash adds the ActionScript that triggers the XMLConnector to your selected location. You can view the Actions panel to see the code that Flash generates. Figure 8-15 shows a frame action in the Actions panel after adding the Behavior. We used a Relative setting in the Trigger Data Source dialog box.

Actions - Frame

```
// Trigger Data Source Behavior
// Macromedia 2003
this.address_xc.trigger();
```

Layer 1 : 1

Line 5 of 5, Col 1

Figure 8-15. The ActionScript generated by Flash

The code to trigger a component is very simple. It consists of the instance name of the XMLConnector and the `trigger` method. In Figure 8-15, it also includes the word `this`. If you're working on the main timeline, you can remove `this` without affecting the `trigger` method.

```
instanceName.trigger();
```

The `trigger` method creates a call to the XML document specified in the Component Inspector. When it completes the call, the `result` event is broadcast. You can use this event to process the results from the loaded XML document with ActionScript. In the first exercise, you'll see how to use this event to display the XML tree in an Output window.

Testing for a loaded XML document

To test whether an XML document has loaded, you'll have to write ActionScript that accesses the results from the XMLConnector. You'll use an event listener to listen for the result event. The results property of the XMLConnector contains the XML document, and you can trace this to see the contents. Be careful not to mix up the result and results keywords—they mean very different things. This code snippet shows an example:

```
var xmlListener:Object = new Object();
xmlListener.result = function(evtObj:Object):Void {
  trace (evtObj.target.results);
};
myXML_xc.addEventListener("result", xmlListener);
myXML_xc.trigger();
```

If you tested this code, you'd see the XML document displayed in an Output window. The listener passes the evtObj object to the event handler function, and you can use evtObj.target.results to display the complete XML document.

Loading an XML document into Flash

A common use for the XMLConnector is to load an external XML document into Flash. You'll drag an XMLConnector component to the Flash movie. You'll then configure the parameters and add a URL for the file that you want to load. If you don't need to update the content in Flash, you can set the direction property to receive on the Parameters tab of the Component Inspector. If you do need to update the content in Flash, you can use the send/receive setting; however, it's more common to use a second XMLConnector to send the updated data from Flash.

While you don't need to use a schema when you load an external XML document, it's a good idea. It makes binding much easier if you can see a visual representation of your element and attribute structure.

So far, I've shown you the theory about how to use the XMLConnector component. Now, let's work through an example that uses the XMLConnector to load an external XML document.

Exercise 1: Loading an external XML document using the XMLConnector component

In this example, we'll load the file address.xml into Flash using the XMLConnector component. We'll add some ActionScript to display the XML content within an Output window.

1. Open Flash and create a new movie.
2. Rename Layer 1 as UI and add another layer called actions.
3. Drag an XMLConnector component to the UI layer. Position it off the Stage.
4. Name the component instance address_xc.
5. Save the file as loadContacts.fla in the same folder as the address.xml file.

6. Select the XMLConnector and show the Component Inspector. Configure the Parameters tab as shown in Figure 8-16.

   The tab shows the settings that will load the file `address.xml`.

7. Click on the Schema tab and import the file `address.xml` to create a schema. You should see the structure of the document displayed in the tab.

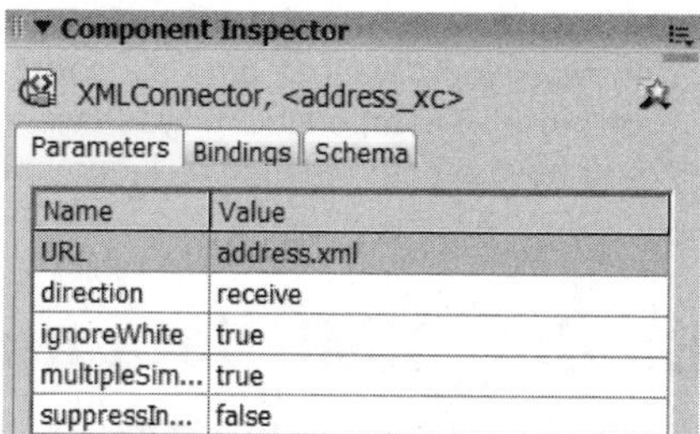

Figure 8-16. The completed Parameters tab

8. Click in frame 1 of the actions layer. If necessary, open the Behaviors panel using the *SHIFT-F3* shortcut.

9. Add a new Behavior to trigger the address_xc component. Click the plus sign in the Behaviors panel, choose the Data category, and select Trigger Data Source.

10. Open the Actions panel with the *F9* shortcut key and modify the code as shown here. The new lines appear in bold.

```
var xmlListener:Object = new Object();
xmlListener.result = function(evtObj:Object):Void {
  trace (evtObj.target.results);
};
address_xc.addEventListener("result", xmlListener);
address_xc.trigger();
```

   The lines create a new listener called `xmlListener`. The listener responds to the `result` event and displays the results of the XMLConnector component called `address_xc`.

11. Test the movie and you should see an Output window displaying the contents of `address.xml`. You can see my Output window in Figure 8-17. I've saved the completed resource file as `loadContacts.fla`.

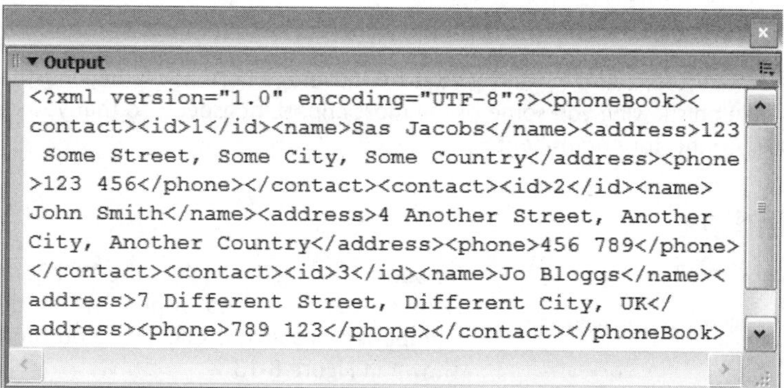

Figure 8-17. Tracing the results property of the XMLConnector

In exercise 1, we used the XMLConnector component to load XML content from the external file `address.xml`. We also added ActionScript so that we could display the XML tree and test that the XML document was successfully loaded.

After you load an XML document, you won't usually display the contents in an Output window. Instead, you'll want to bind the content to other components. You can bind the XML directly to one or more UI components or you can bind to a DataSet component first. In the next section, I'll show you how to bind directly to UI components.

Binding XML data directly to UI components

You use data binding to add the data from your XML document to one or more UI components. This is done visually, through the Component Inspector. Visual data binding is much easier than writing ActionScript to populate UI components. Instead of looping through `childNodes` and using the `addItem` method, you can configure the bindings in Bindings tab of the Component Inspector. For example, you can bind XML directly to the `dataProvider` of a ComboBox or List component.

The Bindings tab of the Component Inspector specifies how data is bound to another component. You will need to bind from the XMLConnector to a data-aware component, such as a List, DataGrid, or ComboBox. You can also use the Bindings tab to specify further bindings between UI components. For example, you could bind a List component to a TextInput component. When you click a List item, further details display in the TextInput component.

You'll need to set the direction for the binding. Bindings involve two directions: the data will come out of one component—the source—and go into another—the target. This is the case where you want to display external data within Flash, without tracking updates. For example, the data could come out of the XMLConnector component into a UI component such as a List or TextInput.

Sometimes you'll have a two-way binding between your components, especially where you want to be able to update your content within Flash. In this case, the content in both components is synchronized, regardless of which component makes the change. You'll see an example of this later, when we bind a DataSet component to UI components using two-way bindings.

It's important to note that you have to add your bindings in the first frame of your Flash movie. They won't work on components that you add later in the timeline. The other restriction is that you can't bind components in multiple scenes in a Flash movie.

Data binding is a huge topic, and I won't give it full coverage here as it's beyond the scope of this book. Instead, I plan on showing you some of the most important aspects so that you can create bindings using the XMLConnector component.

Adding a binding

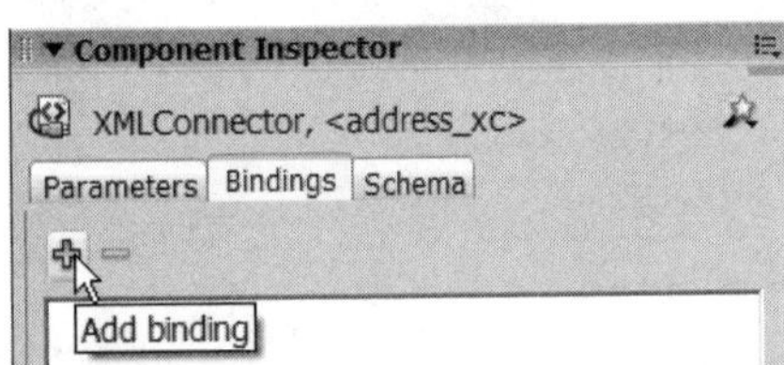

Figure 8-18. The Add binding button in the Bindings tab of the Component Inspector

To add a binding, first select the XMLConnector component on the Stage and display the Bindings tab in the Component Inspector. Click the Add binding button, as shown in Figure 8-18.

You'll need to identify which component property you wish to bind. If you're binding to a data-aware component, you'll usually choose an Array. You might choose a String property if you were binding directly to the text property of a TextInput component.

Select the relevant element from your schema and click OK. Make sure that you've chosen the parent of any items that you want to include within your UI component. Figure 8-19 shows the selection of the contact Array. Choosing the contact element allows us to access the id, name, address, and phone elements.

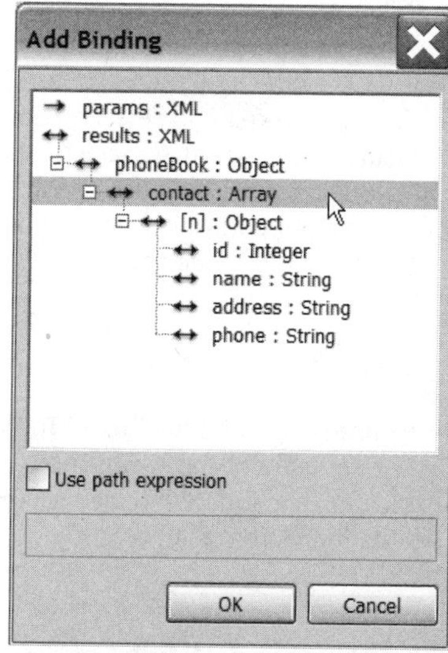

Figure 8-19. Selecting an element for binding

In Figure 8-19, I selected an Array element. This means that I can bind the data to the `dataProvider` of a data-aware component such as a List, ComboBox, or DataGrid.

Once you've added the binding, you'll see it displayed within the Bindings tab, as shown in Figure 8-20. Notice that the path for the binding uses a dot notation to drill down through the elements in the structure.

In Figure 8-20, we're binding to the contact element in the phoneBook element. This element is part of the results property of the XMLConnector component.

After you've added a binding, you'll need to configure the other component involved in the binding.

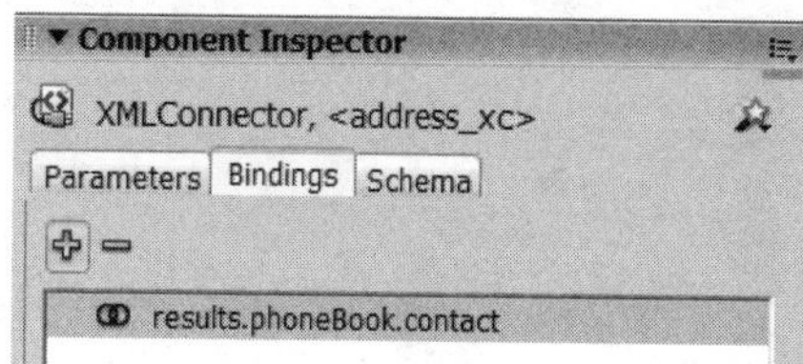

Figure 8-20. A binding in the Bindings tab

Configuring the binding

You can use the Component Inspector to select a direction and a second component for the binding. The direction—in or out—specifies whether the data is sent out of a component or received by a component. You can also change the way that the bound data displays in the component. Table 8-4 summarizes each of the settings in the Bindings tab and explains their purpose.

Table 8-4. Settings for each binding

Setting	Purpose
direction	Specifies whether the binding sends data, receives it, or does both.
bound to	Specifies the other component or target for the binding.
formatter	Lists any formatting to change the display within the target component. Choose from None, Boolean, Compose String, Custom Formatter, Date, Rearrange Fields, and Number Formatter.
formatter options	Lists the options available for the chosen formatter.

You'll learn more about formatters a little later in this chapter.

If you're directly binding from an XMLConnector component to a UI component, you would set the direction to out and select a UI component for binding. If you've chosen an array element from the results, you'll need to select a component capable of displaying more than one value. This could include a ComboBox, List, or DataGrid component. You can then set the array as the `dataProvider` for the component. Alternatively, you could bind to the `selectedIndex` property. You'll see examples of both of these bindings later in this chapter.

When you click in the bound to setting, a magnifying glass button will appear at the right of the field. Click the button to select a target component. Make sure that you have set an instance name for the target.

Figure 8-21 shows the Bound To dialog box. In Figure 8-21, I've selected a List component. Because the List component has a `dataProvider` property, I can select the dataProvider option from the Schema location section of the dialog box. A `dataProvider` is an array, so you can assign the array from the XMLConnector results.

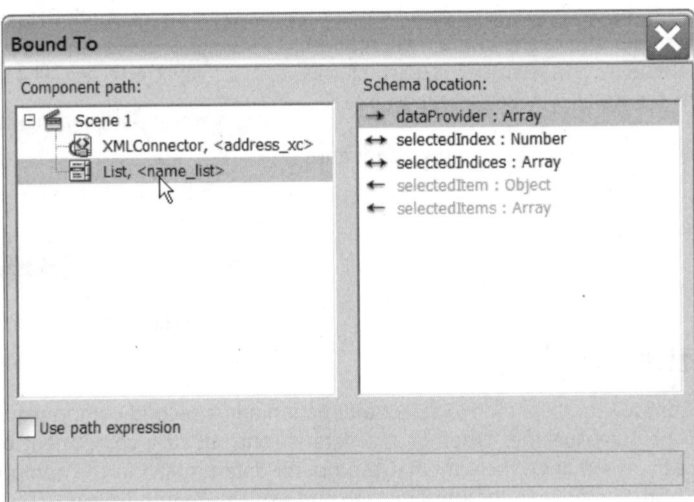

Figure 8-21. A binding in the Bindings tab

You may notice the arrows in Figure 8-21 indicating what directions are available to each binding. The right arrow indicates that the XMLConnector can send data to the dataProvider of the name_list component. This is equivalent to adding the contents from the XML document in the UI component. Because the binding is one way, the UI component can't add a new item to the address_xc component.

If we choose the SelectedIndex location, we can add a two-way binding. This means that selecting an item in the component selects the same item in the XML data. You would use the SelectedIndices item if you were selecting multiple items in the UI component.

Click OK to set the binding. If you select the target UI component on the Stage, you'll see that Flash has added an equivalent binding in the Bindings tab.

If the data has more than one child element, you'll assign all the children to the bound component. For example, if you've bound an array directly to the dataProvider of a component, it will display a list of all values from the array, separated by commas. This is shown in a List component in Figure 8-22.

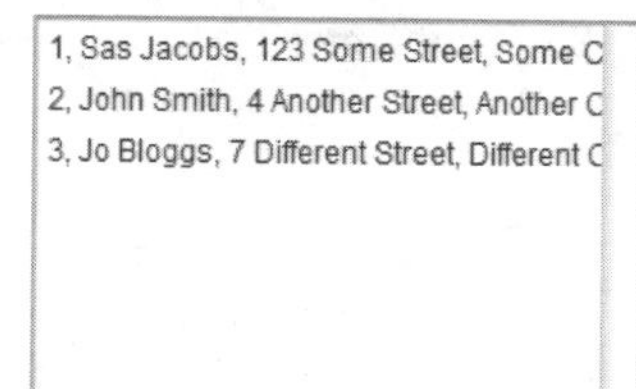

Figure 8-22. Without a formatter, the the child elements display in the component.

You can add a formatter to the binding to choose which element displays in the target component. In Figure 8-22, we could use a Rearrange Fields formatter to assign values to the label and data properties of the List component. This would allow us to display only the name in the List.

To make this clearer, we'll work through an example where we bind the contents of the address.xml file directly to a List component. We'll use a formatter to display the data correctly.

Exercise 2: Binding data to a List component

In exercise 2, we'll use the file from exercise 1 and bind the name element to a List component. If you didn't complete exercise 1, you can use the starter file loadContacts.fla.

1. Open Flash if necessary and open either the starter file loadContacts.fla or your completed file from exercise 1. Make sure the file is in the same folder as the address.xml file.
2. Drag a List component to the UI layer and size it appropriately in the Properties panel. Give it the instance name name_list.
3. Select the XMLConnector component, display the Bindings tab in the Component Inspector, and click the Add binding button.
4. Select the contact array from the XMLConnector schema and bind to the dataProvider of the name_list component. Click OK to create the binding.
5. Select the binding and change the direction to out.
6. Test the movie, and you'll see the complete contact element displayed in the List component. Your movie should look like the image shown in Figure 8-21. We'll need to add a formatter to display only the name.
7. Choose the Rearrange Fields formatter. We'll use this to choose the name element for the label within the list. We can also add a data value at the same time.
8. Click the formatter options setting to show the magnifying glass icon. Click the icon and enter the settings shown in Figure 8-23.

Rearrange Fields
Fields definitions: label=name;data=id
OK Cancel

Figure 8-23. Setting the Rearrange Fields options

We have set the label property of the List items to the name field in the schema and the data to the id field. Click OK to apply the settings.

9. Test the movie and you should see something similar to the screenshot displayed in Figure 8-24. You can see the completed file saved as `loadAddress_Binding.fla` in your resource files.

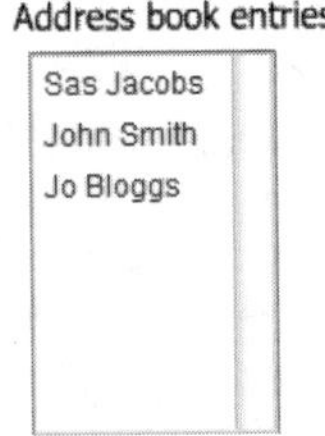

Figure 8-24. The List component showing only the name from the XML document

In this exercise, we bound the data from an XMLConnector component directly to a List component. We added a Rearrange Fields formatter so that we displayed only the name within the List.

We can extend the example so that when we click on the name, the other details will display in UI components. We'll do this by adding more bindings.

Exercise 3: Adding multiple bindings to an XMLConnector component

In this exercise, we'll add multiple bindings so that when we choose an item from the List, the details display in a TextInput and TextArea component. You should complete exercise 2 before you start this exercise, but if you didn't, you can use the starter file `loadAddress_Binding.fla` instead.

1. Open Flash if necessary and open either the starter file `loadAddress_Binding.fla` or your completed file from exercise 2. Again, the file should be in the same folder as `address.xml`.
2. Drag a TextInput component to the UI layer, to the right of the List component. Give it the instance name phone_txt. We'll use this to display the phone number from the XML document.
3. Drag a TextArea component below the TextInput and give it the instance name address_txt. We'll display the address in this component. Figure 8-25 shows my Flash movie at this point. Notice that I've added static text fields with a description to the left of the TextInput and TextArea components. You can also see the XMLConnector component to the left of the Stage.

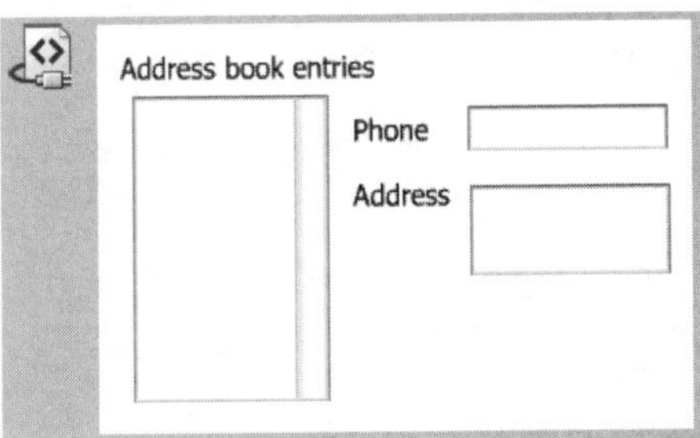

Figure 8-25. The address book interface

4. Select the XMLConnector component and add a new binding to the phone element.

5. Set the direction to out and bind it to the `text` property of the TextInput component. You'll see an additional setting at the bottom of the Bindings tab called Index for 'contact'. Figure 8-26 shows the setting; the value is currently set to 0. This setting shows which value from the array to display in the Text Input component. Currently it is set to display the first element from the array—the element at position 0.

Name	Value
direction	out
bound to	phone_txt:text
formatter	none
formatter options	
Index for 'contact'	0

Figure 8-26. The additional Index for 'contact' setting

6. Click the magnifying glass icon in the Index for 'contact' setting to bring up the Bound Index dialog box. Uncheck the Use constant value check box. Select the List component and choose the selectedIndex : Number option. We've told Flash that the value in the TextInput depends on the item chosen from the List, that is, the `selectedIndex`. Figure 8-27 shows the settings for the Bound Index dialog box.

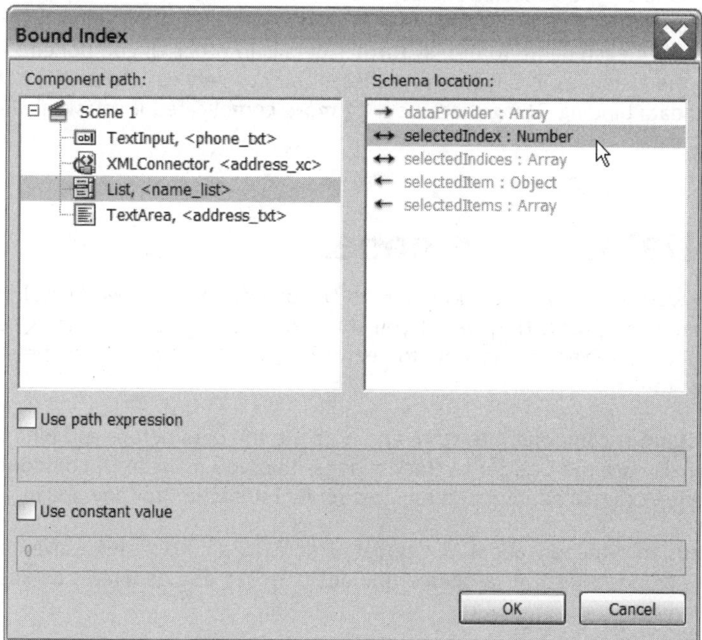

Figure 8-27. The settings for the phone binding

7. Test the movie and check that the phone number displays when you select a name from the List component. We'll repeat the process to bind the address to the TextArea component.

8. Make sure that you select the XMLConnector on the Stage. Add another binding, this time choosing the address element.

9. Set the direction to out and bind the data to the TextArea component. Set the index setting to use the selectedIndex of the List component.
10. Test the movie. You should be able to select an item from the List component and see the relevant values in the TextInput and TextArea components. You may need to resize and rearrange the components on the Stage so that you can display all data. Figure 8-28 shows my completed movie. You can see the completed `loadAddress_multipleBinding.fla` in your resource files.

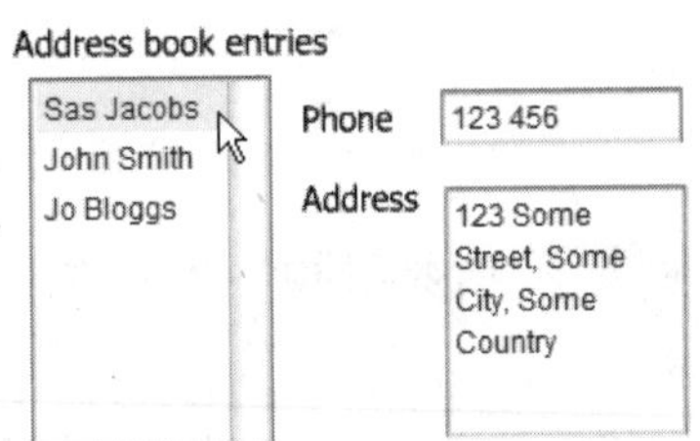

Figure 8-28. The completed phone book application

In the previous examples, you've seen how easy it is to load XML data into an XMLConnector and bind it directly to one or more UI components. We created a very simple application that displays a list of contacts. You can click each name to display further details in other UI components. If you compare this process with the examples in Chapter 4, you'll see that it's very easy to use an XMLConnector, UI components, and data binding. Things become a lot more complicated if you want UI components to update your XML data.

Using the DataSet component

You've seen how we can bind XML data directly to UI components. This works well if you have data that you don't need to update. However, if you want to make changes in Flash, you'll have to add DataSet and XUpdateResolver components to keep track of your updates. Let me say at the outset that this is not for the faint of heart.

You can use the DataSet component to store and organize the data before you bind it to other components. You can also use the DataSet to track changes that you make in UI components. Remember that Flash can't alter external content and requires server interaction for any updates.

The DataSet sends information about the updated data to an XUpdateResolver component in a `deltaPacket`. The XUpdateResolver processes the `deltaPacket` and generates an `xupdatePacket` for use by server-side files.

Figure 8-29. The icon for the DataSet component

Like the XMLConnector, the DataSet has no visual appearance, which means you can place it anywhere in your Flash movie. Figure 8-29 shows the icon for the DataSet component.

Where you need to update data, you'll bind the XMLConnector to a DataSet first. You'll then apply two-way bindings from the DataSet to your UI components. The two-way bindings ensure that the DataSet always contains the updated data from the UI components. You'll also need to add other bindings between the DataSet and XUpdateResolver. I'll take you through this process in the next section.

Binding to a DataSet component

To start with, you'll need to bind data from an XMLConnector component to a DataSet component. The DataSet will keep track of any changes made by the UI components. If you don't use a DataSet component, you won't be able to track updates to the content.

You'll probably want to select an array from the XMLConnector component properties. This will allow you to bind the data directly to the `dataProvider` property of the List, ComboBox, and DataGrid. It's much quicker to use data binding than to write ActionScript. You'll set the direction to out so that the data is sent out of the XMLConnector. Finally, you'll bind the array to the `dataProvider` of the DataSet component.

Figure 8-30 shows the Bound To dialog box for a binding from an XMLConnector to a DataSet.

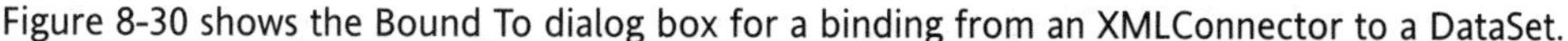

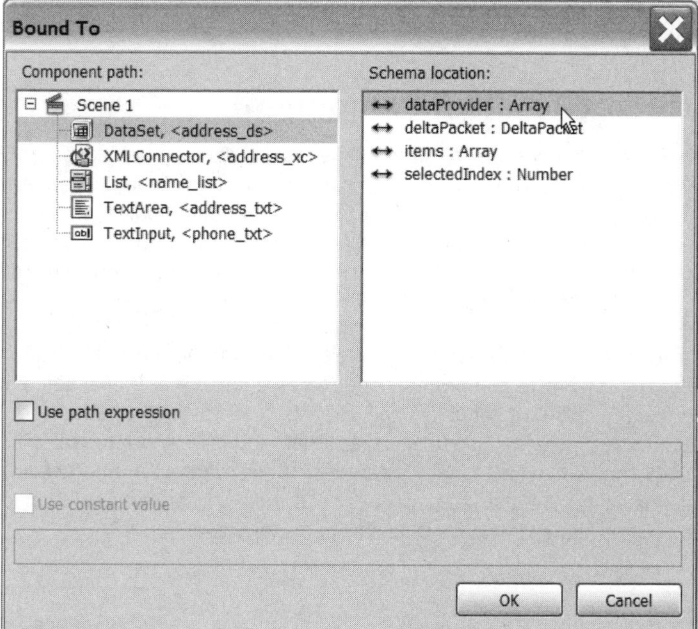

Figure 8-30. Binding to the dataProvider of a DataSet component

Notice that the Schema location section provides a number of different properties that you can use for binding. In addition to the dataProvider, you could bind to the deltaPacket—an XML packet describing changes to the data. You'll see this type of binding a little later. You could also bind to the items in the component or to the selectedIndex. The previous exercise showed an example where we bound data to the `selectedIndex` of a List component.

Next, you'll add bindings from the DataSet to your UI components. Select an in/out binding direction so that the components will inform the DataSet of any changes that a user makes. For list-based components, you'll need to bind both the `dataProvider` and `selectedIndex` properties to synchronize the DataSet and UI component.

You should also create fields in the schema of the DataSet so that the schema matches the exact structure of the results from the XMLConnector component. If you don't do this, the two components won't be identical, and you may have difficulty generating updates later on.

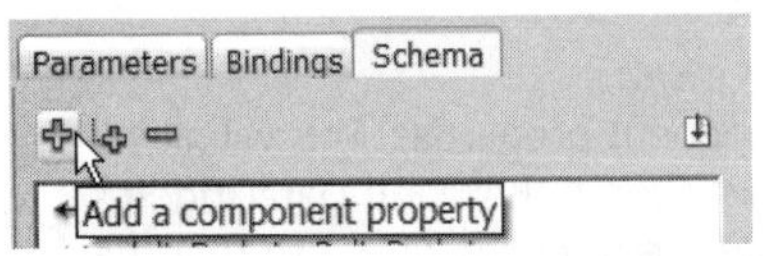

Figure 8-31. Adding a component property to the schema of a DataSet component

You can add fields in the Schema tab of the Component Inspector. Click the leftmost plus sign to add a component property. I've shown this in Figure 8-31.

You can specify the name of the property and its datatype. The name and datatype should be the same as in the XMLConnector schema—that way, you ensure that the two components contain exactly the same content. This is necessary so that you'll be able to update the data correctly.

To capture any changes made to the data, you'll need to add an XUpdateResolver component that binds to the DataSet component.

Adding an XUpdateResolver component

Figure 8-32. The XUpdateResolver icon

An XUpdateResolver component keeps the data in Flash consistent with an external data source. The resolver translates information about changes from a DataSet component into a format that the external data source understands. As with the other data components, the XUpdateResolver has no visual appearance in the finished movie, which means you can position it anywhere. Figure 8-32 shows the XUpdateResolver icon.

The relationship between the DataSet and XUpdateResolver components is a little complicated. The DataSet monitors changes from UI components and stores them in a `deltaPacket`. When you're ready to process these changes, the DataSet sends the `deltaPacket` to the XUpdateResolver. The resolver converts the `deltaPacket` into an `xupdatePacket` that you can send to an XMLConnector. The XMLConnector sends the `xupdatePacket` to a server-side file where the updates are processed. The server-side file returns an `updateResults` packet back to the XMLConnector. This packet may contain updated values for UI components. Figure 8-33 shows the process.

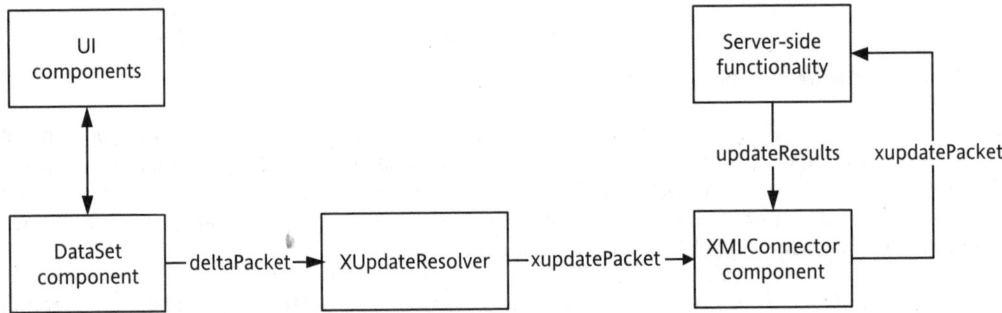

Figure 8-33. The update process using a DataSet and XUpdateResolver

The XUpdateResolver uses XUpdate statements to describe changes that you've made to the data. At the time of writing, XUpdate was a Working Draft from the XML: DB Working Group. You can find out more about XUpdate at `http://xmldb-org.sourceforge.net/xupdate/`.

To make sure that you track all of the changes to your data, you'll need to add two bindings, one for the `deltaPacket` and one for the `xupdatePacket`. The first binding occurs between the `deltaPacket` of the DataSet and the `deltaPacket` of the XUpdateResolver. The `deltaPacket` is generated by the DataSet component to summarize changes made to the XML content. You'll need to set the direction to out for the DataSet and in for the XUpdateResolver. In other words, the DataSet sends the changes in the `deltaPacket` to the XUpdateResolver component.

You'll need to add another binding to the XUpdateResolver so that the `xupdatePacket` is sent out to a second XMLConnector. This XMLConnector sends the `xupdatePacket` to a server-side file for processing. Figure 8-34 shows the settings for this binding.

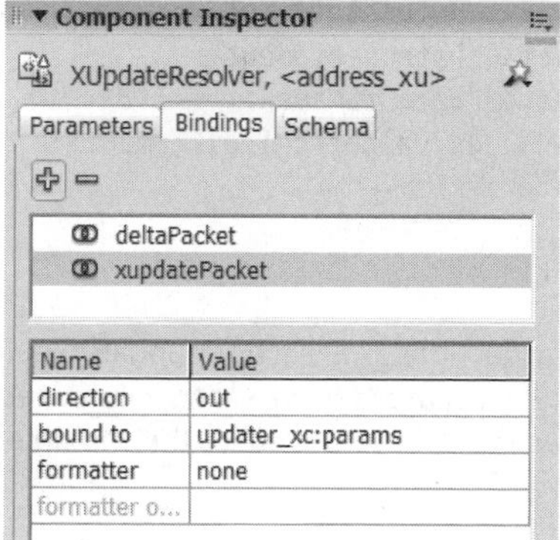

Figure 8-34. Binding to the xupdatePacket of a DataSet component

The XMLConnector will also receive an `updateResults` packet from the server-side file after processing. The server-side page can use the `updateResults` packet to send additional data to Flash.

One crucial step in the process is setting the encoder for the XUpdateResolver `deltaPacket` in the Schema tab of the Component Inspector. You'll need to choose the `DatasetDeltaToXUpdateDelta` encoder and specify the `rowNodeKey` in the encoder options. The `rowNodeKey` is an XPath statement that identifies the path to the rows of data. It's a little like the primary key for a database. The XPath statement also contains a predicate that links the path to the relevant data in the DataSet. Check out Chapter 3 to learn more about XPath.

The following code shows the structure of this setting:

```
XPathStatement/rowNode[keyFieldName='?DSKeyFieldName'
```

The setting includes an XPath expression that identifies the path directly to the `row` node of the data. The predicate, within square brackets, includes the key field from the schema, an equals sign, and the key field from the DataSet, prefaced by a question mark. The DataSet key field name is usually the same as the schema key field. The text to the right of the equals sign is surrounded by single quotes. When Flash creates the `xupdatePacket`, it will convert the apostrophes to the entity `'`.

It's critical that you write this path correctly; otherwise, you won't be able to generate the correct XUpdate statements in your xupdatePacket.

You need to trigger the DataSet to create the deltaPacket by calling the applyUpdates method. The DataSet then generates the deltaPacket containing the changes to the data. The DataSet sends the deltaPacket to the XUpdateResolver, where the contents are converted into XUpdate statements and added to an xupdatePacket.

The following code shows the structure of an xupdatePacket:

```
<?xml version="1.0"?>
<xupdate:modifications version="1.0"
xmlns:xupdate="http://www.xmldb.org/xupdate">
  <xupdate:update select="XPath statement">
  Updated value </xupdate:update>
  <xupdate:remove select="XPath statement "/>
  <xupdate:append select="XPath statement">
    <xupdate:element name="parentEName">
      <child1Element>Updated value</child1Element>
    </xupdate:element>
  </xupdate:append>
</xupdate:modifications>
```

The packet contains three different sections, one each for updates, deletions, and additions to the data. These are the <xupdate:update>, <xupdate:remove>, and <xupdate:append> nodes. You can repeat each of these elements in the xupdatePacket to reflect the multiple additions, updates, or deletions in Flash.

As you can see, things get a lot more complicated when you include DataSet and XUpdateComponents in your Flash movies. We'll work through a detailed example so that you can see this process for yourself.

Putting it all together

In this section we'll put together everything we've covered so far and create a simple application. The application will use a trimmed-down version of our address book XML document, and we'll use Flash to manage changes to the data. We'll use a DataGrid component and create multiple component bindings, and we'll track the changes in a DataSet component.

Exercise 4: A simple address book application

In this exercise, we'll build a simple address book application that will allow us to add, edit, and delete records in Flash. To update the content externally, we'll need to send the data to a server-side file for processing. I won't include this functionality in the example, but you will see the XML content that Flash provides to the server-side file. If you want to add server-side functionality, you'll need to build it yourself using a language like ColdFusion, PHP, or ASP.NET.

We'll use the starter file addressBook.fla and start by adding an XMLConnector.

Configure the XMLConnector

The first stage in this exercise is to open the starter file `addressBook.fla` and add an XMLConnector component. In this exercise, we're using data from the file `address_simple.xml`, so you'll need to make sure that both files are in the same folder.

You can see the file `address_simple.xml` in your resources, and I've shown the XML document here. Notice that this file contains no attributes and only <id>, <name>, and <phone> child elements. I've left out the <address> element so that there aren't too many columns in the DataGrid.

```
<?xml version="1.0" encoding="UTF-8"?>
<phoneBook>
  <contact>
    <id>1</id>
    <name>Sas Jacobs</name>
    <phone>123 456</phone>
  </contact>
  <contact>
    <id>2</id>
    <name>John Smith</name>
    <phone>456 789</phone>
  </contact>
  <contact>
    <id>3</id>
    <name>Jo Bloggs</name>
    <phone>789 123</phone>
  </contact>
</phoneBook>
```

1. Start Flash if necessary and open the starter file addressBook.fla. Figure 8-35 shows the interface. It consists of a DataGrid component, two TextInput components, a TextArea, and three buttons.

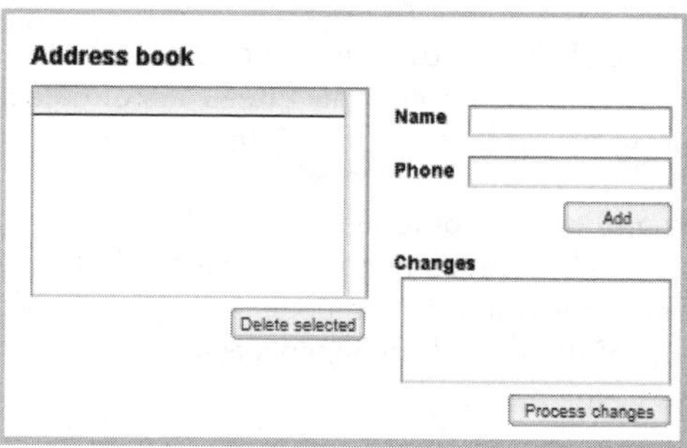

Figure 8-35. The Flash interface for the address book application

I've made the DataGrid component editable, so we can modify the data within each cell. You can use the TextInput components to add new entries, and clicking the Delete selected button will delete the selected row from the DataGrid. When we're ready to process the changes, we'll click the Process changes button. The TextArea component will display the XUpdate statements.

2. Drag an XMLConnector component into the Flash movie and configure it as shown in Figure 8-36. Give it the instance name address_xc.

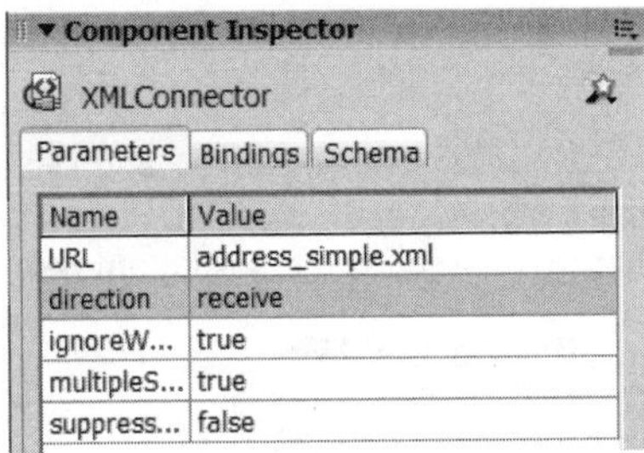

Figure 8-36. Configuring the XMLConnector component

3. In the Schema tab of the Component Inspector, import a schema from the file address_simple.xml. Make sure you select results : XML first. Figure 8-37 shows the imported schema. It replicates the structure from the XML document.

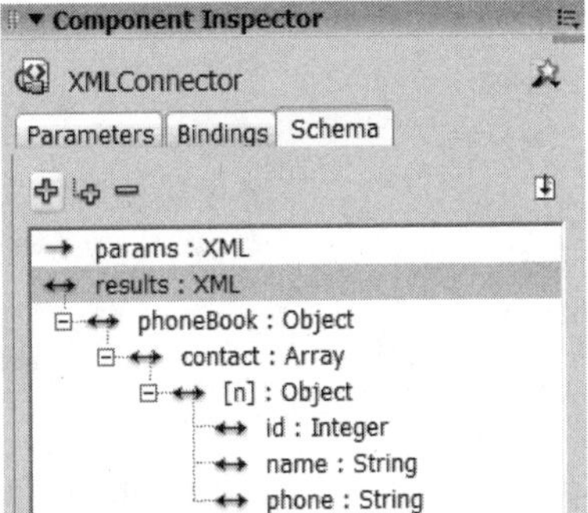

Figure 8-37. The schema created from the file address_simple.xml

You could also have imported a trimmed-down version of the `address_simple.xml` file, providing it contained at least two data rows. As there were only three rows of data in the XML document, there wasn't much advantage in using a shortened version of the XML file.

Add a DataSet component and related bindings

At this point, you'll need to add a DataSet component to the movie and bind it to the XMLConnector. You will also bind the DataSet to the DataGrid component so that the data displays in the interface. It is important that the contents of these two components are identical so that they synchronize whenever the user makes changes to the data.

4. Drag a DataSet component into your movie and give it the instance name address_ds.
5. Add a binding from the XMLConnector to the DataSet. Select the contact array and bind it to the `dataProvider` of the DataSet. Make sure the direction is set to out.
6. Create a new layer called actions and add the following code line on frame 1. The line triggers the XMLConnector to load the external XML document. If you test the movie at this point, nothing will happen because we haven't yet bound the DataSet to the DataGrid component.

```
address_xc.trigger();
```

7. Add two bindings between the DataSet and DataGrid components. Both are in/out bindings. The first should bind the `dataProvider` and the second, the `selectedIndex`. These bindings will keep the DataSet and DataGrid synchronized.

8. We'll need to add component properties to the schema for the DataSet. This will create the correct columns in the DataGrid component. Select the DataSet and click the Schema tab in the Component Inspector. Click the Add a component property button, as shown in Figure 8-38.

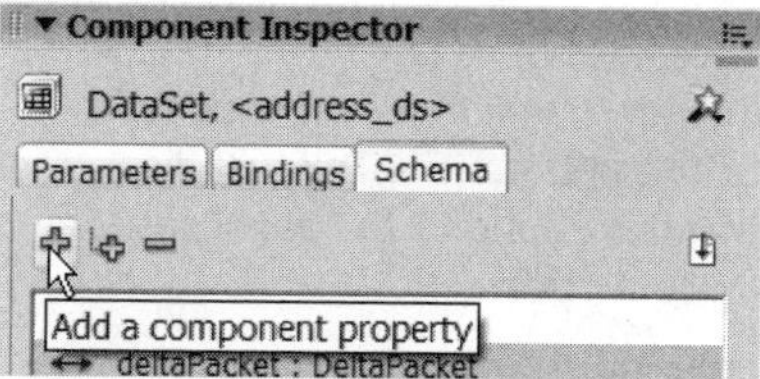

Figure 8-38. Clicking the Add a component property button in the Schema tab

9. Enter the field name id and make sure that you select the datatype Integer. Repeat the process to add the name and phone fields. They are String datatypes. Make sure that the names you use match the names of the elements in the schema. Figure 8-39 shows the completed Schema tab for the DataSet with the new component properties.

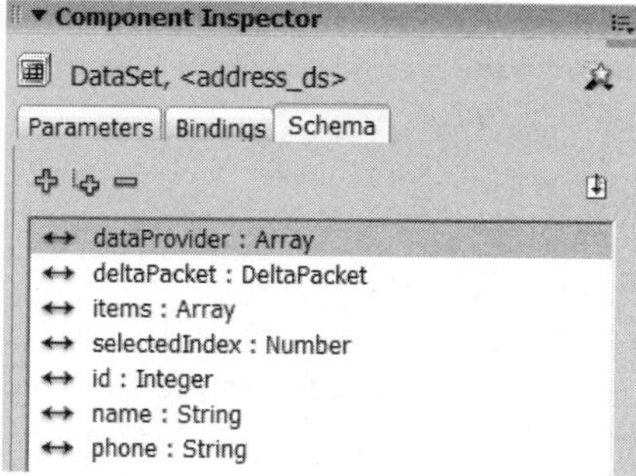

Figure 8-39. The Schema tab showing the new component properties

10. Test the movie and you should see the DataGrid populated with data from the XML document. Figure 8-40 shows the interface at this point. The order of the component properties dictates the order of the columns in the DataGrid.

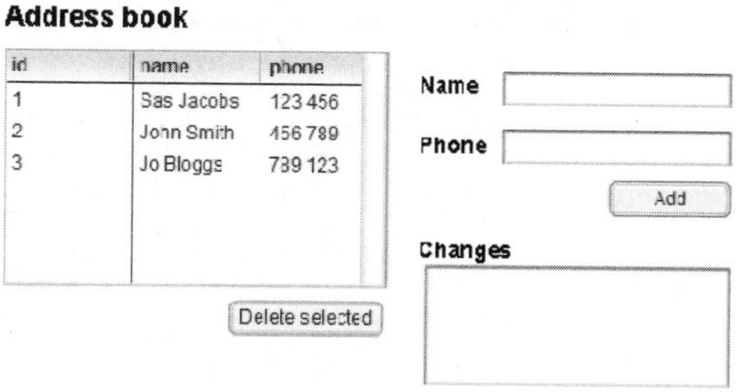

Figure 8-40. The Flash interface showing the populated DataGrid component

At this point, we've bound data from the XMLConnector to a DataSet and then onto the dataProvider of a DataGrid component. We also bound the selectedIndex of the DataSet and DataGrid so that both components always contain the same data. It's critical that you don't forget the second binding.

Configure the Add and Delete buttons
Now we need to modify the DataGrid so that we can add new contacts, as well as edit and delete existing entries.

11. Add the code shown here to the actions layer. This code specifies what happens when you click the Add button. It finds the new name and phone number from the data input fields and adds them to the dataProvider of the DataGrid. This will display the new entry in the DataGrid. The dataProvider of the DataGrid is bound to the dataProvider of the DataSet so the DataSet will be updated with the new information.

```
add_btn.onRelease = function():Void {
  var newName:String = name_txt.text;
  var newPhone:String = phone_txt.text;
  if (newName.length >0 && newPhone.length>0) {
    address_dg.dataProvider.addItem({name:newName, phone:newPhone});
  }
}
```

12. Add the following code to the actions layer. When you click the Delete button, Flash will remove the selected row from the dataProvider of the DataGrid. Again, the binding to the DataSet ensures that Flash also updates the dataProvider for the DataSet.

```
delete_btn.onRelease = function():Void {
  var selRow:Number = address_dg.focusedCell.itemIndex;
  address_dg.dataProvider.removeItemAt(selRow);
}
```

13. Test the movie and check that you can add, edit, and delete data in the DataGrid. The id column will be blank for new entries. This is because your server-side pages would normally generate the id or primary key field.

Add and configure the XUpdateResolver
In order to track the changes to our address book data, we need to generate a deltaPacket from the DataSet component. We'll add an XUpdateResolver to interpret the deltaPacket from the DataSet component and create XUpdate statements.

14. Drag an XUpdateResolver component into your movie and name it address_rs.

15. Bind the deltaPacket from the XUpdateResolver to the deltaPacket of the DataSet component. Set the direction to in so that the XUpdateResolver receives the delta packet from the DataSet.

16. Display the Schema tab and select the deltaPacket from the XUpdateResolver component. Change the encoder setting to DatasetDeltaToXUpdateDelta and enter the following path in the encoder options:

```
phoneBook/contact[id='?id']
```

This is a critical step. If you don't add the correct path, you won't generate the correct XUpdate statements in the xupdatePacket. In our XPath statement, we go to the contact child element of the phoneBook element and set the child id element to the value from the id field in the DataSet.

17. Add a second XMLConnector to your movie and name it sendChanges_xc. You will use this XMLConnector to send the changes from Flash to server-side pages for updating. In this example, we won't configure the XMLConnector since we don't have any server-side pages prepared. You may want to complete these pages yourself.

18. Add another binding to the XUpdateResolver. This time the binding should send the xupdatePacket from the XUpdateResolver to the sendChanges_xc component. You'll notice that you have to select params when you add the binding because the data will be sent out of Flash.

19. We still need to generate the deltaPacket from the DataSet. We'll need to configure the Process changes button to call the applyUpdates method of the DataSet component. Add the following code to your actions layer:

```
change_btn.onRelease = function():Void {
  address_ds.applyUpdates();
}
```

When you click the Process changes button, the DataSet will prepare the deltaPacket. Because we've added a binding to the XUpdateResolver, it will receive the deltaPacket and generate an xupdatePacket.

Displaying the xupdatePacket

If you test the movie at this point, nothing will appear to happen because we haven't configured the sendChanges_xc component. Normally, we would link this to a server-side file to process the XUpdate statements. I'm not going to do that in this exercise, but we will set up another binding so we can see the contents of the xupdatePacket.

20. Add another binding to the XUpdateResolver component. The binding should send the xupdatePacket to the text property of the xupdate_txt component. Set the direction to out. By binding the xupdatePacket to the text property of the TextArea component, we'll be able to display the XUpdate statements in the TextArea.

21. Test the movie and make some additions, edits, and deletions to the data. Click the Process changes button and check the contents of the TextArea. Here is some sample content that I generated:

```
<?xml version="1.0"?>
<xupdate:modifications version="1.0"
xmlns:xupdate="http://www.xmldb.org/xupdate">
  <xupdate:update select="/phoneBook/contact[id=&apos;2&apos;]/name">
  John R Smith</xupdate:update>
  <xupdate:remove select="/phoneBook/contact[id=&apos;3&apos;]"/>
  <xupdate:append select="/phoneBook">
    <xupdate:element name="contact">
      <id/>
      <phone>145 789</phone>
      <name>Roger Rabbit</name>
    </xupdate:element>
```

```
    </xupdate:append>
    <xupdate:append select="/phoneBook">
      <xupdate:element name="contact">
        <id/>
        <phone>987 123</phone>
        <name>Percy Penguin</name>
      </xupdate:element>
    </xupdate:append>
  </xupdate:modifications>
```

In the XML packet shown here, I updated the name of the contact with an id of 2 to John R Smith. I also added two new contacts: Roger Rabbit and Percy Penguin.

You can see the completed addressBook_completed.fla in your resource files.

Points to note from exercise 4

- If you look at the contents generated by the XUpdateResolver, you'll notice that they include XPath statements in the select attribute to identify the elements to update. Here is one example:

  ```
  select="/phoneBook/contact[id=&apos;2&apos;]/name"
  ```

  This XPath statement identifies the <name> element within the <contact> element that has an id of 2. Notice that the statement uses the entity for the apostrophe character—'. You can find out more about XPath expressions in Chapter 3 and the Appendix.
- In the previous example, I used a physical XML document. I could just have easily used a server-side page to generate the XML content. Server-side pages offer one way to connect to a database using XML, and this might be useful in the case of an XML-enabled database. I could also use server-side pages to proxy XML data from a web service. I'll discuss web services in more detail in the next chapter. If you choose a server-side file, don't forget to enter the complete server path in the URL field for the XMLConnector component, for example, http://localhost/XMLApplication/getData.aspx.

In the previous section, we used the Component Inspector to configure the data components in our application. It's also possible to achieve the same functionality using ActionScript. I could go into a lot of detail about how to script bindings; however, that's beyond the scope of this chapter. Instead, in the next section, I'll provide a brief overview of how to script the XMLConnector class and add simple bindings.

The XMLConnector class

The XMLConnector class is the script version of the XMLConnector component. You can use this class to work with external XML documents using ActionScript. You can use ActionScript to bind the contents to other components.

You might want to script the XMLConnector component if you're adding components to the Stage dynamically. Before you can get started, you'll need to have a copy of the XMLConnector in your library. The easiest way to do this is to drag the component to the Stage and delete it again.

You can include the XMLConnector class within your file using the following code line. Using an `import` statement means you won't have to use `mx.data.components.XMLConnector` each time you want to refer to the XMLConnector class.

```
import mx.data.components.XMLConnector;
```

You've already seen some of the scripting that you can use with the XMLConnector component. Earlier, you saw the `trigger` method of the XMLConnector class and you displayed the `results` property in an Output window.

Setting the XMLConnector properties

We'll get started by scripting an XMLConnector that loads an external XML document. You can create a new XMLConnector with this line:

```
var myXMLConnector:XMLConnector = new XMLConnector();
```

You can set the parameters for the XMLConnector with the following code. These are equivalent to the parameters within the Component Inspector; you can see a description of each parameter in Table 8-2.

```
myXMLConnector.URL = "xmlDoc.xml";
myXMLConnector.direction = "receive";
myXMLConnector.ignoreWhite = true;
myXMLConnector.multipleSimultaneousAllowed = true;
myXMLConnector.suppressInvalidCalls = true;
```

Interestingly, even though the `ignoreWhite` parameter is set to true by default in the Component Inspector, it still defaults to false when you script the XMLConnector. Make sure you don't forget this line if you're scripting the XMLConnector; otherwise Flash will include white space in the results.

Once you've configured the parameters, you'll need to trigger the component using this line:

```
myXMLConnector.trigger();
```

Displaying the results

The XMLConnector class broadcasts the `result` event when it completes the call to the XML document. You can use a listener to display the XML content as shown here:

```
var xmlListener:Object = new Object();
xmlListener.result = function(evtObj:Object):Void {
  trace (evtObj.target.results);
};
myXMLConnector.addEventListener("result", xmlListener);
```

You can access the XML document through the `results` property of the XMLConnector. The name is very similar to the `result` event, so make sure you don't confuse the two.

The best way to get started with the XMLConnector class is through an example.

Exercise 5: Using the XMLConnector class to load an XML document

In this exercise, we'll load the file address.xml into Flash using the XMLConnector class.

1. Open Flash and create a new movie. Add a new layer, actions, to the movie.
2. Save the file as `scriptLoadAddress.fla` in the same folder as the `address.xml` file.
3. Add and then delete an XMLConnector component. This adds the XMLConnector component to the library.
4. Select frame 1 of the actions layer and add the following code:

```
import mx.data.components.XMLConnector;
var addressXC:XMLConnector = new XMLConnector();
var xCListener:Object = new Object();
xCListener.result = function(evtObj:Object):Void {
  trace (evtObj.target.results);
};
addressXC.addEventListener("result", xCListener);
addressXC.URL = "address.xml";
addressXC.direction = "receive";
addressXC.ignoreWhite = true;
addressXC.multipleSimultaneousAllowed = true;
addressXC.suppressInvalidCalls = true;
addressXC.trigger();
```

   This code imports the XMLConnector class and creates a new XMLConnector object. It assigns a listener that traces the `results` when the XMLConnector broadcasts the `result` event. The XMLConnector loads the `address.xml` file and sets the relevant properties. The last line triggers the connection.

5. Test the movie and you should see the contents of the XML document in an Output window. You can see the completed file `scriptLoadAddress.fla` saved with your resources.

In exercise 5, you saw how to use ActionScript with the XMLConnector component. You loaded the contents of an XML document into an XMLConnector object called addressXC, set the parameters, and displayed the results in an Output window.

Working with the XML class

You could work with the loaded XML using the XML class. For example, you can set an XML variable to the value of `evtObj.target.results` in the listener function, as shown here:

```
xCListener.result = function(evtObj:Object):Void {
  var myXML:XML = evtObj.target.results;
  var RootNode:XMLNode = myXML.firstChild;
  trace (RootNode.nodeName);
};
addressXC.addEventListener("result", xCListener);
```

You can then work with the resulting XML object using the methods and properties of the XML class. However, this defeats the purpose of the XMLConnector class. One of the main benefits of the XMLConnector class is that you can bind the results to other components. You can do this using the Component Inspector, or you can use the DataBindingClasses component to achieve the same result with ActionScript.

Binding the results to components with ActionScript

The DataBindingClasses component allows you to use ActionScript to set the bindings between components. This is useful if you're dynamically adding components to your Flash movies using the `createClassObject` method. You need to use ActionScript because the components don't exist until you compile the movie.

Including the DataBindingClasses component

To start with, you'll need to include the DataBindingClasses component in your movie. This component is available from the Classes library. You can open this library by choosing Window ➤ Other Panels ➤ Common Libraries ➤ Classes. Drag the DataBindingClasses component to the Stage of your movie and then delete it again. This will add the component to your library. You can check this by opening your library with the *Ctrl-L* (*Cmd-L* for Macintosh) shortcut key. Unlike the data components, the DataBindingClasses component has a visual appearance, so don't forget to delete it from the Stage before you publish your movie.

You can import the relevant classes from the `mx.data.binding` package with this code:

```
import mx.data.binding.*;
```

Table 8-5 shows the classes included in the package. These classes are only available with the Professional version of Flash.

Table 8-5. The classes included within the mx.data.binding package

Class name	Purpose
Binding	Creates a binding between two EndPoint objects
ComponentMixins	Allows you to add data binding to components
CustomFormatter	Allows you to create custom formatter classes
CustomValidator	Allows you to create customer validator classes
DataType	Provides read and write access to the data fields of a component property
EndPoint	Defines a point in the data binding
TypedValue	Provides information about the datatype of a value

In this section, I'll introduce you to the Binding and EndPoint classes. The Binding class creates the binding but it uses the EndPoint class to specify the details for each side of the binding. You'll need two EndPoint objects—one for each component involved in the binding. Each EndPoint object needs information about the component, as well as a component property for binding.

Creating EndPoints

You can create the two EndPoint objects using this code:

```
var fromBinding:EndPoint = new EndPoint();
var toBinding:EndPoint = new EndPoint();
```

You'll need to set two properties for each EndPoint with the following code:

```
EndPoint.component = componentName;
EndPoint.property = "componentProperty";
```

The code sets the `component` property to the instance name of the component. The `property` is a string value that refers to the bindable component property. For example, in a TextInput component, you would set the property to `text`. You'd normally use the `dataProvider` property for data-aware components.

Depending on how you trigger the binding, you may need to set the event property of the source EndPoint as shown here. This code line lists the name of the event that will trigger the binding.

```
EndPoint.event = "triggerEventName";
```

You can leave out this line if you're going to trigger the binding at another time, for example, within an event-handler function.

Creating the binding

To create the binding, you'll need to call the constructor for the Binding class, as shown here:

```
new Binding(fromBinding, toBinding);
```

When you create bindings using ActionScript, they are one-way by default. The component that triggers the binding has an out direction while the other component has an `in` direction.

As you saw a little earlier, you can set the event that will trigger the binding:

```
EndPoint.event = "triggerEventName";
```

This is useful where updating one component should immediately update another, for example, two TextInput components. You could use the change, focusOut, or keyDown events to trigger the updating.

The second approach is to call the `execute` method of the binding in an event-handler function. For example, you could call this method in the `result` event handler of an XMLConnector component. The `execute` method looks like this:

```
var bindingResults:Array = newBinding.execute(reverse);
```

The execute method has one Boolean parameter, `reverse`, that indicates whether to apply the binding in both directions. You can assign the execute method to an array as shown. The array will contain any errors that occur when executing the binding. If there are no errors, it will contain the value `null`.

In the next exercise, I'll show you a simple example of how to script the XMLConnector class.

Exercise 6: Displaying content from an XMLConnector using ActionScript bindings

In this exercise, we'll script an XMLConnector and display the results in a TextArea component.

1. Open Flash if necessary and create a new movie. Save it in the same folder as the `address.xml` file.
2. Rename the first layer actions.
3. Add the DataBindingClasses component to your library by choosing Window ➤ Other Panels ➤ Common Libraries ➤ Classes and dragging the DataBindingClasses component to the Stage. Delete the symbol from the Stage so it doesn't show in the completed movie.
4. Add a TextArea component to the library. Do the same with an XMLConnector component. The library should contain the three items shown in Figure 8-41.

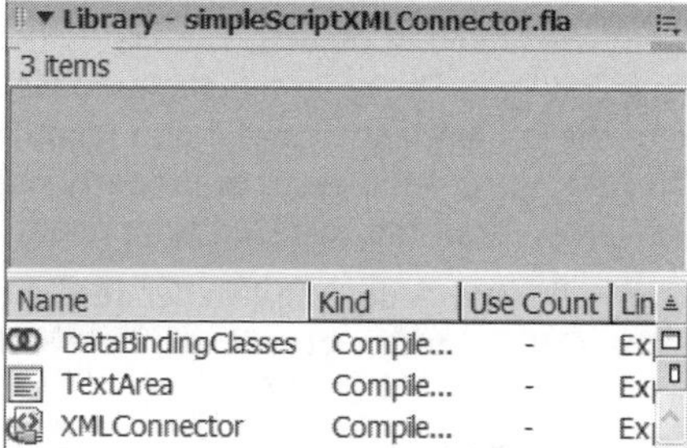

Figure 8-41. The library contents

5. Click on frame 1 of the actions layer and add the following code in the Actions panel. The code imports the binding, TextArea, and XMLConnector classes.

```
import mx.data.binding.*;
import mx.controls.TextArea;
import mx.data.components.XMLConnector;
```

   Importing the classes means that we don't have to use a fully qualified name to refer to the class. We can avoid using `mx.data.component.XMLConnector` each time we refer to the XMLConnector class.

6. Add the following code to the actions layer to create a new XMLConnector object and set values for its properties:

```
var addressXC:XMLConnector = new XMLConnector();
addressXC.URL = "address.xml";
addressXC.direction = "receive";
addressXC.ignoreWhite = true;
addressXC.multipleSimultaneousAllowed = true;
addressXC.suppressInvalidCalls = true;
```

7. Create a TextArea component using ActionScript by adding the following code at the bottom of the actions layer:

```
createClassObject(TextArea," content_ta", this.getNextHighestDepth());
content_ta.moveTo(10,10);
content_ta.setSize(400, 200);
content_ta.wordWrap = true;
```

This code uses the createClassObject method to add a TextArea component called content_ta to the Stage at 10,10. The code also sets the size and wordWrap property of the TextArea.

8. Add this binding at the bottom of the actions layer:

```
var fromBinding:EndPoint = new EndPoint();
var toBinding:EndPoint = new EndPoint();
fromBinding.component = addressXC;
fromBinding.property = "results";
toBinding.component = content_ta;
toBinding.property = "text";
var newBinding:Binding = new Binding(fromBinding, toBinding);
```

In this code, we've created two EndPoint objects. The first is fromBinding, which will send the results to the toBinding EndPoint. The code sets the component properties of each EndPoint by specifying the name of the component to use. It also identifies which component property should be bound. In this case, we use the results property of the addressXC XMLConnector and bind that to the text property of the TextArea component.

9. Create a listener with the following code. The listener responds to the result event of the XMLConnector object. The XMLConnector broadcasts the event after it completes the call to an external XML document.

```
var xCListener:Object = new Object();
xCListener.result = function(evtObj:Object):Void {
  var bindingResults:Array = newBinding.execute(false);
  trace (bindingResults);
};
addressXC.addEventListener("result", xCListener);
```

When the results are received, we call the execute method to apply the binding. The false parameter specifies that the binding is one way. We assign the outcome of the execute method to an array variable called bindingResults. This array contains any errors that Flash encounters when trying to execute the binding. If there are no errors, the word null displays in the Output window.

10. Add the following line at the bottom of the actions layer. This code triggers the XMLConnector component.

```
addressXC.trigger();
```

11. Test the movie and you'll see the results from the binding within an Output window. You should see the word null in the window if there are no errors. When you close the Output window, you should see the same interface as that shown in Figure 8-42.

```
<?xml version="1.0" encoding="UTF-
8"?><phoneBook><contact><id>1</id><name>Sas
Jacobs</name><address>123 Some Street, Some City, Some
Country</address><phone>123
456</phone></contact><contact><id>2</id><name>John
Smith</name><address>4 Another Street, Another City, Another
Country</address><phone>456
789</phone></contact><contact><id>3</id><name>Jo
Bloggs</name><address>7 Different Street, Different City,
UK</address><phone>789 123</phone></contact></phoneBook>
```

Figure 8-42. The completed interface

You can find the completed resource file saved as `simpleScriptXMLConnector.fla`.

In exercise 6, we loaded an external XML document into an XMLConnector object and bound it to a TextArea component. It was a very simple example, but as you can see it took a lot of code to create the bindings.

In the next exercise, we'll look at an alternative method of binding the results of an XMLConnector to a component. Instead of using bindings, we'll use ActionScript to process the results and add them to the `dataProvider` of a List component.

Exercise 7: Using an XMLConnector to populate the `dataProvider` of a List component

In this exercise, we'll use the results from an XMLConnector to populate the `dataProvider` of a List component. The steps outlined in this exercise provide an alternative to the approach in exercise 6, scripting the bindings.

1. Open Flash if necessary and create a new movie. Save it in the same folder as the `address.xml` file and rename Layer 1 as actions.
2. Drag the DataBindingClasses component from Window ➤ Other Panels ➤ Common Libraries ➤ Classes onto the Stage. Delete the symbol so it appears only in the library.
3. Add a List and XMLConnector to the library.
4. Click frame 1 of the actions layer and add the following code to import the List and XMLConnector classes:

```
import mx.controls.List;
import mx.data.components.XMLConnector;
```

5. Add the following code to the actions layer. These lines create a new XMLConnector object that loads the file address.xml.

```
var addressXC:XMLConnector = new XMLConnector();
addressXC.URL = "address.xml";
addressXC.direction = "receive";
addressXC.ignoreWhite = true;
addressXC.multipleSimultaneousAllowed = true;
addressXC.suppressInvalidCalls = true;
```

6. Use the following code to add a List component to the Stage:

```
createClassObject(List,"name_list", this.getNextHighestDepth());
name_list.moveTo(10,10);
name_list.setSize(200,100);
```

7. Create an event listener that listens for the `result` event of the XMLConnector object:

```
var xCListener:Object = new Object();
xCListener.result = function(evtObj:Object):Void {
  trace (evtObj.target.results);
};
addressXC.addEventListener("result", xCListener);
```

8. Add the following line at the bottom of the actions layer. The code triggers the XMLConnector object.

```
addressXC.trigger();
```

9. Test the movie and you'll see the results from the XMLConnector in an Output window.

   So far, we've used the same steps as in the previous example. Now, instead of using the EndPoint and Binding classes, we'll populate the `dataProvider` with ActionScript.

10. Change the event listener function as shown here. The new lines, which appear in bold, add the XML content to an array. We use the array to populate the `dataProvider` of the List component. Note that we can use `evtObj.target.results` to refer to the XML tree loaded into the XMLConnector object.

```
xCListener.result = function(evtObj:Object):Void {
  var len:Number = evtObj.target.results.firstChild.childNodes.length;
  var dp_arr:Array = new Array();
  var childNode:XMLNode, theName:String, theID:Number;
  for (var i:Number = 0; i < len; i++) {
    childNode = evtObj.target.results.firstChild.childNodes[i];
    theName = childNode.childNodes[1].firstChild.nodeValue;
    theID = childNode.childNodes[0].firstChild.nodeValue;
    dp_arr.push({label: theName, data: theID });
  }
  name_list.dataProvider = dp_arr;
};
```

The code creates a variable `len` that finds the number of contacts in the address book. We can find this by counting the number of `childNodes` in the `firstChild`. The code creates an array for the List items as well as supporting variables. We loop through each contact and find the name and id. These values are stored in the variables `theName` and `theID` and added to the array `dp_arr`. The function sets the array as the `dataProvider` for the `name_list` List box.

11. Test the movie and you'll see the interface shown in Figure 8-43. You can also see the completed `scriptLoadAddressNoBinding.fla` in your resource files.

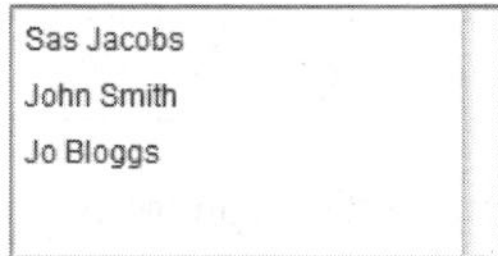

Figure 8-43. The completed interface

Exercise 7 has shown how to add data from an XMLConnector object to a List component without scripting the bindings. It is an alternative method for working with complicated data structures in bindings.

The ActionScript to create multiple bindings can get very involved, especially where you are using an XML document with complicated data structures. The EndPoint class has another property, `location`, which allows you to navigate data structures within the XML document. You can specify the path in many different ways, such as by using XPath statements or ActionScript paths. You then have to use Rearrange Fields, Compose String, or Custom formatters to manipulate the data.

Given the amount of effort involved in creating simple bindings with ActionScript, it's much easier to create these bindings visually using the Component Inspector. I strongly suggest that you configure your bindings through the Component Inspector wherever possible.

Summary of the properties, methods, and events of the XMLConnector class

This section provides a summary of the properties and methods of the XMLConnector class. Table 8-6 shows the only method of the XMLConnector class.

Table 8-6. The only method of the XMLConnector class

Method	Explanation
`trigger`	Triggers the XMLConnector class to process the XML document

Table 8-7 summarizes the properties of the XMLConnector class.

Table 8-7. Summary of properties of the XMLConnector class

Property	Explanation
`direction`	Sets the direction for the data. Either receive, send, or send/receive.
`ignoreWhite`	Determines whether white space is stripped out of XML data. The default setting is `false`.
`multipleSimultaneousAllowed`	Specifies whether multiple XMLConnectors can be triggered at the same time.
`params`	Lists the XML content sent to a server-side page when an XMLConnector triggers.
`results`	Lists the XML data received when an XMLConnector triggers.
`surpressInvalidCalls`	Specifies whether to suppress a call if the parameters are invalid.
`URL`	Specifies the URL for the external XML document.

Table 8-8 lists the events broadcast by the XMLConnector class.

Table 8-8. Summary of events of the XMLConnector class

Event	Explanation
`result`	Broadcasts when an XMLConnector has completed its call, i.e., after successfully triggering the data.
`send`	Broadcasts during the trigger method, when the parameters have been gathered before the call is initiated.
`status`	Broadcasts when the call starts. Provides information on the status on the call.

Summary

In this chapter, you've seen how to use the XMLConnector component to load an external XML document into Flash. You've also learned how to bind XML data to other components. Binding data allows you to associate part of a loaded XML document directly with a UI component. By using visual data binding, you can avoid writing ActionScript code to display the XML data in your movie.

We've completed exercises in this chapter that bind the data from the XMLConnector component directly to one or more UI components. I've also shown you how to bind the XMLConnector to DataSet and XUpdateResolver components so that you can keep track of changes and send them to a server-side page for external processing.

The XMLConnector provides a quick way to create Flash applications. It's easy to learn how to bind data to components, and you can be flexible in the way that you use these bindings. I haven't spent a lot of time exploring the different ways to configure bindings because that's beyond the scope of this book. My main aim was to show you how easy it is to use the data components to work with XML content.

Although you can script the XMLConnector, the code required to create bindings within complicated data structures can be cumbersome, so I suggest that you stick to visual bindings wherever possible. There are several articles about visual data binding at the Macromedia website at www.macromedia.com/devnet/ if you want to find out more.

In the next chapter, I'll look at consuming web services with Flash. I'll show you different ways that you can add content from web services, including the use of the WebService connector for SOAP-based services.

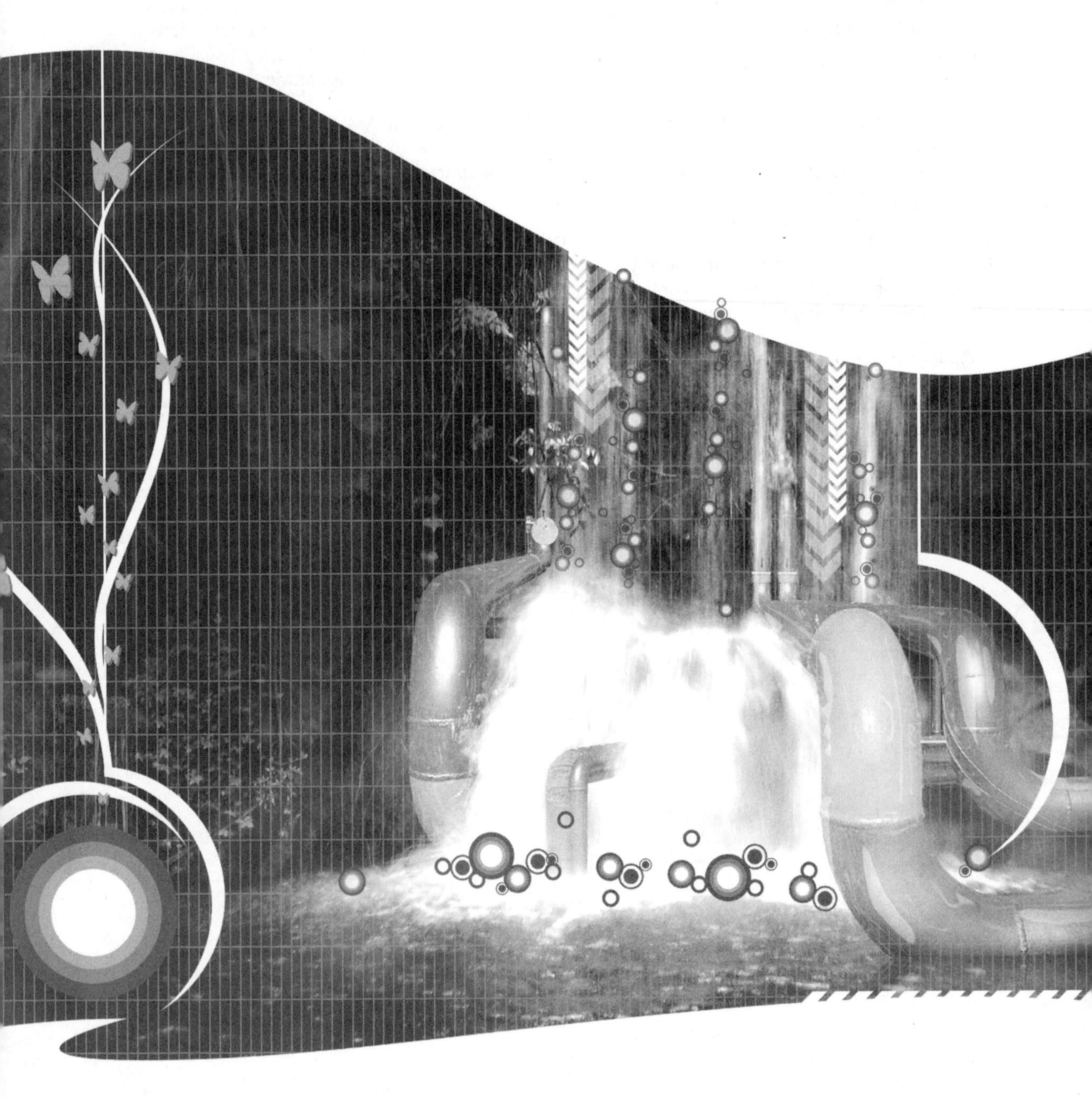

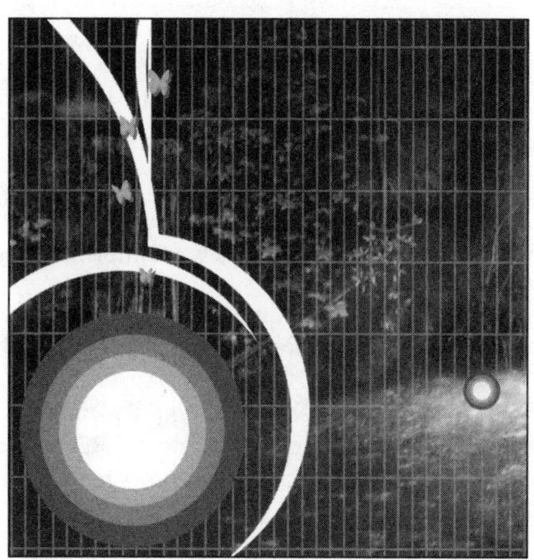

Chapter 9

CONSUMING WEB SERVICES WITH FLASH

Web services allow organizations to provide information to the public using the Internet. Organizations use them so that they can provide information from their own systems in a controlled way. Web services can provide public data but restrict access to sensitive information. Users make a request, and the web service provides the response in an XML document. The response is a stream of information rather than a physical document. This process is referred to as *consuming* a web service.

You can use web services to consume many different types of information, including currency exchange rates, weather information, stock quotes, and Google search results. Imagine being able to create Flash applications that search Google or Amazon, or a Flash-based shopping cart that provides up-to-date exchange rates. You could use Flash to display up-to-the-minute information about your company's stock prices or about the local weather. As an author, I can use Flash to find out the sales ranking and database details for any books I've written.

These are all examples of how you might include web services in your Flash applications. You can search using your favorite search engine to locate public web services. You can also see a list of web services at `www.flash-db.com/services/` and `www.xmethods.com/`.

There are many ways to consume a web service. One option is to display the XML content in a web browser. However, you're more likely to use server-side pages or a web application to process the XML from the web service. Flash can receive the web service response and display the XML data in a movie.

You can find out what web services are available through a company's Universal Description, Discovery, and Integration (UDDI) registry. The UDDI contains a description of the web services that are available and lists the way that you can access them.

Web Services Description Language (WSDL) describes web services in a standard XML format. The WSDL document for a web service explains what operations you can perform, what parameters you need to supply, and what information you'll receive.

There are a number of protocols for accessing web services, including Simple Object Access Protocol (SOAP), Representational State Transfer (REST), and RSS. SOAP uses formatted XML messages to request and receive information from web services. REST is a way to work with web services that allows you to make requests from a web service through a URL. Another option is RSS (which stands for either Rich Site Summary, RDF Site Summary, or Really Simple Syndication). RSS makes information available through XML news feeds using standard XML elements.

At the time of writing, SOAP is the probably the most common protocol for consuming web services. Flash has native support for SOAP-based web services over the HTTP protocol. This means that Flash will generate the SOAP request and process the response automatically. There are two types of SOAP requests: Remote Procedure Call (RPC) and Document. Flash supports both types as long as the web service response includes datatypes that Flash recognizes.

Flash can connect to a WSDL file to find what operations are available through the SOAP web service. You can use the WebServiceConnector data component, or you can write ActionScript to generate the SOAP request. As with the other data components, you'll only have access to the WebServiceConnector if you own Flash Professional. We'll show you how to consume SOAP web services later in this chapter.

You can also consume REST web services in Flash. Because of the security restrictions with the Flash Player, you'll normally do this through a server-side page that proxies the XML data and makes it available locally. Chapter 4 has more information about Flash Player security.

If you want to include content from a web service in Flash, you have several choices:

- Use the WebServiceConnector component.
- Write ActionScript to use either the WebServiceConnector or Web Service classes.
- Write server-side pages to query the web service.
- Use Flash Remoting.

Whichever approach you decide to use, you'll need to consider the security issues with the Flash Player when consuming web services. You may also need to change the Flash publish settings to allow you to access remote networks.

In this chapter, we'll explore all of the alternatives for working with web services except Flash Remoting. We'll start by looking at how you can consume a REST web service using a server-side language. I'll use ASP.NET, but you can use any other language, such as ColdFusion or PHP. We'll also look at consuming an RSS feed without a server-side page. We'll work with the WebServiceConnector component and use it to consume currency exchange rates and weather information. Finally, I'll show you how to use ActionScript to work with the WebServiceConnector and Web Service classes. By the end of this chapter, you'll have built several applications that consume web services.

Consuming REST web services

REST (Representational State Transfer) allows you to request information from a web service through a URL. You make your request by adding the parameters in the URL. Unlike SOAP, REST isn't a standard—rather, it is a description of a style of web service.

A company with a URL at `http://www.mycompany.com` could provide a REST web service about products at the following URL:

```
http://www.mycompany.com/WebServices/Products
```

When a user opened this URL in a web browser, the browser could display an XML document containing the response. The company could refine the process and provide information about a specific product through a more detailed URL, for example:

```
http://www.mycompany.com/WebServices/Products/XA-123
```

You can try a REST-style web service yourself. Enter the following URL in your favorite web browser. The URL points to the Web Developer news web service from Moreover:

```
http://p.moreover.com/cgi-local/page?c=Web%20developer%20news&o=xml
```

Figure 9-1 shows the page open in Internet Explorer.

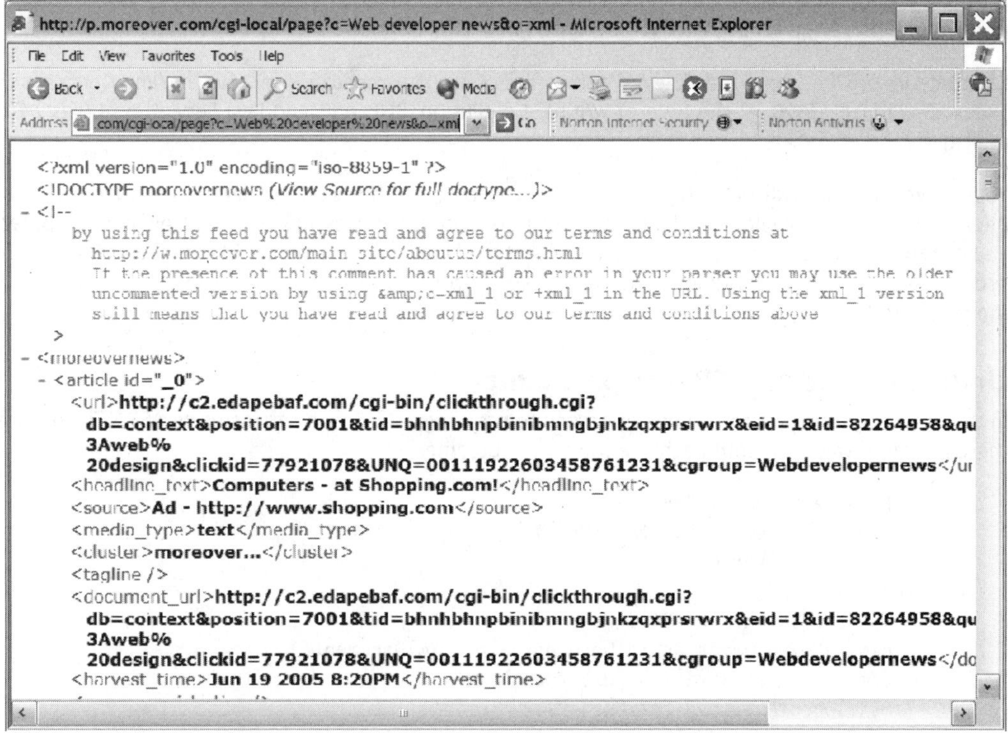

Figure 9-1. Internet Explorer showing the Moreover Web Developer news

You can see that the root node is <moreovernews> and that this element contains a number of <article> elements. Each article has a set of child elements that describe everything from the heading to the URL of the original document. You can find a complete list of Moreover XML news web services at http://w.moreover.com/categories/category_list.html.

RSS is one form of REST web services. However, it provides more strict guidelines about the XML elements used in the response. In the next section, we'll work through two examples, one using a REST web service and the other consuming an RSS news feed.

Using REST in Flash

To consume a REST web service in Flash, you need to know the URL. If the web service has a cross-domain security policy in place, you can request the contents directly within Flash. In most cases, however, that won't be the case, so you'll need to write a server-side page to make the request and provide access to the information locally. This is known as *proxying* the data.

The server-side page will receive the response from the web service and provide it to Flash. Because the server-side page is local to the Flash movie, you won't need to consider Flash Player security. You can include the proxied content by using the XML class or XMLConnector component.

Creating a proxy file

To proxy the XML data, you'll need to create a server-side file that queries the web service and provides the information to Flash. You can write the file in any language familiar to you, including ColdFusion, PHP, or Java. I use ASP.NET because I'm a .NET developer.

Macromedia provide some examples of proxy files at www.macromedia.com/cfusion/knowledgebase/index.cfm?id=tn_16520. At the time of writing, ColdFusion, PHP, ASP, and Java Servlet examples were available.

Your server-side file will need to run through a web server before that data is included in Flash. Because I'm a .NET developer, I have Internet Information Services (IIS) installed on my computer. You'll refer to the file in Flash using its full URL, for example, http://localhost/FOE/proxyWebService.aspx. This allows the web server to process the server-side code before providing the results to Flash.

Understanding an ASP.NET proxy file

In the following code, I've shown one approach to proxying a REST web service using ASP.NET. I'm sure there are other ways you could achieve the same outcome.

```
<%@ Page Language="VB"%>
<%@ import Namespace="System.XML" %>
<script runat="server">
  sub Page_Load
    dim strContents as String
    dim myXmlDocument as XmlDocument = new XmlDocument()
    dim strURL as String = "URL goes here"
    myXmlDocument.load (strURL)
    strContents = myXmlDocument.OuterXML
```

```
    response.write (strContents)
  end sub
</script>
```

This code uses the System.XML namespace. It creates some variables, including a new XmlDocument. It uses the load method of the XmlDocument to load the REST URL and writes the OuterXML content to the browser window. To use this approach, you'll need to replace URL goes here in the code with your own URL.

You can find an example that uses this code saved with your resources as genericWSRequest.aspx. The example file loads the Web Developer news from Moreover. If you open this page in a web browser, you'll see the XML contents displayed. Don't forget to include the full web server path in the address. The URL on my computer is http://localhost/FOE/genericWSRequest.aspx. If you prefer to work with PHP, you can find a PHP version saved in the resource file genericWSRequest.php. Again, you'll need to use the full web server path to test this file.

Consuming the XML content

Once you've gathered the information using your web service proxy, you can include the data in Flash. You could use the XML class to work through the XML document tree and add the content to the relevant parts of the movie. If you have Flash Professional, you can also use the XMLConnector component to load the content. One advantage of this approach is that you can bind the data directly to user interface (UI) components. You can also use the XMLConnector class and script the bindings. Chapter 8 describes this approach in greater detail.

We'll look at an example where we use a proxy file to load a REST-style web service. I'll use the file genericWSRequest.aspx to consume the Web Developer news from Moreover. We'll display the news headings and users will be able to open the news item in a web browser. If you'd prefer to work in PHP, you can use the resource file genericWSRequest.php.

You'll need to have IIS or another web server installed to complete the exercise. If you're working with ASP.NET, you'll also need to have the .NET Framework installed. Make sure you're connected to the Internet before you work through this exercise.

Exercise 1: Consuming Moreover news using the XML class

In this exercise, we'll consume the Web Developer news web service from Moreover and view the news headings in a List component. We'll use the XML class, and you'll be able to click each heading to view the details of the news item in a web browser.

1. Open Flash and create a new movie. If necessary, create a folder called FOE within your web server. I'm running IIS so the path to my folder is C:\Inetpub\wwwroot\FOE. Copy the genericWSRequest.aspx file to the FOE folder. If you'd prefer to work with PHP, you can use the file genericWSRequest.php instead. Save the Flash file as news.fla in the same folder.
2. Rename Layer 1 as UI and add another layer called actions.

3. Add a List component to the UI layer and give it the instance name news_list. Resize it to the width of the movie. Add a static text field with the title Web Developer News. Add a dynamic text field over the List component and enter the text Loading. Name the field error_txt. Make sure the dynamic text field can display two lines of text as it will also display error messages. Figure 9-2 shows the interface.

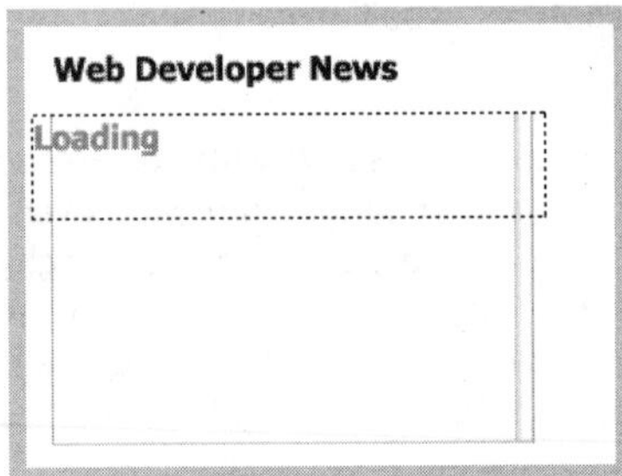

Figure 9-2. The Flash interface for the Web Developer News movie

4. Add the following code to load the XML content into Flash. If you've written your own server-side file or you're using the PHP resource file, change the file name in the load line. Don't forget to include the full server path to the file.

```
news_list.visible = false;
var RootNode:XMLNode;
var News_xml:XML = new XML();
News_xml.ignoreWhite = true;
News_xml.onLoad = FormatXML;
News_xml.load("http://localhost/FOE/genericWSRequest.aspx");
function FormatXML(success:Boolean):Void {
  if (success) {
    error_txt._visible = false;
    RootNode = this.firstChild;
    trace (RootNode);
  }
else {
    error_txt.text = "Could not load news file";
  }
}
```

The code hides the news_list component and loads the XML document. Note that I've included the full path to the server-side file. If this file doesn't load successfully, an error message displays in the error_txt text field. Otherwise, Flash hides the error_txt field and brings up an Output window containing the RootNode variable.

5. Test the movie and you should see an Output window displaying the XML content from the proxy file. If you see an error message, test the server-side file through a web browser to make sure it is correctly loading the XML content.

6. Modify the FormatXML function as shown here. I've indicated the new lines in bold.

```
function FormatXML(success:Boolean):Void {
  if (success) {
    error_txt._visible = false;
    RootNode = this.firstChild;
    var headline_str:String;
    var headingNode:XMLNode;
    for (var i:Number = 0; i < RootNode.childNodes.length; i++) {
      headingNode = RootNode.childNodes[i].childNodes[1];
      headline_str = headingNode.firstChild.nodeValue;
      headline_str = headline_str.substr(0,60) + "... ";
      news_list.addItem({label: headline_str});
    }
    news_list.visible = true;
  }
  else {
    error_txt.text = "Could not load news file";
  }
}
```

In the new lines, we create the new variables `headline_str` and `headingNode`. We loop through each of the `childNodes` of the `RootNode`, that is, each article, and find the `headingNode`. This node is the second child, `childNodes[1]`, of each article. To find the heading text, we use `headingNode.firstChild.nodeValue`. Before adding it as the `label` of the List component, we find the first 60 characters using the `substr` method. We use the `addItem` method to add each heading to the List.

7. Test the movie and you should see something similar to Figure 9-3.

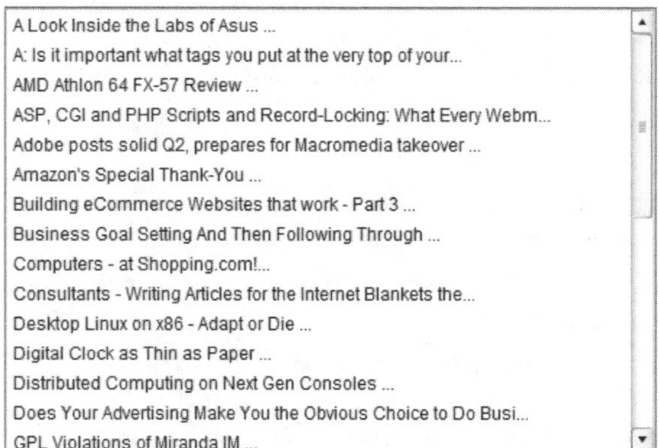

Figure 9-3. The Flash interface showing the loaded Web Developer news

Nothing happens when you click each headline, so we'll need to add an `eventListener` to the List component. The listener will detect when a new selection is made in the List and respond by calling a function.

8. Add the following code above the var RootNode line:

```
var ListListener:Object = new Object();
ListListener.change = function(evtObj:Object):Void{
  var ListNum:Number = evtObj.target.selectedIndex;
  var articleNode:XMLNode = RootNode.childNodes[ListNum];
  var theURL:String = articleNode.childNodes[0].firstChild.nodeValue;
  getURL (theURL);
};
news_list.addEventListener("change", ListListener);
```

This code creates a new listener called ListListener that responds to the change event in the List component. It finds the selectedIndex of the chosen item and stores it in the variable ListNum. The code sets another variable called articleNode, which locates the selected node. A variable called theURL stores the link, and we use the getURL action to display the link.

9. Test the movie and click one of the headlines. You should see the article displayed in a web browser window.

   When we test this movie from within Flash, a new web browser window will open each time we click an article heading. If you test the movie from within a web browser, clicking an article title will replace the Flash movie.

   You can open each article in a new window by adding some JavaScript to the web page hosting the Flash movie and by changing the code in the ListListener object. You'll also need to set your Flash publish settings appropriately.

10. Publish an HTML page from the Flash movie and rename it as newsJS.html. This will prevent you from overwriting the HTML file each time you republish your Flash movie.

11. Open the newsJS.html page in a text or HTML editor and add the following JavaScript function between the <head> </head> tags:

```
<script language="JavaScript">
  function popWin(popName, popPage) {
    var strParams = "width=800,height=600,scrollbars=yes,";
    strParams += "status=no,menubar=no";
    var popWindow=window.open(popPage,popName,strParams);
  }
</script>
```

The function accepts parameters for the name of the new window and the URL. It shows a window 800X600 pixels in size with scroll bars but without a status bar and menu bar.

12. Modify the change function in Flash as shown in the following code. The new line (shown in bold) calls the JavaScript function, passing the window name and the page URL.

```
ListListener.change = function(evtObj:Object):Void{
  var ListNum:Number = evtObj.target.selectedIndex;
  var articleNode:XMLNode = RootNode.childNodes[ListNum];
  var theURL:String = articleNode.childNodes[0].firstChild.nodeValue;
  theURL = "JavaScript:popWin('News','" + theURL + "')";
  getURL (theURL);
};
```

13. To access the web server from the Flash Player, you'll need to change the publish settings in File ➤ Publish Settings ➤ Flash. Change the Local playback security option to Access network only.

14. Open the file `newsJS.html` in a web browser using the web server path—`http://localhost/FOE/newsJS.html`—and click one of the headlines. You should see the news item open in a new web browser window. Note that once you change the theURL variable within Flash, you'll need to test the Flash file from a web browser instead of within Flash. You can view the completed resource files `news.fla` and `newsJS.html`. The resource files `newsPHP.fla` and `newsJSPHP.html` contain the PHP file references.

In this exercise, we used an ASP.NET file to request an XML document from Moreover. The XML document provided content for a List component, and we were able to click the heading to pop up each news item in a new web browser window. The ASP.NET file provided a local copy of the XML document to Flash so we could avoid the security restrictions of the Flash Player. Because we were using the web server, we needed to change the publish settings for the file.

Another application of REST is in RSS news feeds. RSS uses a specific XML vocabulary to share information.

Consuming an RSS feed

As we mentioned earlier, RSS stands for Rich Site Summary, RDF Site Summary, or Really Simple Syndication (depending on which article you read). RSS is an XML vocabulary that describes information about website changes, so this makes it ideal for sharing news. Netscape originally developed it as a way to provide news through different news channels.

RSS comes in a number of versions, each one using slightly different XML elements. Learn more about each version at `www.webreference.com/authoring/languages/xml/rss/1/`.

You need to consider Flash Player security when consuming an RSS feed. If there's a cross-domain policy file on the server providing the feed, you can consume the content directly in a Flash movie. If not, you'll need to use a server-side file to proxy the content locally.

In the next section, we'll look at an example of consuming an RSS feed using the XMLConnector component. You'll need to have Flash Professional and an active Internet connection to complete this exercise. The RSS feed comes from Macromedia and has a cross-domain policy in place, so we don't need to use a server-side file to proxy the data.

Exercise 2: Consuming a news feed using the XMLConnector

In exercise 2, we'll use the XMLConnector component to load the news feed from `http://weblogs.macromedia.com/product_feeds/archives/flash/index.rdf`. This news feed provides information about Flash from the Developer Center. You can find out more about the available Macromedia RSS feeds at `http://weblogs.macromedia.com/notifications/`.

1. Enter the URL http://weblogs.macromedia.com/product_feeds/archives/flash/index.rdf in a web browser. You should see the structure of the XML document in the browser window. In some web browsers, the file may open in a different application. Figure 9-4 shows this XML document open in Internet Explorer.

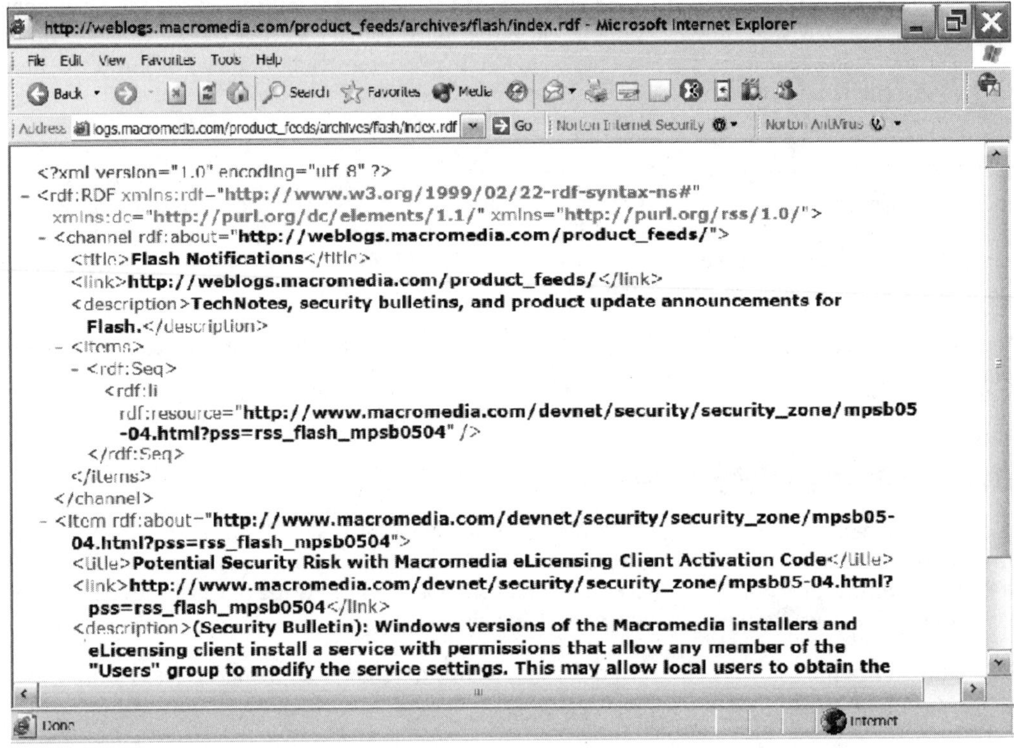

Figure 9-4. The Flash RSS feed

2. Open Flash if necessary and open the starter file `FlashRSS.fla`. Figure 9-5 shows the interface.

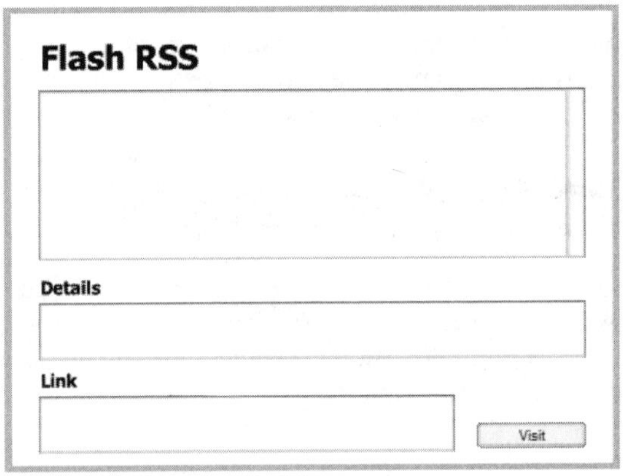

Flash RSS

Details

Link

Visit

Figure 9-5. The Flash RSS interface

The Flash file has a List component and two TextArea components. There is also a button component called `visit_btn`. We'll load the articles into the List component. When we click one of the titles, the details and link will display in the TextArea components. We can view the article in a web browser by clicking the Visit button.

3. Drag an XMLConnector component into the movie and position it off the Stage. Give it the instance name rss_xc.

4. Select the XMLConnector and open the Component Inspector. Enter the URL http://weblogs.macromedia.com/product_feeds/archives/flash/index.rdf and set the direction to receive.

5. Select the Schema tab and choose results. Select the read only setting and choose true. Load a schema from the document `flashRSSSample.xml`. I saved this document from the RSS feed. It contains a trimmed-down version of the data and provides a structure for Flash to use. You can open the file in a text or XML editor if you want to see what it contains. Figure 9-6 shows the schema generated from the file.

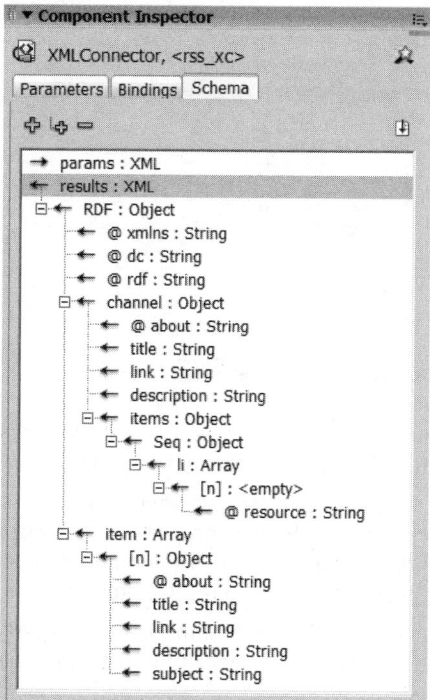

Figure 9-6. The schema imported from flashRSSSample.xml

6. Create a new layer called actions and add the following code on frame 1:

```
rss_xc.trigger();
```

This code triggers the XMLConnector component to load the data from the RSS feed. Once the data is loaded, we'll need to display the headings in the List component. We'll do this by adding a binding.

7. Select the XMLConnector and choose the Bindings tab in the Component Inspector. Click the Add binding button and add a binding from the item array. Set the direction to out and bind the item to the `dataProvider` of the List component. If we want to display multiple values from the results, it's common to bind from an array to the `dataProvider` of a data-aware component such as a List or ComboBox.
8. Choose a Rearrange Fields formatter and add label=title to the formatter options. This specifies what field should display in the List.
9. Test the Flash movie and check that the List component populates correctly. Figure 9-7 shows the interface at this stage.

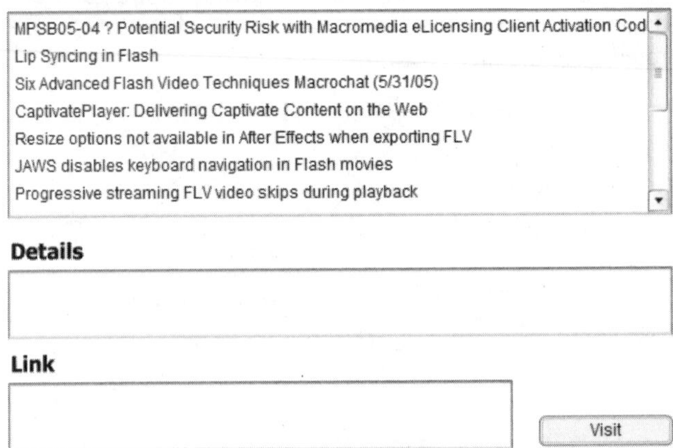

Figure 9-7. The interface with the loaded content

We'll need to add bindings to the TextArea components. When we click a heading, the description should appear in the Details TextArea while the link should display in the Link TextArea.

10. Select the XMLConnector and add a binding from the description element. Set the direction to out and bind the description to the text property of the `details_txt` component. Set the Index to the selectedIndex property of the List component. We've told the XMLConnector to display the description for whichever item is selected in the List.
11. Repeat the process to bind the link element to the text property of the `link_txt` component. Set the Index to the selectedIndex property of the List component.
12. Test the movie. When you select a List item, you should see the description and title within the TextArea components. Figure 9-8 shows the interface.

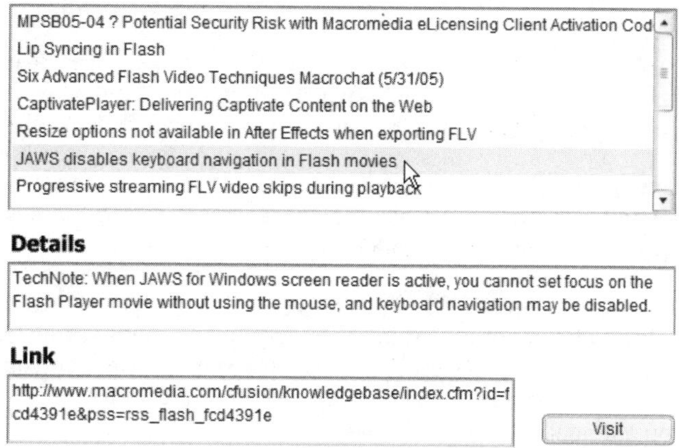

Figure 9-8. The interface showing the bound components

13. The final step is to configure the Visit button so that the selected article displays in a web browser. Add the following code to the actions layer. The code checks to see if there is any text within the `link_txt` component. If so, it loads the link using the `getURL` action.

```
visit_btn.onRelease = function ():Void {
  if (link_txt.text.length > 0) {
    getURL(link_txt.text);
  }
}
```

14. Test the Flash movie. You should be able to select an item from the List component and click the Visit button to open the article in a web browser window. You can see the completed file saved as `FlashRSS_completed.fla`.

Points to note from exercise 2

- When tested from Flash, this movie loads the URL into a new web browser. As with the previous exercise, you could add a JavaScript function to the HTML page hosting the movie so that the link loads in a new browser window. You'd have to call this function from with the `onRelease` function of the Visit button.
- This movie loads data from an external domain directly into Flash. When you test the movie from Flash, you can load the data successfully, even though it is coming from another domain.

  Because this RSS feed has a cross-domain policy in place, you'll be able to load the data into a Flash movie on any web server. If there were no cross-domain policy, you'd need to find a workaround for the Flash player security restrictions. One option would be to proxy the data using a server-side file. You saw an example of how to do this in exercise 1. You can find out more about security in Chapter 4.

So far, we've looked at REST and RSS, and you've created two applications to display data. A more common protocol for web services is SOAP. Flash can automate the process of making a SOAP request for you.

Using the WebServiceConnector with SOAP web services

Simple Object Access Protocol (SOAP) is another protocol for web services. It uses XML to request information from the web service in a SOAP message. It receives an XML document in response. SOAP messages can be sent using HTTP and even by email. Flash only supports HTTP-based SOAP messages.

To consume a web service, a SOAP message containing the request is sent to a receiver. The receiver processes the request and acts upon it, usually running a remote method in a web application. The method returns the results to the requester in XML format.

Web Services Description Language (WSDL) is an XML-based language that describes how to access the web service. The WDSL document for a web service lists the methods or functions that a web service can perform. It specifies how to make the request and what information you'll need to provide. You should consult the WDSL document before you start working with SOAP web services. Luckily, Flash does this for you automatically.

For example, the WSDL file for Google web services lists three methods: `doGetCachedPage`, `doSpellingSuggestion`, and `doGoogleSearch`. You can see the details of these methods if you visit `http://api.google.com/GoogleSearch.wsdl`. Later in this chapter, you'll see how the WebServiceConnector component finds these methods automatically.

Using SOAP in Flash

Flash Professional can work natively with SOAP requests. You can use the WebServiceConnector component to query a WDSL file and generate a SOAP request for you. You can also script the WebServiceConnector class.

Each WebServiceConnector component can work with only one operation at the web service. The connector can call the same operation more than once. You need to add extra WebServiceConnector components if you're calling more than one operation in your application.

Using the WebServiceConnector

Figure 9-9. The WebServiceConnector component icon

The WebServiceConnector is available in Flash Professional. Like the other data components, it has no visual appearance in a compiled Flash movie. When you drag the WebServiceConnector to a movie, Flash displays the icon shown in Figure 9-9.

Configuring the WebServiceConnector

You configure the WebServiceConnector using the Component Inspector panel. To begin, enter the settings in the Parameters tab of the panel. Figure 9-10 shows the panel.

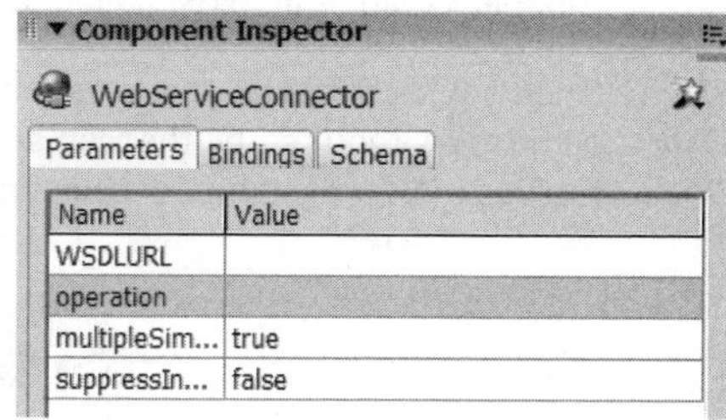

Figure 9-10. The WebServiceConnector parameters

Table 9-1 provides a summary of the parameters in this tab.

Table 9-1. The settings listed in the Parameters tab of the Component Inspector

Parameter	Purpose
WSDLURL	Specifies the path to the WSDL document for the web service.
operation	Contains the name of the remote procedure or method specified within the WSDL.
multipleSimultaneousAllowed	Specifies whether to allow multiple connections. If you set this property to false, when you are triggering one XMLConnector, you can't trigger others.
suppressInvalidCall	Sets the behavior for invalid data parameters. If you set the value to true, the component won't be triggered if the parameters are invalid.

You start by entering the URL for the WSDL document. You can either type the URL or copy and paste it from another location. If you've entered the URL previously, you can also select it from a drop-down list. If Flash finds a valid WSDL document at the URL, it will populate the operation setting with all available procedures for the web service. This may take a few seconds.

Figure 9-11 shows the operations available after entering the Google WSDL URL http://api.google.com/GoogleSearch.wsdl. Google provides three operations through its web services: doGetCachedPage, doSpellingSuggestion, and doGoogleSearch.

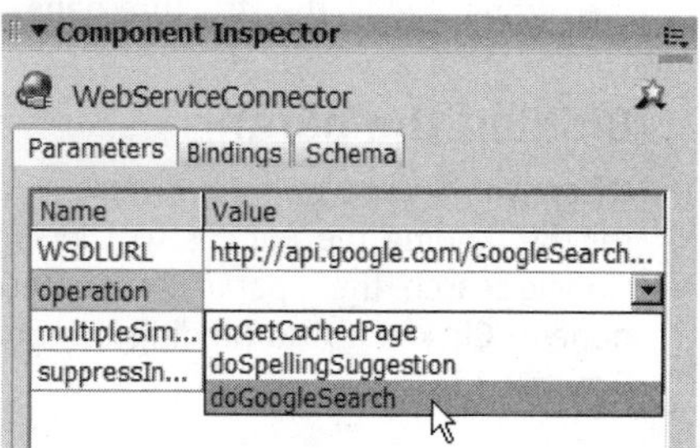

Figure 9-11. The operations available from the Google WSDL document

After you've selected the operation, you don't normally need to change the last two settings in the Parameters tab, multipleSimultaneousAllowed and suppressInvalidCall.

Once you've selected an operation, the Schema tab of the Component Inspector will identify any parameters required by the web service as well as show you the structure of the results. Figure 9-12 shows the Schema tab after selecting the doGoogleSearch operation.

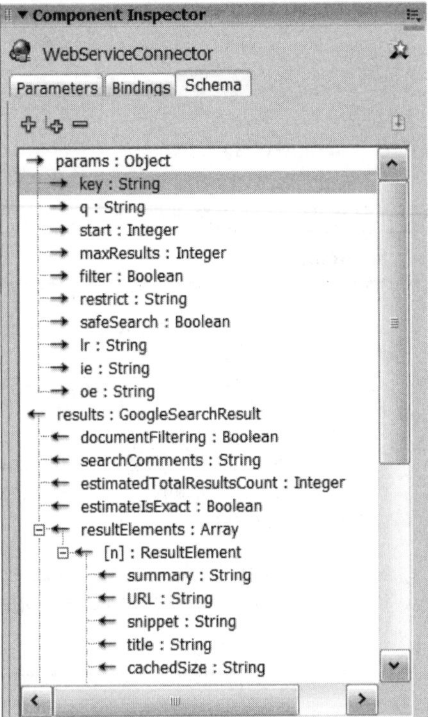

Figure 9-12. The Schema tab available after selecting an operation

The params section identifies information required by Google, and the results section provides the structure for the returned results. You can find out more information about each element by viewing the settings below the structure pane.

Binding the params

Often, you'll need to enter different parameters each time you call the web service. You can achieve this by binding the params to UI components such as TextInputs. For example, in the case of the Google search, the q parameter represents the search query, so you could bind it to a TextInput component. Click the Add binding or + button in the Schema tab and select a parameter, as shown in Figure 9-13.

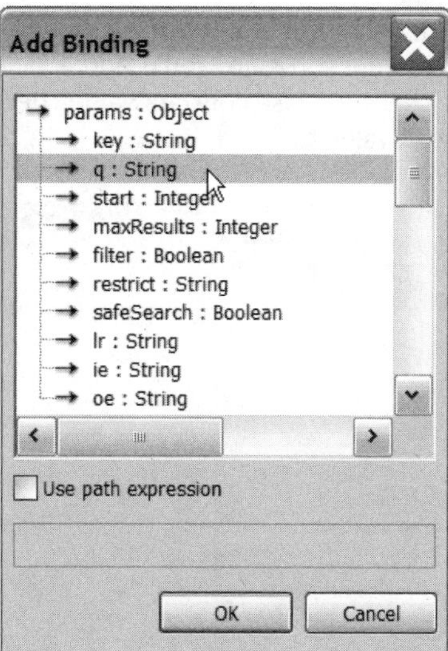

Figure 9-13. Adding a parameter binding

Set the direction to in since the component is sending the value in to the parameter. Then select the UI component that will supply the value for this parameter. In Figure 9-14, we've selected the text property of the search_txt component.

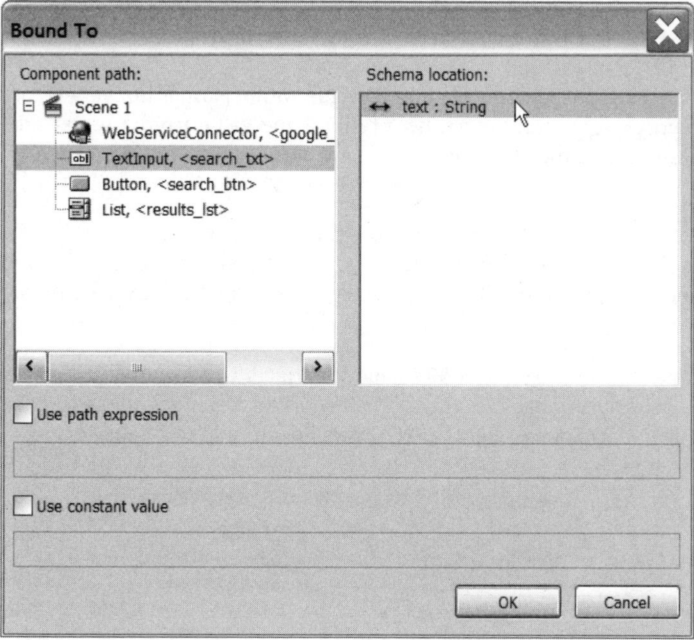

Figure 9-14. Selecting a component for the binding

You can also specify a fixed value for parameters that won't vary. You might do this if you need to send a developer token or ID with your request. Again, you'd add a binding and set the direction to in. Instead of selecting a component, check the Use constant value check box and enter the value. Figure 9-15 shows a binding with a constant value of 10.

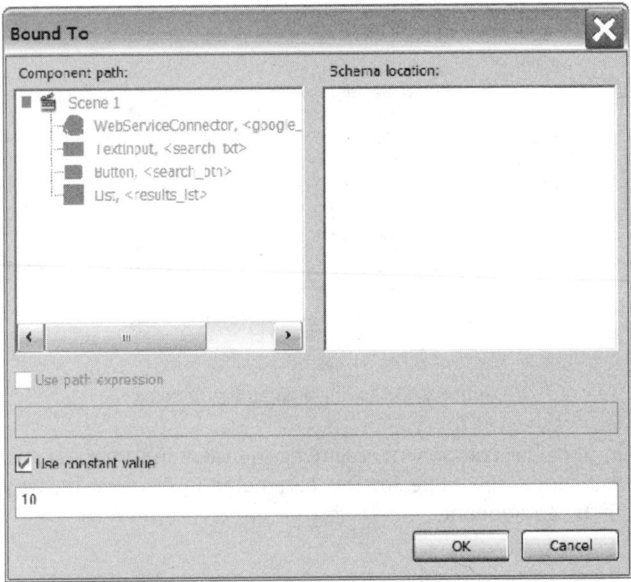

Figure 9-15. Entering a constant value for the binding

Bear in mind that storing a developer token or ID value within Flash is not very secure. If you are concerned about security, a better approach is to request the value from a server-side file or load the token with the page hosting the Flash movie.

Triggering the web services call

Before you receive the results from your request, you must trigger the call to the web service. As with the XMLConnector, you can use the Behaviors panel to generate the ActionScript, or you can add the code yourself.

When you work with web services, you'll often add the trigger to a button instance. Select the instance and bring up the Behaviors panel with the *Shift-F3* shortcut key. Click the Add Behavior button and select Data ➤ Trigger Data Source. Figure 9-16 shows how to add this Behavior.

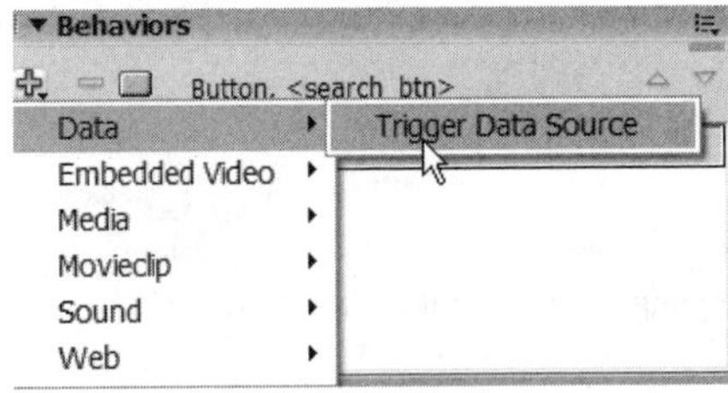

Figure 9-16. Adding a Behavior panel to trigger the WebServiceConnector

You'll need to select the component to trigger from the Trigger Data Source dialog box, as shown in Figure 9-17. You can insert either a Relative or an Absolute path to the WebServiceConnector component. I normally choose a relative path in case I need to rearrange my movie timelines later.

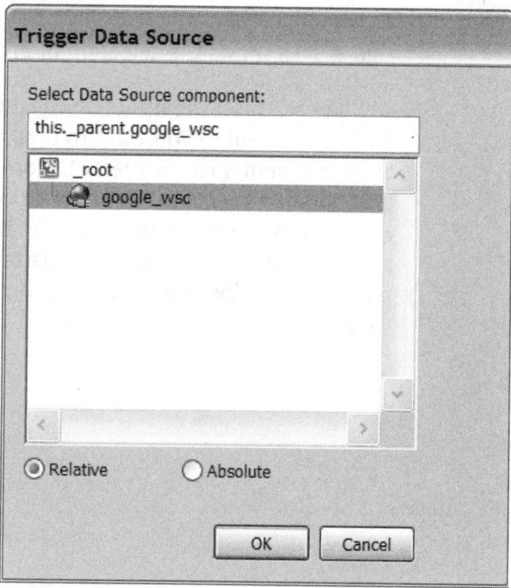

Figure 9-17. Selecting the Data Source component to trigger

In the case of a button instance, Flash will add the following code:

```
on (click) {
  // Trigger Data Source Behavior
  // Macromedia 2003
  this._parent.WSCInstanceName.trigger();
}
```

You could also type this ActionScript yourself or enter an onRelease event handler, as shown in this code snippet:

```
buttonInstance.onRelease = function():Void {
  WSCInstanceName.trigger();
}
```

This code would work where the Button and WebServiceConnector components are in the same timeline.

Binding the results

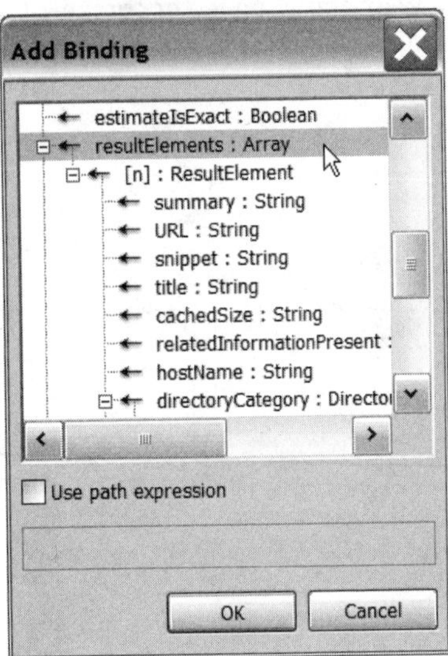

Figure 9-18. Adding a binding for the results

Once you've triggered the component, you'll be able to bind the results of your web service request to one or more UI components. Click the Add binding button in the Bindings tab of the Component Inspector and select one of the resulting elements. Figure 9-18 shows the selection of an Array element.

You'll need to set the direction for the binding to out and select a UI component. If you want to bind the results to a data-aware UI component such as the List, ComboBox, or DataGrid, you'll probably want to select an element with an Array datatype. You can bind the Array to the `dataProvider` for the UI component and use a Rearrange Fields formatter to determine which element to use for the label and data properties. Figure 9-19 shows the Bound To dialog box.

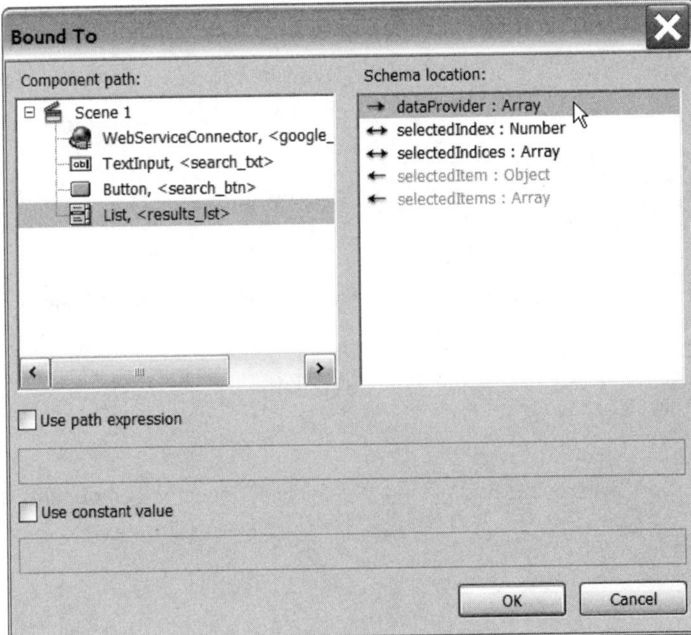

Figure 9-19. Binding to the dataProvider of a List component

If the results array has multiple child elements, you'll see all of the children in the UI component. In the case of a List or ComboBox component, you'll probably need to use a Rearrange Fields formatter so you have more control over which values display.

Select this formatter from the drop-down list in the formatter setting of the Bindings tab. The Rearrange Fields formatter allows you to specify the `label` and `data` properties for a List-based component using the names from the results schema. Click the magnifying glass within the formatter options setting and enter the values.

Figure 9-20 shows a sample Rearrange Fields dialog box. The label comes from the title field and the data associated with each item comes from the URL field, so I've used the setting data=URL;label=title.

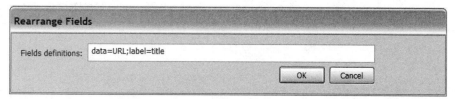

Figure 9-20. Setting the Rearrange Fields formatter options

Once you've added this setting, the data will display correctly in the component.

Viewing the Web Services panel

You can view a list of web services that you've worked with through the Web Services panel. Display the panel by choosing Window ➤ Development Panels ➤ Web Services or by using the *Ctrl-Shift-F10* shortcut (*Cmd-Shift-F10* on a Macintosh). Figure 9-21 shows the Web Services panel.

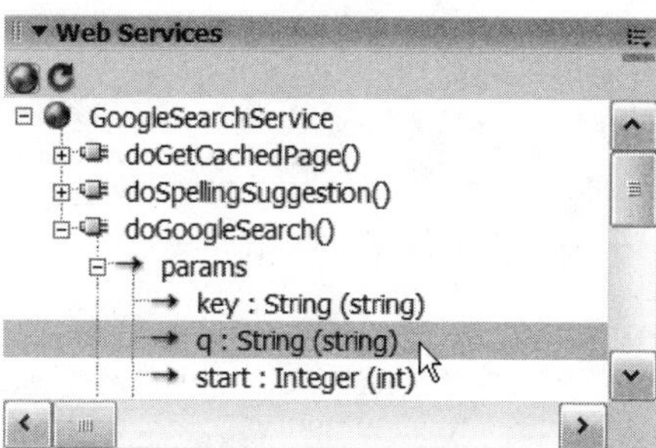

Figure 9-21. The Web Services panel

You can expand each web service listed in the panel to see a list of available operations as well as the schema for the params and results. This provides an alternative to using a WebServiceConnector and viewing the Component Inspector.

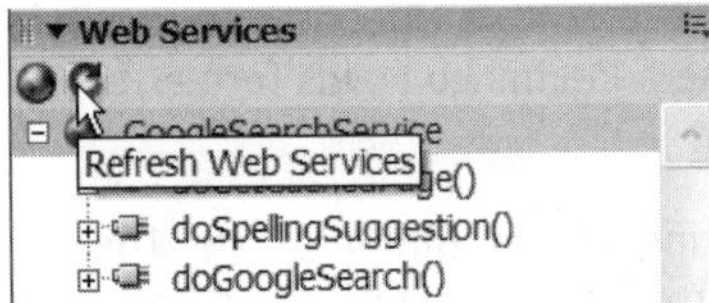

Figure 9-22. Refreshing all web services

You can refresh all web services in the panel by clicking the Refresh Web Services button at the top of the panel, as shown in Figure 9-22. This might be useful if you've entered a WSDL URL but can't see any operations listed in the Parameters tab of the Component Inspector.

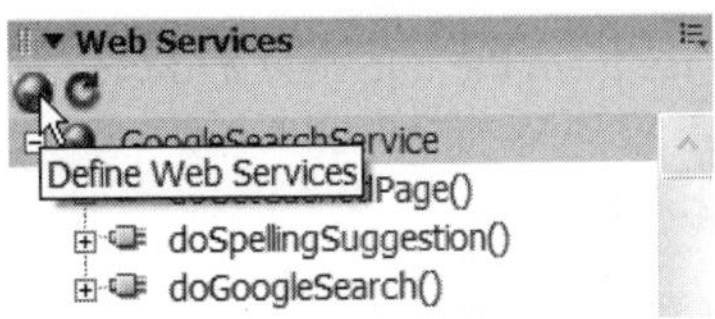

Figure 9-23. Defining web services

You can also manage the web services in the list by clicking the Define Web Services button at the top left of the panel. Figure 9-23 shows this button.

Clicking the button displays the Define Web Services dialog box. You can use the plus and minus buttons at the top of the dialog box to add and remove the URLs for the WSDL documents for each web service. Figure 9-24 shows the Define Web Services dialog box.

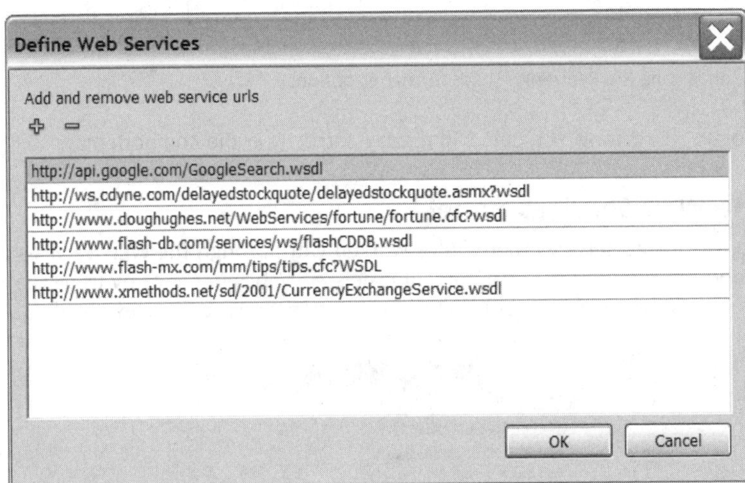

Figure 9-24. The Define Web Services dialog box

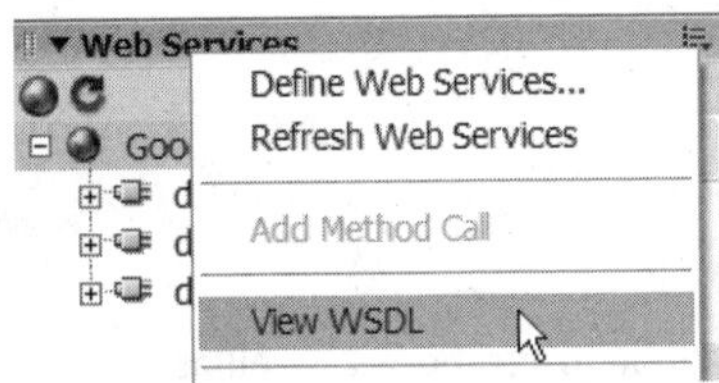

Figure 9-25. Viewing the WSDL through the panel menu

You can use the panel menu to carry out these tasks, as well as to view the WSDL document in a web browser. Figure 9-25 shows how to view the WSDL document using the panel menu.

The WebServiceConnector component will become a lot clearer when we work through a simple example. In the next exercise, we'll create a currency converter that uses rates from a web service. Make sure you have an active connection to the Internet before you start the exercise.

Exercise 3: Creating a currency converter using the WebServiceConnector

In exercise 3, we'll create a currency converter that uses the XMethods currency converter web service. The WSDL is at `www.xmethods.net/sd/2001/CurrencyExchangeService.wsdl`. At the time of writing, you could see details of the web service at `www.xmethods.com/ve2/ViewListing.po?key=uuid:D784C184-99B2-DA25-ED45-3665D11A12E5`.

The web service requires two country names. The parameters are `country1` and `country2`, and both are string values. You can find a valid list of all country names at the XMethods URL given in the previous paragraph. The web service finds the value of the first country's currency expressed in the second country's currency. It returns a floating-point number called `return`.

Because we'll use a WebServiceConnector component to prepare the SOAP request, you'll need Flash Professional to complete this exercise.

1. Open the starter file `currency.fla`. Figure 9-26 shows the interface.

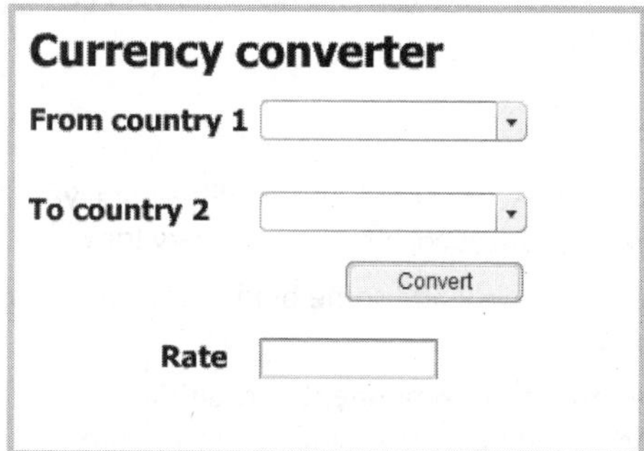

Figure 9-26. The currency converter interface

The movie has two ComboBox components: a Convert button and a TextInput component that will display the exchange rate.

2. Test the movie and check that the ComboBox components populate with the country names. The Combo layer contains the ActionScript used to populate these components. You should see a list of countries in each of the ComboBox components. Figure 9-27 shows `country1_cbo` expanded.

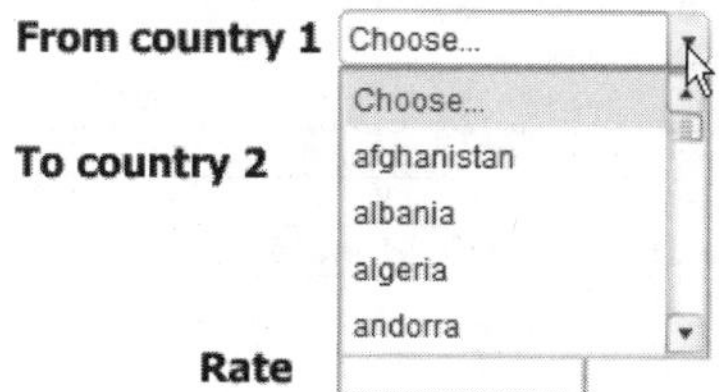

Figure 9-27. The ComboBox components are populated using ActionScript.

3. Drag a WebServiceConnector component to the movie and place it off the Stage. Give it the name converter_wsc.

4. Add the following WSDL for the WSDLURL setting in the Parameters tab of the Component Inspector:

   http://www.xmethods.net/sd/2001/CurrencyExchangeService.wsdl

5. Choose the getRate operation. If you can't see this operation, you may need to wait for a few seconds or refresh the web services in the Web Services panel. Note that you can't proceed unless you are able to choose the getRate operation.

6. Add a new layer called actions and enter the following code. The code finds the values in the two ComboBoxes. If we've selected two countries, that is, the values don't equal Choose, we trigger the WebServiceConnector component.

```
convert_btn.onRelease = function():Void {
  var country1:String = country1_cbo.selectedItem.label;
  var country2:String = country2_cbo.selectedItem.label;
  if (country1<> "Choose..." && country2<> "Choose...") {
    converter_wsc.trigger();
  }
}
```

   I wouldn't normally place my ActionScript on two different layers but if you look at the Combo layer, you'll see that the populateCombo function is very long.

   Before we can test the movie, we'll add some bindings from the ComboBox components to the params of the web service.

7. Select the WebServiceConnector component and display the Bindings tab of the Component Inspector. Click the Add binding button and select country1 : String. Click in the bound to setting, choose the country1_cbo and select the value property. Repeat this process for the country2_cbo ComboBox.

8. Add another binding for the results. Bind it to the text property of the rate_txt TextInput component. Figure 9-28 shows the appearance of the Bindings tab at this point.

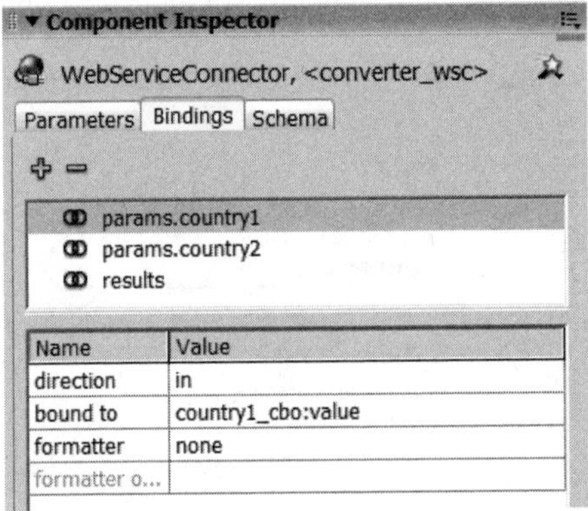

Figure 9-28. The completed bindings for exercise 3

9. We'll add some more ActionScript so we can find out about any errors that might occur when we connect to the web service. Add the following code to the actions layer:

```
var WSCListener:Object = new Object();
WSCListener.result = function(evtObj:Object):Void {
  trace (evtObj.target.results);
}
converter_wsc.addEventListener("result", WSCListener);
```

   The code adds an event listener that responds to the `result` event from the WebServiceConnector. When this event is detected, the event listener function displays the results in an Output window. If an error occurs, we should see an error message in the Output window.

10. Test the movie. Select two countries, and you should see an Output window and a rate displayed in the `rate_txt` TextInput. You'll find the completed file `currency_completed.fla` with your resources. If you don't see a result, check for error messages in the Output window.

You could extend this example so that the user could enter a currency amount. You could then display the rate as well as the converted value.

In exercise 3, we created a simple currency converter using the WebServiceConnector. The WebServiceConnector created the SOAP request and sent through values from two ComboBox components. Flash received a result value, which it displayed in a TextInput component.

You can also use ActionScript to work directly with the content returned by a web service.

Working with XML content from the WebServiceConnector

In a perfect world, all web services would return content with datatypes that Flash can recognize. However, sometimes the content returned by a web service can't be mapped through the Component Inspector. Instead of an XML object, sometimes a web service returns a string representation of an XML object, which means you must use a combination of components and scripting to load the results.

Next we'll work through a more complicated exercise in which we use the WebServiceConnector component with ActionScript to populate an application. The application finds the weather at airports around the world, and returns the content as a string of XML information.

Exercise 4: Displaying airport weather with the WebServiceConnector and ActionScript

In this exercise, we'll use both the WebServiceConnector and the XML class to load the contents from a web service. We'll enter a country and display a list of airports. We'll then choose one of the airports and display the weather conditions. The application will use two WebServiceConnector components because we're requesting two different operations from the web service.

You'll need Flash Professional to work with this exercise because we're using WebServiceConnector components. Make sure you have an active Internet connection before you start.

1. Open the starter file `weather.fla`. Figure 9-29 shows the interface.

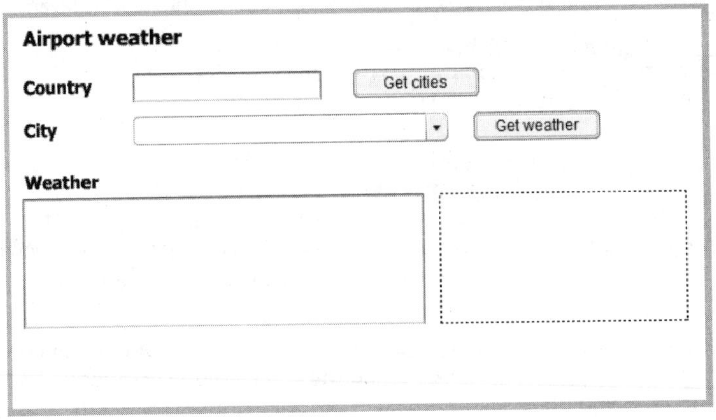

Figure 9-29. The Airport weather interface

The interface shows several UI components and a dynamic text field. We'll use two WebServiceConnector components. The first will get the cities for a selected country and the second will get the weather for the selected city.

Configuring the WebServiceConnector components

2. Drag two WebServiceConnector components to the movie and position them off the Stage. Name them cities_wsc and weather_wsc.
3. Configure both WebServiceConnector components using the WSDLURL http://www.webservicex.com/globalweather.asmx?WSDL. Select the operation GetCitiesByCountry for cities_wsc and GetWeather for weather_wsc. You may need to refresh the Web Services panel if you can't see the operations.
4. Select cities_wsc and add an in binding from the CountryName to the country_txt TextInput component. This will send the value from the TextInput to the WebServiceConnector.
5. Add an out binding from the results string of cities_wsc to the TextArea component. This will allow us to see the content that the web service returns.
6. Select weather_wsc and add an in binding from the CountryName to the country_txt TextInput component. This binding sends the country name as a parameter to the weather_wsc connector. Bind the CityName to the value property of the ComboBox component. The weather_wsc connector receives the selected city as the second parameter.
7. Add another binding from the results to the text property of the TextArea component. Again, this will display the results string in the TextArea.

   If you tested the movie now, nothing would happen because we still need to trigger the components. We'll do that using the two buttons Get cities and Get weather. We'll also add a movie clip to show the user that we're waiting for results from the web service. This is useful as a call to a web service may take several seconds.

Triggering the first WebServiceConnector component

8. Open the Library with the *Ctrl-L* shortcut key (*Cmd-L* on a Macintosh) and drag the loading movie clip to the movie. Place it off the Stage and give it the instance name loading_mc. We'll

use this clip to show the user that we're in the process of requesting information from the web service.

9. Add the following code on frame 1 of the actions layer:

```
cities_btn.onRelease = function():Void {
  error_txt.text = "";
  if (country_txt.text.length > 0) {
    cities_wsc.trigger();
    results_txt.text = "";
    cities_cbo.removeAll();
    showLoading();
  }
  else {
    error_txt.text = "Enter a country";
  }
}
```

This code runs when the user clicks the `cities_btn`. The code resets the `error_txt` text field and checks that the user has entered a country. If not, an error message displays. If the user has entered a country, the function triggers the first WebServiceConnector and resets the `results_txt` TextArea component. It also removes any existing entries in the `cities_cbo` ComboBox component.

Finally, the code calls the showLoading function. This function will place the `loading_mc` on the Stage and disable the two buttons. This shows the user that a call to the web service is in progress.

10. Add the showLoading function to the actions layer:

```
function showLoading():Void {
  loading_mc._x = 170;
  loading_mc._y = 120;
  cities_btn.enabled = false;
  weather_btn.enabled = false;
}
```

11. Test the movie, enter a country, and click the Get cities button. The results will be displayed in the TextArea component. You should see the `loading_mc` clip on the Stage and the buttons should be disabled. Figure 9-30 shows the interface at this point.

Figure 9-30. The results displayed in a TextArea component

You probably noticed that the web service returned the XML results as a string containing white space. One way to access the contents is using the XML class and an event handler for the result event of the WebServiceConnector.

Formatting the cities XML string

12. Add the following event listener function on frame 1 of the actions layer. The code looks more complicated than it is, so I'll explain it after the listing.

```
var CitiesListener:Object = new Object();
CitiesListener.result = function(evtObj:Object):Void {
  hideLoading();
  var CitiesXML:XML = new XML(evtObj.target.results);
  var RootNode:XMLNode;
  var City:String;
  for (var i:Number = 0; i < CitiesXML.childNodes.length; i++) {
    if (CitiesXML.childNodes[i].toString().length > 0) {
      RootNode = CitiesXML.childNodes[i];
    }
  }
  if (RootNode.childNodes.length > 0) {
    var LookupNode:XMLNode;
    for (var i:Number = 0; i < RootNode.childNodes.length; i++) {
      LookupNode = RootNode.childNodes[i];
      for (j:Number = 0; j < LookupNode.childNodes.length; j++) {
        if (LookupNode.childNodes[j].nodeName == "City") {
          City = LookupNode.childNodes[j].firstChild.nodeValue;
          cities_cbo.addItem(City);          }
      }
    }
    cities_cbo.sortItemsBy("label");
  }
  else {
    error_txt.text = "That country could not be found.";
    country_txt.text = "";
  }
};
cities_wsc.addEventListener("result", CitiesListener);
```

The CitiesListener listens for the result event of the WebServiceConnector. When the listener detects this event, it calls a function called hideLoading, which we'll add shortly. It assigns the results from the connector to an XML object called CitiesXML. The code also creates the variables RootNode and City.

The first for loop sets the RootNode. As the white space in the XML string is treated as empty nodes, we have to test for a node that is longer than 0 characters by finding the length. Notice that I used the toString method before finding the value of the length property. This treats the node as a string variable so we can find the length.

The next code block tests for children of the RootNode. If there are no childNodes, no cities were found by the web service and the code will move to the else section, where it will display an error message.

If the web service returns cities, the code loops through them, finds nodes with the name City, and adds the text to the cities_cbo component. The city name is found using LookupNode.childNodes[j].firstChild.nodeValue because text within an element is always the firstChild of that element. Finally, the code sorts the ComboBox component by label.

13. We'll need to create the hideLoading function to enable the buttons and remove the loading_mc movie clip. Otherwise, the user won't be able to use the application. Add the following code to the actions layer:

```
function hideLoading():Void {
  cities_btn.enabled = true;
  weather_btn.enabled = true;
  loading_mc._x = -220;
  loading_mc._y = 0;
}
```

14. Remove the results binding from cities_wsc. We don't need to display the XML string any more since we're processing the content and adding it to a Combo Box component.

15. Test the movie. You should see the ComboBox component populated with the names of the cities of the chosen country. Enter an invalid country name and check that an error message displays.

We'll need to configure the second WebServiceConnector so that the weather for the selected city displays in the TextArea component.

Triggering the second WebServiceConnector component

16. Add the following code to the actions layer:

```
weather_btn.onRelease = function():Void {
  error_txt.text = "";
  results_txt.text = "";
  var numCities:Number = cities_cbo.dataProvider.length;
  if (country_txt.text.length > 0 && numCities > 0) {
    weather_wsc.trigger();
    showLoading ();
  }
}
```

The onRelease event handler clears the values from error_txt and results_txt and finds the number of cities. If there is a country and at least one city, it triggers the WebServiceConnector and calls the showLoading function.

17. Test the movie. You should be able to select a country and choose a city. When you click the Get weather button, the results from the web service should display in the TextArea component, as shown in Figure 9-31.

Figure 9-31. The weather displayed in a TextArea component

The last step is to format the XML string to display the weather details in the TextArea.

Formatting the weather XML string

18. Add the following eventListener on frame 1 of the actions layer. The listener detects the result event from the weather_wsc component. You'll probably want to add the code underneath the CitiesListener code.

```
var WeatherListener:Object = new Object();
WeatherListener.result = function (evtObj:Object):Void {
  hideLoading();
  if (evtObj.target.results == "Data Not Found") {
    error_txt.text = evtObj.target.results;
  }
  else {
    var weatherXML:XML = new XML(evtObj.target.results);
    var RootNode:XMLNode;
    for (var i:Number = 0; i < weatherXML.childNodes.length; i++) {
      if (weatherXML.childNodes[i].toString().length > 0) {
        RootNode = weatherXML.childNodes[i];
      }
    }
    var childNodeName:String = "";
    var Wind:String = "";
    var SkyConditions:String = "";
    var Temperature:String = "";
    var RelativeHumidity:String = "";
    for (var i:Number=0; i< RootNode.childNodes.length; i++) {
      childNodeName = RootNode.childNodes[i].nodeName;
      if (childNodeName == "Wind") {
        Wind = RootNode.childNodes[i].firstChild.nodeValue;
      }
      else if (childNodeName == "SkyConditions") {
        SkyConditions = RootNode.childNodes[i].firstChild.nodeValue;
      }
      else if (childNodeName =="Temperature") {
```

```
          Temperature = RootNode.childNodes[i].firstChild.nodeValue;
        }
        else if (childNodeName =="RelativeHumidity") {
          RelativeHumidity=RootNode.childNodes[i].firstChild.nodeValue;
        }
      }
      var strWeather = "Temp: " + Temperature + "\n";
      strWeather += "Wind: " + Wind + "\n";
      strWeather += "Conditions: " + SkyConditions + "\n";
      strWeather += "Relative humidity: " + RelativeHumidity + "\n";
      results_txt.text = strWeather;
      }
}
weather_wsc.addEventListener("result", WeatherListener);
```

This code is long but it is not difficult to understand. We start by calling the `hideLoading` function to move the `loading_mc` clip and enable the buttons. Then we test for the message Data Not Found. If there is no data, we won't have any XML to process and we need to display the message.

If we have data, we create an XML object called `weatherXML` and find the root node. Then we set some variables for the weather information and add the values from the elements `<Wind>`, `<SkyConditions>`, `<Temperature>`, and `<relativeHumidity>`. A variable called `strWeather` stores these values, and I have used `\n` to create line breaks between each setting. Finally, the `results_txt` TextArea component displays the value from `strWeather`.

19. Test the movie. You should be able to select a country, choose a city, and display the weather conditions, as shown in Figure 9-32. You can view the completed resource file `weather_completed.fla`.

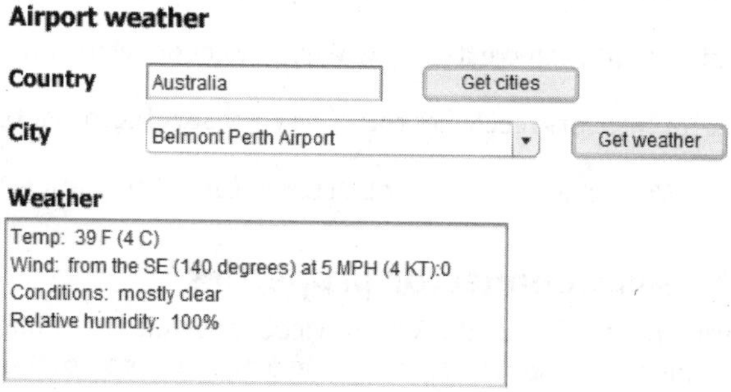

Airport weather

Country Australia Get cities

City Belmont Perth Airport Get weather

Weather

Temp: 39 F (4 C)
Wind: from the SE (140 degrees) at 5 MPH (4 KT):0
Conditions: mostly clear
Relative humidity: 100%

Figure 9-32. The completed Aiport weather application

In this exercise, we used two WebServiceConnector components to request information from a web service. We needed two components because we called two different remote procedures. Because the web service returned the XML results as a string, we used ActionScript to extract the relevant information and add it to the movie interface.

Points to note from exercise 4

- Even though the content returned from the WebServiceConnector components looked like XML, it wasn't recognized that way by Flash. Instead, Flash treated the results as a string variable. By binding the results directly to the `text` property of a TextArea component, we could see the string. This was a useful way to see the data returned by the web service.
- Because we requested two different operations from the web service, we had to use two WebServiceConnector components. Each WebServiceConnector can only call a single operation, although it can call it more than once.
- We didn't know how long it would take to receive the results from the web service. It was useful to change the interface by displaying the `loading_mc` movie clip so that users of the application could see that the call was in progress.

As you'll see in the next section, it's possible to use ActionScript to work with the WebServiceConnector component instead of working with the Component Inspector panel.

The WebServiceConnector class

You can use the WebServiceConnector class to work with web services using ActionScript. It is equivalent to working with the WebServiceConnector component and, as with the XMLConnector, you can use ActionScript to bind the results to other components.

To work with the class, you'll need to have a copy of the WebServiceConnector component in your library. Drag the component to the Stage and delete it again.

You can also include the WebServiceConnector class within your movie by using the following `import` statement. The statement means you won't have to use `mx.data.components.WebServiceConnector` each time you want to refer to the class.

```
import mx.data.components.WebServiceConnector;
```

After adding the `import` line, you can create a new WebServiceConnector with the following code:

```
var myWSConnector:WebServiceConnector = new WebServiceConnector();
```

Once you've created the WebServiceConnector object, you can set the properties using ActionScript.

Setting the WebServiceConnector properties

You can set the following properties for the WebServiceConnector. The properties are equivalent to those available through the Component Inspector. Table 9-1 provides an overview of these properties.

```
myWSConnector.WSDLURL = "http://urltoWSDL/file.wdsl ";
myWSConnector.operation = "NameOfRemoteOperation";
myWSConnector.multipleSimultaneousAllowed = true;
myWSConnector.suppressInvalidCalls = true;
```

If you've added the web service using the Web Services panel, you'll be able to view the schema for the `params` and `results`. You can display this panel with the *Ctl-Shift-F10* shortcut (*Cmd-Shift-F10* on a Macintosh).

Sending data to the web service

You'll need to specify the data that you'll send to the web service. You can find out the requirements in the params section of the web service schema. You may need to send an array of values or an XML document, depending on the requirements of the web service. Most commonly, you'll send an array of values, as shown in the following code. Make sure you use the same order for the values as that listed in the params section of the web service schema.

```
myWSConnector.params =[value1, value2, value3];
```

You could also collect the values from UI components as shown in this code:

```
myWSConnector.params =[TI1_txt.text, TI2_txt.text, TI3_txt.text];
```

You send the request by triggering the component, using the following line. You'll have seen this line earlier in the chapter.

```
myWSConnector.trigger();
```

You can add this code on the timeline so that it processes as soon as the movie loads. However, when you're working with web services, it's more common to trigger the component within a button onRelease handler. This allows you to specify the values that you'll send to the web service using UI components. When you've filled in the values, you can click a button to trigger the call to the web service.

The WebServiceConnector broadcasts the send event during the trigger process. The event occurs after gathering the params but before Flash sends them to the web service. You can use an event listener function to respond to this event as shown here:

```
var WSListener:Object = new Object();
WSListener.send = function(evtObj:Object):Void {
  trace ("sending data");
};
myWSConnector.addEventListener("send", WSListener);
```

You might add a send event handler if you have to format or transform the params before sending them to the web service.

Displaying the results

As with the XMLConnector class, the WebServiceConnector class broadcasts the result event when it receives the results from the web service. You can use a listener to display the results, as shown in the following code:

```
var WSListener:Object = new Object();
WSListener.result = function(evtObj:Object):Void {
  trace (evtObj.target.results);
};
myWSConnector.addEventListener("result", WSListener);
```

Once the WebServiceConnector broadcasts the result event, you can access the results property of the component. The result event sends an event object into the handler function. In the preceding code, I've called the object evtObj. You can refer to the WebServiceConnector using evtObj.target. You can then use the results property to see what the web service has returned to Flash. Make sure you don't confuse the result event with the results property since the terms are so similar.

Let's work through an example so you can see how to use ActionScript with the WebServiceConnector class.

Exercise 5: Consuming a web service with ActionScript and the WebServiceConnector class

In this example, we'll use the WebServiceConnector class to display a Flash product tip from a web service.

1. Open Flash if necessary and create a new file. Save it as FlashTip.fla.
2. Add the WebServiceConnector component to the library. Make sure it is not visible on the Stage.
3. Rename layer 1 as actions and add the following code at frame 1:

```
import mx.data.components.WebServiceConnector;
var tipWS:WebServiceConnector = new WebServiceConnector();
var WSListener:Object = new Object();
WSListener.send = function(evtObj:Object):Void {
  trace ("sending data");
}
WSListener.result = function(evtObj:Object):Void {
  trace (evtObj.target.results);
};
tipWS.addEventListener("send", WSListener);
tipWS.addEventListener("result", WSListener);
tipWS.WSDLURL = "http://www.flash-mx.com/mm/tips/tips.cfc?wsdl";
tipWS.operation = "getTipByProduct";
tipWS.multipleSimultaneousAllowed = false;
tipWS.suppressInvalidCalls = true;
tipWS.params = ["Flash"];
tipWS.trigger();
```

   The code imports the WebServiceConnector class and creates a new WebServiceConnector object called tipWS. We create two functions to listen for the send and result events. We set the WDSLURL, operation, and other parameters. The web service needs a string value that specifies name of a product. In this case, we've used Flash in the params array so we can see Flash tips. Finally, we trigger the component.

4. Test the movie. You should see an Output window containing a tip, similar to the image shown in Figure 9-33. You can see the completed file saved as FlashTip.fla with your resources.

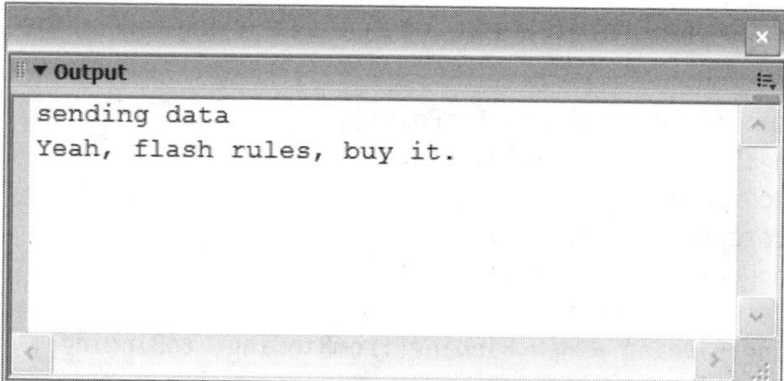

Figure 9-33. The completed tip application

In exercise 5, we were able to connect to a web service using the WebServiceConnector class. We used ActionScript to display the results in an Output window. We'll extend this example so that we bind the results to a TextArea component. I covered the DataBindingClasses component in Chapter 8, so I won't go over it again here. Feel free to turn back to that chapter for a refresher.

Exercise 6: Binding the results from a WebServiceConnector object

In exercise 6, we'll extend the previous example so that we bind the results of our web service call to a TextArea component. We'll add the TextArea component dynamically and use the DataBindingClasses component. You should complete exercise 5 first, but if you haven't, you can use the starter file `tip.fla` from your resources.

1. Open Flash if necessary and open your file from exercise 5 or the starter file FlashTip.fla.
2. Drag a TextArea component to the Stage and delete it again, so that it appears in the library.
3. Add the DataBindingClasses component to your library by opening Window ➤ Other Panels ➤ Common Libraries ➤ Classes and dragging it to the Stage. Delete the symbol from the Stage so it doesn't show in the completed movie. Unlike the data components, this symbol has a visual appearance.
4. Open the Actions panel with the *F9* shortcut and add the following lines at the top of the layer, below the first `import` statement:

```
import mx.controls.TextArea;
import mx.data.binding.*;
```

5. Add the following lines to add a TextArea component to the Stage dynamically. The lines set the size, location, and `wordWrap` properties of the component.

```
var tipTA:TextArea = createClassObject(TextArea, "tip_txt", ➥
this.getNextHighestDepth());
tipTA.setSize(300, 200);
tipTA.move(50, 50);
tipTA.wordWrap = true;
```

6. Create the bindings for the results by adding the following code at the bottom of the actions layer:

```
var fromBinding:EndPoint = new EndPoint();
var toBinding:EndPoint = new EndPoint();
fromBinding.component = tipWS;
fromBinding.property = "results";
toBinding.component = tipTA;
toBinding.property = "text";
var newBinding:Binding = new Binding(fromBinding, toBinding);
```

The code creates two new EndPoint objects for the binding. It binds the `results` from the `tipWS` component to the text property of the `tipTA` component.

7. Modify the result listener function as shown. I've shown the new line in bold.

```
WSListener.result = function(evtObj:Object):Void {
  var bindingResults:Array = newBinding.execute(false);
};
```

This line executes the binding after Flash receives the results from the WebServiceConnector class. You can trace the `bindingResults` variable to see any errors encountered during the binding process. The variable will have a value of null if there were no errors.

8. Test the movie. You should see something similar to the screenshot shown in Figure 9-34. I've saved the resource file as `FlashTip_bound.fla`.

instead of relying on LoadVars and XML, you can
pass values easily in Flash by using the
WebServiceConnector component or using the
WebServiceClasses to pass arrays and objects
between Flash and WebServices.

Figure 9-34. The Tip web service bound to a TextArea component

Exercise 6 showed how to create a simple binding between the results of a web service and a TextArea component. The movie didn't have any visual components although we had to add components to the library. The example shows that it's possible to create a Flash movie that consumes a web service using only ActionScript.

If you weren't able to connect directly to the web service for security reasons, you could use an XMLConnector class with a server-side file that proxies the data. I covered scripting the XMLConnector class in Chapter 8. You can find out more about the security restrictions in the Flash Player in Chapter 4.

Summary of the properties, methods, and events of the WebServiceConnector class

This section summarizes the properties and methods of the WebServiceConnector class. Table 9-2 shows the only method of the WebServiceConnector class.

Table 9-2. The only method of the WebServiceConnector class

Method	Explanation
`trigger`	Triggers the WebServiceConnector class to make the remote call to the web service

Table 9-3 summarizes the properties of the WebServiceConnector class.

Table 9-3. Summary of properties of the XMLConnector class

Property	Explanation
`multipleSimultaneousAllowed`	Specifies whether multiple WebServiceConnectors can be triggered at the same time
`operation`	Specifies the name of the remote operation at the web service
`params`	Specifies the information sent to the web service when the WebServiceConnector triggers
`results`	Contains the information returned from the web service after an WebServiceConnector triggers
`surpressInvalidCalls`	Specifies whether to suppress a call if the parameters are invalid
`WSDLURL`	Specifies the URL for the WSDL document

Table 9-4 lists the events broadcast by the WebServiceConnector class.

Table 9-4. Summary of events of the XMLConnector class

Event	Explanation
`result`	Broadcasts when an WebServiceConnector has completed its call, i.e., after successfully triggering the data
`send`	Broadcasts during the trigger method, when the parameters have been gathered before the call is initiated
`status`	Broadcasts when the call starts and provides information on the status on the call

The Web Service classes

The Web Service classes offer another alternative for consuming SOAP web services within Flash. These classes are only available in Flash Professional. One reason for using them is that they'll create smaller file sizes than if you use data components. Table 9-5 shows the classes included in the services package.

Table 9-5. The classes included in the services package

Class name	Purpose
WebService	Creates a WebService object to manage web service requests and responses. This is different from the WebServiceConnector class.
PendingCall	Returned when you make a web service call. The object manages the response and any faults reported.
Log	Tracks the consumption of a web service.
SOAPCall	Controls the way the web service operates.

Before you can use the Web Service classes, you need to add the WebServiceClasses component to your library. You can find this in Window ➤ Other Panels ➤ Common Libraries ➤ Classes. Drag the WebServiceClasses component to the Stage. Delete it and you'll have added the WebServiceClasses component to your library.

Creating a WebService object

You can create a new WebService object with the following code. Replace URL to WSDL with the full URL to the WSDL document for the web service.

```
var myWS:WebService = new WebService("URL to WSDL");
```

We can then specify the operation using a PendingCall object. You don't need to create it with a constructor method, as you would for other objects. Constructor methods use the keyword new. You create a PendingCall object by specifying the name of the operation and the parameters for the call.

```
var pc:PendingCall = myWS.operationName(param1, param2, param3);
```

The pending call has two event handlers to deal with the results or faults from the web service: `onResult` and `onFault`. You can create a results handler function with the following code:

```
pc.onResult = function(result:Object):Void {
  //do something with the result;
}
```

The result object is the response from the web service, converted into ActionScript. If you are returning a single value, you can refer to it with

```
pc.result
```

If the returned value is an object containing other values, you can access them by using

```
pc.result.propertyName;
```

You can use the Web Services panel to find out about the operations, parameters, and return values that you'll get from the web service. Add the web service to the panel and you'll be able to see the full details, including the operations and schemas for the parameters and results. We discussed this panel earlier in the chapter.

The following code shows how to set up an onFault event handler to track faults returned by the web service:

```
pc.onFault = function(fault:Object):Void {
  //do something with the fault
}
```

You can use the faultString, faultCode, and details properties to find out more information about the fault.

Viewing the raw XML content

If you want to see the request or response XML information, you can use the request and response properties of the pending call:

```
pc.request;
pc.response;
```

You can display the values contained within the response using the onResult handler function:

```
pc.onResult = function(result:Object):Void {
  trace (this.response);
};
```

Logging the details

The Log class allows you to see what's happening during the call to the web service. You can display each message from the web service.

You need to create a Log object using the following code:

```
var WSLog:Log = new Log();
```

You can optionally include the level of logging required—Log.BRIEF, Log.VERBOSE, or Log.DEBUG—as well as a name for a log object, if you're using more than one WebService object. In most cases, using the Log constructor without parameters works well.

The Log object has an onLog event handler that you can use to display messages. In the following example, we use it to display messages in an Output window:

```
WSLog.onLog = function(logInfo:String):Void {
  trace (logInfo);
}
```

You also need to add a reference to the Log object when you create your WebService object:

```
var myWS:WebService = new WebService("URL to WSDL", WSLog);
```

Figure 9-35 shows the type of messages that you could expect to see.

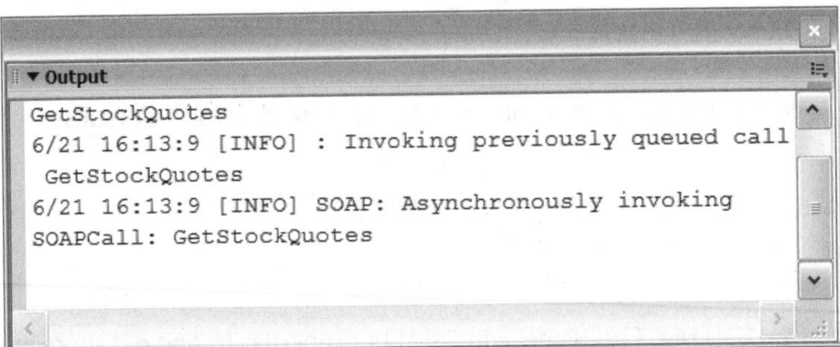

Figure 9-35. Log messages shown in an Output window

We'll use the code discussed in this section to create a simple application for converting temperatures between Celsius and Fahrenheit values.

Exercise 7: Using the Web Service classes to create a temperature converter

In the final exercise for this chapter, we'll use the Web Service classes to create a temperature conversion application. The conversion will use a web service and we'll provide two options: convert Fahrenheit to Celsius and convert Celsius to Fahrenheit.

1. Open Flash if necessary and open the starter file tempConvert.fla. Figure 9-36 shows the interface of the movie.

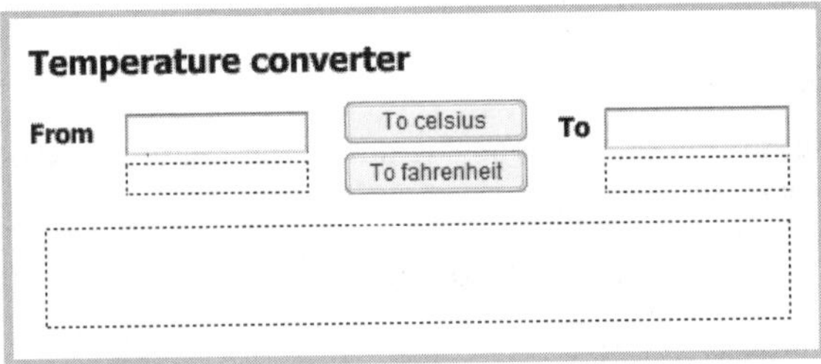

Figure 9-36. The Temperature converter interface

The interface contains two TextInput components and two Buttons. There are also three dynamic text fields for displaying messages.

2. Add the WebServiceClasses component to your library by selecting Window ➤ Other Panels ➤ Common Libraries ➤ Classes and dragging the WebServiceClasses component onto the Stage. Delete the component from the Stage.

3. Create a new layer called actions and add the following line on frame 1 to import the services classes. This will save you from having to use full class names each time you refer to a WebService class in your code.

```
import mx.services.*
```

4. Add the following code on the actions layer:

```
var WSDL_URL:String = "http://developerdays.com/cgi-bin/➥
tempconverter.exe/wsdl/ITempConverter";
var WSLog:Log = new Log();
WSLog.onLog = function(logInfo:String):Void {
  trace (logInfo);
}
```

The code creates a variable for the URL to the WSDL document for the web service. It also creates a new Log object and traces each log message in an Output window.

5. Configure the buttons by adding the following onRelease handler functions to the actions layer:

```
celsius_btn.onRelease = function():Void {
  clearText();
  if (temp_txt.text.length > 0) {
    if (!isNaN(temp_txt.text)) {
      fromUnit_txt.text = "Fahrenheit";
      toUnit_txt.text = "Celsius";
      convertTemp("toC",temp_txt.text);
    }
    else {
      error_txt.text="Enter a valid temperature";
    }
  }
  else {
    error_txt.text="Enter a temperature first";
  }
}
fahrenheit_btn.onRelease = function():Void {
  clearText();
  if (temp_txt.text.length > 0) {
    if (! isNaN(temp_txt.text)) {
      convertTemp("toF",temp_txt.text);
      fromUnit_txt.text = "Celsius";
      toUnit_txt.text = "Fahrenheit";
    }
    else {
    error_txt.text="Enter a valid temperature";
    }
  }
  else {
    error_txt.text="Enter a temperature first";
  }
}
```

The functions call the clearText function first and then validate the data entry. They set the text properties of the fromUnit_txt and toUnit_txt dynamic text fields. The functions either display appropriate error messages or call the convertTemp function. Note that I've used isNaN to check for non-numeric entries.

6. Add the clearText function to the actions layer. This function clears the text showing in the TextInput components and the dynamic text fields.

```
function clearText():Void {
  endTemp_txt.text="";
  error_txt.text="";
  fromUnit_txt.text = "";
  toUnit_txt.text = "";
}
```

7. Create the call to the web service with the following code:

```
function convertTemp(convDir:String, temp:Number):Void {
  var myWS:WebService = new WebService(WSDL_URL, WSLog);
  if (convDir == "toC") {
    var pc:PendingCall = myWS.FtoC(temp);
  }
  else if (convDir == "toF") {
    var pc:PendingCall = myWS.CtoF(temp);
  }
  pc.onResult = function(result:Object):Void {
    endTemp_txt.text = result;
  };
  pc.onFault = function(fault:Object):Void {
    error_txt.text = fault.faultstring;
  };
}
```

The function takes two parameters: the direction of the conversion and the temperature to convert. It creates a new WebService object that uses the WSDL_URL variable for the location of the WSDL document. The WebService will log messages to the WSLog object.

The code creates a PendingCall object that calls either the FtoC or CtoF operation. If the conversion is successful, the converted value displays in the endTemp_txt component; otherwise, the faultstring displays in the error_txt dynamic text field.

8. Test the movie by entering a temperature and clicking one of the conversion buttons. You should see messages displayed in an Output window, as shown in Figure 9-37. You should also see the converted temperature value displayed in the second TextInput component. I've saved the completed resource file under the name tempConvert_completed.fla.

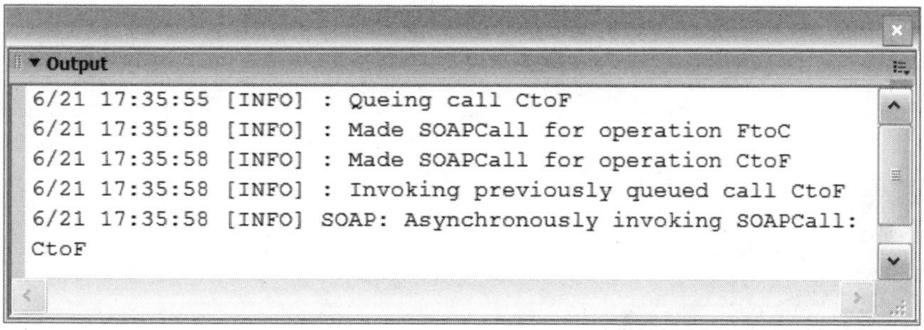

```
Output
6/21 17:35:55 [INFO] : Queing call CtoF
6/21 17:35:58 [INFO] : Made SOAPCall for operation FtoC
6/21 17:35:58 [INFO] : Made SOAPCall for operation CtoF
6/21 17:35:58 [INFO] : Invoking previously queued call CtoF
6/21 17:35:58 [INFO] SOAP: Asynchronously invoking SOAPCall:
CtoF
```

Figure 9-37. Log messages from the temperature conversion web service

In the previous example, we used the Web Service classes to connect to a temperature conversion web service. I showed you how to work with the WebService, PendingCall, and Log classes so that we didn't need to use any data components.

The exercise introduced you to the most common Web Service classes rather than providing a complete reference to all classes. We didn't cover the SOAPCall class or explore the details of all of the methods of each class. You can explore these topics in more detail on your own if you're interested.

Summary

In this chapter, we've looked at the different ways that you can include information from web services in your Flash movies. You can request information from a REST or RSS web service. If there is no cross-domain policy in effect, you may need to use a server-side file to proxy the data locally. After receiving data from these web services, you can use the XML class or XMLConnector component to add the content to a Flash movie.

We also looked at how you could use the WebServiceConnector component to consume a SOAP web service. After specifying a WSDL document, the component finds the operations available at the web service. It also displays schemas for both the request and results. You can use this component to bind data directly to the UI components.

The chapter also introduced you to the WebServiceConnector class and the related ActionScript. We finished by looking at the Web Service classes. Using ActionScript, we were able to consume a SOAP web service and add the contents to a Flash application.

In the next chapter, we'll look briefly at the working with XML sockets. The XMLSocket class allows you to remain connected to an XML data source so that you can work in real time with a persistent connection.

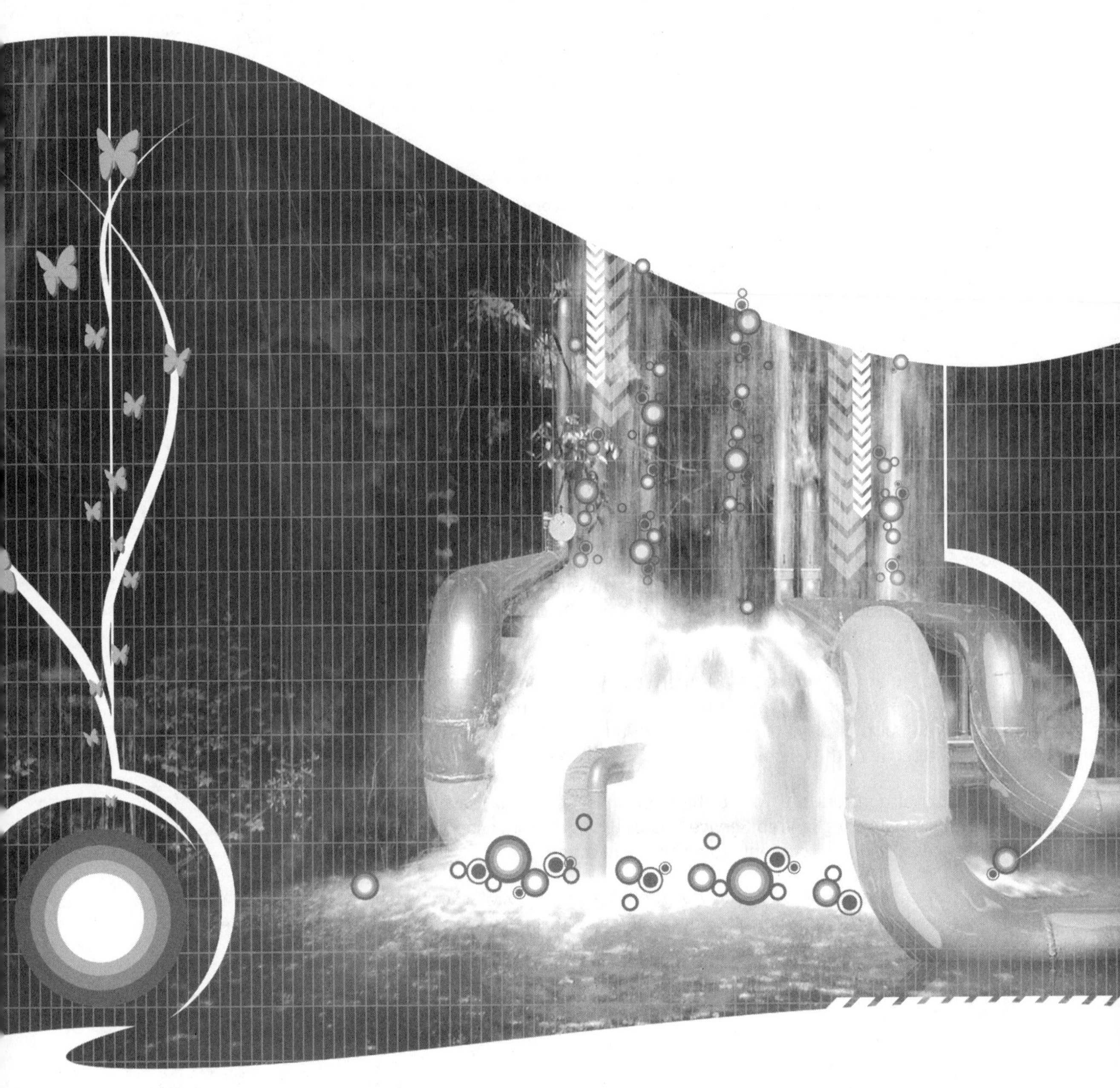

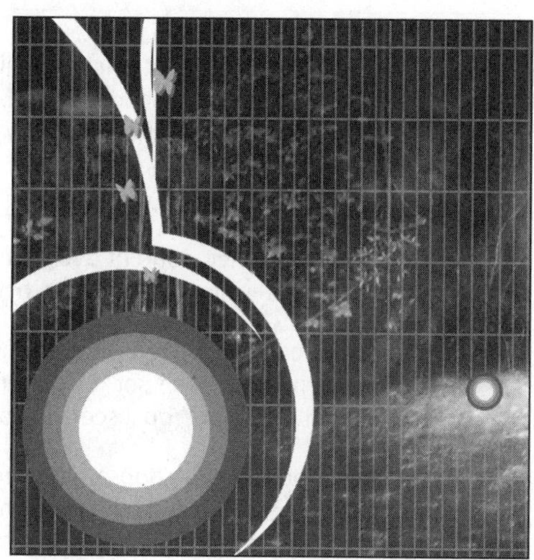

Chapter 10

USING THE XMLSOCKET CLASS

If you've worked through this book, you'll have seen several different ways to include XML content within a Flash movie. In general, we used one of two approaches—writing ActionScript to work with XML or working visually with the data components and Component Inspector panel. In Chapter 4, we explored the methods, properties, and events of the XML and XMLNode classes. We worked with the data components in Chapters 8 and 9. In all the examples, each time we wanted to include XML information in a movie, we had to request it first from an external source.

When you work with the XML class and data components, Flash uses the *request response* model. Flash must request XML information and receive a response before you can include the information in your Flash movie. Flash doesn't remain connected to the XML data. Each time the data changes, the movie won't update until Flash makes another request. If your data changes frequently, Flash will have to keep making requests to make sure that it has up-to-date information. As you can imagine, this is a very inefficient way for Flash to work.

An alternative is to work with the XMLSocket class. This class allows you to keep an open connection with a server. The server can push information into Flash in real time without Flash having to initiate the contact first. If your data changes regularly, XMLSocket objects allow your Flash movie to respond automatically to each change. For example, you could build a news display that always shows the latest news from an XML feed.

XMLSockets also allow multiple users to interact within Flash movies. Users send information to a server, and it is broadcast to the other users. You could use XMLSocket objects with a chat application or a multiplayer game. In this chapter, you'll build a simple chat application.

Computers all over the Internet communicate using sockets. You use a socket every time you connect to another computer or send an email. A socket server is a piece of software installed on a computer, often written in Java or C++. The software listens on a specific port and responds when it receives new information.

For those technically minded readers, socket servers communicate with Flash in a very specific way. They must send their content over a full-duplex TCP/IP stream socket connection. Each message from Flash must be terminated by a zero byte.

Before you can get started with the XMLSocket class, you have to choose and install a socket server. You can write your own socket server using Java, C++, PHP, or ASP.NET. You can also buy a socket server from a vendor. You'll see a list of common socket servers in Table 10-1.

Whichever option you choose, you need to know that installing and working with socket servers can be quite frustrating. Depending on which socket server you choose, you may have to install the Java Runtime Environment (JRE), set up database tables, and configure the socket server settings.

Socket server considerations

You'll need to consider a couple of issues before you select and install a socket server. These include the server environment and security.

Although a socket server can run on its own, you'll usually locate it on the same machine as your web server. If you're working locally, installing a socket server is not likely to be a problem. If you want to distribute your XMLSocket applications via the Web, you'll need to install the socket server on the hosting computer. It may be best to check with your web host first, in case they have restrictions or support a specific socket server.

If you're using a Java-based socket server to develop an XMLSocket application on your computer, you'll need to have the JRE installed. On Windows, you can check by choosing All Programs ➤ Control Panel ➤ Add or Remove Programs. You will see the Java Runtime Environment entry listed if you have a copy installed. If not, you can find the latest version at `http://java.sun.com/j2se/index.jsp`. Flash only uses port numbers from 1024 upward to communicate with a socket server. You'll need to specify the port number when you connect to the socket server. If you have a firewall installed on your computer, you may have to configure it so that it will allow traffic on that port number.

You'll also need to think about Flash Player security. If your users are located in a different domain or subdomain, you'll need to add a policy file so that they can load data into their Flash Player. You can find out more about security in Chapter 4.

What socket servers are available?

Table 10-1 shows some common socket servers that you can download. Some are free, and others you'll have to purchase. Some vendors offer a trial version with limited functionality.

Table 10-1. Common socket servers

Name	Link	Comments
FlashNow	`www.nowcentral.com/`	Available for Windows and Linux. You can download a trial version.
Oregano	`www.oregano-server.org/`	Free Java-based socket server.
Swocket	`http://swocket.sourceforge.net/`	Open source server built in Python.
Unity 2	`www.moock.org/unity/`	Available for Unix, Macintosh OS X, and Windows. You can download a free developer's version of Unity with trial applications for Flash.

Before you purchase a socket server, check that it provides comprehensive documentation about installation and configuration. It will also be useful if the server includes sample applications that you can view or modify.

After you've chosen your socket server, you'll need to install it on your computer. In the example that follows, I'll show you how to download and install the Unity 2 server. You can install Unity on a Windows, Macintosh OS X, or Unix computer. You'll need to have at least Java 1.3 installed before you can run the Unity 2 server. In Windows, you can check this by choosing All Programs ➤ Control Panel ➤ Add or Remove Programs and looking for the entry Java Runtime Environment. The entry should show the version. If necessary, you can download Java from `http://java.sun.com/j2se/downloads/index.html`.

Installing the Unity 2 socket server

We'll work through the following steps to install the Unity 2 socket server:

1. Download the trial version of Unity 2 server.
2. Unpack the files.
3. Change configuration settings (optional).
4. Start the socket server.

Downloading the trial version of Unity 2

You can download a trial version of the Unity 2 server from `http://moock.org/unity/trial/`. You can also download the UClient sample applications from the same location. The trial version of Unity limits you to five users at a time. If you develop a chat application, it will disconnect after 5 minutes. In spite of these restrictions, you should be able to see how the server works using the trial version. If you want to create the chat application later in the chapter, you'll need to download both the Unity 2 Multiuser Server as well as the UClient for Macromedia Flash.

Unpacking the unity files

Once you've downloaded the unity_2.0.1_trial.zip file (Windows) or unity_2.0.1_trial.tar.gz (Macintosh), you'll need to unpack the files. You can choose any location for these files. I downloaded the Windows version and unzipped the files to the C:\ Inetpub > wwwroot folder—my web server. This created a unity folder at that location. I could have unzipped the files to any location on my hard drive.

After extracting the files, view the contents of the unity folder. You'll see several batch files and some subfolders. You'll also see the policy file policy.xml. The policy.xml file provides a cross-domain policy so that users from other domains and subdomains can access data. You can open the file to see the contents. Chapter 4 provides more information about cross-domain policy files.

The unity folder also contains a file called uconfig.xml that contains the settings for the socket server. You may want to change the settings before you start the socket server. For example, you might want to change the port number for the socket server.

Configuring the server

Unity uses the uconfig.xml file to store all the settings for the socket server. If you have to change the settings, you can modify this file in a text or XML editor. You can find the uconfig.xml file in the unity folder located wherever you unzipped your files. My unity folder is located at C:\Inetpub\wwwroot\unity.

If you open the file in a text or XML editor, you'll see the following structure:

```
<UNITY>
  <SERVER>
    <SERVER_PORT>9100</SERVER_PORT>
    <ADMIN_PORT>9101</ADMIN_PORT>
    <ADMIN_PASSWORD>password</ADMIN_PASSWORD>
      <CLIENT_TIMEOUT>100</CLIENT_TIMEOUT>
      <MAX_CLIENTS>400</MAX_CLIENTS>
  </SERVER>
  <TYPES>
  </TYPES>
  <INSTANCES>
  </INSTANCES>
  <UPCROOM_GLOBALS>
    <CREATE_UNITY_ROOM>true</CREATE_UNITY_ROOM>
    <CLIENT_PERMISSIONS>all</CLIENT_PERMISSIONS>
  </UPCROOM_GLOBALS>
</UNITY>
```

The file sets the server and admin ports. The default port number is 9100. If you need to change the port number, you can do so by altering the number in the <SERVER_PORT> element.

If you're building a chat application, the <INSTANCES> element contains all the rooms that are available. In the previous listing, the element is empty so there are no chat rooms. You can add a new room by changing the <INSTANCES> element as shown here. The new element adds a room called ChatRoom.

```
<INSTANCES>
  <ROOM>
    <ID>ChatRoom</ID>
  </ROOM>
</INSTANCES>
```

If the socket server is running, make sure that you stop it before you make changes to the uconfig.xml file. The uconfig.xml file loads when the server starts up so changes won't apply until the next time you start up the server.

Starting the server

Unity runs on Windows, Unix, or Macintosh OS X machines. You start the server by running the appropriate batch file. For Windows computers, use the file startserver.bat; Macintosh OS X and Unix users load the file startserver.sh. You can run the file either from the command prompt or by double-clicking the file name. I like to use the command prompt because it allows me to see any errors. The instructions that follow show how to use the command prompt in Windows.

Use the shortcut key *Windows-R* to bring up a command prompt. The Windows key is between the Ctrl and Alt keys on your keyboard. Figure 10-1 shows the Run dialog box. Type command in the Open field and click OK.

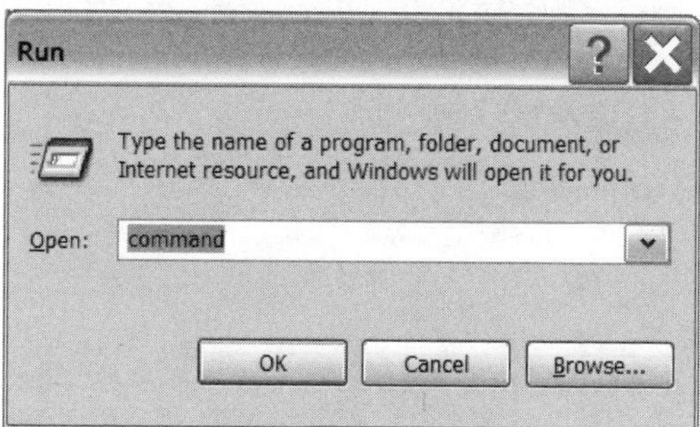

Figure 10-1. The Run dialog box

You should see a Command window open. Change to the unity directory by using the cd command. The cd command is used to change directories. In my case, I typed cd c:\Inetpub\wwwroot\Unity and pressed *Enter*. The prompt will update to show the current directory.

You'll then need to type the name of the start server batch file and press *Enter*. In my case, I'll use the Windows file `startserver.bat`. When you've finished, you should see the message shown in Figure 10-2.

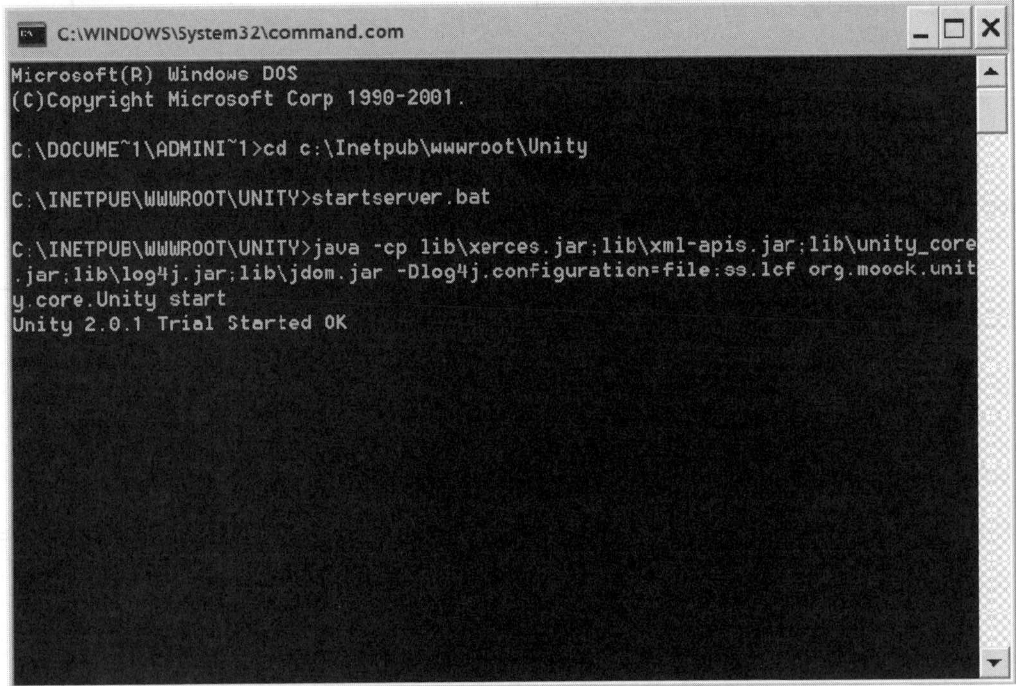

Figure 10-2. The Unity server has been started successfully.

Once you've installed and configured the socket server, you're ready to start working with the XMLSocket class in Flash.

Using the XMLSocket class

You'll use the following steps to work with an XMLSocket object:

1. Create a new XMLSocket object.
2. Set an `onConnect` event handler.
3. Make the connection.
4. Within the `onConnect` event handler, initialize the application.
5. Set up event handlers to respond to new data or an unexpected closing of the connection.
6. Configure the interface to display data.

We'll start by creating an XMLSocket object.

Creating an XMLSocket connection

You can create a new XMLSocket object using this code:

```
var theSocket:XMLSocket = new XMLSocket();
```

After you have created the object, you'll need to create an onConnect event handler. This handler works in a very similar way to the onLoad handler for the XML class. Flash calls the handler function when it connects to the socket server. The event handler receives a Boolean (that is, true or false) value that indicates whether the connection was successful. I've shown an example in the following code:

```
theSocket.onConnect = testConnect;
function testConnect(success:Boolean):Void {
  if (success) {
    trace("connection successful");
  }
  else {
    trace("connection not successful");
  }
}
```

After you've set the onConnect event handler, you can connect to the server using the connect method. If you're not clear about why we set the handler before connecting, you can find an explanation in Chapter 4. You will need to specify the host and the port number for the connection. The host is a string value that indicates the name or IP address for the server. If you're working locally, you can use `localhost` or `127.0.0.1` for the host value.

An XMLSocket object can only connect to a TCP port with a number great than or equal to port 1024. Make sure you choose the same port that you specify in your socket server. The following code shows how to connect to port `1234` of the local server:

```
theSocket.connect("127.0.0.1", 1234);
```

Notice that I've used the IP address `127.0.0.1`. I could have used `localhost` as shown here:

```
theSocket.connect("localhost", 1234);
```

You can also use `null` to indicate that the connection should use the current domain of the Flash movie:

```
theSocket.connect(null, 1234);
```

The connect method returns a Boolean value that tells you whether you connected to the server. This allows you to check that you have correctly installed the server and that Flash can locate it on the port specified. This code shows how you can check this value:

```
if (!theSocket.connect("127.0.0.1", 1234)) {
  trace("Couldn't connect to server");
}
else {
  trace ("connected to server");
}
```

In this code, we add the connect method in an `if` statement. An appropriate message will appear in an Output window, depending on whether Flash makes a connection. If the connection sends a value of `true`, Flash calls the onConnect event handler.

Let's put this code together to test a connection to a socket server. I've assumed that you already have a socket server installed locally. If not, you'll need to install and configure one on your computer. I'm using Unity.

Exercise 1: Connecting to an XMLSocket server

In this exercise, we'll connect to a socket server and test the connection. I've used the Unity server that I described earlier in the chapter. This is set up on port 9100 on my local web server. Make sure you start the server as described earlier before you work through this exercise.

1. Open Flash and create a new movie. Save it as `testconnection.fla`. You don't need to save this file in a folder within your web server.
2. Add the following code to Layer 1 and rename the layer actions. The code creates a new XMLSocket object called theSocket and adds an onConnect event handler. When the movie connects to the server, it will call the testConnect function.

```
var theSocket:XMLSocket = new XMLSocket();
theSocket.onConnect = testConnect;
```

3. You can create the connection with the following code. Add it at the bottom of the actions layer. The code connects to the socket server using port 9100. You'll need to change the port number if you're using something other than the default settings in Unity. I've used the IP address for my local web server. I could also have used `localhost`. If Flash can't make a connection to the socket server, you'll see the message `Couldn't connect to server` in an Output window.

```
if (!theSocket.connect("127.0.0.1", 9100)) {
  trace("Couldn't connect to server");
}
else {
  trace ("connected to server");
}
```

4. Add the following event handler function to the actions layer. If we can connect successfully, we'll see the message connection successful in an Output window.

```
function testConnect(success:Boolean):Void {
  if (success) {
    trace("connection successful");
  }
  else {
    trace("connection not successful");
  }
}
```

5. Test the movie. Figure 10-3 shows the Output window that should display when you connect successfully to the socket server. Notice that we've tested the connection twice. The first test checks for the port number and existence of the socket server. The second test checks that we can actually connect using the supplied settings.

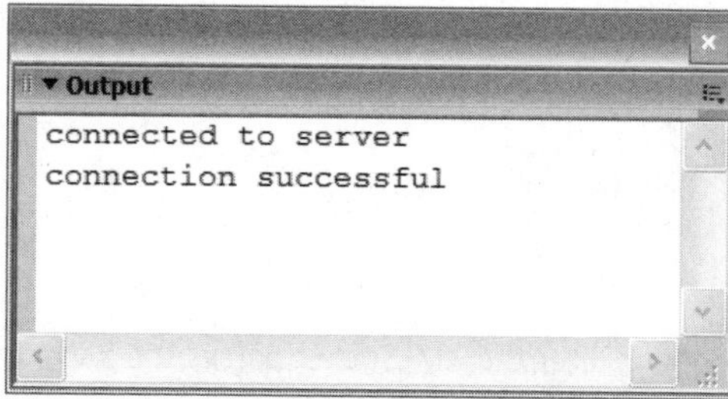

Figure 10-3. An Output window showing the success messages

In this exercise, we tested whether we could connect to a socket server using an XMLSocket object. I've saved the completed example as `testConnection.fla` with your Chapter 10 resource files. I've used the Unity socket server, and you'll notice that I'm connecting to port 9100, the default port, in the example file.

Once you've connected to the socket server, you'll need to be able to send data and respond to incoming data. You'll also need to be able to close down the connection. I'm going to cover the code that you'll use in the next section. However, when we look at an example, we'll simplify the process by using resources provided with the Unity server Flash examples.

Sending data

The XMLSocket object can send information to the socket server using the send method. You need to specify the data that you're sending as an argument. I've shown this in the following code:

```
theSocket.send(someData);
```

If you're sending XML, you may need to create an XML object first:

```
var someXML:XML = new XML(XMLString);
theSocket.send(someXML);
```

Be sure to check on the requirements of your socket server in case you need to use any special settings when sending the data.

You're not limited to sending XML data. You could also use the send method with strings:

```
theSocket.send("some string");
```

When you call the send method, Flash converts the XML object to a string and sends it to the server followed by a zero byte. The zero byte tells the server that the message is complete. The send method doesn't return a value indicating that the data was sent successfully.

Responding to data

The XMLSocket class responds when it receives information from the server. You can use two event handlers to detect new information—onData and onXML. The onData event occurs when the server sends data. This occurs before the XMLSocket parses the data into an XML tree. You could use this event if you want to do something with the raw data from the server or if you're not receiving XML information.

```
theSocket.onData = showData;
function showData(theData:String):Void {
  trace(theData);
}
```

The onXML event handler responds after the XMLSocket parses the XML data. You can use this event if you know you're going to receive XML formatted information.

```
theSocket.onXML = showXML;
function showXML(theXML:String):Void {
  trace(theXML);
}
```

Closing the connection

You can close the connection using the close method. For example, you might add the code shown here in a Log off button:

```
theSocket.close();
```

You can also detect whether the server loses the connection by using the onClose method:

```
theSocket.onClose = showClose;
function showClose():Void {
  trace("The connection was closed");
}
```

You can use this event handler to display an appropriate message to a user in case of accidental loss of connection.

Your use of the XMLSocket class depends on which socket server that you're using. Each socket server has its own requirements and methods of working with Flash. In the example that follows, I'll show you how to create a very simple chat room using Unity. I've based this exercise on one of the sample applications included in the UClient applications download from the Unity web site. You can download these sample files from http://moock.org/unity/trial/.

Exercise 2: Creating a simple chat application

In this exercise, I'll show you how to set up a simple chat application using the Unity socket server. We'll use the starter file chatUnity.fla for this exercise. The example comes from the tutorial at http://moock.org/unity/docs/client/simplechat/as2version/part1.html.

Before you start, make sure that you include the folder org from your Chapter 10 resources in the same folder as your Flash movie. It contains the class file USimpleChat.as, which provides most of the functionality for the chat room. This file comes with the UClient applications download. I've modified the file slightly from the Unity version.

We'll work through these steps:

1. Adding a chat room to Unity
2. Connecting to the socket server
3. Configuring the Talk button to initiate chat

When you've finished the tutorial, you'll have a simple chat application with a single chat room. The tutorial creates the application on your own computer so, unfortunately, you'll only be able to talk to yourself. You'll need to move the application to a shared web server if you want to test the multiuser aspects of the application. You'll also need to add a policy file to allow people from other domains to access the data. You can find out more about policy files in the section on security in Chapter 4.

Adding a chat room

In order to add a chat room, we'll have to change the configuration of the Unity server in the uconfig.xml file. We need to stop the server before we make any changes to the uconfig.xml file.

1. If the Unity server is running, close it down. You can use batch file from the unity folder. In Windows, you can use the file stopserver.bat. Macintosh OS X users can use the file stopserver.sh.
2. Locate the unity directory on your computer and open the file uconfig.xml in a text or XML editor. I installed my unity directory to C:\Inetpub\wwwroot\unity so the uconfig.xml file is in that location.
3. Modify the <INSTANCE> element in the uconfig.xml file as shown here. I've indicated the new lines in bold. This creates a new room called ChatRoom. The <AUTOJOIN>true</AUTOJOIN> setting makes users join the room automatically when they start a chat application.

```
<INSTANCES>
  <ROOM>
    <ID>ChatRoom</ID>
    <AUTOJOIN>true</AUTOJOIN>
  </ROOM>
</INSTANCES>
```

4. Start the Unity server as described earlier in the chapter. Windows users will need to run the file startserver.bat; Macintosh users can run startserver.sh.

   Once you've added a default chat room, you're ready to start creating your chat application. You'll need to connect to the socket server first.

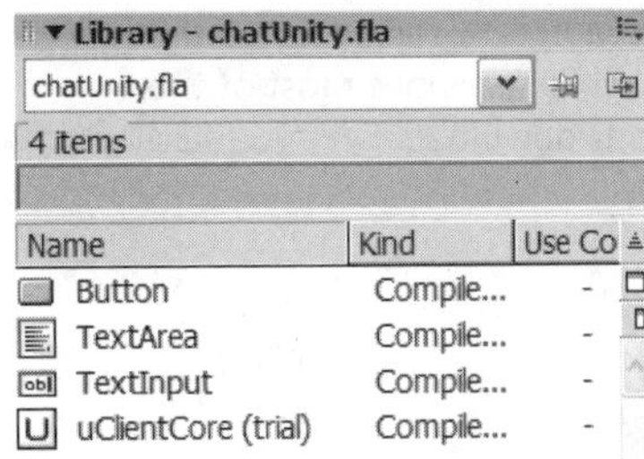

Figure 10-4. The uClientCore component in the library

Connecting to the server

Unity provides some useful tools for working with XMLSockets, including the uClientCore component. This component provides much of the functionality that you'll need to work with chat rooms. You'll need to include this component in any Flash chat application that you create. The starter file `chatUnity.fla` already includes this component. Figure 10-4 shows it in the library, under the name uClientCore (trial).

The sample applications from Unity include a USimpleChat class that you can use to connect to the server and transmit data. I've included the class file USimpleChat.as with your resources in the `org\moock\unity\simplechat\v2` folder. It's important that you don't change the path to this folder. Feel free to open the class file and have a look at the contents.

5. Open the resource file `chatUnity.fla`. Figure 10-5 shows the interface. There is a TextArea component called incoming and a TextInput called outgoing. It's important that you don't change these instance names as they're used in the USimpleChat.as class file. There is also a Talk button. Clicking the Talk button will initiate the chat process.

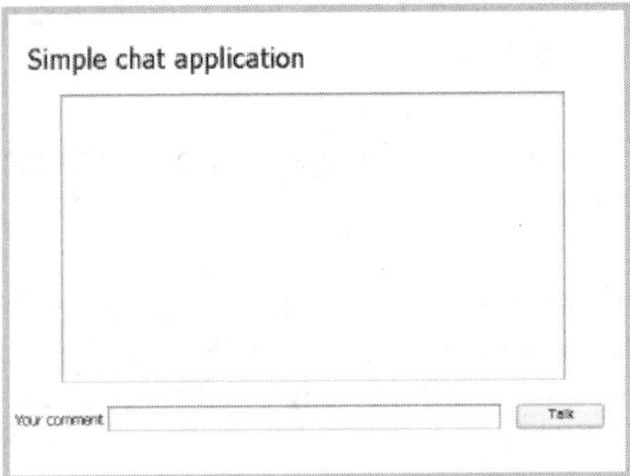

Figure 10-5. The chat application interface

6. Add the following code to the actions layer to create a USimpleChat object and connect to the server:

```
import org.moock.unity.simplechat.v2.USimpleChat;
var chat:USimpleChat = new USimpleChat(this, "localhost", 9100,
null, true);
chat.connect();
```

This code imports the USimpleChat class so that you don't have to use the fully qualified name in your code. It creates a new USimpleChat object called chat. This object manages the chat connections.

The USimpleChat constructor method takes five parameters. The first parameter, `this`, refers to the current timeline. The second and third parameters show the server address and port number. I've used `localhost` because I'm connecting to my local server. I've used port number 9100 as that's the port specified in the `uconfig.xml` file. The last two parameters specify a client configuration file—`null`—and the `true` parameter disables the log.

7. Test the movie. You should see something similar to Figure 10-6. This shows that you've successfully connected to the socket server. If you don't see the message, you'll need to go back through the steps to see where you went wrong.

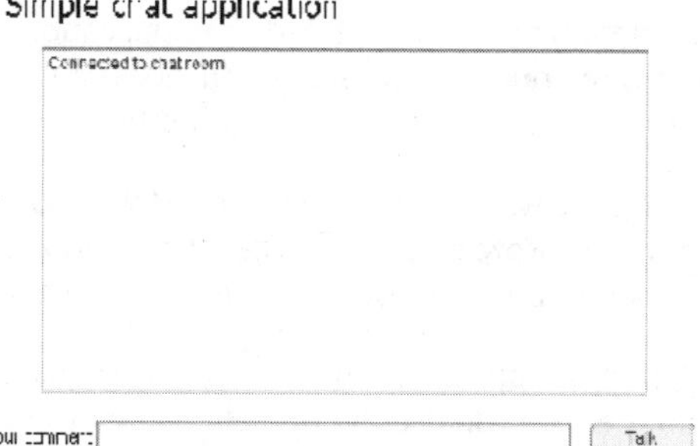

Figure 10-6. Checking the connection to the chat room

Users will enter their comments and click the Talk button, so you'll need this button to send the details to the server.

Configuring the Talk button

The USimpleChat class includes a sendMessage method that sends the message to the socket server. We'll want to use this method after the user has entered text and clicked the Talk button.

8. Add the following code to the actions layer. The code handles the click of the Talk button using the onRelease handler. It checks to see if the user has entered text and, if so, calls the sendMessage method. This method is contained in the class file USimpleChat.as.

```
talk_btn.onRelease = function ():Void {
  if (outgoing.text.length > 0) {
    chat.sendMessage();
  }
}
```

9. Test the movie and enter some text in the comment field. You should be able to see your comment in the TextArea component after you click the Talk button. Because you're testing the file locally, you won't get a response. Figure 10-7 shows a sample interface.

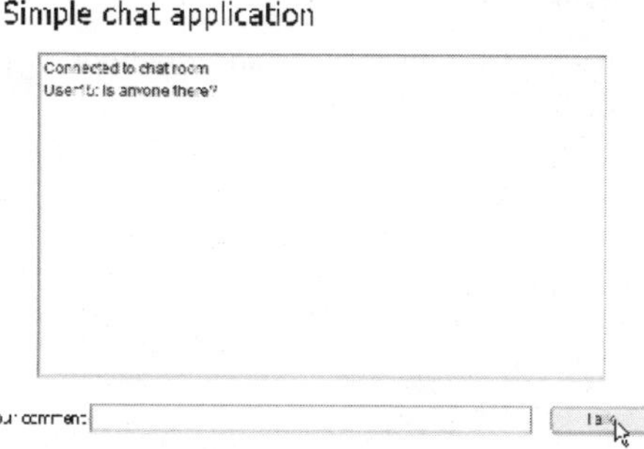

Figure 10-7. A chat message displaying in the application

In this example, we created a simple application that allowed you to chat with other users. We could have extended this example to create multiple chat rooms and add avatars for each user. You can see a demo of the simple chat room at `www.moock.org/unity/clients/uSimpleChat/v4/`. You can also purchase a professional chat client from the site.

If you followed the instructions, you'll have created the application on your local server. That means you'll only be able to chat with yourself. One-sided conversations are quite boring, so you'll need to copy the file to a shared server before you can chat with others.

You'll need to locate a web host with the Unity server installed. Users will then be able to use your chat application through a web browser. Don't forget that if you're using the trial version of Unity, you'll only be able to work with up to five users for a maximum of five minutes.

Before you upload the Flash chat application to the web server, you'll need to change the server path and port number in the movie. You can use the domain name or IP address of the web server for the path. Double-check which port your host has used for the socket server and change it in the `connect` method of the XMLSocket object:

```
theSocket.connect("name or IP address of host", 1234);
```

You should change your publishing settings so that you choose Access network only in the Local playback security settings drop-down box. You'll also need to add a policy file so that users from different domains can share the XML data. The unity server includes a sample policy file `policy.xml`. You'll need to copy this file to the root directory of the web server. You can find out more about policy files in the security section in Chapter 4.

The steps to install the application on an external host are summarized here:

1. Locate a suitable web host and find out the address and port number for the socket server.
2. Modify the `connect` method in your chat application to reference the address and port number provided by the host.
3. Publish the chat application and upload to the web server.
4. Copy the `policy.xml` file from the `unity` folder to the root of the web server.

Summary of the methods and event handlers of the XMLSocket class

This section provides a summary of the properties and methods of the XMLSocket class. Table 10-2 shows the methods of the XMLSocket class.

Table 10-2. Summary of methods of the XMLSocket class

Method	Explanation
`close`	Closes the connection to the socket server.
`connect`	Connects to the socket server. You need to specify the server address and port.
`send`	Sends data to the server. Usually used with XML information.

Table 10-3 lists the event handlers for the XMLSocket class.

Table 10-3. Summary of event handlers for the XMLConnector class

Event	Explanation
`onClose`	Called when the connection to the socket server is closed.
`onConnect`	Called when a connection is made to the socket server.
`onData`	Called when the data is downloaded from the server.
`onXML`	Called when the data has been parsed into an XML object.

Summary

In this chapter, we've looked briefly at the XMLSocket class and the role of socket servers in Flash movies. You'll use a socket server if you need multiuser interaction or a persistent connection to XML information. You don't need to request information from the server continually, as you would with the XML class. As new information becomes available, the socket server will feed it into your movie.

Setting up a socket server can be quite difficult, so don't undertake this process lightly. If you need the type of functionality offered by XMLSockets, you may need to spend some time looking for a socket server that is easy to set up and that provides sample applications and good documentation. You'll also need to locate a web host that supports the socket server.

If you've worked through the book, you'll have seen that there are many different options for working with XML data in Flash movies. In the final chapter, we'll look at some of the decisions to consider when you choose which method you'll use.

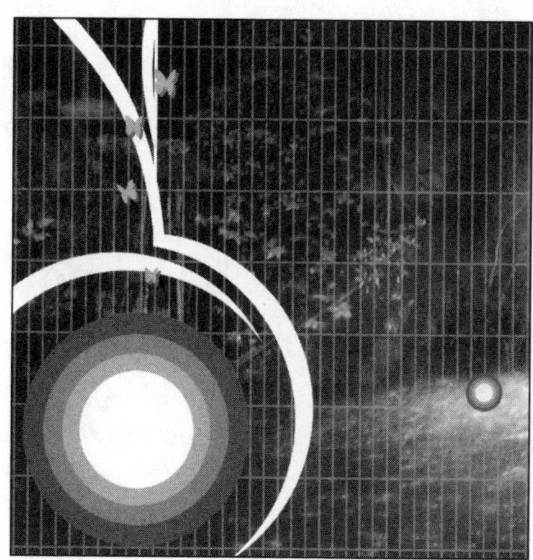

Chapter 11

WHICH XML OPTION IS BEST FOR ME?

After reading this book, you're probably a little overwhelmed by the different choices you have for working with XML. Do you use the XML class or the data components? Should you use the Component Inspector to configure the data components or write ActionScript instead? Do you need to consider the XMLSocket class? In this chapter, I'd like to provide a framework that you can use to make these decisions.

I believe that you face two choices:

1. Decide whether XML is the best choice to provide data for your application.
2. If you choose XML, decide how to include the XML content within Flash.

XML is a very flexible alternative for data exchange, but other options such as using a database or text file may be appropriate, depending on the type of application you're building. You can include XML within Flash by using the XMLSocket class, the XML class, or the data components. You can even script the data components or Web Service classes.

If XML is the best option for your Flash data, you'll need to consider these factors:

- Do you need real-time or multiuser interaction?
- Is timeliness of information a factor?
- Which version of Flash do you own?
- Which Flash players are you targeting?
- Do you prefer to work visually?

The good news is that there isn't a single "correct" way to work with Flash and XML. The choices that you make will depend on the type of application that you're building and your target audience. In this chapter, I'll explore these questions in more detail so that you can make informed decisions about the best way forward.

Is XML the best choice?

To start with, you'll need to consider whether XML is the best choice for your data. By definition, XML is a verbose way to store information; it requires a text-based tag structure to be included in addition to the data. XML documents are likely to take up more space compared with their text file counterparts, which means choosing XML as a data storage medium could affect the size and speed of your application. It's obviously going to be quicker to load a smaller file into Flash. It will also be quicker to extract the information from a smaller file.

For very large amounts of data, storing the information in an XML file may not be practical. Including additional text to describe data structures may affect how quickly the application responds. You can decide whether XML is the best choice by determining whether response speed is critical and considering how the data is currently stored. You should also take into account how the data will be maintained. While you consider whether to use XML, you'll also be able to determine whether you'll need server-side interaction within your application.

Is response speed an issue?

When asked, most people will say that it's important to have a Flash application that works quickly. In most applications, however, a delay of 2 or 10 seconds is unlikely to be significant. Typically, you'll only need to consider response speed if you have large-scale or enterprise-level applications. Large-scale applications have a large number of concurrent users and complex data.

By its very nature, working with XML data in Flash is a slow process. XML information consists of text information sent over HTTP. The larger the XML document, the longer it takes to send. When Flash receives the information, it has to work through the document tree to locate specific information. As a result, you might find that large XML documents or those with a complex structure take many seconds to load and parse in Flash. This may be an unacceptable delay for enterprise-level applications.

If speed is critical, you'll get the fastest response times if you use Flash Remoting to interact with the data. Flash Remoting allows a movie to call remote methods as if they were local. This means that you create your functions using server-side files but call them directly in Flash. Your server-side files process the content and provide the processed information to Flash. Server-side processing is always quicker than processing within Flash, so you'll save time. Flash Remoting is also quicker because it uses Action Message Format (AMF), a compressed binary format. This reduces the size of content sent to Flash.

Another advantage of Remoting is that the variable datatypes are preserved. An array from a server-side file arrives as an array in Flash when you're using Remoting. The movie can use the array without processing it first. This is quite different from using the LoadVars and XML objects, where content arrives as strings. You need to use ActionScript to process the strings and convert them to other types of variables.

The disadvantage of Flash Remoting is that, unlike an XML document, an AMF message can't be read easily by humans. It is also a proprietary Macromedia format, and you'll have to invest money to use it in a commercial environment.

If speed isn't critical in your application, it's worthwhile looking at the current location of the data.

Where is the data stored?

The other important issue to consider is where the data is currently stored. As a general principle, you shouldn't change the data storage mechanism without good reason. Data is usually stored in XML documents, databases, or other software packages.

XML document

If the data is already stored in one or more XML documents, then it makes sense to keep it in that format. This includes information stored in physical files as well as data that exists as an information stream. Web services are an example of a stream of XML data.

If data already exists in XML format, there's no sense in adding another step to the process by transforming the data into a text file or inserting it into a database first. You'll just increase processing time unnecessarily. Bear in mind that it's possible to apply an XSL transformation to change the structure of an existing XML document to one that is more suitable for use in Flash.

Your approach depends on the type of application that you're creating. If the application will run from a CD-ROM in stand-alone mode, you'll only be able to use physical XML documents. When people run applications from CDs, you can't guarantee that they'll have access to the Internet. You've no way of ensuring that they will be able to connect to a web server to request an XML information stream.

You can use a server-side file to save the XML stream as a physical XML document. The stand-alone Flash application can then load the physical XML document without accessing a web server.

If you're consuming web services, you'll also need to consider Flash Player security. You can't consume data from another domain or subdomain in Flash unless the remote application has a policy file in effect. If there is no policy file, you'll need to use a server-side file to proxy the data locally. You can find out more about security in Chapter 4.

Database

If your information is stored in a database, you'll need to use a server-side file to request the content. The server-side file will need to convert the results into a format that Flash can understand. You can generate variable pairs for use with a LoadVars object. You can also generate an XML document. There is no clear advantage in using either approach, so the choice is really up to you.

Some databases support XML queries that return the content in XML format. If this is the case, your server-side file will be able to return XML directly to Flash. Flash can then load the contents into an XML document tree for inclusion in your movie. This is likely to be quicker than using the server-side file to generate the content. If your database provides this functionality, this should be your preferred option.

Again, if your application is running offline, for example, on a CD-ROM, you won't be able to guarantee access to a web server. You'll have to create the content from the database in physical files—either text or XML files.

Other software package

XML is such a pervasive technology that many software packages allow you to import and export data in XML format. As well as popular databases, many survey, e-commerce, and contact management software packages allow you to exchange data in this way.

While other software packages are unlikely to interact directly with Flash, you can use them to generate physical XML files. Flash can then load the content using the XML class or data components. By using physical documents, you'll make your application portable so you can distribute it on a CD-ROM. Using an XML layer between Flash and your enterprise-level applications also provides extra security that prevents users from accessing sensitive corporate information.

If the data is stored in a software package without XML support, you'll need to export it and manipulate the data into a structure that Flash can understand. You could re-create the data using either variable pairs or XML. Again, there's no clear advantage to either approach. You can use a text or XML editor to restructure the data, or you could write a server-side file to automate the process.

Office 2003 document

PC users who have data stored in Office 2003 documents can use Word, Excel, or Access to generate XML content. I covered this in chapters 5, 6, and 7.

Unfortunately, Macintosh Office users don't have access to the same functionality. If you're a Mac user or your data is stored in an earlier version of Office, you'll have to re-create the data for Flash. You could create either an XML file or a text file containing variable pairs.

How will the data be maintained?

It's also important to take into account how you'll maintain the data that you'll use in your Flash application. You saw earlier in this book that it's possible to maintain XML content using Office 2003. If the data already exists in Word, Excel, or Access 2003, it makes sense to use an XML format and thus allow the user to update the content themselves. It may even be possible to create new Office 2003 documents to store the data or transform existing data from other sources. You can find out more about Office 2003 and XML in chapters 5, 6, and 7.

Do you need server-side interaction?

You'll need server-side interaction with your XML Flash movie in the following situations:

- You need to use Flash Remoting to ensure quick response times.
- You need to proxy XML data, that is, there is no policy file for data from a different domain or subdomain.
- You need to update the XML content in a Flash movie.
- You need to create a physical XML document from an XML information stream.

Although it may not change your decision to use XML, you'll need to be aware of the additional requirements of using server-side files in your application. You'll need to install the application on a web server and write the server-side functionality using a language such as ColdFusion, PHP, or ASP.NET. You can't easily distribute applications that use server-side functionality on CD-ROMs.

Making the decision

I've summarized the decision points we've discussed so far in Table 11-1.

Table 11-1. Data storage decision points.

Current Storage Mechanism	Considerations	Decision
Any	Application speed is critical.	Use Flash Remoting and server-side files.
Physical XML document		Use the existing XML document in Flash.
Web service		Consume web service in Flash. If no policy file exists, use a server-side file to proxy the information or save to a physical file for offline applications.
Database	The database supports XML queries.	Use XML information streams generated by a server-side file. Generate a physical XML document for offline applications.
Database	The database doesn't support XML queries.	Transform content into either XML or variable pairs using server-side files. Generate a physical document for offline applications.
Office 2003 (PC)		Export content as XML document(s). Word and Excel are likely to require a schema document to streamline the process.
Office 2003 (PC)	User needs to be able to maintain XML content.	Maintain content in Word, Excel, or Access 2003 and export XML documents for use in Flash. Word and Excel are likely to require a schema document to streamline the process.
Other Office		Create physical text or XML file containing content.
Other application	The software supports XML export.	Export content as XML document(s).
Other application	The software doesn't support XML export.	Create physical text or XML file containing content.

The rest of this chapter assumes that you've decided to use XML to provide data for your Flash application. In the next sections, we'll examine the decisions that you'll need to make when choosing how best to incorporate XML content in Flash.

How should you include the XML content in Flash?

There are several ways to include XML content within a Flash movie and all have different requirements. These options include:

- The XML class
- Data components
- The XMLConnector or WebServiceConnector classes
- The Web Service classes
- The XMLSocket class

I'll look at each of these in turn.

Using the XML class

The XML class has been available within Flash since version 5, with only minor changes. You can use the XML class to load content from external XML documents into Flash. You can also modify XML data and send it from Flash for external updating with server-side files. If you want to work with the XML class, you'll need to write ActionScript. You can find out more about the XML class in Chapter 4 of this book.

Using data components

Flash MX 2004 Professional and Flash Professional 8 include data components that provide a visual mechanism for working with XML documents. You can use the XMLConnector and WebServiceConnector components in your movies. You can drag components into your movie and configure them using the Component Inspector and Behaviors panel.

The data components allow you to bind XML content directly to user interface components. You can populate a ComboBox, List, or DataGrid component using the Component Inspector. You can also bind the content through a DataSet and XUpdateResolver component if you need to capture changes in your XML content. The XUpdateResolver can send changes to a server-side file for processing.

To learn more about the XMLConnector, DataSet, and XUpdateResolver components, see Chapter 8. Chapter 9 covers the WebServiceConnector component.

Using the XMLConnector, WebServiceConnector, and Web Service classes

The XMLConnector and WebServiceConnector classes are the script versions of the XMLConnector and WebServiceConnector data components. You can create and configure these components using ActionScript. This allows you to add the components to your movie entirely through code. You can even script the bindings to other UI components. You can find out more about scripting these components in chapters 8 and 9.

You can also script the Web Service classes to consume web services. This provides a little more control than you'd get with the WebServiceConnector. Chapter 9 contains more information about these classes.

Using the XMLSocket class

The XMLSocket class allows you to remain connected to a socket server. The socket server can then push information into a Flash movie. This stops Flash from having to request information continually, as with the XML class. Chapter 10 covers the XMLSocket class.

Making the decision

With so many options available to you, it can be hard to decide on the appropriate method to use. The choice will depend on several factors:

- Whether you need real-time or multiuser interaction
- Whether the information is time sensitive
- Which version of Flash you own
- Which Flash players you are targeting
- Whether you prefer to work visually or by writing ActionScript

In the next section, I'll cover each of these points. I'll finish by providing a diagram that summarizes these choices.

Do you need real-time interaction?

The first decision is whether you need to provide multiuser or real-time interaction with the XML data. Real-time interaction allows changes made outside of Flash to be fed into your application as they occur. Multiuser interaction enables you to work with multiple users and be notified immediately of changes that they make. In either case, you can achieve this functionality only by using a socket server and the XMLSocket class.

XMLSockets allow a socket server to push data into Flash. This is different from the request and response model of information gathering that Flash uses in the XML class and data components. Learn more about XMLSockets in Chapter 10.

Bear in mind that you're likely to require a financial investment in the socket server. You will also have to spend some time installing and configuring the server. If you're using a public web host, there may also be some issues with installing socket server software.

Is the information time sensitive?

Another reason for using the XMLSocket class with a socket server is if your information is time sensitive. Socket servers push information into Flash in real time so that the application always displays up-to-date data. You might need this functionality for a stock ticker or booking system that requires up-to-the-minute information.

If you don't need to use the XMLSocket class, there are some further decisions to consider when choosing between the XML class, the data components, and the Web Service classes.

Which version of Flash do you own?

You can't include XML content in a version of Flash prior to version 5. If you own either Flash MX 2004 Professional or Flash Professional 8, you'll be able to use any of the methods listed earlier to include XML content. The Professional editions of Flash ship with data components and data-aware UI components that you can use to include XML content. You can either add these to your movie visually or script them.

If you own the basic version of Flash 8, you are limited to using the XML class to include XML content. You'll need to use ActionScript to include and manipulate XML content, and you can use either version 1.0 or version 2.0. The advantage in using version 2.0 is that you can enforce strict typing of variables. This helps you to avoid type mismatch errors and provides code hints.

Which Flash players are you targeting?

If you're targeting Flash players earlier than version 7, you'll have to use the XML class. You have more choices if you're targeting Flash Player 7 and above. In this case, you'll be able to use the data components or the XML class. You can work with the data components visually or by scripting them with ActionScript 2.0.

Do you prefer to work visually?

Your decision about including XML content also depends on how you prefer to work in Flash. Some people prefer to work visually, using the panels in Flash. Others prefer to write ActionScript to achieve the same functionality. If you're a visual developer who owns one of the Professional versions of Flash, you'll probably prefer to use the data components. You can drag them onto the Stage and configure them using the Component Inspector. You can also create bindings using the Component Inspector.

Developers who are more comfortable working in code can achieve the same functionality by scripting the XML class or the data components. You can even script the Web Service classes if you're consuming web services. More experienced developers may wish to develop their own classes for working with XML content.

A decision diagram

Figure 11-1 shows a visual representation of the decision-making process that I've just described. The diagram will help you to decide how best to include XML content in Flash.

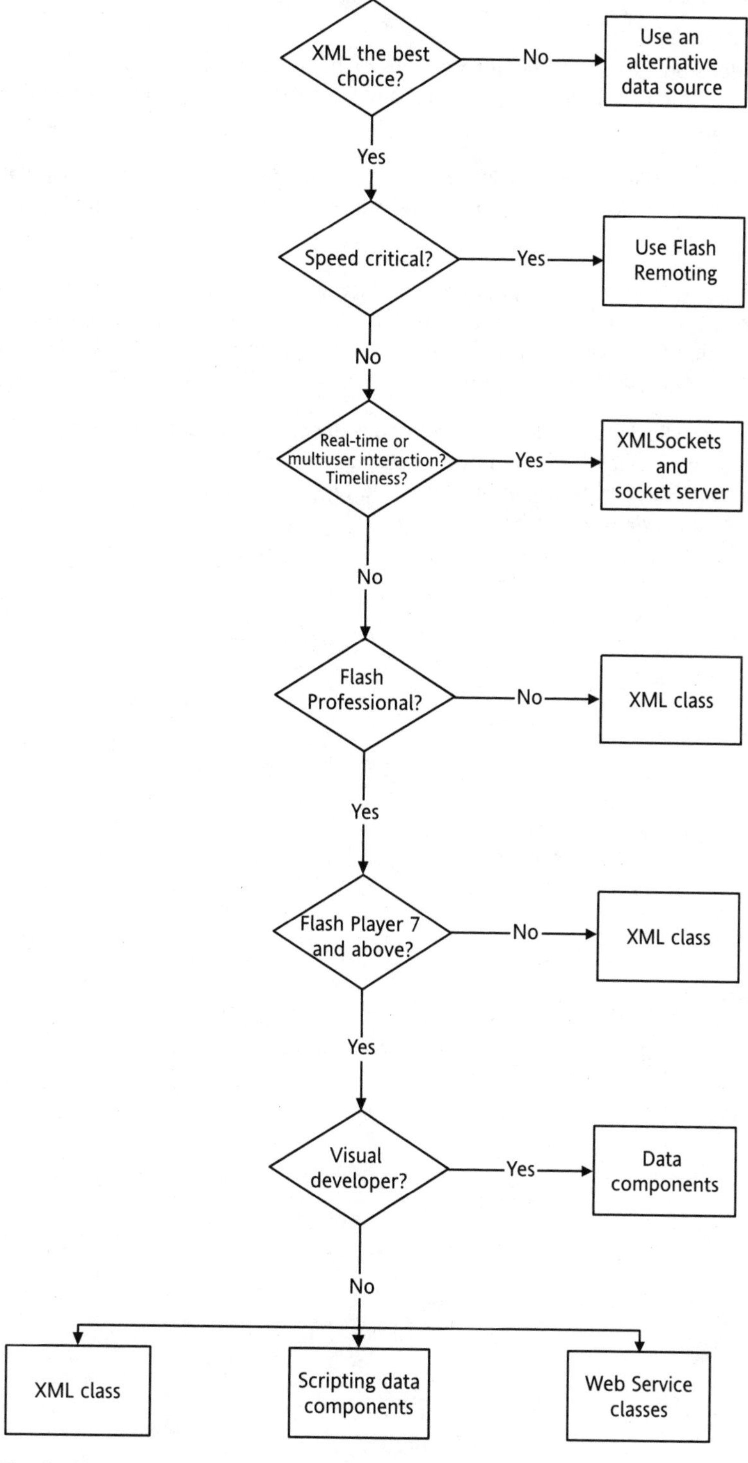

Figure 11-1. The decision-making process

Summary

There are many decisions that you'll need to consider when working with Flash and XML. In this section, I've looked at some of the major points that any Flash developer should address when creating Flash XML applications.

You should start by checking whether XML is the best storage mechanism for your data. You can decide this by considering how important response speed is in the application and where the data is currently stored.

If you decide to go ahead with XML to provide your data, you'll need to determine whether the application requires real-time or multiuser interaction. You should also take into account whether the data is time sensitive. If these considerations are important, you'll need to use the XMLSocket class with a socket server. This means you'll need to purchase, install, and configure a socket server.

If you're not using XMLSockets, you'll be able to choose between the data components and the XML class, depending on your version of Flash, the Flash players you're targeting, and your working style. Developers who own Flash Professional and who are targeting Flash Player 7 and up will have the widest range of choices available to them.

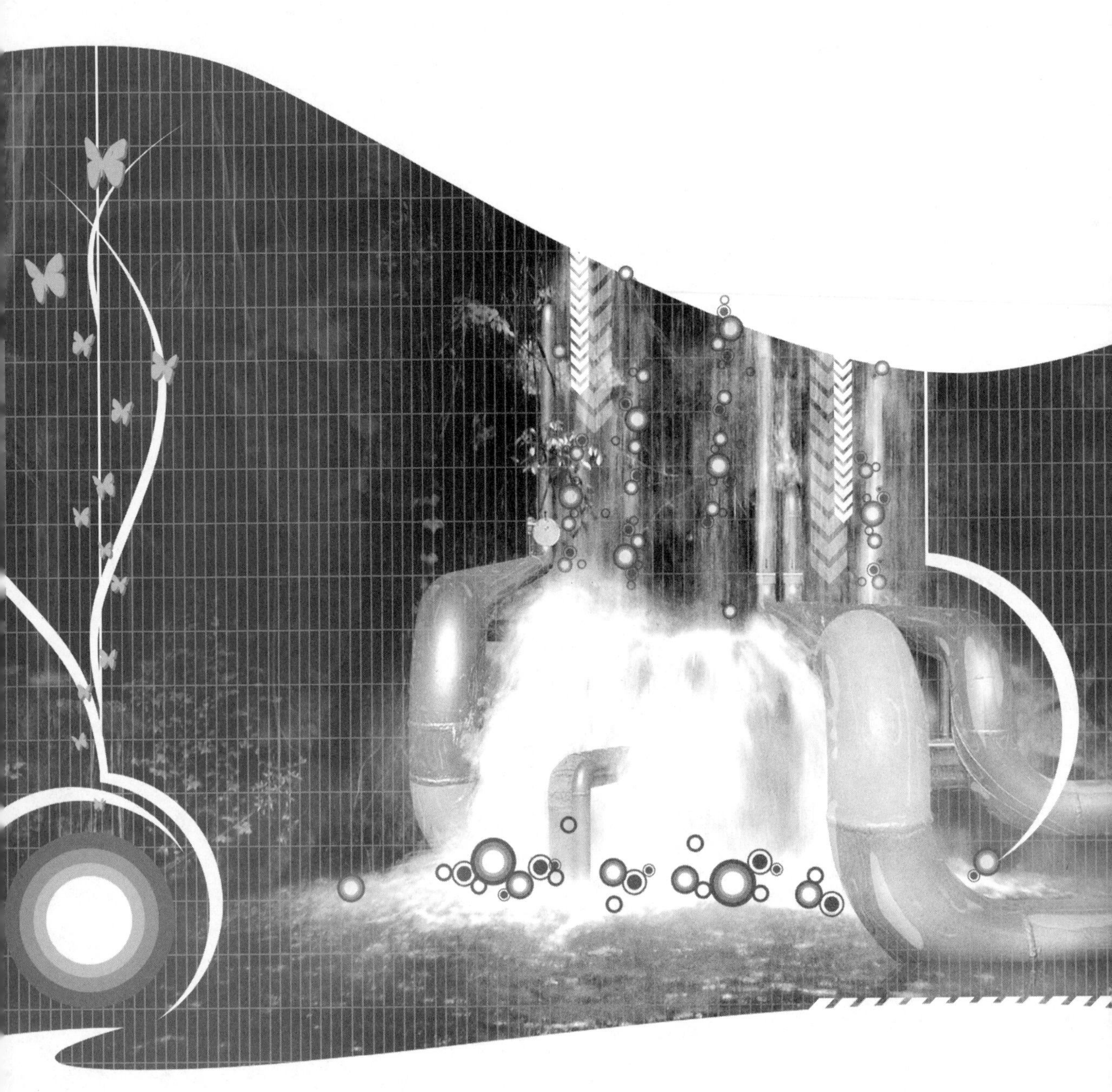

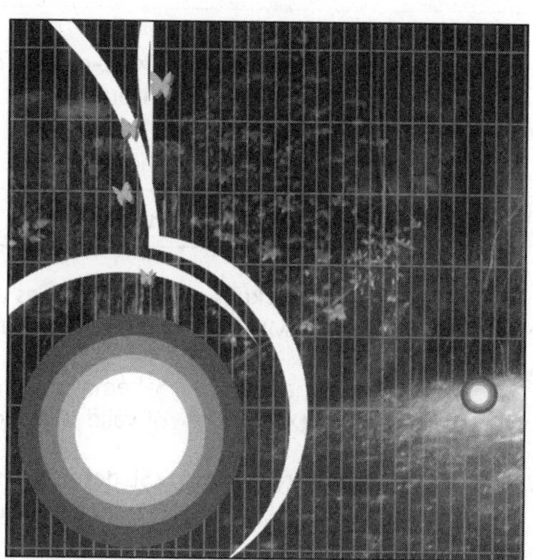

Appendix

USEFUL ONLINE RESOURCES

XML is one recommendation in a family of related recommendations. Together, the recommendations create a framework for designing markup languages. They specify everything from the rules for constructing the language to the styling and querying of XML documents. Many recommendations rely on features from other recommendations for their operations.

The World Wide Web Consortium (W3C) oversees XML and the related recommendations. Each recommendation that W3C releases contains a set of specifications and guidelines, which you can view at the W3C website. Recommendations from the W3C are similar to standards issued by other organizations.

The W3C is an international member organization made up of companies, academics, and other consultants. It also has full-time staff members. The mission of the W3C is

> *"To lead the World Wide Web to its full potential by developing protocols and guidelines that ensure long-term growth for the Web."*

Recommendations start as proposals from members or as notes from nonmembers. At this point, the proposal or note has no backing from the W3C—it is only an idea. If the W3C adopts the idea, it forms a Working Group to create a Working Draft document and oversee the development of technical content.

Working Drafts are released for comment. This may result in the creation of further drafts. Once the draft has been sufficiently refined, the Working Group releases a Proposed Recommendation. This provides the final chance for review of the specification. At this point, the proposal could be returned to Working Draft status or dropped from the W3C activities. If the members agree to accept the proposal, it becomes a recommendation.

Table A-1 shows the main XML-related recommendations and activities at the W3C, their purpose, and the responsible Working Group(s).

Table A-1. XML-related activities at the W3C

Recommendation	Purpose	Main Responsibility
Extensible Markup Language (XML)	XML provides a framework for creating markup languages.	XML Core Working Group
XML Schema Definition (XSD)	Schemas describe the structure and syntax of valid XML documents.	XML Schema Working Group
Extensible Stylesheet Language (XSL)	XSL determines the presentation of XML documents. It uses XSL Transformations (XSLT), the XML Path Language, and XSL Formatting Objects (XSL-FO).	XSL Working Group
XSL Transformations (XSLT)	XSLT transforms one XML document into another XML document.	XSL Working Group
XSL Formatting Objects (XSL-FO)	XSL-FO specifies output formatting for an XML document.	XSL Working Group
XML Path Language (XPath)	XPath navigates or locates specific parts of XML documents.	XSL Working Group, XML Linking Working Group
XML Linking Language (XLink)	XLink describes the links between XML documents.	XML Linking Working Group
XML Pointer Language (XPointer)	XPointer describes references between XML documents so you can use them in links.	XML Linking Working Group
XML Query (XQuery)	XQuery queries XML documents to extract information. At the time of this writing, it was a Working Draft rather than a recommendation of the W3C.	XML Query (XQuery) Working Group
XForms	XForms are an XML-based replacement for XHTML forms.	XForms Working Group
XML Information Set	XML Information Set provides a consistent set of definitions for the other specifications to use when they want to refer to information.	XML Core Working Group
Simple Object Access Protocol (SOAP)	SOAP is a standard format for requesting information from a web service	XML Protocol Working Group
Web Services Description Language (WSDL)	WSDL describes web services using an XML structure.	Web Services Description Working Group, Web Services Addressing Working Group

You can find a summary of the latest recommendations and publications at www.w3.org/TR/.

Table A-2 provides a summary of the W3C URLs for the XML and related recommendations. All URLs were correct at the time of writing.

Table A-2. W3C URLs for XML-related recommendations

Recommendation	URL
Document Type Definitions	Existed prior to XML specification; covered in www.w3.org/TR/REC-xml/
Extensible Markup Language (XML)	www.w3.org/TR/2004/REC-xml-20040204/ (XML 1.0 third edition), www.w3.org/TR/2004/REC-xml11-20040204/ (XML 1.1)
XML Schema	www.w3.org/TR/2004/REC-xmlschema-0-20041028/ (XML Schema Primer), www.w3.org/TR/2004/REC-xmlschema-1-20041028/ (XML Schema Structures), www.w3.org/TR/2004/REC-xmlschema-2-20041028/ (XML Schema Datatypes)
XSL Transformations	www.w3.org/TR/1999/REC-xslt-19991116/
XSL Formatting Objects	www.w3.org/TR/2001/REC-xsl-20011015/
XPath	www.w3.org/TR/1999/REC-xpath-19991116/
XPath 2.0 (Working Draft)	www.w3.org/TR/2005/WD-xpath20-20050404/
XLink	www.w3.org/TR/2001/REC-xlink-20010627/
XPointer	www.w3.org/TR/2003/REC-xptr-element-20030325/ (XPointer element() Scheme), www.w3.org/TR/2003/REC-xptr-framework-20030325/ (XPointer Framework), www.w3.org/TR/2003/REC-xptr-xmlns-20030325/ (XPointer xmlns() Scheme)
XQuery	www.w3.org/TR/2005/WD-xquery-20050404/ (Working Draft)
XForms	www.w3.org/TR/2003/REC-xforms-20031014/ (XForms 1.0 recommendation), www.w3.org/TR/xforms11/ (XForms 1.1 Working Draft)
XML Information Set	www.w3.org/TR/2004/REC-xml-infoset-20040204/ (second edition)
SOAP	www.w3.org/TR/2003/REC-soap12-part0-20030624/ (SOAP 1.2 Primer), www.w3.org/TR/2003/REC-soap12-part1-20030624/ (SOAP 1.2 Messaging Framework), www.w3.org/TR/2003/REC-soap12-part2-20030624/ (SOAP 1.2 Adjuncts), www.w3.org/TR/2003/REC-soap12-testcollection-20030624/ (SOAP 1.2 Specification Assertions and Test Collection)
WDSL	www.w3.org/TR/wsdl (WSDL 1.1 note from Microsoft, Ariba, and IBM), www.w3.org/TR/2004/WD-wsdl20-20040803/ (WSDL 2.0 Core Language – Working Draft), www.w3.org/TR/2004/WD-wsdl20-extensions-20040803/ (WSDL 2.0 Predefined Extensions – Working Draft), www.w3.org/TR/2004/WD-wsdl20-bindings-20040803/ (WSDL 2.0 Bindings – Working Draft)

Table A-3 provides a summary of other XML-related online resources that you might find useful. Again, all URLs were correct at the time of writing.

Table A-3. Useful XML-related websites

Recommendation	URL
XML	www.w3.org/XML/1999/XML-in-10-points.html.en www.w3schools.com/xml/default.asp http://xml.silmaril.ie/ www.xml.com/pub/a/98/10/guide0.html
DTD	www.w3schools.com/dtd/default.asp
XML schema	www.w3schools.com/schema/default.asp lucas.ucs.ed.ac.uk/xml-schema/ www.xml.com/pub/a/2001/06/06/schemasimple.html www.xml.com/pub/a/2000/11/29/schemas/part1.html
XPath	www.w3schools.com/xpath/default.asp www.topxml.com/xsl/xpathref.asp www.oreilly.com/catalog/xmlnut/chapter/ch09.html XSLwww.wdvl.com/Authoring/Languages/XSL/
XSLT	www.topxml.com/xsl/XSLTRef.asp www.w3schools.com/xsl/default.asp www.xml.com/pub/a/2000/08/holman/index.html
XSL-FO	www.w3schools.com/xslfo/default.asp www.renderx.com/tutorial.html www.xml.com/pub/a/2002/03/20/xsl-fo.html
XLink and XPointer	www.w3schools.com/xlink/default.asp www.cafeconleche.org/books/bible2/chapters/ch20.html www.xml.com/pub/a/2000/09/xlink/index.html
XQuery	www.w3schools.com/xquery/default.asp www.xml.com/pub/a/2002/10/16/xquery.html
XForms	www.w3schools.com/xforms/default.asp www.xml.com/pub/a/2001/09/05/xforms.html
Namespaces	www.w3schools.com/xml/xml_namespaces.asp www.rpbourret.com/xml/NamespacesFAQ.htm
Web services	http://webservices.xml.com/pub/a/ws/2001/04/04/webservices/index.html
WSDL	www.w3schools.com/soap/default.asp www.oreilly.com/catalog/webservess/chapter/ch06.html
SOAP	www.w3schools.com/soap/default.asp
REST	www.xfront.com/REST-Web-Services.html

Some of the examples in the book used ASP.NET. I also provided PHP versions of the code with your resources. Table A-4 lists links that might be helpful if you want to learn more about working with ASP.NET and PHP.

Table A-4. Useful ASP.NET and PHP websites

Server-side language	Website

ASP.NET	`www.w3schools.com/aspnet/`
	`www.asp.net/tutorials/quickstart.aspx`
	`www.learnvisualstudio.net`
	`www.asp-visual-basic-csharp-training.net`

PHP	`www.php.net`
	`www.php.net/tut.php`
	`www.w3schools.com/php/default.asp`
	`www.phpbuilder.com`
	`www.devshed.com/c/b/php`
	`www.zend.com/zend/tut/index.php`

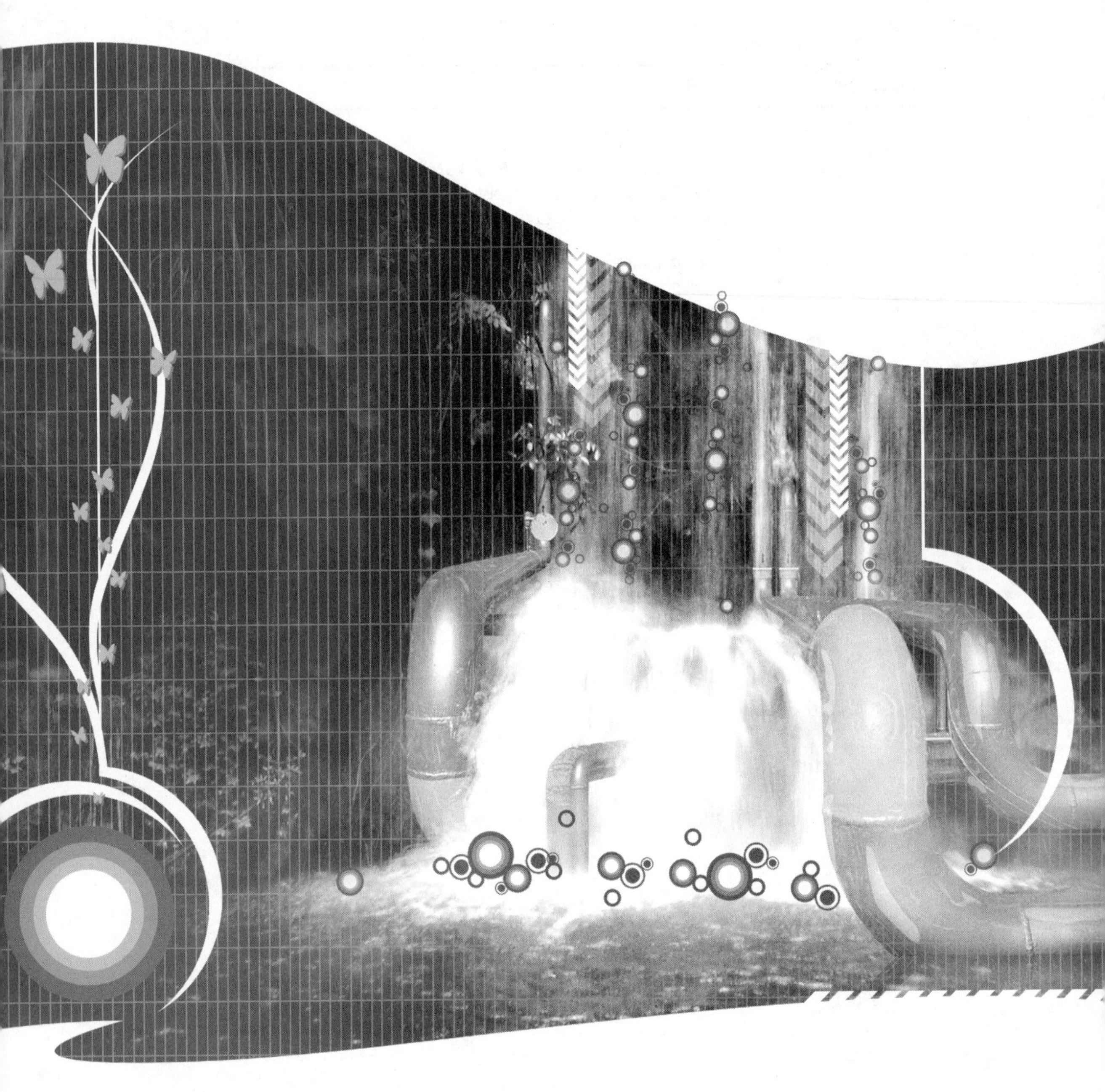

INDEX

Special Characters

A

E

F

G

H

I

N

O

P

T